Strategies for Working the Web

Online databases are a tremendous boon for genealogists, but you could easily spend a lot of time searching the Internet for your family names and come up with nothing. Take the time to learn a few strategies for searching databases, using search engines, and keeping track of your research, and you'll greatly increase your chances of finding useful information.

ASSESSING A DATABASE

Database Characteristics

Before searching a database, try to get a feel for what you can expect to find in it.

What geographic area and time period does the database cover?

The directories in this book indicate the town, county, state, or country and the range of years covered by almost every database. If you know the town where your ancestor lived, search databases for the town, county, and state where it is located, as well as national and international databases. **If you don't know where your ancestor lived, first try databases with broad geographic coverage.**

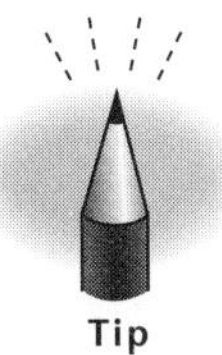

How comprehensive is the database?

Sometimes a database has incomplete coverage of a time period. Read the database description for notes on missing records and planned updates.

Search Capabilities

Can you search for any name or just heads of household?

Most census indexes cover just heads of households, but the 1880 and 1881 censuses of the United States, Canada, and Great Britain on FamilySearch <www.familysearch.org> and the indexes to the 1870 and 1930 U.S. censuses on Ancestry.com covers every name. You can even narrow your search by age and place of birth.

Can you include a middle name in your query?

Databases on Ancestry.com do not have a special box for middle initial or middle name, but you can include a middle initial or name in the same box with the first name. However, the first name, middle name or initial, and last name will not necessarily appear together as part of a single name in the matches.

On the other hand, Genealogy.com's databases *do* have a special box for middle initial or middle name, but anything you enter in it is ignored (except on the World Family Tree). Genealogy.com plans to make it possible to search for middle initials or middle names in other databases.

Does the database have its own customized search form?

Instead of searching all the databases on Ancestry.com or FamilySearch at once, select the individual databases most likely to have information on your family. Many databases have customized search forms with more search options than the generic search form. For example, when searching for a soldier in Ancestry.com's Civil War Pension Index <www.ancestry.com/search/rectype/military/cwpi/main.htm> you can search on place of residence, place of enlistment, and state served. Another option lets you search for a regiment by regiment number, type, or state.

QUERYING A DATABASE

Check name variations.

Search on all possible spellings of a name, like Jonathan and Johnathan, or Myer, Meyer, Meier, and Myers. FamilySearch automatically finds many spelling variations of both first and last names. It doesn't necessarily cover all possibilities, so it's still worth trying other spellings. Ancestry.com supports Soundex searches on surnames so you can find names that sound the same or almost the same, even though they are spelled differently.

You should also try including and excluding middle names and middle initials. My great-grandfather Stephen Armstrong Olmsted was known as Armstrong Olmsted or S.A. Olmsted, so I need to consider several possible variations: Stephen Armstrong Olmsted, Stephen A. Olmsted, S. Armstrong Olmsted, and S.A. Olmsted.

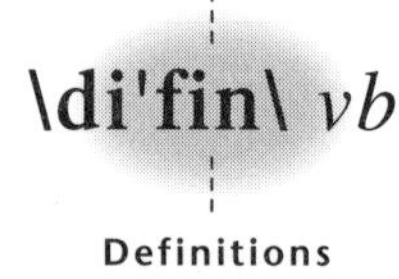

Definitions

SOUNDEX

The Soundex is an indexing system based on how a name sounds. Names that sound alike or almost alike, such as Crume, Croom and Croome, all get the same Soundex code, C650. Even though the name Krume also sounds the same, it gets a different code, K650, because it begins with a different letter.

Try changing the scope of your query.

You can add keywords to narrow your search on Genealogy.com's Family and Local Histories subscription or on Ancestry.com. Matches must contain *all* the terms in your query. If you get too many matches, add more search terms to zero in on better matches. If you get too few matches or none, search on fewer terms or on just a last name, if it's rare.

USING SEARCH ENGINES

This book lists many online and CD-ROM databases, but it's impossible to cover every one, and new ones are released almost daily. You'll find many databases among the more than 200,000 categorized links on Cyndi's List of Genealogy Sites on the Internet <www.cyndislist.com>.

Internet search engines index every word on millions of Web sites and can help you ferret out other databases with indexes, transcribed records, and document images. Keep in mind that Internet search engines do not index all the genealogy data available on the Web. Library catalogs and the databases on FamilySearch, RootsWeb, Ancestry.com, and Genealogy.com are not generally indexed by third-party search engines.

Wording Your Query

By carefully wording your query (the words you type in to search on), you can zero in on the most relevant Web sites. You might search on just a surname if it's rare, on a person's name, or on both a person's name and a place name. Your goal is to come up with a combination of words that uniquely applies to the family you are researching. Some examples:

A rare surname: Schaubhut

If you get too many matches, you can narrow the search by adding another word, such as family, genealogy, ancestry, ancestors, or descendants: Schaubhut genealogy.

A name: "Julius B. Chafee" OR "Julius B. Chaffee" OR "Chafee Julius" OR "Chaffee Julius"

Here quotation marks are used to search on exact phrases. "OR" is used to find either of two spellings of the last name and the name written with either the given name first or the surname first.

A surname and a place name (town, county, state, or country): Robertson "South Worcester"

The names of a husband and wife: "William White" "Ruth Green"

A place name and a subject term: "Bradford County" Pennsylvania cemeteries

You could search on the name of a town, township, county, state, or country and a subject term like these:

adoptions
African American
Afro-American
apprentices
atlas
baptisms
Bible
biography
births
blacks
burials
cemeteries
census
church
Civil War
coat of arms
colonial
Confederacy
Confederate
court
deaths
deeds
directories
divorces
emigrants
emigration
genealogy
gravestones
guardianship
heraldry
history
homestead
immigrants
immigration
land
land grants
Loyalists
maps
marriages
Mayflower
military
militia
missionaries
naturalization
newspapers

nobility
obituaries
passenger lists
patriots
pensions
Pilgrims
probate
Puritans
Revolutionary War
royalty
school
ships
slavery
soldiers
tax
tombstones
Union
vital records
wills

Google

Google <www.google.com> has such an uncanny knack for finding relevant information that it has become the search engine of choice for many researchers (see Figure 1-1 below). When searching Google's index to more than three billion Web pages, don't overlook these useful features:

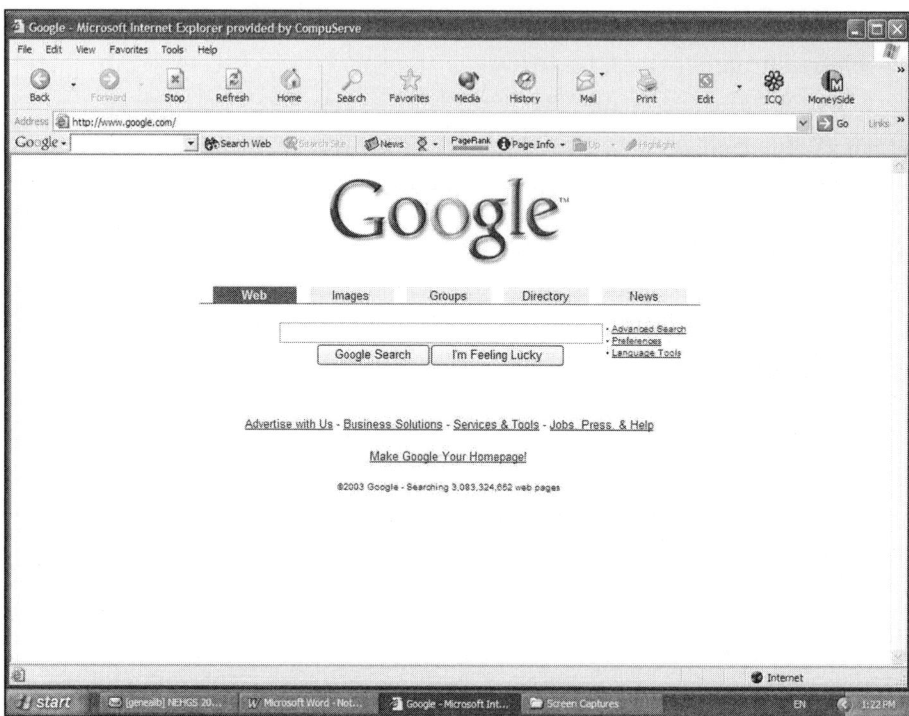

Figure 1-1
The Google Toolbar is also installed.

Site Search: You can limit your Google search to a single Web site. Just precede your query with the word "site" and a colon. To search the Palatine Project Web site <www.palproject.org> for the name Schantz, here's what you type in Google: <site:www.palproject.org Schantz>

You can't limit your search to a specific Web site if the site doesn't have a unique domain name. North Carolina Loyalists During the American Revolution <www.members.aol.com/hoseygen/NCLOYAL.HTML> shares the members.aol.com domain with many other Web sites. A Google search on "site:members.aol.com" would search all of them.

Cached Links: Web sites come and go, but **if you click on a Google match and get a message saying, "The page cannot be found," you still may be able to retrieve the page.** Just go back to the list of Google matches and click on

Cached to view the page as it looked when Google indexed it. If you want to follow a link to a page that has been removed from the Web and you have installed the Google Toolbar (below), right-click on the link and select Cached Snapshot of Page from the pop-up menu.

The Google Toolbar: If you'd like easy access to Google's handy tools from any Web page, download and install the free Google Toolbar <www.toolbar.google.com>. It requires Microsoft Windows 95 or higher and Internet Explorer version 5 or higher.

The Google Toolbar lets you do a Google search from any Web page, translate text and Web pages, search only the pages of the site you're visiting, and find your search terms wherever they appear on the page—all handy features.

Other Search Engines

Google may be the best search engine, but it's still worth trying others, such as these:

- AlltheWeb <www.alltheweb.com>
- AltaVista <www.altavista.com>
- Yahoo! <www.yahoo.com>

RETRIEVING MISSING WEB SITES

If you enter a Web site address and get the message "File not found," you still may be able to retrieve the site.

Try taking off the last part of the Web site address up to the last slash mark, and look for a link to the page. If you still don't find it, keep taking more off the end of the Web site address until you get to the home page.

As noted above, Google may have kept a copy of the page. Use Google to search on the Web page's title, as listed in a directory in this book. Surround the title with quotation marks so you search on the exact phrase. If you find the Web site in Google, but still get the message "Page not found," click on Cached to view the site as it appeared when Google indexed it.

FINDING NEW DATABASES

Reminder

New databases are being published in electronic form every day. You can stay abreast of many of them by subscribing to these newsletters:

- Ancestry Daily News <www.ancestry.com/myaccount/newsletter/newsletter.htm>
- CyndisList Mailing List <www.cyndislist.com/maillist.htm>
- Eastman's Online Genealogy Newsletter <www.eogn.com>
- NEHGS eNews <www.newenglandancestors.org>

The newest additions to these sites are listed online:

- FamilySearch <www.familysearch.org>, click on News.
- Genealogy.com <www.genealogy.com>, click on one of the categories under New Data.

- HeritageQuest Online <www.heritagequestonline.com>, click on "Read what is new."

KEEPING TRACK OF YOUR RESEARCH

With so many ancestors and so little time to find them, you have to work efficiently. You don't want to waste time rechecking the same database unless you have new clues to follow up on or the database has been updated. There are several ways you can keep track of your research:

- Use your genealogy software's research log or research calendar.
- Make notes in the individual records in your genealogy software.
- Keep a word processing document open and make notes of your research as you go. You could record your research in a table with columns for surname, date, database, query, and results. You might create a separate document for each surname and county.
- Print the page describing the database and make notes on the page.
- When logging your research, be sure to include the current date, the database's name and Web site address, what you searched for, and what you found. You might also add the years and places covered by the database.

PUTTING IT ALL IN CONTEXT

Reminder

While the indexes, abstracts, transcriptions, and digitized records described in this book are a tremendous boon for genealogists, **don't neglect other online resources, such as these:**

- **Pedigree databases**, such as the WorldConnect Project <http://worldconnect.rootsweb.com> and the Pedigree Resource File <www.familysearch.org>, as well as Gendex <www.gendex.com>, an index to online family trees.
- **Online library catalogs**, such as those of the Family History Library <www.familysearch.org>, the DAR Library <http://dar.library.net>, the Allen County Public Library <www.acpl.lib.in.us>, and The New York Public Library <http://catnyp.nypl.org>. My own creation, the Genealogical Library Master Catalog, lets you search the holdings of eighteen libraries at once. It's on Ancestry.com at <www.ancestry.com/search/rectype/inddbs/3622.htm> and with more records and enhanced searching capabilities on the CD-ROM version from the National Genealogical Society Bookstore <www.ngsgenealogy.org>.
- **Mailing lists**, such as those sponsored by RootsWeb <www.rootsweb.com>.
- **Message boards**, such as GenForum <www.genforum.com> and those on Ancestry.com <www.ancestry.com>.
- **Surname lists**, such as the RootsWeb Surname List <http://rsl.rootsweb.com>.

- **New and used book dealers,** such as Advanced Book Exchange <www.abebooks.com>, Alibris <www.alibris.com>, Amazon.com <www.amazon.com>, Betterway Books <www.familytreemagazine.com>, BookFinder.com <www.bookfinder.com>, the Genealogical Publishing Company <www.genealogical.com>, Quintin Publications <www.quintinpublications.com>, and Willow Bend Books <www.willowbend.net>.

A lot of family information exists only in family papers or in documents held by county courthouses, state libraries, and national archives. And the only way to verify most information in electronic format is by referring to the original documents or facsimiles.

The Family History Library in Salt Lake City has microfilmed records from around the world, and you can borrow them through a Family History Center in your community. FamilySearch <www.familysearch.org> has a directory of Family History Centers and the Family History Library Catalog, which lists records you can borrow. Click on the Search tab and then on Research Helps to view excellent research outlines for many countries and every U.S. state and Canadian province.

SUGGESTED READING

For More Info

Carmack, Sharon DeBartolo. *Organizing Your Family History Search*. Cincinnati, Ohio: Betterway Books, 1999.

Hendrickson, Nancy. *Finding Your Roots Online*. Cincinnati, Ohio: Betterway Books, 2003.

McClure, Rhonda. *The Genealogist's Computer Companion*. Cincinnati, Ohio: Betterway Books, 2001.

Warren, Paula Stuart, and James W. Warren. *Your Guide to the Family History Library*. Cincinnati, Ohio: Betterway Books, 2001.

Genealogy Megasites

Five key online destinations for genealogists offer a smorgasbord of databases. Finding your ancestors in the billions of names on these sites takes perseverance, but learning a few tips and tricks will improve your chances of success.

Several of these services also publish data on CD-ROM, and these products are listed in this book's database directories.

ANCESTRY.COM

<www.ancestry.com>

Ancestry.com (see Figure 2-1 below), a subscription service from MyFamily-.com, provides access to over 1.2 billion genealogy records, some free, through these online subscriptions:

Historical Newspapers

Search for any word in dozens of newspapers from across the United States and view the actual page images on your computer screen. $12.95/month or $79.95/year.

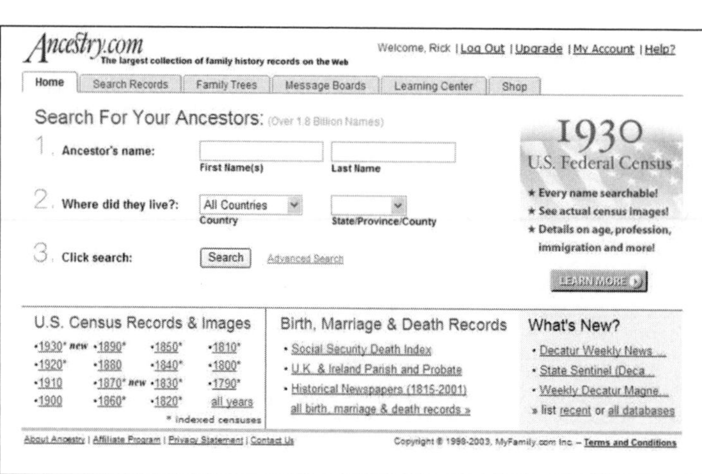

Figure 2-1
Ancestry.com.

U.K. & Ireland Records Collection

Databases include (1) parish and probate records with information on 15 million people from 1538 to 1837, (2) the Pallot Marriage and Baptism Index with 4 million names from England, and (3) an index of 600,000 Irish immigrants arriving in New York between 1846 and 1851. $12.95/month or $99.95/year.

LONG URLS

The URLs (Web site addresses) for Ancestry's databases are long. If you don't want to type them, click on the Search Records tab and click on List All Databases to view an alphabetical list. Then just click on the name of the database.

U.S. Census Images and Indexes

View images of all U.S. federal population census records from 1790 to 1930. Ancestry is creating indexes to the entire collection. $12.95/month or $99.95/year.

U.S. Immigration Collection

Search passenger lists from all major U.S. ports, immigration indexes, and naturalization records. $19.95/month or $79.95/year.

U.S. Records Collection

Search over three thousand databases ranging from military service records to finding aids like the American Genealogical-Biographical Index. $12.95/month or $79.95/year.

The U.S. Federal Census Collection, the U.S. Records Collection, and the U.K. and Ireland Records Collection are also accessible at libraries subscribing to AncestryPlus <www.galegroup.com/AncestryPlus/>, (800) 877-4253, a library version provided by a partnership between Ancestry.com and Gale.

Tips for Searching Ancestry.com

Do a global search if the name is rare.

If you're researching an uncommon name, Ancestry's simple search is an efficient way to search many databases at once. Just type in a first name and a last name and, optionally, select a country and a state, province, or county. For example, search on the name Tobias Schaubhut and all the matches pertain to the only person by that name ever to walk the face of the earth (as far as I know).

USE POST-EMS ON ANCESTRY.COM AND ROOTSWEB TO CONNECT WITH OTHER RESEARCHERS

Some databases on Ancestry.com and RootsWeb <www.rootsweb.com> have a helpful tool to help you make contact with other researchers interested in the same family. For example, do a search in RootsWeb's Social Security Death Index and click on Add Post-em beside a matching name. Just fill in your name, e-mail address, and a note describing your interest in the family. Then click on the Post button to submit the form.

Add a middle initial or middle name and adjust the proximity.
You can include a middle initial or middle name in the First Name box. The Proximity box on the Advanced Search screen lets you specify how close the first and last name must appear in the text—anywhere from one to twenty words. Or you can select no proximity. Sometimes the proximity you specify is ignored and the first and last names appear anywhere on the same page in the matching database.

Limit your search by place and time period.
Searching on even a moderately common name is likely to produce oodles of matches on Ancestry, so you have to modify your search criteria to zero in on the right person. Click on Advanced Search, whose search options include not only name and place, but also year range and record type.

If you search on just the name Jonathan Hall, you'll get thousands of matches—way too many to slog through. Add more search criteria like Country: United States, State: New York, and Year Range: 1810 to 1865, and the list of matches is whittled down to a manageable number. Every match isn't your Jonathan Hall, but it doesn't take long to browse through the list.

Search on a keyword.
Go to Ancestry's home page and click on Advanced Search. You might search on just a keyword or a name combined with one or more keywords:

- *Keyword*: My ancestors in Wales lived in a home called Porthamel, spelled various ways. I could search on each spelling (Porthaml, Porthamel, Porthamal, and Porthamall) or use a wildcard (Portham*l) to cover them all in one search.
- *Name and spouse's name*: Search on a name and, as a keyword, enter the spouse's first name, last name, or both (Stephen Adams and keyword Jane, Bond, or Jane Bond).
- *Name and a town or county*: Search on a name and, as a keyword, enter a town or county (John French and keyword Pittsfield or Berkshire).
- *Name and country*: (John Ferguson and keyword India).
- *Name and subject term*: To find matches for a Loyalist in the Revolutionary War, you might search on the soldier's name and the word Loyalist: James Pennington and keyword Loyalist.

Use the Soundex to find similar spellings.
Advanced Search finds either the exact spelling of a last name or possible spelling variations using the Soundex (see page 4). A Soundex search on my last name (Crume) finds many similar spellings like Crum, Croom, and Croome. However, it doesn't find some spellings I've seen, like Crumes and Croomes, and some matches like Corwin and McCarney aren't even close.

Keep in mind that the Soundex search finds similar spellings for the last name, but not for the first name. So even when using the Soundex be sure to try different spellings of the first name, like Philip and Phillip or Jonathan and Johnathan.

Try different spellings.
The Soundex doesn't catch all possible spellings of a name, so be sure to search on alternate spellings. And when browsing through records, be on the lookout for spellings you might never have imagined.

Use a wildcard.
You can use a wildcard to represent one or more letters. That saves you from doing separate searches on different spellings, and it might even retrieve spellings you wouldn't have thought to try. A question mark represents any letter, so a search on Ev?ns finds Evans, Evens, and Evins. An asterisk substitutes for zero to six letters, so you can search on Phi*ip to find either Philip or Phillip. Keep in mind that an asterisk cannot substitute for any of the first three letters in a name. Joh*n will find John, Johann, or Johnathan, but you can't search on Jo*n to find Jon, John, or Jonathan.

Search a specific database.
Use this book to identify databases for the places where your ancestors lived. To identify other databases, click on the Search Records tab on Ancestry's home page and then on a topic like Military or Immigration/Emigration.

You can also view the databases arranged by place. Click on a state on the U.S. map or on England, Scotland, Wales, or Ireland on the U.K. and Ireland map. Then you can either search all the databases for a state or country or select a single database.

Use all the census search options.
Several of Ancestry.com's census indexes give you many search options so you can find the right person, even if it's a common name. You can search by first name, middle name or middle initial, last name, age, and place of birth. You can also limit the search to a specific state, county, or town.

You don't even need to include a last name, so if you don't know a woman's married name, you can search on just her first name. Narrow down the list of matches by adding other search criteria like age, place of birth, and state of residence.

FAMILYSEARCH

<www.familysearch.org>
This popular free site sponsored by the Church of Jesus Christ of Latter-day Saints (LDS) features nearly a billion names in searchable databases (see Figure 2-2 on page 14). Click on the Search tab to search these key files:

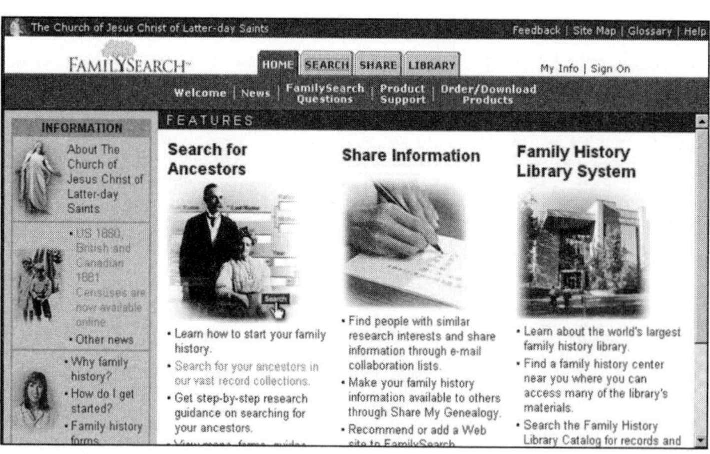

Figure 2-2
FamilySearch.

Census transcriptions and indexes
The 1880 U.S. census (50 million names), the 1881 census of Canada (4.3 million names), and the 1881 census of England and Wales (25 million names).

International Genealogical Index (IGI)
Includes 285 million births and marriages worldwide, either extracted from original records or submitted by church members.

U.S. Social Security Death Index
Death information on adults who had a Social Security number and died in the United States since 1962 (and some earlier). Many women are not listed if they didn't work outside the home.

Tip

Tips for Searching FamilySearch

Search on an exact name.
Check the Use Exact Spelling box to search for the first, middle, and last name exactly as you enter it. If you don't check this box, FamilySearch will find names similar to the first and last names you enter, but will ignore the middle name or middle initial.

Do a parent search.
To search for a couple's children, click on the Search tab, fill in just the father's and mother's first and last names, and click on Search. The mother's last name (her maiden name) is optional.

Search the IGI by batch number.
You can limit a search of the IGI to a U.S. state, a Canadian province, a county in the British Isles, or a region of some other countries. Adding a batch number lets you narrow your search to a specific town or church, especially useful if you're researching a common last name.

Search the IGI for James Snow born in 1756 in Massachusetts, and you'll find three entries for the one born in Haverhill, Essex County, on 21 September

1756. One of the entries was extracted from the original records. The source information for this record identifies the batch number as C502331. Click on the batch number and it is automatically filled in on the IGI search form and North America is selected as the region. Now you can type Snow in the Last Name box and click on the Search button to find other baptismal records for Snows in the same town. Marriages would be in a different batch.

Some tremendously ambitious souls have compiled IGI batch numbers for several countries. The batch numbers for the United States, Canada, and the British Isles are listed at <http://freepages.genealogy.rootsweb.com/~hughwallis/IGIBatchNumbers.htm#Page>. Find the name of a town and click on the batch number for baptisms/births or marriages. Then enter a surname and, optionally, the spouse's surname and click on Submit Query to view the matches.

The batch numbers described above will help you find baptisms and marriages copied from records microfilmed by the Family History Library. Keep in mind that other IGI entries were submitted by LDS church members. Search the IGI by name to find these entries.

Check source microfilms to verify IGI entries.

It's important to check the original records to verify information in the IGI. When you find an IGI entry, click on the Source Call No., and then click on the title to view the Family History Library Catalog's description of the records. Click on View Film Notes to identify the microfilm number. You can borrow most microfilms for a small fee through a Family History Center in your community.

In some cases, the microfilmed church records may give more information than the IGI. A record of baptism may provide the occupation or specific place of residence of the child's father. Very few burials are listed in the IGI, so be sure to look for them in the church records, too.

GENEALOGY.COM

<www.genealogy.com>

Genealogy.com (see Figure 2-3 on page 16), a subscription service from MyFamily.com, provides access to digitized books, passenger lists, and census images through these online subscriptions:

Family and Local Histories

Page images from 7,000 family histories, over 8,000 local histories, and over 165 primary sources. $14.99/month or $49.99/year.

Genealogy Library

Over 1,700 genealogies, more than 250 town and county histories, vital records collections (mostly from Georgia, Idaho, Indiana, and Massachusetts), 1850 census images, and over 35 collections of land, military, marriage, probate, church, and other records. $9.99/month or $79.99/year.

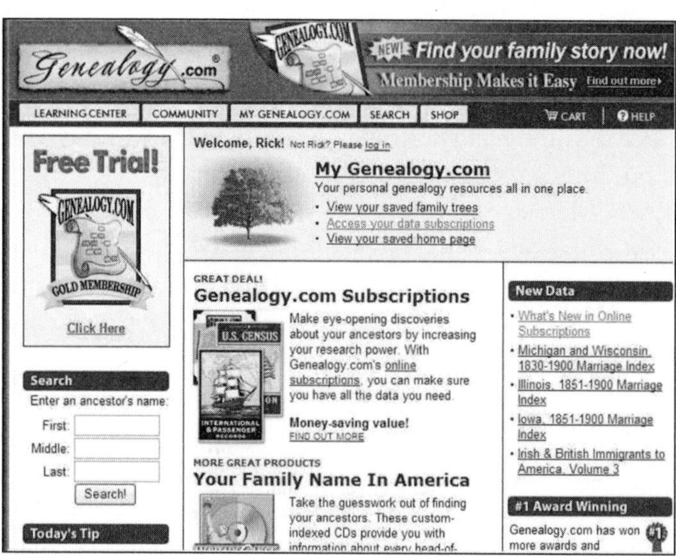

Figure 2-3
Genealogy.com.

International and Passenger Records

Databases naming millions of immigrants from Great Britain, Germany, Italy, Russia, and other countries. $14.99/month or $79.99/year.

U.S. Census Collection

Page images of all U.S. federal censuses from 1790 to 1930 with indexes. $19.99/month or $99.99/year.

Tips for Searching Genealogy.com

General

Search on just a last name and you'll get a list of every match in Genealogy-.com's databases. This is especially helpful if you're not sure of the spelling of the first name.

Family and Local Histories

Many years ago University Microfilms International (UMI) published a huge collection of family and local histories on microfiche. More recently, UMI, now known as ProQuest, converted the whole collection to electronic images and began offering it as a subscription service called HeritageQuest Online <www.heritagequestonline.com> exclusively for libraries. Now Genealogy.com has partnered with the HeritageQuest division of ProQuest to give individual genealogists online access to these valuable books.

Known as Family and Local Histories on Genealogy.com, this subscription features images of over 7.5 million pages from over 7,900 family histories, over 12,000 local histories, and over 250 primary sources. Among them you'll find books like *The Cooley Genealogy*, *History of Delaware County and Border Wars of New York*, *Vital Records of Sturbridge, Massachusetts, to the year 1850*, and *The German Element of the Shenandoah Valley of Virginia*. The collection focuses on U.S. genealogy and local history, but also includes titles from Canada and the British Isles.

The Family and Local Histories Collection will continue to grow. Genealogy.com and HeritageQuest plan to expand the collection to include all 25,000 titles in the microfiche version. Then they'll add about 1,000 titles every year from libraries and genealogical societies across the country.

Full-text searching

Every word in the Family and Local Histories Collection of books is indexed, and that makes it much more useful than the old microfiche version. You have three search options:

1. People: Search on a person's first and last name and you'll find all instances where they appear within five words of each other. By default, matches include similar spellings. Search on Daniel Crume and it will find both Daniel Crume and Daniel Crum. To search on the exact spelling of a word, precede it with exact, e.g., "Daniel exact Crume."

You can add one or more place names or keywords to zero in on relevant matches—a necessity if you're searching on a common name. I'm researching Timothy Murphy, a charismatic frontiersman affectionately known as "the king of Indian hunters." Searching on Timothy Murphy produced 106 matches, and none of the first items on the list seemed to be the right guy. My Timothy Murphy lived at Worcester, New York, so I searched on Timothy Murphy and added Worcester to the Place(s) name box. That narrowed the list of matches to 65, but the top matches still didn't look promising. Finally, I searched on Timothy Murphy near Worcester (typed in the Person Names(s) box) and found a good match in *Town of Worcester, Otsego County, New York*. Adding "near" to your query finds all instances where the two terms appear within ten words of each other and often produces the most relevant matches.

You can search on an exact phrase by enclosing it in quotation marks. Including a middle name or middle initial in your name search is an excellent way to focus on the most relevant matches. Just type a name like Henry J. Hall or John Pugsley Jones in the Person Name(s) box.

2. Places: The Places search gives you the same three search boxes for persons, places, and keywords, but the Place Search box appears first. You might search for the name of a town or county.

3. Publications: This option displays an alphabetical list of all the books in the Family and Local Histories Collection.

Click on Search Publications to browse the list of books by author, title, publisher, place or date of publication, subject, or language. Use the Keyword search to find a word in just one or a few books, rather than in the entire collection. To search *The Cooley Genealogy* for Dennis Nelson Cooley, you might type Cooley Genealogy in the Book or Article Title box and Dennis near Nelson in the Keyword(s) box.

What if you don't have a specific book title, but want to find out if Family and Local Histories has histories of a certain family or county? Click on Search Publications and on the Browse button beside the Subject box. Type a last name or the name of a city, county, state, or country in the Subject box and click on Jump. Click on the boxes beside the relevant subject terms and click on okay. The Subject terms are copied into the Subject search box. Type one or more keywords like a last name in the Keyword(s) box and click on Search to find the keywords in any books with the specified subject terms.

From the search results page, click on View Image to see a book's title page. Then click on the right arrow by the Hit button to go to the next page where your search term appears.

If your search doesn't produce useful information, you might try browsing through a book. With a page from a book displayed, click on View Citation. Then you can jump to any section of the book, including the index if the book has one. To jump to a specific page in a book, click on Browse by Page Number.

Searching an individual database

The URLs for individual databases in Genealogy.com's Family and Local Histories Collection (also known as HeritageQuest Online) are not listed in the database directories in this book because the URLs are very long and, even if you go directly to a database, you can't search it from that Web page.

To search a specific database in the Family and Local Histories Collection, follow these steps:

1. Under Search Books, click on Publications.
2. Click on Search Publications.
3. Type the words you are searching for, such as a last name like Smith or a person's name like Charles J. Hall, in the Keyword(s) box and the first few words of the title, as shown in the database directories in this book, in the Book or Article Title box.
4. Click on Search.
5. Click on View Image.
6. The book's title page will be displayed. Click on the Hit button's right arrow to view the first page where your search terms appear.
7. Click on the Hit button's right arrow again to view the other matches, one by one.

Genealogy Library

While Genealogy Library boasts impressive content, its search functions may leave you confused. You can choose from several search forms, but the sparse instructions don't clearly explain the differences between them or how to use them effectively. Here's a summary of each form's search options and the part of Genealogy Library that it searches:

1. Simple search (first, middle, last name) searches all of Genealogy Library, including Family Books, the 1850 census index, and Historical Records. You'll find the basic search form on the home page of Genealogy Library. This search works fine for rare names, but not for common names since it provides no way to limit your search to a certain place or time period.

2. Advanced search (first, middle, last name; event; location; date or date range) searches Family Books and Historical Records, but the event, loca-

tion, and date or date range searches apply only to Historical Records. The instructions say that it searches the 1850 Census Images, too, but it really searches the index to heads of households in the 1850 census, not the images.

3. Search a group of books (first name, last name, or any word). If you are researching a family that lived in New York, you might select Places from the Family Books & 1850 Census category and then United States and New York, to search only Family Books focusing on that state.

Click on the title of a match to view the whole page of text from the original book. Better yet, click on Show Hits to display the same thing with your search words highlighted. You can page through the book and print any page.

4. Search one book (first name, last name, or any word). Select the database on the Genealogy Library home page. Then either jump to the first page with the surname you specify or search on a first and last name.

5. Search on a keyword. To search on a keyword in the title or description of a book (not in the text of the book), go to the Genealogy Library home page, click on Expanded Directory, and then on Index of Keywords. Click on the keyword's first letter, on the keyword, and then on the book's title.

U.S. Census Collection

Genealogy.com is creating head-of-household indexes to the census images and, so far, has completed indexes to the 1790, 1800, 1810, 1820, 1860, 1870, 1890 (only a small fragment of the original 1890 census records still exists), 1900, and 1910 censuses. Use the Family Finder Index to search the indexed censuses for all states at once. To search the index for a specific state and year, go to the Census Collection page, click on the year, and then select the state. Although the census search page has a link to Advanced Search options, they don't work with the census search.

The 1900 and 1910 census indexes are the first nationwide indexes for these census years. You can search for a first and last name and limit the search to a specific state. Although there's a search box for a middle name or middle initial, the census search ignores middle names and middle initials.

NEW ENGLAND ANCESTORS

<www.newenglandancestors.org>

Members of the New England Historic Genealogical Society have access to dozens of databases on this site, including the full text of *The New England Historical and Genealogical Register*, 1847–1994, *The Great Migration Begins: Immigrants to New England, 1620–1633*, and *Massachusetts Vital Records* to 1850 (see Figure 2-4 on page 20). An annual membership costs $75 and includes subscriptions to *New England Ancestors* and *The Register*.

USGENWEB PROJECT

<www.usgenweb.org>

Through the efforts of many volunteers across the country, this extensive network of free sites has quickly built up an enormous body of genealogical data (see Figure 2-5 on page 20). Don't overlook any of the Project's main parts:

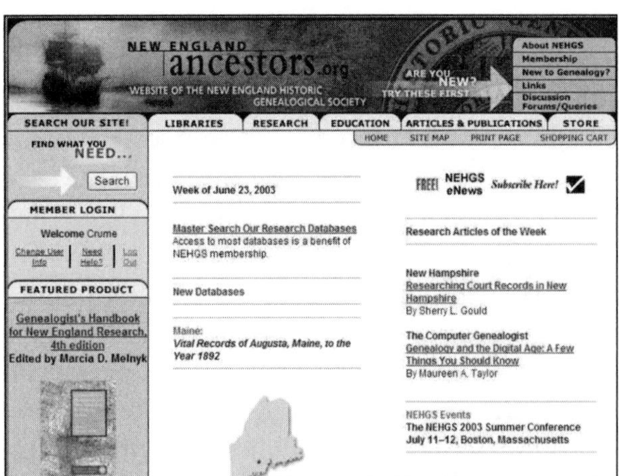

Figure 2-4
New England Ancestors.

State Pages <www.usgenweb.org/thestates.html>
These pages are the jumping-off point to county pages where you'll find gravestone transcriptions, church records, indexes to wills, and much more.

USGenWeb Archives <www.rootsweb.com/~usgenweb/>
Here you can view transcribed records from every state. Be sure to use the search engines to find a name in the files for a specific state or anywhere in the entire collection.

USGenWeb Census Project <www.us-census.org>
The goal of this ambitious volunteer effort is to transcribe all U.S. census records from 1790 to 1930. Some transcriptions include links to page images. A similar but separate undertaking at <www.rootsweb.com/~census> shares the same name and objective.

USGenWeb Tombstone Project <www.rootsweb.com/~cemetery/>
Here you'll find gravestone transcriptions from cemeteries across the country.

Figure 2-5
The USGenWeb Project.

Vital Records

Andrew J. Hall, a good-humored auctioneer with a knack for creative advertising and an entrepreneurial spirit, also operated a grocery and hardware store and was an agent for International Harvester farm machinery. When he died at age 69 in 1936, the local newspaper in the small Minnesota town where he lived carried a detailed obituary, but it was his death certificate that revealed his mother's maiden name—a key piece of information that allowed me to begin researching a whole new branch of my family tree.

Important

Vital records—birth, marriage, divorce, and death records kept by civil governments—are some of the most important documents for genealogical research. Since they usually include the names of the person's parents, both birth records and twentieth-century death records establish a link to a previous generation. Tracking down female lines can be a major challenge, but marriage and divorce records usually reveal the bride's maiden name and sometimes the name of her father or even both parents (see Figure 3-1 on page 22).

Some town clerks in colonial New England recorded vital information, but most states did not create statewide registration systems until the early 1900s.

What vital records are online or on CD-ROM?

States with long runs of vital records widely accessible in electronic databases include Alabama, California, Connecticut, Florida, Georgia, Illinois, Indiana, Kentucky, Louisiana, Maine, Massachusetts, Michigan, Minnesota, Montana, North Carolina, Ohio, Oregon, Rhode Island, South Dakota, Texas, Virginia, Washington, and Wisconsin.

Some vital records databases from the nineteenth century and earlier were compiled from church records and other sources.

What vital records are not online or on CD-ROM?

Few vital records from two large states, New York and Pennsylvania, have been published online or on CD-ROM.

Most vital records online and on CD-ROM are merely indexes or partial

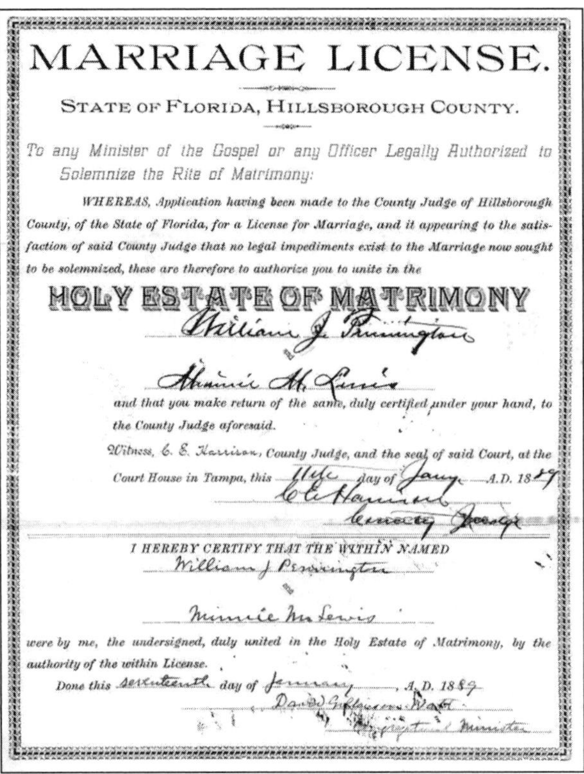

MARRIAGE LICENSE.

STATE OF FLORIDA, HILLSBOROUGH COUNTY.

To any Minister of the Gospel or any Officer Legally Authorized to Solemnize the Rite of Matrimony:

WHEREAS, Application having been made to the County Judge of Hillsborough County, of the State of Florida, for a License for Marriage, and it appearing to the satisfaction of said County Judge that no legal impediments exist to the Marriage now sought to be solemnized, these are therefore to authorize you to unite in the

HOLY ESTATE OF MATRIMONY

William J. Pennington

&

Minnie M. Lewis

and that you make return of the same, duly certified under your hand, to the County Judge aforesaid.

Witness, E. E. Harrison, County Judge, and the seal of said Court, at the Court House in Tampa, this 11th *day of* Jany *A.D. 18*89

E. E. Harrison

County Judge

I HEREBY CERTIFY THAT THE WITHIN NAMED

William J Pennington

&

Minnie M. Lewis

were by me, the undersigned, duly united in the Holy Estate of Matrimony, by the authority of the within License.

Done this seventeenth *day of* January, *A.D. 18*89

Figure 3-1
Hillsborough County (Fla.) Marriage Record <www.lib.usf.edu/ldsu/digitalcollections/H19/images/1889/00008.jpg>, ID 1082. Special Collections Department, University of South Florida Library <www.lib.usf.edu/spccoll>.

transcriptions, not digital images of the actual records. They do not include all the information from the original records.

VERIFYING VITAL RECORDS FROM CD-ROMS AND THE WEB

Important

When you find a birth, marriage, divorce, or death record in a CD-ROM or online database, **always check the original record to make sure the information was copied correctly.** You might also find more details in the original record. Sometimes the database entry includes a complete source citation, including

FIND VITAL RECORDS ON THE WEB

You can use an Internet search engine like Google <www.google.com> to find vital records on the Web. Search on "vital records," "birth records," "marriage records," "divorce records," or "death records" and the name of a county or a state. If the county is a common name you could include both the county and state in the query. You also could search on the name of a town, especially if it's a town in New England. For example, you could search on Marriage Records Spotsylvania to find marriage records in Spotsylvania County, Virginia, or on Death Records San Francisco to find death records in San Francisco.

a book's name, author, publisher, and a page number, or a document's volume and page number and the courthouse or repository that holds it. Unfortunately, electronic databases often provide little or no clue as to where the information was obtained.

If the database doesn't cite an exact source, you may need to do some detective work to verify the information. Here's an example: The Family Tree Maker (Genealogy.com) CD-ROM titled *Maryland, North Carolina, and Virginia, 1624–1915 Marriage Index*, has this marriage: "Samuel Phillips and Elizabeth Brooks, married Mar. 19, 1724, Cecil County, Maryland." Clicking the on-screen tab for the Introduction displays this explanation: "The information on this CD is extracted from original county records, not from a microfilm set. To obtain additional information regarding a marriage, please contact the appropriate county clerk." You could go ahead and contact the county official in Cecil County, Maryland, but first you might check other sources that could verify the information faster and cheaper.

The International Genealogical Index (IGI) <www.familysearch.org>, for example, is a database that contains millions of births and marriages, some of which were extracted from original records and published transcriptions. The IGI has two entries for the Phillips/Brooks marriage:

1. Samuel Phillips, born 30 November 1689 at North Farnham Parish, Richmond, Virginia, was married 19 March 1723 at Saint Maryannes Parish, Cecil County, Maryland, to Ann Elizabeth Brooks, born 1699 in Prince George's County, Maryland. The message with this entry says, "Record submitted after 1991 by a member of the LDS Church. No additional information is available."

2. Samuel Phillips and Elizabeth Brooks were married 19 March 1724 at Saint Maryannes Parish, Cecil County, Maryland. The entry indicates that the source call number is Family History Library microfilm 0013887 item 2. Click on the source call number and then on item 2 and you'll find that the marriage was extracted from this source: Church records, 1718–1799, St. Mary Ann's Parish (Cecil County, Maryland: Protestant Episcopal). You can print this bibliographic reference and take it to a Family History Center where you can order the microfilm on loan and view the original church records when the film arrives.

If the IGI hadn't led you to the source record, you could have looked for it in the Family History Library Catalog <www.familysearch.org>. Under Family History Library System, click on Search the Family History Library Catalog for records and resources. Click on Place Search, and since you know the county, but not the parish, type Cecil in the first box and Maryland in the second box. Then select Maryland, Cecil. Maryland county clerks weren't required to issue marriage licenses until 1777, so church records are the best place to check for a marriage before that year. Click on either Maryland, Cecil—Church Records or Maryland, Cecil—Church Records—Indexes. You'll find that the Family History Library has records from both

St. Mary Ann's Parish and St. Stephen's Parish for the year 1724. You could order those microfilms and search for the marriage of Samuel Phillips and Elizabeth Brooks. Later births and marriages in the IGI might have been abstracted from records kept by government officials. In the Family History Library Catalog, under your locality of interest, check the Vital Records and Vital Records—Indexes headings for those records.

KEY DATABASES

Transcripts and Abstracts

Michigan Genealogical Death Indexing System

<www.mdch.state.mi.us/pha/osr/gendisx/index.htm>

This database contains complete transcriptions of 170,000 death records from 1867 to 1884 (see Figure 3-2 below).

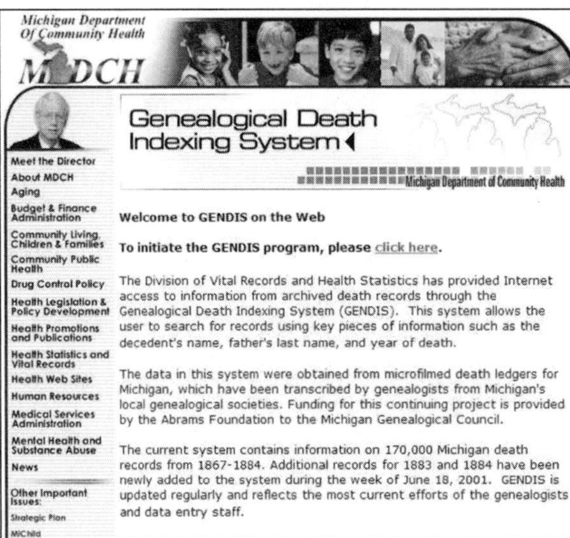

Figure 3-2
Michigan Genealogical Death Indexing System.

South Dakota Birth Records

<www.state.sd.us/doh/VitalRec/birthrecords/index.cfm>

This file has abstracts of more than 100,000 records of births occurring over 100 years ago. The birth certificate may contain more information, and you can request a copy online for $10 (see Figure 3-3 on page 25).

Databases and Indexes

Ancestry.com U.S. Records Collection

Vital records databases on Ancestry.com range from colonial New England town records to 1.8 million nineteenth-century Wisconsin records, and millions of twentieth-century records from Alabama, California, Connecticut, Florida, Georgia, Indiana, Kentucky, Louisiana, Michigan, North Carolina, Ohio, Oregon, Rhode Island, and Texas (see Figure 3-4 on page 25).

Figure 3-3 South Dakota Birth Records.

Ancestry.com.
The No. 1 Source for Family History Online
Home | Search Records | Family Trees | Message Boards | Genealogy Help | Ancestry Shops | ?
Become an Ancestry.com Subscriber
Current Customers Login Here!
Find Your Ancestors Now!
Enter Your Ancestor's Name
Advanced Search
Given Name(s) Last Name
Search ››
Give the Gift of Ancestry.com
Give the next family heirloom....your family history Click here.
Homeland Sweepstakes
Sign up today for a chance to win a trip to your ancestral homeland. Sign up now.
Things to do @ Ancestry.com
Search Historical Records
• U.S. Census Records NEW
• Birth, Marriage & Death Records
• Historical Newspaper Archives
more...
Build A Family Tree
• FREE Genealogy Software
• Online Family Tree
• Ancestry World Tree
more...
Genealogy Search by Location
• US Genealogy Records by State
• UK & Irish Genealogy
Ancestry Message Boards
• Surname Message Boards
• Locality Message Boards
What's New?
WWI Draft Registration Cards
Genetic Genealogy
U.S. Census Records:
• 1930 Census Index (Massachusetts, Michigan, Idaho, Connecticut, Georgia, New Jersey, Rhode Island, New Hampshire, Maine, Missouri, Delaware, Utah, District of Columbia)
• 1930 Census Images (All states)
• 1920 Census Index (All states)
all census years...
New Records Today!
• Marion Star, The (Marion, Ohio)
• Pendleton, Oregon City Directory, 1975
• New York Historic Homes and Family History, Volume I-II

Figure 3-4 Ancestry.com.

FamilySearch
<www.familysearch.org>

This popular Web site from the Church of Jesus Christ of Latter-day Saints features the Internet International Genealogical Index (including over 62 million U.S. birth and marriage records, abstracted from original records or submitted by church members) and the Social Security Death Index (mostly records since 1962) (see Figure 3-5 on page 26). The Vital Records Index North America on CD-ROM covers births and marriages in the United States and Canada from 1631 to 1888, includes 4 million names, and costs $13.50.

Genealogy.com CD-ROMs and Genealogy Library
<www.genealogy.com>

Genealogy.com's databases include indexes to thousands of marriages in Alabama, Indiana, Maryland, Massachusetts, Missouri, New York, Ohio, Tennessee, Texas, and West Virginia (see Figure 3-6 on page 26).

Figure 3-5
FamilySearch.

Figure 3-6
Genealogy.com.

Illinois State Archives Databases
<www.library.sos.state.il.us/departments/archives/databases.html>

Researchers with Illinois ancestry will find a treasure trove of information in these databases. Statewide indexes cover marriages from 1763 to 1900 and deaths to 1950. Indexes to county birth records round out the collection (see Figure 3-7 on page 27).

Library of Virginia Digital Library Program
<www.lva.lib.va.us>

This tremendous site features more than eighty databases, indexes, and finding aids. Key resources include indexes to marriage records from 1630 to 1876 and death records from 1853 to 1896 (see Figure 3-8 on page 27).

Minnesota Death Certificates
<http://people.mnhs.org/dci>

The Minnesota Historical Society's index to Minnesota death certificates

Figure 3-7 Illinois State Archives Databases.

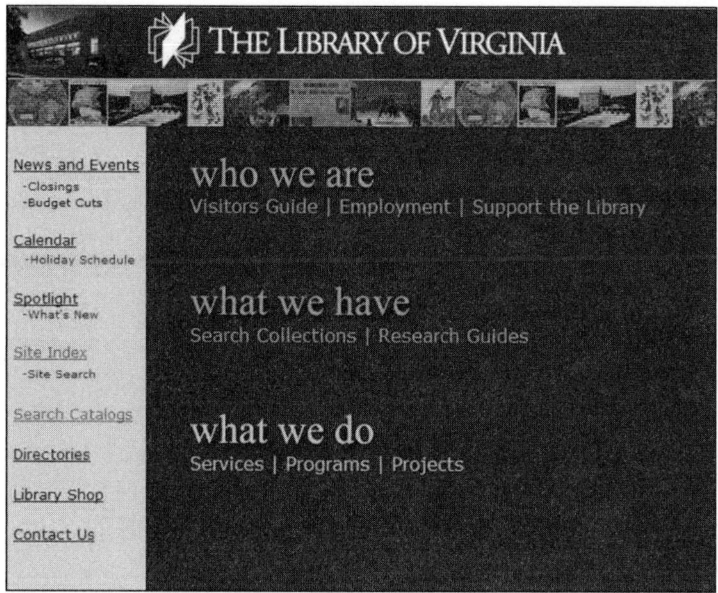

Figure 3-8 Library of Virginia Digital Library Program.

covers the years 1907 through 1996. The Society will provide a copy of a death certificate for $8. You can also borrow microfilmed death records through your local public library for $3 per roll, plus $2.50 for shipping and handling for each order of up to six rolls (see Figure 3-9 on page 28).

New England Marriages Prior to 1700

This CD-ROM, $89.99 from the New England Historic Genealogical Society <www.newenglandancestors.org>, has the complete text of Clarence A. Torrey's twelve-volume manuscript of marriages compiled from many

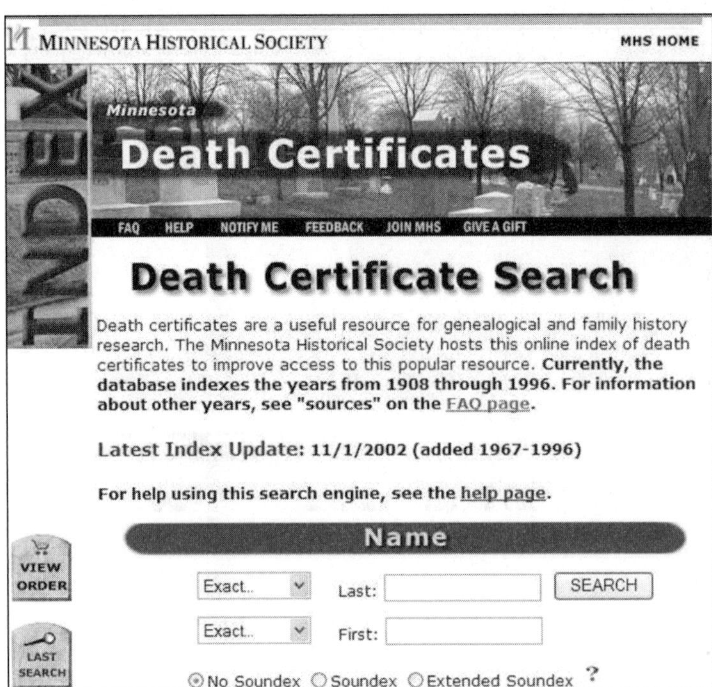

Figure 3-9 Minnesota Death Certificates.

sources. With about 37,000 records, it contains about 99 percent of all marriages of New Englanders before 1700. Unlike the book version, the CD-ROM includes a complete bibliography of source citations.

RootsWeb
<http://searches.rootsweb.com>

Like several other Web sites, RootsWeb has the Social Security Death Index (see below), as well as four large databases of death records: California (over 9 million records from 1940 to 1997), Kentucky (almost 3 million records from 1911 to 2000), Maine (over 400,000 records from 1960 to 1997), and Texas (almost 4 million records from 1964 to 1998). Unfortunately, because of concerns over privacy, RootsWeb has removed the indexes to twentieth-century California and Texas birth records (see Figure 3-10 on page 29).

Social Security Death Index
<www.ancestry.com>, <www.familysearch.org>, <www.familytreelegends.com>, <www.newenglandancestors.org/research/database/ss>, or <http://ssdi.rootsweb.com>

The SSDI lists over 70 million people who had Social Security numbers and whose death was reported to the Social Security Administration (see Figure 3-11 on page 29). The database primarily covers deaths since 1962 when the SSA started computerizing its records, but some date back to the passage of the Social Security Act of 1935. Most entries include an exact date of birth, the month or exact date of death, and the last place of residence. Family Tree Legends' version of the Social Security Death Index offers the most search options.

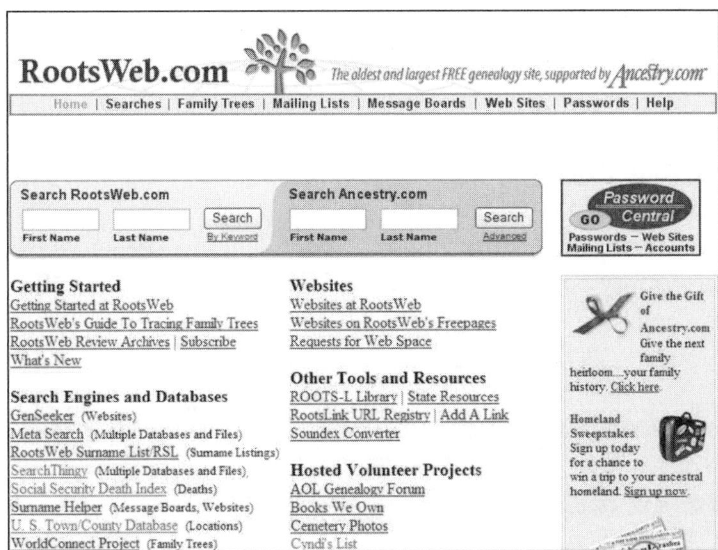

Figure 3-10
RootsWeb.

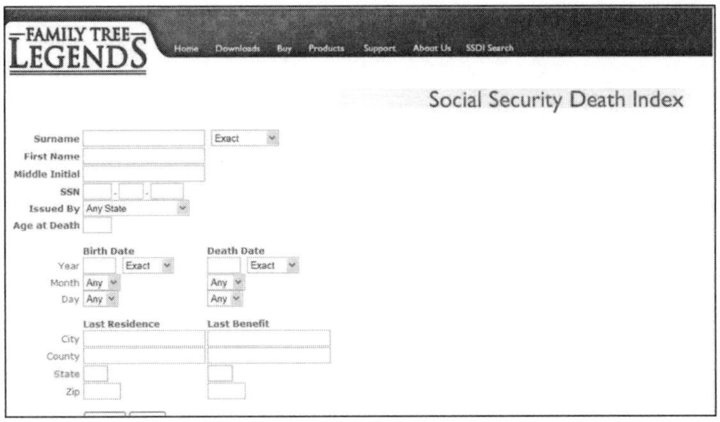

Figure 3-11
Family Tree Legends' Social Security Death Index.

The original Social Security application includes the applicant's date and place of birth, father's name, and mother's maiden name. You can request a copy for $27 and the SSDI search sites on Ancestry.com, Family Tree Legends, and RootsWeb automatically generate letters for you to send to

FIND A WOMAN IN THE SOCIAL SECURITY DEATH INDEX EVEN IF YOU DON'T KNOW HER MARRIED NAME

Whether you search the Social Security Death Index on Ancestry.com, FamilySearch, Family Tree Legends, New England Ancestors, or RootsWeb, you don't need to include a last name in your query. You may get a lot of matches, especially if the first name is common, but you can narrow the search if you know the year of birth or death, the state where the SS number was issued, the last place of residence or the middle initial. (Many records in the SSDI do not include a middle initial.)

the Social Security Administration. You can also use information from the SSDI to request a death certificate, which usually gives the parents' names and more details.

USGenWeb Project State Pages
<www.usgenweb.org/statelinks-table.html>

Researchers have contributed many vital records indexes to USGenWeb's state pages and the county pages linked to them. The records come from a variety of sources, including county records offices and books (see Figure 3-12 below).

The USGenWeb Project

Visit The USGenWeb Project State Pages

Alabama	Alaska	Arizona	Arkansas
California	Colorado	Connecticut	Delaware
District of Columbia	Florida	Georgia	Hawaii
Idaho	Illinois	Indiana	Iowa
Kansas	Kentucky	Louisiana	Maine
Maryland	Massachusetts	Michigan	Minnesota
Mississippi	Missouri	Montana	Nebraska
Nevada	New Hampshire	New Jersey	New Mexico
New York	North Carolina	North Dakota	Ohio
Oklahoma	Oklahoma/Indian Territory	Oregon	Pennsylvania
Rhode Island	South Carolina	South Dakota	Tennessee
Texas	Utah	Vermont	Virginia

Figure 3-12
USGenWeb Project State Pages.

Tip

SEEKING AN ELUSIVE WOMAN?

You can even search for a woman by her maiden name in the Vitalsearch index to California deaths from 1940 to 2000.

Vitalsearch
<www.vitalsearch-worldwide.com>

This massive set of databases indexes over 80 million vital records from nine states. More records are coming, including Alabama deaths from 1941 to 1949. Access to most databases is free. Paying customers ($24.95/quarter

VITALSEARCH VITAL RECORDS INDEXES

STATE	BIRTHS	MARRIAGES	DIVORCES	DEATHS
Alabama				1940
California	1905–2001	1949–1986		1905–2000
Florida		1970–2001	1970–2001	1877–1916, 1999–2001
Georgia		1997–1998		
Kentucky	1911–2002	1973–2002	1999–2002	1900–2002
Oregon		1999–2001	2001	1951–1960, 1999–2001
Texas	1926–1998	1967–2001	1968–2000	1956–2000
Washington				1960–1974
Wisconsin				1959–1979

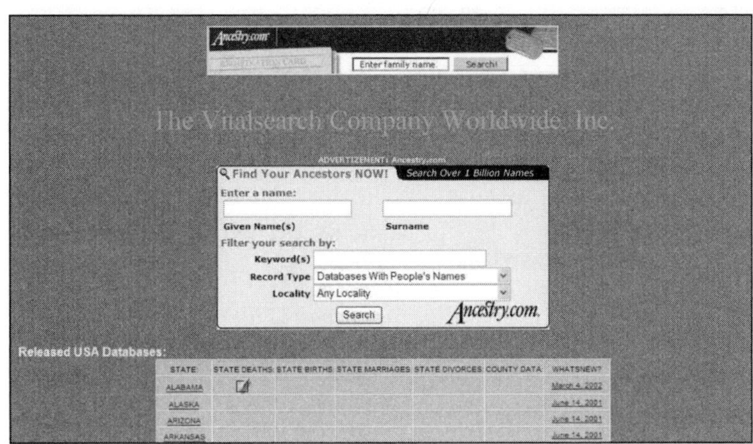

Figure 3-13
Vitalsearch.

or $57.95/year) avoid pop-up ads and can view more indexes (see Figure 3-13 above).

GUIDES AND RESOURCES

Cyndi's List of Genealogy Sites on the Internet

<www.cyndislist.com>
Check especially the categories for Births & Baptisms, Death Records, Marriages, and Vital Records.

Online Searchable Death Indexes for the USA

<home.att.net/~wee-monster/deathrecords.html>
Links to major online death indexes and databases categorized by state.

Vital Records Information, United States

<www.vitalrec.com>
This site tells you where to obtain vital records in U.S. states and territories and how much they cost.

Where to Write for Vital Records

<www.cdc.gov/nchs>
Click on "Help obtaining birth, death, marriage, or divorce certificates." Maintained by the National Center for Health Statistics, this site gives the current fees and addresses for getting copies of vital records in U.S. states and territories.

SUGGESTED READING

Carmack, Sharon DeBartolo. *Your Guide to Cemetery Research*. Cincinnati: Betterway Books, 2002. See especially chapter one, which describes many kinds of records associated with death, including autopsy and coroners' records, obituaries, funeral home records, mortality schedules, and more.

DATABASE DIRECTORY Regional, National, and International Vital Records

These directories do not include URLs for databases in the Family and Local Histories collection. See page 18 for instructions on "searching an individual database" in Family and Local Histories. Entries are arranged by title. **Type**: Digital Images, Transcript, Database, Abstracts, or Index; Births (B), Marriages (M), Divorces (DI), Deaths (D), Burials (BU).

Alabama, Georgia, South Carolina, 1641–1944, Marriage Index
Type: Index; M
Year Range: 1641–1944
CD-ROM: $29.99, Genealogy.com, CD #003
Notes, URL: 379,000 names from church and government sources. <www.genealogy.com/003facd.html>

American Marriages Before 1699
Type: Database; M
Year Range: Up to 1699
Online: Ancestry
Notes, URL: Over 10,000 entries. Mostly from Mass., some from N.Y. and Penn. Original data: Clemens, William Montgomery. *American Marriage Records Before 1699.* <www.ancestry.com/search/rectype/inddbs/2081.htm>

Anybirthday.com
Type: Database; B
Year Range: 1900–pres.
Online: Free
Notes, URL: Birthdays of over 135 million living persons. <www.anybirthday.com>

Arizona, California, Idaho, and Nevada, 1850–1951 Marriage Index
Type: Index; M
Year Range: 1850–1951
CD-ROM: $29.99, Genealogy.com, CD #225
Notes, URL: <www.genealogy.com/225facd.html>

Arkansas, Missouri, Mississippi, Texas, 1766–1981 Marriage Index
Type: Index; M
Year Range: 1766–1981
CD-ROM: $29.99, Genealogy.com, CD #005
Notes, URL: 1,047,000 names from 161 counties. <www.genealogy.com/005facd.html>

AZ, CO, NE, NM, OR, & WA 1727–1900, Marriage Index
Type: Index; M
Year Range: 1727–1900
CD-ROM: $29.99, Genealogy.com, CD #405
Online: Genealogy Library
Notes, URL: 154,000 names. <www.genealogy.com/405facd.html>

The BMD Project
Type: Database; B-M-D
Online: Free
Notes, URL: Births, marriages, and deaths submitted by visitors to the site. Records from Fla., Ga., Ky., Miss., N.Y., N.C., Ohio, Okla., Tenn., Va., & Wis. <www.bmdproject.com>

California, Oregon, Nevada Births and Deaths
Type: Transcripts; B-D
Year Range: 1753–1996
CD-ROM: $69 (Win), Global Data
Notes, URL: Misc. births & deaths in Calif. & Ore., 1753–1988. About 1 million marriages in Las Vegas, Clark Co., Nev., 1983–1996. <www.gencd.com>

Directory of Deceased American Physicians, 1804–1929
Type: Extracts from a book; B-D
Year Range: 1804–1929
CD-ROM: $39.99, Genealogy.com, CD #507
Online: Genealogy Library
Notes, URL: 149,000 physicians who died between 1804 & 1929. From the two-volume set edited by Arthur W. Hafner. <www.genealogy.com/507facd.html>

District of Columbia, Delaware, Maryland, & Virginia, 1740–1920 Marriage Index
Type: Index; M
Year Range: 1740–1920
CD-ROM: $29.99, Genealogy.com, CD #399
Online: Genealogy Library
Notes, URL: 250,000 names. <www.genealogy.com/399facd.html>

Genealogy Today—Online Records
Type: Index; M
Online: Free
Notes, URL: Early marriage records for Ala., Ind., Iowa, Ky., Miss., N. C., Tenn., & W. Va. <www.genealogytoday.com/genealogy/enoch/records.html>

IL, IN, KY, OH, TN, 1720–1926 Marriage Index
Type: Index; M
Year Range: 1720–1926
CD-ROM: $29.99, Genealogy.com, CD #002
Notes, URL: 738,000 names. <www.genealogy.com/002facd.html>

Illinois & Indiana, 1790–1850 Marriage Index
Type: Index; M
Year Range: 1790–1850
CD-ROM: $29.99, Genealogy.com, CD #228
Notes, URL: 380,000 names. <www.genealogy.com/228facd.html>

International Genealogical Index (IGI)
Type: Database; B-M
Year Range: Up to 1920
CD-ROM: Family History Centers
Online: FamilySearch
Notes, URL: About 725 million names. <www.familysearch.org>

KY, NC, TN, VA, and WV, 1728–1850, Marriage Index
Type: Index; M
Year Range: 1728–1850
CD-ROM: $29.99, Genealogy.com, CD #229
Notes, URL: 1,164,000 names from 333 counties. <www.genealogy.com/229facd.html>

Marriages: AR, CA, IA, LA, MN, MO, OR, TX 1728–1850
Type: Index; M
Year Range: 1728–1850
CD-ROM: $15, Global Data
Notes, URL: Misc. marriages. <www.gencd.com>

Maryland, North Carolina, and Virginia, 1624–1915 Marriage Index
Type: Index; M
Year Range: 1624–1915
CD-ROM: $29.99, Genealogy.com, CD #004
Notes, URL: About 500,000 names. <www.genealogy.com/004facd.html>

Mayflower Vital Records, Deeds, and Wills, 1600s–1900s
Type: Digital images of books; B-M-D
Year Range: 1600s–1900s
CD-ROM: $29.99, Genealogy.com, CD #167
Online: Genealogy Library
Notes, URL: Images of pages from five books with 82,000 names. <www.genealo242facd.html>

New England Genealogy By Ray Brown
Type: Transcripts; B-M-D
Year Range: Up to 1886
Online: Free
Notes, URL: Vital records from many New England towns. <www.rays-place.com>

New England Marriages Prior to 1700
Type: Database; M
Year Range: Up to 1699
CD-ROM: $89.99 (Mac/Win), NEHGS
Notes, URL: 37,000 marriages (about 99 percent of all marriages of New Englanders before 1700). The CD includes source references not in the book version. Item SCDTY. <www.newenglandancestors.org>

NY, NJ, PA Marriages 1700s–1893
Type: Index; M
Year Range: 1700s–1893
CD-ROM: $39, Global Data
Notes, URL: Misc. marriages. <www.gencd.com>

Orena V. Grant genealogical collection (marriages and cemetery records): from southeastern, north, and south central states
Type: Digital images of pages containing transcripts; M
Online: F&LH
Notes, URL: Marriage records from Ala., Ind., La., Miss., Ohio, & W. Va.

RootsWeb: Death Records
Type: Index; D
Online: Free
Notes, URL: Over 400,000 records contributed by users. <http://userdb.rootsweb.com/deaths>

RootsWeb: Early Birth Records
Type: Index; B
Online: Free
Notes, URL: About 200,000 records contributed by users. <http://userdb.rootsweb.com/births>

RootsWeb: Marriage Records
Type: Index; M
Online: Free
Notes, URL: Over 500,000 records contributed by users. <http://userdb.rootsweb.com/marriages>

Selected States, 1728–1850 Marriage Index
Type: Index; M
Year Range: 1728–1850
CD-ROM: $19.99, Genealogy.com, CD #227
Notes, URL: 215,000 names from Ark., Calif., Iowa, La., Minn., Mo., Ore., & Tex. <www.genealogy.com/227facd.html>

U.S. and International, 1340–1980 Marriage Records
Type: Index; M
Year Range: 1340–1980
CD-ROM: $29.99, Genealogy.com, CD #403
Online: IPR
Notes, URL: 1.4 million names from the U.S. and 32 other countries. <www.genealogy.com/403facd.html>

United States Marriage Index, 1691–1850
Type: Index; M
Year Range: 1691–1850
CD-ROM: $19.95 (Win), HeritageQuest
Notes, URL: About 584,537 marriages from 18 states and the District of Columbia. <www.heritagequest.com>

U.S. 1850–1880, Mortality Index
Type: Index; D
Year Range: 1850–1880
CD-ROM: $19.99, Genealogy.com, CD #164
Notes, URL: More than 382,000 records. <www.genealogy.com/164facd.html>

USGenWeb Archives Marriage Project
Type: Transcripts; M
Year Range: All dates
Online: Free
Notes, URL: Records submitted by researchers. <www.rootsweb.com/~usgenweb/marriages>

USGenWeb Project State Pages
Type: Transcripts; indexes; B-M-DI-D-BU
Year Range: All dates
Online: Free
Notes, URL: The state pages and county pages linked to them have many vital records. <www.usgenweb.org/statelinks-table.html>

Vital Records Index North America
Type: Index; B-M
Year Range: 1631–1888
CD-ROM: $13.50, FamilySearch
Notes, URL: 4 million names from the U.S. & Canada. <www.familysearch.org>

Western States Marriage Records Index
Type: Index; M
Year Range: Up to 1940 & later
Online: Free
Notes, URL: 270,000 marriage records in Ariz., Idaho, Nev., Utah, Wyo., eastern Wash., eastern Ore., and selected counties in Calif. <http://abish.byui.edu/specialCollections/fhc/gbsearch.htm>

DATABASE DIRECTORY Local and Statewide Vital Records

Arranged by place and year range. **Type:** Digital Images, Transcript, Database, Abstracts, Index; Births (B), Marriages (M), Divorces (DI), Deaths (D), Burials (BU).

Alabama
Type: Index; M
Year Range: Up to 1825
Online: Free
Title: Alabama Marriages before 1825
Notes, URL: <www.censusdiggins.com/alabama_marriages.html>

Alabama
Type: Index; M
Year Range: Up to 1825
CD-ROM: Ancestry
Title: Marriage—Alabama to 1825
Notes, URL: Over 12,000 names. <www.ancestry.com/search/rectype/inddbs/2080a.htm>

Alabama
Type: Index; M
Year Range: 1800–1900
CD-ROM: $29.99, Genealogy.com, CD #248
Online: Genealogy Library
Title: Alabama, 1800–1900 Marriage Index
Notes, URL: 179,000 names from 41 counties. <www.genealogy.com/248facd.html>

Alabama
Type: Transcripts; M
Year Range: 1800–1920
CD-ROM: $26.95 (Win), Ancestry, item 2088, <http://shops.ancestry.com>. Search on "Alabama marriages."
Online: Ancestry
Title: Alabama Vital Records: Marriages, 1808–1920
Notes, URL: Over 162,000 records in 54 of 67 counties. Source: Dodd, Jordan R. *Early American Marriages: Alabama, 1800 to 1920.* <www.ancestry.com/search/rectype/inddbs/4192a.htm>

Alabama
Type: Transcripts; DI
Year Range: 1803–1816
Online: Free
Title: Divorces: Mississippi Territory—Legislative Records Pertaining to Alabama 1803–1816
Notes, URL: <www.trackingyourroots.com/anderson.htm>

Alabama
Type: Transcripts; M
Year Range: 1809–1967
Online: Free
Title: Alabama Marriage Records
Notes, URL: <www.idreamof.com/marriage/al.html>

Alabama
Type: Abstracts; DI
Year Range: 1818–1846
Online: Free
Title: Alabama Acts: Divorces
Notes, URL: <www.trackingyourroots.com/aldivorc.htm> and <www.trackingyourroots.com/aldiv2.htm>

Alabama
Type: Transcript; D
Year Range: 1860
Online: F&LH
Title: Federal death records of Alabama, 1860 (Autauga, Baldwin, Barbour, Bibb, Blount, & Butler Counties)
Notes, URL: Transcript of census mortality schedule.

Alabama
Type: Index; D
Year Range: 1908–1959
CD-ROM: $26.95 (Win), Ancestry, item #2335, <http://shops.ancestry.com>. Search on "Alabama deaths."
Online: Ancestry
Title: Alabama Vital Records: Deaths 1908–59
Notes, URL: 1,363,335 records. <www.ancestry.com/search/rectype/inddbs/5188a.htm>

Alabama
Type: Index; D
Year Range: 1940–1949
Online: Free
Title: The Vitalsearch Company Worldwide, Inc.
Notes, URL: In progress. <www.vitalsearch-worldwide.com>

Alabama, Autauga Co.
Type: Index; M
Year Range: 1832–1897
Online: Free
Title: Autauga County, Alabama Marriages
Notes, URL: <http://searches.rootsweb.com/cgi-bin/autauga/auta-mar.pl>

Alabama, Bibb Co.
Type: Index; M
Year Range: 1820–1862
Online: Free
Title: Bibb County, AL Marriages 1820–1862
Notes, URL: <www.rootsweb.com/~aljeffer/bibb/marriage.html>

Alabama, Clarke Co.
Type: Index; M
Year Range: 1814–1834
Online: Free
Title: Clarke County, Alabama Marriages, 1814–1834
Notes, URL: <www.rootsweb.com/~alclarke/cmariage.htm>

Alabama, Clarke Co.
Type: Index; M
Year Range: 1814–1834
Online: Free
Title: Clarke County, Alabama Marriages
Notes, URL: <http://vidas.rootsweb.com/ClkMar1.html>

Alabama, Dallas Co.
Type: Index; M
Year Range: 1818–1845
Online: Free
Title: Dallas County, Alabama: Marriages—Appearing in Marriage Book I: 1818–1845
Notes, URL: <ftp://ftp.rootsweb.com/pub/usgenweb/al/dallas/vitals/marriages/1818-1845.txt>

Alabama, Escambia Co.
Type: Index; B-M-D
Year Range: 1879–1919
Online: Free
Title: Escambia County Vital Records—Births, Marriages, Deaths
Notes, URL: Births, 1914–1919. Marriages, 1879–1892. Deaths, 1914–1919. <www.rootsweb.com/~usgenweb/al/escambia/vitals.htm>

Alabama, Greene Co.
Type: Index; M
Year Range: 1823–1860
Online: Free
Title: Greene County, AL Marriages 1823–1860

Notes, URL: <www.rootsweb.com/~alpicken/greene/marriage.html>

Alabama, Jackson Co.
Type: Index; M
Year Range: 1851–1871
Online: Free
Title: Jackson County, Alabama Marriages
Notes, URL: Surnames A–C, 1851–1856, 1859–1871. <www.genealogytoday.com/pub/alamarr2.htm>

Alabama, Jackson Co.
Type: Index; M
Year Range: 1851–1871
Online: Free
Title: Jackson County, Alabama Marriages
Notes, URL: Surnames D–H, 1851–1856, 1859–1871. <www.genealogytoday.com/pub/ALAMARR3.HTM>

Alabama, Jefferson Co.
Type: Index; M
Year Range: 1815–1899
Online: Free
Title: Jefferson County, AL Marriages 1815–1899
Notes, URL: <www.rootsweb.com/~aljeffer/jeffco/marriage.html>

Alabama, Lawrence Co.
Type: Index; M
Year Range: 1818–1989
Online: Free
Title: Lawrence Co., Alabama Marriages
Notes, URL: 4,000 marriages. <www.rootsweb.com/~allawren/marriage.htm>

Alabama, Marshall Co.
Type: Index; M
Year Range: 1836–1847
Online: Free
Title: Marshall County Marriages
Notes, URL: <www.rootsweb.com/~almarsha/marriages/marriage.html>

Alabama, Mobile Co.
Type: Digital images of books; M
Year Range: 1700s–1800s
CD-ROM: $29.99, Genealogy.com, CD #527
Online: Genealogy Library
Title: Early Alabama, Arkansas, and Mississippi Settlers, 1700s–1800s
Notes, URL: 12 books, including *Marriages of Mobile County, Alabama, 1813–1855*, by Clinton P. King & Meriem A. Barlow. <www.genealogy.com/527facd.html>

Alabama, Shelby Co.
Type: Index; D
Year Range: 1902–1904
Online: Free
Title: Shelby County Alabama, February 1902–May 1904, Register of Deaths Index
Notes, URL: <www.rootsweb.com/~alshelby/deathIndex1.html>

Alabama, Sumter Co.
Type: Index; M
Year Range: 1833–1850
Online: Free
Title: Sumter County, AL Marriages 1833–1850
Notes, URL: <www.rootsweb.com/~alpicken/sumter/marriage.html>

Alabama, Tuscaloosa Co.
Type: Index; M
Year Range: 1821–1860
Online: Free
Title: Tuscaloosa County, AL Marriages 1821–1860
Notes, URL: <www.rootsweb.com/~aljeffer/tuscal/marriage.html>

Arkansas
Type: Index; M
Year Range: Up to 1850
Online: Ancestry
Title: Marriages—Arkansas to 1850
Notes, URL: Over 18,000 names. <www.ancestry.com/search/rectype/inddbs/2082a.htm>

Arkansas
Type: Index; M
Year Range: 1779–1992
CD-ROM: $29.99 (Win/Power Mac), Genealogy.com, CD #006
Title: Arkansas, 1779–1992 Marriage Index
Notes, URL: 308,000 names. <www.genealogy.com/006facd.html>

Arkansas
Type: Index; M
Year Range: 1793–1910
CD-ROM: $26.95 (Win), Ancestry, item #2289, <http://shops.ancestry.com>. Search on "Arkansas marriages."
Title: Arkansas Vital Records: Marriages
Notes, URL: 277,000 records in 48 counties, 700,000 names. 90% of the records date from 1850 to 1900.

Arkansas
Type: Index; M
Year Range: 1850—1900
CD-ROM: $29.99, Genealogy.com, CD #244
Online: Genealogy Library
Title: Arkansas, 1850–1900 Marriage Index
Notes, URL: 287,000 names. <www.genealogy.com/244facd.html>

Arkansas
Type: Index; M
Year Range: 1851–1900
Online: Ancestry
Title: Arkansas Marriages, 1851–1900
Notes, URL: Records from 40 counties. <www.ancestry.com/search/rectype/inddbs/4383a.htm>

Arkansas, Carroll Co.
Type: Index; M
Year Range: 1869–1930
Online: Free
Title: Carroll County Arkansas Marriage Records, Eastern District Grooms Index, 1869–1930
Notes, URL: Includes links to Eastern District Brides Index & Western District Index. <www.rootsweb.com/~arcchs/MARA.html>

Arkansas, Jackson Co.
Type: Index; DI
Year Range: 1832–1890
Online: Free
Title: Divorces of Jackson Co. 1832–1890
Notes, URL: <www.rootsweb.com/~arjackso/divorces.htm>

Arkansas, Prairie Co.
Type: Index; D
Year Range: 1914–1950
Online: Free
Title: Prairie County, Arkansas, Death Certificates Index
Notes, URL: <www.rootsweb.com/~arprairi/Death/deathltr.htm>

Arkansas, Stone Co.
Type: Index; M-DI
Year Range: 1873–1899
Online: Free
Title: Stone County Arkansas Genealogical Society
Notes, URL: Marriages, 1873–1874. Divorces, 1874–1899. <www.rootsweb.com/~arscgs>

California
Type: Index; D
Year Range: Up to 1905
Online: Free
Title: California Pre 1905 Death Index
Notes, URL: Selected counties. <www.rootsweb.com/~cabf1905>

California
Type: Index; B

Year Range: 1905–1910
Online: Ancestry (free)
Title: California Birth Index, 1905–10
Notes, URL: Records kept by the state registrar of vital statistics. <www.ancestry.com/search/rectype/inddbs/5247.htm>

California
Type: Index; B
Year Range: 1905–1919
CD-ROM: $49, Global Data
Title: California State Birth Index 1905–1919
Notes, URL: <www.gencd.com>

California
Type: Index; B-M-D
Year Range: 1905–2000
Online: Vitalsearch (free/subscription)
Title: Vitalsearch—California (USA): California State Vital Records
Notes, URL: Over 24 million births, 1905–1999. Over 4 million marriages, 1949–1986. Over 12 million deaths, 1905–2000. <www.vitalsearch-ca.com>

California
Type: Index; B
Year Range: 1940–1949
CD-ROM: $98, Global Data
Title: California State Birth Index 1940–1949
Notes, URL: 1,875,584 births. <www.gencd.com>

California
Type: Index; D
Year Range: 1940–1997
Online: Free
Title: California Death Records
Notes, URL: 9,366,786 records. <http://userdb.rootsweb.com/ca/death/search.cgi> or <http://vitals.rootsweb.com/ca/death/search.cgi?>

California
Type: Index; D
Year Range: 1940–1997
Online: Ancestry
Title: California Death Index, 1940–1997
Notes, URL: <www.ancestry.com/search/rectype/inddbs/5180.htm>

California, Calaveras Co., San Andreas
Type: Transcript; B
Year Range: 1874–1911
Online: Free
Title: San Andreas, Calaveras County, California—Births
Notes, URL: <ftp://ftp.rootsweb.com/pub/usgenweb/ca/calaveras/vitals/births.txt>

California, Madera Co.
Type: Index; M
Year Range: 1893–1905
Online: Free
Title: Madera County, California GenWeb: Madera Marriages 1893–1905
Notes, URL: <www.cagenweb.com/madera/MadMarriages.htm>

California, Mendocino Co., Mendocino
Type: Transcripts; B-M-D
Year Range: 1889–1979
CD-ROM: $29.50 (Mac or Win), Heritage Books
Title: HB Archives: Births, Deaths and Marriages on California's Mendocino Coast, Vols. 1-4
Notes, URL: Graphic image CD-ROM, 1,301 pp. Also, records of Mendocino Co. men in WWI. <www.heritagebooks.com>

California, Merced Co.
Type: Index; D
Year Range: 1852–1999
Online: Ancestry
Title: Merced County, California Deaths, 1852–1999
Notes, URL: Over 52,600 names. <www.ancestry.com/search/rectype/inddbs/4390.htm>

California, Napa Co.
Type: Index; B
Year Range: 1873–1905
Online: Free
Title: Index of births registered in Napa Co., CA, through 1905
Notes, URL: <www.napanet.net/~nvgbs/BIRTHS.htm>

California, Shasta Co.
Type: Index; M
Year Range: 1852–1904
Online: Ancestry
Title: Shasta County, California Marriages, 1852–1904
Notes, URL: 3,248 marriages. <www.ancestry.com/search/rectype/inddbs/3862.htm>

California, Sonoma Co.
Type: Transcripts; D
Year Range: 1873–1905
CD-ROM: $28.50 (Mac or Win), Heritage Books
Title: Heritage Books Archives: Sonoma County [CA] Records Volume I
Notes, URL: 6 books, including cemetery & death records, reconstructed 1890 census & homestead declarations. <www.heritagebooks.com>

California, Trinity Co.
Type: Index; B-M-D
Year Range: 1948–1999
Online: Free
Title: Trinity County Vital Records
Notes, URL: <http://halfile.trinitycounty.org>

California, Tulare Co.
Type: Index; M
Year Range: 1852–1893
Online: Free
Title: Tulare County Marriages 1852 to June, 1893
Notes, URL: <www.cagenweb.com/cpl/tulare/tckcm.htm>

California, Tulare Co.
Type: Index; M
Year Range: 1893–1909
Online: Free
Title: Tulare County Marriages July 1, 1893 to Dec. 31, 1909
Notes, URL: <www.cagenweb.com/cpl/tulare/tcm.htm>

Colorado
Type: Index; M
Year Range: 1859–1900
Online: Ancestry
Title: Colorado Marriages, 1859–1900
Notes, URL: Nearly 900 records from Arapahoe, Boulder, and Mesa Counties. <www.ancestry.com/search/rectype/inddbs/4364.htm>

Colorado
Type: Transcript; D
Year Range: 1870–1963
Online: Free
Title: Colorado Mining Fatalities (pre-1963)
Notes, URL: <www.denver.lib.co.us/ebranch/whg/datafile.html>

Colorado, Gilpin Co.
Type: Index; M
Year Range: 1864–1944
Online: Free
Title: Gilpin County Brides' And Groom's Marriage Index 1864–1944
Notes, URL: <www.colorado.gov/dpa/doit/archives/marriage/gilpin_index.htm>

Colorado, Kit Carson Co.
Type: Index; D
Year Range: 1893–1907
Online: Free
Title: Kit Carson County Death Register, 1893–1907
Notes, URL: 94 names. <www.colorado.gov/dpa/doit/archives/deaths/>

Colorado, Mineral Co.
Type: Indexes; B-M-DI-D
Year Range: 1892–1972
Online: Free
Title: Resources
Notes, URL: Births, 1892–1901. Marriages, 1893–1972. Divorces, 1892–1951. Deaths, 1896–1901, 1918. <www.comineral.homestead.com/resources.html>

Colorado, Rio Grande Co.
Type: Extracts; B-D
Year Range: 1885–1899
Online: Free
Title: Resources for Rio Grande County
Notes, URL: Misc. births, 1893–1898, & deaths, 1895–1899. 1885 mortality index. <www.riograndeco.homestead.com/resources.html>

Connecticut
Type: Index; M
Year Range: Up to 1850
Online: Ancestry
Title: Connecticut Marriages to 1850
Notes, URL: Records for Redding, Fairfield Co., & Mansfield, Tolland Co. <www.ancestry.com/search/rectype/inddbs/5318.htm>

Connecticut
Type: Indexes; M-D
Year Range: Up to 1996
CD-ROM: $26.95 (Win), Ancestry, item #2087, <http://shops.ancestry.com>. Search on "Connecticut marriages and deaths."
Online: Ancestry
Title: Connecticut Vital Records: Marriages & Deaths, Selected Years
Notes, URL: 57,700 marriages to 1800. Death Index 1949–1996 (1,258,000).

Connecticut
Type: Index; M
Year Range: 1635–1860
CD-ROM: $29.99
Online: Genealogy Library
Title: Connecticut, 1635–1860 Marriage Index
Notes, URL: 134,000 names. <www.genealogy.com/397facd.html>

Connecticut
Type: Abstracts; DI
Year Range: 1740–1922
CD-ROM: $37.50 (Mac or Win), Heritage Books
Title: HB Archives: Connecticut Vol. 2
Notes, URL: Includes divorces in Litchfield Co., 1752–1922, & Hartford Co., 1740–1849. <www.heritagebooks.com>

Connecticut
Type: Index; D
Year Range: 1949–2001
Online: Ancestry
Title: Connecticut Death Index, 1949–2001
Notes, URL: 1.4 million names. <www.ancestry.com/search/rectype/inddbs/4124a.htm>

Connecticut
Type: Index; M
Year Range: 1959–2001
Online: Ancestry
Title: Connecticut Marriage Index, 1959–2001
Notes, URL: <www.ancestry.com/search/rectype/inddbs/7158.htm>

Connecticut, Fairfield Co., Greenwich
Type: Abstracts; B-M-D
Year Range: 1670–1847
Online: NEHGS
Title: Vital Records of Greenwich, Connecticut, 1670–1847
Notes, URL: <www.newenglandancestors.org/research/database/vital_records_gr>

Connecticut, Fairfield Co., Newtown
Type: Transcript; B-M-D
Year Range: 1701–1891
Online: NEHGS
Title: Vital Records of Newtown, Connecticut, 1701–1891
Notes, URL: <www.newenglandancestors.org/research/database/newtonct>

Connecticut, Middlesex Co., Saybrook
Type: Text of a book; B-M-D
Year Range: 1647–1834
Online: Genealogy Library
Title: Saybrook, CT-Vital Records
Notes, URL: Select Records | Vital Records | Connecticut.

Connecticut, New Haven Co., Derby
Type: Transcript; B-M
Year Range: 1655–1710
Online: Ancestry
Title: Derby, Connecticut Town Records, 1655–1710
Notes, URL: Original Data: Sarah Riggs Humphrey Chapter, DAR. *Town records of Derby, Connecticut, 1655–1710.* <www.ancestry.com/search/rectype/inddbs/4730.htm>

Connecticut, New Haven Co., Guilford
Type: Transcript; D
Year Range: 1883–1890
Online: NEHGS
Title: Record of Deaths in Guilford, Connecticut, 1883–1890
Notes, URL: <www.newenglandancestors.org/research/database/guilforddeaths>

Connecticut, New Haven Co., Madison
Type: Transcript; B-M-D
Year Range: 1718–1890
Online: NEHGS
Title: Vital Records of Madison, Connecticut, 1718–1890
Notes, URL: <www.newenglandancestors.org/research/database/madisonvr>

Connecticut, New Haven Co., New Haven
Type: Abstracts; B-M-D
Year Range: 1649–1850
CD-ROM: $19.95, Willow Bend, #A0792QP
Title: Vital Records of New Haven, Connecticut, 1649–1850
Notes, URL: <www.willowbend.net>

Connecticut, New London Co., New London
Type: Transcript; B-M-D
Year Range: 1644–1780
Online: Free
Title: New London Vital Statistics from the Collated Copy from the Original Records, Vol. 1.
Notes, URL: <www.rootsweb.com/~ctcnewlo/nl1.html>

Connecticut, New London Co., New London
Type: Transcript; B-M-D
Year Range: 1709–1779
Online: Free
Title: New London—Connecticut Town Records. Book Second
Notes, URL: <www.rootsweb.com/~ctcnewlo/nl2.html>

Connecticut, New London Co., Voluntown
Type: Index; B-M-D
Year Range: 1708–1850
Online: Free
Title: Connecticut Vital Records, Voluntown, Births—Marriages—Deaths, 1708–1850
Notes, URL: <www.idreamof.com/marriage/ct.html>

Connecticut, Tolland Co., Bolton
Type: Abstracts; B-M-D
Year Range: 1704–1859
Online: NEHGS
Title: Vital Records of Bolton, Connecticut, 1704–1859

Notes, URL: <www.newenglandancestors.org/research/database/boltonvr/>

Connecticut, Tolland Co., Coventry
Type: Text of a book; B-M-D
Year Range: 1711–1844
Online: Genealogy Library
Title: Births, Marriages, Baptisms, and Deaths in Coventry, Connecticut
Notes, URL: Text of the published vital records. Select Records | Vital Records | Connecticut.

Connecticut, Tolland Co., Vernon
Type: Abstracts; B-M-D
Year Range: Up to 1852
Online: NEHGS
Title: Vital Records of Vernon, Connecticut, to 1852
Notes, URL: <www.newenglandancestors.org/rs1/research/database/vernonvr>

Connecticut, Windham Co.
Type: Transcript, index; B-M-D
Year Range: 1850–1915
Online: Free
Title: Selected Windham Vital Records
Notes, URL: About 400 vital records from Windham (Town) and Willimantic, Conn. <www.angelfire.com/ct3/windhamvitals/>

District of Columbia, Washington
Type: Index; M
Year Range: Up to 1825
Online: Ancestry
Title: Marriages—Washington DC to 1825
Notes, URL: Over 9,000 names up to 1825. <www.ancestry.com/search/rectype/inddbs/2084a.htm>

District of Columbia, Washington
Type: Index; D
Year Range: 1801–1878
Online: F&LH
Title: Historical court records of Washington, District of Columbia: death records of Washington, D.C., 1801 to 1878, as taken from Administration of estates records group no. 21 . . .

District of Columbia, Washington
Type: Index; M
Year Range: 1806–1850
Online: Genealogy Library
Title: Washington DC Marriages from 1806 to 1850
Notes, URL: 15,902 marriages. Select Records | Marriage | District of Columbia.

District of Columbia, Washington
Type: Abstract; M
Year Range: 1811–1858
Online: F&LH
Title: Historical court records of Washington, District of Columbia
Notes, URL: Includes names of bride & groom & the date of marriage.

Florida
Type: Index; M
Year Range: 1822–1850
Online: Ancestry
Title: Florida Marriages, 1822–1850
Notes, URL: 7,000 names. <www.ancestry.com/search/rectype/inddbs/4019.htm>

Florida
Type: Indexes; M-D
Year Range: 1877–2001
Online: Vitalsearch (free/subscription)
Title: Florida State Deaths Database
Notes, URL: Over 45,000 death entries, 1877–1916. Also, marriages and divorces, 1970–2001, & deaths, 1999–2001. <www.vitalsearch-worldwide.com>

Florida
Type: Index; D
Year Range: 1936–1998
Online: Ancestry
Title: Florida Death Index
Notes, URL: Click on the Search Records tab, the letter *F*, and then on a year.

Florida, Alachua Co.
Type: Index; M
Year Range: 1837–1973
Online: Free
Title: Alachua County Archives: Marriage Records
Notes, URL: Over 43,000 marriages. <www.clerk-alachua-fl.org/archive/default.cfm>

Florida, Baker Co.
Type: Index; M
Year Range: 1877–1930
Online: Free
Title: Baker County Marriages 1877–1930
Notes, URL: <www.rootsweb.com/~flbaker/mgs.html>

Florida, Charlotte Co.
Type: Index; D
Year Range: 1925–1931
Online: Free
Title: Charlotte County Death Index
Notes, URL: <www.rootsweb.com/~flcharlo/dimain.htm>

Florida, Desoto Co.
Type: Index; M
Year Range: 1887–1910
Online: Free
Title: Marriages, Desoto Co., FLGenWeb Project
Notes, URL: <www.rootsweb.com/~fldesoto/marriages.htm>

Florida, Escambia Co., Pensacola
Type: Transcript; B
Year Range: 1891–1898
Online: Free
Title: Pensacola Florida Birth Index
Notes, URL: <www.anzwers.org/trade/research/pers.html>

Florida, Gadsden Co.
Type: Index; M
Year Range: 1851–1875
Online: Ancestry
Title: Florida Marriages, 1851–1875
Notes, URL: <www.ancestry.com/search/rectype/inddbs/5323.htm>

Florida, Hillsborough Co.
Type: Digital images; M
Year Range: 1846–1988
Online: Free
Title: Hillsborough County Marriage Records
Notes, URL: Click on "Search this collection." <www.lib.usf.edu/ldsu/index2.html?f=13771>

Florida, Leon Co.
Type: Index; M
Year Range: 1864–pres.
Online: Free
Title: Leon County Clerk of Courts
Notes, URL: <http://cvweb.clerk.leon.fl.us/index_marriage.html>

Florida, Miami-Dade Co.
Type: Index; D
Year Range: 1974–2003
Online: Free
Title: Miami-Dade County Clerk, County Recorder's Record Search
Notes, URL: Select Standard Record Search & then Death Certificate from the Document Type pull-down menu. <www.co.miami-dade.fl.us/public-records/pubsearch.asp>

Florida, Suwannee Co.
Type: Transcript; B
Year Range: 1878–1936
Online: Free
Title: Suwannee County, Florida—Delayed Birth Certificates Book 1

Notes, URL: <www.rootsweb.com/~flsuwann/Archives.htm>

Georgia
Type: Index; M
Year Range: 1754–1850
CD-ROM: $19.99, Genealogy.com
Title: Georgia, 1754–1850 Marriage Index
Notes, URL: 169,000 names. <www.genealogy.com/226facd.html>

Georgia
Type: ; M
Year Range: 1775–1900
CD-ROM: $26.95 (Win), Ancestry Item #2151, <http://shops.ancestry.com>. Search on "Georgia marriages."
Title: Georgia Vital Records: Marriages 1775–1900 (Selected Counties)
Notes, URL: Data covers about 60% of the state.

Georgia
Type: Index; M
Year Range: 1851–1900
CD-ROM: $29.99, Genealogy.com, CD #237
Online: Genealogy Library
Title: Georgia, 1851–1900 Marriage Index
Notes, URL: 277,000 names. <www.genealogy.com/237facd.html>

Georgia
Type: Index; D
Year Range: 1919–1929
Online: Vitalsearch (free subscription)
Title: Georgia State Death Index
Notes, URL: <www.vitalsearch-cd.com/gen/GAcompstat.htm>

Georgia
Type: Index; D
Year Range: 1919–1998
Online: Ancestry
Title: Georgia Deaths, 1919-98
Notes, URL: More than 2.7 million records. <www.ancestry.com/search/rectype/inddbs/5426a.htm>

Georgia
Type: Index; M
Year Range: 1997–1998
Online: Vitalsearch (free subscription)
Title: Vitalsearch: Georgia State Marriages
Notes, URL: <www.vitalsearch-worldwide.com>

Georgia, Calhoun Co.
Type: Abstracts; B
Year Range: Up to 1911
Online: Free
Title: Calhoun Co. GA Births before 1911
Notes, URL: <ftp.rootsweb.com/pub/usgenweb/ga/calhoun/vitals/births/birtcalh.txt>

Georgia, Cherokee Co.
Type: Index; D
Year Range: 1920–1946
Online: Free
Title: Cherokee County, Georgia Death Index
Notes, URL: <www.rootsweb.com/~gacherok/death.htm>

Idaho
Type: Index; D
Year Range: 1911–1951
Online: Ancestry
Title: Idaho Death Index, 1911–51
Notes, URL: <www.ancestry.com/search/rectype/inddbs/6856.htm>

Idaho
Type: Index; D
Year Range: 1911–1951
Online: Free
Title: Idaho Death Index
Notes, URL: RootsWeb. <www.rootsweb.com/~idgenweb/deaths/search.htm>

Idaho
Type: Index; D
Year Range: 1911–1951
Online: Free
Title: State of Idaho Death Index
Notes, URL: <http://abish.byui.edu/specialCollections/fhc/Death/searchForm.cfm>

Illinois
Type: Index; M
Year Range: 1763–1900
Online: Free
Title: Illinois Statewide Marriage Index, 1763–1900
Notes, URL: Not all counties are complete. <www.cyberdriveillinois.com/departments/archives/marriage.html> or <www.sos.state.il.us/cgi-bin/archives/marriages>.

Illinois
Type: Index; M
Year Range: 1791–1900
CD-ROM: $26.95 (Win), Ancestry Item #2308, <http://shops.ancestry.com>. Search on "Illinois marriages."
Title: Illinois Vital Records: Marriages 1791–1900
Notes, URL: Over 271,000 marriage records from 78 of Illinois's 102 counties. 542,346 total names.

Illinois
Type: Index; M
Year Range: 1851–1900
CD-ROM: $29.99, Genealogy.com, CD #250
Online: Genealogy Library
Title: Illinois, 1851–1900 Marriage Index
Notes, URL: 707,000 names. <www.genealogy.com/250facd.html>

Illinois
Type: Index; D
Year Range: 1916–1950
Online: Free
Title: Database of Illinois Death Certificates, 1916–1950
Notes, URL: <www.cyberdriveillinois.com/departments/archives/idphdeathindex.html>. See <www.rootdig.com/adn/illinoisdeathindex.html> for tips on searching this index.

Illinois, Adams Co., Camp Point
Type: Abstracts; B-D
Year Range: 1873–1903
CD-ROM: $33, Heritage Books, item #2205
Title: Heritage Books Archives: Births and Deaths Abstracted from The Camp Point Journal, Camp Point, Adams County, Illinois, 1873–1903
Notes, URL: Graphic image CD-ROM, 1,393 pp. <www.heritagebooks.com>. Click on Search and search for "2205."

Illinois, Coles Co., Mattoon
Type: Index; D
Year Range: 1899–1918
Online: Free
Title: City of Mattoon (Coles County), Death Certificate Registers Index, 1899–1918
Notes, URL: Nearly 3,600 death records. <www.cyberdriveillinois.com/departments/archives/matdth.html>

Illinois, Cook Co.
Type: Index; D
Year Range: 1872–1911
Online: Free
Title: Cook County Coroner's Inquest Record Index, 1872–1911
Notes, URL: 74,160 records. <www.cyberdriveillinois.com/departments/archives/cookinqt.html>

Illinois, Cook Co., Chicago
Type: Index; D
Year Range: 1870–1930
Online: Free
Title: Chicago Police Department Homicide Record Index, 1870–1930

Notes, URL: 12,705 records. <www.cyberdriveillinois.com/departments/archives/homicide.html>

Illinois, De Witt Co.
Type: Index; D
Year Range: 1878–1917
Online: Free
Title: Index to Death Records
Notes, URL: <www.rootsweb.com/~ildewitt/deathrecords/deathrecordindex.htm>

Illinois, Gallatin Co., Shawneetown
Type: Abstracts; M
Year Range: 1859–1897
Online: Free
Title: Kentucky Residents Married in Shawneetown, Illinois
Notes, URL: <www.rootsweb.com/~kyhender/ill.htm>

Illinois, Jo Daviess Co.
Type: Index; M
Year Range: 1855–1865
Online: Free
Title: Jo Daviess Co., IL Marriage Records Index
Notes, URL: <www.members.tripod.com/~Chemingway/Mrg.html>

Illinois, Kankakee Co.
Type: Index; D
Year Range: 1877–1916
Online: Free
Title: KVGS County Records Death Index
Notes, URL: <www.kvgs.org/deathindex/>

Illinois, Kendall Co.
Type: Abstracts; B-M-D
Year Range: 1837–1997
Online: Free
Title: Kendall County, Illinois Home Page
Notes, URL: Births, 1887–1903. Marriages 1837–1920. Deaths, 1855–1997. <www.rootsweb.com/~ilkendal/>

Illinois, Menard Co.
Type: Abstracts; D
Year Range: 1877–1900
Online: Free
Title: Menard County, Illinois Deaths, 1877–1900
Notes, URL: <www.rootsweb.com/~ilmenard/deathindex.html>

Illinois, Piatt Co.
Type: Transcripts; M
Year Range: 1841–1853
Online: Ancestry
Title: Piatt County, Illinois Marriage and Cemetery Records, 1841–53
Notes, URL: Source: Richart, Fern J., *Piatt County, Illinois, Marriage Records 1841–1853 and Cemetery Records.* <www.ancestry.com/search/rectype/inddbs/3248.htm>

Illinois, Saline Co.
Type: Abstracts; B
Year Range: 1877–1916
Online: Free
Title: Saline County Illinois Birth Records 1877–19—
Notes, URL: <www.rootsweb.com/~ilsaline/sabirths.txt>

Illinois, Schuyler Co.
Type: Abstracts; D
Year Range: 1877–1903
Online: Free
Title: Schuyler County, Illinois, Death Records
Notes, URL: <www.rootsweb.com/~ilschuyl/DeathRecords/Deathrecordsindexpage.html>

Illinois, St. Clair Co.
Type: Index; D
Year Range: Up to 1882
Online: Free
Title: Proof of Death Index, 1870–1880, St. Clair County, Illinois
Notes, URL: 1,911 records. <www.compu-type.net/rengen/stclair/prd1.htm>

Indiana
Type: Abstracts; M
Year Range: Up to 1850
Online: Free
Title: Genealogy Division Database of Indiana Marriages Through 1850
Notes, URL: <www.statelib.lib.in.us/www/isl/indiana/genealogy/mirr.html>

Indiana
Type: Index; M-D
Year Range: Up to 1977
CD-ROM: $26.95 (Win), Ancestry, Item #2093, <http://shops.ancestry.com>. Search on "Indiana vital records."
Title: Indiana Vital Records: Selected Counties & Years
Notes, URL: 200,000 marriages up to 1850 in 84 of 92 counties. Jasper County marriage index, 1850–1920, and deaths, 1921–1977.

Indiana
Type: Index; D
Year Range: 1800–1941
CD-ROM: $19.95 (Win), HeritageQuest
Title: Indiana Vital Records Death Index, 1800–1941
Notes, URL: 867,134 death entries in 67 counties. <www.heritagequest.com>

Indiana
Type: Indexes; B-M-D
Year Range: 1824–1941
Online: Genealogy Library
Title: Indiana Vital Records Indexes
Notes, URL: Mostly 1882–1920. Select Records | Vital Records | Indiana.

Indiana
Type: Abstracts; M
Year Range: 1836–1855
Online: Free
Title: Indiana Marriage Records
Notes, URL: Miscellaneous records. <www.genealogytoday.com/pub/indmarr.htm>

Indiana
Type: Transcript; M
Year Range: 1845–1920
Online: Ancestry
Title: Indiana Marriages, 1845–1920
Notes, URL: Records from 71 counties. <www.ancestry.com/search/rectype/inddbs/5059a.htm>

Indiana
Type: Index; B
Year Range: 1850–1920
CD-ROM: $24.95 (Win), HeritageQuest
Title: Indiana Vital Records Birth Index, 1850–1920
Notes, URL: 1,530,485 birth records in 68 counties. <www.heritagequest.com>

Indiana
Type: Index; M
Year Range: 1850–1920
CD-ROM: $49.95 (Win), HeritageQuest
Title: Indiana Vital Records Marriage Index, 1850–1920
Notes, URL: 3,042,781 marriage entries in 68 Indiana counties. <www.heritagequest.com>

Indiana
Type: Index; M
Year Range: 1851–1900
CD-ROM: $29.99, Genealogy.com, CD #243
Online: Genealogy Library
Title: Indiana, 1851–1900 Marriage Index
Notes, URL: 292,000 names. <www.genealogy.com/243facd.html>

Indiana
Type: Index; B
Year Range: 1880–1920
Online: Ancestry
Title: Indiana Births, 1880–1920
Notes, URL: Records from 31 counties indexed by the WPA. <www.ancestry.com/search/rectype/inddbs/4745a.htm>

Indiana
Type: Index; D
Year Range: 1882–1920
CD-ROM: $29.99, Genealogy.com, CD #216
Title: Indiana Deaths, 1882–1920 Vital Records
Notes, URL: 886,000 names from 67 of Indiana's 92 counties. Indexed by the WPA. <www.genealogy.com/216facd.html>

Indiana, Bartholomew Co.
Type: Index; B
Year Range: 1883–1920
Online: Ancestry
Title: Bartholomew County, Indiana Index to Birth Records, 1883–1920, Volumes I-II
Notes, URL: <www.ancestry.com/search/rectype/inddbs/6400.htm>

Indiana, Cass Co.
Type: Index; D
Year Range: 1870–1920
Online: Free
Title: Cass Co., Indiana, WPA Death Record Index for 1882–1920
Notes, URL: <www.rootsweb.com/~incass/deathidx.html>

Indiana, Clinton Co.
Type: Database; M
Year Range: 1834–1941
Online: Free
Title: Clinton County, Indiana Marriages
Notes, URL: <www.rootsweb.com/~inclinto/marriages.html>

Indiana, Clinton Co.
Type: Index; B
Year Range: 1882–1920
Online: Ancestry
Title: Clinton County, Indiana Index to Birth Records, 1882–1920, Volume I-II
Notes, URL: The Indiana WPA created this index. <www.ancestry.com/search/rectype/inddbs/6409.htm>

Indiana, Elkhart Co.
Type: Index; B
Year Range: 1882–1920
Online: Ancestry
Title: Elkhart County, Indiana Index to Birth Records, 1882–1920
Notes, URL: <www.ancestry.com/search/rectype/inddbs/6590.htm>

Indiana, Elkhart Co., Goshen
Type: Index; D
Year Range: 1882–1920
Online: Ancestry
Title: Goshen, Elkhart County, Indiana Index to Death Records, 1882–1920
Notes, URL: <www.ancestry.com/search/rectype/inddbs/6782.htm>

Indiana, Elkhart Co., Nappanee
Type: Abstracts; B
Year Range: 1907–1920
Online: Ancestry
Title: Nappanee, Elkhart County, Indiana Index to Birth Records, 1907-20
Notes, URL: Includes the child's name & date of birth, the father's full name, & the mother's maiden name. <www.ancestry.com/search/rectype/inddbs/6787.htm>

Indiana, Greene Co.
Type: Index; B
Year Range: 1885–1920
Online: Ancestry
Title: Greene County, Indiana Index to Birth Records, 1885–1920
Notes, URL: <www.ancestry.com/search/rectype/inddbs/6709.htm>

Indiana, Harrison Co.
Type: Index; D
Year Range: 1882–1920
Online: Ancestry
Title: Harrison County, Indiana Index to Death Records, 1882–1920
Notes, URL: By the Indiana WPA. <www.ancestry.com/search/rectype/inddbs/6498.htm>

Indiana, Jasper Co.
Type: Abstracts; M
Year Range: 1850–1920
Online: Ancestry
Title: Jasper County, Indiana Marriages, 1850–1920
Notes, URL: Contains the names of over 13,500 men and women. <www.ancestry.com/search/rectype/inddbs/3745.htm>

Indiana, Jasper Co.
Type: Index; D
Year Range: 1882–1920
Online: Ancestry
Title: Jasper County, Indiana Index to Death Records, 1882–1920
Notes, URL: <www.ancestry.com/search/rectype/inddbs/6721.htm>

Indiana, Jasper Co.
Type: Abstracts; D
Year Range: 1921–1977
Online: Ancestry
Title: Jasper County, Indiana Deaths, 1921–77
Notes, URL: 9,000 names. <www.ancestry.com/search/rectype/inddbs/3939.htm>

Indiana, Jefferson Co.
Type: Index; D
Year Range: 1879–1905
Online: Free
Title: Jefferson County Death Records
Notes, URL: <www.myindianahome.net/gen/jeff/records/death/index.html>

Indiana, Johnson Co.
Type: Index; D
Year Range: 1882–1920
Online: Ancestry
Title: Johnson County, Indiana Index to Death Records, 1882–1920
Notes, URL: <www.ancestry.com/search/rectype/inddbs/6814.htm>

Indiana, Lake Co.
Type: Index; B
Year Range: 1882–1920
Online: Ancestry
Title: Lake County, Indiana Index to Birth Records, 1882–1920
Notes, URL: <www.ancestry.com/search/rectype/inddbs/6634.htm>

Indiana, Lake Co.
Type: Index; B
Year Range: 1921–1941
Online: Ancestry
Title: Lake County and Crown Point, Indiana Index to Birth Records, 1921-41
Notes, URL: <www.ancestry.com/search/rectype/inddbs/6475.htm>

Indiana, Lake Co., Gary
Type: Index; D
Year Range: 1908–1920
Online: Ancestry
Title: Gary, Lake County, Indiana Index to Death Records, 1908–1920
Notes, URL: <www.ancestry.com/search/rectype/inddbs/6609.htm>

Indiana, Lake Co., Hammond
Type: Index; D
Year Range: 1882–1920

Online: Ancestry
Title: Hammond, Lake County, Indiana Index to Death Records, 1882–1920
Notes, URL: <www.ancestry.com/search/rectype/inddbs/6795.htm>

Indiana, Lake Co., Whiting
Type: Index; B
Year Range: 1899–1920
Online: Ancestry
Title: Whiting, Lake County, Indiana Index to Birth Records, 1899–1920
Notes, URL: <www.ancestry.com/search/rectype/inddbs/6494.htm>

Indiana, Montgomery Co.
Type: Index; B
Year Range: 1882–1920
Online: Ancestry
Title: Montgomery County, Indiana Index to Birth Records, 1882–1920
Notes, URL: <www.ancestry.com/search/rectype/inddbs/7006.htm>

Indiana, Orange Co.
Type: Index; D
Year Range: 1882–1920
Online: Ancestry
Title: Orange County, Indiana Index to Death Records, 1882–1920
Notes, URL: <www.ancestry.com/search/rectype/inddbs/6734.htm>

Indiana, Porter Co.
Type: Abstracts; M
Year Range: 1836–1850
Online: Free
Title: Genealogy in Porter County, Indiana
Notes, URL: <www.members.aol.com/kjtcet2/porter.htm>

Indiana, Starke Co.
Type: Index; D
Year Range: 1894–1938
Online: Ancestry
Title: Starke County, Indiana Index to Death Records, 1894–1938
Notes, URL: <www.ancestry.com/search/rectype/inddbs/6491.htm>

Indiana, Tipton Co.
Type: Index; D
Year Range: 1882–1896
Online: Ancestry
Title: Tipton County, Indiana Death Records Index, 1882–96
Notes, URL: <www.ancestry.com/search/rectype/inddbs/6461.htm>

Indiana, Warren Co.
Type: Index; D
Year Range: 1882–1920
Online: Ancestry
Title: Warren County, Indiana Index to Death Records, 1882–1920
Notes, URL: <www.ancestry.com/search/rectype/inddbs/6624.htm>

Indiana, Washington Co.
Type: Index; D
Year Range: 1882–1920
Online: Ancestry
Title: Washington County, Indiana Index to Death Records, 1882–1920
Notes, URL: <www.ancestry.com/search/rectype/inddbs/6699.htm>

Indiana, Wayne Co.
Type: Index; M
Year Range: 1811–1903
Online: Free
Title: Wayne County Indiana Marriage License Database
Notes, URL: <www.co.wayne.in.us/marriage/retrieve.cgi>

Indiana, Wayne Co.
Type: Index; D
Year Range: 1882–1920
Online: Ancestry
Title: Wayne County, Indiana Death Records Index, 1882–1920
Notes, URL: <www.ancestry.com/search/rectype/inddbs/6989.htm>

Indiana, Wells Co.
Type: Index; D
Year Range: 1883–1920
Online: Ancestry
Title: Wells County, Indiana Index to Death Records, 1883–1920
Notes, URL: <www.ancestry.com/search/rectype/inddbs/6730.htm>

Indiana, Whitley Co.
Type: Index; M
Year Range: 1905–1907
Online: Free
Title: Index to Marriage Applications, Book 1–April 1905–March 1907
Notes, URL: <http://home.whitleynet.org/genealogy/gswc_i1.htm>

Iowa
Type: Index; M
Year Range: 1835–1900
CD-ROM: $26.95 (Win), Ancestry Item #2287, <http://shops.ancestry.com>. Search on "Iowa marriages."
Title: Iowa Vital Records: Marriages 1835–1900
Notes, URL: 164,058 names in 52 counties.

Iowa
Type: Index; M
Year Range: 1851–1900
CD-ROM: $29.99, Genealogy.com
Online: Genealogy Library
Title: Iowa, 1851–1900 Marriage Index
Notes, URL: 157,000 names. <www.genealogy.com/222facd.html>

Iowa, Calhoun Co.
Type: Index; D
Year Range: 1898–1996
Online: Free
Title: Calhoun County, Iowa, Death Index
Notes, URL: <www.rootsweb.com/~usgenweb/ia/calhoun/death.htm>

Iowa, Story Co.
Type: Index; D
Year Range: 1904–1916
Online: Free
Title: State of Iowa Death Certificates for Story County
Notes, URL: Partial index mid-1904 through 1916. Surnames A through I only. <www.genloc.com/DCerts/>

Kansas
Type: Index; M
Year Range: 1854–1873
Online: Ancestry
Title: Kansas Marriage Index, 1854–73
Notes, URL: Nearly 22,000 records. <www.ancestry.com/search/rectype/inddbs/3444.htm>

Kansas, Anderson Co.
Type: Transcript; M
Year Range: 1857–1894
Online: Ancestry
Title: Anderson County, Kansas Marriages, 1857–94
Notes, URL: Nearly 3,000 records. <www.ancestry.com/search/rectype/inddbs/3461.htm>

Kansas, Franklin Co.
Type: Indexes; B-M-DI
Year Range: 1858–1917
Online: Free
Title: Franklin County Kansas Indexes
Notes, URL: Births, 1890s to early 1900s; marriages, 1858–1895; divorces, 1860–1917. <www.ku.edu/heritage/chs/franklin/indexes/>

Kansas, Johnson Co.
Type: Index; DI
Year Range: 1853–1882
Online: Free

Title: Divorces on File at Johnson County Archives in Olathe, KS
Notes, URL: <http://skyways.lib.ks.us/genweb/johnson/divorces.txt>

Kansas, Leavenworth Co.
Type: Index; B
Year Range: 1891–1900
Online: Ancestry
Title: Leavenworth County, Kansas Births, 1891–1900
Notes, URL: 10,000 names. <www.ancestry.com/search/rectype/inddbs/4493.htm>

Kansas, Leavenworth Co.
Type: Abstracts; D
Year Range: 1891–1911
Online: Ancestry
Title: Leavenworth County, Kansas Deaths, 1891–1911
Notes, URL: <www.ancestry.com/search/rectype/inddbs/4605.htm>

Kansas, Leavenworth Co.
Type: Index; M
Year Range: 1900–1920
Online: Ancestry
Title: Leavenworth County, Kansas, Marriage Records, 1900–20
Notes, URL: <www.ancestry.com/search/rectype/inddbs/6267.htm>

Kansas, Leavenworth Co.
Type: Transcripts; BU
Year Range: 1954–1970
Online: Ancestry
Title: Leavenworth County, Kansas Burials, 1954–58, 1963–70
Notes, URL: Compiled by the Leavenworth County Genealogical Society. <www.ancestry.com/search/rectype/inddbs/4578.htm>

Kansas, Leavenworth Co., Leavenworth
Type: Index; B
Year Range: 1832–1895
Online: Ancestry
Title: Leavenworth, Kansas Births, 1832–95
Notes, URL: 200 births. <www.ancestry.com/search/rectype/inddbs/3418.htm>

Kansas, Leavenworth Co., Leavenworth
Type: Database; D
Year Range: 1840–1935
Online: Ancestry
Title: Leavenworth, Kansas Deaths, 1840–1935
Notes, URL: Nearly 700 names. <www.ancestry.com/search/rectype/inddbs/3396.htm>

Kansas, Leavenworth Co., Leavenworth
Type: Index; D
Year Range: 1870–1920
Online: Ancestry
Title: Leavenworth, Kansas Death Index, 1870–1920
Notes, URL: Over 1,400 names. <www.ancestry.com/search/rectype/inddbs/3405.htm>

Kansas, Leavenworth Co., Leavenworth
Type: Index; D
Year Range: 1923–1930
Online: Ancestry
Title: Leavenworth, Kansas Deaths, 1923–30
Notes, URL: Over 5,600 names. <www.ancestry.com/search/rectype/inddbs/3410.htm>

Kansas, Lyon Co.
Type: Indexes; B-M-D
Year Range: 1856–1967
Online: Free
Title: Lyon County, Kansas Vital Records
Notes, URL: Births, 1885–1892. Marriages, 1856–1919, 1954, 1965–1967. Deaths, 1885–1899. <www.rootsweb.com/~ksfhgslc/vital.html>

Kansas, Miami Co.
Type: Indexes; B-M-DI-D
Year Range: 1835–1951
Online: Free
Title: KSGenWeb Digital Library, Miami County, Kansas
Notes, URL: Births, 1835–1951. Marriages & divorces, 1856–1943. Deaths, 1885–1911. <http://skyways.lib.ks.us/genweb/miami/library/index.html#vitalrecords>

Kansas, Sedgwick Co.
Type: Index; D
Year Range: 1887–1910
Online: Free
Title: Wichita Death Index, 1887–1910
Notes, URL: <http://skyways.lib.ks.us/genweb/sedgwick/death.html>

Kentucky
Type: Abstracts; M
Year Range: Up to 1850
Online: Ancestry
Title: Kentucky Marriages to 1850
Notes, URL: 145,000 names. <www.ancestry.com/search/rectype/inddbs/2089a.htm>

Kentucky
Type: Abstracts; M
Year Range: 1780–1920
CD-ROM: $26.95 (Win), Ancestry Item #2105, <http://shops.ancestry.com>. Search on "Kentucky marriages."
Title: Kentucky Vital Records: Marriages 1780–1920 (Selected Counties)
Notes, URL: Over 212,000 marriage records from 75 of 120 counties.

Kentucky
Type: Abstracts; M
Year Range: 1795–1850
Online: Ancestry
Title: Northern Kentucky Marriages, 1795–1850
Notes, URL: Records from Boone, Campbell, and Kenton Counties. <www.ancestry.com/search/rectype/inddbs/3455.htm>

Kentucky
Type: Abstracts; M
Year Range: 1795–1850
Online: Genealogy Library
Title: Marriages of Campbell, Boone, and Kenton Counties, Kentucky, 1795–1850
Notes, URL: Select Records | Marriage | Kentucky.

Kentucky
Type: Abstracts; M
Year Range: 1797–1865
CD-ROM: $29.99, Genealogy.com, CD #519
Online: Genealogy Library
Title: Early Kentucky Settlers, 1700s–1800s
Notes, URL: Includes about 8,000 names from *Kentucky Marriages, 1797–1865*, by G. Glenn Clift, & 50,000 names from *Kentucky Marriage Records*. <www.genealogy.com/519facd.html>

Kentucky
Type: Digital images of books; B-M-D
Year Range: 1839–1910
CD-ROM: $26.50 (Mac or Win), Heritage Books
Title: HB Archives: Kentucky Vol. 1
Notes, URL: Includes Lee Co. births, marriages, & deaths, 1874–1878 & 1900–1910. Breathitt Co. marriages, 1839–1873. <www.heritagebooks.com>

Kentucky
Type: Index; M
Year Range: 1851–1900
CD-ROM: $29.99, Genealogy.com, CD #233
Online: Genealogy Library
Title: Kentucky 1851–1900 Marriage Index

Notes, URL: 317,000 names from 62 counties. <www.genealogy.com/233facd.html>

Kentucky
Type: Abstracts; M
Year Range: 1851–1900
Online: Ancestry
Title: Kentucky Marriages, 1851–1900
Notes, URL: Records from 35 counties. <www.ancestry.com/search/rectype/inddbs/4428a.htm>

Kentucky
Type: Indexes; B-M-D
Year Range: 1900–2002
Online: Vitalsearch (free subscription)
Title: VitalSearch—Kentucky (USA): Kentucky State Vital Records
Notes, URL: Over 5.5 million births, 1911–2002. 1.1 million marriages, 1973–2002. Over 2.6 million death entries, 1900–2002. Divorces, 1999–2002. <www.vitalsearch-worldwide.com>

Kentucky
Type: Indexes; M-DI-D
Year Range: 1911–1993
Online: Free
Title: Kentucky Vital Records Index
Notes, URL: Marriages and divorces, 1973–1993. Deaths, 1911–1986, 1987–1992. <http://ukcc.uky.edu/~vitalrec/>

Kentucky
Type: Indexes; M-D
Year Range: 1911–2000
Online: Free
Title: Kentucky Vital Statistics Records
Notes, URL: Kentucky Birth Index 1911–1912, Kentucky Death Index 1911–2000, Kentucky Marriages 1973–2000. <www.kygenweb.net/vitals/index.html>

Kentucky
Type: Index; D
Year Range: 1911–2000
Online: Free
Title: Kentucky Death Records
Notes, URL: 2,921,383 records. <http://vitals.rootsweb.com/ky/death/search.cgi> or <http://userdb.rootsweb.com/ky/death/search.cgi>

Kentucky
Type: Index; D
Year Range: 1911–2000
CD-ROM: $26.95 (Win), Ancestry (Kentucky Vital Records: Deaths 1911–1993), item #2226, <http://shops.ancestry.com>. Search on "Kentucky deaths."
Online: Ancestry
Title: Kentucky Death Index, 1911–2000
Notes, URL: 2,700,000 records from all 120 counties. The online version covers 1911–2000. <www.ancestry.com/search/rectype/inddbs/3077a.htm>

Kentucky
Type: Index; M
Year Range: 1973–2000
Online: Free
Title: Kentucky Records: Marriage Records
Notes, URL: 1,213,864 records. <http://userdb.rootsweb.com/ky/marriage/search.cgi>

Kentucky, Butler Co.
Type: Transcript; B-M-D
Year Range: 1820–1884
Online: Free
Title: Butler County, KY GenWeb Project
Notes, URL: Births, 1852–1859. Marriages, 1820–1884 (various years). Deaths, 1852. <www.rootsweb.com/~kybutler>

Kentucky, Christian Co.
Type: Index; B
Year Range: 1911–1930
Online: Free
Title: Christian County, Kentucky Birth Index 1911–1930
Notes, URL: <www.kyseeker.com/christian/birth/birthindex.html>

Kentucky, Fulton Co.
Type: Index; M
Year Range: 1861–1867
Online: Free
Title: Fulton County, Kentucky Marriage Records Index January 1861–March 1867
Notes, URL: <www.genealogytoday.com/pub/Fulton.htm>

Kentucky, Greenup
Type: Index; M
Year Range: 1904–1920
Online: Free
Title: Greenup County, Kentucky Marriage Records
Notes, URL: <www.genealogytoday.com/pub/GREENUP.HTM>

Kentucky, Hickman Co.
Type: Index; M
Year Range: 1852–1858
Online: Free
Title: Hickman County, Kentucky Marriage Records 1852
Notes, URL: <www.genealogytoday.com/pub/Hickman.htm>

Kentucky, Johnson Co.
Type: Database; B
Year Range: 1852–1904
Online: Free
Title: Kentucky Birth Records
Notes, URL: Births, 1852–1904 (various years). <www.idreamof.com/birth/ky.html>

Kentucky, Knott Co.
Type: Digital images; M
Year Range: 1884–1905
Online: Free
Title: Knott County GenWeb Project: Marriage Records
Notes, URL: Marriages, 1884–1898, 1902–1905. <www.rootsweb.com/~kyknott/marriages.html>

Kentucky, Lawrence Co.
Type: Index; M
Year Range: 1822–1854
Online: Free
Title: Lawrence County, Kentucky Marriage Records
Notes, URL: <www.genealogytoday.com/pub/LWCOKY.HTM>

Kentucky, Metcalfe Co.
Type: Index; B
Year Range: 1852–1911
Online: Free
Title: Metcalfe Co., Ky. Births 1852–1911 various years
Notes, URL: <ftp://ftp.rootsweb.com/pub/usgenweb/ky/metcalfe/vitals/births.txt>

Kentucky, Ohio Co.
Type: Index; M
Year Range: 1799–1840
Online: Free
Title: Ohio County, Kentucky Marriage Records
Notes, URL: <www.genealogytoday.com/pub/OHCOKY.HTM>

Kentucky, Perry Co.
Type: Index; M
Year Range: 1821–1846
Online: Free
Title: Perry County Marriage Index 1821 to around 1846
Notes, URL: <www.rootsweb.com/%7Ekyknott/pmarr.html>

Kentucky, Pulaski Co.
Type: Index; B-M-D

Year Range: 1852–1859
Online: Free
Title: Pulaski County, KY Archives
Notes, URL: <www.rootsweb.com/~usgenweb/ky/pulaski>

Kentucky, Shelby Co.
Type: Transcripts; M
Year Range: 1792–1800
Online: Ancestry
Title: Shelby County, Kentucky Marriage Bonds: 1792–1800
Notes, URL: <www.ancestry.com/search/rectype/inddbs/6063.htm>

Kentucky, Trigg Co.
Type: Transcripts; M
Year Range: 1830–1905
Online: Free
Title: Trigg County Marriages, 1830, 1871–1905
Notes, URL: <www.kyseeker.com/trigg/marriages.html>

Louisiana
Type: Abstracts; M
Year Range: Up to 1850
Online: Ancestry
Title: Marriages—Louisiana to 1850
Notes, URL: Over 29,000 names. <www.ancestry.com/search/rectype/inddbs/2090a.htm>

Louisiana
Type: Index; M
Year Range: 1718–1925
CD-ROM: $29.99, Genealogy.com, CD #001
Title: Louisiana, 1718–1925 Marriage Index
Notes, URL: 570,000 names. <www.genealogy.com/001facd.html>

Louisiana
Type: Index; M
Year Range: 1851–1900
Online: Ancestry
Title: Louisiana Marriage Records, 1851–1900
Notes, URL: Records for Bienville, Bossier, Caldwell, Jackson, Lincoln, Ouachita, and Sabine parishes. <www.ancestry.com/search/rectype/inddbs/5228.htm>

Louisiana
Type: Index; D
Year Range: 1900–1949
Online: Ancestry
Title: Louisiana Statewide Death Index, 1900–49
Notes, URL: <www.ancestry.com/search/rectype/inddbs/6697.htm>

Louisiana, Orleans Parish
Type: Index; D
Year Range: 1804–1876
Online: Free
Title: Orleans Parish Death Index
Notes, URL: <www.rootsweb.com/~usgenweb/la/orleans/death_index1.htm>

Louisiana, Orleans Parish, New Orleans
Type: Abstracts; M
Year Range: 1720–1733
CD-ROM: $29.99, Genealogy.com, CD #525
Online: Genealogy Library
Title: Early Louisiana Settlers, 1600s–1800s
Notes, URL: Includes *The New Orleans French, 1720–1733: A Collection of Marriage Records Relating to the First Colonists of the Louisiana Province*, by Winston De Ville. <www.genealogy.com/525facd-long.html>

Louisiana, Orleans Parish, New Orleans
Type: Index; B
Year Range: 1790–1899
Online: Ancestry
Title: New Orleans, Louisiana Birth Records Index, 1790–1899
Notes, URL: <www.ancestry.com/search/rectype/inddbs/6587.htm>

Louisiana, Orleans Parish, New Orleans
Type: Index; D
Year Range: 1804–1949
Online: Ancestry
Title: New Orleans, Louisiana Death Records Index, 1804–1949
Notes, URL: <www.ancestry.com/search/rectype/inddbs/6606.htm>

Louisiana, Orleans Parish, New Orleans
Type: Index; M
Year Range: 1831–1925
Online: Ancestry
Title: New Orleans, Louisiana Marriage Records Index, 1831–1925
Notes, URL: <www.ancestry.com/search/rectype/inddbs/6500.htm>

Maine
Type: Index; M
Year Range: Up to 1875
Online: Ancestry
Title: Maine Marriages to 1875
Notes, URL: Covers Belfast (Waldo County), Hallowell (Kennebec County), and Pittsdon (Kennebec County). <www.ancestry.com/search/rectype/inddbs/5266.htm>

Maine
Type: Index; M
Year Range: 1743–1891
CD-ROM: $29.99, Genealogy.com, CD #404
Online: Genealogy Library
Title: Maine, 1743–1891 Marriage Index
Notes, URL: About 115,000 marriages in select Maine counties. <www.genealogy.com/404facd.html>

Maine
Type: Transcript; M
Year Range: 1892–1966
CD-ROM: $59, Picton Press
Title: Maine Marriage Returns 1892–1966
Notes, URL: 625,000 marriages. <www.pictonpress.com>

Maine
Type: Abstracts; M
Year Range: 1892–1996
Online: Ancestry
Title: Maine Marriages, 1892–1996
Notes, URL: Excludes the years 1967–1976. <www.ancestry.com/search/rectype/inddbs/6904.htm>

Maine
Type: Abstracts; M
Year Range: 1892–1996
Online: Free
Title: Maine State Archives—Marriage History Search Form
Notes, URL: <http://thor.dafs.state.me.us/pls/archives/archdev.marriage_archive.search_form>

Maine
Type: Index; D
Year Range: 1960–1996
Online: Free
Title: Maine State Archives—Death History Search Form
Notes, URL: <http://thor.dafs.state.me.us/pls/archives/archdev.death_archive.search_form>

Maine
Type: Index; D
Year Range: 1960–1997
Online: Ancestry
Title: Maine Death Index, 1960–97
Notes, URL: <www.ancestry.com/search/rectype/inddbs/6703.htm>

Maine
Type: Index; D

Year Range: 1960–1997
Online: Free
Title: Maine Death Records
Notes, URL: 401,960 records. <http://vitals.rootsweb.com/me/death/search.cgi>

Maine
Type: Index; B-M-D
Year Range: All dates
Online: Free
Title: World Genealogy Project: Maine Vital Records
Notes, URL: <www.worldgenealogyproject.com/everynameindexproject.htm>

Maine, Franklin Co., Farmington
Type: Transcripts; B-M-D
Year Range: 1784–1890
Online: NEHGS
Title: Vital Records of Farmington, Maine, 1784–1890
Notes, URL: <www.newenglandancestors.org/research/database/vrfarmington>

Maine, Hancock Co., Brooksville
Type: Transcripts; B-M-D
Year Range: 1767–1913
Online: NEHGS
Title: Vital Records of the Town of Brooksville, Hancock County, Maine
Notes, URL: <www.newenglandancestors.org/rs0/research/database/BrooksvilleME>

Maine, Hancock Co., Castine
Type: Transcripts; M
Year Range: 1892–1960
Online: Free
Title: Castine Marriages 1892–1960
Notes, URL: <www.kalama.com/~mariner/casmarry.htm>

Maine, Kennebec Co., Augusta
Type: Abstracts; B-M-D
Year Range: Up to 1892
Online: NEHGS
Title: Vital Records of Augusta, Maine to the Year 1892
Notes, URL: <www.newenglandancestors.org/research/database/augusta/>

Maine, Kennebec Co., Gardiner
Type: Database; B-D
Year Range: 1800–1892
Online: Ancestry
Title: Gardiner, Kennebec County Maine, Birth & Death records 1800–1892
Notes, URL: Over 10,000 records. <www.ancestry.com/search/rectype/inddbs/5529.htm>

Maine, Oxford Co., Andover
Type: Transcripts; B-M-D
Year Range: 1795–2001
Online: Free
Title: Welcome to Andover, Maine
Notes, URL: Births, 1795–1930. Marriages, 1805–1944. Deaths, up to 2001. <http://andovermaine.tripod.com/index.html>

Maine, Oxford Co., Rumford
Type: Transcript from a book; M
Year Range: 1801–1869
Online: Free
Title: Marriage Intentions, 1801–1869
Notes, URL: Source: *History of Rumford, Oxford County, Maine, From its First Settlement in 1779 to the Present Time*, by William B. Lapham. <www.rootsweb.com/~meoxford/rumintro.htm>

Maine, Penobscot Co., Springfield
Type: Abstracts; B-M
Year Range: 1834–1891
Online: NEHGS
Title: Some Early Records of the Town of Springfield, Maine, 1834–1891
Notes, URL: <www.newenglandancestors.org/research/database/springfieldme/default.asp>

Maine, Waldo Co., Belfast
Type: Database; B-D
Year Range: 1743–1892
Online: Ancestry
Title: Waldo County, Maine Births, 1743–1892: Belfast
Notes, URL: More than 5,500 births. Source: *Vital Records of Belfast, ME, Vol. 1, Births.* <www.ancestry.com/search/rectype/inddbs/5283.htm>.

Maine, Waldo Co., Belfast
Type: Database; B-D
Year Range: 1743–1892
Online: Ancestry
Title: Waldo County, Maine Deaths, 1743–1892: Belfast
Notes, URL: More than 5,500 deaths. Source: *Vital Records of Belfast, ME: Vol. 2, Marriages and Deaths.* <www.ancestry.com/search/rectype/inddbs/5298.htm>

Maine, York Co., Wells
Type: Transcript; B-M-D
Year Range: 1737–1836
Online: NEHGS
Title: Vital Records of Wells, Maine
Notes, URL: <www.newenglandancestors.org/rs0/research/database/JoshuaHubbard/Default.asp>

Maryland
Type: Index; M
Year Range: 1649–1816
Online: Free
Title: Maryland Indexes, Maryland Marriage References, by Robert Barnes, MSA S 1527
Notes, URL: Marriages abstracted from materials at the Maryland State Archives, including Hodges' Marriage References, diaries, Bible records, & the private marriage registers of ministers. <www.mdarchives.state.md.us/msa/stagser/s1500/s1527/html/ssi1527.html>

Maryland
Type: Index; M
Year Range: 1655–1850
CD-ROM: $29.99, Genealogy.com, CD #224
Online: Genealogy Library
Title: Maryland, 1655–1850 Marriage Index
Notes, URL: 258,000 names. <www.genealogy.com/224facd.html>

Maryland
Type: Index; D
Year Range: 1662–1967
Online: Free
Title: Maryland Church Records, Deaths and Burials Index
Notes, URL: <www.mdarchives.state.md.us/msa/stagser/s1400/s1402/html/ssi1402.html>

Maryland
Type: Index; M
Year Range: 1667–1899
Online: Ancestry
Title: Maryland Marriages, 1667–1899
Notes, URL: Records from 17 counties. <www.ancestry.com/search/rectype/inddbs/4729.htm>

Maryland
Type: Digital images of a book containing abstracts; D
Year Range: 1736–1737
Online: F&LH
Title: Maryland death records as taken from Maryland account book no. 15: dated 1736 to 1737
Notes, URL: A book by Annie Walker Burns.

Maryland
Type: Index, transcript; M
Year Range: 1774–1886

CD-ROM: $29.99, Genealogy.com, CD #521
Online: Genealogy Library
Title: Maryland Settlers & Soldiers, 1700s–1800s
Notes, URL: Includes *Index of Marriage Licenses, Prince George's County, Maryland 1777–1886,* by Helen W. Brown, & *Marriage Licenses of Caroline County, Maryland, 1774–1815,* by Henry Downes Cranor. <www.genealogy.com/521facd.html>

Maryland, Baltimore City
Type: Index; D
Year Range: 1875–1880
Online: Free
Title: Maryland State Archives, Death Records
Notes, URL: <www.mdarchives.state.md.us/msa/stagser/s1400/s1483/html/ssi1483a.html>

Maryland, Baltimore City
Type: Index; D
Year Range: 1943–1949
Online: Free
Title: Maryland State Archives, Death Records
Notes, URL: <www.mdarchives.state.md.us/msa/stagser/s1400/s1483/html/ssi1483b.html>

Maryland, Baltimore County
Type: Index; M
Year Range: 1823–1826
Online: F&LH
Title: Marriage records of Baltimore County, Maryland, for the period of 1823 to 1826
Notes, URL: A book by Annie Walker Burns.

Maryland, Caroline Co.
Type: Digital images of a transcript; M
Year Range: 1774–1815
CD-ROM: $29.99, Genealogy.com, CD #521
Online: Genealogy Library
Title: Maryland Settlers & Soldiers, 1700s–1800s
Notes, URL: More than 2,000 marriage licenses. <www.genealogy.com/521facd.html>

Maryland, Caroline Co.
Type: Abstracts; M
Year Range: 1774–1815
Online: Ancestry
Title: Caroline County, Maryland Marriages, 1774–1815
Notes, URL: Original data: Cranor, Henry Downes. *Marriage Licenses of Caroline County, Maryland, 1774–1815.* <www.ancestry.com/search/rectype/inddbs/4707.htm>

Maryland, Prince George's Co.
Type: Abstracts; M
Year Range: 1777–1836
Online: F&LH
Title: Marriage records, Prince George's Co., Maryland, 1777 to 1836
Notes, URL: A book by Sylvia Gorman Greene.

Maryland, Prince George's Co.
Type: Digital images of an index; M
Year Range: 1777–1886
CD-ROM: $29.99, Genealogy.com, CD #521
Online: Genealogy Library
Title: Maryland Settlers & Soldiers, 1700s–1800s
Notes, URL: Nearly 7,000 marriage licenses. <www.genealogy.com/521facd.html>

Maryland, Talbot Co.
Type: Abstracts; M
Year Range: 1796–1810
Online: F&LH
Title: The marriage licenses of Talbot County, Maryland, from 1796–1810

Massachusetts
Type: Database; M
Year Range: Up to 1800
Online: Ancestry
Title: Massachusetts Marriages to 1800
Notes, URL: Over 29,000 names. Source: Bailey, Frederic W. *Early Massachusetts Marriages Prior to 1800.* <www.ancestry.com/search/rectype/inddbs/2091.htm>

Massachusetts
Type: Transcripts; B-M-D
Year Range: Up to 1850
Online: Ancestry
Title: Massachusetts Town Vital Records Collection
Notes, URL: Published vital records for 49 towns. <www.ancestry.com/search/rectype/vital/massrecords/main.htm>

Massachusetts
Type: Transcripts; B-M-D
Year Range: Up to 1850
Online: F&LH
Title: Vital Records of Massachusetts to 1850
Notes, URL: Published vital records for over 115 towns (in separate databases).

Massachusetts
Type: Transcript; B-M-D
Year Range: Up to 1850
Online: NEHGS
Title: Massachusetts Vital Records to 1850
Notes, URL: Originally published as 140 volumes. <www.newenglandancestors.org/rs0/research/database/vital_records/>.

Massachusetts
Type: Transcript; B-M-D-BU
Year Range: Up to 1850
CD-ROM: $39.95/CD or $195 for set of 9 (Mac/Win), Search & ReSearch
Title: Early Vital Records of the Commonwealth of Massachusetts to about 1850
Notes, URL: <www.searchresearchpub.com/multipack.html>

Massachusetts
Type: Abstracts; B-M-D-BU
Year Range: Up to 1850
CD-ROM: $39.99, Genealogy.com, CD #220
Online: Genealogy Library
Title: Massachusetts, 1600s–1800s Vital Records
Notes, URL: Published vital records for 193 towns. 1,350,000 names. <www.genealogy.com/220facd.html>

Massachusetts
Type: Transcripts; B-M-D
Year Range: 1600s–1900s
CD-ROM: $29.99, Genealogy.com, CD #502
Online: Genealogy Library
Title: Massachusetts, 1600s–1900s Probate, Town, & Vital Records
Notes, URL: Vital records for more than 160,000 people in Barnstable, Eastham, Fairhaven, Middleborough, Orleans, Plymouth, & Sandwich. <www.genealogy.com/502facd.html>

Massachusetts
Type: Digital images of books; B-M-D
Year Range: 1630–1809
CD-ROM: $39.99, Genealogy.com, CD #526
Online: Genealogy Library
Title: Massachusetts, 1600s–1800s Genealogical Records
Notes, URL: Includes *Early Massachusetts Marriages Prior to 1800; Boston Births, Baptisms, Marriages, and Deaths, 1630–1699, Volume 1; Boston Births, 1700–1800, Volume 2; Boston Marriages from 1700–1809, Vol. 1 (1700–1751) &*

Vol. 2 (1752–1809). <www.genealogy.com/526facd.html>

Massachusetts
Type: Text of books; B-M-D-BU
Year Range: 1633–1689
CD-ROM: $39.99, Genealogy.com, CD #023
Online: Genealogy Library
Title: Pilgrim Genealogies and Histories, 1600s–1900s
Notes, URL: Includes *Records of Plymouth Colony Births, Deaths, Burials, and Other Records, 1633–1689*. <www.genealogy.com/023facd-long.html>

Massachusetts
Type: Database; M
Year Range: 1633–1850
Online: Genealogy Library
Title: Massachusetts, 1633–1850 Marriage Index
Notes, URL: 838,000 names from Family History Library microfilms. <www.genealogy.com/231facd.html>

Massachusetts
Type: Abstracts; B-M-D
Year Range: 1690–1890
CD-ROM: $26.95 (Win), Ancestry Item #2230 <http://shops.ancestry.com>. Search on "Massachusetts vital."
Title: Massachusetts Vital Records 1690–1890
Notes, URL: Over a million records from all 14 counties. Collected by NEHGS. Most are pre-1850.

Massachusetts
Type: Transcripts; M
Year Range: 1841–1850
Online: Free
Title: Massachusetts Genealogy: Marriages 1841–1850
Notes, URL: Records from 119 towns. <www.angelfire.com/ma2/massmarriages/index.html>

Massachusetts
Type: Transcripts; D
Year Range: 1843–1844
Online: Ancestry
Title: Massachusetts Deaths, 1844: Vol. 8, Barnstable to Hampshire; Volume 9, Middlesex to Worcester
Notes, URL: Deaths outside Boston, from 1 May 1843 to 30 April 1844. <www.ancestry.com/search/rectype/inddbs/5973.htm>

Massachusetts, Barnstable Co.
Type: Digital images of original manuscripts; B-M-D-BU
Year Range: 1637–1892
CD-ROM: $78 (2 CDs), Archive Publishing
Title: Massachusetts Town & Vital Records, 1620–1910: Orleans/Eastham 1637–1892
Notes, URL: Also includes church records, 1772–1835, & gravestone inscriptions, 1709–1880. <www.archivepublishing.com/cd_titles.htm>

Massachusetts, Barnstable Co., Barnstable
Type: Transcript; B-M-D
CD-ROM: $39.99, NEHGS (Mac/Win)
Title: Records of Barnstable, Massachusetts
Notes, URL: Early vital & town records, as well as cemetery & church records. <www.newenglandancestors.org>

Massachusetts, Barnstable Co., Provincetown
Type: Transcript; B-M-D
Year Range: 1698–1859
Online: NEHGS
Title: Records of Provincetown, Massachusetts 1698–1859
Notes, URL: <www.newenglandancestors.org/research/database/ptown_vital records>

Massachusetts, Barnstable Co., Wellfleet
Type: Digital images of original manuscripts; B-M-D
Year Range: 1763–1910
CD-ROM: $78 (2 CDs), Archive Publishing
Title: Massachusetts Town & Vital Records 1620–1910: Wellfleet 1763–1910
Notes, URL: <www.archivepublishing.com/cd_titles.htm>

Massachusetts, Berkshire Co., Pittsfield
Type: Transcript; D
Year Range: 1886–1941
Online: Free
Title: Pittsfield Deaths
Notes, URL: About 20,000 names. <www.rootsweb.com/~maberksh/towns/pittsfield/pitt_deaths/index.html>

Massachusetts, Bristol Co., Dartmouth
Type: Text of a book containing transcripts; B
Year Range: Up to 1850
Online: Genealogy Library
Title: Vital Records of Dartmouth Massachusetts to the year 1850 volume I—Births
Notes, URL: Select Records I Birth Records I Massachusetts.

Massachusetts, Bristol Co., Easton
Type: Transcript; M
Year Range: 1725–1802
Online: NEHGS
Title: Marriages at Easton, Massachusetts, 1725–1802
Notes, URL: <www.newenglandancestors.org/rs0/research/database/EastonMA/>

Massachusetts, Bristol Co., Freetown
Type: Transcript; B-M-D
Year Range: 1686–1890
CD-ROM: $43 (Mac/Win), Heritage Books
Title: HB Archives: Bristol County, Mass.
Notes, URL: Includes *Vital Records of the Town of Freetown, Massachusetts, 1686–1890*, by Helen Gurney Thomas (1988). <www.heritagebooks.com>

Massachusetts, Bristol Co., Rehoboth
Type: Transcript; B-M-D
Year Range: 1642–1896
Online: Ancestry
Title: Rehoboth, Massachusetts, Vital Records, 1642–1896
Notes, URL: Original data: Arnold, James N. *Vital Record of Rehoboth, 1642–1896*. <www.ancestry.com/search/rectype/inddbs/4824.htm>

Massachusetts, Bristol Co., Rehoboth
Type: Transcript; B-M-D
Year Range: 1642–1896
Online: F&LH
Title: Vital record of Rehoboth, 1642–1896
Notes, URL: Source: Arnold, James N. *Vital record of Rehoboth, 1642–1896.*

Massachusetts, Bristol Co., Rehoboth
Type: Transcript; B-M-D
Year Range: 1642–1896
Online: NEHGS
Title: Vital Records of Rehoboth, Massachusetts, 1642–1896
Notes, URL: <www.newenglandancestors.org/research/database/vital_records_rehoboth>

Massachusetts, Dukes Co., Tisbury
Type: Index; M
Year Range: 1844–1940
Online: Free
Title: Index to Marriages in Tisbury by Bride's Name 1844–1940
Notes, URL: Has a link to the grooms' index. <www.history.vineyard.net//bridesi.htm>

Massachusetts, Dukes Co., Tisbury
Type: Index; M
Year Range: 1850–1875
Online: Free
Title: Every Name Index to Town Marriage Records in Tisbury, MA 1850–1875
Notes, URL: <www.history.vineyard.net//tmindex.htm>

Massachusetts, Essex Co., Beverly
Type: Transcript; B-M-D
Year Range: 1650–1704
Online: F&LH
Title: Early records of the Town of Beverly, Essex County, Mass.
Notes, URL: A book published in 1907.

Massachusetts, Essex Co., Lynn
Type: Digital images of a book containing transcripts; B-M-D
Year Range: 1707–1764
Online: F&LH
Title: Extracts from the records of the town of Lynn
Notes, URL: Births & deaths, 1707–1764. Marriages, 1727–1764.

Massachusetts, Franklin Co., Shelburne
Type: Abstracts; B-M-D
Year Range: 1768–1849
Online: Ancestry
Title: Shelburne, Massachusetts Vital Records
Notes, URL: Source: Essex Institute, Rhonda Marquess, ed. *Vital Records of Shelburne, Massachusetts.* <www.ancestry.com/search/rectype/inddbs/3495.htm>

Massachusetts, Hampden Co., Springfield
Type: Transcripts; B-M-D-BU
Year Range: Up to 1850
CD-ROM: $39.99 (Mac/Win), NEHGS, Item #SCD-SVR
Title: Vital Records of Springfield, Massachusetts to 1850
Notes, URL: Includes information from town records, 21 cemeteries, 10 churches, 11 newspapers, & state vital records. <www.newenglandancestors.org>

Massachusetts, Hampshire Co., Northampton
Type: Transcript; D
Year Range: 1653–1824
Online: F&LH
Title: Register of the deaths in Northampton, from the first settlement of the town in 1653, to August 1824
Notes, URL: A book published in 1824.

Massachusetts, Middlesex Co., Groton
Type: Transcript; B-M-D
Year Range: Up to 1810
Online: Ancestry
Title: Groton, Massachusetts Vital Records
Notes, URL: Source: Butler, Caleb. *History of the Town of Groton, Including Pepperell and Shirley.* <www.ancestry.com/search/rectype/inddbs/1047.htm>

Massachusetts, Middlesex Co., Lexington
Type: Transcript; B-M-D
Year Range: Up to 1898
Online: NEHGS
Title: Lexington, Mass. Record of Births, Marriages, and Deaths to January 1, 1898
Notes, URL: <www.newenglandancestors.org/research/database/vital_records3>

Massachusetts, Middlesex Co., Natick
Type: Transcript; B-M-D
Year Range: 1874–1913
Online: Free
Title: Town of Natick, Middlesex Co., Massachusetts 1874–1913 Vital Records
Notes, URL: <http://freepages.genealogy.rootsweb.com/~searchinglinane>

Massachusetts, Middlesex Co., Tewksbury
Type: Abstracts; B-M-D
Year Range: 1734–1850
Online: Ancestry
Title: Tewksbury, Massachusetts Vital Records
Notes, URL: Over 2,000 records with nearly 5,000 names. <www.ancestry.com/search/rectype/inddbs/3459.htm>

Massachusetts, Middlesex Co., Watertown
Type: Transcript; B-M-D-BU
Year Range: 1630–1693
Online: Ancestry
Title: Watertown, Massachusetts Records of Births, Deaths, and Marriages, 1630–1693
Notes, URL: Original data: *Watertown Records*, by Fred G. Baker. <www.ancestry.com/search/rectype/inddbs/6298.htm>

Massachusetts, Middlesex Co., Watertown
Type: Transcript; B-M-D-BU
Year Range: 1630–1737
Online: Ancestry
Title: Watertown, Massachusetts, various Town Records through 1737
Notes, URL: Original data: *Watertown Records*, by Fred G. Baker. <www.ancestry.com/search/rectype/inddbs/4748.htm>

Massachusetts, Middlesex Co., Watertown
Type: Transcript; B-M-D-BU
Year Range: 1693–1822
Online: Ancestry
Title: Watertown, Massachusetts Records of Births, Deaths, and Marriages, 1693–1822
Notes, URL: Original data: *Watertown Records*, by Fred G. Baker. <www.ancestry.com/search/rectype/inddbs/6310.htm>

Massachusetts, Middlesex Co., Woburn
Type: Transcript; B-M-D
Year Range: 1640–1900
Online: F&LH
Title: Woburn records of births, deaths, and marriages
Notes, URL: A book by Edward F. Johnson.

Massachusetts, Norfolk Co., Braintree
Type: Transcript; B-M-D
Year Range: 1640–1793
Online: Free
Title: Vital Records of Braintree, Massachusetts 1640–1793 Edited by Samuel A. Bates 1886
Notes, URL: <http://freepages.genealogy.rootsweb.com/~dyer/braintre.htm>

Massachusetts, Norfolk Co., Franklin
Type: Transcript; B-M-D
Year Range: 1778–1872
Online: F&LH
Title: The record of births, marriages, and deaths in the town of Franklin, from 1778 to 1872
Notes, URL: Orestes T. Doe, ed.

Massachusetts, Norfolk Co., Walpole
Type: Transcript; B-M-D
Year Range: 1724–1850
Online: Free
Title: Vital Records of Walpole to 1850
Notes, URL: Text of the published records. <www.walpole.ma.us/hhisdocvitalrecords.htm>

Massachusetts, Plymouth Co., Abington
Type: Text of a book containing transcripts; B
Year Range: Up to 1850
Online: Genealogy Library
Title: Vital Records of Abington, Massachusetts to the year 1850 volume I—Births

Notes, URL: Select Records | Birth Records | Massachusetts.

Massachusetts, Plymouth Co., Bridgewater
Type: Transcript; M
Year Range: 1670–1722
Online: Free
Title: Marriages in the Town of Bridgewater Previous to its Division
Notes, URL: From *The New England Historical and Genealogical Register*, vol. 21 [July 1867], pp. 225-228. <www.rootsweb.com/~mabridge/nehgr/nehgr.html>

Massachusetts, Plymouth Co., Hanover
Type: Transcript; B-M-D
Year Range: 1717–1787
Online: F&LH
Title: A copy of the records of births, marriages, and deaths, and of intentions of marriage of the town of Hanover, Mass., 1717–1787
Notes, URL: Published in 1898.

Massachusetts, Plymouth Co., Marshfield
Type: Transcript; D
Year Range: 1658–1666
Online: F&LH
Title: Thunder & lightning and deaths at Marshfield in 1658 & 1666
Notes, URL: A book by Nathaniel Bradstreet Shurtleff

Massachusetts, Plymouth Co., Middleborough
Type: Transcript; B-M-D
Year Range: 1669–1845
CD-ROM: $49.99 Genealogy.com. CD #203
Online: Genealogy Library
Title: The Complete Mayflower Descendant. Vols. 1-46 & Other Sources
Notes, URL: Includes *Middleborough, Massachusetts Vital Records, Volumes 1-2.* <www.genealogy.com/203facd.html>

Massachusetts, Suffolk Co., Boston
Type: Transcript; B-M-D
Year Range: 1630–1699
Online: Ancestry
Title: Boston Vital Records, 1630–99
Notes, URL: Over 30,000 vital records plus baptisms at the Boston First Church. Original data: Appleton, William S., ed. *Boston Births, Baptisms, Marriages, and Deaths 1630–1699.* <www.ancestry.com/search/rectype/inddbs/1021.htm>

Massachusetts, Suffolk Co., Boston
Type: Transcript; B
Year Range: 1700–1800
Online: Ancestry
Title: Boston Births, 1700–1800
Notes, URL: Over 15,000 birth records. Largely complete up to 1745. Original data: Boston Registry Department. Boston Births from A.D. 1700 to A.D. 1800. <www.ancestry.com/search/rectype/inddbs/1021.htm>

Massachusetts, Suffolk Co., Boston
Type: Transcript; M
Year Range: 1700–1809
Online: Ancestry
Title: Boston, Massachusetts Marriages, 1700–1809
Notes, URL: Original data: Boston, Massachusetts Registry Department. *Boston Marriages from 1700 to 1751* and *Boston Marriages from 1752–1809.* <www.ancestry.com/search/rectype/inddbs/5208.htm>

Massachusetts, Suffolk Co., Boston
Type: Transcript; M
Year Range: 1752–1809
Online: F&LH
Title: Boston marriages from 1752 to 1809
Notes, URL: Published in 1903.

Massachusetts, Worcester Co., Fitchburg
Type: Transcript; B-M-D
Year Range: 1789–1859
CD-ROM: $33.50 (Mac/Win), Heritage Books, item #1824
Title: Heritage Books Archives: The Old Records of the Town of Fitchburg [MA] Volumes 1-8
Notes, URL: Includes town records, 1764–1859. Compiled by Walter A. Davis. <www.heritagebooks.com>. Search on "Fitchburg."

Massachusetts, Worcester Co., Milford
Type: Abstracts; B-M-D
Online: F&LH
Title: [Register of births, marriages, and deaths in the town of Milford, Massachusetts]

Michigan
Type: Index; M
Year Range: Up to 1850
Online: Ancestry
Title: Marriages—Michigan to 1850
Notes, URL: 13,000 names. <www.ancestry.com/search/rectype/inddbs/2092a.htm>

Michigan
Type: Index; M
Year Range: 1840–1899
Online: Genealogy Library
Title: Michigan Marriages from 1840 to 1899
Notes, URL: 54,402 marriages. Select Records | Marriage | Michigan.

Michigan
Type: Abstracts; M
Year Range: 1847–1849
Online: Free
Title: Early Marriages by Albertus C. Van Raalte, From Southern Ottawa County Michigan, and Northern Allegan County Michigan.
Notes, URL: <www.macatawa.org/~devries/Earlym.htm>

Michigan
Type: Transcripts; B-M-D
Year Range: 1850–1859
Online: F&LH
Title: Michigan vital records from the Michigan Christian Herald: 1850–[1859]

Michigan
Type: Index; M
Year Range: 1851–1875
Online: Ancestry
Title: Michigan Marriages, 1851–1875
Notes, URL: Branch, Hillsdale, Jackson, Kent, and Wayne counties. <www.ancestry.com/search/rectype/inddbs/5299.htm>

Michigan
Type: Transcript; D
Year Range: 1867–1897
Online: Free
Title: Michigan Department of Community Health, Genealogical Death Indexing System
Notes, URL: 170,000 records through 1884. <www.mdch.state.mi.us/pha/osr/gendisx/search2.htm>

Michigan
Type: Index; D
Year Range: 1971–1996
CD-ROM: $29.95 (Win), Ancestry, itm #2353, <http://shops.ancestry.com>. Search on "Michigan deaths."
Online: Ancestry
Title: Michigan Vital Records: Deaths 1971–1996
Notes, URL: An index of over 2.75 million death records from all counties. Compiled by the Michigan Department

of Vital and Health Records. <www.ancestry.com/search/rectype/inddbs/3171a.htm>

Michigan, Alpena Co.
Type: Abstracts; M
Year Range: 1869–1872
Online: Free
Title: Early Alpena County Marriages 1871
Notes, URL: <www.rootsweb.com/~mialpena/early.htm>

Michigan, Branch Co.
Type: Index; D
Year Range: 1867–pres.
Online: Free
Title: Branch County Clerk's Office, Search for a Death Record
Notes, URL: <www.co.branch.mi.us/deathsearch.taf>

Michigan, Eaton Co., Vermontville
Type: Transcripts; B-D
Year Range: 1900–1964
Online: Free
Title: Birth and Death Records for Vermontville, Eaton County, Michigan
Notes, URL: <ftp://ftp.rootsweb.com/pub/usgenweb/mi/eaton/multiple/index/i53212.txt>

Michigan, Genesee Co.
Type: Index; M-D
Year Range: 1930–pres.
Online: Free
Title: Genesee County Clerk's Public Access Web Service
Notes, URL: Marriages, 1963 to present. Deaths, 1930 to present. <www.co.genesee.mi.us/vitalrec/>

Michigan, Grand Traverse Co.
Type: Index; M-D
Year Range: 1853–pres.
Online: Free
Title: Grand Traverse County Records
Notes, URL: Marriage records from 1853. Death records from 1867. <www.tcnet.org/gtcounty/index.html>

Michigan, Ionia Co.
Type: Abstracts; M
Year Range: 1832–1932
Online: Free
Title: Ionia County, Michigan—Early Marriage Records—Indexed by Groom
Notes, URL: <www.rootsweb.com/~miionia/more.txt>

Michigan, Kalkaska Co.
Type: Abstracts; M
Year Range: 1871–1875
Online: Free
Title: Marriages in Kalkaska County, Michigan 1871–1875
Notes, URL: <www.members.aol.com/kingsley/kas-mar.html>

Michigan, Kent Co.
Type: Abstracts; M
Year Range: 1845–1870
Online: Free
Title: Marriage Records I Kent County, Michigan I 1845–1870
Notes, URL: <www.rootsweb.com/~mikent/marriages/court/1845-1870/>

Michigan, Kent Co., Grand Rapids
Type: Transcript; M
Year Range: 1837–1889
Online: Free
Title: Early Marriages and Deaths of Village Residents
Notes, URL: Source: *History of the City of Grand Rapids, Michigan,* by Albert Baxter. Includes marriages, 1837–1850, & golden wedding anniversaries, 1859–1889. <www.wellswooster.com/grmarr.txt>

Michigan, Livingston Co.
Type: Index; D
Year Range: 1867–1948
Online: Free
Title: Livingston County Michigan Death Index
Notes, URL: <www.livgenmi.com/deathlisting.htm>

Michigan, Macomb Co.
Type: Index; D
Year Range: 1904–pres.
Online: Free
Title: Macomb County Database Direct—Death Records
Notes, URL: <www.macomb.mcntv.com/deathrecords/>

Michigan, Muskegon Co.
Type: Index; D
Year Range: 1867–1965
Online: Free
Title: Muskegon County Genealogical Death Indexing System
Notes, URL: <www.co.muskegon.mi.us/clerk/websearch.cfm>

Michigan, Newaygo Co.
Type: Abstracts; M
Year Range: Early
Online: Free
Title: Early Marriages Newaygo County: The Dibean Collection
Notes, URL: <www.rootsweb.com/~minewayg/dibean.html>

Michigan, Oakland Co.
Type: Compiled research; B-M-D
Year Range: 1800–1917
Online: Ancestry
Title: Oakland County, Michigan Vital Records, 1800–1917
Notes, URL: 215,500 names. Source: Martha Baldwin. *Our Pioneers: Families of Early Oakland County, Michigan.* <www.ancestry.com/search/rectype/inddbs/4404.htm>

Michigan, Saginaw Co.
Type: Index; M-D
Year Range: 1995–pres.
Online: Free
Title: Saginaw, MI, County Clerk, Death Certificates Index
Notes, URL: <www.saginawcounty.com/clerk/search/index.html>

Michigan, St. Clair Co.
Type: Transcripts; M-D
Year Range: 1838–1974
Online: Free
Title: St. Clair County, Michigan Marriages & Deaths
Notes, URL: Marriages, 1838–1898. Deaths, 1868–1974. <www.rootsweb.com/~mistcla2>

Michigan, St. Joseph Co.
Type: Index; M
Year Range: 1832–1887
Online: Free
Title: Indexes of Marriages in St. Joseph County 1832 through 1887
Notes, URL: <www.members.tripod.com/~tfred/marrind.html>

Michigan, St. Joseph Co.
Type: Index; D
Year Range: 1867–1929
Online: Free
Title: St. Joseph County Death Index 1867–1929
Notes, URL: <www.members.tripod.com/~tfred/67-29ind.html>

Michigan, Tuscola Co.
Type: Index; D
Year Range: 1867–1903
Online: Free
Title: Tuscola County, MI, Death Records Master Index

Notes, URL: <www.usgennet.org/usa/mi/county/tuscola/deaths/deathsindex.htm>

Minnesota
Type: Index; D
Year Range: 1907–1996
Online: Free
Title: Minnesota Death Certificate Index
Notes, URL: <http://people.mnhs.org/dci/Search.cfm>

Minnesota, Norman Co.
Type: Index; D
Year Range: 1871–1981
Online: Free
Title: Norman County Minnesota Death Record Index
Notes, URL: <www.rootsweb.com/~mnnorman/death.htm>

Minnesota, Olmsted Co., Rochester
Type: Index; D
Year Range: 1871–1940
Online: Free
Title: Rochester Death Records Index
Notes, URL: <www.selco.lib.mn.us/apps/ochs/rocdeath.cfm>

Minnesota, Pipestone Co.
Type: Index; M
Year Range: 1879–1891
Online: Free
Title: Pipestone County Museum Marriage Records: Pipestone County Marriage Records, 1879–1891
Notes, URL: <www.pipestoneminnesota.com/museum/marria~1.htm>

Minnesota, Rice Co.
Type: Database; M
Year Range: 1860–1869
Online: Ancestry
Title: Rice County, Minnesota Marriages, 1860–69
Notes, URL: Nearly 800 names. <www.ancestry.com/search/rectype/inddbs/3754.htm>

Minnesota, Rice Co.
Type: Transcript; B
Year Range: 1870–1874
Online: Ancestry
Title: Rice County, Minnesota Births, 1870–74
Notes, URL: 2,100 births. <www.ancestry.com/search/rectype/inddbs/3735.htm>

Minnesota, St. Louis Co.
Type: Index; D
Year Range: 1870–2000
Online: Free
Title: St. Louis County, Minnesota, Death Records Index
Notes, URL: <www.rootsweb.com/~mnstloui/slcmndin.htm>

Minnesota, Wadena Co.
Type: Index; D
Year Range: 1880–1994
Online: Free
Title: Wadena County Death Index (1880–February 1994)
Notes, URL: <www.rootsweb.com/~mnwadena/deathpage.htm>

Minnesota, Waseca Co.
Type: Index; D
Year Range: 1870–1989
Online: Free
Title: Minnesota Death Records, Waseca Co. Death Index
Notes, URL: <www.idreamof.com/death/mn.html>

Minnesota, Washington Co.
Type: Abstracts; B
Year Range: 1870–1910
Online: Free
Title: Washington County Births 1870–1910
Notes, URL: In progress. <www.rootsweb.com/~mnwashin/birthindex.htm>

Mississippi
Type: Abstracts; M
Year Range: Up to 1825
Online: Ancestry
Title: Marriages—Mississippi to 1825
Notes, URL: Over 8,500 names. <www.ancestry.com/search/rectype/inddbs/2093a.htm>

Mississippi
Type: Index; M
Year Range: 1809–1925
Online: Free
Title: Mississippi Connections
Notes, URL: Marriages. <www.mississippiconnections.nisa.com/marriageindex.html>

Mississippi
Type: Abstracts; M
Year Range: 1826–1850
Online: Ancestry
Title: Mississippi Marriages, 1826–50
Notes, URL: Over 22,000 names. <www.ancestry.com/search/rectype/inddbs/3739.htm>

Mississippi
Type: Abstracts; M
Year Range: 1826–1900
Online: Ancestry
Title: Mississippi Marriages, 1826–1900
Notes, URL: <www.ancestry.com/search/rectype/inddbs/4585.htm>

Mississippi
Type: Abstracts; M
Year Range: 1829–1900
Online: Genealogy Library
Title: Mississippi Marriages from 1829 to 1900
Notes, URL: An index to 76,891 marriages. Select Records I Marriage I Mississippi.

Mississippi
Type: Transcript; M
Year Range: 1870–1925
Online: Free
Title: CensusDiggins.com: Mississippi Marriage Records Database
Notes, URL: Over 3,000 marriages. <www.censusdiggins.com/mississippi_marriages.html>

Mississippi, Rankin Co.
Type: Abstracts; M
Year Range: 1828–1865
Online: Free
Title: Rankin County, Mississippi Marriage Records
Notes, URL: <www.genealogytoday.com/pub/rankin.htm>

Missouri
Type: Abstracts; B-M-D
Year Range: Up to 1839
CD-ROM: $28.50 (Mac/Win), Heritage Books
Title: HB Archives: Missouri, Vol. 3
Notes, URL: 6 volumes of the Missouri Genealogical Records & Abstracts series by Sherida K. Eddlemon. <www.heritagebooks.com>

Missouri
Type: Abstracts; M
Year Range: Up to 1840
CD-ROM: $29.99, Genealogy.com
Online: Genealogy Library
Title: Midwest Pioneers, 1600s–1800s
Notes, URL: Includes *Missouri Marriages Before 1840* with 16,000 marriage records. <www.genealogy.com/508facd.html>

Missouri
Type: Abstracts; B-D
Year Range: Up to 1909
Online: Free

Title: Missouri Birth & Death Records Database
Notes, URL: Over 185,000 records from 87 counties. <www.sos.mo.gov/archives/resources/birthdeath>

Missouri
Type: Abstracts; M
Year Range: 1767–1900
CD-ROM: $26.95 (Win), Ancestry, item #2310, <http://shops.ancestry.com>. Search on "Missouri marriages."
Title: Missouri Vital Records: Marriages 1767–1900
Notes, URL: 115,322 records with the names of 310,273 men and women in 88 counties.

Missouri
Type: Index; D
Year Range: 1816–2000
Online: Free
Title: MO Death Index
Notes, URL: Over 35,000 names submitted by researchers. <http://freepages.genealogy.rootsweb.com/~nettimae/modeaths>

Missouri
Type: Index; M
Year Range: 1851–1900
CD-ROM: $29.99 (Mac/Win), Genealogy.com, CD #234
Online: Genealogy Library
Title: Missouri, 1851–1900 Marriage Index
Notes, URL: 409,000 names. <www.genealogy.com/234facd.html>

Missouri
Type: Abstracts; M
Year Range: 1851–1900
Online: Ancestry
Title: Missouri Marriages, 1851–1900
Notes, URL: Records from 31 counties. <www.ancestry.com/search/rectype/inddbs/4474a.htm>

Missouri, Buchanan Co.
Type: Abstracts; M
Year Range: 1839–1855
Online: Ancestry
Title: Buchanan County, Missouri Marriages: 1839–55
Notes, URL: Original data: Ellsberry, Elizabeth Prather, comp. *Buchanan County, Missouri Marriage Records 1839–1855.* <www.ancestry.com/search/rectype/inddbs/6017.htm>

Missouri, Butler Co.
Type: Index; M
Year Range: 1848–1996
Online: Free
Title: Butler Co., Missouri Marriage Index
Notes, URL: <www.rootsweb.com/~mobutle2/marriage/ndx-ndx.htm>

Missouri, Caldwell Co.
Type: Abstracts; M
Year Range: 1845–1871
Online: Ancestry
Title: Caldwell County, Missouri Marriages, 1845–71
Notes, URL: Original data: Ellsberry, Elizabeth Prather. *Caldwell County, Missouri Marriages, 1845–1871.* <www.ancestry.com/search/rectype/inddbs/5172.htm>

Missouri, Caldwell Co.
Type: Transcripts; M
Year Range: 1861–1880
Online: Free
Title: Caldwell County Missouri Marriage Records
Notes, URL: <www.surnamearchive.com/document/caldwell1.htm>

Missouri, Carter Co.
Type: Abstracts; M
Year Range: 1860–1881
Online: Free
Title: Carter County, Missouri Marriages—Book 1: 1860–1881
Notes, URL: <ftp://ftp.rootsweb.com/pub/usgenweb/mo/carter/marriage/1860-81a.txt>

Missouri, Carter Co.
Type: Abstracts; M
Year Range: 1881–1890
Online: Free
Title: Marriage Records Carter County, Missouri Book "A", 1881–1890
Notes, URL: <ftp://ftp.rootsweb.com/pub/usgenweb/mo/carter/marriage/1881-90a.txt>

Missouri, Carter Co.
Type: Abstracts; M
Year Range: 1890–1898
Online: Free
Title: Carter County Missouri Marriage Book "B" 1890–1898
Notes, URL: <ftp://ftp.rootsweb.com/pub/usgenweb/mo/carter/marriage/1890-98b.txt>

Missouri, Carter Co.
Type: Abstracts; M
Year Range: 1898–1927
Online: Free
Title: Carter County Marriages 1898–1927
Notes, URL: <www.rootsweb.com/~mocarter/marrges.htm>

Missouri, Christian Co.
Type: Abstracts; M
Year Range: 1859–1940
Online: Free
Title: Christian County, Missouri Marriages—1859–1940
Notes, URL: <www.rootsweb.com/~moccl/marriages.htm>

Missouri, Dade Co.
Type: Database; M
Year Range: 1841–1953
Online: Free
Title: Dade County Marriage Records
Notes, URL: <www.rootsweb.com/~modade/mgrec.htm>

Missouri, Daviess Co.
Type: Abstracts; M
Year Range: 1838–1866
Online: Free
Title: Daviess County Missouri Marriages 1838–1866
Notes, URL: <www.rootsweb.com/~modavies/marriages.htm>

Missouri, Dent Co.
Type: Abstracts; D
Year Range: 1883–1885
Online: Free
Title: Dent County, Missouri Deaths 1883–1885
Notes, URL: <www.rootsweb.com/~modent/dd.htm>

Missouri, Greene Co.
Type: Index; D
Year Range: 1875–1972
Online: Free
Title: Greene County Records: Index to Coroner's Record Books
Notes, URL: Suspicious, unnatural, or unattended deaths. <http://thelibrary.springfield.missouri.org/lochist/records/index.html#coroner>

Missouri, Grundy Co.
Type: Abstracts; M
Year Range: 1841–1850
Online: Free
Title: Grundy Co., MO. Marriages, 1841–1850
Notes, URL: <www.rootsweb.com/~mogrundy/marriages.html>

Missouri, Henry Co.
Type: Abstracts; M

Year Range: 1835–1861
Online: Free
Title: Henry County Marriage Records 1835–1861
Notes, URL: <www.kcnet.com/~denis/rela ted/genealog/marriage.htm>

Missouri, Hickory Co.
Type: Transcripts; B
Year Range: 1883–1891
Online: Free
Title: Hickory Co., Mo. Births
Notes, URL: <ftp://ftp.rootsweb.com/pub/ usgenweb/mo/hickory/vitals/hick brth.txt>

Missouri, Jackson Co.
Type: Transcripts; D
Year Range: 1908–1909
Online: Free
Title: Jackson County Death Records
Notes, URL: <www.genealogytoday.com/ genealogy/enoch/records.html>

Missouri, Livingston Co.
Type: Abstracts; M
Year Range: 1837–1863
Online: Ancestry
Title: Livingston County, Missouri Marriages: 1837–63
Notes, URL: Compiled by Elizabeth Prather Ellsberry. <www.ancestry.com/search/ rectype/inddbs/6033.htm>

Missouri, Livingston Co.
Type: Transcripts; D
Year Range: 1883–1890
Online: Ancestry
Title: Livingston County, Missouri Death Records, 1883–90 and Agency Roll of Pensioners of Missouri
Notes, URL: Compiled by Elizabeth Prather Ellsberry. Includes more than 740 deaths. <www.ancestry.com/search/rec type/inddbs/5644.htm>

Missouri, Livingston Co.
Type: Transcript; B
Year Range: 1883–1891
Online: Ancestry
Title: Livingston County, Missouri Birth Records, 1883–84, 1888–91 Volume I & III
Notes, URL: Compiled by Elizabeth Prather Ellsberry. <www.ancestry.com/search/ rectype/inddbs/5552.htm>

Missouri, Mississippi Co.
Type: Index; M
Year Range: 1845–1885
Online: Free
Title: Mississippi Co., Missouri Marriage Index
Notes, URL: <www.rootsweb.com/~momis sis/marriage/ndx-ndx.htm>

Missouri, Morgan Co.
Type: Transcripts; M
Year Range: 1833–1893
CD-ROM: $29.50 (Mac/Win), Heritage Books, item #1369
Title: HB Archives: Missouri Vol. 1
Notes, URL: Includes Morgan County, MO Marriage Records 1833–1893, by Sherida K. Eddlemon (1990). <www.her itagebooks.com>. Search on "1369."

Missouri, New Madrid Co.
Type: Transcripts; M
Year Range: 1864–1874
Online: Ancestry
Title: New Madrid, Missouri Cemetery Records, and Marriage Records, 1864–1874
Notes, URL: More than 800 entries. Compiled by Elizabeth Prather Ellsberry. <www.ancestry.com/search/rectype/ inddbs/5822.htm>

Missouri, Polk Co.
Type: Transcript; M
Year Range: 1835–1889
Online: Free
Title: Polk County, Missouri Marriages
Notes, URL: <www.rootsweb.com/~mop olk/polkmarr.htm>

Missouri, Polk Co.
Type: Transcript; B
Year Range: 1867–1900
Online: Free
Title: Polk Co., Mo Birth Records
Notes, URL: <ftp://ftp.rootsweb.com/pub/ usgenweb/mo/polk/vitals/births.txt>

Missouri, Reynolds Co.
Type: Transcript; M
Year Range: 1870–1891
Online: Free
Title: Reynolds County Marriage Records 1870–1891
Notes, URL: <www.rootsweb.com/~morey nol/reymarge.htm>

Missouri, Ripley Co.
Type: Abstracts; M
Year Range: 1833–1860
Online: Free
Title: Ripley County Missouri Marriage Records {1833–1860}
Notes, URL: <www.members.tripod.com/~t msnyder/Ripley.htm_>

Missouri, Ripley Co.
Type: Abstracts; M
Year Range: 1833–1900
Online: Free
Title: Ripley County Marriages
Notes, URL: <www.rootsweb.com/~morip ley/marry.htm>

Missouri, Saline Co.
Type: Abstracts; M
Year Range: 1820–1881
Online: Ancestry
Title: Saline County, Missouri Marriages, 1820–81, Vols. 1–4
Notes, URL: More than 4,400 marriage records. Compiled by Elizabeth Prather Ellsberry. <www.ancestry.com/search/ rectype/inddbs/5495.htm>

Missouri, St. Clair Co.
Type: Transcripts; M
Year Range: 1855–1951
Online: Free
Title: St. Clair County, Missouri
Notes, URL: Mostly 1855–1859. <http://fre epages.genealogy.rootsweb.com/~cb ell/>

Missouri, St. Louis (city)
Type: Abstracts; M
Year Range: 1754–1835
Online: Free
Title: St. Louis Marriages (1754–1835)
Notes, URL: Over 4,200 names. <www.gene alogyinstlouis.accessgenealogy.com/ stlmarr.htm>

Missouri, St. Louis (city)
Type: Abstracts; M
Year Range: 1804–1876
Online: Ancestry
Title: St. Louis, Missouri Marriages, 1804–76
Notes, URL: Almost 77,000 marriages. Original data: St. Louis Genealogical Society. *St. Louis Marriage Index, 1804–76*. <www.ancestry.com/search/ rectype/inddbs/5413.htm>

Missouri, St. Louis (city)
Type: Index; D
Year Range: 1850–1908
Online: Ancestry
Title: St. Louis City Death Records, 1850–1908
Notes, URL: <www.ancestry.com/search/re ctype/inddbs/5696.htm>

Missouri, Wright Co.
Type: Abstracts; M
Year Range: 1897–1900

Online: Ancestry
Title: Wright County, Missouri: Marriages (1897–1900) & Wills (1859–1874)
Notes, URL: Compiled by Elizabeth Prather Ellsberry. <www.ancestry.com/search/rectype/inddbs/6045.htm>

Montana
Type: Index; D
Year Range: 1954–2002
Online: Ancestry
Title: Montana Death Index, 1954–2002
Notes, URL: <www.ancestry.com/search/rectype/inddbs/5437.htm>

Montana, Butte Co.
Type: Index; B-M-D
Online: Free
Title: Butte County Recorder's Office: Vital Records Database Inquiry
Notes, URL: <http://clerk-recorder.buttecounty.net/RiimsWeb/ASP/VTInquiry.asp>

Nevada
Type: Index; DI
Year Range: 1968–2002
CD-ROM: $15 (Win), Global Data
Title: Nevada Divorces
Notes, URL: <http://stores.shopforge.com/gencd/StoreFront.bok>

Nevada
Type: Index; M
Year Range: 1968–2002
CD-ROM: $15/day
Title: Nevada Marriages online search
Notes, URL: <http://stores.shopforge.com/gencd/StoreFront.bok>

Nevada, Clark Co.
Type: Index; M
Year Range: 1984–pres.
Online: Free
Title: Clark County, Nevada, Recorder: Marriage Inquiry System
Notes, URL: Includes marriages in Las Vegas. <www.co.clark.nv.us/recorder/mar_srch.htm>

Nevada, Douglas Co.
Type: Abstracts; B-M-D
Year Range: 1862–1923
Online: Ancestry
Title: Douglas County, Nevada Vital Records, 1862–1923
Notes, URL: Birth records, 1885–1900; marriage records, 1862–1919; death records, 1887–1923. <www.ancestry.com/search/rectype/inddbs/5013.htm>

Nevada, Storey Co.
Type: Transcript; B-D
Year Range: 1862–1903
Online: Ancestry
Title: Storey County Nevada Death & Birth records, 1862–1903
Notes, URL: Over 6,700 birth and death records. <www.ancestry.com/search/rectype/inddbs/6084.htm>

Nevada, Storey Co.
Type: Transcript; M
Year Range: 1874–1885
Online: Ancestry
Title: Storey County Nevada marriage records, 1874–85
Notes, URL: Over 2,600 marriage applications. <www.ancestry.com/search/rectype/inddbs/5829.htm>

New Hampshire, Carroll Co., Madison
Type: Transcript; B
Year Range: 1887–1901
Online: Free
Title: Madison Births, 1887–1901
Notes, URL: <http://conwayhistorical.tripod.com/Madison_Vitals_Births_1887–1901.htm>

New Hampshire, Grafton Co., Bath
Type: Transcript; B
Year Range: 1807–1857
Online: NEHGS
Title: Record of Births Attended by Dr. John French in Bath, New Hampshire and Surrounding Towns, 1807–1857
Notes, URL: Names of 2,336 fathers & the dates of birth of their children. Includes births in Landaff, Lisbon, Lyman, Benton, & Haverhill. <www.newenglandancestors.org/research/database/johnfrench>

New Hampshire, Grafton Co., Enfield
Type: Transcript; B-M-D
Year Range: 1761–1940
Online: NEHGS
Title: Vital Records of the Town of Enfield, Grafton County, New Hampshire, 1761–1940
Notes, URL: Compiled from various sources. <www.newenglandancestors.org/research/database/enfieldnh/Default.asp>

New Hampshire, Merrimack Co., Hopkinton
Type: Transcript; B-M-D
CD-ROM: $30 (Mac/Win), Heritage Books, item #1416
Title: HB Archives: New Hampshire, Vol. 4
Notes, URL: Includes *Hopkinton, New Hampshire, Vital Records* (Vols. 1& 2), by Pauline J. Oesterlin. <www.heritagebooks.com>. Search on 1416.

New Hampshire, Rockingham Co., Londonderry
Type: Digital images of pages containing transcripts; B-M-D
Year Range: 1719–1910
CD-ROM: $29.99, Genealogy.com, CD #523
Online: Genealogy Library
Title: Maine & New Hampshire Settlers, 1600s–1900s
Notes, URL: Includes *Vital Records of Londonderry, New Hampshire, 1719–1910.* <www.genealogy.com/genealogy/523facd.html>

New Hampshire, Rockingham Co., Londonderry
Type: Transcript; B-M-D
Year Range: 1722–1910
Online: Ancestry
Title: Londonderry, New Hampshire Vital Records, 1722–1910
Notes, URL: Records for 40,000 people. Source: Annis, Daniels. *Vital Records of Londonderry, New Hampshire.* <www.ancestry.com/search/rectype/inddbs/3710.htm>

New Hampshire, Rockingham Co., Plaistow
Type: Abstracts; B-M-D
Year Range: 1726–1871
Online: NEHGS
Title: Plaistow, New Hampshire, Vital Records, 1726–1871
Notes, URL: <www.newenglandancestors.org/research/database/plaistownh>

New Hampshire, Rockingham Co., Rye
Type: Transcript; B-M-D
Year Range: Up to 1890
CD-ROM: $29.50 (Mac/Win), Heritage Books, item #1165
Title: HB Archives: New Hampshire, Vol. 1
Notes, URL: Includes *Vital Records of Rye, New Hampshire,* by Kathleen E. Hosier. <www.heritagebooks.com>. Search on "1165."

New Hampshire, Rockingham Co., Salem
Type: Transcript; B-M-D
Year Range: 1760–?
CD-ROM: $30 (Mac/Win), Heritage Books, item #1416
Title: HB Archives: New Hampshire, Vol. 4
Notes, URL: Includes *History of Salem, New*

Hampshire (Parts 1 & 2), by Edgar Gilbert. <www.heritagebooks.com>. Search on 1416.

New Hampshire, Strafford Co., Dover
Type: Transcript; D
Year Range: 1708–1802
Online: NEHGS
Title: Bill of Mortality for Dover, New Hampshire—Deaths from 1708 to 1802
Notes, URL: 653 deaths from *Bill of Mortality for the Society of Friends in Dover, N.H. . . .* by James K. Remich. <www.newengland ancestors.org/research/database/ dovernh>

New Jersey
Type: Abstracts; M
Year Range: 1665–1800
Online: Ancestry
Title: New Jersey Marriages, Colonial Era, 1665–1800
Notes, URL: 45,000 names. Source: Nelson, William. *Documents Relating to the Colonial History of the State of New Jersey: Vol. XXII, Marriage Records 1665–1800.* <www.ancestry.com/search/rectype/ inddbs/2095.htm>

New Jersey
Type: Abstracts; M
Year Range: 1680–1900
CD-ROM: $29.99 (Mac/Win), Genealogy.com, CD #240
Online: Genealogy Library
Title: New Jersey, 1680–1900 Marriage Index
Notes, URL: 179,000 names. <www.geneal ogy.com/240facd.html>

New Jersey
Type: Abstracts; M
Year Range: 1684–1895
Online: Ancestry
Title: New Jersey Marriages, 1684–1895
Notes, URL: Records from 10 counties. Source: original microfilmed documents. <www.ancestry.com/sea rch/rectype/inddbs/4480.htm>

New Jersey
Type: Transcript; M
Year Range: 1707–1800
Online: F&LH
Title: South Jersey marriages: supplementing the Cape May, Cumberland, Gloucester, and Salem County marriage records
Notes, URL: By H. Stanley Craig.

New Jersey, Atlantic Co.
Type: Abstracts; M
Year Range: 1805–1880
Online: F&LH
Title: Atlantic County, New Jersey marriage records
Notes, URL: Compiled by H. Stanley Craig.

New Jersey, Atlantic Co.
Type: Abstracts; M
Year Range: 1837–1880
Online: Ancestry
Title: Atlantic County, New Jersey Marriages, 1837–1880
Notes, URL: Nearly 5,700 names. Original data: Craig, H. Stanley. *Atlantic County, New Jersey Marriage Records.* <www.anc estry.com/search/rectype/inddbs/ 3970.htm>

New Jersey, Bergen Co.
Type: Index; M
Year Range: 1796–1878
Online: F&LH
Title: Index of Bergen County marriages
Notes, URL: Index to Bergen County, New Jersey, Marriage records, by Frances A. Westervelt.

New Jersey, Bergen Co.
Type: Transcripts; M
Year Range: 1796–1878
Online: F&LH
Title: Bergen County, New Jersey marriage records
Notes, URL: By Frances A. Westervelt.

New Jersey, Camden Co.
Type: Abstracts; M
Year Range: 1837–1910
Online: Ancestry
Title: Camden County, New Jersey Marriages, 1837–1910
Notes, URL: Over 6,000 records. Original data: Craig, H. Stanley. *Camden County New Jersey Marriages.* <www.ancestry. com/search/rectype/inddbs/3725 .htm>

New Jersey, Cape May Co.
Type: Abstracts; M
Year Range: 1727–1796
Online: F&LH
Title: Cape May County records
Notes, URL: By H. Stanley Craig. *Marriages from Liber A of deeds and miscellaneous records, printed marriage licenses, archives of New Jersey, Book A of marriages, and Liber B of marriages.*

New Jersey, Cumberland Co.
Type: Transcripts; M
Year Range: 1740–1910
Online: Ancestry
Title: Cumberland County, New Jersey Marriages, 1740–1910
Notes, URL: Over 12,000 records. Source: Craig, Stanley H., comp. *Cumberland County Marriages.* <www.ancestry.com/ search/rectype/inddbs/4090.htm>

New Jersey, Gloucester Co.
Type: Transcripts; M
Year Range: 1688–1891
Online: F&LH
Title: Bible records, marriage certificates indexed, place names bibliography

New Jersey, Hunterdon Co.
Type: Transcripts; M
Year Range: 1795–1875
Online: Ancestry
Title: Hunterdon County, New Jersey Marriages, 1795–1875
Notes, URL: Over 40,000 names. Originally published in the *Hunterdon County Democrat.* <www.ancestry.com/search/ rectype/inddbs/4353.htm>

New Jersey, Salem Co.
Type: Transcripts; M
Year Range: 1686–1830
Online: F&LH
Title: Salem County (New Jersey) marriage records
Notes, URL: By Stanley H. Craig.

New Jersey, Salem Co.
Type: Compiled research; B-M-D
Year Range: 1801–1900
Online: Ancestry
Title: Salem County, New Jersey Genealogical Records
Notes, URL: Over 10,000 names. By Stanley H. Craig. <www.ancestry.com/search/ rectype/inddbs/3959.htm>

New Jersey, Somerset Co., Bernards
Type: Transcripts; B
Year Range: 1850–1904
Online: F&LH
Title: Return of births in the township of Bernards, county of Somerset, state of New Jersey: typescript (photocopy)
Notes, URL: By Mrs. Edmund M. Oehlers.

New Jersey, Sussex Co.
Type: Transcripts; B-M-D
Year Range: 1665–1874
Online: Free
Title: Nancy Pascal's Genealogy Page

Notes, URL: Births & deaths, 1848–1867. Marriages, 1665–1874. <www.gate.net/~pascalfl/index.html>

New Mexico
Type: Transcripts; M
Year Range: 1868–1904
Online: Free
Title: New Mexico Genealogical Society
Notes, URL: Marriages in Colfax County, 1889–1893, 1897–1901; Grant County, 1868–1872, 1909–1910; Mora County, 1875–1890; Rio Arriba County, 1902–1904. <www.nmgs.org/znmgs.htm>

New Mexico
Type: Index; D
Year Range: 1899–1940
Online: Free
Title: New Mexico Death Index Project (1899–1940)
Notes, URL: <www.rootsweb.com/~usgenweb/nm/nmdi.htm>

New Mexico, Lincoln Co.
Type: Transcripts; D
Year Range: 1913–1919
Online: Free
Title: Lincoln County Deaths 1913–1919
Notes, URL: <www.usgennet.org/usa/nm/county/lincoln/lcdmain.htm>

New Mexico, Valencia Co.
Type: Transcripts; D
Year Range: 1907–1909
Online: Free
Title: New Mexico Genealogical Society: Valencia County Death Register 1907–1909
Notes, URL: <www.nmgs.org/znmgs.htm>

New York
Type: Compiled research; B-M-D
Year Range: 1613–1674
CD-ROM: $29.99, Genealogy.com
Online: IPR
Title: New Netherlands, Vital Records 1600s
Notes, URL: Indexed images of 1,793 family group records. Source: *Genealogical and Biographical Directory to Persons in New Netherland, From 1613 to 1674. Volumes I-IV.* <www.genealogy.com/011facd.html>

New York
Type: Transcripts; M
Year Range: 1639–1786
Online: Free
Title: Family Researcher: Early N.Y. Marriages
Notes, URL: <www.familyresearcher.net/US/NY/marriages.cfm>

New York
Type: Transcripts; M
Year Range: 1639–1786
Online: Free
Title: NY Marriage Licenses
Notes, URL: <http://homepages.rootsweb.com/~rbillard/ny_marriage_licenses.htm>

New York
Type: Abstracts; M
Year Range: 1639–1786
Online: Free
Title: Long Island Genealogy: Province of New York—Marriage Licenses
Notes, URL: Source: O'Callaghan, E.B. *New York Marriages Previous to 1784.* <www.longislandgenealogy.com>

New York
Type: Index; M
Year Range: 1639–1916
CD-ROM: $29.99, Genealogy.com
Title: Selected Areas of New York, 1639–1916 Marriage Index
Notes, URL: 216,000 names. <www.genealogy.com/401facd.html>

New York
Type: Abstracts; M
Year Range: 1664–1784
Online: Ancestry
Title: New York Marriages to 1784
Notes, URL: Source: O'Callaghan, E.B. *New York Marriages Previous to 1784.* <www.ancestry.com/search/rectype/inddbs/3177.htm>

New York
Type: Index; M
Year Range: 1740s–1880s
CD-ROM: $29.99, Genealogy.com, CD #402
Online: Genealogy Library
Title: New York #2, 1740s–1880s Marriage Index
Notes, URL: Nearly 100,000 names from church records, censuses, vital records, magazines, journals, and newspapers. <www.genealogy.com/402facd.html>

New York
Type: Abstracts; B-D
Year Range: 1800s–1992
CD-ROM: $98, Global Data
Title: NY Births & Deaths 2-CD set 1800s–1992
Notes, URL: Misc. births & deaths. <www.gencd.com>

New York, New York (City)
Type: Transcript; D
Year Range: 1814–1816
Online: Ancestry
Title: New York City Deaths, 1814–16
Notes, URL: Nearly 3,000 names. Source: *Longworth's 1815 New York City Directory.* <www.ancestry.com/search/rectype/inddbs/4256.htm>

New York, New York (City)
Type: Transcripts; M
Year Range: 1830–1854
Online: F&LH
Title: Marriages performed by the various mayors and aldermen of the city of New York, as well as justices of the peace, etc.: 1830–1854
Notes, URL: By Ray C. Sawyer.

New York, New York (City)
Type: Index; M
Year Range: 1865–1890
CD-ROM: $29.99, Genealogy.com, CD #239
Online: Genealogy Library
Title: New York City, 1600s–1800s Marriage Index
Notes, URL: More than 410,000 names, mostly 1865–1890. <www.genealogy.com/239facd.html>

New York, New York (City)
Type: Index; B
Year Range: 1891–1902
Online: Ancestry
Title: New York City Births, 1891–1902
Notes, URL: <www.ancestry.com/search/rectype/inddbs/5157a.htm>

New York, New York (City)
Type: Index; D
Year Range: 1892–1902
Online: Ancestry
Title: New York City Deaths, 1892–1902
Notes, URL: <www.ancestry.com/search/rectype/inddbs/6492.htm>

New York, Ontario Co.
Type: Index; B-M-D
Year Range: 1882–1935
Online: Free
Title: Ontario County Records and Archives Center
Notes, URL: Town vital records, 1882–1913. Marriage records, 1908–1935. <www.raims.com>

New York, Otsego Co., Worcester
Type: Transcript; D
Year Range: 1818–1842
Online: Free
Title: Deaths and Burials in Worcester, New York
Notes, URL: Taken from the records of Dr. Uriah Bigelow. <www.newyorkstateresearch.com/deaths_and_burials.html>

New York, Saratoga Co., Saratoga Springs
Type: Transcript; D
Year Range: 1888
Online: Free
Title: Deaths from Kerwin's 1888 Saratoga Springs City Directory
Notes, URL: <www.bfn.org/~ae487/1888.html>

New York, Suffolk Co., Huntington
Type: Index; B-M-D
Year Range: 1653–1975
CD-ROM: $19.50 (Mac/Win), Long Island Genealogy
Title: Huntington Town Records, History & Family Stories CD
Notes, URL: Includes an index to the Huntington Town Records, including Babylon, Long Island, N.Y., 1653–1873. <http://genealogycds.com/sales/HuntingtonBabylon.htm>

New York, Suffolk Co., Southold
Type: Transcript; M-D
Year Range: 1696–1811
CD-ROM: $19.50 (Mac/Win), Long Island Genealogy
Title: The Salmon records: a private register of marriages and deaths of the residents of the town of Southold, Suffolk County, N.Y.
Notes, URL: <http://genealogycds.com/sales/salmon.htm>

New York, Suffolk Co., Southold
Type: Transcript; M-D
Year Range: 1696–1811
Online: F&LH
Title: The Salmon records: a private register of marriages and deaths of the residents of the town of Southold, Suffolk County, N.Y.

New York, Tompkins Co., Ithaca
Type: Transcripts; B-M-D
Year Range: Up to 1880
Online: F&LH
Title: Unpublished records of births, baptisms, confirmations, marriages, deaths
Notes, URL: By Edna May Gross.

New York, Ulster Co., New Paltz
Type: Transcripts; B-M-D
Year Range: 1847–1850
Online: F&LH
Title: Births, marriages, deaths, New Paltz, Ulster County, New York: 1847–1850

New York, Warren Co., Bolton
Type: Transcripts; M
Year Range: 1840–1870
Online: Free
Title: Marriages Performed by George B. Reynolds, Justice of the Peace, Town of Bolton, Warren County, N.Y.
Notes, URL: <www.inet-1.com/~markham/marriages.htm>

New York, Westchester Co.
Type: Indexes; M
Year Range: 1908–1928
Online: Free
Title: Westchester County Archives, Indexes to Online Series
Notes, URL: <www.co.westchester.ny.us/wcarchives/ind.html>

New York, Westchester Co., New Rochelle
Type: Transcripts; D
Year Range: 1853–1881
Online: F&LH
Title: New Rochelle, New York deaths, 1853–1881: Copied from the New Rochelle press almanacs, 1879–1882, and records of deaths in New Rochelle from account books of Cornelius Seacord, coffin maker

North Carolina
Type: Abstracts; M
Year Range: Up to 1825
Online: Ancestry
Title: North Carolina Marriages to 1825
Notes, URL: Over 103,000 names. <www.ancestry.com/search/rectype/inddbs/2096.htm>

North Carolina
Type: Abstracts; B-M-D
Year Range: 1700s–1900s
CD-ROM: $29.99, Genealogy.com, CD #524
Online: Genealogy Library
Title: Early North Carolina Settlers, 1700s–1900s
Notes, URL: Includes records from 11 volumes of the *North Carolina Historical and Genealogical Register*. <www.genealogy.com/524facd.html>

North Carolina
Type: Abstracts; M
Year Range: 1741–1868
Online: Ancestry
Title: North Carolina Marriage Bonds, 1741–1868
Notes, URL: 170,000 marriage bonds. <www.ancestry.com/search/rectype/inddbs/4802a.htm>

North Carolina
Type: Transcripts; M
Year Range: 1744–1900
CD-ROM: $26.95 (Win), Ancestry Item #2171, <http://shops.ancestry.com>. Search on "North Carolina marriages."
Title: North Carolina Vital Records: Marriages 1744–1900 (Select Counties & Years)
Notes, URL: 137,000 records from 44 of 100 counties.

North Carolina
Type: Abstracts; M
Year Range: 1827–1900
Online: Ancestry
Title: North Carolina Marriages, 1827–1900
Notes, URL: <www.ancestry.com/search/rectype/inddbs/3975.htm>

North Carolina
Type: Index; M
Year Range: 1850–1900
CD-ROM: $29.99, Genealogy.com, CD #245
Online: Genealogy Library
Title: North Carolina, 1850–1900 Marriage Index
Notes, URL: About 126,000 names. <www.genealogy.com/245facd.html>

North Carolina
Type: Abstracts; D
Year Range: 1968–1996
CD-ROM: $35.95 (Win), Ancestry Item #2172, <http://shops.ancestry.com>. Search on "North Carolina deaths."
Title: North Carolina Vital Records CD: Deaths 1968–1996
Notes, URL: Nearly 1.4 million Health Dept. records from all 100 counties. On two CDs.

North Carolina, Buncombe Co.
Type: Abstracts; M
Year Range: 1808–1937
Online: Free
Title: Marriage Records
Notes, URL: <www.obcgs.com/wedindx.htm>

North Carolina, Catawba Co.
Type: Abstracts; M
Year Range: 1842–1880
CD-ROM: $35 (Mac or Win), Heritage Books, item #1749
Title: HB Archives: North Carolina Vol. 1
Notes, URL: Includes *Catawba Co., North Carolina, Marriages, 1842 [50]-1880, Vol. 1*, by Elizabeth Bray Sherrill. <www. heritagebooks.com>. Search on "Catawba."

North Carolina, Macon Co.
Type: Index; D
Year Range: 1913–1978
Online: Free
Title: Macon County Death Index 1913–1978
Notes, URL: Indexing in progress. <www.ge ocities.com/Heartland/Prairie/7305/ macon_county_death_index.htm>

North Carolina, Madison Co.
Type: Abstracts; M
Year Range: 1831–1868
Online: Free
Title: Madison County, NC Marriage Bonds
Notes, URL: <www.obcgs.com/madi-bonds .htm>

North Carolina, Nash Co.
Type: Abstracts; B-M-D
Year Range: Up to 1909
Online: Ancestry
Title: Nash County, North Carolina Vital Records Abstracts
Notes, URL: 30,000 names. Source: *Families of Early North Carolina*, publ. in 1909. <www.ancestry.com/search/rectype/ inddbs/4682.htm>

North Carolina, Rowan Co.
Type: Abstracts; M
Year Range: 1762–1826
Online: Free
Title: Rowan County Marriages from the Duncan Collection at OBCGS
Notes, URL: <www.obcgs.com/rowanmarr. htm>

North Carolina, Rowan Co.
Type: Index; M
Year Range: 1901–1949
Online: Genealogy Library
Title: Marriages of Rowan County North Carolina 1901–1925, 1925–1949
Notes, URL: By Robert H. Knotts Jr. Select Records I Vital Records I North Carolina.

North Carolina, Washington Co.
Type: Index; D
Year Range: 1913–1980
Online: Free
Title: Death Records Index of Washington County, North Carolina 1913–1980
Notes, URL: <www.rootsweb.com/~ncwas hin/WASHDTH.HTM>

North Dakota
Type: Index; D
Year Range: 1903–1997
Online: Free
Title: Red River Valley Genealogical Society, Funeral Home Indexes
Notes, URL: Covers eastern counties of N.Dak. <www.fargocity.com/~rrvgs/ht mls/indexes.htm>

North Dakota, Cass Co.
Type: Index; M
Year Range: 1872–1944
Online: Free
Title: Cass County (N.D.) Marriage License Index
Notes, URL: Over 15,000 marriages. <h ttp://dp3.lib.ndsu.nodak.edu/ marriage>

Ohio
Type: Abstracts; M
Year Range: 1750s–1880s
CD-ROM: $29.99, Genealogy.com, CD #177
Online: Genealogy Library
Title: Ohio, 1750s–1880s Vital Records #2
Notes, URL: 70,000 names from gravestone inscriptions, marriage records, local histories, newspaper abstracts, and land records. From articles in *The "Old Northwest" Genealogical Quarterly* and *The Ohio Genealogical Quarterly*. <www. genealogy.com/117facd.html>

Ohio
Type: Abstracts; B-M-D
Year Range: 1755–1900
CD-ROM: $26.95 (Win), Ancestry Item #2288, <http://shops.ancestry.com>. Search on "Ohio marriages."
Title: Ohio Vital Records: Marriages Selected Counties
Notes, URL: 149,636 marriage records, 1800–1900, with 302,430 names in court records from 14 counties. Birth & death records from 1755 for Knox & Morrow Counties.

Ohio
Type: Index; M
Year Range: 1789–1850
CD-ROM: $29.99, Genealogy.com, CD #400
Online: Genealogy Library
Title: Selected Counties of Ohio, 1789–1850 Marriage Index
Notes, URL: 303,000 marriage records from 85 counties. <www.genealogy.com/40 0facd.html>

Ohio
Type: Abstracts; M-D-DI
Year Range: 1790s–1870s
CD-ROM: $29.99, Genealogy.com, CD #175
Online: Genealogy Library
Title: Ohio, 1790s–1870s Vital Records #1
Notes, URL: More than 93,000 names from marriage, death, cemetery, divorce, and naturalization records. From the two-volume book *Gateway to the West*. <ww w.genealogy.com/175facd.html>

Ohio
Type: Abstracts; M
Year Range: 1790–1897
CD-ROM: $29.99, Genealogy.com, CD #528
Online: Genealogy Library
Title: Early Ohio Settlers, 1700s–1900s
Notes, URL: Names 10,000 brides & grooms extracted from *The "Old Northwest" Genealogical Quarterly*. <www.genealog y.com/528facd.html>

Ohio
Type: Index; M
Year Range: 1803–1899
Online: Free
Title: Miami Valley Genealogical Index
Notes, URL: Includes indexes to marriage records for Butler, Clark, Darke, Greene, Miami, Montgomery, Preble, Shelby, & Warren Counties. <www.pcdl.lib.oh.us/ miami/miami.htm>

Ohio
Type: Abstracts; M
Year Range: 1803–1900
Online: Ancestry
Title: Ohio Marriages, 1803–1900
Notes, URL: Records from 36 counties. <ww w.ancestry.com/search/rectype/ inddbs/5194a.htm>

Ohio
Type: Index; M
Year Range: 1851–1900
CD-ROM: $29.99, Genealogy.com, CD #236
Online: Genealogy Library
Title: Ohio, 1851–1900 Marriage Index
Notes, URL: About 272,000 names. <www. genealogy.com/236facd.html>

Ohio
Type: Index; D
Year Range: 1913–1937
Online: Free
Title: Ohio Death Certificate Index 1913–1937
Notes, URL: <www.ohiohistory.org/dindex/search.cfm>

Ohio
Type: Index; D
Year Range: 1958–1969
Online: Ancestry
Title: Ohio Deaths, 1958–69
Notes, URL: Over 1 million names. <www.ancestry.com/search/rectype/inddbs/3221.htm>

Ohio
Type: Index; D
Year Range: 1958–2000
Online: Ancestry
Title: Ohio Deaths, 1958–2000
Notes, URL: Over 3.1 million names. <www.ancestry.com/search/rectype/inddbs/5763.htm>

Ohio
Type: Index; B
Year Range: 1959–1996
CD-ROM: $98, Global Data
Title: Ohio Birth Index 1959–1996
Notes, URL: Over 5 million births on 2 CDs. Supplemental CD, $75, has "special births," 1959–1996, useful for adoption research. <www.gencd.com/ohbirth.htm>

Ohio
Type: Index; D
Year Range: 1970–1988
Online: Ancestry
Title: Ohio Deaths, 1970–88
Notes, URL: Over 1.5 million names. <www.ancestry.com/search/rectype/inddbs/5748a.htm>

Ohio
Type: Index; D
Year Range: 1989–1991
Online: Ancestry
Title: Ohio Deaths, 1989–91
Notes, URL: Over 50,000 names. <www.ancestry.com/search/rectype/inddbs/3401.htm>

Ohio
Type: Index; D
Year Range: 1992
Online: Ancestry
Title: Ohio Deaths, 1992
Notes, URL: Over 15,000 names. <www.ancestry.com/search/rectype/inddbs/3412.htm>

Ohio, Allen Co.
Type: Index; D
Year Range: 1909–1953
Online: Free
Title: Delphos, Ohio & Marion Twp, Allen County Deaths 1909–1953
Notes, URL: <www.delphos-ohio.com/history/death.htm>

Ohio, Coshocton Co.
Type: Abstracts; M
Year Range: 1811–1930
Online: F&LH
Title: Marriages, Coshocton County, Ohio, 1811–1930: compiled from marriage records, Probate Court, Coshocton County, Ohio
Notes, URL: Includes names of bride & groom & date of marriage.

Ohio, Cuyahoga Co.
Type: Index; M
Year Range: 1810–1998
Online: Free
Title: Probate Court of Cuyahoga County, Ohio, Historical Marriage License Index
Notes, URL: Includes Cleveland. <http://probate.cuyahogacounty.us/ml>

Ohio, Cuyahoga Co.
Type: Index; D
Year Range: 1867–1890
Online: Free
Title: Cuyahoga County Deaths 1867–1890
Notes, URL: <www.rootsweb.com/~ohcuyah2/deaths/coarch/part1/>

Ohio, Fayette Co.
Type: Indexes; B-D
Year Range: 1867–1999
Online: Free
Title: Fayette County Births 1909–1999, Fayette Co. Archive 1867–1908 Death Index
Notes, URL: <www.washington-ch.lib.oh.us/GenealogyLinks.asp>

Ohio, Geauga Co.
Type: Abstracts; B
Year Range: 1867–1907
Online: Free
Title: Births—Geauga County, Ohio—1867–1907
Notes, URL: <ftp://ftp.rootsweb.com/pub/usgenweb/oh/geauga/vitals/birthalp.txt>

Ohio, Lake Co.
Type: Transcripts; D
Year Range: 1867–1875, 1876–1908 forthcoming
Online: Free
Title: Lake County Probate Death Records
Notes, URL: <www.rootsweb.com/~ohlake/vitalrec/probated.html>

Ohio, Lawrence Co.
Type: Indexes; M
Year Range: 1816–1945
Online: Free
Title: Lawrence County, Ohio Marriages
Notes, URL: <www.lawrencecountyohio.com>

Ohio, Lawrence Co.
Type: Indexes; D
Year Range: 1850–2001
Online: Free
Title: Lawrence County, Ohio Vital Statistics
Notes, URL: Death records from various sources. <www.lawrencecountyohio.com>

Ohio, Licking Co.
Type: Transcript; B
Year Range: 1864–1922
Online: Free
Title: Licking County (Ohio) Probate Court, Record of Registrations or Corrections of Births, Volumes 1–19
Notes, URL: <www.kinfinder.com/births/BirthRegisterIntro.htm>

Ohio, Licking Co.
Type: Transcript; D
Year Range: 1874–1908
Online: Free
Title: Licking County, Ohio, Death Records, 1874–1908 Registered in Probate Court Office
Notes, URL: <www.kinfinder.com/deaths/LickCoDeaths.htm>

Ohio, Lucas Co., Toledo
Type: Index; B
Year Range: 1888–1890
Online: Ancestry
Title: Lucas County, Toledo Ohio Birth Records: 1888–1890
Notes, URL: <www.ancestry.com/search/rectype/inddbs/6090.htm>

Ohio, Lucas Co., Toledo
Type: Index; B
Year Range: 1891–1895
Online: Ancestry
Title: Lucas County, Toledo Ohio Birth Records: 1891–1895

Notes, URL: <www.ancestry.com/search/rectype/inddbs/6085.htm>

Ohio, Lucas Co., Toledo
Type: Index; D
Year Range: 1894–1897
Online: Ancestry
Title: Lucas County, Toledo Ohio Death Index, 1894–1897
Notes, URL: 7,388 deaths. <www.ancestry.com/search/rectype/inddbs/5585.htm>

Ohio, Marion Co.
Type: Abstracts; M
Year Range: 1824–1902
Online: Free
Title: Early Marion County Marriages
Notes, URL: <www.heritagepursuit.com/Marion/Marriages/marrt.htm>

Ohio, Montgomery Co.
Type: Abstracts; M-DI
Year Range: 1803–1827
CD-ROM: $34.50 (Mac/Win), Heritage Books
Title: HB Archives: Ohio Vol. 2
Notes, URL: Source: *Early Settlers of Montgomery County, Ohio, Vols. 1–3,* by Shirley Keller Mikesell. <www.heritagebooks.com>

Ohio, Richland Co.
Type: Index, transcripts; M
Year Range: 1813–1940
Online: Free
Title: Richland Co., Ohio Marriage Records
Notes, URL: <www.rootsweb.com/~ohricha/MarriageRecords.htm>

Ohio, Scioto Co.
Type: Abstracts; D
Year Range: 1803–1860
Online: Free
Title: Death records of Scioto County, Ohio 1803–1860
Notes, URL: <www.Scioto.org/Scioto/Death/WLP/introduction.html>

Oklahoma
Type: Abstracts; M
Year Range: 1820–1995
Online: Free
Title: Oklahoma Marriages, OKGenWeb Project
Notes, URL: Various counties. <http://marti.rootsweb.com/okmarr/marriage.htm>

Oklahoma
Type: Transcript; M
Year Range: 1895–1929
Online: Free
Title: Mary Turner Kinard Archives
Notes, URL: Marriages of Cleveland Co. (1895–1901), Garvin & McClain Cos. (1907–1929) & Stephens Co. (1907–1912). <www.rootsweb.com/~okgarvin/kinard/kinard.htm>

Oklahoma, Greer Co.
Type: Index; DI
Year Range: 1901–1930
Online: Free
Title: Greer County, Oklahoma, *Selected Civil* Cases 1901–1930
Notes, URL: <http://marti.rootsweb.com/greer/greercva.html>

Oklahoma, Greer Co.
Type: Index; D
Year Range: 1912–1918
Online: Free
Title: Greer County Oklahoma 1912–1918 Death Index
Notes, URL: <http://marti.rootsweb.com/greer/greerdnx.html>

Oklahoma, Le Flore Co.
Type: Transcript; M
Year Range: 1907–1910
Online: Free
Title: LeFlore County Marriage Books 1 & 2, 1907–1910
Notes, URL: <www.rootsweb.com/~okgarvin/kinard/leflore.txt>

Oklahoma, Payne Co.
Type: Abstracts; M
Year Range: 1894–1899
Online: Ancestry
Title: Payne County, Oklahoma Marriages, 1894–1899
Notes, URL: 6,100 names. <www.ancestry.com/search/rectype/inddbs/3925.htm>

Oregon
Type: Index; M
Year Range: 1806–1850
Online: Genealogy Library
Title: Oregon Marriages From 1806 to 1850
Notes, URL: An index to 18,434 marriages. Select Records | Marriage | Oregon.

Oregon
Type: Index; B-M-DI-D
Year Range: 1842–1956
Online: Free
Title: Oregon Historical Records Index
Notes, URL: Records from various counties. <http://arcweb.sos.state.or.us/banners/genlist.htm>

Oregon
Type: Index; D
Year Range: 1903–1930
Online: Free
Title: Heritage Trail Press: Oregon Death Index
Notes, URL: Over 140,000 names. 1921–1930 in progress. <www.heritagetrailpress.com/Death_Index/>

Oregon
Type: Index; D
Year Range: 1903–1998
CD-ROM: $26.95 (Win), Ancestry, item #2351, <http://shops.ancestry.com>. Search on "Oregon deaths."
Online: Ancestry
Title: Oregon Vital Records: Deaths 1903–1998
Notes, URL: Over 1.4 million records taken from the Oregon Center for Health Statistics. <www.ancestry.com/search/rectype/inddbs/5254a.htm>

Oregon
Type: Index; M
Year Range: 1906–1920
Online: Ancestry
Title: Oregon Marriages, 1906–20
Notes, URL: Over 400,000 records. <www.ancestry.com/search/rectype/inddbs/5193.htm>

Oregon
Type: Index; M-DI-D
Year Range: 1951–2001
Online: VitalSearch (free/subscription)
Title: VitalSearch—Oregon (USA): Oregon State
Notes, URL: Marriages, 1999–2001. Divorces, 2001. Over 170,000 deaths, 1951–1960. Over 35,000 deaths, 1999–2001. <www.vitalsearch-ca.com/gen/or>

Oregon, Clatsop Co.
Type: Index; DI
Year Range: 1850s–1913
Online: Free
Title: Divorces in Clatsop County, Oregon, From the 1850s to 1913
Notes, URL: <www.rootsweb.com/~orclatso/divorceind.htm>

Oregon, Multnomah Co., Portland
Type: Index; B-D
Year Range: 1881–1917
Online: Free
Title: Oregon State Archives: Genealogy Records
Notes, URL: Births, 1881–1901. Deaths,

1881–1917. Click on "Oregon Historical Records Index." <http://arcweb.sos.state.or.us/banners/genealogy.htm>

Oregon, Multnomah Co., Portland
Type: Index; D
Year Range: 1915–1924
Online: Ancestry
Title: Portland, Oregon Deaths, 1915–1924
Notes, URL: Over 4,000 names. <www.ancestry.com/search/rectype/inddbs/4479.htm>

Panama Canal Zone
Type: Database; D
Year Range: 1906–1991
Online: Free
Title: Index to the Gorgas Hospital Mortuary Death Records
Notes, URL: 26,213 U.S. military soldiers and officers, employees of the Panama Canal Commission, and Canal Zone civilians who died 1906–1991. <www.archives.gov/aad>. Click on Search I People.

Pennsylvania
Type: Abstracts; M
Year Range: Up to 1790
Online: Ancestry
Title: Pennsylvania Marriages to 1790
Notes, URL: 31,000 names. Source: *Names of Persons for whom Marriage Licenses Were Issued in the Province of Pennsylvania Previous to 1790.* Comp. John B. Linn and William H. Egle. (Originally published as Volume II, Second Series, Pennsylvania Archives). <www.ancestry.com/search/rectype/inddbs/2097.htm>

Pennsylvania
Type: Transcript; M
Year Range: Up to 1790
Online: Free
Title: Pennsylvania Archives, Second Series: Marriage Licenses . . . Issued in the Province of Pennsylvania Previous to 1790
Notes, URL: <www.rootsweb.com/%7Eusgenweb/pa/1pa/paarchivesseries/series2/vol2/pass2-00.html>

Pennsylvania
Type: Abstracts; M
Year Range: Up to 1810
Online: Ancestry
Title: Pennsylvania Marriages to 1810
Notes, URL: Almost 35,000 marriages. Source: *Record of Pennsylvania Marriages Prior to 1810*, 2 vols. (Originally published as Volume VIII, Second Series, Pennsylvania Archives). <www.ancestry.com/search/rectype/inddbs/2098.htm>

Pennsylvania
Type: Abstracts; M
Year Range: 1700s–1896
Online: Global Data
Title: Pennsylvania Marriages 1700s–1896
Notes, URL: Misc. marriages. <www.gencd.com>. $35 download.

Pennsylvania
Type: Abstracts; B-M-D
Year Range: 1701–1882
CD-ROM: $29.99, Genealogy.com, CD #172
Online: Genealogy Library
Title: Pennsylvania, 1700s–1800s Vital Records
Notes, URL: 87,000 names from *The Pennsylvania Magazine of History and Biography* and the *Pennsylvania Genealogical Magazine.* <www.genealogy.com/172facd.html>

Pennsylvania
Type: Abstracts; DI
Year Range: 1786–1867
CD-ROM: $24 (Mac/Win), Heritage Books, item #1160
Title: Pennsylvania Divorces, by Eugene F. Throop
Notes, URL: Divorces in Cumberland Co., 1789–1860; Dauphin Co., 1788–1867; Lancaster Co., 1786–1832; York Co., 1790–1860. <www.heritagebooks.com>. Search on "1160."

Pennsylvania, Berks Co.
Type: Indexes; B-M-D
Year Range: 1852–pres.
Online: Free
Title: Register of Wills, Berks Co., PA
Notes, URL: Berks Co. births index 1894–1906, marriage index 1885–pres., and death index 1852–1855, 1894–1906. City of Reading birth index 1876–1905, marriage index 1876–1885, and death register 1873–1905. <www.berksregofwills.com>

Pennsylvania, Berks Co.
Type: Index; D
Year Range: 1852–1906
Online: Ancestry
Title: Berks County, Pennsylvania Deaths, 1852–55, 1894–1906
Notes, URL: Over 12,000 deaths. <www.ancestry.com/search/rectype/inddbs/3833.htm>

Pennsylvania, Berks Co.
Type: Index; B
Year Range: 1876–1906
Online: Ancestry
Title: Berks County, Pennsylvania Births 1876–1906
Notes, URL: Over 24,000 births. <www.ancestry.com/search/rectype/inddbs/3831.htm>

Pennsylvania, Berks Co.
Type: Index; M
Year Range: 1885–1929
Online: Ancestry
Title: Berks County, Pennsylvania Marriages, 1885–1929
Notes, URL: Over 130,000 marriage licenses. <www.ancestry.com/search/rectype/inddbs/3829.htm>

Pennsylvania, Berks Co.
Type: Index; B
Year Range: Before 1906
Online: Ancestry
Title: Berks County, Pennsylvania Delayed Births
Notes, URL: 4,200 births. <www.ancestry.com/search/rectype/inddbs/3828.htm>

Pennsylvania, Berks Co., Reading
Type: Index; D
Year Range: 1873–1905
Online: Ancestry
Title: Reading, Pennsylvania Deaths, 1873–1905
Notes, URL: 39,000 deaths. <www.ancestry.com/search/rectype/inddbs/3834.htm>

Pennsylvania, Berks Co., Reading
Type: Index; M
Year Range: 1876–1884
Online: Ancestry
Title: Reading, Pennsylvania Marriages, 1876–84
Notes, URL: 9,700 marriages. <www.ancestry.com/search/rectype/inddbs/3830.htm>

Pennsylvania, Berks Co., Reading
Type: Index; B
Year Range: 1876–1905
Online: Ancestry
Title: Reading, Pennsylvania Births, 1876–1905
Notes, URL: 49,000 births. <www.ancestry.

com/search/rectype/inddbs/3832.htm>

Pennsylvania, Fayette Co.
Type: Abstracts; B-M-D
Year Range: 1750–1890
Online: Ancestry
Title: Fayette County, Pennsylvania Vital Records, 1750–1890
Notes, URL: 9,200 records. <www.ancestry.com/search/rectype/inddbs/4112.htm>

Pennsylvania, Northampton Co.
Type: Abstracts; M
Year Range: 1772–1836
Online: Ancestry
Title: Northampton County, Pennsylvania, Marriage Licenses issued by Isaac Hicks, 1772–74 and 1824–36
Notes, URL: <www.ancestry.com/search/rectype/inddbs/6008.htm>

Pennsylvania, Schuylkill Co.
Type: Abstracts; B
Year Range: 1893–1895
Online: Free
Title: Schuylkill County, PA—1893–1895 Birth Registrations
Notes, URL: <ftp://ftp.rootsweb.com/pub/usgenweb/pa/schuylkill/vitals/birth/reg/brth9395.txt>

Pennsylvania, Schuylkill Co.
Type: Abstracts; B
Year Range: 1895–1897
Online: Free
Title: Schuylkill County, PA—Birth Registrations 1895–1897
Notes, URL: <ftp://ftp.rootsweb.com/pub/usgenweb/pa/schuylkill/vitals/birth/reg/brthbk1b.txt>

Pennsylvania, Washington, Cross Creek
Type: Abstracts; D
Year Range: 1810–1890
Online: Ancestry
Title: Cross Creek, Pennsylvania Deaths, 1810–90
Notes, URL: Over 1,000 records. <www.ancestry.com/search/rectype/inddbs/4053.htm>

Pennsylvania, Wyoming Co.
Type: Abstracts; M-D
Year Range: 1810–1832
Online: Free
Title: Marriages and Deaths from Vol. X of Proceedings & Collections of Wyoming Historical & Geological Society
Notes, URL: Surnames A-D. Includes records from Bradford, Luzerne, & Susquehanna Cos., Pa. <www.geocities.com/Heartland/Plains/3558/admarrig.htm>

Pennsylvania, Wyoming Co.
Type: Abstracts; M-D
Year Range: 1811–1830
Online: Free
Title: Marriages and Deaths from Vol. X of Proceedings & Collections of Wyoming Historical & Geological Society
Notes, URL: Surnames E-G. Includes records from Bradford, Luzerne, & Susquehanna Cos., Pa. <www.geocities.com/Heartland/Plains/3558/egmarrig.htm>

Rhode Island
Type: Abstracts, transcripts; B-M-D
Year Range: 1500s–1900s
CD-ROM: $39.99, Genealogy.com, CD #215
Online: Genealogy Library
Title: Rhode Island Vital Records, 1500s–1900s
Notes, URL: 550,000 names. Images of pages in 20 volumes of the *Rhode Island Genealogical Register* and 13 volumes of *Rhode Island Vital Records, New Series.* <www.genealogy.com/215facd.html>

Rhode Island
Type: Abstracts, transcripts; B-M-D
Year Range: 1600s–1800s
CD-ROM: $29.99, Genealogy.com, CD #180
Online: Genealogy Library
Title: Rhode Island Family Histories #1, 1600s–1800s (aka Rhode Island Genealogies #1, 1600s–1800s)
Notes, URL: 46,000 names. Digital images of *Genealogies of Rhode Island Families,* vols. 1–2. <www.genealogy.com/180facd.html>

Rhode Island
Type: Abstracts; B-M-D
Year Range: 1630–1930
Online: Ancestry
Title: Rhode Island Vital Records
Notes, URL: <www.ancestry.com/search/rectype/vital/rivitals/main.htm>

Rhode Island
Type: Transcript; B-M-D
Year Range: 1636–1850
CD-ROM: $49 (Mac/Win), NEHGS
Online: NEHGS
Title: Vital Record of Rhode Island, 1636–1850
Notes, URL: From the books by James N. Arnold. <www.newenglandancestors.org/research/database/vital_records_ri/>

Rhode Island
Type: Index; M
Year Range: 1696–1850
Online: Free
Title: Index for 3,000+ Rhode Island Marriages Alphabetical order by groom From 1696 to 1850
Notes, URL: <www.yeoldedirectoryshoppe.com/oldcitydirectories/marriages/RI.html>

Rhode Island
Type: Index; M
Year Range: 1744–1850
Online: Genealogy Library
Title: Rhode Island Marriages From 1744 to 1850
Notes, URL: An index to 3,068 marriages. Select Records | Marriage | Rhode Island.

Rhode Island, Bristol Co.
Type: Transcript; DI
Year Range: 1819–1893
Online: NEHGS
Title: Bristol County, Rhode Island, Divorces, 1819–1893
Notes, URL: <www.newenglandancestors.org/research/database/bristoldivorces>

South Carolina
Type: Abstracts; M
Year Range: 1641–1929
Online: Free
Title: SCGenWeb Archives: Marriage Records
Notes, URL: More than 23,000 marriages. <www.rootsweb.com/~usgenweb/sc/sca_marr.html>

South Carolina
Type: Abstracts; D
Year Range: 1917–1992
Online: Free
Title: Various Death Certificates from Upstate SC
Notes, URL: <www.scgenealogy.com/pickens/records/obits/index.htm>

South Carolina, Horry Co.
Type: Abstracts; D
Year Range: 1916–1943
Online: Free
Title: Horry County Death Certificates
Notes, URL: 64 records. <www.hchsonline.org/deathcertificates/scarchives.html>

South Carolina, Spartanburg Co., Spartanburg

Type: Index; D
Year Range: 1895–1914
Online: Free
Title: Register of Deaths of Spartanburg, SC
Notes, URL: 1895–1896, 1903–1914. <www.spt.lib.sc.us/obits/citydeath/index.html>

South Dakota
Type: Abstracts; B
Year Range: Up to 1900
Online: Free
Title: South Dakota Records: Birth Records
Notes, URL: 86,115 records. <http://userdb.rootsweb.com/sd/birth/search.cgi>

South Dakota
Type: Abstracts; B
Year Range: Up to 1903
Online: Free
Title: Birth Record Search Site For South Dakota Birth Records With Birth Dates Over 100 Years
Notes, URL: 99,461 records. <www.state.sd.us/doh/VitalRec/birthrecords/index.cfm>

South Dakota
Type: Abstracts; B
Year Range: 1856–1903
Online: Ancestry
Title: South Dakota Births, 1856–1903
Notes, URL: Records from the South Dakota Health Department. <www.ancestry.com/search/rectype/inddbs/6996.htm>

South Dakota, Bon Homme Co.
Type: Index; B
Year Range: 1867–1899
Online: Free
Title: Delayed Birth Registrations, Bon Homme Co., SD
Notes, URL: <ftp://ftp.rootsweb.com/pub/usgenweb/sd/bonhomme/vitals/birth.txt>

South Dakota, Yankton Co.
Type: Index; B
Year Range: 1866–1899
Online: Free
Title: Delayed Birth Registrations, Yankton Co., SD
Notes, URL: <ftp://ftp.rootsweb.com/pub/usgenweb/sd/yankton/vitals/birth.txt>

Tennessee
Type: Index; M
Year Range: Up to 1825
Online: Ancestry
Title: Marriages—Tennessee to 1825
Notes, URL: Over 45,000 names. <www.ancestry.com/search/rectype/inddbs/2099a.htm>

Tennessee
Type: Abstracts; B-M-D
Year Range: 1720–1890
Online: Ancestry
Title: Tennessee Marriage and Bible Records
Notes, URL: Over 25,000 records from family Bibles, church, court, and county records. Source: Acklen, Robert. *Tennessee Records, Bible Records and Marriage Bonds.* <www.ancestry.com/search/rectype/inddbs/3186.htm>

Tennessee
Type: Abstracts; M
Year Range: 1733–1898
Online: Free
Title: Tennessee Marriages from USGenWeb
Notes, URL: <www.members.tripod.com/~rosters/index-8.html>

Tennessee
Type: Abstracts; M
Year Range: 1787–1866
CD-ROM: $39.99, Genealogy.com, CD #407
Online: Genealogy Library
Title: Tennessee, 1787–1866 Marriages
Notes, URL: 278,000 names from 21 counties. <www.genealogy.com/407facd.html>

Tennessee
Type: Index; M
Year Range: 1851–1900
CD-ROM: $26.95 (Win), Ancestry, item #2235, <http://shops.ancestry.com>. Search on "Tennessee marriages."
Online: Ancestry
Title: CD: Tennessee Vital Records: Marriages CD (Selected Counties & Years—Win). Online: Tennessee Marriages, 1851–1900.
Notes, URL: An index of 168,272 names from 36 of the 95 counties. <www.ancestry.com/search/rectype/inddbs/4125a.htm>

Tennessee
Type: Index; M
Year Range: 1851–1900
CD-ROM: $29.99, Genealogy.com, CD #235
Online: Genealogy Library
Title: Tennessee, 1851–1900 Marriage Index
Notes, URL: 439,000 names. <www.genealogy.com/235facd.html>

Tennessee
Type: Index; D
Year Range: 1908–1925
Online: Free
Title: Index to Tennessee Death Records
Notes, URL: 1908–1912, 1914–1925 (partial). <www.state.tn.us/sos/statelib/pubsvs/intro.htm#vital_records>

Tennessee, Bedford Co.
Type: Abstracts; M
Year Range: 1853–1878
Online: Free
Title: Bedford County, Tennessee Marriage Records
Notes, URL: <www.genealogytoday.com/pub/bedfrdtn.htm>

Tennessee, Davidson Co., Nashville
Type: Index; M
Year Range: 1864–1905
Online: Free
Title: Nashville Local History Indexes: Marriages Recorded in Nashville, 1864–1905
Notes, URL: <http://wendy.nashv.lib.tn.us:82/>

Tennessee, Franklin Co.
Type: Abstracts; M
Year Range: 1838–1874
Online: Free
Title: Franklin County, Tennessee Marriage Records
Notes, URL: <www.genealogytoday.com/pub/frankltn.htm>

Tennessee, Gibson Co.
Type: Abstracts; M
Year Range: 1845–1851
Online: Free
Title: Gibson County, Tennessee Marriage Records
Notes, URL: <www.genealogytoday.com/pub/gibsontn.htm>

Tennessee, Greene Co.
Type: Abstracts; M
Year Range: 1783–1824
Online: Free
Title: Greene County, Tennessee Marriage Records
Notes, URL: <www.genealogytoday.com/pub/greenetn.htm>

Tennessee, Grundy Co.
Type: Abstracts; M
Year Range: 1850–1874
Online: Free
Title: Grundy County, Tennessee Marriage Records

Notes, URL: <www.genealogytoday.com/pub/grundytn.htm>

Tennessee, Lawrence Co.
Type: Abstracts; M
Year Range: 1818–1845
Online: Free
Title: Lawrence County, Tennessee Marriages
Notes, URL: <www.genealogytoday.com/pub/tennmarr.htm>

Tennessee, Polk Co.
Type: Abstracts; M
Year Range: 1894–1898
Online: Free
Title: Polk County, Tennessee Marriage Records
Notes, URL: <www.genealogytoday.com/pub/polktn.htm>

Tennessee, Rutherford Co.
Type: Abstracts; M
Year Range: 1717–1858
Online: Free
Title: Rutherford County, Tennessee Marriage Records
Notes, URL: <www.genealogytoday.com/pub/ruthertn.htm>

Tennessee, Shelby Co.
Type: Index; D
Year Range: 1848–1945
Online: Free
Title: Memphis/Shelby County Death Index (1848–1945)
Notes, URL: <http://history.memphislibrary.org/>

Texas
Type: Index; M
Year Range: 1823–1998
Online: Free
Title: Texas Marriage Records
Notes, URL: Links to sites with marriage records for 20 counties. <www.idreamof.com/marriage/tx.html>

Texas
Type: Abstracts; M
Year Range: 1824–1900
CD-ROM: $26.95 (Win), Ancestry Item #2311, <http://shops.ancestry.com>. Search on "Texas marriages."
Online: Ancestry
Title: Texas Vital records: Marriages 1824–1900
Notes, URL: 73,660 records with 147,290 names from 90 of 256 counties.

Texas
Type: Index; M
Year Range: 1851–1900
CD-ROM: $29.99, Genealogy.com, CD #398
Online: Genealogy Library
Title: Texas, 1851–1900 Marriage Index
Notes, URL: 272,000 names. <www.genealogy.com/398facd.html>

Texas
Type: Index; B-M-DI-D
Year Range: 1926–2001
Online: Vitalsearch (free/subscription)
Title: Vitalsearch—Texas (USA): Texas State Vital Records
Notes, URL: 15 million births, 1926–1998. Over 5 million marriages, 1967–2001. Divorces, 1968–2000. Deaths, 1956–2000. $57.95 per year or $24.95 per quarter to view marriages, 1999–2001, & deaths, 1999–2000. <www.vitalsearch-ca.com/gen/tx>

Texas
Type: Index; D
Year Range: 1964–1998
CD-ROM: $26.95 (Win), Ancestry Item #2354, <http://shops.ancestry.com>. Search on "Texas deaths."
Online: Ancestry
Title: Texas Vital Records: Deaths 1964–1998
Notes, URL: 3,963,456 records compiled by the Texas Department of Health. <www.ancestry.com/search/rectype/inddbs/4876a.htm>

Texas
Type: Index; D
Year Range: 1964–1998
Online: Free
Title: Texas Death Records
Notes, URL: 3,963,456 records compiled by the Texas Department of Health. <http://vitals.rootsweb.com/tx/death/search.cgi?> or <http://userdb.rootsweb.com/tx/death/search.cgi?>

Texas
Type: Index; M-DI
Year Range: 1966–2001
Online: Free
Title: Texas Marriage and Divorce Records
Notes, URL: Downloadable marriage indexes, 1966–2001 and divorce indexes, 1968–2001. <www.tdh.state.tx.us/bvs/registra/mdindx.htm>

Texas, Bosque Co.
Type: Transcript; M
Year Range: 1860–1928
Online: Free
Title: Bosque County, Texas, Marriage Index 1860–1928
Notes, URL: <www.rootsweb.com/~okgarvin/kinard/bostxmarriageindex.htm>

Texas, El Paso Co.
Type: Index; M
Year Range: 1963–pres.
Online: Free
Title: El Paso County Clerk Marriage Records Search
Notes, URL: <www.co.el-paso.tx.us/clerk/marriagesearch.htm>

Texas, Hood Co.
Type: Index; M
Year Range: 1854–1900
Online: Free
Title: Hood County Texas Genealogical Society, Index of Records
Notes, URL: Source: *Hood County Marriages 1875 to 1900*, by Geraldine Elkins Cook, Talmadge Hawthorne, & R.R. Massegee. <www.granburydepot.org/MainIndex.htm>

Texas, Houston Co.
Type: Transcript; M
Year Range: 1882–1917
Online: Free
Title: Houston County, Texas, Marriage Index, 1882–1917
Notes, URL: <www.rootsweb.com/~okgarvin/kinard/houtxmarriageindex.htm>

Texas, Johnson Co.
Type: Abstracts; M
Year Range: 1854–1866
Online: Free
Title: 1854–1866 Marriage Records, Johnson County, Texas
Notes, URL: <www.granburydepot.org/mar/1854to1866Marriages.htm>

Texas, Johnson Co.
Type: Index; M
Year Range: 1854–1872
Online: Ancestry (free)
Title: Johnson County, Texas, Marriages, 1854–72
Notes, URL: <www.ancestry.com/search/rectype/inddbs/5665.htm>

Texas, Johnson Co.
Type: Abstracts; B-M-D
Year Range: 1854–1943
Online: Free
Title: Johnson County Texas Records
Notes, URL: Births, 1873–1943; marriages, 1854–1893; deaths, 1934–1939. <www

.angelfire.com/ny/LesleysWorld/Johnson.html>

Texas, Rusk Co.
Type: Abstracts; B-M
Year Range: 1873–1875
Online: Free
Title: Rusk County, TXGenWeb
Notes, URL: Births, 1873–1875. <www.ladytexian.com/txrusk/>

Texas, Tom Green Co.
Type: Abstracts; B-M-DI-D
Year Range: 1926–2001
Online: Free
Title: Tom Green County, TX
Notes, URL: Births, 1926–1995. Marriages, 1966–2001. Divorces, 1968–2001. Deaths, 1964–1999. <www.rootsweb.com/~txtomgre>

Utah
Type: Index; M
Year Range: 1800s–1992
CD-ROM: $125 (Win), Global Data
Title: Utah Marriages CD 1800s–1992
Notes, URL: Marriages from the county clerks of Salt Lake, Davis, & Utah counties. <www.gencd.com>

Utah
Type: Index; B-DI-D
Year Range: 1875–1905
Online: Free
Title: Utah State Archives: Indexes of Record Series at the Archives
Notes, URL: Birth records for several counties & death records for Beaver County, mostly 1897–1905. Davis County divorces, 1875–1886. <www.archives.utah.gov/silverstream.htm>

Utah
Type: Transcript; B
Year Range: 1895–1905
Online: Ancestry
Title: Utah Births, 1895–1905
Notes, URL: <www.ancestry.com/search/rectype/inddbs/6899.htm>

Utah
Type: Index; D
Year Range: 1905–1951
Online: Ancestry
Title: Utah Death Index, 1905–1951
Notes, URL: <www.ancestry.com/search/rectype/inddbs/6967.htm>

Utah, Davis Co.
Type: Index; DI
Year Range: 1875–1886
Online: Ancestry
Title: Davis County, Utah Divorce Case Files, 1875–1886
Notes, URL: <www.ancestry.com/search/rectype/inddbs/7155.htm>

Utah, Davis Co.
Type: Index; DI
Year Range: 1877–1880
Online: Ancestry
Title: Davis County, Utah Divorce Registers of Actions, 1877, 1880
Notes, URL: <www.ancestry.com/search/rectype/inddbs/7154.htm>

Utah, Weber Co.
Type: Index; M
Year Range: 1972–1996
Online: Global Data
Title: Weber County, Utah Marriages 1972–1996
Notes, URL: <www.gencd.com>. $49 download.

Vermont
Type: Index; D
Year Range: 1989–1998
Online: Ancestry
Title: Vermont Death Index, 1989–1998
Notes, URL: Over 38,000 entries. <www.ancestry.com/search/rectype/inddbs/3269.htm>

Virginia
Type: Abstracts; M
Year Range: Up to 1800
Online: Ancestry
Title: Marriages—Virginia to 1800
Notes, URL: Over 85,000 names. <www.ancestry.com/search/rectype/inddbs/3002a.htm>

Virginia
Type: Abstracts; M
Year Range: Up to 1824
Online: Ancestry
Title: Virginia Marriages before 1824
Notes, URL: Over 9,000 names. Source: Crozier, William Armstrong. *Early Virginia Marriages*. <www.ancestry.com/search/rectype/inddbs/3001.htm>

Virginia
Type: Abstracts, transcripts; B-M-D
Year Range: 1600s–1800s
CD-ROM: $39.99, Genealogy.com, CD #174
Online: Genealogy Library
Title: Virginia, 1600s–1800s Vital Records #1
Notes, URL: Over 138,000 names from the *Virginia Magazine of History and Biography, The William and Mary College Quarterly*, and *Tyler's Quarterly*. <www.genealogy.com/174facd.html>

Virginia
Type: Abstracts?; M
Year Range: 1607–1800
CD-ROM: $29.99, Genealogy.com, CD #510
Online: Genealogy Library
Title: Colonial Virginia Source Records, 1600s–1700s
Notes, URL: Includes the book *Marriages of Some Virginia Residents, 1607–1800*, by Dorothy Ford Wulfeck. <www.genealogy.com/510facd.html>

Virginia
Type: Index; M
Year Range: 1630–1876
Online: Free
Title: Library of Virginia: Marriage Records
Notes, URL: <http://lvaimage.lib.va.us/collections/MG.html>

Virginia
Type: Abstracts; B
Year Range: 1656–1896
CD-ROM: $26.95 (Win), Ancestry Item #2109, <http://shops.ancestry.com>. Search on "Virginia births."
Title: Virginia Vital Records: Births 1656–1896 (Selected Counties)
Notes, URL: Over 317,000 records from 21 counties.

Virginia
Type: Abstracts; D
Year Range: 1660–1896
CD-ROM: $26.95 (Win), Ancestry Item #2106, <http://shops.ancestry.com>. Search on "Virginia deaths."
Title: Virginia Vital Records: Deaths 1660–1896 (Selected Counties)
Notes, URL: Over 73,000 records from 10 counties.

Virginia
Type: Abstracts; M
Year Range: 1670–1929
CD-ROM: $26.95 (Win), Ancestry Item #2108, <http://shops.ancestry.com>. Search on "1670–1929."
Title: Virginia Vital Records: Marriages 1670–1929
Notes, URL: Over 426,000 records from 80 of 94 counties.

Virginia
Type: Transcript; M
Year Range: 1722–1900
CD-ROM: $30 (Mac/Win), Heritage Books, item #2373
Title: Virginia Marriage Records
Notes, URL: These 4 volumes of marriage records compiled by Therese A. Fisher cover the city of Fredericksburg, 1722–1900; & the counties of Floyd, Giles, & Montgomery, 1772–1850; Fauquier, 1759–1854; Orange, 1722–1867; Pulaski, 1772–1850; Spotsylvania, 1722–1900; Stafford, 1722–1900. <www.heritagebooks.com>. Search on "2373."

Virginia
Type: Abstracts; M
Year Range: 1740–1850
Online: Ancestry
Title: Virginia Marriages, 1740–1850
Notes, URL: Over 300,000 names. <www.ancestry.com/search/rectype/inddbs/3723a.htm>

Virginia
Type: Abstracts; M
Year Range: 1778–1872
CD-ROM: $27.50 (Mac/Win), Heritage Books, item #1259
Title: HB Archives: Virginia Vol. 2
Notes, URL: Includes *Marriages of Alleghany Co., Virginia: 1822–1872*, by Carletta Lanear Nelson; *A History of Rockingham Co., Virginia*, by John W. Wayland, (marriage records, 1778–1820); and *Annals of Bath County, Virginia*, by Oren F. Morton. <www.heritagebooks.com>. Search on "1259."

Virginia
Type: Abstracts; M
Year Range: 1851–1900
Online: Ancestry
Title: Virginia Marriages, 1851–1900
Notes, URL: Marriages from 15 counties. <www.ancestry.com/search/rectype/inddbs/4498.htm>

Virginia
Type: Abstracts; M
Year Range: 1851–1929
Online: Ancestry
Title: Virginia Marriages, 1851–1929
Notes, URL: 57,000 names in 6 counties and 2 cities. <www.ancestry.com/search/rectype/inddbs/3976.htm>

Virginia
Type: Index; D
Year Range: 1853–1896
Online: Free
Title: Library of Virginia: Death Records Indexing Project
Notes, URL: Over 46,000 entries. <www.lva.lib.va.us/whatwehave/vital>

Virginia, Augusta Co.
Type: Abstracts; M
Year Range: 1639–1850
CD-ROM: $39.99, Genealogy.com, CD #513
Online: Genealogy Library
Title: Virginia Land, Marriage, and Probate Records, 1639–1850
Notes, URL: <www.genealogy.com/513facd.html>

Virginia, Augusta Co.
Type: Transcript; M
Year Range: 1785–1813
Online: F&LH
Title: First marriage record of Augusta County, Virginia, 1785–1813
Notes, URL: Publ. by the Col. Thomas Hughart Chapter, D.A.R.

Virginia, Augusta Co.
Type: Transcript; M
Year Range: 1785–1813
Online: Genealogy Library
Title: First Marriage Record of Augusta County, Virginia
Notes, URL: Publ. by the Col. Thomas Hughart Chapter, D.A.R. Select Records | Marriage | Virginia.

Virginia, Bedford Co.
Type: Transcript; M
Year Range: 1755–1800
Online: F&LH
Title: Marriage bonds of Bedford County, Virginia, 1755–1800
Notes, URL: By Earle S. Dennis.

Virginia, Botetourt Co.
Type: Abstracts; B
Year Range: 1885–1896
Online: Ancestry
Title: Botetourt County, Virginia Births, 1885–96
Notes, URL: More than 2,800 births. <www.ancestry.com/search/rectype/inddbs/5353.htm>

Virginia, Brunswick Co.
Type: Abstracts; B
Year Range: 1853–1862
Online: Ancestry
Title: Brunswick County, Virginia Births, 1853–62
Notes, URL: 5,500 birth records. <www.ancestry.com/search/rectype/inddbs/4692.htm>

Virginia, Brunswick Co.
Type: Abstracts; B
Year Range: 1865–1873
Online: Ancestry
Title: Brunswick County, Virginia Births, 1865–73
Notes, URL: 3,000 birth records. <www.ancestry.com/search/rectype/inddbs/4678.htm>

Virginia, Brunswick Co.
Type: Abstracts; B
Year Range: 1874–1879
Online: Ancestry
Title: Brunswick County, Virginia Births, 1874–79
Notes, URL: 3,200 birth records. <www.ancestry.com/search/rectype/inddbs/4664.htm>

Virginia, Brunswick Co.
Type: Abstracts; B
Year Range: 1880–1896
Online: Ancestry
Title: Brunswick County, Virginia Births, 1880–96
Notes, URL: 10,000 birth records. <www.ancestry.com/search/rectype/inddbs/4637.htm>

Virginia, Caroline Co.
Type: Abstracts; B
Year Range: 1859–1868
Online: Ancestry
Title: Caroline County, Virginia Births, 1859–68 (except 1863)
Notes, URL: <www.ancestry.com/search/rectype/inddbs/4862.htm>

Virginia, Caroline Co.
Type: Abstracts; B
Year Range: 1870–1880
Online: Ancestry
Title: Caroline County, Virginia Births, 1870–1880
Notes, URL: <www.ancestry.com/search/rectype/inddbs/4728.htm>

Virginia, Caroline Co.
Type: Abstracts; B
Year Range: 1881–1896
Online: Ancestry
Title: Caroline County, Virginia Births, 1881–96
Notes, URL: <www.ancestry.com/search/rectype/inddbs/4649.htm>

Virginia, Craig Co.
Type: Abstracts; B
Year Range: 1853–1896
Online: Ancestry
Title: Craig County, Virginia Births, 1853–96
Notes, URL: 7,300 records. <www.ancestry.com/search/rectype/inddbs/3989.htm>

Virginia, Craig Co.
Type: Abstracts; D
Year Range: 1853–1896
Online: Ancestry
Title: Craig County, Virginia Deaths, 1853–96
Notes, URL: <www.ancestry.com/search/rectype/inddbs/4103.htm>

Virginia, Essex Co.
Type: Abstracts; M
Year Range: 1655–1900
Online: Ancestry
Title: Essex County, Virginia Marriages, 1655–1900
Notes, URL: Over 3,000 names. Source: Wilkerson, Eva Eubank. *Index to Marriages of Old Rappahannock and Essex Counties, Virginia, 1655–1900.* <www.ancestry.com/search/rectype/inddbs/4033.htm>

Virginia, Essex Co.
Type: Abstracts; B
Year Range: 1856–1862
Online: Free
Title: Essex Co, VA Births
Notes, URL: <ftp://ftp.rootsweb.com/pub/usgenweb/va/essex/vitals/br56-58.txt>

Virginia, Fauquier Co.
Type: Abstracts; M
Year Range: 1759–1854
CD-ROM: $25 (Mac/Win), Heritage Books, item #1128
Title: Fauquier County, Virginia
Notes, URL: Includes *Fauquier County, Virginia: Marriage Bonds (1759–1854)* and *Marriage Returns (1785–1848)*, by John K. Gott. <www.heritagebooks.com>. Search on "1128."

Virginia, Frederick Co.
Type: Abstracts; M
Year Range: 1771–1825
Online: F&LH
Title: Frederick County, Virginia, marriages, 1771–1825
Notes, URL: By Eliza Timberlake Davis.

Virginia, Frederick Co.
Type: Abstracts; B
Year Range: 1855–1896
Online: Ancestry
Title: Frederick County Virginia Birth Records, 1855–96
Notes, URL: 9,600 records. <www.ancestry.com/search/rectype/inddbs/5572.htm>

Virginia, Gloucester Co., Kingston Parish
Type: Abstracts; B-M-D
Year Range: 1749–1827
Online: Ancestry
Title: Kingston Parish, Virginia Register, 1749–1827
Notes, URL: Records for over 6,500 people. Source: Matheny, Emma R., Helen K. Yates, comp. *Kingston Parish Register.* <www.ancestry.com/search/rectype/inddbs/3987.htm>

Virginia, Grayson Co.
Type: Abstracts; B
Year Range: 1853–1854
Online: Free
Title: Grayson Co., Va. birth records
Notes, URL: <ftp://ftp.rootsweb.com/pub/usgenweb/va/grayson/vitals/births.txt>

Virginia, Hanover Co.
Type: Abstracts; B
Year Range: 1853–1896
Online: Ancestry
Title: Hanover County Virginia Birth Records, 1853–1896
Notes, URL: Over 14,800 records. <www.ancestry.com/search/rectype/inddbs/6091.htm>

Virginia, Highland Co.
Type: Abstracts; B
Year Range: 1853–1896
Online: Ancestry
Title: Highland County Virginia Birth Records, 1853–1896
Notes, URL: Nearly 4,200 records. <www.ancestry.com/search/rectype/inddbs/5736.htm>

Virginia, Isle of Wight Co.
Type: Abstracts; B
Year Range: 1867–1896
Online: Ancestry
Title: Isle of Wight County Virginia Birth Records, 1867–96
Notes, URL: Over 7,800 records. <www.ancestry.com/search/rectype/inddbs/6018.htm>

Virginia, James City Co.
Type: Abstracts; B
Year Range: 1853–1896
Online: Ancestry
Title: James City County Virginia Birth Records, 1853–96
Notes, URL: Over 3,600 records. <www.ancestry.com/search/rectype/inddbs/5832.htm>

Virginia, King George Co.
Type: Abstracts; D
Year Range: 1853–1896
CD-ROM: $29.50 (Mac/Win), Heritage Books, item #1270
Title: HB Archives: Virginia Vol. 3
Notes, URL: Includes *King George County, Virginia, Death Records, 1853–1896*, by Elizabeth Nuckols Lee. Slave deaths are also recorded. <www.heritagebooks.com>. Search on "1270."

Virginia, Lancaster Co.
Type: Abstracts; M
Year Range: 1701–1848
Online: Genealogy Library
Title: The Marriage License Bonds of Lancaster County, Virginia
Notes, URL: Nearly 2,000 bonds. By Stratton Nottingham. Select Records | Vital Records | Virginia.

Virginia, Loudoun Co.
Type: Transcripts; B
Year Range: 1853–1866
Online: Free
Title: Loudoun County, Virginia—1853–1866 Births
Notes, URL: <ftp://ftp.rootsweb.com/pub/usgenweb/va/loudoun/vitals/births01.txt>

Virginia, Mecklenburg Co.
Type: Abstracts; M
Year Range: 1765–1810
Online: Genealogy Library
Title: The Marriage License Bonds of Mecklenburg County, Virginia
Notes, URL: About 2,000 marriages. By Stratton Nottingham. Select Records | Vital Records | Virginia.

Virginia, Mecklenburg Co.
Type: Abstracts; B
Year Range: 1866–1885
Online: Ancestry
Title: Mecklenburg County Virginia Birth Records, 1866–85
Notes, URL: Over 6,600 births. <www.ancestry.com/search/rectype/inddbs/6103.htm>

Virginia, Pittsylvania Co., Danville
Type: Abstracts; B
Year Range: 1853–1896
Online: Ancestry
Title: Danville, Pittsylvania County, Virginia Births, 1853–96
Notes, URL: 5,400 records. <www.ancestry.com/search/rectype/inddbs/4791.htm>

Virginia, Powhatan Co.
Type: Abstracts; B
Year Range: 1853–1896
Online: Ancestry
Title: Powhatan County, Virginia Births, 1853–96
Notes, URL: More than 21,000 names. <www.ancestry.com/search/rectype/inddbs/5305.htm>

Virginia, Russell Co.
Type: Abstracts; D
Year Range: 1853–1929
Online: Free
Title: Russell County Deaths, 1853–1896, 1912–1929
Notes, URL: <www.rootsweb.com/~varussel/vitals/deaths>

Virginia, Shenandoah Co.
Type: Transcript; M
Year Range: 1773–1915
Online: Free
Title: Shenandoah County Marriage Records
Notes, URL: Over 26,500 records. <www.rootsweb.com/~vashenan/cem/marrndx.html>

Virginia, Shenandoah Co.
Type: Abstracts; B
Year Range: 1853–1871
Online: Ancestry
Title: Shenandoah County, Virginia Births, 1853–71
Notes, URL: 12,000 records. <www.ancestry.com/search/rectype/inddbs/4769.htm>

Virginia, Shenandoah Co.
Type: Abstracts; B
Year Range: 1872–1877
Online: Ancestry
Title: Shenandoah County, Virginia Births, 1872–77
Notes, URL: 12,000 records. <www.ancestry.com/search/rectype/inddbs/5075.htm>

Virginia, Shenandoah Co.
Type: Abstracts; B
Year Range: 1878–1890
Online: Ancestry
Title: Shenandoah County, Virginia Births, 1878–90
Notes, URL: 12,000 records. <www.ancestry.com/search/rectype/inddbs/5074.htm>

Virginia, Shenandoah Co.
Type: Abstracts; B
Year Range: 1891–1896
Online: Ancestry
Title: Shenandoah County, Virginia Births, 1891–96
Notes, URL: 2,500 records. <www.ancestry.com/search/rectype/inddbs/5018.htm>

Virginia, Smyth Co.
Type: Abstracts; B
Year Range: 1875–1878
Online: Ancestry
Title: Smyth County, Virginia Births, 1875–78
Notes, URL: 2,500 records. <www.ancestry.com/search/rectype/inddbs/4198.htm>

Virginia, Smyth Co.
Type: Abstracts; B
Year Range: 1879–1884
Online: Ancestry
Title: Smyth County, Virginia Births, 1879–84
Notes, URL: 3,200 records. <www.ancestry.com/search/rectype/inddbs/4186.htm>

Virginia, Smyth Co.
Type: Abstracts; B
Year Range: 1885–1896
Online: Ancestry
Title: Smyth County, Virginia Births, 1885–96
Notes, URL: 4,000 records. <www.ancestry.com/search/rectype/inddbs/4155.htm>

Virginia, Spotsylvania Co.
Type: Abstracts; M
Year Range: Up to 1873
Online: Free
Title: Spotsylvania Marriage Records Search
Notes, URL: <www.historiccourtrecords.org/spotsymarriages.asp>

Virginia, Warren Co.
Type: Abstracts; M
Year Range: 1836–1853
CD-ROM: $31 (Mac/Win), Heritage Books, item #1522
Title: HB Archives: Virginia Vol. 5
Notes, URL: Includes *Marriage Records of Warren County, Virginia, 1836–1853; Including Marriage Bonds and Minister's Returns*, by Good & Hackett. <www.heritagebooks.com>. Search on "1522."

Virginia, Washington Co.
Type: Transcripts; D
Year Range: 1853–1885
Online: Ancestry
Title: Washington County, Virginia Deaths, 1853–85
Notes, URL: Over 7,200 names. <www.ancestry.com/search/rectype/inddbs/4073.htm>

Virginia, Washington Co.
Type: Transcripts; B
Year Range: 1853–1896
Online: Ancestry
Title: Washington County, Virginia Births, 1889–96
Notes, URL: 4,300 names. <www.ancestry.com/search/rectype/inddbs/4784.htm>

Virginia, Washington Co.
Type: Transcripts; D
Year Range: 1886–1896
Online: Ancestry
Title: Washington County, Virginia Deaths, 1886–96
Notes, URL: Over 7,300 names. <www.ancestry.com/search/rectype/inddbs/4047.htm>

Virginia, Winchester (city)
Type: Indexes, abstracts; B-M-D
Year Range: 1783–1937
CD-ROM: $23 (Mac/Win), Heritage Books, item #1413
Title: HB Archives: Winchester, Virginia
Notes, URL: Books by Dola S. Tylor. Births, 1853–1860, 1865–1891. Marriages, 1783–1937. Deaths, 1871–1891. <www.heritagebooks.com>. Search on "1413."

Virginia, York Co., Charles Parish
Type: Abstracts; B-D
Year Range: 1648–1789
Online: Ancestry
Title: Charles Parish Records, York County, Virginia, 1648–1789
Notes, URL: Birth and death information for nearly 5,000 people. <www.ancestry.com/search/rectype/inddbs/3479.htm>

Washington
Type: Index; M
Year Range: 1803–1899
Online: Genealogy Library
Title: Washington Marriages From 1803 to 1899
Notes, URL: 4,749 marriages. Select Records | Marriage | Washington.

Washington
Type: Abstracts; B
Year Range: 1907–1919
Online: Ancestry
Title: Washington State Birth Index 1907–1919
Notes, URL: <www.ancestry.com/search/rectype/inddbs/6493.htm>

Washington
Type: Index; D
Year Range: 1940–1996
Online: Ancestry
Title: Washington Death Index, 1940–1996
Notes, URL: Created by the Washington State Health Department. <www.ancestry.com/search/rectype/inddbs/6716.htm>

Washington
Type: Index; D
Year Range: 1960–1974
Online: Vitalsearch
Title: Washington State Deaths Database
Notes, URL: Death entries, 1960–1974. <www.vitalsearch-worldwide.com>

Washington, Stevens Co.
Type: Abstracts; D
Year Range: 1891–1907
Online: Free
Title: Stevens County Death Register, 1891–1907
Notes, URL: <ftp://ftp.rootsweb.com/pub/usgenweb/wa/stevens/vital/death.txt>

West Virginia
Type: Abstracts; B-M-D
Year Range: 1778–2000
Online: Free
Title: The West Virginia Genealogy Guide
Notes, URL: Births, 1810–1969. Marriages, 1784–2000. Deaths, 1778–1998. <www.usgenealogyguide.com/westvirginia/>

West Virginia
Type: Abstracts; M
Year Range: 1781–1915
CD-ROM: $29.99, Genealogy.com, CD #520
Online: Genealogy Library
Title: Early West Virginia Settlers, 1600s–1900s
Notes, URL: Includes about 6,000 marriages of Berkeley County, (West) Virginia, 1781–1854, & more than 11,000 marriages in Mason County, West Virginia, 1806–1915. <www.genealogy.com/520facd.html>

West Virginia
Type: Abstracts; M
Year Range: 1784–1799
Online: Free
Title: West Virginia Marriage Records
Notes, URL: <www.genealogytoday.com/pub/wvrec.htm>

West Virginia
Type: Index; M
Year Range: 1863–1900
CD-ROM: $29.99, Genealogy.com, CD #241
Online: Genealogy Library
Title: West Virginia, 1863–1900 Marriage Index
Notes, URL: About 177,000 names. <www.genealogy.com/241facd.html>

West Virginia
Type: Abstracts; M
Year Range: 1863–1900
Online: Ancestry
Title: West Virginia Marriage Records, 1863–1900
Notes, URL: Marriage records from 25 counties. <www.ancestry.com/search/rectype/inddbs/4484.htm>

West Virginia, Brooke Co.
Type: Abstracts; M
Year Range: 1797–1874
CD-ROM: $29 (Mac/Win), Heritage Books Item #1361
Title: HB Archives: West Virginia Vol. 3
Notes, URL: Includes *Brooke County Virginia/West Virginia Licenses and Marriages 1797–1874*, by Renee Britt Sherman (1991). 5000 names. <www.heritagebooks.com>. Search on "1361."

West Virginia, Fayette Co.
Type: Abstracts; B
Year Range: 1866–1880
Online: Ancestry
Title: Fayette County, West Virginia, Births, 1866–1880
Notes, URL: 2,400 records. <www.ancestry.com/search/rectype/inddbs/6062.htm>

West Virginia, Fayette Co.
Type: Abstracts; B
Year Range: 1881–1887
Online: Ancestry
Title: Fayette County, West Virginia Births 1881–87
Notes, URL: 7,100 records. <www.ancestry.com/search/rectype/inddbs/4983.htm>

West Virginia, Fayette Co.
Type: Abstracts; B
Year Range: 1888–1893
Online: Ancestry
Title: Fayette County, West Virginia Births, 1888–93
Notes, URL: 7,100 records. <www.ancestry.com/search/rectype/inddbs/4798.htm>

West Virginia, Hancock Co.
Type: Abstracts; B
Year Range: 1803–1937
Online: Free
Title: West Virginia Birth Records
Notes, URL: <www.idreamof.com/birth/wv.html>

West Virginia, Kanawha Co.
Type: Abstracts; M
Year Range: 1792–1869
Online: Genealogy Library
Title: Kanawha County Marriages
Notes, URL: By Julia Wintz. Select Records | Marriage | West Virginia.

West Virginia, Mason Co.
Type: Abstracts; M
Year Range: 1806–1915
CD-ROM: $29.99, Genealogy.com, CD #520
Online: Genealogy Library
Title: Early West Virginia Settlers, 1600s–1900s
Notes, URL: 11,000 marriages. <www.genealogy.com/520facd.html>

West Virginia, Pleasants Co.
Type: Abstracts; B-M-D
Year Range: 1853–1920
Online: Free
Title: Pleasants County WVGenWeb Archives
Notes, URL: Births, 1873–1891. Marriages, 1853–1899. Deaths, 1853–1920. <www.rootsweb.com/usgenweb/wv/pleasant.htm>

West Virginia, Raleigh Co.
Type: Abstracts; B
Year Range: 1853–1875

Online: Ancestry
Title: Raleigh County, West Virginia Birth Records, 1853–75
Notes, URL: 2,479 births. <www.ancestry.com/search/rectype/inddbs/4866.htm>

West Virginia, Upshur Co.
Type: Abstracts; B-D
Year Range: 1853–1928
CD-ROM: $25.50 (Mac/Win), Heritage Books Item #1159
Title: HB Archives, West Virginia, Vol. 1: Upshur
Notes, URL: Includes: Births, 1853–1897. Deaths, 1853–1928. Source: Books by Paul C. & Judith Hawkins, Billie Faye Drost, and Karon Janel King. <www.heritagebooks.com>. Search on "1159."

Wisconsin
Type: Index; B
Year Range: Up to 1907
Online: Free
Title: Index to Wisconsin Delayed and Affidavit Birth Registrations Prior to 1 October 1907
Notes, URL: Over 27,000 entries. <www.rootsweb.com/~wsgs/delayed_birth.htm>

Wisconsin
Type: Index; M
Year Range: Up to 1907
Online: Ancestry
Title: Wisconsin Marriages, Pre-1907
Notes, URL: Over 920,000 names in marriage records. <www.ancestry.com/search/rectype/inddbs/4997a.htm>

Wisconsin
Type: Index; B
Year Range: 1820–1907
Online: Ancestry
Title: Wisconsin Births, 1820–1907
Notes, URL: Over 985,000 births. <www.ancestry.com/search/rectype/inddbs/4750a.htm>

Wisconsin
Type: Index; M-D
Year Range: 1820–1907
Online: Ancestry
Title: Wisconsin Deaths, 1820–1907
Notes, URL: Over 435,000 deaths. <www.ancestry.com/search/rectype/inddbs/4984.htm>

Wisconsin
Type: Abstracts; M-D
Year Range: 1835–1900
Online: Ancestry
Title: Wisconsin Marriages, 1835–1900
Notes, URL: Marriage records from Grant (1891–1900), Jackson, and Monroe counties. <www.ancestry.com/search/rectype/inddbs/5230.htm>

Wisconsin
Type: Index; D
Year Range: 1859–1979
Online: Vitalsearch (free/subscription)
Title: VitalSearch: Wisconsin State Deaths
Notes, URL: 820,000 records. <www.vitalsearch-worldwide.com>

Wisconsin, Kenosha Co.
Type: Abstracts; M
Year Range: 1846–1996
Online: Free
Title: Kenosha County, Wisconsin Marriages
Notes, URL: Misc. marriages submitted by researchers. <www.rootsweb.com/~wikenosh/marriage.htm>

Wisconsin, Richland Co.
Type: Index; D
Year Range: Up to 1998
Online: Free
Title: Thompson's Richland County, Wisconsin Death Index (To 1998)
Notes, URL: <www.rootsweb.com/~wiricha/deadintr.htm>

Wisconsin, Sheboygan Co.
Type: Indexes; B-M-D
Year Range: 1841–1912
Online: Free
Title: Sheboygan County Vital Records Indexes
Notes, URL: <http://freepages.genealogy.rootsweb.com/~sheboygan/11.htm>

Wyoming, Sheridan Co.
Type: Index; M
Year Range: 1888–1925
Online: Free
Title: Sheridan County Wyoming USGenWeb Project: Sheridan County Marriages
Notes, URL: <www.rootsweb.com/~wysherid/index.html>

Census Records

The 1880 census shows that Viola Myers, age 25, was an "exhibitor" living with showmen and actors on Coney Island. By 1920 she had moved to Pennsylvania, where the census shows her age as 65 and occupation as planet reading. (Does that mean she was a fortune-teller?) Nationwide census indexes made it easy for me to find these tantalizing bits of information on Viola, and now I can't wait to learn more.

Conducted every ten years since 1790, U.S. federal censuses are generally regarded as the most important records for researching American family history. The population schedules are used most often, but don't overlook censuses of manufactures and mortality, agriculture, industrial, and veterans' schedules. The earliest census records list only heads of household. Beginning in 1850 they cover all free persons and include names, ages, occupations, places of birth, and more.

Figure 4-1
Hooper family in 1860 census of Pittsfield, Otsego County, New York. Ancestry.com, U.S. Census Images and Indexes. Copyright 2003, MyFamily.com, Inc. Used by permission, all rights reserved. For further family history resources visit <www.ancestry.com>.

What census records are online or on CD-ROM?

Ancestry.com, Genealogy.com, and HeritageQuest Online have put images of virtually all U.S. federal population census records from 1790 through 1930 online (see Figure 4-1 above). All three services are also creating indexes linked to the digital images. Ancestry.com has already created every-name indexes for several years, and more are in the works.

If you have a dial-up Internet connection, viewing census images online can be a slow process. Instead, you might opt for HeritageQuest's CD-ROMs with images of all U.S. federal census records from 1790 to 1930. They're great for browsing, but don't include indexes.

FamilySearch has published a transcription and every-name index of the 1880 U.S. federal census in both online and CD-ROM versions. You'll also find various census indexes and transcriptions on Ancestry.com, Genealogy-.com, the USGenWeb Project, and other Web sites.

What census records are not online or on CD-ROM?

Most of the 1890 U.S. federal census was destroyed and is not available anywhere, online or offline. Since they are confidential for seventy-two years, U.S. census records taken after 1930 have not yet been released to the public. Some states conducted their own censuses at various times, but few of these records have been published online or on CD-ROM.

KEY RESOURCES

Digital Images

Ancestry.com: U.S. Census Images and Indexes

This tremendous resource (see Figure 4-2 below) features images of all U.S. federal census images from 1790 to 1930. Every-name indexes to the 1870, 1880, and 1930 censuses and head-of-household indexes to the 1790 through 1850 and 1920 censuses are linked to census images. The index to the 1860 census is partially completed and indexes to the remaining years will follow.

To find everyone with a certain last name in a state, just fill in the last name and state. Add a county or a county and a town or township to narrow the scope. You can even search on just a first name. That's especially useful when you're searching the 1930 census and don't know a woman's married name, but do have her year and place of birth.

Ancestry.com's census indexes include several search options that help

CHECK FOR NEW INDEXES

Ancestry.com, Genealogy.-com, and HeritageQuest Online continue to create new census indexes, so be sure to check their Web sites regularly for the latest years and states available.

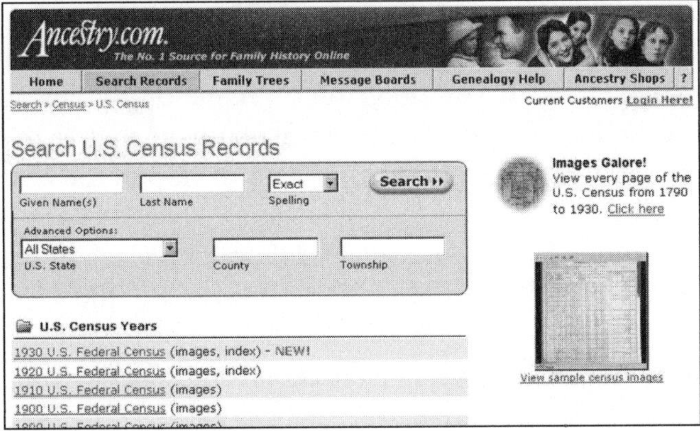

Figure 4-2
Ancestry.com's US Census Images and Indexes.

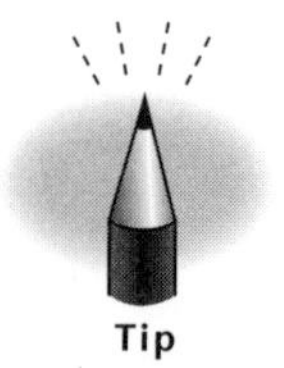

Tip

OPEN NEW WINDOWS

If you open a census image from Ancestry.com in a new window, you can refer back to the index while you still have the census image open. In Windows right-click on View Image Online and select Open in New Window.

you zero in on the right person. When searching any census year you can include a middle initial, do a Soundex search to find similar spellings (just in case the last name is spelled wrong on the census or transcribed wrong in the index) and limit the search to a specific town or county. And as with all databases on Ancestry.com, you can use a wildcard character. A question mark substitutes for a single letter and an asterisk for zero to six letters.

You can also search the 1870, 1880, 1920, and 1930 census indexes by age and place of birth—especially useful if you're searching on a common name. All index entries don't include an age and place of birth, so if you include an age or a place of birth in your search and don't find the right person, try searching on just the name.

A subscription to Ancestry.com's U.S. Census Images and Indexes costs $39.95 for three months or $99.95 a year.

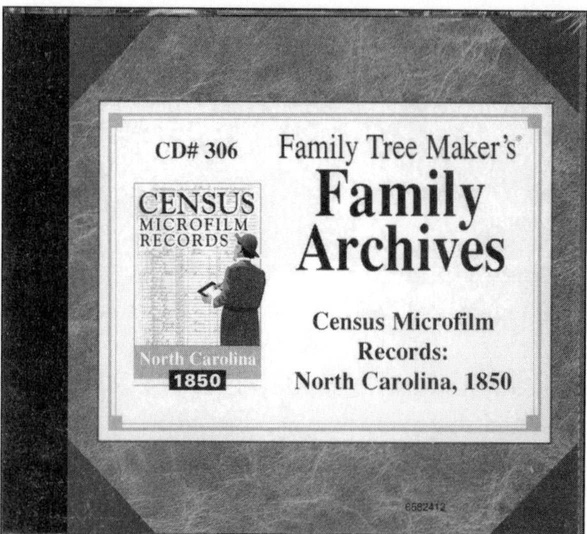

Figure 4-3
Genealogy.com's 1850 census index and images on CD-ROM.

Genealogy Library: 1850 Census Images

Click on 1850 Census Microfilm Images to search head-of-household indexes linked to census images for twenty-two of the thirty-seven states covered by the 1850 census. The index results are hard to browse, so you might find it helpful to use your Web browser to search for a town or county on the page. In Internet Explorer select Find from the Edit menu or hold down the Ctrl key and press the F key. If you don't find a name on the linked census image page, click on Image 2 of 2 to view the next page that shares the same number. Click on Next Page only if you want to skip to the next numbered page.

A subscription to Genealogy Library <www.genealogy.com/glsub.html> is $9.99 for one month or $49.99 for a year. You can also buy the 1850 census index and images on CD-ROM from Genealogy.com for $49.99 each or $79.99 for Pennsylvania <http://familytreemaker.genealogy.com/cenmicro.html> (see Figure 4-3 above).

Genealogy.com: U.S. Census Collection

This collection (see Figure 4-4 below) features images of all U.S. federal census images from 1790 to 1930. Head-of-household indexes have been completed for 1790, 1800, 1810, 1820, 1860, 1870, 1890, 1900, and 1910, and more are in the works.

Use the Family Finder Index to search the indexed censuses for all states at once. To search the index for a specific state and year, go to the Census Collection page, click on the census year, and then select a state.

You can also search on a last name and browse through the list of persons with that name in a specific census year and state. Enter the surname in the box after "Jump to page containing surname" and click on the Go button.

Although the census search page has a link to Advanced Search options, they don't work with the census search. And although there's a search box for a middle name or middle initial, whatever you type in the box is ignored.

Hint: Save census images from Genealogy.com as TIFF files, not JPEG files. The JPEG files are huge!

U.S. Census Collection <www.genealogy.com/uscensussub.html>, $19.99 a month or $99.99 a year, Genealogy.com, (800) 548-1806.

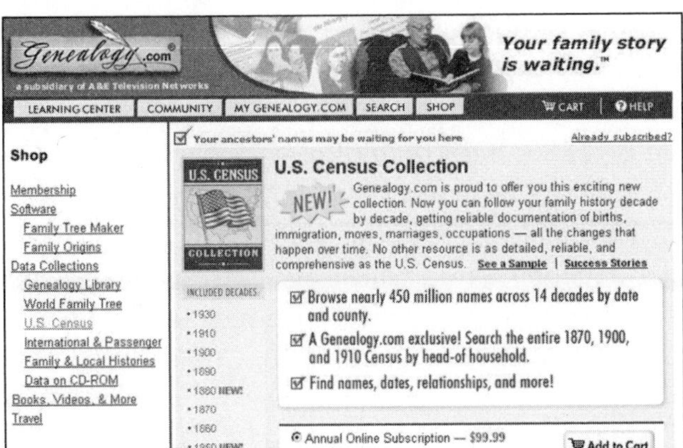

Figure 4-4
Genealogy.com's US Census Collection.

HeritageQuest Online: U.S. Federal Census, 1790–1930

Geared toward libraries, this database features digital images of all the U.S. federal census records from 1790 to 1930. Head-of-household indexes are being created for the entire collection, and the years 1790 through 1820, 1860, 1870, 1890, and 1920 were completed first. You can search by name, place of birth, age, ethnicity, and other variables. HeritageQuest Online <www.heritagequestonline.com>.

Transcripts

FamilySearch: 1880 U.S. Census and National Index

The culmination of 11.5 million hours of work carried out over a period of seventeen years, this database includes not only an every-name national index, but also all the most important details from the census records (see Figure 4-5 on page 76). The 1880 census covers thirty-eight states and eight

Figure 4-5
FamilySearch.

territories as of June 1880. No federal census was taken in Indian Territory (present-day Oklahoma). You can also search this index on Ancestry.com.

Tip

A few tips:

- *Try alternate spellings.* The index usually finds all likely spelling variations of both first and last names. Search on my name (Crume) and matches will include Crume, Croom, Krume, Crumes, and Crooms. However, a search for Crow doesn't find Crowe, and a search for Robertson doesn't find Robinson or Robison. So be sure to try various spellings.
- *Search on just a first name.* You don't even need a last name to find someone in the index. I suspected that my widowed ancestor Lucy Myers had remarried by 1880, but I didn't know her new married name. So I searched for a Lucy born in 1801 and living in upstate New York and found Lucy Hummel, age 79, now widowed again and living with the family of her daughter Sarah whose age corresponded with early censuses, but whose married name was also new to me. Lucy Myers's gravestone says she died on 2 April 1896. Confirmation that she and Lucy Hummel were the same person came with a death notice in a local newspaper, "Hummell, Lucy M., 1896, 04/02, 94 years 10 months." Sometimes this technique also works when you can't find a person whose surname is spelled in a way you hadn't considered.
- *Check the original census records.* Once you find your family in the transcription, look up the original census record to make sure everything was copied correctly and to find additional details like street address, literacy, disability, and school attendance. The 1880 U.S. census transcriptions on FamilySearch are linked to images of the census pages on Ancestry.com. You'll need a subscription to Ancestry.com's U.S. Census Images and Indexes to view the images.

You can search the 1880 U.S. Census for free on FamilySearch <www.familysearch.org> or buy the set of fifty-five CDs for $49 (item 50168). The online and CD-ROM versions are very similar, but you can search the 1880 U.S. census and the 1881 censuses of the British Isles and Canada all at once with the online version. FamilySearch <www.familysearch.org> or Salt Lake Distribution Center, (800) 537-5971. The program requires Windows 95 or higher and 35MB of hard disk space.

USGenWeb Project State Pages

<www.usgenweb.org/statelinks-table.html>. Researchers have contributed many census record indexes and transcriptions to USGenWeb's state pages and the county pages linked to them. Sometimes they include state census records that are not included on the commercial sites.

Indexes

Ancestry.com: (AIS) U.S. Federal Census Indexes Online

<www.ancestry.com/search/rectype/census/ais/main.htm>, or select Search Records | Census | U.S. Federal Census Indexes.

Part of Ancestry.com's U.S. Records Collection, the Accelerated Indexing Systems (AIS) index covers federal censuses from 1790 to 1850 and some later years, such as Minnesota (1870), Colorado (1880), and Hawaii (1910). While it's not linked to images of census pages, this index can be searched by page number. Once you find someone in the index, you can search on the place and page number to identify the person's neighbors. My ancestor Jonathan Hall appears on page 253 of the 1840 census of South Bristol, Ontario County, New York. If I search the AIS census index and just fill in the state (*New York*), county (*Ontario*), year (*1840*), and page (*253*), the results show Jonathan and his neighbors. Family members often lived close together, so some of his neighbors could turn out to be relatives.

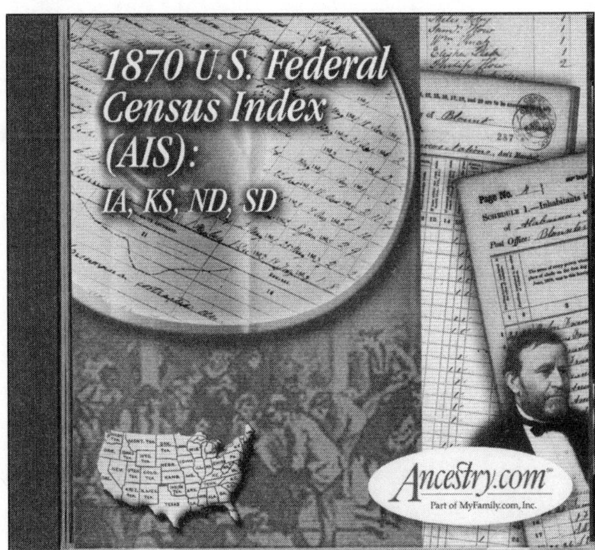

Figure 4-6
Ancestry.com's U.S. Federal Census Indexes (AIS) on CD-ROM.

Ancestry.com: U.S. Federal Census Indexes (AIS) on CD-ROM

<www.ancestry.com> Click on Shop and search on "AIS." You can also buy the AIS census indexes on CD-ROM (see Figure 4-6 above). This series of twenty-seven CDs includes one CD for tax lists before 1790, one CD for each U.S. federal census from 1790 to 1840, seven CDs for 1850, and another seven for 1860. The 1870 indexes, on five CDs, cover only selected states, and a partial index to the 1880 census is on one CD.

Most of these indexes list only heads of household, but a few cover every person. Most are $19.95 each.

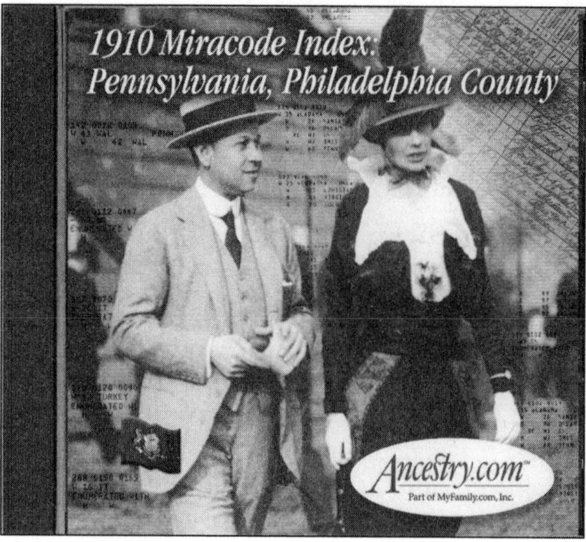

Figure 4-7
Ancestry.com's 1910 U.S. Miracode Census Index.

Ancestry.com: 1910 U.S. Miracode Census Indexes
<www.ancestry.com> Click on Shop and search on "Miracode." These CDs index not just heads of household, but everyone listed in the census (see Figure 4-7 above). The first states covered were Kentucky, Ohio, Pennsylvania, and Virginia. Each state's index is published on two or more CDs. Most CDs are $26.95 each.

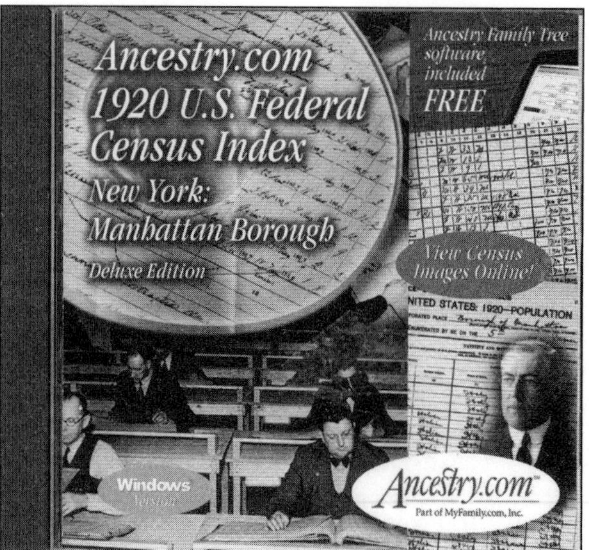

Figure 4-8
Ancestry.com's 1920 U.S. Federal Census Index.

Ancestry.com: 1920 U.S. Federal Census Index
<www.ancestry.com> Click on Shop and search on "1920." These CDs have indexes to heads of household. $19.95. The Deluxe Edition CDs, with links to online census images, are $49.95 (see Figure 4-8 above).

Ancestry.com: 1930 U.S. Federal Census Index
<**www.ancestry.com**> Click on Shop and search on "1930." These CDs, $19.95 each, index every name in the census. The Deluxe Edition CDs have links to the census images online and cost $49.95 each.

Genealogy.com: 1790 to 1910 Census Indexes
<**http://familytreemaker.genealogy.com/census.html**>. This series of twenty-five CDs (see Figure 4-9 below) includes one CD for tax lists before 1790 and one CD for each of the eight U.S. federal censuses from 1790 to 1860. The CDs index all the states through 1850, but only selected states after that year. Most of these CDs list only heads of household, but the 1870 Massachusetts index and the 1910 Idaho index list every person. All the 1870 indexes except Massachusetts include place of birth. The 1860 Indiana index covers every person and includes all information in the original census. Mac/Power Mac or Windows. $19.99 to $49.99 each.

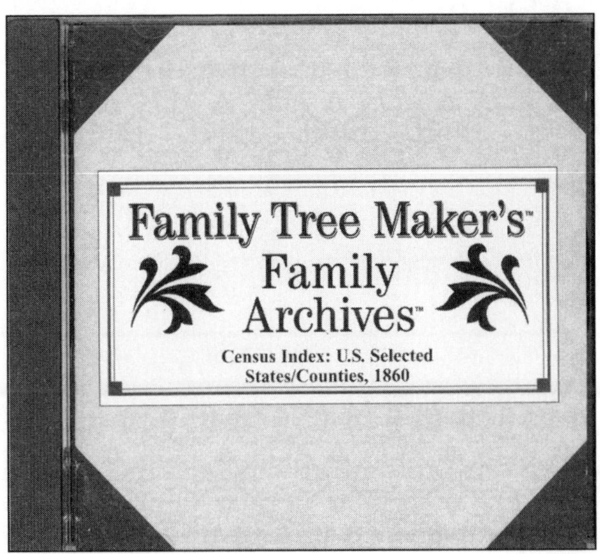

Figure 4-9
Genealogy.com's Census Index on CD-ROM.

Genealogy Library: Census Indexes
<**www.genealogy.com**> Select Records | Census Records to search census indexes, mostly from 1790 to 1880. $9.99/month or $49.99/year.

HeritageQuest: 1870 Census Indexes
<**www.heritagequest.com/html/indexlist.html**>. This series of twenty-five CDs (see Figure 4-10 on page 80) covers heads of household in the entire United States. Also included are every male over age fifty, every female over age seventy, and anyone with a different surname than the head of household. These indexes include age, race, and place of birth. Windows. $19.95 or $24.95 each.

HeritageQuest: 1870 Index of Origin and World Immigration Series
Similar to HeritageQuest's regular 1870 census indexes, these CDs list everyone anywhere in the country who was *born* in a particular state, region or

country: New England, Indiana, New York, Ohio, Pennsylvania, Canada, Europe, Germany, Great Britain, Ireland, Latin America, or Scandinavia. Other CDs list African Americans (including mulattos and natives of Africa); and Asians, Australians, Mideasterners, and Africans. Windows. $19.95 to $24.95 each. HeritageQuest <www.heritagequest.com/html/indexlist.html>.

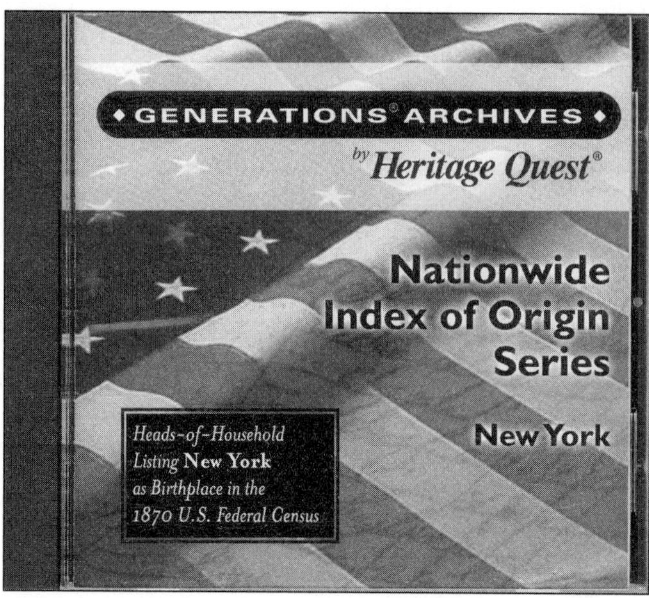

Figure 4-10
Heritage Quest's Index of Origin CD-ROM.

HeritageQuest: 1910 World Immigration Series
These CDs list everyone anywhere in the country who was nonwhite or foreign-born. The CDs cover African Americans; Asians, Mideasterners and Africans; British, Australians and New Zealanders; Canadians; Western Europeans; Germans; Irish; Latin and South Americans; Scandinavians; and Russians and Eastern Europeans. Windows. $19.95 to $34.95 each. HeritageQuest <www.heritagequest.com/html/indexlist.html>.

HeritageQuest: Your Family Name in 1870 or 1910 America
You specify a surname and receive a custom nationwide listing of every head of household in the 1870 or 1910 census with that surname, plus all Soundex variations. The index includes age, race, and place of birth. Windows. $19.95. HeritageQuest <www.heritagequest.com/html/indexlist.html>.

HeritageQuest: 1910 U.S. Census Indexes
Both heads of household and anyone with a different surname than the head's are indexed on these CDs (see Figure 4-11 on page 81). References include age and place of birth. Windows. $29.95 to $49.95 each. HeritageQuest <www.heritagequest.com/html/indexlist.html>.

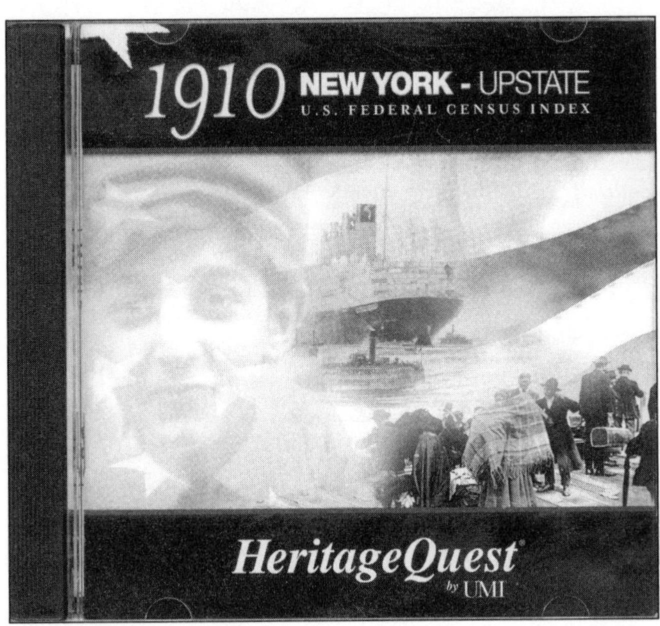

Figure 4-11
HeritageQuest's 1910 U.S. Census Index.

LINKS

Census Finder

<www.censusfinder.com>
More than 10,000 links to free census records on the Web.

Census Links

<www.censuslinks.com>
A directory of census transcriptions published on the Internet.

Census Online

<www.census-online.com>
A directory of census transcriptions published on the Internet and on CD-ROM.

City Directories of the United States of America

<www.uscitydirectories.com>
Links to online, microfilm, and print city directories.

Cyndi's List of Genealogy Sites on the Internet: U.S. Census

<www.cyndislist.com/census.htm>
Links to census indexes, records, and forms.

SUGGESTED READING

Hinckley, Kathleen W. *Your Guide to the Federal Census*. Cincinnati: Betterway Books, 2002.

DATABASE DIRECTORY Census Records

Also includes tax and voters' lists. **Type:** Digital Images, Transcript, Database, Abstracts, or Index.

United States
Type: Index
CD-ROM: Free
Online: RootsWeb.com: Tax and Voter Lists
Title: Over 14,000 records. <http://userdb.rootsweb.com/tax_voter>

United States
Type: Digital images
Year Range: 1790–1890
CD-ROM: $9.95
Title: Census View
Notes, URL: These CDs cover selected counties in 30 states. Most CDs cover a single county and year. Census View <www.censusview.org>, (800) 959-9968.

United States
Type: Digital images
Year Range: 1790–1930
CD-ROM: $20 each
Title: SK Publications Census CD-ROMs
Notes, URL: Each of these CDs covers the records for one county in one census year. Only selected counties are covered so far. SK Publications <www.skcensus.com>, (888) 705-4887. Most of these census images are also on RootsWeb.

United States
Type: Digital images
Year Range: 1790–1930
Online: Free
Title: USGenWeb Archives Census Project—Census Images Table of Contents
Notes, URL: <www.rootsweb.com/~usgenweb/cen_img.htm>

United States
Type: Transcripts
Year Range: 1790–1930
Online: Free
Title: USGenWeb Census Project
Notes, URL: Two separate projects, both named USGenWeb Census Project, to transcribe census records. <www.rootsweb.com/~census> & <www.us-census.org>

United States
Type: Transcripts & indexes
Year Range: 1790–1944
Online: Free
Title: RootsWeb.com: Census Records
Notes, URL: Over 390,000 records from state and federal censuses. <http://userdb.rootsweb.com/census/index>

United States
Type: Transcript
Year Range: 1850–1880
CD-ROM: $19.99, Genealogy.com, CD #164
Title: U.S. 1850–1880, Mortality Index
Notes, URL: More than 382,000 records. <www.genealogy.com/164facd.html>

Arizona
Type: Index
Year Range: 1831–1880
Online: Ancestry
Title: Arizona Census, 1831–80
Notes, URL: 1831 (St. Cruz Co. only); 1862, 1864, 1866, 1867, 1870, 1880. <www.ancestry.com/search/rectype/inddbs/3533.htm>

Arizona
Type: Excerpts
Year Range: 1860–1870
Online: Ancestry
Title: Arizona and New Mexico Territories Census, Late 1800s
Notes, URL: 1860 census of Arizona Co., in the Territory of New Mexico. 1870 census of the Territory of Arizona. Special Territorial Census of 1864 taken in Arizona. Over 12,000 records. <www.ancestry.com/search/rectype/inddbs/3085.htm>

Arizona
Type: Transcript
Year Range: 1864
Online: Ancestry
Title: Arizona Territory Census, 1864
Notes, URL: 4,187 names. <www.ancestry.com/search/rectype/inddbs/3121.htm>

Arizona, Navajo Co.
Type: Index
Year Range: 1910
Online: Ancestry
Title: Navajo County, Arizona Census, 1910
Notes, URL: <www.ancestry.com/search/rectype/inddbs/4180.htm>

Arizona, Yavapai Co.
Type: Index
Year Range: 1870–1920
Online: Free
Title: Sharlot Hall Museum Censuses
Notes, URL: 1870, 1880, 1900, & 1920 censuses. <www.sharlot.org/archives/census/index.html>

Arkansas
Type: Indexes
Year Range: 1819–1870
Online: Ancestry
Title: Arkansas Census, 1819–70
Notes, URL: <www.ancestry.com/search/rectype/inddbs/3534a.htm>

Colorado
Type: Transcript
Year Range: 1861
Online: Free
Title: Colorado 1861 Territorial Election
Notes, URL: <www.denver.lib.co.us/ebranch/whg/datafile.html#election>

Colorado
Type: Index
Year Range: 1870
Online: Free
Title: Colorado State Archives, 1870 Federal Census Index: Colorado
Notes, URL: <www.colorado.gov/dpa/doit/archives/1870/index.htm>

Colorado
Type: Transcript
Year Range: 1885
Online: Ancestry
Title: Colorado State Census, 1885
Notes, URL: <www.ancestry.com/search/rectype/inddbs/6837.htm>

Dakota Territory
Type: Transcript
Year Range: 1860
Online: Free
Title: Dakota Territory 1860 Census—Interactive Search
Notes, URL: <www.rootsweb.com/cgi-bin/sdcensus/sd1860cen.pl>

Dakota Territory
Type: Digital images
Year Range: 1880
Online: Free
Title: North Dakota Census Online: ND Territory 1880 Census Sites
Notes, URL: Dakota Territory counties in present-day North Dakota. <http://free

pages.genealogy.rootsweb.com/~cat s61/ndcensus/1880_census.htm>

Illinois
Type: Transcripts
Year Range: 1787–1930
Online: Free
Title: Illinois Trails Census
Notes, URL: <www.iltrails.org/ilcens.htm>

Illinois
Type: Digital images of a book containing transcripts
Year Range: 1810–1820
CD-ROM: $29.99, Genealogy.com, CD #508
Online: Genealogy Library
Title: Midwest Pioneers, 1600s–1800s
Notes, URL: Includes Illinois census returns, 1810, 1818, & 1820. <www.genealogy.com/508facd.html>

Illinois, Hancock Co., Nauvoo
Type: Transcript
Year Range: 1842
Online: Ancestry
Title: Nauvoo, Illinois Tax Index, 1842
Notes, URL: <www.ancestry.com/search/rectype/inddbs/4221.htm>

Illinois, Putnam Co.
Type: Digital images
Year Range: 1835
CD-ROM: $19.95/CD, FamilyToolbox.net
Online: Free
Title: Sources2Go.com: Census Records: 1835 Illinois State Census, Putnam County
Notes, URL: <www.sources2go.com>

Indiana, Morgan Co.
Type: Index
Year Range: 1850–1910
Online: Free
Title: Morgan County Public Library, Morgan County Census Records
Notes, URL: <www.scican.net/~morglib/genasist/genasist.html>

Indiana, Porter Co.
Type: Index
Year Range: 1930
Online: Free
Title: Porter Co. Public Library System
Notes, URL: <www.pcpls.lib.in.us>. Click on "Genealogy Department."

Iowa
Type: Index
Year Range: 1838–1870
Online: Ancestry
Title: Iowa Census, 1838–70
Notes, URL: Censuses of 1838, 1840, 1841–1849, 1850, 1851, 1852, 1860, 1870. <www.ancestry.com/search/rectype/inddbs/3547a.htm>

Iowa
Type: Transcript
Year Range: 1885
Online: Ancestry
Title: Iowa State Census 1885
Notes, URL: <www.ancestry.com/search/rectype/inddbs/6812.htm>

Kansas
Type: Transcript
Year Range: 1854–1856
Online: Ancestry
Title: Kansas Voter Registration Lists, 1854–56
Notes, URL: Over 16,000 names. <www.ancestry.com/search/rectype/inddbs/3961.htm>

Kansas
Type: Index
Year Range: 1855
Online: Ancestry
Title: Kansas Territorial Census, 1855
Notes, URL: Over 3000 names. <www.ancestry.com/search/rectype/inddbs/4056.htm>

Kansas
Type: Digital images of a book containing an index
Year Range: 1860
CD-ROM: $29.99, Genealogy.com, CD #508
Online: Genealogy Library
Title: Midwest Pioneers, 1600s–1800s
Notes, URL: Natives of Tennessee, Virginia, North Carolina, & South Carolina in the Kansas territorial census of 1860. <www.genealogy.com/508facd.html>

Kansas
Type: Index
Year Range: 1895
Online: Free
Title: 1895 Kansas State Census
Notes, URL: <www.kshs.org/genealogists/census/kansas/census1895ks.htm>

Kansas, Leavenworth Co.
Type: Index
Year Range: 1865
Online: Ancestry
Title: Leavenworth, Kansas State Census, 1865
Notes, URL: Over 7,600 names. <www.ancestry.com/search/rectype/inddbs/3995.htm>

Kansas, Leavenworth Co.
Type: Transcript
Year Range: 1895–1900
Online: Ancestry
Title: Leavenworth, Kansas Tax List, 1895–97, 1899–1900
Notes, URL: Over 3,100 names. <www.ancestry.com/search/rectype/inddbs/3499.htm>

Kansas, Leavenworth Co., Leavenworth
Type: Transcript
Year Range: 1859
Online: Ancestry
Title: Leavenworth, Kansas Voter Registration, 1859
Notes, URL: Nearly 3,000 names. <www.ancestry.com/search/rectype/inddbs/3489.htm>

Kansas, Riley Co.
Type: Transcript
Year Range: 1865
Online: Ancestry
Title: Riley county, Kansas State Census, 1865
Notes, URL: 1,809 names. <www.ancestry.com/search/rectype/inddbs/5976.htm>

Kansas, Riley Co.
Type: Transcript
Year Range: 1875
Online: Ancestry
Title: Riley County, Kansas Census, 1875
Notes, URL: Nearly 9,000 names. <www.ancestry.com/search/rectype/inddbs/5072.htm>

Kansas, Riley Co.
Type: Transcript
Year Range: 1885
Online: Ancestry
Title: Riley county, Kansas, 1885 State Census
Notes, URL: <www.ancestry.com/search/rectype/inddbs/6074.htm>

Kansas, Riley Co.
Type: Abstracts
Year Range: 1905
Online: Ancestry
Title: Riley county, Kansas, 1905 State Census
Notes, URL: 13,738 names. <www.ancestry.com/search/rectype/inddbs/5956.htm>

Kansas, Riley Co.
Type: Abstracts
Year Range: 1915
Online: Ancestry
Title: Riley County, Kansas State Census, 1915
Notes, URL: 16,507 names. <www.ancestry.com/search/rectype/inddbs/5292.htm>

Kansas, Riley Co.
Type: Abstracts
Year Range: 1925
Online: Ancestry
Title: Riley County Kansas 1925 Decennial Agricultural State census
Notes, URL: <www.ancestry.com/search/rectype/inddbs/6105.htm>

Kentucky
Type: Transcript
Year Range: 1800–1880
CD-ROM: $26.50 (Mac/Win), Heritage Books, CD #1374
Title: HB Archives: Kentucky Vol. 1
Notes, URL: Includes the 1880 census of Lee County annotated with birth, marriage, & death data from 45 sources. Also, the 1800 census of Owsley County annotated with data from 57 sources. <www.heritagebooks.com>. Search on "1374."

Louisiana
Type: Transcript
Year Range: 1699–1820
CD-ROM: $29.99, Genealogy.com, CD #525
Online: Genealogy Library
Title: Early Louisiana Settlers, 1600s–1800s
Notes, URL: Includes *Louisiana Census Records* (Avoyelles & St. Landry Parishes, 1810 & 1820; Iberville, Natchitoches, Pointe Coupee, & Rapides Parishes, 1810 & 1820). Also, *The Census Tables for the French Colony of Louisiana from 1699 Through 1732*. <www.genealogy.com/525facd.html>

Maine
Type: Transcript
Year Range: 1790
CD-ROM: $29.99, Genealogy.com, CD #523
Online: Genealogy Library
Title: Maine & New Hampshire Settlers, 1600s–1900s
Notes, URL: Includes the 1790 census of Maine. Select Genealogical Records: Maine & New Hampshire Settlers, 1600s–1900s. <www.genealogy.com/523facd.html>

Maine, York Co.
Type: Transcript
Year Range: 1850–1920
Online: Free
Title: York County Genealogy and Virtual Cemeteries
Notes, URL: Censuses of 1850, 1904/1905, and 1920 for various towns. <www.knights.hls-inc.net/>

Maryland
Type: Transcript
Year Range: 1776
Online: Ancestry
Title: Maryland Colonial Census, 1776
Notes, URL: Over 17,100 names. <www.ancestry.com/search/rectype/inddbs/4247.htm>

Massachusetts
Type: Transcript, index
Year Range: 1790–1800
CD-ROM: $39.99, Genealogy.com, CD #526
Online: Genealogy Library
Title: Massachusetts, 1600s–1800s Genealogical Records
Notes, URL: Includes a transcript of the 1790 census & an index of the 1800 census. Also, Missouri histories. <www.genealogy.com/526facd.html>

Massachusetts, Barnstable Co.
Type: Transcript
Year Range: 1855
Online: Ancestry
Title: Barnstable County Massachusetts 1855 Census
Notes, URL: <www.ancestry.com/search/rectype/inddbs/4815.htm>

Massachusetts, Suffolk Co., Boston
Type: Transcript
Year Range: 1707
Online: Ancestry
Title: Boston, Massachusetts, Census, 1707
Notes, URL: <www.ancestry.com/search/rectype/inddbs/6363.htm>

Massachusetts, Suffolk Co., Boston
Type: Transcript
Year Range: 1831
Online: NEHGS
Title: Boston Tax List, 1831
Notes, URL: From *List of persons, co-partnerships, and corporations who were taxed twenty-five dollars and upwards, in the city of Boston, in the year 1831*. <www.newenglandancestors.org/research/database/boston_tax>

Michigan
Type: Index
Year Range: 1827–1870
Online: Ancestry
Title: Michigan Census, 1827–70
Notes, URL: An index to the censuses of 1827, 1837, 1840, 1845, 1850, 1860, & 1870. <www.ancestry.com/search/rectype/inddbs/3554a.htm>

Michigan
Type: Index, images
Year Range: 1870
Online: Free
Title: Library of Michigan 1870 Census Index
Notes, URL: The index to heads of households is linked to images of the census pages. <http://envoy.libraryofmichigan.org/1870_census>

Minnesota
Type: Index
Year Range: 1835–1890
Online: Ancestry
Title: Minnesota Census, 1835–90
Notes, URL: Indexes to the 1835–1839 tax lists, the 1849, 1850, 1860, 1870, & 1880 censuses & the 1890 veterans schedule. <www.ancestry.com/search/rectype/inddbs/3555a.htm>

Minnesota, Rice Co.
Type: Abstract
Year Range: 1900–1910
Online: Ancestry
Title: Rice County, Minnesota Census, 1900–10
Notes, URL: <www.ancestry.com/search/rectype/inddbs/3743.htm>

Minnesota, Rice Co.
Type: Abstract
Year Range: 1920
Online: Ancestry
Title: Rice County, Minnesota Census, 1920
Notes, URL: <www.ancestry.com/search/rectype/inddbs/4188.htm>

Mississippi
Type: Index
Year Range: 1805–1890
Online: Ancestry
Title: Mississippi Census, 1805–90
Notes, URL: Index to the censuses of 1805, 1810, 1818, 1822, 1823, 1824, 1825, 1830, 1837, 1840, 1841, 1845, 1850, 1853, 1860, 1866, 1870, & 1890. <ww

w.ancestry.com/search/rectype/inddbs/3556a.htm>

Missouri, Miller Co.
Type: Transcript with annotations
Year Range: 1840
CD-ROM: $41 (Mac/Win), Heritage Books, CD #1520
Title: HB Archives: Missouri Vol. 2
Notes, URL: Includes a transcript of the 1840 census of Miller Co. plus 350 pages of census annotations. <www.heritagebooks.com>. Search on "1520."

Missouri, Saline Co.
Type: Transcript
Year Range: 1876
Online: Ancestry
Title: Saline County, Missouri: 1876 Taxpayers and Biographies
Notes, URL: From Elizabeth Prather Ellsberry, *1876 Taxpayers and Biographies for Saline County, Missouri.* <www.ancestry.com/search/rectype/inddbs/6055.htm>

Nebraska
Type: Index
Year Range: 1854–1870
Online: Ancestry
Title: Nebraska Census, 1854–70
Notes, URL: 1854, 1855, & 1856 territorial censuses & 1870 federal census. <www.ancestry.com/search/rectype/inddbs/3559.htm>

Nebraska
Type: Transcript
Year Range: 1885
Online: Ancestry
Title: Nebraska State Census 1885
Notes, URL: <www.ancestry.com/search/rectype/inddbs/6585.htm>

Nevada
Type: Transcript
Year Range: 1875
Online: Ancestry
Title: Nevada State Census, 1875
Notes, URL: More than 51,000 names. <www.ancestry.com/search/rectype/inddbs/4873.htm>

Nevada
Type: Transcript
Year Range: 1913–1918
Online: Ancestry
Title: Nevada Car Registration Records, 1913–18
Notes, URL: Over 24,500 names. <www.ancestry.com/search/rectype/inddbs/4328.htm>

New Hampshire
Type: Transcript
Year Range: 1790
CD-ROM: $29.99, Genealogy.com, CD #523
Online: Genealogy Library
Title: Maine & New Hampshire Settlers, 1600s–1900s
Notes, URL: Includes the 1790 census of New Hampshire. Select Genealogical Records: Maine & New Hampshire Settlers, 1600s–1900s. <www.genealogy.com/523facd.html>

New Hampshire, Hillsborough Co.
Type: Transcript
Year Range: 1850
CD-ROM: $28.50 (Mac/Win), Heritage Books, item #1358
Title: HB Archives: New Hampshire Vol. 2
Notes, URL: Includes a transcript of the 1850 census of Hillsborough Co., N.H., & *The History of New Hampshire.* <www.heritagebooks.com>. Search on "1358."

New Jersey
Type: Index
Year Range: 1772–1890
Online: Ancestry
Title: New Jersey Census, 1772–1890
Notes, URL: Covers tax lists, 1772–1822. <www.ancestry.com/search/rectype/inddbs/3562a.htm>

New Mexico
Type: Excerpts
Year Range: 1860
Online: Ancestry
Title: Arizona and New Mexico Territories Census, Late 1800s
Notes, URL: 1860 census of Arizona Co., in the Territory of New Mexico. Over 12,000 records. <www.ancestry.com/search/rectype/inddbs/3085.htm>

New York
Type: Transcript
Year Range: 1689–1720
Online: Free
Title: New York State Census
Notes, URL: Links to the 1720 census of Albany County, 1714 census of Dutchess County, 1702 census of Orange County, & 1689 census of Ulster County. <www.frontiernet.net/~halsey1/ny/ny-census.htm>

New York, Albany Co., Albany
Type: Index
Year Range: 1915
Online: Ancestry
Title: Albany, New York State Census, 1915
Notes, URL: 108,000 names from wards 1-8. <www.ancestry.com/search/rectype/inddbs/3958.htm>

New York, Albany Co., Berne
Type: Transcript
Year Range: 1790–1925
Online: Free
Title: Berne Historical Project
Notes, URL: <www.bernehistory.org/census/census.htm>

New York, Allegany Co.
Type: Transcript
Year Range: 1850–1900
Online: Free
Title: Painted Hills Genealogy Society: Allegany: Census
Notes, URL: Various towns. <www.paintedhills.org/allco.html>

New York, Cattaraugus Co.
Type: Indexes
Year Range: 1820–1892
Online: Free
Title: Painted Hills Genealogy Society: Cattaraugus: Census
Notes, URL: Indexes to the 1820, 1835, 1850, 1855, 1865, 1870, 1875, 1880, & 1892 censuses. <www.paintedhills.org/cattco.html>

New York, Delaware Co.
Type: Digital images of books
Year Range: 1800–1855
CD-ROM: $24.50 (Mac/Win), Long Island Genealogy
Title: Vital Records Collection from Delaware County, New York
Notes, URL: Includes 1800 and 1855 census. <http://genealogycds.com/sales/Delaware.htm>

New York, New York (City)
Type: Index
Year Range: 1890
Online: Ancestry
Title: New York City Police Census, 1890
Notes, URL: Incomplete. More than 5,000 names. <www.ancestry.com/search/rectype/inddbs/3519.htm>

New York, Ontario Co.
Type: Index
Year Range: 1790–1900
Online: Free

Title: Historical Census Records for Ontario County
Notes, URL: Census indexes for 1790, 1820, 1845, 1850, 1855, 1860, 1865, 1870, 1875 & 1900. <www.raims.com/censusmenu.html>

New York, Steuben Co., Troupsburg
Type: Transcript, index
Year Range: 1855
Online: Free
Title: Painted Hills Genealogy Society: Steuben: Census
Notes, URL: 1855 Troupsburg Census. <www.paintedhills.org/steuben.html>

New York, Suffolk Co.
Type: Transcript
Year Range: 1778
Online: Free
Title: Suffolk County, Long Island, New York, 1778 Census
Notes, URL: <www.longislandgenealogy.com/1778Census/IndexPage.html>

North Carolina, Pitt Co.
Type: Transcript
Year Range: 1900
Online: Free
Title: Pitt County Census Information
Notes, URL: <www.lib.ecu.edu/exhibits/tobacco/Census.html>

North Dakota (see also Dakota Territory)
Type: Transcript
Year Range: 1885
Online: Free
Title: Dakota Territory 1885 Census Database
Notes, URL: Over 132,000 names, which is more than two-thirds of the total population for the northern half of Dakota Territory at that time. <www.lib.ndsu.nodak.edu/ndirs/bio&genealogy/dakterr1885census.html>

North Dakota
Type: Transcript
Year Range: 1900
Online: Free
Title: North Dakota Census Online
Notes, URL: <http://freepages.genealogy.rootsweb.com/~cats61/ndcensus/1900_census.htm>

North Dakota
Type: Digital images
Year Range: 1910–1930
Online: Free
Title: North Dakota Census Online
Notes, URL: Censuses of 1910, 1920, & 1930. <http://freepages.genealogy.rootsweb.com/~cats61/ndcensus/censusonline.htm>

Ohio, Wayne Co.
Type: Transcript
Year Range: 1913–1916
Online: Ancestry
Title: Wayne County, Ohio Tax Lists, 1913, 1914, and 1916
Notes, URL: From *Assessment of Real Estate and Improvements Wayne County Ohio 1913, 1914, part of 1916*. <www.ancestry.com/search/rectype/inddbs/3944.htm>

Oklahoma
Type: Transcript
Year Range: 1860
Online: Free
Title: 1860 Lands West of Arkansas
Notes, URL: Covers white & free inhabitants, not Indians. <www.rootsweb.com/~okgarvin/kinard/1860index.htm>

Oklahoma
Type: Index
Year Range: 1890
Online: Free
Title: 1890 Oklahoma Territory Census Index
Notes, URL: <www.ok-history.mus.ok.us/lib/1890/1890index.htm>

Oklahoma
Type: Transcript
Year Range: 1910–1920
Online: Free
Title: Mary Turner Kinard Archives
Notes, URL: 1910 & 1920 censuses of Garvin Co. & 1920 census of McClain Co. <www.rootsweb.com/~okgarvin/kinard/kinard.htm>

Oklahoma, Logan Co.
Type: Transcript
Year Range: 1890
Online: Free
Title: Mary Turner Kinard Archives
Notes, URL: <www.rootsweb.com/~okgarvin/kinard/okla1890census.htm>

Oklahoma, Muskogee Co.
Type: Transcript
Year Range: 1910
Online: Ancestry
Title: Muskogee County, Oklahoma Census, 1910
Notes, URL: <www.ancestry.com/search/rectype/inddbs/4177.htm>

Oregon
Type: Index
Year Range: 1865–1895
Online: Free
Title: Oregon Historical Records Index
Notes, URL: Indexes to census records from Lake, Marion, Morrow, Multnomah, & Umatilla Counties. <http://arcweb.sos.state.or.us/banners/genlist.htm>

Pennsylvania
Type: Index
Year Range: 1772–1890
Online: Ancestry
Title: Pennsylvania Census, 1772–1890
Notes, URL: Includes the 1772 tax list of Northampton County & the 1842 & 1857 census indexes of Chester County. <www.ancestry.com/search/rectype/inddbs/3570a.htm>

Pennsylvania, McKean Co.
Type: Transcript
Year Range: 1810–1930
Online: Free
Title: Painted Hills Genealogy Society: McKean: Census
Notes, URL: Various towns. <www.paintedhills.org/mckeanco.html>

Pennsylvania, Potter Co.
Type: Transcripts
Year Range: 1840–1920
Online: Free
Title: Painted Hills Genealogy Society: Potter: Census
Notes, URL: The 1840, 1850, 1860, 1870, 1880, & 1920 censuses of various towns. <www.paintedhills.org/potterco.html>

Pennsylvania, Susquehanna Co., Silver Lake Township
Type: Transcript
Year Range: 1878–1879
Online: Ancestry (free)
Title: Susquehanna County, Silver Lake Township, Pennsylvania, 1878–79 tax rolls
Notes, URL: From Silver Lake Township Tax Rolls, Higginson Book Company. <www.ancestry.com/search/rectype/inddbs/5766.htm>

Rhode Island
Type: Transcript
Year Range: 1774
Online: Ancestry
Title: Rhode Island Census, 1774
Notes, URL: Over 9,000 records. <www.anc

estry.com/search/rectype/inddbs/3081.htm>

South Carolina, Charleston Co., Charleston
Type: Transcript
Year Range: 1861
Online: Free
Title: Census of the City of Charleston, South Carolina, For the Year 1861
Notes, URL: Text of the book by Frederick A. Ford. <http://docsouth.unc.edu/imls/census/census.html>

South Dakota
Type: Index
Year Range: 1885
Online: Ancestry
Title: South Dakota Territorial Census, 1885
Notes, URL: <www.ancestry.com/search/rectype/inddbs/6247.htm>

South Dakota
Type: Index
Year Range: 1895
Online: Ancestry
Title: South Dakota State Census, 1895
Notes, URL: Covers Beadle, Butte, Pratt (now Jones), Presho (now Lyman), Campbell, & Charles Mix Counties. <www.ancestry.com/search/rectype/inddbs/6120.htm>

South Dakota (see Dakota Territory)

Tennessee
Type: Index
Year Range: 1810–1891
Online: Ancestry
Title: Tennessee Census, 1810–91
Notes, URL: Covers the 1891 Voters List. <www.ancestry.com/search/rectype/inddbs/3574a.htm>

Tennessee
Type: Index
Year Range: 1820
CD-ROM: $29.99, Genealogy.com, CD #511
Online: Genealogy Library
Title: Early Tennessee Settlers, 1700s–1900s
Notes, URL: Includes an index to the 1820 census of Tennessee & a list of residents of Davidson, Sumner, & Tennessee Counties, 1770–1790. <www.genealogy.com/511facd.html>

Texas
Type: Transcript
Year Range: 1867
CD-ROM: $33 (Mac/Win), Heritage Books, item #1354
Title: An Index to the 1867 Voters' Registration of Texas
Notes, URL: Digital images of a book by Donaly E. Brice & John C. Barron. This CD is "the first statewide listing showing the names of newly freed slaves in TX." <www.heritagebooks.com>. Search on "1354."

Utah
Type: Index
Year Range: 1850–1880
Online: Free
Title: Utah Census Search
Notes, URL: <www.xmission.com/~nelsonb/census_search.htm>

Virgin Islands (U.S.)
Type: Transcript
Year Range: 1722
Online: Free
Title: HGS: U.S. Virgin Islands
Notes, URL: Inhabitants of St. John, then the Danish West Indies. English translation. <www.horlacher.org/usviris/>

Virginia, Shenandoah Co.
Type: Transcript
Year Range: 1860–1870
CD-ROM: $32 (Mac/Win), Heritage Books, item #1951
Title: HB Archives: Virginia Vol. 7
Notes, URL: Includes *Shenandoah County, Virginia: A Study of the 1860 Census, Volumes 1-4* (with a transcript & detailed biographies) & *Shenandoah County: The 1870 Census*, by Marvin J. Vann. <www.heritagebooks.com>. Search on "1951."

Washington
Type: Transcript, digital images.
Year Range: 1851–1889
Online: Free
Title: Washington Secretary of State: Washington History, Historical Records Search
Notes, URL: Transcript & images of 1851 census of Lewis County. Transcripts of 1857 census of King Co., 1871 census of Yakima Co., & 1885, 1887, & 1889 censuses of Skagit Co. <www.secstate.wa.gov/history/search.aspx>

West Virginia, Lewis Co.
Type: Transcript with annotations
Year Range: 1850
CD-ROM: $26 (Mac/Win), Heritage Books, item #1598
Title: The People of Lewis County, (West) Virginia, in 1850
Notes, URL: Images of a book by Crystal V. Wagoner, which builds on the census data with cemetery inscriptions, military records, & information from other sources. <www.heritagebooks.com>. Search on "1598."

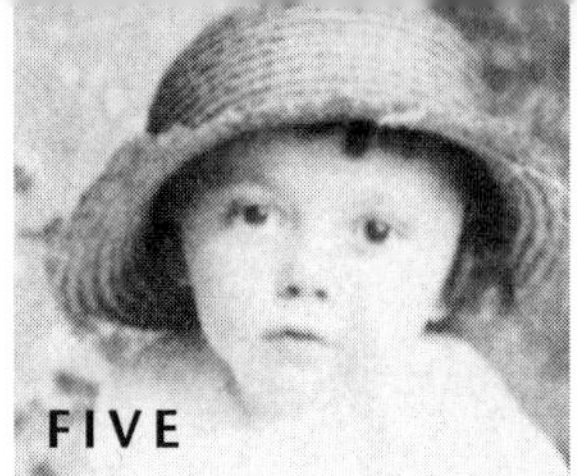

Will, Probate, and Court Records

Reminder

WHAT IF SOMEONE DIED WITHOUT A WILL?

A person who left a will died testate, while someone who died without a will died intestate. In either case, valuable records may have been created to document the distribution of the deceased's property.

Carriage, $10. Bay horse, $20. Red cow with white face, $40. Corn in field, $250. Watch, $2. Book-case, $2. In 1897 Stephen S. Olmsted died at age 85 in Victoria, Knox County, Illinois, and these are some of the dozens of items recorded in the inventory of his estate. In addition to the fascinating list of articles in his home and on his farm, the probate file also provides his date of death and names his heirs.

Wills, probate records, and court records all provide useful information for genealogists. A last will and testament tells how someone wishes to have his property distributed after his death. Probate records are court records created regarding the distribution of a deceased person's property. They may provide a date of death, and, like wills, they may name family members. Other court records can also help establish family relationships and may reveal places of residence, occupations, and other interesting details.

What will, probate, and court records are online or on CD-ROM?
You'll find many indexes, some abstracts, and a few digital images of these records from all over the United States (see Figure 5-1 below).

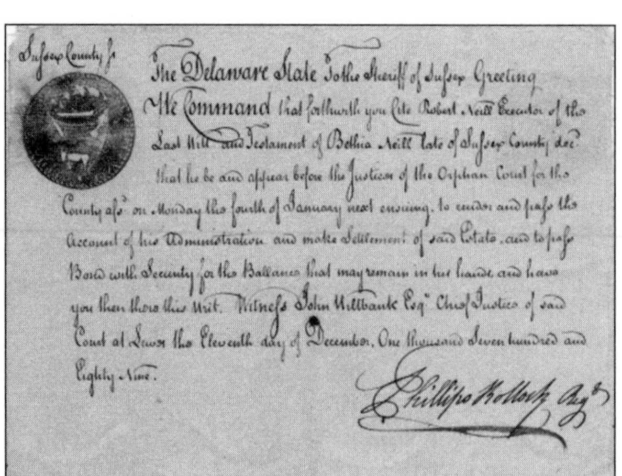

Sussex County ss

The Delaware State To the Sheriff of Sussex Greeting

We Command that forthwith you Cite Robert Neill Executor of the Last Will and Testament of Bethia Neill late of Sussex County dec'd that he be and appear before the Justices of the Orphans Court for the County afs'd on Monday the fourth of January next ensuing, to render and pass the Account of his Administration and make Settlement of said Estate, and to pass Bond with Security for the Ballance that may remain in his hands and have you then there this Writ. Witness John Wiltbank Esq. Chief Justice of said Court at Lewes the Eleventh day of December, One thousand Seven hundred and Eighty Nine.

Phillips Kollock Reg.

Figure 5-1
Bethia Neill court case, 1788-89, Sussex County (Delaware), Orphans Court Case Files, Delaware Public Archives <www.state.de.us/sos/dpa/exhibits/Orphans/index.htm>.

What will, probate, and court records are not online or on CD-ROM?
Few digital images of these records are online or on CD-ROM. When you find a promising reference in an index or abstract, be sure to get a copy of the original record.

PROBATE AND LIVING INDIVIDUALS

If someone is deemed mentally unfit, a court may issue commitment papers and oversee the distribution of the person's property. You may find these records in court or probate files.

KEY RESOURCES

Indexes

Sampubco

<www.sampubco.com>

Searchable databases include indexes to over 300,000 wills in Alabama, Georgia, Idaho, Iowa, Kansas, Maryland, Massachusetts, New York, Ohio, Oregon, Pennsylvania, Rhode Island, Tennessee, Virginia, and Wisconsin (see Figure 5-2 below). Indexes to guardianship records in New York and naturalization records in Iowa, Massachusetts, Missouri, New York, Oregon, Pennsylvania, and Wisconsin are being added. You can request a copy of most wills for $14 and guardianship and naturalization records for $5.

SAMPUBCO
Gateway to the Indexes
All Absolute FREE to browse
Latest SAMPUBCO NEWS . Follow the single link bottom if you don't want news and don't want to know about new additions.
(Wills News Update 31 Jan 2003)
(Naturalizations and Intentions News Update 8 Jan 2003)
(Guardianships News Update 08 Jan 2003)
Effective IMMEDIATELY! No orders without email addresses listed will be accepted including the checks. They will be destroyed and no acknowledgement of such orders will be provided. The requirement is imposed to protect the safety of your mail. You are notified by email when your order is on way to you. Please make sure you do not forget to list your email address on your order. | Privacy Statement |
All Absolute FREE to browse!
Who will be lucky 5,000th customer? The milestone will be hit sometime during February 2003.

Figure 5-2
Sampubco.

USGenWeb Project State Pages

<www.usgenweb.org/statelinks-table.html>

Researchers have contributed many indexes of will, probate, and court records to USGenWeb's state pages and the county pages linked to them. Most of these databases are not listed in the directory below, so be sure to check USGenWeb for the counties where your family lived.

LINKS

Cyndi's List of Genealogy Sites on the Internet: Wills & Probate

<www.cyndislist.com/wills.htm>

DATABASE DIRECTORY Will, Probate, and Court Records

This directory does not include URLs for databases in the Family and Local Histories collection. See page 18 for instructions on "Searching an Individual Database" in Family and Local Histories. Claims (CL), Court (CT), Guardianships (G), Legislative Journals (LJ), Orphans (OR), Poor (PO), Probate (PR), Wills (W). **Type**: Digital Images, Transcript, Database, Abstracts, or Index.

United States
Type: Index; W
Year Range: 1629–1965
Online: Free
Title: Sampubco
Notes, URL: Indexes to wills in 15 states. Go to <www.sampubco.com/wills/search.htm> & click on Search Engine or a 2-letter state abbreviation.

United States
Type: Transcripts; W
Year Range: 1699–1896
Online: Free
Title: Cindy's Delmarva Wills
Notes, URL: Covers the peninsula divided between Delaware, eastern Maryland and Accomack Co., Virginia. <www.shoreweb.com/cindy/wills.htm>

United States
Type: Database; CL
Year Range: 1790–1851
Online: Ancestry
Title: U.S. House of Representative Private Claims, Vol. 3
Notes, URL: Nearly 20,700 names in claims to the House of Representatives. <www.ancestry.com/search/rectype/inddbs/4565.htm>

United States
Type: Database; CL
Year Range: 1799–1850
Online: Ancestry
Title: U.S. House of Representative Private Claims, Vol. 1
Notes, URL: Nearly 23,000 names in claims to the House of Representatives. <www.ancestry.com/search/rectype/inddbs/4519.htm>

United States
Type: Database; CL
Year Range: 1799–1850
Online: Ancestry
Title: U.S. House of Representative Private Claims, Vol. 2
Notes, URL: Nearly 18,300 names in claims to the House of Representatives. <www.ancestry.com/search/rectype/inddbs/4544.htm>

Alabama, Bibb Co.
Type: Index; PR
Year Range: 1834–1839
Online: F&LH
Title: Index of Book A, Minutes of Probate Court, Bibb County, Alabama

Arkansas
Type: Index; CT
Year Range: 1863–1906
Online: Free
Title: RootsWeb.com Court Records
Notes, URL: Over 15,000 records. Mostly criminal cases from Arkansas. <http://userdb.rootsweb.com/courtrecords>

Arkansas, Sebastian Co., Fort Smith
Type: Index; CT
Year Range: 1866–1900
Online: Free
Title: Fort Smith Arkansas Criminal Case Files
Notes, URL: <www.archives.gov/research_room/arc/arc_info/genealogy_search_hints.html#smith>

Colorado
Type: Index; CT
Year Range: 1871–1973
Online: Free
Title: Colorado State Archives: Colorado State Penitentiary Prisoner Index 1871–1973
Notes, URL: <www.colorado.gov/dpa/doit/archives/pen/index.htm>

Colorado
Type: Index; PR
Year Range: 1876–1953
Online: Free
Title: Colorado State Archives: County Probate Records
Notes, URL: Various counties. <www.colorado.gov/dpa/doit/archives/probate/>

Colorado
Type: Index; CT
Year Range: 1887–1939
Online: Free
Title: Denver Public Library: Colorado State Reformatory Records 1887–1939
Notes, URL: <www.denver.lib.co.us/ebranch/whg/datafile.html>

Colorado
Type: Index; PR
Year Range: 1907–1956
Online: Free
Title: Colorado State Archives: Inheritance Tax Records
Notes, URL: Various counties. <www.colorado.gov/dpa/doit/archives/inh_tax/index.html>

Colorado, Adams Co.
Type: Index; W
Year Range: 1903–1938
Online: Free
Title: Adams County Will Records 1903–1938
Notes, URL: <www.colorado.gov/dpa/doit/archives/wills/1adams.html>

Colorado, Clear Creek Co.
Type: Index; W
Year Range: 1950–1964
Online: Free
Title: Clear Creek County Will Records 1950–1964
Notes, URL: <www.colorado.gov/dpa/doit/archives/wills/1clear_creek.html>

Colorado, Custer Co.
Type: Index; W
Year Range: 1887–1966
Online: Free
Title: Custer County Will Records 1887–1966
Notes, URL: <www.colorado.gov/dpa/doit/archives/wills/1custer.html>

Colorado, Douglas Co.
Type: Index; W
Year Range: 1886–1961
Online: Free
Title: Douglas County Will Records 1886–1961
Notes, URL: <www.colorado.gov/dpa/doit/archives/wills/1douglas.html>

Colorado, Elbert Co.
Type: Index; W
Year Range: 1887–1966
Online: Free
Title: Elbert County Will Records 1887–1966

Notes, URL: <www.colorado.gov/dpa/doit/archives/wills/1elbert.html>

Colorado, Gilpin Co.
Type: Index; CT
Year Range: 1862–1878
Online: Free
Title: Gilpin County Chancery Cases
Notes, URL: <www.colorado.gov/dpa/doit/archives/chancery/index.html>

Colorado, Logan Co.
Type: Index; PR
Year Range: 1913–1942
Online: Free
Title: Logan County Inheritance Tax Record 1913–1942
Notes, URL: <www.colorado.gov/dpa/doit/archives/inh_tax/logan/>

Colorado, Park Co.
Type: Index; W
Year Range: 1892–1925
Online: Free
Title: Park County Will Records 1892–1925
Notes, URL: <www.colorado.gov/dpa/doit/archives/wills/1park.html>

Colorado, Routt Co.
Type: Index; W
Year Range: 1888–1905
Online: Free
Title: Routt County Will Records 1888–1905
Notes, URL: <www.colorado.gov/dpa/doit/archives/wills/1routt.html>

Connecticut
Type: Abstracts; PR
Year Range: 1635–1650
Online: Ancestry
Title: Hartford, Connecticut Probate Records, 1635–50
Notes, URL: <www.ancestry.com/search/rectype/inddbs/4337.htm>

Connecticut
Type: Abstracts; PR
Year Range: 1635–1750
CD-ROM: $32 (Mac/Win), Heritage Books, CD #2174
Title: A Digest of the Early Connecticut Probate Records, Volumes 1-3, 1635–1750
Notes, URL: <www.heritagebooks.com>. Search on "2174."

Connecticut, Hartford Co., Wethersfield
Type: Abstracts; CT
Year Range: 1800–1903
Online: Free
Title: Wethersfield Prison Records
Notes, URL: <www.cslib.org/wethers.asp>

Connecticut, Litchfield, Westmoreland
Type: Transcript; PR
Year Range: 1777–1783
Online: Genealogy Library
Title: The records of the probate court of Westmoreland
Notes, URL: Click on Records I Court and Civil Proceedings.

Connecticut, New Haven Co., New Haven
Type: Index; PR
Year Range: 1647–about 1730
Online: Free
Title: New Haven Probate Index, Volumes I-V
Notes, URL: <www.chedsey.com/probate/index.htm>

Delaware
Type: Index; PR
Year Range: 1680–1925
Online: Free
Title: Delaware Public Archives: Probate Database Search
Notes, URL: <www.state.de.us/sos/dpa/collections/probate.shtml>

Delaware, Kent Co.
Type: Abstracts; PR
Year Range: 1680–1800
Online: Ancestry
Title: Kent County, Delaware Probate Records, 1680–1800
Notes, URL: <www.ancestry.com/search/rectype/inddbs/4020.htm>

Delaware, Kent Co.
Type: Abstracts; PR
Year Range: 1680–1800
Online: F&LH
Title: Calendar of Kent County, Delaware probate records, 1680–1800

Delaware, New Castle Co.
Type: Abstracts; W
Year Range: 1682–1800
Online: Ancestry
Title: Calendar of Delaware Wills, New Castle County, 1682–1800
Notes, URL: <www.ancestry.com/search/rectype/inddbs/6282.htm>

Delaware, New Castle Co.
Type: Abstracts; W
Year Range: 1682–1800
Online: Ancestry
Title: New Castle County, Delaware Wills, 1682–1800
Notes, URL: About 7000 names in nearly 1700 entries. <www.ancestry.com/search/rectype/inddbs/4245.htm>

Delaware, Sussex Co.
Type: Abstracts; PR
Year Range: 1680–1800
CD-ROM: $30 (Mac/Win), Heritage Books, CD #1473
Title: Heritage Books Archives: Delaware & Pennsylvania
Notes, URL: Also includes land records & biographies. <www.heritagebooks.com>. Search on "1473."

Delaware, Sussex Co.
Type: Abstracts; PR
Year Range: 1680–1800
Online: Ancestry
Title: Sussex County, Delaware Probate Records, 1680–1800
Notes, URL: Over 10,000 names. <www.ancestry.com/search/rectype/inddbs/4295.htm>

Delaware, Sussex Co.
Type: Digital images; CT
Year Range: 1773–1937
Online: Free
Title: Delaware Public Archives: Sussex County Orphans Court Case Files
Notes, URL: <www.state.de.us/sos/dpa/exhibits/document/orphans/>

Florida, Alachua Co.
Type: Index; PR-G
Year Range: 1828–1957
Online: Free
Title: Alachua County Archives: Probate Records
Notes, URL: Over 27,000 total entries. <www.clerk-alachua-fl.org/archive/default.cfm>

Illinois, Will Co., Joliet
Type: Transcripts; CT
Year Range: 1847–1889
Online: Free
Title: Illinois Trails History & Genealogy Presents The Joliet, Illinois Prison Convict Register
Notes, URL: <www.iltrails.org/convicts/convictregister.htm>

Indiana, Dearborn Co.
Type: Transcripts; PR
Year Range: 1836–1859
Online: Free
Title: Dearborn County Indiana Transcribed Probate Inventories
Notes, URL: <http://departments.mwc.

edu/hipr/www/inventories/dearborn/19cindea.htm>

Indiana, Franklin Co.
Type: Transcripts; PR
Year Range: 1811–1860
Online: Free
Title: Franklin County Indiana Transcribed Probate Inventories
Notes, URL: <http://departments.mwc.edu/hipr/www/inventories/franklin/19cinfra.htm>

Indiana, Kosciusko Co.
Type: Index; W
Year Range: 1844–1920
Online: Free
Title: Kosciusko County, Indiana Index to the Early Wills 1844–1920
Notes, URL: <www.rootsweb.com/~inkosciu/willsndx.htm>

Indiana, Ripley Co.
Type: Transcripts; PR
Year Range: 1833–1856
Online: Free
Title: Ripley County Indiana Transcribed Probate Inventories
Notes, URL: <http://departments.mwc.edu/hipr/www/inventories/ripley/19cinrip.htm>

Kentucky
Type: Abstracts; CT-W
Year Range: 1725–1875
CD-ROM: $29.99, Genealogy.com, CD #519
Online: Genealogy Library
Title: Early Kentucky Settlers, 1700s–1800s
Notes, URL: Select Genealogical Records: Early Kentucky Settlers, 1700s–1800s. Includes *Kentucky Court and Other Records*, vols. 1-2, & *Abstract of Early Kentucky Wills and Inventories.* <www.genealogy.com/519facd.html>

Kentucky
Type: Index; W
Year Range: 1795–1849
Online: Ancestry
Title: Kentucky Will Index, vol. 1 & 2
Notes, URL: Covers Cumberland, Christian, Fleming, Harrison, Logan, Russell, Todd, Trigg, & Nicholas Counties. <www.ancestry.com/search/rectype/inddbs/5661.htm>

Kentucky
Type: Index; W
Year Range: 1815–1840
Online: Ancestry
Title: Kentucky Will Index, Vol. 2
Notes, URL: Covers Cumberland, Christian, Logan, Russell, Todd, & Trigg Counties. <www.ancestry.com/search/rectype/inddbs/5168.htm>

Kentucky, Barren Co.
Type: Abstracts; W
Year Range: 1800–1824
Online: Ancestry
Title: Barren County, Kentucky Wills, 1800–24
Notes, URL: <www.ancestry.com/search/rectype/inddbs/5668.htm>

Kentucky, Bath Co.
Type: Abstracts; W
Year Range: 1811–1824
Online: Ancestry
Title: Bath County, Kentucky Wills, 1811–24
Notes, URL: <www.ancestry.com/search/rectype/inddbs/5700.htm>

Kentucky, Clark Co.
Type: Abstracts; W
Year Range: 1792–1826
Online: Ancestry
Title: Clark County, Kentucky Wills 1792–1826, Vol. 1-2
Notes, URL: <www.ancestry.com/search/rectype/inddbs/5721.htm>

Kentucky, Fayette Co.
Type: Abstracts; W
Year Range: 1794–1818
Online: Ancestry
Title: Fayette County, Kentucky Wills 1794–1818
Notes, URL: <www.ancestry.com/search/rectype/inddbs/5765.htm>

Kentucky, Green Co.
Type: Abstracts; W
Year Range: 1796–1824
Online: Ancestry
Title: Green County, Kentucky Wills 1796–1824
Notes, URL: <www.ancestry.com/search/rectype/inddbs/5773.htm>

Kentucky, Greenup Co.
Type: Abstracts; W
Year Range: 1822–1843
Online: Ancestry
Title: Greenup County, Kentucky Will Records: 1822–1843
Notes, URL: <www.ancestry.com/search/rectype/inddbs/5790.htm>

Kentucky, Henry Co.
Type: Abstracts; W
Year Range: 1800–1821
Online: Ancestry
Title: Henry County, Kentucky Will Records for 1800 to July 1821
Notes, URL: <www.ancestry.com/search/rectype/inddbs/6007.htm>

Kentucky, Lincoln Co.
Type: Abstracts; W
Year Range: 1870–1890
Online: Ancestry
Title: Lincoln County, Kentucky Wills and Administrations, Vol. 1
Notes, URL: <www.ancestry.com/search/rectype/inddbs/5806.htm>

Kentucky, Mercer Co.
Type: Abstracts; W
Year Range: 1818–1826
Online: Ancestry
Title: Mercer County, Kentucky Wills 1818–26
Notes, URL: <www.ancestry.com/search/rectype/inddbs/5794.htm>

Kentucky, Montgomery Co.
Type: Abstracts; W
Year Range: 1796–1821
Online: Ancestry
Title: Montgomery County, Kentucky Wills: 1796–1821
Notes, URL: <www.ancestry.com/search/rectype/inddbs/5831.htm>

Kentucky, Scott Co.
Type: Abstracts; W
Year Range: 1794–1820
Online: Ancestry
Title: Scott County, Kentucky Wills: 1794–1820
Notes, URL: <www.ancestry.com/search/rectype/inddbs/6083.htm>

Kentucky, Shelby Co.
Type: Abstracts; W
Year Range: 1794–1817
Online: Ancestry
Title: Shelby County, Kentucky Wills: 1794–1817
Notes, URL: <www.ancestry.com/search/rectype/inddbs/5988.htm>

Maine
Type: Abstracts; W
Year Range: 1640–1760
Online: Ancestry
Title: Maine Will Abstracts, 1640–1760
Notes, URL: Nearly 500 wills with about 2000 names. <www.ancestry.com/search/rectype/inddbs/4368.htm>

Maine
Type: Abstracts; W
Year Range: 1640–1760
CD-ROM: $29.99, Genealogy.com, CD #523
Online: Genealogy Library
Title: Maine & New Hampshire Settlers, 1600s–1900s
Notes, URL: Includes *Maine Wills, 1640–1760* with 471 wills. Select Places | United States | Maine. Or select Genealogical Records: Maine and New Hampshire Settlers, 1600s–1900s. <www.genealogy.com/523facd.html>

Maine
Type: Index; CT
Year Range: 1686–1854
Online: Free
Title: Maine Court Page
Notes, URL: Kennebec County court index, 1799–1854. Washington County court index, 1839–1845. York County court index, 1686–1760. <www.rootsweb.com/~usgenweb/me/mecourt.html>

Maine
Type: Index; CT
Year Range: 1696–1854
Online: Ancestry
Title: Maine Court Records, 1696–1854
Notes, URL: Original record: *York County Court of Common Pleas (1696–1760), Kennebec County Supreme Court (1799–1854) & Washington County District Court (1839–46).* <www.ancestry.com/search/rectype/inddbs/6888.htm>

Maine, Lincoln Co.
Type: Abstracts; PR
Year Range: 1760–1800
Online: Ancestry
Title: Lincoln County, Maine: Probates, 1760–1800
Notes, URL: Includes full transcripts of some wills. <www.ancestry.com/search/rectype/inddbs/6034.htm>

Maine, Lincoln Co.
Type: Digital images of pages containing abstracts; PR
Year Range: 1760–1800
CD-ROM: $29.99, Genealogy.com, CD #523
Online: Genealogy Library
Title: Maine & New Hampshire Settlers, 1600s–1900s
Notes, URL: Includes *The Probate Records of Lincoln County, Maine, 1760 to 1800.* <www.genealogy.com/523facd.html>

Maryland
Type: Abstracts; W
Year Range: 1635–1685
Online: Ancestry
Title: Maryland Calendar of Wills
Notes, URL: <www.ancestry.com/search/rectype/inddbs/3250.htm>

Maryland
Type: Transcripts; W-PR
Year Range: 1670–1899
Online: Free
Title: Baltimore & Anne Arundel County Last Will and Testaments & Other Probate/Estate Related Documents
Notes, URL: <www.rootsweb.com/~mdbaltim/wills/xxwills.htm>

Maryland
Type: Index; CT
Year Range: 1713–1853
Online: Free
Title: Chancery Court (Chancery Papers)
Notes, URL: <www.mdarchives.state.md.us/msa/refserv/stagser/ssu500/html/ssu0512.html>

Maryland
Type: Index; CT
Year Range: 1775–1897
Online: Free
Title: Maryland Indexes (Maryland State Papers, Index) 1775–1897
Notes, URL: <www.mdarchives.state.md.us/msa/stagser/s1400/s1484/html/ssu1484.html>

Maryland
Type: Index; CT
Year Range: 1776–1812
Online: Free
Title: Index to Admiralty Court (Court Papers) 1776–1812
Notes, URL: <www.mdarchives.state.md.us/msa/stagser/s1400/s1471/html/ssi1471.html>

Maryland, Anne Arundel Co.
Type: Index; W
Year Range: 1777–1917
Online: F&LH
Title: General index of wills of Anne Arundel County, Maryland, 1777–1917

Maryland, Charles Co.
Type: Index; CT
Year Range: 1658–1741
Online: F&LH
Title: Index to court records, Charles County, Maryland

Maryland, Frederick Co.
Type: Abstracts; CT
Year Range: 1782–1950s
Online: Free
Title: Early Frederick County, Maryland: County Records
Notes, URL: Court records, 1782–1950s.<http://midmdroots.freewebspace.com/frederick/Probate.html>

Maryland, St. Mary's Co.
Type: Index; W
Year Range: 1633–1900
Online: F&LH
Title: General index of wills of St. Mary's County, Maryland, 1633–1900

Maryland, St. Mary's Co.
Type: Index; CT
Year Range: 1815–1851
Online: Free
Title: St. Mary's County Court (Equity Papers)
Notes, URL: <www.mdarchives.state.md.us/msa/refserv/coagser/sm/html/sm1591.html>

Massachusetts
Type: Transcripts; W
Year Range: 1621–1704
Online: Free
Title: Wills of *Mayflower* Passengers
Notes, URL: <www.members.aol.com/mayflo1620/wills.html>

Massachusetts
Type: Abstracts; CT
Year Range: 1647–1697
Online: Ancestry
Title: Salem Witches
Notes, URL: Over 200 individuals accused of witchcraft in Salem & other towns in Mass. & elsewhere in New England. <www.ancestry.com/search/rectype/inddbs/5141.htm>

Massachusetts
Type: Index; W-PR
Year Range: 1670–1685
Online: Free
Title: The Plymouth Colony Archive Project: Index to Plymouth Colony Wills and Inventories, 1670–1685
Notes, URL: <http://etext.lib.virginia.edu/users/deetz/Plymouth/willsindex00.html>

Massachusetts, Essex Co.
Type: Digital images of a book containing transcripts; PR
Year Range: 1635–1681

Online: Ancestry
Title: Essex County, Massachusetts Probate Records, 1635–81
Notes, URL: <www.ancestry.com/search/rectype/inddbs/6593.htm>

Massachusetts, Essex Co.
Type: Abstracts; CT
Year Range: 1636–1686
Online: Ancestry
Title: Essex County, Massachusetts Depositions, 1636–86
Notes, URL: <www.ancestry.com/search/rectype/inddbs/5342.htm>

Massachusetts, Essex Co.
Type: Index; PR
Year Range: 1636–1694
Online: Ancestry
Title: Essex County, Massachusetts Probate Records, Supplement
Notes, URL: Over 2,000 names. <www.ancestry.com/search/rectype/inddbs/3357.htm>

Massachusetts, Essex Co.
Type: Index; PR
Year Range: 1638–1840
Online: Ancestry
Title: Essex, Massachusetts Probate Records, 1638–1840
Notes, URL: <www.ancestry.com/search/rectype/inddbs/4592.htm>

Massachusetts, Essex Co.
Type: Index; PR
Year Range: 1775–1850
Online: Ancestry
Title: Essex County, Massachusetts Probate Records, Part 1
Notes, URL: Over 1,200 people whose surnames begin with *P.* <www.ancestry.com/search/rectype/inddbs/3361.htm>

Massachusetts, Middlesex Co.
Type: Index; PR
Year Range: 1648–1870
Online: Ancestry
Title: Middlesex County, Massachusetts Probate Index, 1648–1870
Notes, URL: Over 52,000 wills, administrations of wills, guardianships, & adoptions. <www.ancestry.com/search/rectype/inddbs/4775.htm>

Massachusetts, Middlesex Co.
Type: Index; CT
Year Range: 1649–1700
Online: Ancestry
Title: Middlesex County, Massachusetts Deponents, 1649–1700
Notes, URL: Names more than 5,200 deponents. <www.ancestry.com/search/rectype/inddbs/5233.htm>

Massachusetts, Middlesex Co.
Type: Index; PR
Year Range: 1871–1909
Online: Ancestry
Title: Middlesex County, Massachusetts Probate Index, 1871–1909 (Part A-K)
Notes, URL: <www.ancestry.com/search/rectype/inddbs/4892.htm>

Massachusetts, Norfolk Co.
Type: Index; PR
Year Range: 1793–1900
Online: Ancestry
Title: Norfolk County, MA Probate Index 1793–1900
Notes, URL: Over 20,000 entries. <www.ancestry.com/search/rectype/inddbs/5656.htm>

Massachusetts, Norfolk Co., Dedham
Type: Transcript; CT
Year Range: 1635–1673
Online: F&LH
Title: The early records of the town of Dedham, Massachusetts, 1659–1673
Notes, URL: Includes General Court records 1635–1673.

Massachusetts, Plymouth Co.
Type: Transcripts; W
Year Range: 1621–1704
Online: Free
Title: All Known Wills of the *Mayflower* Passengers
Notes, URL: <www.mayflowerhistory.com/PrimarySources/WillsAndProbates/WillsIndex.php>

Massachusetts, Plymouth Co.
Type: Abstracts; CT
Year Range: 1686–1859
CD-ROM: $39.99 (Mac/Windows), NEHGS, item #SCD-PCC
Title: Plymouth [County] Court Records 1686–1859
Notes, URL: Records of the Court of General Sessions, 1686–1827, & the Court of Common Pleas, 1686–1859. <www.newenglandancestors.org>

Massachusetts, Plymouth Co., Marshfield
Type: Transcript; CT
Year Range: 1877
Online: F&LH
Title: Memorial of owners of reclaimed and of cultivated lands, etc., to the General Court of Massachusetts in 1877

Massachusetts, Suffolk Co.
Type: Transcript; PR
Year Range: 1639–1799
Online: F&LH
Title: Registers of probate for the county of Suffolk, Massachusetts: 1639–1799

Massachusetts, Worcester Co.
Type: Index; PR
Year Range: 1731–1881
Online: Ancestry
Title: Worcester County, Massachusetts, Probate Index, Vol. 1 & 2 A-Z, July 1731–1881
Notes, URL: About 35,700 events are recorded in this database. <www.ancestry.com/search/rectype/inddbs/5189.htm>

Michigan, Grand Traverse Co.
Type: Index; PR
Year Range: 1853–1883
Online: Free
Title: Grand Traverse County Probate Files
Notes, URL: <http://freepages.genealogy.rootsweb.com/~jayhomer/Probateintro.htm>

Michigan, Iosco Co.
Type: Index; PO
Year Range: 1869–1934
Online: Ancestry
Title: Iosco County, Michigan Paupers, 1869–1934
Notes, URL: <www.ancestry.com/search/rectype/inddbs/5243.htm>

Mississippi
Type: Index; CT
Year Range: 1799–1835
Online: Ancestry
Title: Mississippi Court Records, 1799–1835
Notes, URL: <www.ancestry.com/search/rectype/inddbs/3184.htm>

Mississippi
Type: Abstracts; W
Year Range: 1800–1900
CD-ROM: $25.50 (Win), Heritage Books, CD #2325
Title: Early Mississippi Records
Notes, URL: Includes records from Carroll and Holmes Counties. <www.heritagebooks.com>. Search on "2325."

Mississippi, Jefferson Co.
Type: Abstracts; W
Year Range: 1800–1833
Online: Ancestry
Title: Jefferson County, Mississippi Wills, 1800–33

Notes, URL: Over 1,500 names. <www.ancestry.com/search/rectype/inddbs/3691.htm>

Mississippi, Madison Co.
Type: Index; W
Year Range: 1828–1892
Online: Free
Title: General Index to Wills
Notes, URL: <www.rootsweb.com/~msmadiso/willindex/qryindex.htm>

Missouri, Carroll Co.
Type: Abstracts; W
Year Range: 1834–1870
Online: Ancestry
Title: Carroll County, Missouri Wills and Administrations, 1834–70
Notes, URL: <www.ancestry.com/search/rectype/inddbs/5147.htm>

Missouri, Chariton Co.
Type: Abstracts; W
Year Range: 1861–1875
Online: Ancestry
Title: Chariton County, Missouri Wills and Administrations, 1861–75
Notes, URL: <www.ancestry.com/search/rectype/inddbs/5489.htm>

Missouri, Jasper Co.
Type: Abstracts; W
Year Range: 1842–1890
Online: Ancestry
Title: Jasper County, Missouri Wills 1842–90
Notes, URL: <www.ancestry.com/search/rectype/inddbs/5713.htm>

Missouri, Linn Co.
Type: Abstracts; W
Year Range: 1820–1878
Online: Ancestry
Title: Linn County, Missouri Wills, 1820–78
Notes, URL: <www.ancestry.com/search/rectype/inddbs/5687.htm>

Missouri, Livingston Co.
Type: Abstracts; PR
Year Range: 1837–1918
Online: Ancestry
Title: Livingston County, Missouri Probate Records, Volumes I, III, V, and VII-XIII
Notes, URL: More than 2,300 probate records. <www.ancestry.com/search/rectype/inddbs/5409.htm>

Missouri, Livingston Co.
Type: Abstracts; W
Year Range: 1837–1870
Online: Ancestry
Title: Livingston County, Missouri Wills and Administrations 1837–1870
Notes, URL: <www.ancestry.com/search/rectype/inddbs/5547.htm>

Missouri, Macon Co.
Type: Abstracts; W
Year Range: 1838–1880
Online: Ancestry
Title: Macon County, Missouri, Will Records & Marriage Records: 1838–80
Notes, URL: <www.ancestry.com/search/rectype/inddbs/5833.htm>

Missouri, Madison Co.
Type: Index; W
Year Range: 1822–1855
Online: Free
Title: A List of Wills, Madison County, Missouri 1822–1855
Notes, URL: <www.genealogymagazine.com/madisoncounty1.html>

Missouri, Marion Co.
Type: Abstracts; W
Year Range: 1853–1887
Online: Ancestry
Title: Marion County, Missouri Wills: 1853–87
Notes, URL: <www.ancestry.com/search/rectype/inddbs/5816.htm>

Missouri, Nodaway Co.
Type: Abstracts; W
Year Range: 1845–1880
Online: Ancestry
Title: Nodaway County, Missouri Wills and Administrations 1845–80
Notes, URL: <www.ancestry.com/search/rectype/inddbs/5566.htm>

Missouri, Pettis Co.
Type: Index; PR
Year Range: 1833–1875
Online: Ancestry
Title: Pettis County, Missouri: Index to the General Probate Index, 1833–1875
Notes, URL: <www.ancestry.com/search/rectype/inddbs/6059.htm>

Missouri, Ralls Co.
Type: Abstracts; W
Year Range: 1824–1872
Online: Ancestry
Title: Ralls County, Missouri Wills, Volume I, 1824–1872
Notes, URL: <www.ancestry.com/search/rectype/inddbs/5582.htm>

Missouri, Ralls Co.
Type: Abstracts; CT
Year Range: 1832–1853
CD-ROM: $29.50 (Mac/Win), Heritage Books, CD #1369
Title: Heritage Books Archives: Missouri Vol. 1
Notes, URL: Includes Ralls County, MO Settlement Records 1832–1853. <www.heritagebooks.com>. Search on "1369."

Missouri, Randolph Co.
Type: Abstracts; W
Year Range: 1836–1858
Online: Ancestry
Title: Randolph County, Missouri Administration and Wills: 1836–1858
Notes, URL: <www.ancestry.com/search/rectype/inddbs/6073.htm>

Missouri, Randolph Co.
Type: Index; PR
Year Range: 1840–1853
CD-ROM: $29.50 (Mac/Win), Heritage Books, CD #1369
Title: Heritage Books Archives: Missouri Vol. 1
Notes, URL: Also includes other records from Randolph County & material from Cooper, Morgan, Ralls, & Randolph Counties. <www.heritagebooks.com>. Search on "1369."

Missouri, St. Louis (Independent City)
Type: Digital images; PR
Year Range: 1802–1900
Online: Free
Title: St. Louis Probate Court Digitization Project: 1802–1900
Notes, URL: Over 2 million images of case documents. <www.sos.mo.gov/archives/stlprobate/>

Missouri, Sullivan Co.
Type: Abstracts; W
Year Range: 1849–1880
Online: Ancestry
Title: Sullivan County, Missouri Wills, 1849–1880
Notes, URL: <www.ancestry.com/search/rectype/inddbs/5600.htm>

Nevada
Type: Transcript; OR
Year Range: 1870–1920
Online: Ancestry
Title: Nevada Orphan's Home Records, 1870–1920
Notes, URL: <www.ancestry.com/search/rectype/inddbs/3347.htm>

New Hampshire
Type: Extracts; PR
Year Range: 1635–1753
Online: Ancestry
Title: New Hampshire Probate Records, 1635–1753
Notes, URL: Original data: Batchellor, Albert Stillman, ed. *Probate Records of the Province of New Hampshire 1635–1717.* Vols. 1-4. <www.ancestry.com/search/rectype/inddbs/7089.htm>

New Hampshire
Type: Transcripts of wills, abstracts of other files; PR
Year Range: 1635–1771
CD-ROM: $49.50 (Mac/Win), Heritage Books, Item #1163
Title: Heritage Books Archives: New Hampshire Provincial Probate Records, 1635–1771
Notes, URL: Digital images of 9 volumes, each with names and place indexes. <www.heritagebooks.com>. Search on "1163."

New Hampshire
Type: Abstracts; PR
Year Range: 1742
CD-ROM: $30 (Mac/Win), Heritage Books, item #1416
Title: HB Archives: New Hampshire, Vol. 4
Notes, URL: Also includes Rockingham Co., N.H., paupers, etc. <www.heritagebooks.com>. Search on "1416."

New Hampshire, Hillsborough Co.
Type: Abstracts; CT
Year Range: 1772–1799
CD-ROM: $30 (Mac/Win), Heritage Books, item #1416
Title: HB Archives: New Hampshire, Vol. 4
Notes, URL: Also includes Rockingham Co., N.H., paupers, etc. <www.heritagebooks.com>. Search on "1353."

New Hampshire, Rockingham Co.
Type: Abstracts; PR
Year Range: 1771–1799
CD-ROM: $29 (Mac/Win), Heritage Books, item #1353
Title: Abstracts of the Probate Records of Rockingham County
Notes, URL: Also available in book form (2 volumes), item #E1477. <www.heritagebooks.com>. Search on "1353" or "E1477."

New Jersey
Type: Index; W
Year Range: Up to 1901
Online: F&LH
Title: Index of wills, inventories, etc., in the Office of the Secretary of State prior to 1901

New Jersey
Type: Index; W-PR-G
Year Range: 1670–1760
Online: Ancestry
Title: Calendar of New Jersey Wills, 1670–1760
Notes, URL: <www.ancestry.com/search/rectype/inddbs/4723.htm>

New Jersey
Type: Abstracts; W-PR-G
Year Range: 1670–1760
CD-ROM: $29 (Mac/Win), Heritage Books, item #1171
Title: HB Archives: Calendar of New Jersey Wills
Notes, URL: Reprints of 3 volumes by William Nelson & A. Van Doren Honeyman. <www.heritagebooks.com>. Search on 1171.

New Jersey
Type: Index; W
Year Range: 1804–1830
Online: F&LH
Title: Index of wills, Office of Secretary of State, State of New Jersey, 1804–1830

New Jersey, Gloucester Co.
Type: Transcript; CT
Year Range: 1686–1687
Online: F&LH
Title: The Organization and minutes of the Gloucester County Court, 1686–7
Notes, URL: "Some loose papers pertaining to our earliest court. Also, Gloucester County ear mark book, 1686–1728."

New Jersey, Gloucester Co.
Type: Transcript; W
Year Range: About 1815–1825
Online: F&LH
Title: Copies of wills taken from will book B, Gloucester County, New Jersey Surrogate's Office at Woodbury, New Jersey, 1952

New Jersey, Monmouth Co.
Type: Transcript; W
Year Range: 1676–1742
Online: Genealogy Library
Title: Unrecorded Wills and Inventories Monmouth County, New Jersey
Notes, URL: Select Places | United States.

New Jersey, Salem Co.
Type: Abstracts; W
Year Range: 1801–1860
Online: F&LH
Title: Salem County wills: recorded in the Office of the Surrogate at Salem, New Jersey

New Jersey, Salem Co.
Type: Index; G
Year Range: 1802–1899
Online: F&LH
Title: Petitions for guardians: from the minutes of the Salem County, New Jersey, Orphans' Court

New Jersey, Sussex Co.
Type: Index; W
Year Range: 1763–1886
Online: Free
Title: Sussex County Will Abstracts Index
Notes, URL: <www.gate.net/~pascalfl/wlabsdex.html>

New York
Type: Images of printed abstracts; W
Year Range: 1626–1836
Online: Ancestry
Title: New York Wills, 1626–1836
Notes, URL: <www.ancestry.com/search/rectype/inddbs/6393.htm>

New York
Type: Transcripts; W
Year Range: 1665–1776
Online: Free
Title: Long Island Wills and Death Notes
Notes, URL: <www.longislandgenealogy.com/death.html>

New York
Type: Index; CT
Year Range: 1824–1911
Online: Ancestry
Title: New York Supreme Court Plaintiffs, 1824–1911
Notes, URL: About 20,400 corporate plaintiffs. <www.ancestry.com/search/rectype/inddbs/5460.htm>

New York, Cayuga Co.
Type: Index; G
Year Range: 1804–1852
Online: Free
Title: New York Counties: Gateway to Indexes
Notes, URL: <www.sampubco.com/guard//ny/newyork.htm>

New York, Chemung Co.
Type: Abstracts; W
Year Range: 1836–1850
Online: F&LH

Title: Abstracts of wills of Chemung County, N.Y.: from 1836 to 1850

New York, Chenango Co.
Type: Index; W
Year Range: 1797–1850
Online: F&LH
Title: Index of wills of Chenango County, New York, from 1797–1850

New York, Chenango Co.
Type: Index; W
Year Range: 1851–1875
Online: F&LH
Title: Index to wills of Chenango County, N.Y.

New York, Columbia Co.
Type: Abstracts; W
Year Range: 1786–1851
Online: F&LH
Title: Calendar of wills of Columbia County, New York

New York, Delaware Co.
Type: Transcript; PR
Year Range: 1797–1875
Online: F&LH
Title: Letters of administration of Delaware County, New York

New York, Delaware Co.
Type: Digital images of books; PR
Year Range: 1797–1875
CD-ROM: $24.50 (Mac/Win), Long Island
Title: Vital Records Collection from Delaware County, New York
Notes, URL: Includes letters of administration and abstracts of wills, by Gertrude A. Barber. <http://genealogycds.com/sales/Delaware.htm>

New York, Dutchess Co.
Type: Index; W
Year Range: 1812–1832
Online: F&LH
Title: Index to wills of Dutchess County, N.Y.: from 1812–1832

New York, Greene Co.
Type: Abstracts; W
Year Range: 1800–1900
Online: F&LH
Title: Abstract of wills of Greene County, New York

New York, Kings Co.
Type: Index; W
Year Range: 1850–1890
Online: F&LH
Title: Index of wills probated in Kings County, New York

New York, Kings Co.
Type: Index; W
Year Range: 1850–1890
CD-ROM: $24.50 (Mac/Win), Long Island Genealogy
Title: Kings County, NY Index of wills probated
Notes, URL: By Gertrude A. Barber.

New York, Monroe Co.
Type: Abstracts; W
Year Range: 1821–1847
Online: F&LH
Title: Monroe County, New York, abstracts of wills

New York, New York (City)
Type: Abstracts; W
Year Range: Up to 1790
Online: Genealogy Library
Title: Abstracts of Unrecorded Wills Vol. XI Prior to 1790
Notes, URL: Wills filed in the Surrogates Office. In the Subject Directory select Places | United States | New York.

New York, New York (City)
Type: Index; W
Year Range: 1662–1850
Online: F&LH
Title: Index of wills for New York County (New York City) from 1662–1850

New York, New York (City)
Type: Abstracts; W
Year Range: 1665–1707
Online: Ancestry
Title: New York City Wills, 1665–1707
Notes, URL: <www.ancestry.com/search/rectype/inddbs/3476.htm>

New York, New York (City)
Type: Abstracts; W
Year Range: 1665–1800
Online: Genealogy Library
Title: Abstracts of Wills Vols. I-XVII
Notes, URL: Select Places | United States | New York.

New York, New York (City)
Type: Transcript; CT
Year Range: 1680–1701
Online: Genealogy Library
Title: Court Records 1680–1682 and 1693–1701
Notes, URL: Preceedings of the General Court of Assizes, 1680–1862, & minutes of the Supreme Court of Judicature, 1693–1701. In the Subject Directory select Records | Court Records | New York.

New York, New York (City)
Type: Abstracts; W
Year Range: 1706–1790
Online: Ancestry
Title: New York City Wills, 1706–90
Notes, URL: Nearly 700 records. <www.ancestry.com/search/rectype/inddbs/3699.htm>

New York, New York (City)
Type: Abstracts; W
Year Range: 1708–1728
Online: Ancestry
Title: New York City Wills, 1708–28
Notes, URL: Nearly 5000 records. <www.ancestry.com/search/rectype/inddbs/3491.htm>

New York, New York (City)
Type: Abstracts; W
Year Range: 1730–1744
Online: Ancestry
Title: New York City Wills, 1730–44
Notes, URL: Nearly 5000 records. <www.ancestry.com/search/rectype/inddbs/3509.htm>

New York, New York (City)
Type: Abstracts; W
Year Range: 1744–1758
Online: Ancestry
Title: New York City Wills, 1744–58
Notes, URL: Over 5000 records. <www.ancestry.com/search/rectype/inddbs/3526.htm>

New York, New York (City)
Type: Abstracts; W
Year Range: 1754–1760
Online: Ancestry
Title: New York City Wills, 1754–60
Notes, URL: Over 5000 records. <www.ancestry.com/search/rectype/inddbs/3590.htm>

New York, New York (City)
Type: Abstracts; W
Year Range: 1760–1766
Online: Ancestry
Title: New York City Wills, 1760–66
Notes, URL: Over 5000 records. <www.ancestry.com/search/rectype/inddbs/3616.htm>

New York, New York (City)
Type: Abstracts; W
Year Range: 1766–1771

Online: Ancestry
Title: New York City Wills, 1766–71
Notes, URL: About 1500 records. <www.ancestry.com/search/rectype/inddbs/3633.htm>

New York, New York (City)
Type: Abstracts; W
Year Range: 1771–1776
Online: Ancestry
Title: New York City Wills, 1771–76
Notes, URL: About 1600 records. <www.ancestry.com/search/rectype/inddbs/3643.htm>

New York, New York (City)
Type: Abstracts; W
Year Range: 1777–1783
Online: Ancestry
Title: New York City Wills, 1777–83
Notes, URL: About 1000 records. <www.ancestry.com/search/rectype/inddbs/3673.htm>

New York, New York (City)
Type: Abstracts; W
Year Range: 1780–1782
Online: Ancestry
Title: New York City Wills, 1780–82
Notes, URL: Nearly 800 records. <www.ancestry.com/search/rectype/inddbs/3686.htm>

New York, New York (City)
Type: Abstracts; W
Year Range: 1819–1892
Online: F&LH
Title: Abstract of wills probated in the Common Pleas Court: . . . of New York County, New York City, N.Y.

New York, New York (City)
Type: Index; W
Year Range: 1851–1875
Online: F&LH
Title: Index of wills for New York County, New York from 1851 to 1875, inclusive

New York, Oneida Co.
Type: Abstracts; W
Year Range: 1798–1848
Online: F&LH
Title: Abstracts of wills of Oneida County, N.Y.

New York, Ontario Co.
Type: Index; CT
Year Range: 1789–1926
Online: Free
Title: Ontario County, Surrogate Records Index
Notes, URL: <www.raims.com/surrogate.html>

New York, Ontario Co.
Type: Index; CT
Year Range: 1789–1960
Online: Free
Title: Listing of 19th Century Court Records of Ontario County, New York
Notes, URL: <www.raims.com/Courtrecords.html>

New York, Ontario Co.
Type: Transcript; CT
Year Range: 1801–1843
Online: Free
Title: Jury List, Ontario County
Notes, URL: <www.raims.com/jury.html>

New York, Ontario Co.
Type: Index; CT
Year Range: 1832–1886
Online: Free
Title: Sample of 19th Century Arrest Warrants and Crimes, Ontario County, NY
Notes, URL: <www.raims.com/crime.html>

New York, Ontario Co.
Type: Abstracts; W
Year Range: 1848–1850
Online: F&LH
Title: Abstracts of wills of Ontario County, New York, 1848–1849–1850: Volume 12 (XII) (Liber D)

New York, Otsego Co.
Type: Digital images of a book containing an index & abstracts; W
Year Range: 1792–1850
CD-ROM: $24.50 (Mac/Win), Long Island Genealogy
Title: Otsego County, NY, Graveyards inscriptions plus more
Notes, URL: Also includes vital records from newspapers & church records. All by Gertrude A. Barber. <http://genealogycds.com/sales/Otsego.htm>

New York, Otsego Co.
Type: Index; W
Year Range: 1792–1850
Online: F&LH
Title: Index of wills of Otsego County, New York, from 1792–1850

New York, Otsego Co.
Type: Abstracts; W
Year Range: 1794–1851
Online: F&LH
Title: Abstracts of wills of Otsego County, N.Y.

New York, Queens Co.
Type: Abstracts; W
Year Range: 1680–1781
Online: F&LH
Title: Records in the office of the county clerk at Jamaica, Long Island, New York: 1680–1781: wills and administrations, guardians, and inventories

New York, Queens Co., Newtown
Type: Abstracts; CT
Year Range: 1656–1690
Online: F&LH
Title: Minutes of the town courts of Newtown: 1656–1690

New York, Rensselaer Co.
Type: Transcript; CT
Year Range: 1648–1652
Online: F&LH
Title: Minutes of the Court of Rensselaerswyck, 1648–1652
Notes, URL: English translation.

New York, Rensselaer Co.
Type: Abstracts; W
Year Range: 1791–1850
Online: F&LH
Title: Abstracts of wills of Rensselaer County, New York

New York, Richmond Co., Staten Island
Type: Abstracts; W-PR
Year Range: 1670–1800
CD-ROM: $33 (Mac/Win), Heritage Books, item #1153
Title: HB Archives: New York Vol. 1
Notes, URL: Includes *Staten Island Wills and Letters of Adminstration, Richmond County, New York, 1670–1800*, by Charlotte Megill Hix. <www.heritagebooks.com>. Search on "1153."

New York, Rockland Co.
Type: Abstracts; W
Year Range: 1786–1845
Online: F&LH
Title: Abstracts of wills of Rockland County, New York, 1786–1845

New York, Rockland Co.
Type: Abstracts; W
Year Range: 1845–1870
Online: F&LH
Title: Abstracts of wills of Rockland County, New York

New York, Saratoga Co.
Type: Abstracts; W
Year Range: 1796–1805
Online: Ancestry
Title: Saratoga County, New York Wills, 1796–1805
Notes, URL: <www.ancestry.com/search/rectype/inddbs/5614.htm>

New York, Schenectady Co.
Type: Abstracts; W
Year Range: 1809–1845
Online: F&LH
Title: Abstracts of wills of Schenectady County, N.Y.

New York, Suffolk Co.
Type: Digital images containing transcripts of wills; W
Year Range: 1691–1703
CD-ROM: $24.50 (Mac/Win), Long Island Genealogy
Online: Free
Title: Early Long Island wills of Suffolk county, 1691–1703
Notes, URL: Includes *Early Long Island wills of Suffolk county, 1691–1703*, by William Smith Pelletreau. <www.longislandgenealogy.com/EarlyWills/MainIndex.html>. Purchase the CD at <http://genealogycds.com/sales/suffolkrecordscombo.htm>.

New York, Suffolk Co., Brookhaven
Type: Digital images containing abstracts; W
Year Range: 1704–1769
Online: Free
Title: Abstracts of Brookhaven (L.I.) Wills
Notes, URL: <www.longislandgenealogy.com/brookhaven/brookhaven1.html>

New York, Sullivan Co.
Type: Index; PR
Year Range: 1811–1909
Online: F&LH
Title: Index to proceedings in administration of interstates [*sic*] estates: 1811–1909, A-K: Sullivan County, New York Courts, Surrogate Court, Monticello, New York

New York, Sullivan Co.
Type: Index; W
Year Range: 1876–1909
Online: F&LH
Title: Index of wills of Sullivan County, New York

New York, Ulster Co.
Type: Abstracts; PR
Year Range: 1665–early 1800s
CD-ROM: $35 (Mac/Win), Heritage Books, item #1960
Title: Heritage Books Archives: New York, Vol. 6
Notes, URL: Includes images of Ulster County, New York, Probate Records, Vols. 1-2, by Gustave Anjou. <www.heritagebooks.com>. Search on "1960."

New York, Washington Co.
Type: Index, abstracts; W
Year Range: 1786–1850
CD-ROM: $24.50 (Mac/Win) Long Island Genealogy
Title: Washington County, N.Y. Genealogical and historical info.
Notes, URL: Index and abstracts of wills by Gertrude A. Barber. <http://genealogycds.com>.

New York, Washington Co.
Type: Abstracts; W
Year Range: 1788–1825
Online: F&LH
Title: Abstracts of wills of Washington County, New York

New York, Washington Co.
Type: Index; W
Year Range: 1825–1850
Online: F&LH
Title: Index of wills of Washington County, N.Y. from 1825–1850

New York, Wayne Co.
Type: Abstracts; W
Year Range: 1823–1849
Online: F&LH
Title: Abstracts of wills of Wayne County, N.Y.: Surrogate's Office, Lyons, N.Y.

New York, Westchester Co.
Type: Abstracts; W
Year Range: 1664–1784
Online: F&LH
Title: Early wills of Westchester County, New York: from 1664 to 1784
Notes, URL: "A careful abstract of all wills (nearly 800) recorded in New York Surrogate's Office and at White Plains, N.Y. from 1664 to 1784."

New York, Westchester Co.
Type: Pages images containing indexes & abstracts; PR-W
Year Range: 1664–1784
CD-ROM: $24.50 (Mac/Win), Long Island Genealogy
Title: Early wills of Westchester County, New York
Notes, URL: Includes indexes to wills & letters of administration. By F.P. Harper, et al. <http://genealogycds.com/sales/westchestercoll.htm>.

New York, Westchester Co., New Rochelle
Type: Transcripts; W
Year Range: 1784–1830
Online: F&LH
Title: Old wills of New Rochelle: copies of wills by citizens of New Rochelle, N.Y., 1784–1830

North Carolina
Type: Index, abstracts; W
Year Range: 1663–1900
CD-ROM: $29.99, Genealogy.com, CD #509
Online: Genealogy Library
Title: North Carolina Wills, 1665–1900
Notes, URL: Includes: *North Carolina Wills: A Testator Index, 1665–1900*, by Thornton W. Mitchell (75,000 names). *North Carolina Wills and Inventories*, (the full text of 200 wills & 50 inventories). *Abstract Of North Carolina Wills, 1663–1760* (20,000 names). *An Abstract of North Carolina Wills from About 1760 to About 1800.*

North Carolina
Type: Abstracts; W
Year Range: 1690–1760
Online: F&LH
Title: Abstract of North Carolina wills compiled from original and recorded wills in the office of the secretary of state

North Carolina
Type: Abstracts; W
Year Range: 1733–1773
Online: Ancestry
Title: North Carolina Wills and Inventories
Notes, URL: <www.ancestry.com/search/rectype/inddbs/6223.htm>

North Carolina
Type: Abstracts; W
Year Range: 1733–1773
Online: F&LH
Title: North Carolina Wills and Inventories

North Carolina
Type: Abstracts; W
Year Range: 1760–1800
Online: Ancestry
Title: North Carolina Will Abstracts, 1760–1800
Notes, URL: Nearly 50,000 names in over 10,000 entries. <www.ancestry.com/search/rectype/inddbs/3945.htm>

North Carolina
Type: Index; PR
Year Range: 1764–1969
Online: Free
Title: Original County Estates Papers
Notes, URL: <www.ah.dcr.state.nc.us/sections/archives/arch/FindingAids/Estates.htm>

North Carolina, Bute Co.
Type: Abstracts; CT
Year Range: 1767–1779
Online: Ancestry
Title: Bute County, North Carolina Court Minutes, 1767–79
Notes, URL: <www.ancestry.com/search/rectype/inddbs/5420.htm>

North Carolina, Catawba Co.
Type: Abstracts; W
Year Range: 1817–1867
CD-ROM: $35 (Mac/Win), Heritage Books, item #1749
Title: HB Archives: North Carolina Vol. 1
Notes, URL: Includes *Catawba Co., North Carolina, Will Book 1,* by Elizabeth Bray Sherrill. <www.heritagebooks.com>. Search on "1749."

North Carolina, Tryon Co.
Type: Abstracts; CT
Year Range: 1769–1779
Online: Ancestry
Title: Tryon County, North Carolina Court Minutes, 1769–79
Notes, URL: Includes lists of wills proved & administrations on intestate estates. <www.ancestry.com/search/rectype/inddbs/5255.htm>

Ohio
Type: Abstracts; W
Year Range: 1803–1850
Online: F&LH
Title: Miami Valley will abstracts: from the counties of Miami, Montgomery, Warren, & Preble in the state of Ohio, 1803–1850

Ohio, Darke Co.
Type: Index; W
Year Range: 1818–1900
Online: F&LH
Title: Index to Darke County, Ohio, wills: 1818–1900 inclusive

Ohio, Fayette Co.
Type: Abstracts; CT
Year Range: 1828–1878
Online: F&LH
Title: Chancery and Common Pleas Court records, Fayette County, Ohio: 1828–1878

Oregon
Type: Index; PR
Year Range: 1842–1953
Online: Free
Title: Oregon Historical Records Index
Notes, URL: <http://arcweb.sos.state.or.us/banners/genlist.htm>

Pennsylvania, Bedford Co.
Type: Index; W
Year Range: 1770–1849
Online: F&LH
Title: Index to wills, Bedford County, Pennsylvania : books 1, 2, 3, etc.

Pennsylvania, Berks Co.
Type: Index; W-PR
Year Range: 1752–1850
Online: F&LH
Title: Index of Berks County, Pennsylvania, wills and administration records, 1752–1850

Pennsylvania, Berks Co.
Type: Index; PR
Year Range: 1752–1914
Online: Ancestry
Title: Berks County, Pennsylvania Estate Records, 1752–1914
Notes, URL: An index to nearly 37,000 estate files. <www.ancestry.com/search/rectype/inddbs/3827.htm>

Pennsylvania, Berks Co.
Type: Index; PR
Year Range: 1752–pres.
Online: Free
Title: Berks County Register of Wills
Notes, URL: Covers wills, inventories, accounts, & guardianship appointments. <www.berksregofwills.com/>

Pennsylvania, Berks Co.
Type: Abstracts; W
Year Range: 1785–1825
Online: Genealogy Library
Title: Abstracts of Berks Co., PA Wills 1785–1800, 1800–1825
Notes, URL: Select Records I United States I Pennsylvania.

Pennsylvania, Bucks Co.
Type: Transcript; CT
Year Range: 1684–1700
Online: F&LH
Title: Records of the Courts of Quarter Sessions and Common Pleas of Bucks County, Pennsylvania, 1684–1700

Pennsylvania, Bucks Co.
Type: W
Year Range: 1684–1850
Online: F&LH
Title: Index of Bucks County, Pennsylvania, wills and administration records, 1684 to 1850

Pennsylvania, Bucks Co.
Type: Abstracts; W
Year Range: 1685–1825
Online: Genealogy Library
Title: Abstracts of Bucks Co., PA Wills 1685–1785, 1785–1825
Notes, URL: Select Records I United States I Pennsylvania.

Pennsylvania, Chester Co.
Type: Transcript; CT
Year Range: 1681–1761
Online: F&LH
Title: Records of the courts of Chester County, Pennsylvania

Pennsylvania, Chester Co.
Type: Abstracts; W
Year Range: 1713–1825
CD-ROM: $26.95 (Win), Ancestry.com, item #2333, CD. "Pennsylvania Wills: Selected Counties and Years." <http://shops.ancestry.com>. Search on "Pennsylvania Wills."
Online: Ancestry
Title: Chester County, Pennsylvania Wills, 1713–1825
Notes, URL: The CD also has records for Philadelphia & York Cos., Pa. <www.ancestry.com/search/rectype/inddbs/4895.htm>

Pennsylvania, Chester Co.
Type: Abstracts; W
Year Range: 1713–1825
Online: Genealogy Library
Title: The Wills of Chester County, Pennsylvania, 1713–1825
Notes, URL: Select Records I United States I Pennsylvania.

Pennsylvania, Chester Co.
Type: Index; W-PR
Year Range: 1713–1850
Online: F&LH
Title: Index to Chester County, Pennsylvania wills and intestate records, 1713–1850

Pennsylvania, Cumberland Co.
Type: Abstracts; W

Year Range: 1750–1825
Online: Genealogy Library
Title: Abstracts of Cumberland Co. Wills, 1750–1785, 1785–1825
Notes, URL: Select Records | United States | Pennsylvania.

Pennsylvania, Delaware Co.
Type: Abstracts; W
Year Range: 1789–1835
Online: Genealogy Library
Title: Abstracts of Delaware Co. Wills, 1789–1835
Notes, URL: Select Records | United States | Pennsylvania.

Pennsylvania, Lancaster Co.
Type: Index; W
Year Range: 1729–1850
Online: Ancestry
Title: Lancaster, Pennsylvania Probate Index, 1729–1850
Notes, URL: Over 15,000 names. <www.ancestry.com/search/rectype/inddbs/2042.htm>

Pennsylvania, Lancaster Co.
Type: Abstracts; W
Year Range: 1732–1820
Online: Genealogy Library
Title: Abstracts of Lancaster Co. Wills, 1732–1785, 1786–1820
Notes, URL: Select Records | United States | Pennsylvania.

Pennsylvania, Montgomery Co.
Type: Abstracts; W
Year Range: 1784–1823
Online: Genealogy Library
Title: Abstracts of Montgomery Co., PA, Wills & Admins, 1784–1823
Notes, URL: Select Records | United States | Pennsylvania.

Pennsylvania, Montgomery Co.
Type: Index; W-PR
Year Range: 1784–1850
Online: F&LH
Title: Index of wills & estate settlements, Montgomery County, Pennsylvania, 1784–1850

Pennsylvania, Northumberland Co.
Type: Index, abstracts; W-PR
Year Range: 1772–1859
Online: Free
Title: Northumberland Archives—Wills
Notes, URL: Will index, 1772–1859. Index of letters of administration 1772–1813. Also includes some will abstracts. <www.rootsweb.com/~usgenweb/pa/northumberp/wills.htm>

Pennsylvania, Philadelphia Co.
Type: Abstracts; W
Year Range: 1682–1819
CD-ROM: $29.95 (Win), Ancestry.com, item #2333 CD. "Pennsylvania Wills: Selected Counties and Years," <http://shops.ancestry.com>. Search on "Pennsylvania Wills."
Online: Ancestry
Title: Philadelphia County, Pennsylvania Wills, 1682–1819
Notes, URL: The CD also has records for Chester & York Cos., Pa. <www.ancestry.com/search/rectype/inddbs/4695.htm>

Pennsylvania, Philadelphia Co.
Type: Abstracts; W
Year Range: 1682–1825
Online: Genealogy Library
Title: Abstracts of Philadelphia Co Wills, 1682–1825
Notes, URL: Select Records | United States | Pennsylvania.

Pennsylvania, Venango Co.
Type: Index; W
Year Range: 1819–?
Online: F&LH
Title: County of Venango, state of Pennsylvania, will book number 1

Pennsylvania, Washington Co.
Type: Abstracts; PR
Year Range: 1781–1796
Online: F&LH
Title: Estate records, 1781–96, and deed records, 1782–85, in Washington County, Pennsylvania
Notes, URL: Both the 1967 & 1977 versions of the book by Raymond Martin Bell.

Pennsylvania, Westmoreland Co.
Type: Abstracts; W
Year Range: 1773–1906
Online: F&LH
Title: Abstracts of wills, Bible records

Pennsylvania, York Co.
Type: Abstracts; W
Year Range: 1749–1819
CD-ROM: $29.95 (Win), Ancestry.com, item #2333 CD. "Pennsylvania Wills: Selected Counties and Years," <http://shops.ancestry.com>. Search on "Pennsylvania Wills."
Online: Ancestry
Title: York County, Pennsylvania Wills, 1749–1819
Notes, URL: The CD also has records for Chester & Philadelphia Cos., Pa. <www.ancestry.com/search/rectype/inddbs/4899.htm>

Pennsylvania, York Co.
Type: Abstracts; W
Year Range: 1749–1819
Online: Genealogy Library
Title: Abstracts of York Co. Wills, 1749–1819
Notes, URL: Select Records | United States | Pennsylvania.

Rhode Island
Type: Transcript; CT
Year Range: 1647–1662
Online: F&LH
Title: Rhode Island court records: records of the Court of Trials of the Colony of Providence Plantations, 1647–1662

Rhode Island, Newport Co., Little Compton
Type: Abstracts; PR
Year Range: 1700–1875
Online: NEHGS
Title: Little Compton, Rhode Island, Wills
Notes, URL: <www.newenglandancestors.org/research/database/lcompton/default.asp>

Rhode Island, Providence Co., Providence
Type: Index; PR
Year Range: 1646–1899
Online: NEHGS
Title: Index to Providence, Rhode Island Probate, 1646–1899
Notes, URL: <www.newenglandancestors.org/research/database/ri_probate>

South Carolina
Type: Index; W
Year Range: 1766–1864
CD-ROM: $29.99, Genealogy.com, CD #517
Online: Genealogy Library
Title: Early South Carolina Settlers, 1600s–1800s
Notes, URL: Includes the book, *Indexes to the County Wills of South Carolina*. <www.genealogy.com/517facd.html> See Genealogical Records: Early South Carolina Settlers, 1600s–1800s.

South Carolina
Type: Transcript; CT
Year Range: 1778–1779

CD-ROM: $29.99, Genealogy.com, CD #517
Online: Genealogy Library
Title: Early South Carolina Settlers, 1600s–1800s
Notes, URL: Includes *Jury Lists of South Carolina, 1778–1779.* See Genealogical Records: Early South Carolina Settlers, 1600s–1800s. <www.genealogy.com/517facd.html>

South Carolina, Barnwell Co.
Type: Abstract; CT-PR
Year Range: 1785–1791
CD-ROM: $24 (Mac/Win), Heritage Books, item #1164
Title: HB Archives: South Carolina, Vol. 1
Notes, URL: Includes *Winton (Barnwell) County, South Carolina, Minutes of the County Court, and Will Book 1, 1785–1791,* by Brent H. Holcomb. <www.heritagebooks.com>. Search on "1164."

South Carolina, Charleston Co.
Type: Index; W
Year Range: 1671–1868
CD-ROM: $29.99, Genealogy.com, CD #517
Online: Genealogy Library
Title: Early South Carolina Settlers, 1600s–1800s
Notes, URL: Includes *Index to Wills of Charleston County, South Carolina, 1671–1868* (about 10,000 names). See Genealogical Records: Early South Carolina Settlers, 1600s–1800s. <www.genealogy.com/517facd.html>

South Carolina, Charleston Co., Charleston
Type: Transcript; PR
Year Range: 1786–1822
Online: Free
Title: Charleston City Inventories
Notes, URL: <http://departments.mwc.edu/hipr/www/inventories/CharlestonSC_room_by_room.inventories>

South Carolina, Edgefield Co.
Type: Index; W
Year Range: 1836–1853
Online: Ancestry
Title: Edgefield County, South Carolina Wills, Books 1-2
Notes, URL: <www.ancestry.com/search/rectype/inddbs/5390.htm>

South Carolina, Kershaw Co.
Type: Abstract; CT-PR
Year Range: 1791–1799
CD-ROM: $24 (Mac/Win), Heritage Books, item #1164
Title: Heritage Books Archives: South Carolina, Vol. 1
Notes, URL: Includes *Kershaw County, South Carolina, Minutes of the County Court, 1791–1799,* by Brent H. Holcomb. <www.heritagebooks.com>. Search on "1164."

South Carolina, Richland Co.
Type: Index; W
Year Range: 1787–1864
Online: Free
Title: Richland County Will Index
Notes, URL: <www.sciway3.net/clark/richland/wills.html>

Tennessee
Type: Abstracts; CT
Year Range: 1796–1836
CD-ROM: $30 (Mac/Win), Heritage Books, item #1367
Title: Heritage Books Archives: Tennessee Vol. 2
Notes, URL: Contains 7 books of court minutes by Carol Wells: Dickson Co., 1816–1828; Giles Co., 1810–1816; Rhea Co., 1815–1836; Robertson Co., 1796–1807; Williamson Co., 1806–1815.<www.heritagebooks.com>. Search on "1367."

Tennessee, Davidson Co.
Type: Abstracts; CT
Year Range: 1783–1803
CD-ROM: $26.50 (Mac/Win), Heritage Books, item #1359
Title: Heritage Books Archives: Tennessee Vol. 1, by Carol Wells
Notes, URL: Covers 3 volumes of county court minutes originally published by Heritage Books. <www.heritagebooks.com>. Search on "1359."

Tennessee, Giles Co.
Type: Transcript; W
Year Range: 1830–1886
Online: Free
Title: Giles County: Wills Index
Notes, URL: <www.rootsweb.com/~tngiles/wills/index.htm>

Tennessee, Henry Co.
Type: Abstracts, indexes; W-CT
Year Range: 1700s–1900s
CD-ROM: $29.99, Genealogy.com, CD #511
Online: Genealogy Library
Title: Early Tennessee Settlers, 1700s–1900s
Notes, URL: Will abstracts & indexes to will books (1856–1863 & 1879–1902), estate abstracts, guardianship records, & court orders. Select Genealogical Records: Early Tennessee Settlers, 1700s–1900s. <www.genealogy.com/511facd.html>

Tennessee, Lincoln Co.
Type: Index; W
Year Range: 1864–1873
Online: Free
Title: A List of Wills, Lincoln County, Tennessee, Feb. 1864–Mar. 1873
Notes, URL: <www.genealogymagazine.com/intolincount.html>

Tennessee, Maury Co.
Type: Abstracts; W-PR
Year Range: 1807–1824
Online: F&LH
Title: Maury County, Tennessee wills and settlements, 1807–1824 and 1820 census

Tennessee, Shelby Co.
Type: Digital images; CT
Year Range: 1820–1824
CD-ROM: $9.95 (Mac/Win), AncestorStuff.com, item #0001-1001
Title: Minutes of the County Court of Shelby County, Tennessee, Book No. 1, 1820–1824
Notes, URL: <www.ancestorstuff.com>

Tennessee, Sumner Co.
Type: Abstracts; W
Year Range: 1788–1842
CD-ROM: $29.99, Genealogy.com, CD #511
Online: Genealogy Library
Title: Early Tennessee Settlers, 1700s–1900s
Notes, URL: Select Genealogical Records: Early Tennessee Settlers, 1700s–1900s. <www.genealogy.com/511facd.html>

Texas
Type: Index; PR
Year Range: 1840–1940
Online: Free
Title: The Index to Texas Probate Records
Notes, URL: An index to 26,000 probate cases in 11 counties. <www.three-legged-willie.org/texas.htm>

Utah
Type: Index; CT
Year Range: 1852–1915
Online: Free
Title: Division of State Archives: Indexes of Record Series at the Archives

Notes, URL: Indexes to civil & criminal cases in several counties. <www.archives.utah.gov/silverstream.htm>

Utah
Type: Index; CT
Year Range: 1882–1896
Online: Ancestry
Title: Utah Third District Court, Territorial Criminal Case Files Index, 1882–96
Notes, URL: <www.ancestry.com/search/rectype/inddbs/6895.htm>

Utah, Salt Lake Co.
Type: Index; PR
Year Range: 1852–1881
Online: Ancestry
Title: Salt Lake County, Index to Probate Case Files, 1852–81
Notes, URL: <www.ancestry.com/search/rectype/inddbs/6907.htm>

Utah, Salt Lake Co.
Type: Index; CT
Year Range: 1852–1887
Online: Ancestry
Title: Salt Lake County, Utah Civil and Criminal Case Files, 1852–1887
Notes, URL: <www.ancestry.com/search/rectype/inddbs/7074.htm>

Utah, Salt Lake Co.
Type: Index; PR
Year Range: 1852–1896
Online: Free
Title: Division of State Archives: Indexes of Record Series at the Archives
Notes, URL: <www.archives.utah.gov/silverstream.htm>

Utah, Weber Co.
Type: Index; CT
Year Range: 1852–1887
Online: Ancestry
Title: Weber County, Utah Civil and Criminal Case Files, 1852–1887
Notes, URL: <www.ancestry.com/search/rectype/inddbs/6999.htm>

Vermont
Type: Transcript; CT
Year Range: 1850–1852
Online: F&LH
Title: Reports of cases argued and determined in the Supreme Court of the state of Vermont

Virgin Islands (U.S.)
Type: Index; PR-W
Year Range: 1671–1848
Online: Free
Title: HGS: US Virgin Islands
Notes, URL: Chancery Records & Index to Wills 1671–1848. St. Thomas & St. John, Index to Probate Records 1717–1814. Formerly the Danish West Indies. <www.horlacher.org/usviris/index.html>

Virginia
Type: Abstracts; W
Year Range: Up to 1799
Online: F&LH
Title: Virginia wills before 1799

Virginia
Type: Abstracts; W
Year Range: 1600s–1700s
CD-ROM: $29.99, Genealogy.com, CD #503
Online: Genealogy Library
Title: Virginia Colonial Records, 1600s–1700s
Notes, URL: Includes *Virginia Gleanings in England: Abstracts of 17th And 18th Century English Wills and Administrations Relating to Virginia and Virginians.* <www.genealogy.com/503facd.html>

Virginia
Type: CT
Year Range: 1616–1625
CD-ROM: $33.50 (Mac/Win), Heritage Books, item #1170
Title: Records of the Virginia Company of London
Notes, URL: Includes 4 books by Susan Myra Kingsbury, including *The Court Book, Volumes 1 and 2.* <www.heritagebooks.com>. Search on "1170."

Virginia
Type: Abstracts; W
Year Range: 1624–1800
Online: Ancestry
Title: Virginia County Records, Volume VI
Notes, URL: Includes wills from Elizabeth City, Rappahannock County, York County, & Hanover County. <www.ancestry.com/search/rectype/inddbs/6280.htm>

Virginia
Type: Index; W-PR
Year Range: 1628–1898
Online: Free
Title: Library of Virginia: Index to Wills and Administrations
Notes, URL: <www.lva.lib.va.us/whatwehave/local/>

Virginia
Type: Index; W-PR
Year Range: 1628–1898
Online: Free
Title: Library of Virginia: Index to Wills and Administrations

Virginia
Type: Transcript; PR
Year Range: 1647–1699
Online: Free
Title: An Index of Seventeenth-Century Virginia Room by Room Inventories
Notes, URL: <http://departments.mwc.edu/hipr/www/inventories/virginia/17cva.htm>

Virginia
Type: Abstracts; W
Year Range: 1679–1708
Online: Ancestry
Title: Virginia County Records, Volume VII
Notes, URL: Includes wills from Richmond & Rappahannock Counties. <www.ancestry.com/search/rectype/inddbs/6286.htm>

Virginia
Type: Transcript; PR
Year Range: 1700–1800
Online: Free
Title: An Index of Eighteenth-Century Virginia Room by Room Inventories
Notes, URL: <http://departments.mwc.edu/hipr/www/inventories/virginia/18cva.htm>

Virginia
Type: Transcript; LJ
Year Range: 1727–1776
CD-ROM: $32 (Mac/Win), Heritage Books, item #1547
Title: Heritage Books Archives: Journals of the House of Burgesses of Virginia, Vol. 1
Notes, URL: Graphic images of 6 vols. published 1905–1909. <www.heritagebooks.com>. Search on "1547."

Virginia
Type: Abstracts; W
Year Range: 1743–1825
CD-ROM: $39.99, Genealogy.com, CD #513
Online: Genealogy Library
Title: Virginia Land, Marriage, and Probate Records, 1639–1850
Notes, URL: Includes wills from Augusta County, 1743–1800; Isle of Wight County, 1647–1800, & Norfolk County, 1752–1825. <www.genealogy.com/513facd.html>

Virginia
Type: Transcript; CT
Year Range: 1775–1780
CD-ROM: $29.99, Genealogy.com, CD #512
Online: Genealogy Library
Title: Pennsylvania Colonial Records, 1600s–1800s
Notes, URL: Includes *Virginia Court Records in Southwestern Pennsylvania, Records of the District of West Augusta and Ohio and Yohogania Counties, Virginia, 1775–1780.* <www.genealogy.com/512facd.html>

Virginia
Type: Transcript; PR
Year Range: 1800–1860
Online: Free
Title: An Index of Nineteenth Century Virginia Room by Room Inventories
Notes, URL: <http://departments.mwc.edu/hipr/www/inventories/virginia/19cva.htm>

Virginia, Accomack Co.
Type: Abstracts; CT
Year Range: 1663–1710
CD-ROM: $33 (Mac/Win), Heritage Books, item #1838
Title: Accomack County, Virginia Court Order Abstracts, 1663–1710, Volumes 1-10
Notes, URL: Contains the 10 volumes by JoAnn Riley McKey. Includes tax lists, wills, & deeds. <www.heritagebooks.com>. Search on "1838."

Virginia, Augusta Co.
Type: Text of books containing transcripts; CT
Year Range: 1745–1800
Online: Free
Title: Chronicles of the Scotch-Irish Settlement in Virginia
Notes, URL: Extracted from the Original Court Records of Augusta County 1745–1800, by Lyman Chalkley, vols. 1-3. <www.rootsweb.com/~chalkley>

Virginia, Augusta Co.
Type: Text of a book containing transcripts; CT
Year Range: 1745–1800
Online: Ancestry
Title: Scots-Irish in Virginia, Vol. 1
Notes, URL: Compiled from court records & other records. From Lyman Chalkley, *Scotch-Irish Settlement in Virginia, volume 1 (Records of Augusta County, Virginia, 1745–1800).* <www.ancestry.com/search/rectype/inddbs/3051.htm>

Virginia, Augusta Co.
Type: Text of a book containing transcripts; CT
Year Range: 1745–1800
Online: Ancestry
Title: Scots-Irish in Virginia, Vol. 2
Notes, URL: Compiled from court records & other records. From Lyman Chalkley, *Scotch-Irish Settlement in Virginia, volume 2 (Records of Augusta County, Virginia, 1745–1800).* <www.ancestry.com/search/rectype/inddbs/3053.htm>

Virginia, Augusta Co.
Type: Text of a book containing transcripts; CT
Year Range: 1745–1800
Online: Ancestry
Title: Scots-Irish in Virginia, Vol. 3
Notes, URL: Compiled from court records & other records. From Lyman Chalkley, *Scotch-Irish Settlement in Virginia, volume 3 (Records of Augusta County, Virginia, 1745–1800).* <www.ancestry.com/search/rectype/inddbs/3071.htm>

Virginia, Fauquier Co.
Type: Abstract; CT
Year Range: 1759–1871
CD-ROM: $25 (Mac/Win) Heritage Books, item #1128
Title: Fauquier County, Virginia
Notes, URL: Includes *Fauquier County, Virginia: Guardian Bonds 1759–1871 & Court Records 1776–1782*, by John K. Gott. <www.heritagebooks.com>. Search on "1128."

Virginia, Franklin Co.
Type: Transcript; CT
Year Range: 1786–1789
Online: F&LH
Title: An old Virginia court: being a transcript of the records of the first court of Franklin County, Virginia, 1786–1789.

Virginia, Fredericksburg
Type: Index; W
Year Range: 1727–1920
Online: Free
Title: Introduction to the Embrey Grantor Index
Notes, URL: Also covers wills through Will Book J, page 404. <http://departments.mwc.edu/hipr/www/Fredericksburg/embreyintro.htm>

Virginia, Goochland Co.
Type: Index; W
Online: F&LH
Title: The Douglas register: an index of Goochland Wills.

Virginia, Norfolk Co.
Type: Abstracts; W
Year Range: 1710–1753
Online: Ancestry
Title: Norfolk County, Virginia Will Abstracts, 1710–53
Notes, URL: Over 7000 names. <www.ancestry.com/search/rectype/inddbs/3838.htm>

Virginia, Northampton Co.
Type: Abstracts; W
Year Range: 1713–1728
Online: Ancestry
Title: Virginia County Records, Volume IX
Notes, URL: Also includes land grants & marriage bonds from other Va. counties. <www.ancestry.com/search/rectype/inddbs/6293.htm>

Virginia, Prince William Co.
Type: Index; W
Year Range: 1734–1920
Online: Ancestry
Title: Prince William County, Virginia Wills, Part 2, 1734–1920
Notes, URL: Over 2800 names. <www.ancestry.com/search/rectype/inddbs/3898.htm>

Virginia, Prince William Co.
Type: Index; W
Year Range: 1734–1925
Online: Ancestry
Title: Prince William County, Virginia Wills, Part 1, 1734–1925
Notes, URL: Over 2000 names. <www.ancestry.com/search/rectype/inddbs/3882.htm>

Virginia, Princess Anne Co.
Type: Abstracts; CT-W
Year Range: 1691–1871
CD-ROM: $25 (Mac/Win), Heritage Books, item #1098
Title: Princess Anne County, Virginia, Deeds, Wills, and Guardianships. Abstracted by Anne E. Maling
Notes, URL: Images of 3 books: *Princess Anne County, Virginia, Land and Probate Records Abstracted from Deed Books One to Eighteen, 1691–1783*; *Princess Anne County, Virginia Wills, 1783–1871*; & *Guardian Accounts of Princess Anne County, Virginia, 1736–1871*. <www.heritagebooks.com>. Search on "1098."

Virginia, Shenandoah Co.
Type: Abstracts; W
Year Range: 1771–1791
Online: Ancestry
Title: Shenandoah County, Virginia Wills, 1771–1791
Notes, URL: <www.ancestry.com/search/rectype/inddbs/5625.htm>

Virginia, Spotsylvania Co.
Type: Abstracts; W
Year Range: 1721–1800
Online: Ancestry
Title: Spotsylvania, Virginia County Records, 1721–1800
Notes, URL: Includes wills, deeds, administrators' & guardians' bonds, marriage licenses, & lists of Revolutionary War pensioners. <www.ancestry.com/search/rectype/inddbs/1039.htm>

Virginia, Westmoreland Co.
Type: Abstracts; W
Year Range: 1654–1800
Online: Ancestry
Title: Westmoreland County, Virginia Wills, 1654–1800
Notes, URL: <www.ancestry.com/search/rectype/inddbs/4900.htm>

Virginia, Westmoreland Co.
Type: Abstracts; W
Year Range: 1654–1800
CD-ROM: $26 (Mac/Win), Heritage Books, item #1270
Title: Heritage Books Archives: Virginia Vol. 3
Notes, URL: Includes *Wills of Westmoreland County Virginia 1654–1800*, by Augusta B. Fothergill. <www.heritagebooks.com>. Search on "1270."

Virginia, Westmoreland Co.
Type: Abstracts; W
Year Range: 1655–1794
Online: Ancestry
Title: Virginia County Records: Westmoreland County, Vol. I
Notes, URL: Includes wills, land grants, and militia records. <www.ancestry.com/search/rectype/inddbs/6277.htm>

Virginia, Williamsburg
Type: Abstracts; W
Year Range: Up to 1906
CD-ROM: $30.50 (Mac/Win), Heritage Books, item #1448
Title: Heritage Books Archives: Virginia Vol. 4
Notes, URL: Includes *Virginia County Records Volume III: Willamsburg Wills, being Transcriptions from the Original Files at the Chancery Court of Williamsburg*, by William Armstrong Crozier. <www.heritagebooks.com>. Search on "1448."

Virginia, Winchester
Type: Abstracts; W
Year Range: 1794–1894
CD-ROM: $23 (Mac/Win), Heritage Books, item #1413
Title: Heritage Books Archives: Winchester, Virginia
Notes, URL: Includes *Winchester, Virginia, Will Abstracts, 1794–1894*, by Dola S. Tylor. <www.heritagebooks.com>. Search on "1413."

West Virginia
Type: Index; W
Year Range: Up to 1850
CD-ROM: $29.99, Genealogy.com, CD #520
Online: Genealogy Library
Title: Early West Virginia Settlers, 1600s–1900s
Notes, URL: Includes *West Virginia Estate Settlements*, by Ross B. Johnston, an index to 25,000 names in wills, inventories, appraisements, land grants, & surveys up to 1850. <www.genealogy.com/520facd.html>

West Virginia, Hampshire Co.
Type: Abstracts; W
Year Range: 1770s–1860s
CD-ROM: $29.99, Genealogy.com, CD #520
Online: Genealogy Library
Title: Early West Virginia Settlers, 1600s–1900s
Notes, URL: Includes *Early Records, Hampshire County, Virginia*, by Sage and Jones. <www.genealogy.com/520facd.html>

West Virginia, Ohio Co.
Type: Index; W
Year Range: 1776–1835
Online: Free
Title: Index of Ohio County, WV Wills, Through 1835
Notes, URL: <www.rootsweb.com/~wvmarsha/ohiowill.txt>

West Virginia, Wood Co.
Type: Index; W
Year Range: 1787–1854
Online: Free
Title: Wood County Wills
Notes, URL: <www.rootsweb.com/~wvwood/wdwills.htm>

Cemeteries and Tombstone Inscriptions

A few years ago I discovered the names of several family members in the gravestone transcriptions of Scribner Cemetery in New Berlin, Chenango County, New York. The records revealed that Seth Hooper, a farmer and chair maker, died on 10 May 1863, at age 91, and his wife Betsey died on 21 June 1853, at age 70. Buried nearby are a son, a grandson, and a great-grandson Everett D. Hooper, who was "killed at Quaker Street, Schenectady Co., N.Y., Nov. 2, 1886, 21 yr 11 mo." Of course, now I'd like to find out what caused Everett's death at such a young age. Was he trampled by a spooked horse? The slower draw in a duel? I can imagine many scenarios straight out of a Western movie.

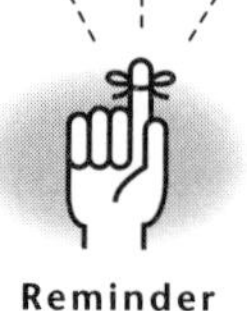

Reminder

Unlike most people, genealogists jump at the chance to visit an old family cemetery. And with good reason. If you're researching someone who died before the state began keeping death records and you can't find an obituary, a family Bible, or church records, **a gravestone inscription may be the only existing evidence of the person's life and death.** Gravestones also reveal dates and places of birth and the names of parents and spouses and other relatives. If you are extremely lucky, they may also include a juicy tidbit about your ancestors occupation, cause of death, or other revealing facts.

What cemetery records are online or on CD-ROM?

You'll find many gravestone transcriptions and sometimes even photographs of tombstones. See Figure 6-1 on page 107.

What cemetery records are not online or on CD-ROM?

Many gravestones have not been transcribed or no longer exist. You should keep in mind that the writing on an old gravestone may have been misread and that the transcription may not include everything written on the stone.

Figure 6-1
Gravestone of Hannah Paine, 1713, Truro Old North Burying Ground. 17th, 18th & 19th Century Cape Cod Gravestones <www.capecodgravestones.com>. *Photo by Robert Carlson.*

KEY RESOURCES

Transcripts

Cemetery Junction

<www.cemeteryjunction.com>

Links to gravestone transcriptions from thousands of cemeteries in the United States, Canada, and Australia. See Figure 6-2 below.

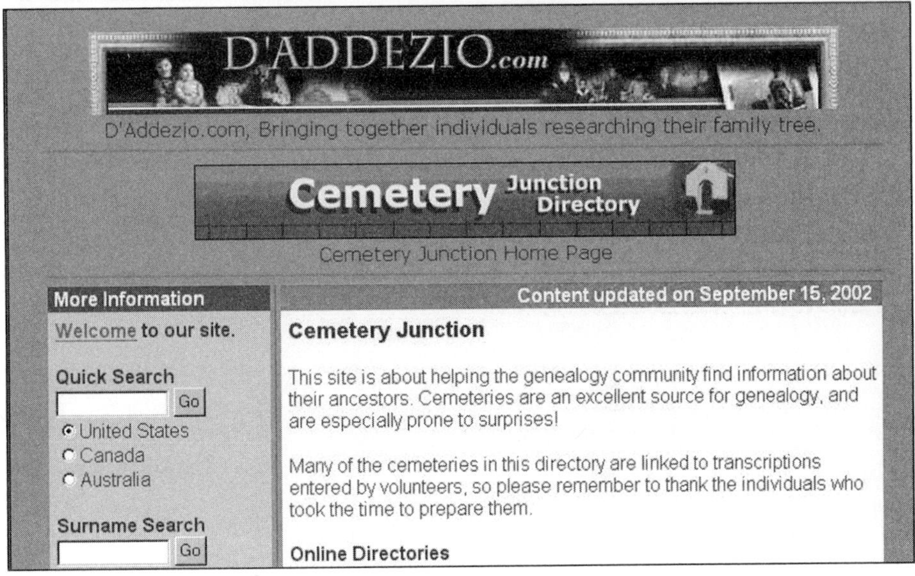

Figure 6-2
Cemetery Junction.

Find a Grave

<www.findagrave.com>

Ever wonder where Elvis Presley or Marilyn Monroe is buried? You'll find their final resting places on this site, along with over 4.7 million other grave

Figure 6-3
Find a Grave.

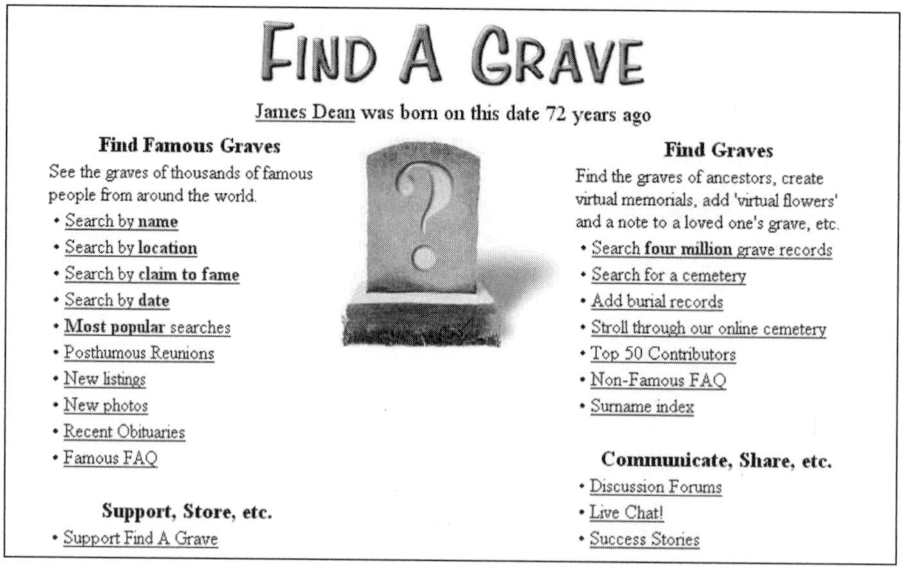

FIND A GRAVE

James Dean was born on this date 72 years ago

Find Famous Graves

See the graves of thousands of famous people from around the world.

- Search by **name**
- Search by **location**
- Search by **claim to fame**
- Search by **date**
- **Most popular** searches
- Posthumous Reunions
- New listings
- New photos
- Recent Obituaries
- Famous FAQ

Support, Store, etc.

- Support Find A Grave

Find Graves

Find the graves of ancestors, create virtual memorials, add 'virtual flowers' and a note to a loved one's grave, etc.

- Search **four million** grave records
- Search for a cemetery
- Add burial records
- Stroll through our online cemetery
- Top 50 Contributors
- Non-Famous FAQ
- Surname index

Communicate, Share, etc.

- Discussion Forums
- Live Chat!
- Success Stories

records from across the United States. You can submit gravestone transcriptions and photos of people or graves, along with your contact information. You can even "visit" a grave and leave flowers and notes. See Figure 6-3 above.

Interment.net

<www.interment.net>

This database contains more than 3.2 million cemetery records from more than 6,000 cemeteries around the world. You can browse cemetery transcriptions by county. The site also has links to gravestone transcriptions on other Web sites. See Figure 6-4 below.

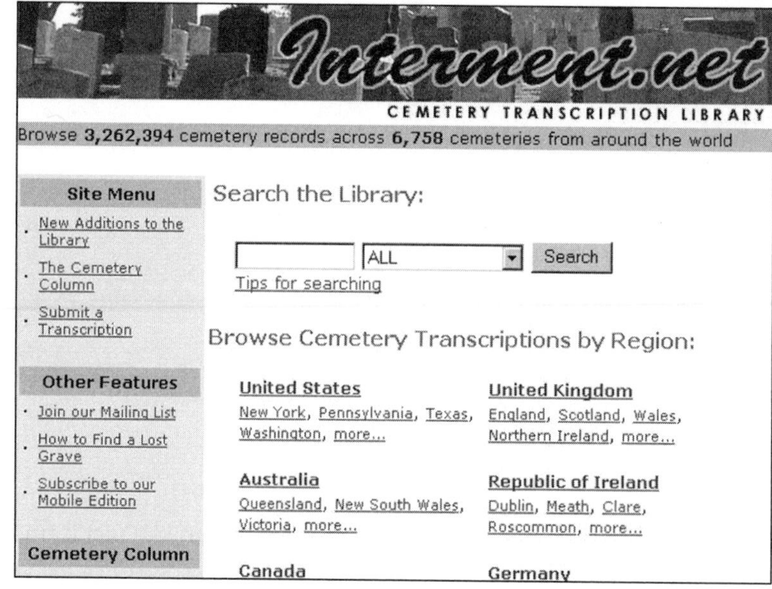

Figure 6-4
Interment.net.

RootsWeb.com Cemetery Records
<http://userdb.rootsweb.com/cemeteries>

Transcripts of over 635,000 cemetery records. See Figure 6-5 below.

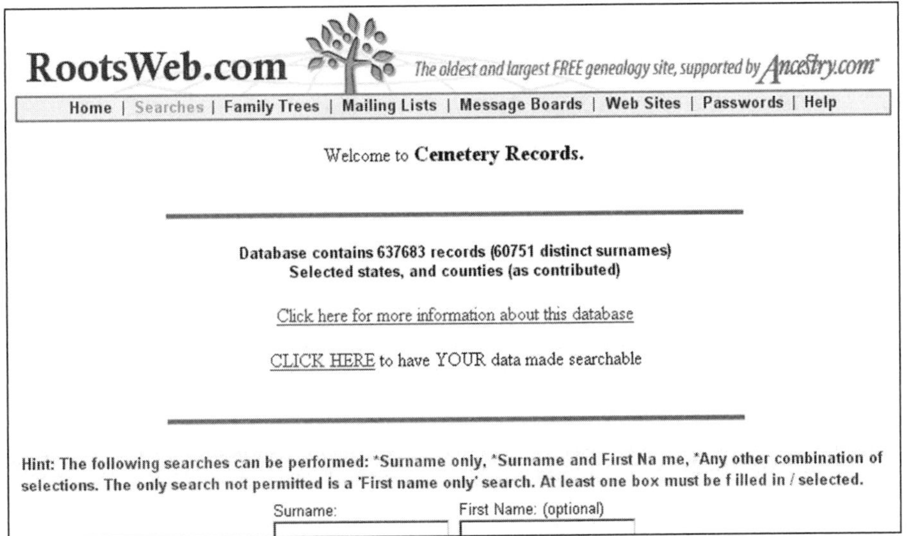

Figure 6-5
RootsWeb Cemetery Records.

USGenWeb Project State Pages
<www.usgenweb.org/statelinks-table.html>

Researchers have contributed many gravestone transcriptions to USGenWeb's state pages and the county pages linked to them. Most of these databases are not listed in the directory below, so be sure to check USGenWeb for the counties where your family lived.

LINKS

Metis Genealogy: Cemeteries
<www.metisgenealogy.com/datacemtrylnks.htm>

Cyndi's List of Genealogy Sites on the Internet: Cemeteries & Funeral Homes
<www.cyndislist.com/cemetery.htm>

SUGGESTED READING

Carmack, Sharon DeBartolo. *Your Guide to Cemetery Research*. Cincinnati: Betterway Books, 2002.

DATABASE DIRECTORY Cemeteries and Tombstone Inscriptions

This directory does not include URLs for databases in the Family and Local Histories Collection. See page 18 for instructions on "Searching an Individual Database" in Family and Local Histories. **Type**: Digital Images, Transcript, Database, Abstracts, or Index.

United States
Type: Transcript
Online: NEHGS
Title: Cemetery Transcriptions from the NEHGS Manuscript Collections
Notes, URL: Transcriptions from all over New England, as well as Canada & even India. <www.newenglandancestors.org/research/database/cemeteries>

United States
Type: Index
Online: Free
Title: DAR GRC Index
Notes, URL: An index to over 7 million names in unpublished genealogical materials, largely Bible and cemetery transcriptions, in 180,000 volumes of Genealogical Records Committee Reports. <www.dar.org>. Click on "DAR Library" and then on "GRC National Index."

United States
Type: Digital images of pages containing transcripts
Online: F&LH
Title: Orena V. Grant genealogical collection (marriages and cemetery records)
Notes, URL: Cemetery records from Ind., Ky., La., Mich., Miss., & Tenn.

United States
Type: Transcripts & photos
Online: Free
Title: Virtual Cemetery (Genealogy.com)
Notes, URL: Tombstone photographs submitted by visitors to the Web site. <www.genealogy.com/vcem_welcome.html>

Alabama, Barbour Co.
Type: Digital images of a book containing transcripts
Online: F&LH
Title: Cemetery records, Barbour County, Alabama
Notes, URL: By the Church of Jesus Christ of Latter-day Saints, Genealogical Society.

Alabama, Blount Co.
Type: Digital images of a book containing transcripts
Online: F&LH
Title: Cemetery records, Blount County, Alabama
Notes, URL: By the Church of Jesus Christ of Latter-day Saints. Gadsden Branch.

Alabama, Bullock Co.
Type: Digital images
Online: F&LH
Title: Bullock Co., AL, Old Confederate Cemetery

Alabama, Choctaw Co.
Type: Digital images of a book containing transcripts
Online: F&LH
Title: Cemetery records of Choctaw County, Alabama
Notes, URL: By the Church of Jesus Christ of Latter-day Saints. Southern States Mission.

Alabama, Conecuh Co.
Type: Digital images of a book containing transcripts
Online: F&LH
Title: The Evergreen Old Historical Cemetery in Evergreen, Alabama, Conecuh County
Notes, URL: By Elizabeth Riley.

Alabama, Covington Co.
Type: Digital images of 6 pages containing transcripts
Online: F&LH
Title: Covington Co., AL, Bushfield Cemetery
Notes, URL: By Edith Odom.

Alabama, Dale Co.
Type: Digital images of a book containing transcripts
Online: F&LH
Title: Cemetery records of Dale County, Alabama
Notes, URL: Church of Jesus Christ of Latter-day Saints. Southern States Mission.

Alabama, Dale Co.
Type: Digital images of a book containing transcripts
Online: F&LH
Title: Inscriptions from the cemeteries of Dale County, Alabama
Notes, URL: A book by E. Howard Hayes, et al.

Alabama, DeKalb Co.
Type: Digital images of books containing transcripts
Online: F&LH
Title: Cemetery records of DeKalb County, Alabama
Notes, URL: 5 vols. by the Church of Jesus Christ of Latter-day Saints. Gadsden Branch.

Alabama, Etowah Co.
Type: Digital images of books containing transcripts
Online: F&LH
Title: Cemetery survey, Etowah County, Alabama
Notes, URL: 2 vols. by the Church of Jesus Christ of Latter-day Saints. Gadsden Branch.

Alabama, Etowah Co.
Type: Digital images of a book containing transcripts
Online: F&LH
Title: Etowah County, Alabama cemetery records
Notes, URL: By the Church of Jesus Christ of Latter-day Saints. Southern States Mission.

Alabama, Fayette Co.
Type: Digital images of a book containing transcripts
Online: F&LH
Title: Cemetery records, Fayette County, Alabama: and neighboring counties
Notes, URL: A book by Herbert M. & Jeanie P. Newell.

Alabama, Greene Co.
Type: Digital images of a book containing transcripts
CD-ROM: $28 (Mac/Win), Heritage Books, item #1418
Title: Heritage Books Archives: Alabama Vol. 1
Notes, URL: Includes inscriptions for 47 cemeteries in Greene County, Ala., & 5 cemeteries in Miss. <www.heritagebooks.com> Search on "1418."

Alabama, Jefferson Co.
Type: Images of pages containing transcripts
Online: F&LH
Title: Cemetery records of Jefferson County, Alabama
Notes, URL: By the Church of Jesus Christ of Latter-day Saints. Southern States Mission.

Alaska, Fairbanks Co., Fairbanks
Type: Transcript
Online: Ancestry (free)
Title: Fairbanks, Alaska Cemetery Records
Notes, URL: Over 5,600 names. <www.ancestry.com/search/rectype/inddbs/4044.htm>

California
Type: Images of pages containing transcripts
Online: F&LH
Title: Cemetery inscription [*sic*] in California counties of Plumas, Alpine, and Sierra

California, Butte Co.
Type: Images of pages containing transcripts
Online: F&LH
Title: Some small Butte Co., Calif. cemeteries
Notes, URL: By Daughters of the American Colonists, Bidwell Chapter.

California, Calaveras Co.
Type: Transcript
Online: Free
Title: Calaveras County Cemeteries and More
Notes, URL: <www.geocities.com/calcems2002>

California, Madera Co., Oakhurst
Type: Transcript
Online: Ancestry
Title: Oakhill Cemetery Inscriptions, Oakhurst, California
Notes, URL: <www.ancestry.com/search/rectype/inddbs/3463.htm>

Colorado, Denver Co., Denver
Type: Transcript
Online: Free
Title: Fort Logan National [Veterans] Cemetery
Notes, URL: 73,640 listings. <www.interment.net/data/us/co/denver/logan/index.htm>

Colorado, El Paso Co.
Type: Transcripts
CD-ROM: $10 (Win)
Title: Pikes Peak Genealogical Society Publications: Tombstone Inscriptions of El Paso County, Colorado
Notes, URL: 76,000 names. <www.rootsweb.com/~coelpaso/ppgspubs.htm>

Connecticut, Hartford Co., Wethersfield
Type: Pages images of a book containing transcripts
Online: F&LH
Title: Wethersfield inscriptions
Notes, URL: By Edward S. Tillotson.

Connecticut, Litchfield Co., Sharon
Type: Digital images containing transcripts
Online: F&LH
Title: Burying Grounds of Sharon, Connecticut, Amenia and North East New York
Notes, URL: By L. Van Alystyne.

Connecticut, Litchfield Co., Sharon
Type: Transcript
Online: Ancestry
Title: Sharon, Connecticut, Burying Grounds
Notes, URL: From L. Van Alystyne, *Burying Grounds of Sharon, Connecticut, Amenia and North East New York*. <www.ancestry.com/search/rectype/inddbs/4823.htm>

Connecticut, New London Co.
Type: Transcript
Online: Ancestry
Title: New London County, Connecticut, Cemetery Records, Vols. I and II
Notes, URL: More than 3,600 entries. <www.ancestry.com/search/rectype/inddbs/5564.htm>

Connecticut, Windham Co.
Type: Transcript
Online: Ancestry
Title: Windham County, Connecticut, Cemetery Records, Vol. I
Notes, URL: More than 2,020 entries. From Elizabeth Prather Ellsberry, *Cemetery Records of Windham County, Connecticut Volume I*. <www.ancestry.com/search/rectype/inddbs/5576.htm>

Connecticut, Windham Co., Windham
Type: Transcript
Online: Free
Title: Windham Center Cemetery Inscriptions
Notes, URL: Enos, Joel N., "Connecticut Cemetery Inscriptions," NEHGR. <www.rootsweb.com/~ctcwindh/windhaminscriptions.html>

Florida
Type: Index
Online: Free
Title: State Library of Florida: Florida Cemeteries
Notes, URL: <http://dlis.dos.state.fl.us/stlib/genealres.html>

Georgia, Fulton Co., Atlanta
Type: Transcript
Online: Ancestry
Title: Oakland Cemetery, Atlanta, Georgia
Notes, URL: Over 40,000 names. <www.ancestry.com/search/rectype/inddbs/4105.htm>

Georgia, Upson Co.
Type: Transcript
Year Range: Up to 1968
Online: Genealogy Library
Title: White Cemeteries of Upson County
Notes, URL: Text of the book by Robert L. Carter. Select Records | Magazine | Georgia.

Idaho, Idaho Co., Grangeville
Type: Transcript
Year Range: 1870–1995
Online: Ancestry
Title: Prairie View Cemetery Inscriptions, Grangeville, Idaho
Notes, URL: 4500 records. <www.ancestry.com/search/rectype/inddbs/4212.htm>

Illinois
Type: Digital images of a book containing transcripts
Online: F&LH
Title: Miscellaneous records of families, Bibles, cemeteries
Notes, URL: By the DAR, Illinois Society.

Illinois, Brown Co.
Type: Index
Year Range: 1825–1972
Online: Free
Title: Brown County Permanent Residents Index
Notes, URL: An index of the Recorded Burial sections of the book *Cemeteries of Brown County, Illinois, 1825–1972*. <www.rootsweb.com/~ilbrown/Cemeteries-html/Brown_Cemetery_index.html>

Illinois, Cook Co., Chicago
Type: Transcript
Year Range: 1864–1984

Online: Ancestry
Title: Wunders Cemetery, Chicago, Illinois
Notes, URL: From *A Transcription of Wunders Cemetery, Chicago, Illinois.* <www.ancestry.com/search/rectype/inddbs/5738.htm>

Illinois, Madison Co., Glen Carbon
Type: Transcript
Year Range: 1908–1979
Online: Free
Title: Glen Carbon Cemetery Listing
Notes, URL: Burials, 1908–1979. <http://freepages.genealogy.rootsweb.com/~ltreat/cemetery/gravlist.htm>

Illinois, Piatt Co.
Type: Transcript
Year Range: 1841–1853
Online: Ancestry
Title: Piatt County, Illinois Marriage and Cemetery Records, 1841–53
Notes, URL: From Fern J. Richart, *Piatt County, Illinois, Marriage Records 1841–1853 and Cemetery Records.* <www.ancestry.com/search/rectype/inddbs/3248.htm>

Illinois, Vermillion Co.
Type: Transcript
Year Range: 1871–1989
Online: Ancestry
Title: East Lynn & Rankin Union Cemeteries: Vermillion County, IL
Notes, URL: 1,995 names. <www.ancestry.com/search/rectype/inddbs/5655.htm>

Indiana, Adams Co.
Type: Digital images of books
Online: F&LH
Title: Cemetery records of Adams County, Indiana
Notes, URL: 3 vols. by Carrie Behrman, et al.

Indiana, Fountain Co.
Type: Digital images of a book
Online: F&LH
Title: Fountain County, Indiana, cemetery inscriptions
Notes, URL: By Daughters of the American Revolution, Quibache Chapter (Attica, Ind.), et al.

Indiana, Madison Co.
Type: Abstracts
Online: Free
Title: Madison County Area Cemetery Database
Notes, URL: 70,000 names from 98 cemeteries. <www.and.lib.in.us/cemetery/cemeterysearch.asp>

Indiana, Porter Co., Boone Township
Type: Digital images of a book
Online: F&LH
Title: Cornell Cemetery records, Boone Township, Porter County, Indiana
Notes, URL: A book by Mary D. Craigmile, et al.

Indiana, Warren Co., Newtown
Type: Digital images of a book containing transcripts
Online: F&LH
Title: Newtown Cemetery, Newtown, Indiana
Notes, URL: A book by Daughters of the American Revolution. Ouibache Chapter (Attica, Ind.).

Indiana, Wayne Co.
Type: Transcript
Year Range: Up to 1968
Online: Genealogy Library
Title: Tombstone Inscriptions in Wayne County, Indiana, Volumes II–IV
Notes, URL: Text of the books by Beverly Yount. Select Records I Cemetery I W.

Iowa
Type: Transcript
Year Range: Up to 1930s
Online: Ancestry
Title: Iowa Cemetery Records
Notes, URL: WPA transcripts from 76 counties. <www.ancestry.com/search/rectype/inddbs/4711a.htm>

Kansas, Leavenworth Co.
Type: Transcript
Year Range: 1954–1970
Online: Ancestry
Title: Leavenworth County, Kansas Burials, 1954–58, 1963–70
Notes, URL: <www.ancestry.com/search/rectype/inddbs/4578.htm>

Kansas, Leavenworth Co., Leavenworth
Type: Index
Year Range: 1942–1954
Online: Ancestry
Title: Leavenworth, Kansas Funeral Home Records, 1942–54
Notes, URL: <www.ancestry.com/search/rectype/inddbs/4689.htm>

Kansas, Riley Co.
Type: Abstracts
Year Range: 1960–1995
Online: Ancestry
Title: Riley County, Kansas Funeral Cards, 1960–95
Notes, URL: <www.ancestry.com/search/rectype/inddbs/4504.htm>

Kansas, Shawnee Co., Topeka
Type: Index
Year Range: 1872–1997
Online: Free
Title: Topeka State Hospital Cemetery
Notes, URL: 1,157 names. <www.kshs.org/genealogists/vital/topekastatehospitalcemetery.htm>

Kentucky
Type: Transcripts
Online: Free
Title: Kentucky Cemetery Records Database
Notes, URL: 179,750 grave records from 3,170 cemeteries as of Sept. 2002. <http://catalog.kyhistory.org/help/Cemetery_Database.htm>

Kentucky, Mason Co.
Type: Transcript
Online: Ancestry
Title: Mason County, Kentucky, Cemetery Records, Volume I
Notes, URL: More than 1,450 entries. <www.ancestry.com/search/rectype/inddbs/5587.htm>

Maine, Hancock Co.
Type: Transcripts
Online: Ancestry
Title: Hancock County, Maine, Cemetery Records, Volume I
Notes, URL: More than 1,100 entries. <www.ancestry.com/search/rectype/inddbs/5598.htm>

Maine, Kennebec Co.
Type: Transcripts
Year Range:
CD-ROM: $99.50, MOCA
Title: Kennebec County CD
Notes, URL: 135,000 names from 345 cemeteries. Maine Old Cemetery Assn. <www.rootsweb.com/~memoca/moca.htm>. Click on Projects and Research.

Maine, Oxford Co., Andover
Type: Transcripts
Year Range: 1801–2002
Online: Free
Title: Welcome to Andover, Maine: Andover Cemetery Inscriptions, 1801 to 2002
Notes, URL: <http://andovermaine.tripod.com/index.html>

Maine, York Co.
Type: Photographs
Online: Free
Title: York County Genealogy and Virtual Cemeteries
Notes, URL: <www.knights.hls-inc.net/>

Maryland, Baltimore City
Type: Digital images of pages containing transcripts
Year Range: 1838–1938
Online: F&LH
Title: Green Mount Cemetery one hundredth anniversary: 1838–1938.
Notes, URL: By Gerald W. Johnson, et al.

Maryland, Baltimore City
Type: Digital images of pages containing transcripts
CD-ROM: $29.99, Genealogy.com, CD #521
Online: Genealogy Library
Title: Maryland Settlers & Soldiers, 1700s–1800s
Notes, URL: Includes *A Record of Interments at the Friends Burial Ground, Baltimore, Maryland & Civil War Burials in Baltimore's Loudon Park Cemetery*. In Genealogy Library, select Genealogical Records: Maryland Settlers & Soldiers, 1700s–1800s. <www.genealogy.com/521facd.html>

Massachusetts
Type: Digital images of a book containing transcripts
Online: F&LH
Title: Epitaphs from graveyards in Wellesley (formerly West Needham), North Natick, and Saint Mary's churchyard in Newton Lower Falls, Massachusetts
Notes, URL: By George K. Clarke.

Massachusetts
Type: Digital images of pages containing transcripts
Online: F&LH
Title: Family records: cemetery and Bible records, mainly Michigan and Massachusetts
Notes, URL: By Maurine C. Johannesen et al.

Massachusetts
Type: Digital images of pages containing transcripts
CD-ROM: $31.50 (Mac/Win), Heritage Books, CD #1449
Title: Heritage Books Archives: Massachusetts Cemetery Inscriptions, Vol. 1
Notes, URL: 2,307 pages of transcriptions cemeteries in Boston, Bridgewater, Dedham, Deerfield, Lexington, & many other towns. <www.heritagebooks.com>. Search on "1449."

Massachusetts, Barnstable Co.
Type: Transcripts, photos
Year Range: 1683–1860
Online: Free
Title: 17th, 18th & 19th Century Cape Cod Gravestones
Notes, URL: About 20,000 names from about 130 cemeteries. <www.capecodgravestones.com>

Massachusetts, Barnstable Co., Truro
Type: Digital images of pages containing transcripts
Year Range: 1713–1840
Online: F&LH
Title: Inscriptions from gravestones in the Old North Cemetery, Truro, Mass.
Notes, URL: By John B. Dyer et al.

Massachusetts, Barnstable Co., Yarmouth
Type: Digital images of pages containing transcripts
Online: F&LH
Title: Gravestone records in the ancient cemetery and the Woodside Cemetery Yarmouth, Massachusetts
Notes, URL: A book by George E. Bowman, et al.

Massachusetts, Berkshire Co., Lee
Type: Digital images of pages containing transcripts
Year Range: 1801–1825
Online: F&LH
Title: Gravestone inscriptions, Lee, Mass.: including all extant of the quarter century 1801–1825
Notes, URL: By Dorvil M. Wilcox.

Massachusetts, Berkshire Co., Lee
Type: Digital images of pages containing transcripts
Online: F&LH
Title: Records of the Town of Lee from its incorporation to A.D. 1801: . . . also inscriptions from the cemeteries . . .

Massachusetts, Bristol Co., Acushnet
Type: Images of pages containing transcripts
Online: F&LH
Title: Acushnet Cemetery: memorial record of the dead of families of the early settlers interred in the old colonial burying ground, . . .

Massachusetts, Bristol Co., Berkley
Type: Digital images of pages containing transcripts
CD-ROM: $43 (Mac/Win), Heritage Books, CD #1848
Title: Heritage Books Archives: Bristol County, Mass.
Notes, URL: Covers 24 cemeteries. The CD also includes several town histories. <www.heritagebooks.com>. Search on "1848."

Massachusetts, Bristol Co., Fairhaven
Type: Digital images of a book containing transcripts
Online: F&LH
Title: An address delivered on Sunday evening, July 7th, 1850 at the consecration of the River-side Cemetery in Fairhaven, Mass.
Notes, URL: By Thomas Dawes.

Massachusetts, Essex Co., Lynn
Type: Digital images
Online: F&LH
Title: An address delivered at the consecration of the Pine Grove Cemetery, July 24, 1850
Notes, URL: By Charles C. Shackford.

Massachusetts, Essex Co., Newburyport
Type: Images of pages containing transcripts
Online: F&LH
Title: Respect for the remains of the dead: an address; Address delivered at the consecration of Oak Hill Cemetery in Newburyport.
Notes, URL: By Jonathan F. Stearns.

Massachusetts, Essex Co., Rowley
Type: Transcript
Year Range: Up to 1892
Online: Ancestry
Title: Rowley, Essex County, Massachusetts: Cemetery Inscriptions
Notes, URL: From Geo. B. Blodgette, *Inscriptions from the Old Cemetery in Rowley, Massachusetts*. <www.ancestry.com/search/rectype/inddbs/6056.htm>

Massachusetts, Middlesex Co., Cambridge
Type: Digital images
Online: F&LH
Title: A concise history of and guide through Mount Auburn: with a catalogue of lots laid out in that cemetery, . . .
Notes, URL: By Nathaniel Dearborn.

Massachusetts, Middlesex Co., Cambridge
Type: Transcript
Online: Ancestry
Title: Massachusetts: Middlesex County, Cambridge, Mt. Auburn Cemetery
Notes, URL: More than 16,000 names. <www.ancestry.com/search/rectype/inddbs/4397.htm>

Massachusetts, Middlesex Co., Lexington
Type: Transcript
Online: Ancestry
Title: Lexington, Massachusetts Cemetery Records
Notes, URL: Nearly 1,000 names. <www.ancestry.com/search/rectype/inddbs/3871.htm>

Massachusetts, Middlesex Co., Medford
Type: Digital images of a book containing transcripts
Online: F&LH
Title: Address delivered in Oak-Grove Cemetery, Medford, Mass., Sept. 6, 1866
Notes, URL: By Charles Brooks.

Massachusetts, Norfolk Co., Dedham
Type: Digital images of a book containing transcripts
Online: F&LH
Title: The record of baptisms, marriages and deaths and admissions to the church and dismissals therefrom, transcribed from the church records in the town of Dedham, Massachusetts, 1638–1845
Notes, URL: "Also all the epitaphs in the ancient burial place in Dedham, together with the other inscriptions before 1845 in the three parish cemeteries." By Don Gleason Hill.

Massachusetts, Plymouth Co., Hingham
Type: Digital images
Year Range: Up to 1842
Online: F&LH
Title: Our old burial grounds

Massachusetts, Plymouth Co., Kingston
Type: Digital images containing transcripts
Online: F&LH
Title: Death records from the ancient burial ground at Kingston, Massachusetts
Notes, URL: By Thomas B. Drew, et al.

Massachusetts, Plymouth Co., Plymouth
Type: Transcript
Year Range: 1657–1892
Online: Ancestry
Title: Epitaphs from Burial Hill, Plymouth, Massachusetts, 1657–1892
Notes, URL: Over 2,000 epitaphs. <www.ancestry.com/search/rectype/inddbs/6241.htm>

Massachusetts, Plymouth Co., Plymouth
Type: Digital images of pages containing transcripts
Year Range: 1657–1892
CD-ROM: $39.99, Genealogy.com, CD #526
Online: Genealogy Library
Title: Massachusetts, 1600s–1800s Genealogical Records
Notes, URL: Transcriptions from Burial Hill. <www.genealogy.com/526facd.html>

Massachusetts, Suffolk Co., Boston
Type: Digital images
Online: F&LH
Title: Mount Hope Cemetery in Dorchester and West Roxbury

Massachusetts, Worcester Co., Grafton
Type: Digital images
Online: F&LH
Title: An address delivered at the consecration of the Riverside Cemetery in Grafton: April 29, 1851
Notes, URL: By E.B. Willson.

Massachusetts, Worcester Co., Worcester
Type: Images of pages containing transcripts
Online: F&LH
Title: An address delivered on the consecration of the Worcester Rural Cemetery, September 8, 1838
Notes, URL: By Levi Lincoln.

Massachusetts, Worcester Co., Worcester
Type: Images of pages containing transcripts
Online: F&LH
Title: Epitaphs from the cemetery on Worcester Common
Notes, URL: By W.S. Barton.

Massachusetts, Worcester Co., Worcester
Type: Transcripts
Year Range: 1727–1859
Online: Ancestry
Title: Worcester, Massachusetts Burials, 1727–1859
Notes, URL: From Worcester Society of Antiquity, *Inscriptions from the Old Burial Grounds in Worcester, Massachusetts from 1727 to 1859.* <www.ancestry.com/search/rectype/inddbs/4821.htm>

Michigan
Type: Digital images of a book
Online: F&LH
Title: A Compilation of Bible-marriage-family-and-cemetery records relating to Michigan pioneer families
Notes, URL: A book by John C. Kreger, et al.

Michigan
Type: Digital images of pages containing transcripts
Online: F&LH
Title: Family records: cemetery and Bible records, mainly Michigan and Massachusetts
Notes, URL: By Maurine C. Johannesen, et al.

Michigan, Iosco Co.
Type: Transcripts
Year Range: 1901–1999
Online: Ancestry (free)
Title: Iosco County, Michigan, 1901–99: Esmond-Evergreen Cemetery
Notes, URL: Nearly 2,000 records. <www.ancestry.com/search/rectype/inddbs/5492.htm>

Minnesota
Type: Index
Online: Ancestry
Title: Minnesota Cemetery Inscription Index (Eleven Counties)
Notes, URL: Over 263,000 names from cemeteries in Rice, Le Sueur, Scott, Goodhue, Dakota, Steele, Dodge, Blue Earth, Waseca, & Olmsted Counties. <www.ancestry.com/search/rectype/inddbs/3775.htm>

Minnesota, Becker Co.
Type: Transcripts
Online: Free
Title: Becker County Historical Society: Cemetery Database
Notes, URL: About 90 cemeteries. <www.beckercountyhistory.org/>

Minnesota, Benton Co.
Type: Transcripts
CD-ROM: $20 (Win)
Title: St. Cloud Area Genealogists, Inc.: Index to Gravestones of Benton County, Minnesota
Notes, URL: <www.rootsweb.com/~mnscag/SCAG/>

Minnesota, Stearns Co.
Type: Transcripts

CD-ROM: $20 (Win)
Title: St. Cloud Area Genealogists, Inc.: Index to Gravestones of Stearns County, Minnesota
Notes, URL: <www.rootsweb.com/~mnscag/SCAG/>

Mississippi, Madison Co.
Type: Transcripts
Online: Free
Title: Madison County, Mississippi Cemeteries
Notes, URL: Over 16,800 names. <www.rootsweb.com/~msmadiso/cemetery/cemindex.htm>

Missouri, Barton Co.
Type: Transcripts
Online: Ancestry
Title: Barton County, Missouri, Cemetery Records, Vol. I
Notes, URL: More than 1,100 names. <www.ancestry.com/search/rectype/inddbs/5610.htm>

Missouri, Bates Co.
Type: Transcripts
Online: Ancestry
Title: Bates County, Missouri, Cemetery Records, Vol. 1-4, 5 (Part 1), 6 (Parts 1 & 2), 7, 8 (Parts 1-3).
Notes, URL: More than 15,600 entries. <www.ancestry.com/search/rectype/inddbs/5639.htm>

Missouri, Boone Co.
Type: Transcripts
Online: Ancestry
Title: Boone County, Missouri, Cemetery Records Vol. 2 (Part 1 & 2), 5, 6, 7, 8 (Part 1 & 2)
Notes, URL: More than 11,500 entries. <www.ancestry.com/search/rectype/inddbs/5659.htm>

Missouri, Caldwell Co.
Type: Transcripts
Online: Ancestry
Title: Caldwell County, Missouri, Cemetery Records, Vol. 6
Notes, URL: More than 1,600 entries. <www.ancestry.com/search/rectype/inddbs/5670.htm>

Missouri, Callaway Co.
Type: Transcripts
Online: Ancestry
Title: Callaway County, Missouri, Cemetery Records, Vol. 1-3, 6
Notes, URL: More than 4,900 entries. <www.ancestry.com/search/rectype/inddbs/5666.htm>

Missouri, Camden Co.
Type: Transcripts
Online: Ancestry
Title: Camden County, Missouri, Cemetery Records, Vol. 1
Notes, URL: More than 940 entries from the Breckenridge Cemetery. <www.ancestry.com/search/rectype/inddbs/5674.htm>

Missouri, Cape Girardeau Co.
Type: Transcripts
Online: Ancestry
Title: Cape Girardeau and Adjoining Counties, Missouri, Cemetery Records
Notes, URL: More than 3,200 entries from about 120 cemeteries. <www.ancestry.com/search/rectype/inddbs/5678.htm>

Missouri, Carroll Co.
Type: Transcripts
Online: Ancestry
Title: Carroll County, Missouri, Cemetery Records, Vols. I, III-IV
Notes, URL: More than 4,350 entries. <www.ancestry.com/search/rectype/inddbs/5732.htm>

Missouri, Cass Co.
Type: Transcripts
Year Range: Up to 2001
CD-ROM: $20/each (vols. 1-8), $80 (vols. 1-10)
Title: Cass Mo Find: Cass County, Missouri Cemeteries—Researched Edition
Notes, URL: Master index online. CDs combine information from gravestones, obituaries, vital records, etc. <http://members.fortunecity.com/cassmofind>

Missouri, Cass Co.
Type: Transcript
Online: Ancestry
Title: Cass County, Missouri, Cemetery Records, Vol. 1
Notes, URL: More than 3,200 entries. <www.ancestry.com/search/rectype/inddbs/5684.htm>

Missouri, Cedar Co.
Type: Transcript
Online: Ancestry
Title: Cedar County, Missouri, Cemetery Records, Vol. 2
Notes, URL: More than 1,400 entries. <www.ancestry.com/search/rectype/inddbs/5688.htm>

Missouri, Chariton Co.
Type: Transcript
Online: Ancestry
Title: Chariton County, Missouri, Cemetery Records, Vols. 1 & 2
Notes, URL: More than 2,700 entries. <www.ancestry.com/search/rectype/inddbs/5691.htm>

Missouri, Clay Co.
Type: Transcript
Online: Ancestry
Title: Clay County, Missouri Cemetery Records, Vols. I-II
Notes, URL: More than 3,000 entries. <www.ancestry.com/search/rectype/inddbs/5440.htm>

Missouri, Cooper Co.
Type: Transcript
Online: Ancestry
Title: Cooper County, Missouri, Cemetery Records, Vols. 1-12
Notes, URL: More than 19,000 entries from almost 100 cemeteries. <www.ancestry.com/search/rectype/inddbs/5701.htm>

Missouri, Daviess Co.
Type: Transcript
Online: Ancestry
Title: Daviess County, Missouri, Cemetery Records, Vol. 2
Notes, URL: More than 2,000 entries. <www.ancestry.com/search/rectype/inddbs/5707.htm>

Missouri, Grundy Co.
Type: Transcript
Online: Ancestry
Title: Grundy County, Missouri, Cemetery Records, Vols. 3 & 6
Notes, URL: More than 3,200 entries. <www.ancestry.com/search/rectype/inddbs/5716.htm>

Missouri, Henry Co.
Type: Transcript
Online: Ancestry
Title: Henry County, Missouri, Cemetery Records, Vol. 2 (Calhoun Cemetery)
Notes, URL: More than 1,400 entries. <www.ancestry.com/search/rectype/inddbs/5722.htm>

Missouri, Lafayette Co.
Type: Transcript
Online: Ancestry
Title: Lafayette County, Missouri, Cemetery Records, Vol. I
Notes, URL: More than 1,000 entries. <www

.ancestry.com/search/rectype/inddbs/5741.htm>

Missouri, Linn Co.
Type: Transcript
Online: Ancestry
Title: Linn County, Missouri, Cemetery Records, Vols. 2 & 8
Notes, URL: <www.ancestry.com/search/rectype/inddbs/5747.htm>

Missouri, Livingston Co.
Type: Transcript
Online: Ancestry
Title: Livingston County, Missouri, Cemetery Records, Vols. 1, 3-5
Notes, URL: <www.ancestry.com/search/rectype/inddbs/5768.htm>

Missouri, Macon Co.
Type: Transcript
Online: Ancestry
Title: Macon County, Missouri, Cemetery Records, Vols. 1-11
Notes, URL: More than 19,200 entries. <www.ancestry.com/search/rectype/inddbs/5782.htm>

Missouri, Marion Co.
Type: Transcript
Online: Ancestry
Title: Marion County, Missouri, Cemetery Records, Vols. 1-2
Notes, URL: More than 3,500 entries. <www.ancestry.com/search/rectype/inddbs/5787.htm>

Missouri, Miller Co.
Type: Transcript
Online: Ancestry
Title: Miller County, Missouri, Cemetery Records, Vol. 1
Notes, URL: More than 800 entries. <www.ancestry.com/search/rectype/inddbs/5792.htm>

Missouri, Montgomery Co.
Type: Transcript
Online: Ancestry
Title: Montgomery County, Missouri, Cemetery Records, Vols. 1-2
Notes, URL: More than 1,900 entries. <www.ancestry.com/search/rectype/inddbs/5796.htm>

Missouri, New Madrid Co., New Madrid
Type: Transcript
Online: Ancestry
Title: New Madrid, Missouri Cemetery Records, and Marriage Records, 1864–1874
Notes, URL: More than 800 entries. <www.ancestry.com/search/rectype/inddbs/5822.htm>

Missouri, Pettis Co.
Type: Transcript
Online: Ancestry
Title: Pettis County, Missouri Cemetery Records, Vol. 1
Notes, URL: More than 1,800 entries. <www.ancestry.com/search/rectype/inddbs/5804.htm>

Missouri, Ralls Co.
Type: Transcript
Online: Ancestry
Title: Ralls County, Missouri Cemetery Records, Vol. 1
Notes, URL: More than 800 names. <www.ancestry.com/search/rectype/inddbs/5810.htm>

Missouri, Randolph Co.
Type: Transcript
Online: Ancestry
Title: Randolph County, Missouri Cemetery Records, Vol. 3
Notes, URL: <www.ancestry.com/search/rectype/inddbs/5814.htm>

Missouri, Randolph Co.
Type: Transcript
Online: Ancestry
Title: Randolph County, Missouri, Cemetery Records and Histories, Vol. IV (1-6) & Vol. V (1-2)
Notes, URL: From books by Elizabeth Prather Ellsberry. <www.ancestry.com/search/rectype/inddbs/5762.htm>

Missouri, Ray Co.
Type: Transcript
Online: Ancestry
Title: Ray County, Missouri Cemetery Records, Vol. I-III
Notes, URL: More than 5,300 entries from the volume by Elizabeth Prather Ellsberry. <www.ancestry.com/search/rectype/inddbs/5416.htm>

Missouri, Ray Co.
Type: Transcript
Online: Ancestry
Title: Ray County, Missouri Cemetery Records, Vols. IV-VI
Notes, URL: More than 5,300 entries from the volume by Elizabeth Prather Ellsberry. <www.ancestry.com/search/rectype/inddbs/5818.htm>

Missouri, St. Clair Co., Appleton
Type: Transcript
Online: Ancestry
Title: Appleton City, St. Clair County, Missouri Cemetery Records, Vol. 1
Notes, URL: <www.ancestry.com/search/rectype/inddbs/6078.htm>

Missouri, St. Louis (Independent City)
Type: Index
Year Range: 1780–2002
CD-ROM: $30 (Mac/Windows)
Title: St. Louis Catholic Burials
Notes, URL: 488,000 records. <www.stlgs.org/cd-cathbur-order.htm>

Missouri, Saline Co.
Type: Transcript
Online: Ancestry
Title: Saline County, Missouri Cemetery Records, Vols. 2-7
Notes, URL: More than 5,600 entries. From Elizabeth Prather Ellsberry, *Cemetery Records of Saline County, Missouri, Volumes II-VII.* <www.ancestry.com/search/rectype/inddbs/5800.htm>

Missouri, Saline Co., Marshall
Type: Transcript
Online: Ancestry
Title: Saline County, Missouri: Ridge Park Cemetery Records
Notes, URL: More than 4,500 entries. From Elizabeth Prather Ellsberry, *Ridge Park Cemetery of Marshall, Saline County, Missouri Part I & Ridge Park Cemetery Association of Marshall, Saline County, Missouri Part II.* <www.ancestry.com/search/rectype/inddbs/5798.htm>

Missouri, Sullivan Co.
Type: Transcript
Online: Ancestry
Title: Sullivan County, Missouri Cemetery Records, Vols. 1-5
Notes, URL: 8,004 entries. From Elizabeth Prather Ellsberry, *Cemetery Inscriptions of Sullivan County, Missouri Volumes 1-5.* <www.ancestry.com/search/rectype/inddbs/6064.htm>

Montana, Ravalli Co.
Type: Transcript
Year Range: Late 1800s to 2000
Online: Ancestry
Title: Missoula and Ravalli County, Montana Cemeteries
Notes, URL: More than 4,800 names. <www.ancestry.com/search/rectype/inddbs/5449.htm>

Montana, Ravalli Co., Stevensville
Type: Transcript

Year Range: 1800s–1900s
Online: Ancestry
Title: Stevensville, Ravalli County, Montana Cemeteries
Notes, URL: <www.ancestry.com/search/rectype/inddbs/4354.htm>

Nevada, Washoe Co., Reno
Type: Abstract
Year Range: 1904–1919
Online: Ancestry
Title: Ross-Burke Funeral Records, Reno, Nevada, 1904–19
Notes, URL: Over 2,200 entries. <www.ancestry.com/search/rectype/inddbs/3625.htm>

New Hampshire
Type: Digital images of pages containing transcripts
Year Range: 1600s–1900s
CD-ROM: $29.99, Genealogy.com, CD #523
Online: Genealogy Library
Title: Maine & New Hampshire Settlers, 1600s–1900s
Notes, URL: Includes *Colonial Gravestone Inscriptions in the State of New Hampshire* containing 12,500 names. <www.genealogy.com/523facd.html>

New Hampshire, Merrimack Co., Concord
Type: Digital images
Online: F&LH
Title: Religious services and address of William L. Foster, at the consecration of Blossom Hill Cemetery, Concord, N.H., Friday, July 13, 1860

New Hampshire, Rockingham Co., New Castle
Type: Transcript
Year Range: 1742–1956
Online: NEHGS
Title: Record Book of New Castle, New Hampshire
Notes, URL: New Castle Cemetery Inscriptions. <www.newenglandancestors.org/research/database/vr_newcastle/Default.asp>

New Jersey, Essex Co.
Type: Images of pages containing transcriptions
Year Range: Before 1800
Online: F&LH
Title: Bloomfield and Montclair cemetery inscriptions before 1800
Notes, URL: By David R. Anderson.

New Jersey, Essex Co., Glen Ridge
Type: Images of pages containing transcriptions
Online: F&LH
Title: Glen Ridge cemetery
Notes, URL: By the Glen Ridge Cemetery Assn.

New Jersey, Essex Co., Irvington
Type: Images of pages containing transcriptions
Year Range: 1842–1971
Online: F&LH
Title: Clinton Cemetery, Irvington, New Jersey, 1842–1971: history-register of lots-inscriptions

New Jersey, Morris Co.
Type: Images of pages containing transcriptions
Online: F&LH
Title: Inscriptions on the tomb stones and monuments in the grave yards at Whippany and Hanover, Morris County, N.J., 1894

New Jersey, Morris Co.
Type: Transcript
Year Range: Up to 1894
Online: Ancestry
Title: Morris County, New Jersey Cemetery Inscriptions
Notes, URL: Over 2,000 names. <www.ancestry.com/search/rectype/inddbs/4763.htm>

New Jersey, Passaic Co., Paterson
Type: Digital images of a book
Online: F&LH
Title: History and description of Cedar Lawn Cemetery at Paterson, New Jersey
Notes, URL: A book by William Nelson.

New Jersey, Somerset, Bernardsville
Type: Digital images
Online: F&LH
Title: Methodist Cemetery, Bernardsville, N.J.: 151 graves

New Jersey, Sussex Co., Sparta
Type: Images of pages containing transcripts
Year Range: 1787–1924
Online: F&LH
Title: Behold and see, as you pass by: epitaphs in the old cemetery, 1787–1924, of the First Presbyterian Church of Sparta
Notes, URL: By Mary E. Eppler.

New Jersey, Union Co., Rahway
Type: Digital images
Online: F&LH
Title: Descriptive sketch of the Rahway Cemetery

New Jersey, Union Co., Scotch Plains
Type: Digital images
Online: F&LH
Title: Cemetery inscriptions: old part of the Baptist Church cemetery, Scotch Plains, New Jersey
Notes, URL: Typescript by Josephine M. Hollingsworth, et al.

New Jersey, Union Co., Scotch Plains
Type: Images of pages containing transcripts
Online: F&LH
Title: God's acre: a study of selected gravestones in the Baptist Church cemetery Scotch Plains, New Jersey
Notes, URL: By the Scotch Plains-Fanwood High School (N.J.). Chapter of the Distributive Education Clubs of America.

New Jersey, Union Co., Westfield
Type: Images of pages containing transcripts
Online: F&LH
Title: Inscriptions from the cemetery of the Presbyterian Church at Westfield in New Jersey from the year 1740 to the year 1899
Notes, URL: By George W. Thomas.

New Jersey, Union Co., Westfield
Type: Digital images of a book containing transcripts
Online: F&LH
Title: The Revolutionary cemetery in Westfield, New Jersey
Notes, URL: By Henry C. Hamilton.

New York
Type: Digital images of a book containing transcripts
Online: F&LH
Title: Cemeteries in Kings and Queens Counties, Long Island, New York
Notes, URL: By William A. Eardeley.

New York
Type: Digital images of a book containing transcripts
Online: Free
Title: Cemeteries in Kings and Queens Counties, Long Island, New York
Notes, URL: By William A. Eardeley. <http://freepages.genealogy.rootsweb.com/~longislandgenealogy/CemeteriesKingsQueens.pdf>

New York
Type: Images of pages containing transcripts
Online: F&LH
Title: Essex and Warren County cemetery records
Notes, URL: By Frank Haviland.

New York
Type: Images of pages containing transcripts
Online: F&LH
Title: Inscriptions from Quaker burying grounds with notes: Purchase, West Chester Co., Chappaqua, West Chester Co., Pawling, Dutchess Co., (Quaker Hill), Bethel, Dutchess Co., index
Notes, URL: By Francis F. Spies.

New York
Type: Photos, transcripts
Online: Free
Title: Long Island Genealogy: Long Island Cemetery Information
Notes, URL: <www.longislandgenealogy.com>

New York, Albany Co.
Type: Digital images
Online: F&LH
Title: A hand book for the Albany Rural Cemetery: with an appendix on emblems
Notes, URL: By Edward Fitzgerald.

New York, Albany Co., Berne
Type: Transcript
Online: Free
Title: Berne Historical Project
Notes, URL: <www.bernehistory.org>

New York, Allegany Co.
Type: Digital images of a book containing transcripts
Online: F&LH
Title: Gravestone inscriptions in Allegany Co., New York: including cemeteries in Granger, East Canadea, Allen Center, Canadea, Hume, Houghton, and Centerville
Notes, URL: By Gertrude A. Barber.

New York, Allegany Co.
Type: Digital images of a book containing transcripts
Online: F&LH
Title: Gravestone inscriptions of Allegany County, N.Y.: including cemeteries in Filmore and Hume, N.Y.
Notes, URL: By Gertrude A. Barber.

New York, Allegany Co.
Type: Transcript
Online: Free
Title: Painted Hills Genealogy Society: Allegany Co., NY, Cemeteries
Notes, URL: Several cemeteries. <www.paintedhills.org/allco.html>

New York, Bronx Co., Kings Bridge
Type: Digital images containing transcripts
Online: F&LH
Title: Burials in the Dyckman-Nagel burial ground and the Berrian graveyards near Kingsbridge, New York City
Notes, URL: By Fred C. Haacker.

New York, Cattaraugus Co.
Type: Transcripts
Online: Free
Title: Painted Hills Genealogy Society: Cattaraugus Co., NY, Cemeteries
Notes, URL: <www.paintedhills.org/cattco.html>

New York, Cattaraugus Co.
Type: Images of pages containing transcripts
Online: F&LH
Title: Gravestone inscriptions in Cattaraugus Co., New York: including cemeteries in the towns of Freedom, Franklinville, and Yorkshire
Notes, URL: 4 vols. by Gertrude A. Barber.

New York, Cayuga Co., Throop
Type: Digital images of a book containing transcripts
Online: F&LH
Title: Inscriptions on gravestones in Pine Hill Cemetery, town of Throop, Cayuga County, N.Y.
Notes, URL: By R.F. Keeler.

New York, Chautauqua Co.
Type: Digital images of a book containing transcripts
Online: F&LH
Title: Gravestone inscriptions of Chautauqua Cemetery, Chautauqua, N.Y.: Hunt family private cemetery, Chautauqua, N.Y., Magnolia Cemetery, Magnolia Springs, N.Y., Bemus Point, N.Y.
Notes, URL: A book by Minnie Cohen.

New York, Chautauqua Co.
Type: Transcripts
Online: Free
Title: Painted Hills Genealogy Society: Chautauqua Co., N.Y., Cemeteries
Notes, URL: <www.paintedhills.org/chautco.html>

New York, Chautauqua Co., Jamestown
Type: Digital images of a book containing transcripts
Online: F&LH
Title: The organization and dedication ceremonies of Lake-View Cemetery

New York, Chautauqua Co., Sherman
Type: Digital images of a book containing transcripts
Online: F&LH
Title: Yorker cemetery record, Sherman, New York
Notes, URL: By the French Creek Yorkers.

New York, Columbia Co.
Type: Digital images of transcripts
Online: F&LH
Title: Gravestone inscriptions of Columbia County, New York
Notes, URL: By Minnie Cohen.

New York, Columbia Co.
Type: Digital images of a book containing transcripts
Online: F&LH
Title: Gravestone inscriptions of the Esselstyne Farm on road from Martindale to Harlemville, . . . : all in Columbia County, N.Y.
Notes, URL: A book by Minnie Cohen with inscriptions from several cemeteries.

New York, Columbia Co.
Type: Digital images of a book containing transcripts
Online: F&LH
Title: Gravestone inscriptions of the Village Cemetery, Hillsdale, . . . all in Columbia County, N.Y.
Notes, URL: A book by Minnie Cohen with inscriptions from several cemeteries.

New York, Columbia Co.
Type: Digital images of a book containing transcripts
Online: F&LH
Title: Gravestone inscriptions of the Boston Corners Cemetery, Boston Corners, . . . all in Columbia County, N.Y.
Notes, URL: A book by Minnie Cohen with inscriptions from several cemeteries.

New York, Columbia Co.
Type: Digital images of a book containing transcripts
Online: F&LH
Title: Gravestone inscriptions of the cemetery adjoining the Reformed Church of Linlithgo, town of

Livingston . . . all in Columbia County, N.Y.
Notes, URL: A book by Minnie Cohen with inscriptions from several cemeteries.

New York, Columbia Co.
Type: Images of pages containing transcripts
Online: F&LH
Title: Inscriptions from graveyards in the northern part of Columbia County, New York, in the vicinity of Chatham, New Britain, Malden Bridge, etc.
Notes, URL: By Ralph D. Phillips.

New York, Columbia Co., Germantown
Type: Images of pages containing transcripts
Online: F&LH
Title: Gravestone inscriptions of the Germantown Reformed Church Cemetery, Germantown
Notes, URL: By Minnie Cohen.

New York, Columbia Co., Hillsdale
Type: Images of typed pages
Online: F&LH
Title: Cemetery records of Old Orchard Cemetery, Hillsdale, Columbia County, N.Y.
Notes, URL: By Harriet M. Wiles.

New York, Columbia Co., Hillsdale
Type: Digital images
Online: F&LH
Title: A History of the establishment of the Hillsdale Rural Cemetery Association: its proceedings, and their results

New York, Columbia Co., Hudson
Type: Digital images of a book containing transcripts
Online: F&LH
Title: Gravestone inscriptions of the Hudson City cemetery, Hudson, Columbia County, N.Y.
Notes, URL: By Minnie Cohen.

New York, Cortland Co.
Type: Digital images
Online: F&LH
Title: Rules, regulations and by-laws: together with a brief historical sketch of Cortland Rural Cemetery Association

New York, Delaware Co., Stamford
Type: Images of pages containing transcripts
Online: F&LH
Title: Tombstone inscriptions in some old cemeteries near Stamford, Delaware County, New York
Notes, URL: By Don McPherson.

New York, Dutchess Co.
Type: Digital images containing transcripts
Online: F&LH
Title: Burying Grounds of Sharon, Connecticut, Amenia and North East New York
Notes, URL: By L. Van Alystyne.

New York, Dutchess Co.
Type: Images of pages containing transcripts
Year Range: 1733–1895
Online: F&LH
Title: Dutchess County, New York cemeteries
Notes, URL: 5 vols. By William A. Eardeley.

New York, Dutchess Co., Fishkill
Type: Images of pages containing transcripts
Online: F&LH
Title: Some of the oldest in the rural cemetery—Fishkill, Dutchess Co., N.Y.
Notes, URL: By William P. Horton.

New York, Erie Co.
Type: Digital images containing transcripts
Online: F&LH
Title: Gravestone inscriptions from cemeteries in Erie County, New York
Notes, URL: By Gertrude A. Barber.

New York, Erie Co., Buffalo
Type: Transcript
Year Range: 1875–1920
Online: Free
Title: Concordia Cemetery Burial Records (Buffalo, NY)
Notes, URL: 8,400 burials. <http://freepages.genealogy.rootsweb.com/~jillaine/concordia/>

New York, Essex Co.
Type: Digital images of a book containing transcripts
Online: F&LH
Title: Essex County cemetery inscriptions
Notes, URL: By Laura O. Jennings.

New York, Genesee Co.
Type: Digital images of a book containing transcripts
Online: F&LH
Title: Tombstone inscriptions from the abandoned cemeteries and farm burials of Genesee County
Notes, URL: By LaVerne C. Cooley.

New York, Kings Co., Brooklyn
Type: Digital images of a book containing transcripts
Online: F&LH
Title: Dutch Reformed Cemetery, Flatbush, Kings County, New York: 1754 per 1913
Notes, URL: By William A. Eardeley.

New York, Kings Co., Brooklyn
Type: Digital images
Online: F&LH
Title: Green-Wood Cemetery: a history of the institution from 1838 to 1864
Notes, URL: By N. Cleaveland.

New York, Madison Co.
Type: Digital images of a book containing transcripts
Online: F&LH
Title: Cemetery inscriptions of Madison Co., N.Y.
Notes, URL: By Mary K. Meyer, et al.

New York, Nassau Co.
Type: Digital images of a book containing transcripts
Year Range: 1832–1898
Online: F&LH
Title: Bethpage and Farmingdale, town of Oyster Bay, Queens County, now Nassau County, Long Island, New York: three cemeteries, 1832–1898
Notes, URL: By William A. Eardeley.

New York, Nassau Co., Freeport
Type: Digital images of a book containing transcripts
Online: F&LH
Title: Village of Freeport, town of Hempstead, county of Nassau, Long Island, New York, Presbyterian Cemetery around the church
Notes, URL: By William A. Eardeley.

New York, Nassau Co., Hempstead
Type: Digital images of a book containing transcripts
Online: F&LH
Title: Cemetery Inscriptions from Hempstead, Long Island, New York
Notes, URL: By Josephine C. Frost.

New York, Nassau Co., Hempstead
Type: Digital images of a book containing transcripts
Online: Free
Title: Cemetery Inscriptions from Hempstead, Long Island, New York
Notes, URL: By Josephine C. Frost. <http://freepages.genealogy.rootsweb.com/

~longislandgenealogy/cemHempstead.pdf>

New York, Nassau Co., Manhasset
Type: Digital images of a book containing transcripts
Online: F&LH
Title: Cemetery inscriptions from Episcopal and Dutch Reformed church yards at Manhasset, Long Island
Notes, URL: By Josephine C. Frost.

New York, New York (City)
Type: Images of pages containing transcripts
Online: F&LH
Title: Gravestone inscriptions of Trinity Cemetery, New York City, New York
Notes, URL: 2 vols. by Ray C. Sawyer.

New York, New York (City)
Type: Transcript
Year Range: 1830–1937
Online: Ancestry (free)
Title: Marble Cemetery Records, New York City, New York, 1830–1937
Notes, URL: 2,060 names. <www.ancestry.com/search/rectype/inddbs/4645.htm>

New York, Oneida Co., Whitesboro
Type: Digital images
Online: F&LH
Title: Historical incidents relating to the Whitesboro Cemetery, Whitesboro, N.Y., 1879

New York, Onondaga Co., Skaneateles
Type: Transcript
Year Range: 1796–1988
Online: Free
Title: The Skaneateles Historical Society
Notes, URL: 3,000 records from St. Mary's Cemetery & over 7,900 records from the Lakeview Cemetery. <www.skaneateles.com/historical/index.shtml>

New York, Onondaga Co., Syracuse
Type: Digital images of a book containing transcripts
Online: F&LH
Title: History of Oakwood Cemetery
Notes, URL: By H.P. Smith.

New York, Ontario Co.
Type: Digital images of a book containing transcripts
Online: F&LH
Title: Inscriptions from Farmington cemetery (Friends Cemetery)
Notes, URL: A book by the Perinton Historical Society (Monroe County, N.Y.).

New York, Ontario Co., East Bloomfield
Type: Digital images of a book containing transcripts
Online: F&LH
Title: East Bloomfield Cemetery
Notes, URL: By Virginia Moscrip, et al.

New York, Ontario Co., Shortsville
Type: Digital images of a book containing transcripts
Online: F&LH
Title: The old Shortsville Cemetery: also known as the Theophilus Short Cemetery, and Evergreen Cemetery . . . burials from 1828–1907
Notes, URL: A book by James DeVoll.

New York, Orange Co.
Type: Digital images of a book containing transcripts
Online: F&LH
Title: Graveyard inscriptions of Orange County, N.Y.: v. 1-2
Notes, URL: By Gertrude A. Barber.

New York, Orange Co.
Type: Digital images of a book containing transcripts
Year Range:
CD-ROM: $24.50 (Mac/Win), Long Island Genealogy
Title: Genealogy and History of Orange County, New York
Notes, URL: Graveyard inscriptions. Orange County Patriot, marriages & deaths, 1828–1831. St. James Protestant Episcopal Church records, Goshen. All by Gertrude A. Barber. <http://genealogycds.com/sales/Orange.htm>

New York, Orange Co., Montgomery
Type: Digital images of a book containing transcripts
Online: F&LH
Title: Inscriptions of German Reformed Cemetery at Montgomery, Orange County, New York
Notes, URL: By Lila J. Roney.

New York, Otsego Co.
Type: Digital images of a book containing transcripts
Year Range:
CD-ROM: $24.50 (Mac/Win), Long Island Genealogy
Title: Deaths, Marriages, and Wills from Otsego County, New York
Notes, URL: Catholic Cemetery at Richfield Springs, Exeter Cemetery at Exeter & Lake View Cemetery (Protestant) near Richfield Springs. All by Gertrude A. Barber. <http://genealogycds.com/sales/Otsego.htm>

New York, Otsego Co.
Type: Digital images of a book containing transcripts
Online: F&LH
Title: Tombstone inscriptions in the Catholic Cemetery at Richfield Springs, N.Y. and also in the Exeter Cemetery at Exeter, N.Y.: both located in Otsego County, N.Y.
Notes, URL: A book by Gertrude A. Barber.

New York, Otsego Co., Richfield Springs
Type: Digital images of a book containing transcripts
Online: F&LH
Title: Tombstone inscriptions in the Lake View Cemetery (Protestant) near Richfield Springs: Otsego County, New York
Notes, URL: By Gertrude A. Barber.

New York, Putnam Co.
Type: Digital images of a book containing transcripts
Online: F&LH
Title: Cemetery inscriptions of Putnam County, N.Y.
Notes, URL: By William P. Horton.

New York, Putnam Co.
Type: Digital images of a book containing transcripts
Year Range: 1794–1914
Online: F&LH
Title: Putnam County, New York cemeteries: 1794–1914
Notes, URL: By William A. Eardeley.

New York, Queens Co., Jamaica
Type: Digital images of a book containing transcripts
Online: F&LH
Title: Springfield, Jamaica, Queens County, Long Island, New York Cemetery: 1735 or 1760 to 1909
Notes, URL: By William A. Eardeley.

New York, Queens Co., Queens
Type: Digital images of a book containing transcripts
Online: F&LH
Title: Description of private and family cemeteries in the borough of Queens
Notes, URL: By Charles U. Powell, et al.

New York, Rensselaer Co.
Type: Images of pages containing transcripts

Online: F&LH
Title: Some Rensselaer County gravestone inscriptions
Notes, URL: By Charles Shepard, et al.

New York, Rensselaer Co., Lansingburgh
Type: Images of pages containing transcripts
Online: F&LH
Title: The burial grounds of Lansingburgh, Rensselaer County, New York
Notes, URL: By Frances D. Broderick.

New York, Rensselaer Co., Nassau
Type: Images of pages containing transcripts
Online: F&LH
Title: Complete list of all gravestone inscriptions in Nassau-Schodack Cemetery at Nassau, Rensselaer County, N.Y.
Notes, URL: By Ralph D. Phillips.

New York, Rockland Co., Nyack
Type: Digital images containing transcripts
Online: F&LH
Title: Gravestone inscriptions of the Oak Hill Cemetery, Nyack, N.Y.
Notes, URL: By Gertrude A. Barber.

New York, Saint Lawrence Co., Canton
Type: Digital images of a book containing transcripts
Online: F&LH
Title: Inscriptions from the Silas Wright Cemetery and St. Mary's Old Cemetery, Canton, N.Y.
Notes, URL: A book by Edward F. Heim.

New York, Saratoga Co.
Type: Transcript
Online: Ancestry
Title: Saratoga County, New York, Cemetery Records, Volume I
Notes, URL: More than 2,400 entries. From Elizabeth Prather Ellsberry, *Cemetery Records of Saratoga County, New York, Volume I.* <www.ancestry.com/search/rectype/inddbs/5540.htm>

New York, Saratoga Co.
Type: Digital images of a book containing transcriptions
Online: F&LH
Title: Sweetman and West Charlton Cemeteries: Saratoga County, New York
Notes, URL: By the Federal Writers' Project.

New York, Saratoga Co., Clifton Park
Type: Digital images of a book containing transcriptions
Online: F&LH
Title: Town of Clifton Park cemetery epitaphs: Saratoga County, New York State.
Notes, URL: By Howard I. Becker.

New York, Saratoga Co., Half Moon
Type: Digital images containing transcripts
Online: F&LH
Title: Town of Half Moon cemeteries
Notes, URL: By Henry C. Ritchie.

New York, Schuyler Co., Reading
Type: Digital images
Year Range: 1813–1897
Online: F&LH
Title: Cemetery and other records, 1813–1897

New York, Seneca Co.
Type: Digital images of a book containing transcriptions
Online: F&LH
Title: Mac Neal Dutch Reformed Cemetery, Seneca County, N.Y.: vital records
Notes, URL: By Helen H. Ellis.

New York, Steuben Co.
Type: Transcript
Online: Free
Title: Painted Hills Genealogy Society: Steuben Co., NY, Cemeteries
Notes, URL: <www.paintedhills.org/steuben.html>

New York, Suffolk Co., Amityville
Type: Digital images
Online: F&LH
Title: Amityville, Town of Babylon, Suffolk County, Long Island, New York: formerly in the Town of Huntington, Suffolk County, Long Island, New York: Cemeteries and Bible Records
Notes, URL: By William A. Eardeley.

New York, Suffolk Co., Amityville
Type: Digital images
Year Range: 1813–1913
CD-ROM: $24.50 (Mac/Win), Long Island-Genealogy
Online: Free
Title: Amityville, L.I., N.Y. Cemeteries and Bible Records—by William Applebie Eardeley
Notes, URL: Includes some Bible records. Online at <www.longislandgenealogy.com/Amityville/css/Amityville.htm>; CD at <http://genealogycds.com/sales/Amityville.htm>

New York, Sullivan Co.
Type: Digital images of a book containing transcriptions
Online: F&LH
Title: Graveyard inscriptions of Baptist Church Cemetery, Parksville, . . . all located in Sullivan County, New York
Notes, URL: A book by Gertrude A. Barber with inscriptions from several cemeteries.

New York, Sullivan Co.
Type: Digital images of a book containing transcriptions
Online: F&LH
Title: Gravestone inscriptions of Gonsalus Farm Cemetery, Wurtsboro, N.Y., . . . all located in Sullivan County
Notes, URL: A book by Gertrude A. Barber with inscriptions from several cemeteries.

New York, Sullivan Co.
Type: Digital images of a book containing transcriptions
Online: F&LH
Title: Graveyard inscriptions of New Vernon Cemetery, also known as Old Baptist School Cemetery, New Vernon, . . . all located in Sullivan County, New York
Notes, URL: A book by Gertrude A. Barber with inscriptions from several cemeteries.

New York, Sullivan Co.
Type: Digital images of a book containing transcriptions
Online: F&LH
Title: Graveyard inscriptions of Old Bethel Cemetery, . . . all located in Sullivan County, New York
Notes, URL: A book by Gertrude A. Barber with inscriptions from several cemeteries.

New York, Sullivan Co.
Type: Digital images of a book containing transcriptions
Online: F&LH
Title: Gravestone inscriptions of Grahamsville Reformed Dutch Church, Grahamsville, N.Y. . . . all located in Sullivan County, N.Y.
Notes, URL: A book by Gertrude A. Barber with inscriptions from several cemeteries.

New York, Sullivan Co.
Type: Digital images of a book containing transcriptions
Online: F&LH
Title: Graveyard inscriptions of Callicoon Centre Cemetery, Callicoon Centre, Rock Ridge Cemetery, Thompson, Old Youngsville Cemetery, Youngsville, all

located in Sullivan County, New York
Notes, URL: A book by Gertrude A. Barber with inscriptions from several cemeteries.

New York, Sullivan Co.
Type: Digital images of a book containing transcriptions
Online: F&LH
Title: Gravestone inscriptions of Bridgeville Cemetery, Bridgeville, Old Fulton or Fraser Cemetery, Ferndale, Old Fallsburg (Palen's) Cemetery, Fallsburg, all located in Sullivan County, New York
Notes, URL: A book by Gertrude A. Barber with inscriptions from several cemeteries.

New York, Sullivan Co.
Type: Digital images of a book containing transcriptions
Online: F&LH
Title: Gravestone inscriptions of Liberty Town Cemetery (old section) Liberty, Old Moulthrop Cemetery, Kenoza Lake, formerly known as Pike Pond, located in Sullivan County, New York
Notes, URL: A book by Gertrude A. Barber with inscriptions from several cemeteries.

New York, Sullivan Co., Cochecton
Type: Digital images
Online: F&LH
Title: Graveyards of Cohecton [*sic*]
Notes, URL: By Charles T. Curtis.

New York, Sullivan Co., Wurtsboro
Type: Digital images of a book containing transcriptions
Online: F&LH
Title: Gravestone inscriptions, Stanton or Centennial Cemetery, of Wurtsboro of Sullivan County—New York
Notes, URL: By Gertrude A. Barber.

New York, Tioga Co., Spencer
Type: Digital images of a book containing transcriptions
Year Range: 1795–1906
Online: F&LH
Title: Cemetery inscriptions, town of Spencer, New York, 1795–1906
Notes, URL: By Mary F. Hall.

New York, Tompkins Co., Dryden
Type: Images of pages containing transcripts
Online: F&LH
Title: The old cemetery at Dryden, Tompkins County, New York: records of inscriptions and genealogical notes
Notes, URL: By Charles M. Sandwick.

New York, Ulster Co.
Type: Digital images of a book containing transcriptions
Online: F&LH
Title: Old gravestones of Ulster County, New York: twenty-two-thousand inscriptions
Notes, URL: By J. Wilson Poucher, et al.

New York, Ulster Co.
Type: Digital images of a book
CD-ROM: $24.50 (Mac/Win), Long Island Genealogy
Title: Ulster County N.Y. Genealogical and Historical Information
Notes, URL: Includes *Old Gravestones of Ulster County, New York*: twenty-two-thousand inscriptions, by J. Wilson Poucher. <http://genealogycds.com/sales/Ulster.htm>

New York, Ulster Co., New Paltz
Type: Digital images of a book containing transcriptions
Year Range: 1860–1962
Online: F&LH
Title: New Paltz rural cemetery records, 1860–1962
Notes, URL: By Ruth P. Heidgerd.

New York, Wayne Co., Lyons
Type: Digital images of a book containing transcriptions
Online: F&LH
Title: Marriages and deaths from the Lyons Republican and inscriptions from the Lyons Rural Cemetery: Nelson, N.Y. and Aurora, N.Y.
Notes, URL: By Harriett M. Wiles.

New York, Wayne Co., Newark
Type: Digital images of a book containing transcriptions
Online: F&LH
Title: Cemetery records from the Willow Avenue Cemetery, Newark, Wayne County, New York
Notes, URL: A book by Harriet M. Wiles.

New York, Westchester Co.
Type: Digital images of a book containing transcriptions
Online: F&LH
Title: Cemetery inscriptions of Westchester County, N.Y.
Notes, URL: 2 vols. by William P. Horton.

New York, Westchester Co.
Type: Digital images of a book containing transcriptions
CD-ROM: $24.50 (Mac/Win), Long Island Genealogy
Title: Cemetery inscriptions of Westchester County, N.Y.
Notes, URL: Books by William P. Horton and Francis F. Spies. <http://genealogycds.com/sales/WestchesterColl.htm>

New York, Westchester Co., Bedford
Type: Digital images of a book containing transcriptions
Online: F&LH
Title: Inscriptions copied from graveyards in Bedford, Westchester County, New York: with genealogical notes
Notes, URL: By Francis F. Spies.

New York, Westchester Co., Larchmont
Type: Digital images of a book containing transcriptions
Online: F&LH
Title: Names on stones in Quaker Cemetery on Post Road, Larchmont, N.Y.

New York, Westchester Co., Mount Kisco
Type: Digital images of a book containing transcriptions
Online: F&LH
Title: St. Mark's Episcopal Cemetery, Mt. Kisco, N.Y.
Notes, URL: A book by William A. Eardeley, et al.

New York, Westchester Co., Mount Vernon
Type: Digital images of a book containing transcriptions
Online: F&LH
Title: St. Paul's Church, Eastchester N.Y.: situated near South Columbus Avenue and South Third Avenue, Mount Vernon, N.Y.: gravestone inscriptions, with genealogical notes
Notes, URL: By Francis F. Spies.

New York, Westchester Co., New Rochelle
Type: Digital images of a book containing transcriptions
Online: F&LH
Title: New Rochelle, New York, cemeteries: part 1, inscriptions from graveyards of Trinity Church, First Methodist Episcopal Church, Methodist Episcopal churchyard on Main Street, Coutant Yard: part 2, Beechwoods Cemetery
Notes, URL: A book by Francis F. Spies.

New York, Westchester Co., Pound Ridge
Type: Digital images
Year Range: 1860–1871
Online: F&LH
Title: Burials in and around Pound Ridge, N.Y.: 1860 to 1871
Notes, URL: By Mildred E. Struble, et al.

New York, Westchester Co., Pound Ridge
Type: Digital images of a book containing transcriptions
Online: F&LH
Title: Tombstone records of eighteen cemeteries in Poundridge, Westchester County, N.Y.
Notes, URL: By Mable L. Jordan, et al.

New York, Westchester Co., Rye
Type: Digital images of a book containing transcriptions
Online: F&LH
Title: The Jay Cemetery, Rye, New York: established 1815, incorporated 1906 under New York law as a family cemetery corporation.

New York, Westchester Co., Tarrytown
Type: Digital images
Online: F&LH
Title: Sleepy Hollow Cemetery at Tarrytown

New York, Westchester Co., Yonkers
Type: Digital images of a book containing transcriptions
Online: F&LH
Title: Inscriptions copied from gravestones in Yonkers, N.Y.: Oakland Cemetery
Notes, URL: By Francis F. Spies.

New York, Westchester Co., Yonkers
Type: Digital images of a book containing transcriptions
Online: F&LH
Title: Inscriptions copied from the gravestones in St. John's Cemetery, Yonkers, N.Y.
Notes, URL: By Francis F. Spies.

New York, Westchester Co., Yonkers
Type: Digital images of a book containing transcriptions
Online: F&LH
Title: Inscriptions from graveyards in Yonkers & Inwood, N.Y.
Notes, URL: By Francis F. Spies.

New York, Wyoming Co.
Type: Digital images of a book containing transcriptions
Online: F&LH
Title: Gravestone inscriptions of Wyoming County, N.Y.: including cemeteries in Sheldon and Bennington, N.Y.
Notes, URL: By Gertrude A. Barber.

New York, Wyoming Co.
Type: Digital images of a book containing transcriptions
Online: F&LH
Title: Gravestone inscriptions of Wyoming County, N.Y.: including cemeteries in Silver Springs, Hermitage, and Genesee Falls
Notes, URL: By Gertrude A. Barber.

New York, Wyoming Co.
Type: Digital images of a book containing transcriptions
Online: F&LH
Title: Tombstone inscriptions from cemeteries located in Wyoming County, New York
Notes, URL: By Gertrude A. Barber.

New York, Yates Co.
Type: Digital images of a book containing transcriptions
Online: F&LH
Title: Inscriptions from three abandonded [*sic*] cemeteries in Yates County, New York
Notes, URL: *Friends Burying Ground, Stoddard Family Cemetery, Thomas Family Cemetery*. A book by Stafford E. Cleveland, et al.

North Carolina, Cabarrus Co.
Type: Images of pages containing transcripts
Online: F&LH
Title: Tombstone records of St. John's Lutheran Graveyard, Cabarrus County, North Carolina from the 18th century to June, 1936
Notes, URL: By Ruth Blackwelder, et al.

North Carolina, Edgecombe Co.
Type: Transcripts
Year Range: 1720–1880
Online: Ancestry
Title: Edgecombe County, North Carolina Vital Records, 1720–1880
Notes, URL: Over 10,000 marriage records, obituaries, & gravestone inscriptions. *From Early Families of Edgecombe County, North Carolina, Its Past and Present.* <www.ancestry.com/search/rectype/inddbs/4990.htm>

North Carolina, Forsyth Co.
Type: Digital images
Online: F&LH
Title: Graveyard register of Friedland Moravian Church, Forsyth County, N.C.
Notes, URL: By Adelaide L. Fries.

North Carolina, Iredell Co.
Type: Digital images of a book containing transcripts
Online: F&LH
Title: Lewis grave yard with mention of some early settlers along Fifth Creek, Iredell County, N.C.

North Dakota, Morton Co.
Type: Abstracts
Online: Free
Title: Morton County N.D. Cemeteries
Notes, URL: <http://pixel.cs.vt.edu/pub/cemeteries/nodak/mortonnd.txt>

Ohio, Delaware Co.
Type: Transcript
Online: Free
Title: Delaware County Ohio Cemeteries
Notes, URL: <http://delcohist.tripod.com/burials.htm>

Ohio, Franklin Co.
Type: Transcripts, photos
Online: Free
Title: Franklin County, Ohio, Gravestone Photos & Etc.
Notes, URL: <http://homepages.rootsweb.com/~rocky/Franklin_Cemeteries/index.html>

Ohio, Hamilton Co., Cincinnati
Type: Digital images of a book
Online: F&LH
Title: Address delivered on the consecration of the Spring Grove Cemetery, near Cincinnati: August 20th, 1845
Notes, URL: By John McLean.

Ohio, Hamilton Co., Cincinnati
Type: Digital images
Online: F&LH
Title: Charter and by-laws of the Cemetery of Spring Grove: with the revised rules and regulations: adopted A.D. 1886.

Ohio, Licking Co.
Type: Transcripts
Year Range: 1807–2001
Online: Free
Title: Donald Davis Young's Home Page
Notes, URL: Gravestone transcriptions from 3 cemeteries. <www.kinfinder.com>

Ohio, Lucas Co.
Type: Transcript
Year Range: Up to 1971

Online: Ancestry
Title: Swan Creek Cemetery Inscriptions, Monclova, Ohio
Notes, URL: <www.ancestry.com/search/rectype/inddbs/4216.htm>

Ohio, Ottawa Co.
Type: Digital images of a book containing transcripts
Online: F&LH
Title: Cemetery inscriptions of Ottawa County, Ohio
Notes, URL: By the Ohio Genealogical Society, Ottawa County Chapter.

Oklahoma, Payne Co., Yale
Type: Transcript
Online: Ancestry
Title: Lawson Cemetery Records, Payne County, Oklahoma
Notes, URL: Over 3,500 names. <www.ancestry.com/search/rectype/inddbs/3902.htm>

Oregon, Clackamas Co.
Type: Digital images
Online: F&LH
Title: Collection of data on cemeteries of Clackamas County
Notes, URL: By the Clackamas County Pomona Grange.

Oregon, Harney Co.
Type: Transcript
Online: Ancestry
Title: Harney County, Oregon, Cemetery Records
Notes, URL: Over 4,600 names. <www.ancestry.com/search/rectype/inddbs/4957.htm>

Pennsylvania
Type: Transcript
Online: Free
Title: PA Roots
Notes, URL: 87,570 cemetery transcripts from Armstrong, Clarion, Clearfield, Forest, Indiana, Jefferson, Lancaster, and Westmoreland counties. <www.pa-roots.com/cemetery.html>

Pennsylvania
Type: Photographs of gravestones
Year Range: 1740s–late 1800s
Online: Free
Title: Stones of Faith: Pennsylvania Germans and Their Gravestones
Notes, URL: Graveyards in Lancaster, Berks, Lehigh, Lebanon, Northampton, & Bucks Counties. <www.pagstones.com>

Pennsylvania, Armstrong Co.
Type: Digital images of a book containing inscriptions
Online: F&LH
Title: Armstrong County cemetery records
Notes, URL: By Phyllis M. Gumbert, et al.

Pennsylvania, Beaver Co.
Type: Digital images of a book containing inscriptions
Online: F&LH
Title: Beaver County cemetery records
Notes, URL: A book by Harvey E. Faulk, et al., with inscriptions from several cemeteries.

Pennsylvania, Berks Co., Centre Township
Type: Digital images
Online: F&LH
Title: A directory of burials on Salem Belleman's graveyard, 1746–1972
Notes, URL: By Milton K. & Luella E. Blatt.

Pennsylvania, Chester Co., Brandywine
Type: Digital images
Online: F&LH
Title: Brandywine Manor Church Cemetery: an address
Notes, URL: By John F. Lewis.

Pennsylvania, Chester Co., Cheyney Station
Type: Text of a book containing transcripts
Online: F&LH
Title: The Cheyney burial ground on Concord Road, north of Cheyney Station, Chester County, Pa.

Pennsylvania, Cumberland Co., Carlisle
Type: Digital images
Online: F&LH
Title: Historical address, the Meeting House Springs graveyard
Notes, URL: By Allan D. Thompson.

Pennsylvania, Cumberland Co., Carlisle
Type: Page images containing transcripts
Year Range: As of 1898
Online: F&LH
Title: Memories of Carlisle's old graveyard
Notes, URL: By Sarah W. Parkinson.

Pennsylvania, Cumberland Co., Carlisle
Type: Text of a book containing inscriptions
Year Range: As of 1898
Online: Genealogy Library
Title: Memories of Carlisle's Old Graveyard
Notes, URL: By Sarah Woods Parkinson. Select Subjects | Records | Cemetery | Pennsylvania.

Pennsylvania, Indiana Co.
Type: Images of pages from a book containing transcripts
Online: F&LH
Title: Cemetery records of Indiana County, Pennsylvania
Notes, URL: By Almetta P. Gay, et al.

Pennsylvania, Lancaster Co., Penryn
Type: Images of pages from a book containing transcripts
Year Range: Before 1928
Online: F&LH
Title: Burials in Penryn Cemetery, Penryn, Pa.: list compiled May 30, 1928.

Pennsylvania, McKean Co.
Type: Transcripts
Online: Free
Title: Painted Hills Genealogy Society: McKean Co., PA, Cemeteries
Notes, URL: <www.paintedhills.org/mckeanco.html>

Pennsylvania, Northampton Co.
Type: Images of pages from a book containing transcripts
Online: F&LH
Title: The old graveyards of Northampton and adjacent counties in the state of Pennsylvania
Notes, URL: Only gravestones of persons born before 1780.

Pennsylvania, Northampton Co., Centerville
Type: Images of pages from a book containing transcripts
Online: F&LH
Title: Inscriptions alphabetically arranged of the tombstones in the old cemetery at Stone Church, Northampton County, Pa.
Notes, URL: By Kathryn & William Atchley.

Pennsylvania, Northampton Co., Kreidersville
Type: Images of pages from a book containing transcripts
Online: F&LH
Title: Burial record of Zion's (Stone) Church graveyard and cemetery, near Kreidersville, Northampton Co., Pa.

Pennsylvania, Philadelphia Co., Philadelphia
Type: Images of pages from a book containing transcripts
Year Range: 1721–1863
Online: Ancestry
Title: Philadelphia, Tombstone Inscriptions from Christ Church

Notes, URL: From Edward L. Clark, *Record of the Inscriptions on the Tablets and Gravestones in the Burial-Grounds of Christ Church, Philadelphia.* <www.ancestry.com/search/rectype/inddbs/6413.htm>

Pennsylvania, Potter Co.
Type: Transcripts
Online: Free
Title: Painted Hills Genealogy Society: Potter Co., PA, Cemeteries
Notes, URL: <www.paintedhills.org/potterco.html>

Pennsylvania, Somerset Co.
Type: Images of pages containing transcripts.
Online: F&LH
Title: Tombstone inscriptions of cemeteries, Somerset County, Pa.
Notes, URL: By Della R. Fischer.

Pennsylvania, Washington Co., Cross Creek
Type: Transcript
Year Range: Up to 1894
Online: Ancestry
Title: Cross Creek, Pennsylvania Cemetery History
Notes, URL: Over 1,000 names. <www.ancestry.com/search/rectype/inddbs/4616.htm>

Pennsylvania, Westmoreland Co.
Type: Digital images of a book containing transcripts
Online: F&LH
Title: Tombstone inscriptions of cemeteries in Cook, Donegal, East Huntington, Hempfield, Mount Pleasant, and Unity Townships, Westmoreland County, Pennsylvania
Notes, URL: By Charlotte Hay Beard, et al.

Pennsylvania, Westmoreland Co., Mount Pleasant Township
Type: Images of a book containing transcripts
Online: F&LH
Title: Tombstone inscriptions, cemeteries, Mount Pleasant Township, Westmoreland County, Pennsylvania
Notes, URL: A book by Elizabeth H. Christner, et al.

Pennsylvania, Westmoreland Co., Unity Township
Type: Images of pages containing transcripts
Online: F&LH
Title: Inscriptions of the Unity Presbyterian Church cemetery, Unity Township, Westmoreland County, Pa.
Notes, URL: By Della R. Fischer.

Rhode Island, Bristol Co., Bristol
Type: Digital images of a book
Online: F&LH
Title: The Juniper Hill Cemetery: in Bristol, R.I.
Notes, URL: By Henry Wadsworth Longfellow.

Rhode Island, Washington Co.
Type: Digital images of a book
Online: F&LH
Title: Inscriptions on the gravestones in the old churchyard of St. Paul's Narragansett: North Kingstown, Rhode Island: with a record of the inscriptions in the graveyard of the old church at Wickford

South Carolina, Aiken Co.
Type: Transcript
Online: Ancestry
Title: Aiken County, South Carolina Cemetery Inscriptions
Notes, URL: 5,900 names from 5 cemeteries. <www.ancestry.com/search/rectype/inddbs/4437.htm>

South Carolina, Aiken Co.
Type: Transcript
Online: Ancestry (free)
Title: Aiken County, South Carolina Cemetery Inscriptions: Graniteville
Notes, URL: Over 4,500 names. <www.ancestry.com/search/rectype/inddbs/6082.htm>

South Carolina, Aiken Co.
Type: Transcript
Online: Ancestry (free)
Title: Aiken County, South Carolina: Cemetery Records
Notes, URL: Over 1,400 names. <www.ancestry.com/search/rectype/inddbs/6020.htm>

South Carolina, Laurens Co., Duncan's Creek
Type: Transcript
Online: Ancestry
Title: Duncan's Creek, South Carolina Church Cemetery Records
Notes, URL: Over 500 names. <www.ancestry.com/search/rectype/inddbs/3371.htm>

South Carolina, Pickens Co.
Type: Transcripts
Online: Free
Title: Pickens County South Carolina Genealogy
Notes, URL: <www.scgenealogy.com/pickens/>

Tennessee
Type: Digital images of a book containing transcripts
CD-ROM: $29.99, Genealogy.com, CD #511
Online: Genealogy Library
Title: Early Tennessee Settlers, 1700s–1900s
Notes, URL: Includes *Tennessee Records: Tombstone Inscriptions and Manuscripts.* <www.genealogy.com/511facd.html>

Tennessee, Greene Co.
Type: Transcript
Year Range: Up to 1935
Online: Ancestry
Title: Greene County, Tennessee Cemetery Records
Notes, URL: <www.ancestry.com/search/rectype/inddbs/4334.htm>

Tennessee, Loudon Co.
Type: Transcript
Online: Ancestry
Title: Loudon County, Tennessee Cemetery Inscriptions
Notes, URL: Over 6,200 names. <www.ancestry.com/search/rectype/inddbs/3442.htm>

Texas
Type: Transcripts, photos
Year Range: 1851–pres.
Online: Free
Title: Texas State Cemetery Database
Notes, URL: The burial place for notable citizens. <www.cemetery.state.tx.us/pub/database.htm>

Texas, Cooke Co.
Type: Transcript
Online: Free
Title: Texas Trails
Notes, URL: 99 cemeteries. <http://freepages.genealogy.rootsweb.com/~texastrails/index/>

Texas, Hood Co.
Type: Transcript
Online: Free
Title: Hood County Texas Genealogical Society: Hood County Cemeteries & Headstone Records
Notes, URL: <www.granburydepot.org/MainIndex.htm>

Texas, Johnson Co.
Type: Transcript
Online: Ancestry (free)
Title: Johnson County, Texas, Cemetery Inscriptions
Notes, URL: <www.ancestry.com/search/rectype/inddbs/5652.htm>

Texas, Upshur Co., Pritchett
Type: Transcript
Year Range: mid-1800s–1998
Online: Ancestry
Title: Pleasant Hill Cemetery Inscriptions, Pritchett, Texas
Notes, URL: Over 1,000 names. <www.ancestry.com/search/rectype/inddbs/3355.htm>

Texas, Williamson Co.
Type: Transcript
Online: Free
Title: Cemeteries in Williamson County, Texas
Notes, URL: 200 cemeteries. <www.three-legged-willie.org/cemetery.htm>

Utah
Type: Transcript
Online: Ancestry
Title: Utah Cemetery Inventory
Notes, URL: 350,000 burial records from 250 cemeteries. <www.ancestry.com/search/rectype/inddbs/5232.htm>

Utah
Type: Transcripts
Online: Free
Title: Utah State History: Burials and Cemeteries Database
Notes, URL: Over 400,000 burial records from more than 300 cemeteries. <http://history.utah.gov/library/burials.html>

Utah, Tooele Co., Grantsville
Type: Transcript
Year Range: 1846–1999
Online: Ancestry
Title: Grantsville, Tooele County, Utah Cemetery, 1846–1999
Notes, URL: <www.ancestry.com/search/rectype/inddbs/5098.htm>

Utah, Utah Co.
Type: Abstracts
Online: Ancestry
Title: Utah County, Utah Cemetery Index
Notes, URL: 80,000 entries. <www.ancestry.com/search/rectype/inddbs/3169a.htm>

Vermont, Bennington Co., Bennington
Type: Transcript
Online: Ancestry
Title: Bennington, Vermont Cemetery Inscriptions
Notes, URL: Nearly 12,000 records. <www.ancestry.com/search/rectype/inddbs/3990.htm>

Vermont, Bennington Co., Shaftsbury
Type: Digital images of a book
Online: F&LH
Title: The gravestone records of Shaftsbury, Bennington County,Vermont
Notes, URL: By Levi H. Elwell.

Vermont, Rutland Co.
Type: Digital images of a book containing transcripts
Online: F&LH
Title: Gravestone inscriptions
Notes, URL: By Fannie S. Spurling.

Vermont, Washington Co., Montpelier
Type: Images of pages containing transcripts
Online: F&LH
Title: Services at the dedication of Green Mount Cemetery, Montpelier, Vt., Sept. 15, 1855

Virginia, Page Co., Luray
Type: Transcript
Online: Ancestry
Title: Page County, Virginia, Cemetery Records, Vol. I (Luray Cemetery)
Notes, URL: More than 1,100 names. <www.ancestry.com/search/rectype/inddbs/5757.htm>

Virginia, Shenandoah Co.
Type: Transcript
Online: Ancestry
Title: Shenandoah County, Virginia, Cemetery Records, Vol. 1 (Woodstock)
Notes, URL: More than 1,500 entries. From Elizabeth Prather Ellsberry, *Cemetery Records of Shenandoah County, Virginia Volume I Woodstock, Virginia*. <www.ancestry.com/search/rectype/inddbs/5726.htm>

Virginia, Warren Co., Front Royal
Type: Transcript
Year Range: Early 1800s–1900s
Online: Ancestry
Title: Prospect Hill Cemetery Inscriptions, Front Royal, Virginia
Notes, URL: Over 6,900 records. <www.ancestry.com/search/rectype/inddbs/3436.htm>

Washington, King Co., Seattle
Online: Free
Title: Associated Catholic Cemeteries, Archdiocese of Seattle
Notes, URL: Covers Calvary, Gethsemane, Holyrood, & St. Patrick Cemeteries. <www.acc-seattle.com/accrsrch1.html>

Washington, Whatcom Co.
Type: Transcripts, images
Year Range: Up to 1985
CD-ROM: $15 (Mac/Win)
Title: Cemetery Records of Whatcom County, Washington, Series II, Volumes 1-12 & Master Index
Notes, URL: Records from all 56 cemeteries. Images of Japanese tombstones in Bayview Cemetery. <www.members.aol.com/whatcom59/cemcd.htm>

West Virginia
Type: Transcripts
Online: Ancestry
Title: West Virginia Cemetery Readings, 1941
Notes, URL: Over 5,200 entries. From Historical Records Survey. *Cemetery Readings in West Virginia*. Charleston, W. Va. <www.ancestry.com/search/rectype/inddbs/4266.htm>

Wisconsin, Milwaukee Co.
Type: Transcripts
Year Range: Late 1700s–late 1900s
CD-ROM: $28.50 (Mac/Win), Heritage Books, item #1267
Title: Heritage Books Archives: Wisconsin Vol. 1
Notes, URL: Includes *Old Cemetery Burials of Milwaukee County, Wisconsin, Vols. 1-2*. <www.heritagebooks.com>. Search on "1267."

Military Records

John R. Olmsted's Civil War pension file reveals a wealth of interesting details about his military service (enrolled on 19 September 1861 in Company K, 9th Regiment, Illinois Cavalry), physical appearance (5′11″ tall, light complexion, blue eyes, brown hair), occupation (farmer), family (wife Sarah E. and six children, all named, with dates of birth), and much more.

Military records identify people who were eligible for military service or actually served in the armed forces (see Figure 7-1 below). They can give places of residence, names of family members, dates and places of birth, marriage, and death, even a physical description.

Every war in American history from King William's War (1689–1697) to

(Spanish War.)
A | 1 Cav. | U.S.Vols.
Charles G. Abbott
Pvt., Co. F, 1 Reg't U.S. Vol. Cavalry.
Appears on
Company Muster-in Roll
of the organization named above. Roll dated
Santa Fe, N.M., May 6, 1898.
Mustered in May 6, 1898.
Age 28 yrs; height 5 feet 4½ inches.
Complexion ruddy; eyes gray; hair dk. brn.
Where born Portsmouth, N.H.
Occupation Miner
Joined for duty and enrolled:
When May 6, 1898.
Where Santa Fe, N.M.
Period 2 years.
Travel from residence to place of rendezvous:
Residence
No. of miles
Married or single
If single, name and address of parent or guardian;
Remarks:
Book mark:
J. H. Fearer
(602) Copyist.

Figure 7-1
Compiled military service record of Charles G. Abbott documenting service in the 1st U.S. Volunteer Cavalry (Rough Riders) during the Spanish-American War. National Archives <www.archives.gov/research_room/arc/arc_info/genealogy_search_hints.html#spanish>.

the Persian Gulf War (1990–1991) produced records such as muster rolls, service records, and pension applications. The federal and state governments issued bounty land warrants to soldiers for service in the Revolutionary War, the War of 1812, the Indian wars, and the Mexican War.

What military records are online or on CD-ROM?
Many indexes and transcriptions of military records have been published online and on CD-ROM. You'll even find digital images of some military records. Some of the most important military records in electronic form include images of Revolutionary War pension files, indexes to Civil War pension applications, abstracts of some WWI draft registrations, and casualty lists from WWII and the Korean and Vietnam wars.

What military records are *not* online or on CD-ROM?
Most military records online and on CD-ROM are merely indexes or transcriptions. **It's important to obtain and view the original records to verify that the information was copied correctly and to find additional details.**

Important

KEY RESOURCES

Digital Images

Heritage Books Archives: New Hampshire Revolutionary War Rolls
This CD <www.heritagebooks.com> (search on 1172) features digital images of five volumes of rolls and documents of New Hampshire men in the Revolutionary War, a master index, and thirty pages of French and Indian War rolls (see Figure 7-2 below). Typical references, like those to Stephen Adams, tell when he enlisted (6 March 1781) and the supplies and compensation he had received (after three months and three days of service, Stephen Adams, a corporal, had been given a coat and blanket and was paid wages of 7 pounds, 17 shillings, and 2 pence).

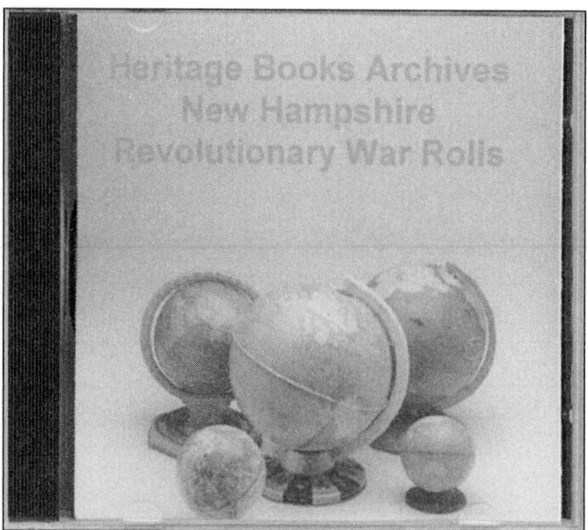

Figure 7-2
Heritage Books Archives: New Hampshire Revolutionary War Rolls.

Revolutionary War Pension Files
<www2.heritagequest.com/qsearch/sr.asp?s=M805>

HeritageQuest has published images of the Revolutionary War Pension and Bounty Land Warrant Applications Files on 898 CD-ROMs, and plans to make them available through libraries subscribing to HeritageQuest Online <www.heritagequestonline.com>. This series is equivalent to National Archives Microfilm Publication M805 which reproduces all records from files containing up to ten pages of records, but only significant genealogical documents from larger files. They are indexed on a CD-ROM called Revolutionary War Pension and Bounty-Land Warrent Index.

The entire contents (not just up to ten pages per file) of the Revolutionary War Pension and Bounty-Land Warrant Application Files are published on National Archives Microfilm Publication M804 (2,670 microfilms). You can order the microfilms through your local public library or Family History Center for a small fee. Search the Family History Library Catalog <www.familysearch.org> for microfilm #970001, the first one in the series. If you don't have an index reference, you can still determine which microfilm would have the files for a specific name because pension files are arranged alphabetically on the microfilms (and CD-ROMs).

Revolutionary War Pension Lists, Military Records
$39.99, Genealogy.com <www.genealogy.com/145facd.html>

This CD features digital images of 12 volumes of Revolutionary War pension records and an index of 110,000 names (see Figure 7-3 below). Just double-click on a name to view the associated page image. Both accepted and rejected pension applications are referenced: Zalmon Hooper's application, for example, was rejected because "he did not serve six months in a military capacity." Once you find a name on this CD, it's worthwhile to consult the original pension application for more details.

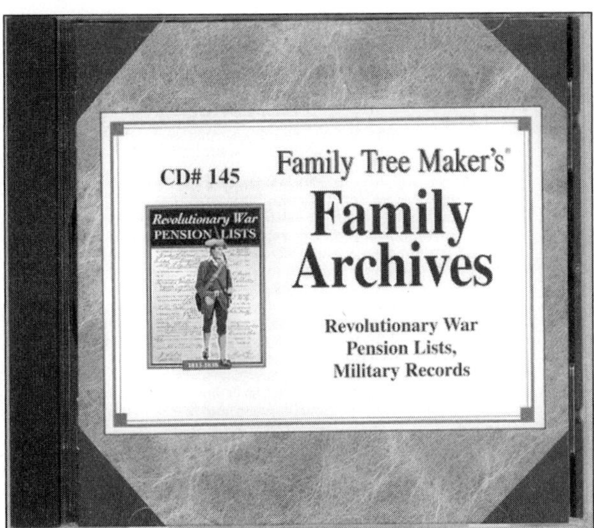

Figure 7-3
Revolutionary War Pension Lists, Military Records.

Databases and Indexes

American Civil War Research Database

<www.civilwardata.com>

This database (see Figure 7-4 below) was created to bring together information on every soldier in the Civil War. So far, it has records of over 2.6 million of the 4 million soldiers in the conflict. Most of this data comes from state rosters. Other sources include regimental histories, Rolls of Honor, and the 1890 census of veterans and widows. A visitor's pass costs $10, and an annual subscription is $25. The database is also part of Ancestry.com's U.S. Records Collection, where it is called Civil War Research Database <www.ancestry.com/search/rectype/military/cwrd/main.htm>.

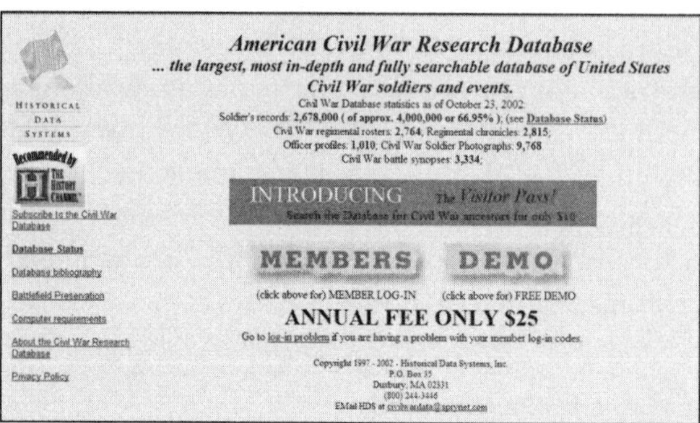

Figure 7-4
American Civil War Research Database.

Ancestry.com U.S. Records Collection

<www.ancestry.com>

Ancestry.com features several large databases of military records, including service records from the Revolutionary War, the War of 1812, and the Civil War; World War I civilian draft registration cards; and casualty lists from the Korean and Vietnam Wars. A subscription costs $12.95 a month or $79.95 a year, but access to some databases is free.

Birth Info in WWI Civilian Draft Registrations

<www.members.aol.com/Rayhbanks/cos.html>

If you have male ancestors who were eligible to serve the United States in World War I, you'll want to check this database (see Figure 7-5 below).

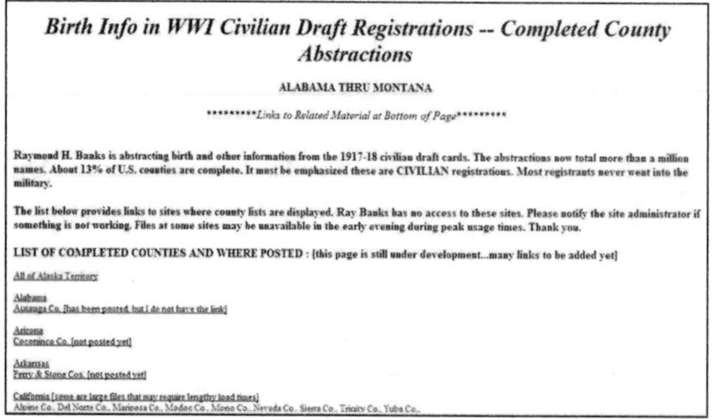

Figure 7-5
Birth Info in WWI Civilian Draft Registrations.

Even though most of them did not ultimately serve, men born between 1873 and 1900, even immigrants not yet naturalized, had to register for the draft in 1917 and 1918. So far, this database has data from more than 1.2 million of the 24 million draft registration cards. Entries include full name and date and place of birth. You can also search the database on RootsWeb <http://userdb.rootsweb.com/ww1/draft/search.cgi> and with a subscription to Ancestry.com.

Civil War Pension Index
<www.ancestry.com/search/rectype/military/cwpi/main.htm>

Ancestry.com's Civil War Pension Index covers nearly 2.5 million pension application cards filed by Union veterans. You can also order the index on microfilm through a public library (*General Index to Pension Files, 1861–1934*, National Archives Microfilm Publication T288) or Family History Center (search the Family History Library Catalog <www.familysearch.org> for microfilm number 540757, the first one of 544 films).

Civil War pension files for Union soldiers have not been microfilmed, but you can get photocopies from the National Archives through Order Online! <https://eservices.archives.gov/orderonline/>. Now you can order copies of federal military pension application files online. To order by mail, you'll need NATF Form 85, and you can request the form by sending an e-mail message to inquire@nara.gov or by filling out the form at <www.archives.gov/global_pages/inquire_form.html>. Copies of all the papers in a pension file now cost $37. If your ancestors fought on the Union side, be sure to read Cyndi Howells's article, "How To Order Military & Pension Records for Union Civil War Veterans from the National Archives" <www.oz.net/~cyndihow/pensions.htm>.

The former Confederate states granted pensions to Confederate veterans, widows, and orphans. You can search online indexes to Confederate pension application files in Alabama, Florida, Georgia, Louisiana, Oklahoma, Tennessee, Texas, and Virginia, and view online images of pension records of Civil War veterans and their widows from Florida and Georgia. These databases are listed in this chapter's database directory.

Civil War Service Records (aka Civil War Muster Rolls)
$49.95 (Windows CD-ROM), Ancestry.com, or online through Ancestry.com's U.S. Subscription <www.ancestry.com/search/rectype/inddbs/4284.htm>

Unlike pension files, service records don't usually name family members, but they may give the soldier's place of birth and dates of enlistment and discharge, and describe wounds received during battle or hospitalization for injury or illness.

This index lists 5.3 million Civil War service records. Names between Sloat and Ticher are missing from the index. Once you find a name in the index, you can request paper copies of the service records from the National Archives. You'll need NATF Form 86, and you can get it by sending an e-mail message to inquire@nara.gov or by filling out the form at <www.archives.gov/global_pages/inquire_form.html>.

Civil War Soldiers and Sailors System
<www.itd.nps.gov/cwss>

Compiled from records in the National Archives, this database (see Figure 7-6 below) has information on over 5 million soldiers who served on both sides in the Civil War. Another 400,000 names will be added, along with regimental histories, battle descriptions, prisoner-of-war records, and cemetery records.

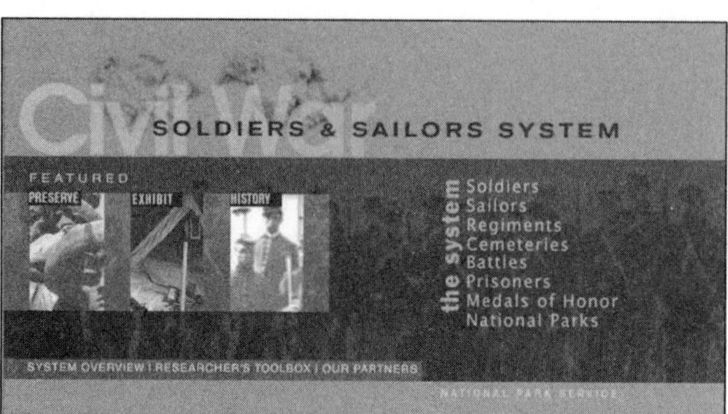

Figure 7-6
Civil War Soldiers and Sailors System.

Illinois State Archives Databases
<www.library.sos.state.il.us/departments/archives/databases.html>

Researchers with Illinois ancestry will find a treasure trove of information in these databases (see Figure 7-7 below). Military databases contain names of Illinois veterans of the War of 1812, the Winnebago War, the Black Hawk War, the Mexican War, the Civil War, and the Spanish-American War.

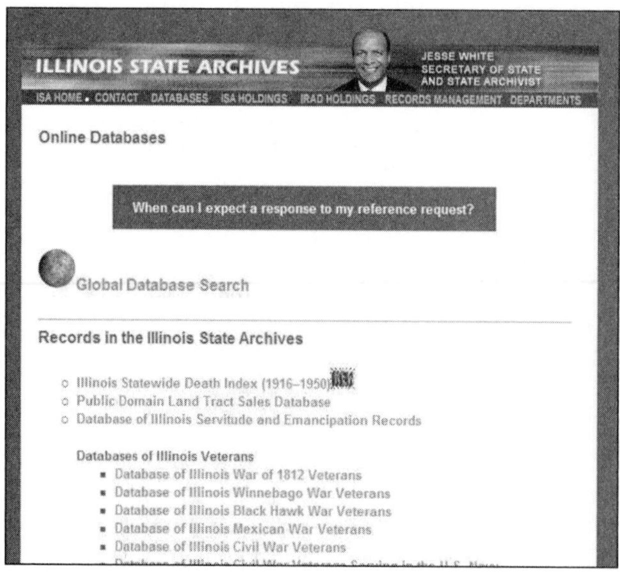

Figure 7-7
Illinois State Archives Databases.

Library of Virginia Digital Library Program
<www.lva.lib.va.us>

This tremendous site features more than eighty databases, indexes, and finding aids (see Figure 7-8 below). Extensive military indexes cover Revolutionary Bounty Warrants, War of 1812 Pay Rolls, Muster Rolls, and Confederate Pension Rolls.

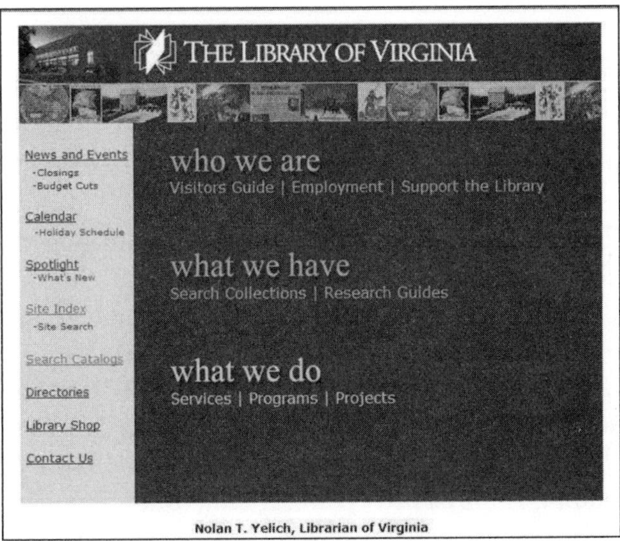

Figure 7-8
Library of Virginia Digital Library Program.

The On-Line Institute for Advanced Loyalist Studies
<www.royalprovincial.com>

If you have ancestors who remained loyal to the British Crown during the Revolutionary War, be sure to check out this Web site (see Figure 7-9 below). In addition to an index to Loyalist muster rolls, you'll find regimental documents, land petitions, and postwar settlement documents.

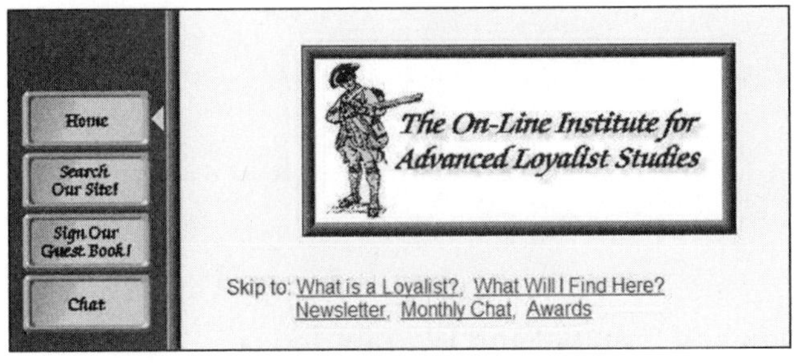

Figure 7-9
The On-Line Institute for Advanced Loyalist Studies.

Pennsylvania's Digital State Archives
<www.digitalarchives.state.pa.us>

Databases on this site (see Figure 7-10 on page 134) focus on Pennsylvania soldiers in the Revolutionary War, Mexican War, Civil War, Spanish-American War, and World War I. About 600,000 records are online.

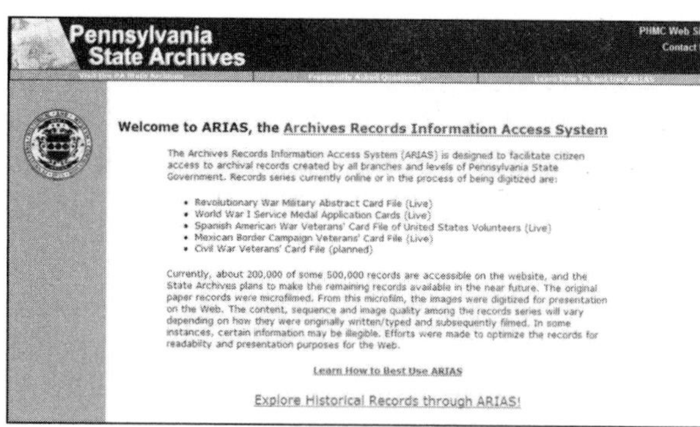

Figure 7-10
Pennsylvania's Digital State Archives.

Military Records: Revolutionary War Muster Rolls

$35.95 (Windows), Ancestry, item #2017

This CD-ROM (see Figure 7-11 below) indexes 426,000 names in the Revolutionary War muster rolls in National Archive microfilm publication M246. Each entry includes the soldier's name, rank, unit, and the National Archives microfilm number, such as "Roll-Box: 36, Roll-Rec: 200." To view the original records, you would order microfilm series M246, roll 36 (sometimes written as M246-36). Then find page 200 on the microfilm. The Family History Library has these microfilms, but the index on this CD-ROM doesn't give the corresponding Family History Library microfilm numbers.

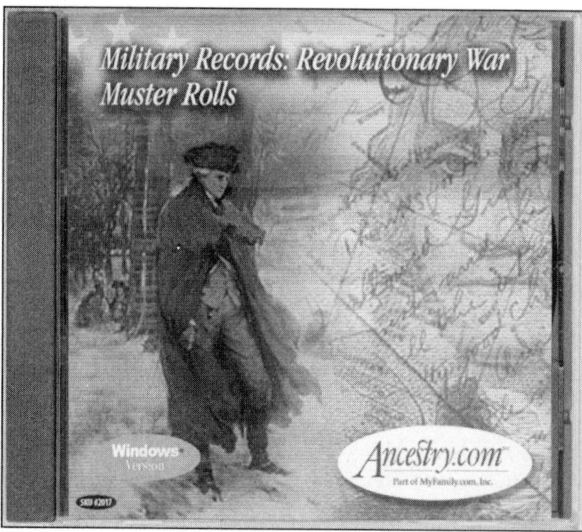

Figure 7-11
Revolutionary War Muster Rolls.

Revolutionary War Pension and Bounty-Land Warrant Index

$19.95 (Windows), HeritageQuest, <www.heritagequest.com>. Search on "warrant index."

This CD-ROM (see Figure 7-12 on page 135) indexes National Archives Series M805 records, a set of 898 microfilms with genealogically important pages from the Revolutionary War pension files. HeritageQuest has publis hed the entire set on 898 CD-ROMs <www2.heritagequest.com/qsearch/sr.asp?s=M805>.

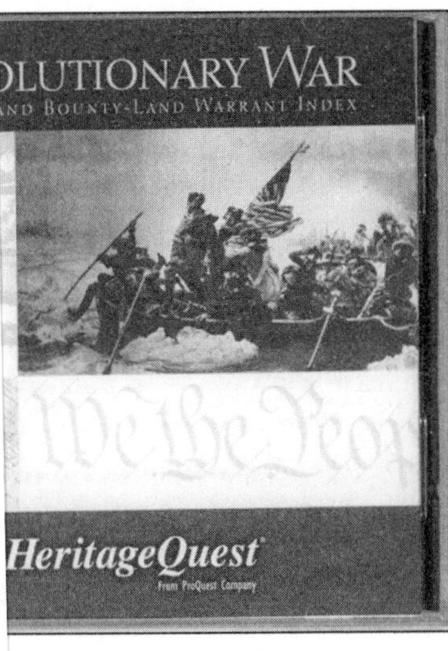

Figure 7-12
Revolutionary War Pension and Bounty-Land Warrant Index.

that another microfilming of the records on 2,670 micro-
04) reproduces all pages in the files, not just those deemed
nportant. If you use the microfilm numbers in the index
M when you order microfilmed pension files on interli-
ugh your public library, be sure to specify Series M805.
ory Library has copies of microfilms in Series M804, but

x Edition III

rs), Progeny Software <www.sar.org/pat_idx>
hing and the National Society of the Sons of the American
borated to produce this CD (see Figure 7-13 below) with
history records of patriots and their descendants. The CD
evolutionary War patriots but also their families, and traces

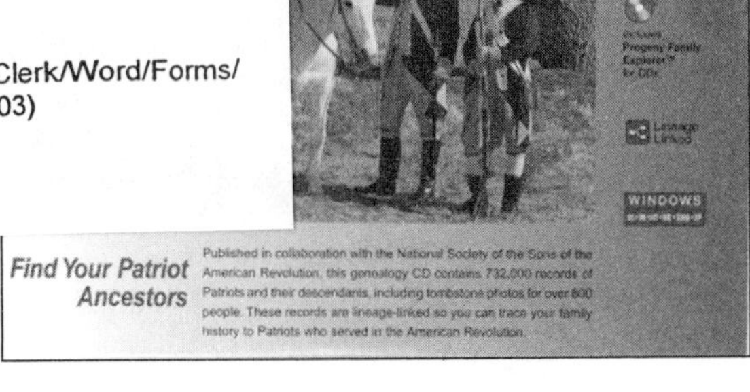

Figure 7-13
SAR Patriot Index, Edition III

some descendants to the twentieth century. Source notes for each patriot cite original SAR membership applications, and you can request copies at <www.sar.org/pat_idx> for a $5 fee.

The latest edition of the CD features more than eight hundred tombstone photographs, and you are invited to submit pictures of your patriot ancestors' tombstones for future editions. See the instructions at <www.sar.org/pat_idx>.

SAR Revolutionary War Graves Register, 2000 Edition
$29.95 (Windows), Progeny Software <www.sar.org/geneal/rwgraves.htm>

More than twice as large as the first edition, this CD (see Figure 7-14 below) has over 140,000 names and burial locations of soldiers, sailors, and civilian patriots, and many of their spouses. Most records also provide details on birth, death, type of service, state served, and place of residence. Advanced search features let you find all Revolutionary War graves in a specific city or state or even cemetery.

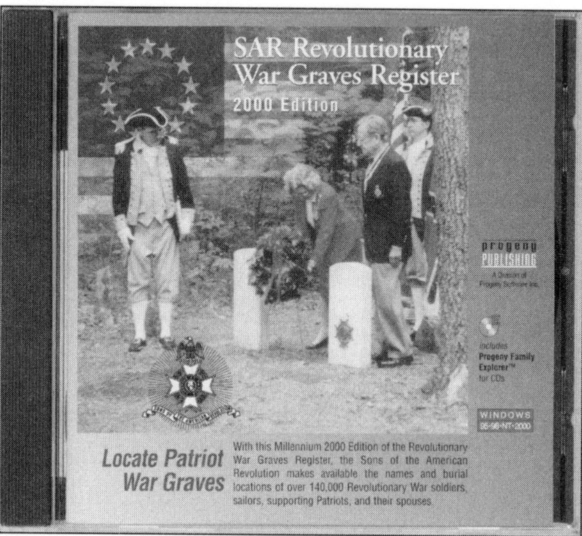

Figure 7-14
SAR Revolutionary War Graves Register, 2000 edition.

USGenWeb Project State Pages
<www.usgenweb.org/statelinks-table.html>

Researchers have contributed many indexes and abstracts of military records to USGenWeb's state pages and the county pages linked to them.

GUIDES AND RESOURCES

Access Genealogy Military Resource Center
<www.accessgenealogy.com/military>
This site has records, research guides, and links.

The American Civil War Homepage
<http://sunsite.utk.edu/civil-war>
This large directory of Civil War resources includes links to many rosters, regimental histories, and battle histories.

Cyndi's List of Genealogy Sites on the Internet

<www.cyndislist.com>

Under Military Resources Worldwide, check especially the categories for Military—World War II <www.cyndislist.com/worldwar2.htm>, U.S.—Civil War (War for Southern Independence) <www.cyndislist.com/cw.htm>, U.S.—Military <www.cyndislist.com/military.htm>, and the links to Regimental Rosters & Histories within the Civil War category. Also, see the separate category for Loyalists.

FamilySearch Research Helps

<www.familysearch.org>

Click on the Search tab, Research Helps, then Sorted by Subject, and click on *M* to view a list of research outlines covering military records. Note especially the U.S. Military Records Research Outline. Then click on the title to view the outline onscreen, on [PDF] to print a copy, or on the item number to order a printed copy.

National Archives Research in Military Records

<www.archives.gov/research_room/genealogy/research_topics/military.html>

An overview of the military records held by the National Archives.

The United States Civil War Center

<www.cwc.lsu.edu>

This site maintained by Louisiana State University includes many links to Civil War battlefield and cemetery Web sites, as well as the guide, "Researching People of the Civil War Era."

For More Info

SUGGESTED READING

Neagles, James C. *U.S. Military Records: A Guide to Federal and State Sources, Colonial America to the Present.* Salt Lake City: Ancestry, ca. 1994.

DATABASE DIRECTORY Military Records

This directory does not include URLs for databases in the Family and Local Histories collection. See page 18 for instructions on "Searching an individual database" in Family and Local Histories. Databases arranged by place and time. Nationwide databases appear first. **Type**: Digital Images, Transcript, Database, Abstracts, or Index; Colonial (**CO**) (ca. 1600–1775), King Philip's (**KP**) (1675–1676), French & Indian (**FI**) (1754–1763), Dunmore's (**DU**) (1774), Revolutionary (**REV**) (1775–1783), War of 1812 (**1812**) (1812–1815), Seminole Indian (**SI**) (1817–1818), Winnebago (**WW**) (1827), Black Hawk (**BH**) (1832), 2d Seminole (**SW**) (1836–1843), Aroostook (**AR**) (1839), Mexican (**MX**) (1846–1848), Civil War (**CW**) (1861–1865), Indian Wars (**IN**) (1865–1890), Spanish-American (**SA**) (1898), Philippine Insurrection (**PI**) (1899–1902), Mexican Border (**MXB**) (1916), World War I (**WWI**) (1917–1918, U.S. participation), World War II (**WWII**) (1941–1945, U.S. participation), Cold War (**CD**) (1945–1991), Korean (**KO**) (1950–1953), Vietnam (**VN**) (1965–1973), Persian Gulf (**PG**) (1991), All Wars (**ALL**) (ca. 1600–2004).

Canada
Type: Abstracts; CW
Online: Free
Title: Canadians in the American Civil War
Notes, URL: 3,427 Civil War soldiers, either natives, residents, or enlistees from what is now Canada. <www.geocities.com/cancivwar/cancivwar.html>

United States
Type: Database; ALL
Year Range: Up to pres.
Online: Free
Title: RootsWeb.com Military Rosters
Notes, URL: Over 81,000 records. <http://userdb.rootsweb.com/military> For a list of the databases searched, see <http://userdb.rootsweb.com/regional.html>.

United States
Type: Database; ALL
Year Range: Up to pres.
Online: Free
Title: The Veteran Ancestor Registry
Notes, URL: Over 7,000 entries. <www.migrations.org/vetreg/search.php3>

United States
Type: Index; REV
Year Range: 1774–1783
CD-ROM: $25 (Mac/Win)
Title: Carleton's Loyalist Index and The Book of Negroes
Notes, URL: "A Select Index to Names of Loyalists and their Associates Contained in the British Headquarters Papers, New York City 1774–1783, The Carleton Papers." <www2.magmacom.com/~ekipp/kingname.htm>

United States
Type: Text of the books; REV
Online: Ancestry
Title: Daughters of the American Revolution Lineage Books (152 Vols.)
Notes, URL: Nearly 2.4 million names. <www.ancestry.com/search/rectype/inddbs/3174.htm>

United States
Type: Compiled research; REV
CD-ROM: $23 (Mac/Win), Heritage Books, item #1123
Title: The Hessian Collection, Volume 1
Notes, URL: Digital images of 4 volumes, including biographies of soldiers from Waldeck, Germany. <www.heritagebooks.com>. Search on "1123."

United States
Type: Index; REV
Online: Free
Title: An index to the book *Revolutionary War Period Bible, Family & Marriage Records*
Notes, URL: <www.dhc.net/~revwar>

United States
Type: Abstracts; REV
Online: Ancestry
Title: American Revolutionary War Rejected Pensions
Notes, URL: 8,600 names. Source: *Rejected or Suspended Applications for Revolutionary War Pensions.* <www.ancestry.com/search/rectype/inddbs/4329.htm>

United States
Type: Index; REV
Online: Genealogy Library
Title: Index of the Rolls of Honor Ancestor's Index in the Lineage Books of DAR Volumes 1-4
Notes, URL: Select Records I Military I Pennsylania.

United States
Type: Compiled research; REV
CD-ROM: $29.99, Genealogy.com, CD #144
Online: Genealogy Library
Title: Loyalists in the American Revolution
Notes, URL: 13 volumes naming 87,000 soldiers loyal to Great Britain. <www.genealogy.com/144facd.html>

United States
Type: Compiled research; REV
Online: Ancestry
Title: Loyalists in the American Revolution: Miscellaneous Records
Notes, URL: <www.ancestry.com/search/rectype/inddbs/6134.htm>

United States
Type: Text of a book containing transcripts of records; REV
Online: Ancestry
Title: United Empire Loyalists, Parts I-II
Notes, URL: From *Second Report of the Bureau of Archives for the Province of Ontario*, by Alexander Fraser. <www.ancestry.com/search/rectype/inddbs/1016.htm>

United States
Type: Compiled research; REV
CD-ROM: $29.99, Genealogy.com, CD #508
Online: Genealogy Library
Title: Midwest Pioneers, 1600s–1800s
Notes, URL: Revolutionary War soldiers buried in Illinois, Indiana, & Michigan. <www.genealogy.com/508facd.html>

United States
Type: Compiled research; REV
CD-ROM: $29.99, Genealogy.com, CD #133
Title: Maryland and Delaware Revolutionary Patriots, 1775–1783 Military Records
Notes, URL: Contains images of 11 books on military records with 104,000 names. <www.genealogy.com/133facd.html>

United States
Type: Indexes; REV

CD-ROM: $39.99, Genealogy.com, CD #145
Title: Revolutionary War Pension Lists Military Records
Notes, URL: Digital images from 12 volumes of Revolutionary War pension records with 110,000 names. <www.genealogy.com/145facd.html>

United States
Type: Index; REV
Online: Free
Title: The On-Line Institute for Advanced Loyalist Studies: Index to Loyalist Muster Rolls
Notes, URL: <www.royalprovincial.com/military/musters/mustlist.htm>

United States
Type: Digital images; REV
CD-ROM: $19.95 each, HeritageQuest
Title: Selected Records from Revolutionary War Pension & Bounty-Land Warrant Application Files
Notes, URL: Scanned images on 898 CD-ROMs. <www2.heritagequest.com/qsearch/sr.asp?s=M805>

United States
Type: Compiled research; REV
Online: Genealogy Library
Title: The Refugees of 1776 from Long Island to Connecticut
Notes, URL: More than 5,000 refugees who fled after the Battle of Long Island in 1776. A book by Frederic Gregory Mather. Select Records I Military I New York.

United States
Type: Index; REV
Online: Ancestry
Title: Revolutionary War Courts-Martial
Notes, URL: 3,315 men brought before military courts-martial. Source: Neagles, James C. *Summer Soldiers, A Survey & Index of Revolutionary War Courts-Martial.* <www.ancestry.com/search/rectype/inddbs/1045.htm>

United States
Type: Compiled research; REV
Online: Ancestry
Title: Revolutionary War Officers
Notes, URL: Over 14,000 listings. Source: Heitman, Francis B. *Historical Register of Officers of the Continental Army During the War of the Revolution.* <www.ancestry.com/search/rectype/inddbs/2030.htm>

United States
Type: Index; REV
CD-ROM: $19.95 (Win), HeritageQuest
Title: Revolutionary War Pension and Bounty-Land Warrant Index
Notes, URL: Over 90,000 entries for pensioners and their dependents. <www2.heritagequest.com/hq/sw.asp?Z_ID=ACD-0111>

United States
Type: Index; REV
Online: Ancestry
Title: Revolutionary War Pension Index
Notes, URL: Over 1,700 names. <www.ancestry.com/search/rectype/inddbs/4691.htm>

United States
Type: Index; REV
Year Range: 1775–1783
CD-ROM: $39.95 (Win), Ancestry
Online: Ancestry
Title: Revolutionary War Service Records, 1775–83
Notes, URL: Nearly 426,000 names. <www.ancestry.com/search/rectype/inddbs/4282a.htm>. The CD is called *Military Records: Revolutionary War Muster Rolls.*

United States
Type: Index, photos; REV
CD-ROM: $39.95 (Win), Progeny Software
Title: SAR Patriot Index Edition III
Notes, URL: 732,000 family history records of Patriots and their descendants, plus tombstone photos for more than 800 people. <www.progenysoftware.com/cdroms.html>

United States
Type: Database; REV
CD-ROM: $29.95 (Win), Progeny Software
Title: SAR Revolutionary War Graves Register
Notes, URL: Over 140,000 names & burial locations of soldiers, sailors, & civilian patriots & many of their spouses. <www.progenysoftware.com/cdroms.html>

United States
Type: Text of a book; REV
Online: Ancestry
Title: Sons of the American Revolution
Notes, URL: A list of all SAR members through 1901 with their lines of descent from Revolutionary War ancestors. From A. Howard Clark, *A National Register of the Society Sons of the American Revolution.* <www.ancestry.com/search/rectype/inddbs/3072.htm>

United States
Type: Transcript; REV
Year Range: 1783–1790
CD-ROM: $29.95, Willow Bend, item #2331QP
Title: United Empire Loyalist: Enquiry into the Losses and Services in Consequence of Their Loyalty
Notes, URL: "Evidence in Canadian Claims, Second Report of the Bureau of Archives for the Province in Ontario." Contains the record of claims for losses for more than 1,200 persons who fled to Canada during and immediately after the American Revolutionary War. <www.willowbendbooks.com>

United States
Type: Digital images; REV
Year Range: 1829–1832
Online: NEHGS
Title: U.S. Revolutionary War Naval Pensioners' Receipts, 1829–1832
Notes, URL: <www.newenglandancestors.org/research/database/naval_pensions>

United States
Type: Abstracts; REV
Year Range: 1840
Online: Free
Title: 1840 Census of Pensioners, Revolutionary or Military Services
Notes, URL: <www.usgennet.org/usa/topic/colonial/census/1840/index.html>

United States
Type: Index
Year Range: 1784–1811
CD-ROM: $39.99, Genealogy.com, CD #146
Title: U.S. Soldiers, 1784–1811 Military Records
Notes, URL: Service records of 21,000 soldiers who served from 22 states and territories. <www.genealogy.com/146facd.html>

United States
Type: Digital images of a book
Year Range: 1789–1853
Online: F&LH
Title: A dictionary of all officers who have been commissioned, or have been appointed and served, in the Army of the United States, since the inauguration of their first president in 1789, to the first January, 1853
Notes, URL: A book by Charles K. Gardner.

United States
Type: Abstracts

Year Range: 1789–1903
Online: Ancestry
Title: U.S. Army Historical Register, 1789–1903, Vol. 1
Notes, URL: "Over 17,500 officers who served in the United States Army from 1789–1903." Source: Heitman, Francis B. *Historical Register and Dictionary of the United States Army, 1789–1903*, Volume 1. <www.ancestry.com/search/rectype/inddbs/3122.htm>

United States
Type: Abstracts
Year Range: 1789–1903
Online: Ancestry
Title: U.S. Army Historical Register, 1789–1903, Vol. 2
Notes, URL: "Over 48,000 officers who served in the United States Army from 1789–1903." Source: Heitman, Francis B. *Historical Register and Dictionary of the United States Army, 1789–1903*, Volume 2. <www.ancestry.com/search/rectype/inddbs/3167.htm>

United States
Type: Abstract; 1812
Year Range: 1811–1814
Online: Free
Title: 41st Regiment of Foot: Deserters and/or settlers in North America
Notes, URL: <http://freepages.history.rootsweb.com/~british41st/41stregt_deserters.htm>

United States
Type: Abstracts; 1812
CD-ROM: $39.95, Willow Bend, item #5792AP
Title: Military Records: War of 1812 Muster Rolls
Notes, URL: 58,000 records. <www.willowbendbooks.com>

United States
Type: Transcript; 1812
Online: Free
Title: Naval History Center: Officers of the U.S. Navy and Marine Corps in the War of 1812
Notes, URL: Source: *Naval Register: Printed by Order of the Secretary of the Navy. August 1st, 1815.* <www.history.navy.mil/wars/war1812/1815list.htm>

United States
Type: Transcript; 1812
Online: Free
Title: Veterans of the War of 1812 listed in the 1903 Membership Roll, Pennsylvania Society of the War of 1812
Notes, URL: It's not known if these veterans had lived in Pennsylvania. <www.geneasearch.com/genealogy/1812veterans.htm>

United States
Type: Digital images; 1812
CD-ROM: $13.95/CD, FamilyToolbox
Online: Free
Title: Sources2Go.com: War of 1812 Military Bounty Land Warrants, 1815–1858
Notes, URL: <www.sources2go.com>

United States
Type: Index; 1812
CD-ROM: $39.95 (Win), Ancestry, item #2019, <http://shops.ancestry.com>. Search on "Military Records: War of 1812."
Online: Ancestry
Title: War of 1812 Service Records
Notes, URL: Nearly 580,000 names. <www.ancestry.com/search/rectype/inddbs/4281a.htm>. The CD-ROM is called *Military Records: War of 1812 Muster Rolls.*

United States
Type: Digital images; 1812
Year Range: 1815–1858
CD-ROM: $378, Willow Bend, item #A1757FB
Title: War of 1812 Military Land Warrants, 1815–1858
Notes, URL: A 28-CD set containing images of warrants issued to War of 1812 veterans & their heirs principally in the public domain land areas of Arkansas, Illinois, & Missouri. <www.willowbendbooks.com>

United States
Type: Transcripts
Year Range: 1813
Online: Free
Title: 1813 Invalid Pensioners
Notes, URL: Mostly veterans of the Revolutionary War and the War of 1812. <www.arealdomain.com/invalid.html>

United States
Type: Abstract
Year Range: 1820
Online: Free
Title: Military Research Room: 1820 Pension List
Notes, URL: <www.lineages.com/military/mil_rw.asp>

United States
Type: Transcript
Year Range: 1846
Online: Free
Title: U.S. Mormon Battalion, Inc.
Notes, URL: Five companies with over 500 men mustered at Council Bluffs, Iowa, marched 2,000 miles to San Diego, California. <www.mormonbattalion.com>

United States
Type: Index; CW
Year Range: 1861–1895
CD-ROM: Historical Data Systems
Title: American Civil War Research Database
Notes, URL: Records of over 2,700,000 of 4,000,000 soldiers, compiled mostly from state rosters. Visitor's pass, $10- Annual, $25. <www.civilwardata.com>. This is the same as the Civil War Research Database on Ancestry.com.

United States
Type: Photos; CW
Year Range: 1861–1865
Online: Free
Title: American Memory, Library of Congress, Selected Civil War Photographs, 1861–1865
Notes, URL: 1,118 photographs. <http://memory.loc.gov/ammem/cwarquery.html>

United States
Type: Database; CW
Online: Free
Title: Macon County, Georgia: Andersonville Prisoner Lookup
Notes, URL: <www.maconcountyga.org>. Click on "Andersonville National Cemetery and Historic Site."

United States
Type: Database; CW
Year Range: 1863–1865
Online: Ancestry
Title: Andersonville Prisoners of War
Notes, URL: Records of 37,000 out of about 45,000 Union soldiers captured by the Confederate States of America. <www.ancestry.com/search/rectype/inddbs/3708.htm>

United States
Type: Compiled research; CW
CD-ROM: $35, Eastern Digital Resources
Title: Black Civil War Soldiers
Notes, URL: Includes rosters of officers & enlisted men and biographies & genealogies of black soldiers who served

in the war. <www.researchonline.net/cwblack/order.htm>

United States
Type: Abstracts; CW
Online: Free
Title: Black Sailors Research Project, Howard University.
Notes, URL: 18,000 men (& more than a dozen women) of African descent who served in the U.S. Navy. <www.civilwar.nps.gov/cwss/sailors.htm>

United States
Type: Digital images of books; CW
CD-ROM: $69.95, Eastern Digital Resources
Title: The Official Records of the American Civil War (The Civil War CD)
Notes, URL: Contains all 128 volumes of the Official Records of the Civil War (without indices). Includes names of soldiers who were killed, captured, wounded, missing, drafted, & pensioned. <www.researchonline.net/or>

United States
Type: Digital images books; CW
Online: Free
Title: The War of Rebellion: A Compilation of the Official Records of the Union and Confederate Armies; The Official Records of the Union and Confederate Navies in the War of Rebellion
Notes, URL: Search for the name of a soldier, his regiment, and the names of captains and colonels who commanded the soldier's units. Part of Cornell University's Making of America site. <http://cdl.library.cornell.edu/moa/moa_browse.html>

United States
Type: Index; CW
Online: Ancestry
Title: Civil War Pension Index
Notes, URL: An index to nearly 2.5 million pension application cards filed by Union veterans. <www.ancestry.com/search/rectype/military/cwpi/main.htm>

United States
Type: Index; CW
Year Range: 1861–1865
CD-ROM: $89.95 (Win), Ancestry, item #2967. <http://shops.ancestry.com>. Search on "Civil War Research." The CD is called "American Civil War Research Database."
Online: Ancestry
Title: Civil War Research Database
Notes, URL: Search for soldiers, regiments, or officers. A work in progress, this database includes "2,660,000 soldiers (out of approx. 4,000,000 who served), 2,742 regimental chronicles, 2,815 officer profiles, 3,343 battle synopses, & 1,012 soldier photographs." <www.ancestry.com/search/rectype/military/cwrd/main.htm>

United States
Type: Index; CW
CD-ROM: $12, Willow Bend, item #A2619ED
Title: Civil War Research Consolidated Index
Notes, URL: <www.willowbendbooks.com>

United States
Type: Index; CW
CD-ROM: $49.95 (Win), Ancestry, item #2020, <http://shops.ancestry.com>. Search on "Civil War Service."
Online: Ancestry
Title: Civil War Service Records (aka Civil War Muster Rolls)
Notes, URL: Over 5.3 million records on 3 CDs. <www.ancestry.com/search/rectype/inddbs/4284.htm>

United States
Type: Index; CW
Online: Free
Title: Civil War Soldiers and Sailors System
Notes, URL: When completed, the Names Index Project will include the names and basic information from 5.4 million soldier records in the National Archives. <www.itd.nps.gov/cwss>

United States
Type: Abstracts; CW
Online: Free
Title: Confederate Cemetery List
Notes, URL: Links to over 2,400 cemetery listings with Confederate burials. <www.geocities.com/CollegePark/Grounds/7235>

United States
Type: CW
CD-ROM: $69.95, Willow Bend, item #A1625GN
Title: Confederate Dead Database
Notes, URL: <www.willowbendbooks.com>

United States
Type: Database; CW
CD-ROM: $10.99, Southern History Unlimited
Title: Confederate Death Records
Notes, URL: Over 20,000 battle and war-related deaths. <www.southernhistory.netfirms.com/confederate_death_records.htm>

United States
Type: Index; CW
Online: Ancestry
Title: Confederate States Field Officers
Notes, URL: Over 5,000 names. Source: *Memorandum of Field Officers in the Confederate States Service.* <www.ancestry.com/search/rectype/inddbs/4537.htm>

United States
Type: Compiled research; CW
Online: Free
Title: Galvanized Tars: Confederate POWs Who Enlisted in the Union Navy
Notes, URL: <http://home.ozconnect.net/tfoen/galvanizedtars.htm>

United States
Type: Index; CW
Online: Free
Title: MHI Photograph Database
Notes, URL: A catalog of Civil War photographs at the U.S. Army Military History Institute. You can order copies. <http://carlisle-www.army.mil/usamhi/PhotoDB.html>

United States
Type: Digital images; CW
Year Range: 1861–1865
CD-ROM: $29.99, Genealogy.com, CD #119
Title: Confederate Soldiers, 1861–1865 Military Records
Notes, URL: 24,000 soldiers who died in federal prisons and military hospitals in the North. Source: Indexed images of National Archives microfilm roll M918, *Register of Confederate Soldiers, Sailors, and Citizens Who Died in Federal Prisons and Military Hospitals in the North 1861–1865.* <www.genealogy.com/119facd.html>

United States
Type: Photos; CW
Online: Free
Title: Photos of Confederate Soldiers and Sailors
Notes, URL: <www.geocities.com/coh41/home.html>

United States
Type: Digital images of books; CW

CD-ROM: $49.99, Genealogy.com, CD #351
Online: Genealogy Library
Title: Roll of Honor: Civil War Union Soldiers
Notes, URL: Names of about 236,000 Union soldiers. <www.genealogy.com/351/fa cd.html>

United States
Type: Index; CW
CD-ROM: $450 (Win), Broadfoot
Title: Roster of Confederate Soldiers 1861–1865
Notes, URL: 1,500,000 names. <www.broa dfootpublishing.com/civ_bks2. htm#cd>

United States
Type: Index; CW
CD-ROM: $650 (Win), Broadfoot
Title: Roster of Union Soldiers 1861–1865
Notes, URL: Over 3,000,000 names. <www. broadfootpublishing.com/civ_bks2.h tm#cd>

United States
Type: Database; CW
Online: Free
Title: Rosters Database
Notes, URL: 35,627 records. <http://userdb. rootsweb.com/rosters>

United States
Type: Index; CW
Online: Free
Title: U.S. Civil War Generals
Notes, URL: "A concise index to the Generals who fought on both sides of the U.S. Civil War." <www.sunsite.utk. edu/civil-war/generals.html>

United States
Type: Various; CW
Online: Free
Title: U.S. Civil War Navies. A Collection of Articles, Muster Rolls, and Images of the Union and Confederate Naval Services.
Notes, URL: <http://hub.dataline.net.au/~tf oen>

United States
Type: ; CW
CD-ROM: $200 (Win), Broadfoot
Title: U.S. Colored Troops in the Civil War
Notes, URL: Over 200,000 names. <www.br oadfootpublishing.com/civ_bks2.ht m#cd>

United States
Type: Transcripts; CW
Online: Free
Title: Wagonmasters Serving the Union During the Civil War
Notes, URL: <www.archives.gov/research_r oom/genealogy/military/union_wagon masters.html>

United States
Type: Transcripts
Year Range: 1863–1979
Online: Free
Title: U.S. Army Center of Military History: Full-text Listings of Medal of Honor Citations
Notes, URL: More than 3,400 names. Source: *Medal of Honor Recipients: 1863–1973.* <www.army.mil/cmh-pg/ moh1.htm>

United States
Type: Transcripts
Year Range: 1883
Online: Free
Title: 1883 Pensioners Online
Notes, URL: Union veterans from the Civil War and survivors of the War of 1812 receiving pensions for war service. <ww w.arealdomain.com/pensioners1883. html>

United States
Type: Index
Year Range: 1883
CD-ROM: $14.95 (Win), HeritageQuest
Title: Pensioners Roll of 1883
Notes, URL: An index of 277,702 individuals or their widows entitled to pensions for their service in all previous wars, including the Revolutionary War, War of 1812, Cherokee Removal, Mexican War, and the Civil War. <www.heritagequest. com>. Search on "1883."

United States
Type: Transcripts
Year Range: 1890
Online: Free
Title: 1890 Veterans and Widows Special Census
Notes, URL: Links to transcriptions. <www.a realdomain.com/vetcensus.html>

United States
Type: Digital images
Year Range: 1890
CD-ROM: $19.95 each (Win), HeritageQuest
Title: 1890 Veterans & Widows of Veterans Census Schedules
Notes, URL: 118 CD-ROMs. <www.heritage quest.com>. Search on "M123."

United States
Type: Index
Year Range: 1890
CD-ROM: $29.99, Genealogy.com, CD #131
Online: Genealogy Library
Title: Veterans' Schedules—U.S. Selected States, 1890 Military Records
Notes, URL: "An index of approximately 385,000 war veterans and veterans' widows who were enumerated in the special veterans' schedule of the 1890 United States census." <www.genealog y.com/131facd.html>

United States
Type: Transcript
Year Range: 1895
Online: Ancestry
Title: National Home for Disabled Volunteer Soldiers
Notes, URL: Completed for the fiscal year ending 30 June 1895, this report lists soldiers admitted to various homes across the U.S. <www.ancestry.com/sea rch/rectype/inddbs/6258.htm>

United States
Type: Transcripts; SA
Online: Free
Title: Researching a Spanish American War Veteran
Notes, URL: Rosters of military units. <www. spanamwar.com/geneaol.htm>

United States
Type: Index; SA
Year Range: 1898
Online: Free
Title: Genealogy Quest: Rough Riders
Notes, URL: <www.genealogy-quest.com/ cgi-bin/genealogy-quest/trooper.cgi>

United States
Type: Digital images; SA
Online: Free
Title: Spanish-American War Compiled Military Service Records for 1,235 "Rough Riders"
Notes, URL: <www.archives.gov/research_r oom/arc/arc_info/genealogy_search_ hints.html#spanish>

United States
Type: Database
Year Range: 1906–1991
Online: Free
Title: Index to the Gorgas Hospital Mortuary Death Records
Notes, URL: 26,213 U.S. military soldiers and officers, employees of the Panama

Canal Commission and its predecessors, and Canal Zone civilians processed through the Gorgas Hospital Mortuary. <www.archives.gov/aad>. Click on Search | People.

United States
Type: Transcript
Year Range: 1907
Online: Free
Title: Men on Board Ships of the Atlantic Fleet Bound for the Pacific December 16, 1907
Notes, URL: Over 14,000 sailors. <www.searchforancestors.com/military/atlanticfleet/>

United States
Type: Transcript
Year Range: 1907
Online: Ancestry
Title: U.S. Military: Great White Fleet (Atlantic Fleet bound for the Pacific, 16 December 1907)
Notes, URL: Men on 16 new battleships in the Atlantic Fleet that sailed from Hampton Roads, Va. <www.ancestry.com/search/rectype/inddbs/5542.htm>

United States
Type: Database; WWI-WWII-KO-VN
Online: Free
Title: American Battle Monuments Commission
Notes, URL: Persons interred at American military cemeteries overseas or missing in action. <www.abmc.gov>

United States
Type: Transcripts
Year Range: 1915–1968
Online: Free
Title: Lost Boats
Notes, URL: Crew lost on sunken submarines. <www.subnet.com/MEMORIAL/lostboat.htm>

United States
Type: Abstracts; WWI
Year Range: 1917–1918
Online: Free
Title: Birth Info in WWI Civilian Draft Registrations—Completed County Abstractions: Alabama thru Montana
Notes, URL: More than a million names from the 1917–18 civilian draft cards. About 13% of U.S. counties are complete. <www.members.aol.com/Rayhbanks/cos.html>

United States
Type: Abstracts; WWI
Year Range: 1917–1918
Online: Free
Title: Birth Info in WWI Civilian Draft Registrations—Completed County Abstractions, Nebraska thru Wyoming
Notes, URL: More than a million names from the 1917–18 civilian draft cards. About 13% of U.S. counties are complete. <www.members.aol.com/Rayhbanks/cos2.html>

United States
Type: Abstracts; WWI
Year Range: 1917–1918
Online: Ancestry
Title: WWI Civilian Draft Registrations
Notes, URL: 1.2 million out of 24 million men, born between 1873 & 1900, who completed draft registration cards in 1917 & 1918. In progress. <www.ancestry.com/search/rectype/inddbs/3172a.htm>

United States
Type: Abstracts; WWI
Year Range: 1917–1918
Online: Free
Title: WWI Draft Registrations: Civilian Draft Registration Database
Notes, URL: Over 1.2 million records, including all registrants born 1872–1900 from about 15% of U.S. counties. <http://userdb.rootsweb.com/ww1/draft/search.cgi>

United States
Type: Database; WWI
Year Range: 1917–1919
Online: Ancestry
Title: U.S. Naval Deaths, World War I
Notes, URL: Death records for over 7,200 sailors. <www.ancestry.com/search/rectype/inddbs/4022.htm>

United States
Type: Abstracts
Year Range: 1925
Online: Ancestry
Title: U.S. Military Records, 1925: Official National Guard Register
Notes, URL: "Officers and sergeant instructors of the National Guard for all the states . . . Birth dates range from 1862 through 1904." <www.ancestry.com/search/rectype/inddbs/4996.htm>

United States
Type: Abstracts; WWI
Year Range: 1930
Online: Ancestry
Title: U.S. World War I Mothers' Pilgrimage, 1930
Notes, URL: Nearly 11,000 mothers & widows of soldiers killed in World War I. <www.ancestry.com/search/rectype/inddbs/4224.htm>

United States
Type: Abstracts; WWII-KO
Year Range: 1940–1995
CD-ROM: $35.95 (Win), Ancestry, item #2018, <http://shops.ancestry.com>. Search on "Overseas."
Online: Ancestry
Title: World War II and Korean Conflict Veterans Interred Overseas
Notes, URL: Nearly 160,000 records from 1940–1995 (152,448 from 1941–46 & 6,038 from 1950–53). <www.ancestry.com/search/rectype/inddbs/4283a.htm>

United States
Type: Digital images; WWII
Online: Free
Title: Archival Research Catalog: World War II Casualty Lists
Notes, URL: Includes casualties in 1946. <www.archives.gov/research_room/arc/>

United States
Type: Database; WWII
Year Range: 1942–1947
Online: Free
Title: World War II Prisoners of War File, ca. 1942–ca. 1947
Notes, URL: 143,374 records. <www.archives.gov/aad>. Click on Search | People.

United States
Type: Database
Year Range: 1941–pres.
Online: Free
Title: U.S. Navy Memorial Foundation: Navy Log
Notes, URL: A register of the names and service information of 250,000 naval service personnel, living or deceased. <www.lonesailor.org/log.php>

United States
Type: Database; CD-KO-VN
Online: Free
Title: RootsWeb.com: POW-MIA Records
Notes, URL: 11,848 records. <www.userdb.rootsweb.com/pow_mia>

United States
Type: Index; KO

Online: Ancestry
Title: Korean Conflict Death Index
Notes, URL: Over 33,000 records. <www.ancestry.com/search/rectype/inddbs/1033.htm>

United States
Type: Database; KO
CD-ROM: MilitaryUSA.com
Online: Database
Title: Korean War Casualty Database
Notes, URL: <www.militaryusa.com>. $9.95/week, $19.95/month, or $39.95/year.

United States
Type: Database; KO
Online: Free
Title: Korean War Databases: KIA MIA Search
Notes, URL: Database of soldiers killed or missing in action. <www.koreanwar.org/html/korean_war_databases.html>

United States
Type: Database; KO
Year Range: 1950–1953
Online: Free
Title: Korean War Casualty File
Notes, URL: 27,727 officers and soldiers who died and 82,248 who were wounded. <www.archives.gov/aad>. Click on Search | People.

United States
Type: Database; KO
Year Range: 1950–1953
Online: Free
Title: Korean War File of American Prisoners of War, ca. 1950–ca. 1953
Notes, URL: 4,714 records. <www.archives.gov/aad>. Click on Search | People.

United States
Type: Database; KO
Year Range: 1950–1954
Online: Free
Title: Repatriated Korean Conflict Prisoners of War File
Notes, URL: 4,447 former POWs. <www.archives.gov/aad>. Click on Search | People.

United States
Type: Database; KO
Year Range: 1950–1957
Online: Free
Title: Korean Conflict Casualty File
Notes, URL: 33,642 records. <www.archives.gov/aad>. Click on Search | People.

United States
Type: Database; VN
Year Range: 1956–1998
Online: Free
Title: Combat Area Casualties Database
Notes, URL: 58,965 U.S. military officers and soldiers who died or who were missing in action or prisoners of war in Southeast Asia during and after the Vietnam War. <www.archives.gov/aad>. Click on Search | People.

United States
Type: Database; VN
Year Range: 1961–1981
Online: Free
Title: Data File from the Casualty Information System
Notes, URL: 293,858 members of the U.S. Army and their dependents who were killed, injured, or missing in action anywhere in the world. About 85% of the records relate to the Vietnam War, 1961 to 1975. <www.archives.gov/aad>. Click on Search | People.

United States
Type: Database; VN
Online: Free
Title: State-Level Casualty Lists for the Vietnam Conflict, Sorted Alphabetically by Last Name
Notes, URL: <www.archives.gov/research_room/research_topics/vietnam_war_casualty_lists/state_level_index_alphabetical.html>

United States
Type: Database; VN
Online: Free
Title: The Vietnam Casualty Search Engine
Notes, URL: <www.no-quarter.org>

United States
Type: Index; VN
Online: Ancestry
Title: Vietnam Casualty Index
Notes, URL: 58,000 names. <www.ancestry.com/search/rectype/inddbs/3095.htm>

United States
Type: Index; VN
Online: Free
Title: Vietnam-Era Prisoner-of-War/Missing-in-Action Database
Notes, URL: <http://lcweb2.loc.gov/pow/powhome.html>

United States
Type: Database; VN
Online: MilitaryUSA.com
Title: Vietnam Veterans Casualty Database
Notes, URL: <www.militaryusa.com>. $9.95/week, $19.95/month, or $39.95/year.

United States
Type: Database; VN
Online: MilitaryUSA.com
Title: Vietnam Veterans Database
Notes, URL: Over 2.7 million names. <www.militaryusa.com/>. $9.95/week, $19.95/month, or $39.95/year.

United States
Type: Transcripts; VN
Online: Free
Title: The Vietnam Veterans Memorial Wall Page
Notes, URL: 58,229 names listed on the Memorial. <www.thewall-usa.com/>

United States
Type: Transcripts; VN
Online: Free
Title: The Wall on the Web
Notes, URL: 58,169 names listed on the Vietnam Veterans Memorial Wall. <www.vietvet.org/thewall/thewallm.html>

United States
Type: Database; VN
Online: Free
Title: Vietnam War Medal of Honor Recipients (A-L)
Notes, URL: <www.army.mil/cmh-pg/mohviet.htm>

United States
Type: Database; VN
Online: Free
Title: Vietnam War Medal of Honor Recipients (M-Z)
Notes, URL: <www.army.mil/cmh-pg/mohviet2.htm>

United States
Type: Database; PG
Year Range: 1990–1991
Online: MilitaryUSA.com
Title: Desert Storm Casualty Database
Notes, URL: <www.militaryusa.com/desert_casulties.cfm>. $9.95/week, $19.95/month, or $39.95/year.

Alabama
Type: Abstracts; REV
Online: Ancestry
Title: Alabama Revolutionary War Soldiers
Notes, URL: Source: Alabama Department of Archives and History and Thomas M.

Owen, comp. *Revolutionary Soldiers in Alabama.* <www.ancestry.com/search/rectype/inddbs/4237.htm>

Alabama
Type: Compiled research; REV
CD-ROM: $28 (Mac/Win), Heritage Books, item #1418
Title: Heritage Books Archives: Alabama Volume 1
Notes, URL: Includes *Revolutionary Soldiers in Alabama,* which contains brief biographies. <www.heritagebooks.co m>. Search on "1418."

Alabama
Type: Index; CW
Online: Free
Title: Alabama Civil War Service Database
Notes, URL: <www.archives.state.al.us/civil war/index.cfm>

Arizona
Type: Transcript; 1812-CW
Online: Free
Title: 1883 Pensioners on the Roll: Arizona Territory
Notes, URL: <http://homepages.rootsweb.com/~godwin/reference/arizona 1883.html>

Arizona, Pima Co., Tucson
Type: Transcript
Year Range: 1791
Online: Free
Title: Río Nuevo Archaeology and History: The 1791 Tucson Presidio Roster
Notes, URL: List of soldiers at the Spanish Presidio of Tucson. <www.rio-nuevo.org/rionuevo/people/records/tucson_1791.htm>

Arkansas
Type: Index
Year Range: 1866–1900
Online: Ancestry
Title: Ft. Smith Criminal Case Files, 1866–1900
Notes, URL: 50,000 cases. <www.ancestry.com/search/rectype/inddbs/3119 .htm>

Arkansas
Type: Database; CW
Year Range: 1890–1963
Online: Free
Title: Arkansas History Commission: Arkansas Confederate Home
Notes, URL: A home for indigent Confederate soldiers & their widows. <http://arkansashistory.arkansas.com/resource_types/military_records>

California, Los Angeles Co., Los Angeles
Type: Index; CW-SA-WWI
Year Range: 1888–1933
Online: Free
Title: Sawtelle Disabled Veterans Home, Los Angeles, Case Files, 1888–1933
Notes, URL: Veterans of the Civil War, Spanish-American War, various Indian conflicts, Pershing's incursion into Mexico, or the First World War. <www.a rchives.gov/facilities/ca/laguna_niguel/disabled_veterans_files.html>

Colorado
Type: Index
Year Range: 1862–1949
Online: Free
Title: Colorado Veterans' Grave Registrations 1862–1949
Notes, URL: <www.colorado.gov/dpa/doit/archives/military/graves/index.html>

Colorado
Type: Index; CW
Online: Free
Title: Colorado Civil War Casualties Index
Notes, URL: <www.colorado.gov/dpa/doit/archives/ciwardea.html>

Colorado
Type: Index; CW
Online: Free
Title: Colorado Civil War Grand Army of the Republic, Civil War Veterans
Notes, URL: <www.denver.lib.co.us/ebra nch/whg/datafile.html>

Colorado
Type: Index; CW
Year Range: 1861–1865
Online: Free
Title: Colorado Volunteers Transcript of Records Index
Notes, URL: <www.colorado.gov/dpa/doit/archives/military/trans/>

Colorado
Type: Index; SA
Year Range: 1898
Online: Free
Title: Colorado Volunteers in the Spanish American War (1898)
Notes, URL: <www.colorado.gov/dpa/doit/archives/military/span_am_war/>

Colorado
Type: Database; WWI
Online: Ancestry
Title: Colorado Soldiers in WWI, 1917–18
Notes, URL: More than 43,000 names. Source: *Roster of Men and Women Who Served in the World War from Colorado, 1917–18.* <www.ancestry.com/search/rectype/inddbs/5442.htm>

Colorado, Conejos Co.
Type: Index; WWI
Year Range: 1917–1918
Online: Free
Title: Conejos County WWI Enlistments 1917–1918
Notes, URL: <www.colorado.gov/dpa/doit/archives/military/enlistments/conejos _county.html>

Connecticut
Type: Transcript; FI
Year Range: 1755–1762
Online: Ancestry
Title: Connecticut Soldiers, French and Indian War, 1755–62
Notes, URL: Over 29,000 names. Source: Bates, Albert C., ed. *Rolls of Connecticut Men in the French and Indian War, 1755–1762.* <www.ancestry.com/sea rch/rectype/inddbs/3983.htm>

Connecticut
Type: Digital images of books; FI-REV
Year Range: 1755–1783
CD-ROM: $28.50 (Mac/Win), Heritage Books, item #1360
Title: Heritage Books Archives: Rolls and Lists of Connecticut Men
Notes, URL: 4 volumes with rolls of Connecticut men in the French and Indian War & the Revolutionary War, compiled by the Connecticut Historical Society. <www.heritagebooks.com>. Search on "1360."

Connecticut
Type: Digital images of books containing transcripts; FI-REV
Year Range: 1700s–1800s
CD-ROM: $29.99, Genealogy.com
Online: Genealogy Library
Title: Connecticut Officers and Soldiers, 1700s–1800s Military Records
Notes, URL: 4 books with 167,000 names. <www.genealogy.com/120facd.html>

Connecticut
Type: Abstracts; REV
Year Range: 1775–1783
Online: Ancestry
Title: Connecticut Revolutionary War Military Lists, 1775–83
Notes, URL: Almost 13,000 names. Source:

Johnston, Henry P., and Iris Rose Guertin, eds. *Collections of the Connecticut Historical Society Revolution Rolls and Lists, 1775–1783, Vol. VIII.* <www.ancestry.com/search/rectype/inddbs/3779.htm>

Connecticut
Type: Abstracts
Year Range: 1835
Online: Ancestry
Title: Connecticut Pensioners, 1835
Notes, URL: <www.ancestry.com/search/rectype/inddbs/3209.htm>

Connecticut
Type: Abstracts; SA
Online: Ancestry
Title: Connecticut Servicemen, Spanish American War
Notes, URL: Over 3,800 names. <www.ancestry.com/search/rectype/inddbs/3803.htm>

Connecticut
Type: Digital images of a book; CW
CD-ROM: $29.95, Willow Bend, item #A0791QP
Online: F&LH
Title: Record of Service of Connecticut Men in the Army and Navy of the United States During the War of the Rebellion
Notes, URL: <www.willowbendbooks.com>

Connecticut
Type: Transcript
Year Range: 1901
Online: Ancestry
Title: Connecticut, Adjutant-General Report, 1901
Notes, URL: Includes members of the Connecticut National Guard. <www.ancestry.com/search/rectype/inddbs/6416.htm>

Connecticut, New London Co., Norwich
Type: Abstracts; CW
Online: Free
Title: Civil War—Norwich, Connecticut: Norwich Volunteers
Notes, URL: Includes rosters. <http://bruceb ouley15.tripod.com/>

Dakota Territory
Type: Abstracts; CW
Online: Free
Title: Dakota Territory During the Civil War
Notes, URL: Includes a roster of all known 1st Dakota Cavalry personnel. <www.rootsweb.com/~usgenweb/sd/military/cw.htm>

Delaware
Type: Abstracts
Year Range: 1835
Online: Ancestry
Title: Delaware Pensioners, 1835
Notes, URL: <www.ancestry.com/search/rectype/inddbs/3228.htm>

Delaware
Type: Digital images; CW
Year Range: 1862–1865
Online: Free
Title: Civil War Records
Notes, URL: Includes lists of Colored Troops. <www.state.de.us/sos/dpa/exhibits/document/civil%20war/>

Delaware
Type: Database; CW
Online: Free
Title: Delaware Roster of Union Soldiers
Notes, URL: <www.bitsofblueandgray.com/roster.htm>

Florida
Type: Abstract
Year Range: 1836–1842
Online: Ancestry
Title: Florida War Death List, 1836–42
Notes, URL: Source: *The Origin, Progress and Conclusion of the Florida War*, by John Sprague. <www.ancestry.com/search/rectype/inddbs/5760.htm>

Florida
Type: Transcripts; CW
Online: Free
Title: Civil War
Notes, URL: Includes muster rolls. <http://mailer.fsu.edu/~rthompso/csa-page.html>

Florida
Type: Transcripts; CW
Online: Free
Title: Florida Civil War Soldiers Index
Notes, URL: Links to regimental rosters. <www.researchonline.net/flcw/mastindx.htm>

Florida
Type: Digital images; CW
Online: Free
Title: Florida Confederate Pension Application Files
Notes, URL: Includes images of about 14,000 pension applications. <http://dlis.dos.state.fl.us/barm/PensionFiles.html>

Florida, Saint Johns Co., Saint Augustine
Type: Digital images of a book; SW
Year Range: 1835–1842
Online: F&LH
Title: Ponce de Leon land and Florida war record
Notes, URL: By George M. Brown. Lists soldiers who were killed.

Georgia
Type: Transcript; REV
Online: Free
Title: Georgia Loyalists
Notes, URL: <www.rootsweb.com/~gagenweb/records/loyalist.htm>

Georgia
Type: Transcript; REV
Year Range: 1769–1785
CD-ROM: $36.50 (Mac/Win), Heritage Books, item #1849
Title: Heritage Books Archives: Georgia Volume 1
Notes, URL: Includes *Revolutionary Records of Georgia*, vols. 1-3, & *History of Georgia*, vols. 1-2. <www.heritagebooks.com>. Search on "1849."

Georgia
Type: Digital images of a book containing an index; REV
Year Range: 1820–1832
Online: Free
Title: Georgia Land Lottery Grants to Revolutionary Veterans
Notes, URL: Source: Hitz, Alex M., comp. *Authentic List of All Land Lottery Grants Made to Veterans of the Revolutionary War by the State of Georgia.* <www.sos.state.ga.us/archives/oe/rv_summary.htm>

Georgia
Type: Digital images of a book containing an index; REV
Year Range: 1820–1832
Online: Ancestry
Title: Land Grants to Georgia Revolutionary War Veterans
Notes, URL: Original data: Hitz, Alex M., comp. *Authentic List of All Land Lottery Grants Made to Veterans of the Revolutionary War by the State of Georgia.* <www.ancestry.com/search/rectype/inddbs/7186.htm>

Georgia
Type: Books; CW

CD-ROM: $35, Eastern Digital Resources
Title: The Civil War in Georgia
Notes, URL: Includes rosters of officers & enlisted men and biographies & genealogies of men from Georgia who served in the war. <www.researchonline.net/catalog/cdindx.htm>

Georgia
Type: Digital images; CW
Online: Free
Title: Georgia Civil War Pension Records
Notes, URL: Images of pension records of Georgia Confederate Civil War veterans & their widows. <http://docuweb.gsu.edu/CivilWar.htm>

Georgia
Type: Index; CW
CD-ROM: $12, Eastern Digital Resources
Online: Free
Title: Georgia Civil War Soldiers Index
Notes, URL: 272,000 names. <www.researchonline.net/gacw>

Georgia
Type: Digital images of books; CW
CD-ROM: $89.95, Eastern Digital Resources
Title: Roster of the Confederate Soldiers of Georgia
Notes, URL: 85,000 names in 6 vols. <www.researchonline.net/catalog/cdindx.htm>

Georgia, Bartow Co., Cassville
Type: Abstracts; CW
Year Range: 1863–1864
Online: Free
Title: List of Deaths of CS Army Personnel at Cassville, Georgia, Hospitals
Notes, URL: From the Atlanta newspaper, the *Southern Confederacy*. <http://hub.dataline.net.au/~tfoen/cassville.htm>

Georgia, Campbell Co.
Type: Text of a book; CW
Online: Genealogy Library
Title: Campbell County Georgia Confederate Pension Roll
Notes, URL: By Nancy Jones Cornell. Select Records | Military | Georgia.

Georgia, Dade Co.
Type: Abstracts; WWI
Year Range: 1917–1918
Online: Free
Title: Birth Information: Residents of Dade County, GA in 1917–18, and Persons with Links to This County
Notes, URL: Information abstracted from civilian registration cards completed in 1917–1918. <ftp://ftp.rootsweb.com/pub/usgenweb/ga/dade/vitals/dadedrft.txt>

Hawaii
Type: Database; WWII
Year Range: 1941
Online: Free
Title: Military Research Room: Pearl Harbor Casualties (U.S.)
Notes, URL: <www.lineages.com/military/PearlHarbor.asp>

Hawaii
Type: Transcript; WWII
Year Range: 1941
Online: Free
Title: Pearl Harbor Casualty List
Notes, URL: <ftp://ftp.rootsweb.com/pub/usgenweb/hi/military/pearl.txt>

Hawaii
Type: Transcript; WWII
Year Range: 1941
Online: Free
Title: Full Pearl Harbor Casualty List, December 7, 1941
Notes, URL: <www.usswestvirginia.org/fulllist.htm>

Hawaii
Type: Transcript; WWII
Year Range: 1941
Online: Free
Title: Comprehensive List of Pearl Harbor Casualties: Civilian and Military Deaths on Oahu, Hawaii, Dec. 7, 1941
Notes, URL: <www.newbie.net/PearlHarbor/casualties.html>

Illinois
Type: Transcripts; REV-1812-CW-WWII-KO
Online: Free
Title: Illinois Trails Military Databases
Notes, URL: Includes several large databases. <www.iltrails.org/military.htm>

Illinois
Type: Text of a book; REV
Online: Ancestry
Title: Illinois Revolutionary War Veteran Burials
Notes, URL: Nearly 1,000 names. Source: *Revolutionary Soldiers Buried in Illinois*. <www.ancestry.com/search/rectype/inddbs/4508.htm>

Illinois
Type: Digital images of a book of compiled information; REV
Online: F&LH
Title: A list of officers of the Illinois Regiment, and of Crockett's Regiment, who have received land for their services . . .

Illinois
Type: Digital images of a book of compiled information; REV
CD-ROM: $29.99, Genealogy.com, CD #508
Online: Genealogy Library
Title: Midwest Pioneers, 1600s–1800s
Notes, URL: About 700 Revolutionary War soldiers buried in Illinois. <www.genealogy.com/508facd.html>

Illinois
Type: Text of a book; REV
Online: Ancestry
Title: Illinois Society of the S.A.R. Yearbook, 1896
Notes, URL: Over 5,000 records. <www.ancestry.com/search/rectype/inddbs/3205.htm>

Illinois
Type: Index; 1812-WW-BH-MX-CW-SA
Online: Free
Title: Illinois State Archives: Databases of Illinois Veterans
Notes, URL: Illinois war veterans plus the 1929 Illinois Roll of Honor & Illinois Soldiers' and Sailors' Home Residents. <www2.sos.state.il.us/departments/archives/databases.html>

Illinois
Type: Transcript; 1812
Online: Free
Title: War of 1812: Bounty Land Grants in the Illinois Military Tract
Notes, URL: Source: House Document No. 262, "Lands in Illinois to Soldiers of Late War," 26th Congress, 1st Session (1840). <www.lineages.com/vault/BountyLands.asp>

Illinois
Type: Abstracts
Year Range: 1840–1847
Online: Ancestry
Title: LDS Military Records, 1840–47
Notes, URL: Nearly 1,000 members of the Nauvoo Legion (part of the Illinois Militia) & the Mormon Battalion. <www.ancestry.com/search/rectype/inddbs/4233.htm>

Illinois
Type: Index; CW

Online: Free
Title: Database of Illinois Civil War Veterans
Notes, URL: 250,000 names. Source: *Report of the Adjutant General of the State of Illinois*, vols. 1-8. <www.sos.state.il.us/departments/archives/datcivil.html>

Illinois
Type: Index; CW
Online: Free
Title: Database of Illinois Civil War Veterans of Missouri Units
Notes, URL: 5,610 names. <www.sos.state.il.us/departments/archives/missouri.html>

Illinois
Type: Index; CW
Online: Free
Title: Database of Illinois Civil War Veterans Serving in the U.S. Navy
Notes, URL: 3,000 names. <www.sos.state.il.us/departments/archives/ilnavy.html>

Illinois
Type: Index; SA
Online: Free
Title: Database of Illinois Spanish-American War Veterans
Notes, URL: 11,000 names. <www.sos.state.il.us/departments/archives/spanam.html>

Illinois, Knox Co.
Type: Index; WWI
Online: Free
Title: Knox County, Illinois, Genealogy & History: 1917–1919 Knox County Honor Roll Service Record
Notes, URL: 3,443 people who assisted in the WWI effort through the military & on the home front. <www.rootsweb.com/~ilknox/records/records.htm>

Illinois, Madison Co., Alton
Type: Abstracts; CW
Online: Free
Title: Alton in the Civil War: Alton Prison
Notes, URL: Confederate Soldiers who died at the Alton Prison. <www.altonweb.com/history/civilwar/confed/index.html>

Illinois, Richland Co.
Type: Transcript; CW
Online: Free
Title: Names of Richland County, Illinois Soldiers Who Participated in the Siege of Vicksburg, Ms.
Notes, URL: Names inscribed on a memorial. <www.geocities.com/CapitolHill/Congress/5574/names.html>

Illinois, Rock Island Co., Rock Island
Type: Abstracts; CW
Online: Free
Title: Confederate POW's Listed in Arkansas Units Who Died in Rock Island, IL Prison Camp
Notes, URL: Source: *Register of Confederate Dead Rock Island Illinois*. <www.couchgenweb.com/civilwar/rockisld.htm>

Illinois, Rock Island Co., Rock Island
Type: Abstracts; CW
Online: Free
Title: Confederate POW's Listed in Kentucky Units Who Died in Rock Island, IL Prison Camp
Notes, URL: Source: *Register of Confederate Dead Rock Island Illinois*. <http://home.hiwaay.net/~woliver/JeanSmallwood/KentuckyPage.html#kypow>

Indiana
Type: Digital images of a book of compiled information; REV
CD-ROM: $29.99, Genealogy.com, CD #508
Online: Genealogy Library
Title: Midwest Pioneers, 1600s–1800s
Notes, URL: Revolutionary War soldiers buried in Indiana or who had lived in Indiana. <www.genealogy.com/508facd.html>

Indiana
Type: Transcripts; 1812
Year Range: 1811
Online: Free
Title: War of 1812 Roster Lists
Notes, URL: <www.genealogytoday.com/pub/1812rost.htm>

Indiana
Type: Index; CW
Online: Free
Title: Civil War—Indiana
Notes, URL: Click on "Soldier Search." <http://civilwarindiana.com>

Indiana
Type: Abstracts; CW
Online: Free
Title: Pensioners on the Roll: January 1, 1883
Notes, URL: Carroll, Cass, Clinton, Grant, Howard, Miami, & Tipton Counties. <www.kokomo.lib.in.us/genealogy/pensidx.html>

Indiana
Type: Text of a book; SA
Online: Ancestry
Title: Indiana Spanish American War Records
Notes, URL: Over 7,800 names. Source: Gore, James K, Gen. *Record of Indiana Volunteers in the Spanish-American War.* <www.ancestry.com/search/rectype/inddbs/4305.htm>

Indiana
Type: Text of a book; WWI
Year Range: 1914–1918
Online: Ancestry
Title: Indiana Gold Star Honor Roll, 1914–18
Notes, URL: 10,500 soldiers from Indiana who died in World War I. Source: Indiana Historical Commission. <www.ancestry.com/search/rectype/inddbs/5182.htm>

Indiana
Type: Index; WWII
Year Range: 1942–1946
Online: Free
Title: Indiana World War II Servicemen Database, Indiana State Library
Notes, URL: An index of 26,058 names in the three major Indianapolis daily newspapers (*News*, *Star*, and *Times*) for notices of casualties, prisoners, etc. <http://199.8.200.90:591/wwii.html>

Indiana, Marion Co., Indianapolis
Type: Digital images of a book; CW
Online: F&LH
Title: Indianapolis and the Civil War
Notes, URL: By John H. Holliday.

Indiana, Morgan Co.
Type: Abstracts; CW
Year Range: 1890
Online: Free
Title: Morgan County Indiana 1890 Enrollment of Soldiers
Notes, URL: Soldiers or their heirs eligible for government pensions. <www.scican.net/~morglib/genasist/enrl1890.html>

Iowa
Type: Books; CW
Online: Ancestry
Title: Iowa Union Soldier Burial Records
Notes, URL: More than 5,000 names. <www.ancestry.com/search/rectype/inddbs/3854.htm>

Iowa, Keokuk Co.
Type: Transcript; CW

Online: Free
Title: Keokuk County Civil War Soldiers from the *1880 History of Keokuk County Iowa*
Notes, URL: <www.rootsweb.com/~iakeokuk/civilwar.html>

Iowa, Muscatine Co.
Type: Abstracts; CW
Online: Ancestry
Title: Muscatine County, Iowa Civil War Soldiers
Notes, URL: Over 2,300 names. <www.ancestry.com/search/rectype/inddbs/3639.htm>

Kansas
Type: Abstracts; CW
Online: Ancestry
Title: Kansas Civil War Soldiers
Notes, URL: Over 20,000 names. <www.ancestry.com/search/rectype/inddbs/3916.htm>

Kansas
Type: Books; CW
Online: Free
Title: Kansas in the Civil War
Notes, URL: Includes a list of veterans buried in Kansas. <http://skyways.lib.ks.us/kansas/genweb/civilwar/index.html>

Kansas
Type: Abstracts; CW
Year Range: 1863–1865
Online: Free
Title: Kansas Prisoners of War at Camp Ford, Texas 1863–1865
Notes, URL: <http://history.cc.ukans.edu/heritage/research/campford.html>

Kansas
Type: Transcript; CW
Year Range: 1883
Online: Free
Title: Pensioners on the Roll: January 1, 1883
Notes, URL: Civil War veterans & a few veterans of the War of 1812. <http://skyways.lib.ks.us/genweb/archives/pensions.htm>

Kansas
Type: Abstracts; WWI
Online: Free
Title: 1917–18 Civilian Draft Registration Cards
Notes, URL: <http://skyways.lib.ks.us/genweb/archives/regcards.htm>

Kansas
Type: Abstracts; WWI
Online: Ancestry
Title: Kansas 353rd Infantry Regiment in World War I
Notes, URL: Source: *They're from Kansas (353rd Infantry Regiment, 89th Division in World War I.)* <www.ancestry.com/search/rectype/inddbs/5695.htm>

Kansas, Leavenworth Co., Leavenworth
Type: Transcript
Year Range: 1915–1916
Online: Ancestry
Title: Leavenworth, Kansas Veterans, 1915–16
Notes, URL: Source: *R.L. Polk City Directory of Leavenworth, Kansas.* <www.ancestry.com/search/rectype/inddbs/4367.htm>

Kentucky
Type: Digital images of books; REV-1812
CD-ROM: $29.99, Genealogy.com, CD #519
Online: Genealogy Library
Title: Early Kentucky Settlers, 1700s–1800s
Notes, URL: Includes *Revolutionary Soldiers in Kentucky, Kentucky Soldiers of the War of 1812, Kentucky in the War of 1812, Remember the Raisin, & Kentucky Pension Roll for 1835.* <www.genealogy.com/519facd.html>

Kentucky
Type: Digital images of a book; 1812
Online: Ancestry
Title: Kentucky Soldiers of the War of 1812
Notes, URL: Source: *Report of the Adjutant General of the State of Kentucky: Soldiers of the War of 1812.* <www.ancestry.com/search/rectype/inddbs/6341.htm>

Kentucky
Type: Transcripts; CW
Online: Free
Title: Civil War: Kentucky's Civil War Pension Applications
Notes, URL: <www.rootsweb.com/~usgenweb/pensions/civilwar/kyindex.htm>

Kentucky
Type: Digital images of a book; CW
Year Range: 1861–1866
Online: Ancestry
Title: Kentucky Civil War Union Volunteers
Notes, URL: Original data: *Report of the Adjutant General of the State of Kentucky. Vols. 1-2.* <www.ancestry.com/search/rectype/inddbs/7082.htm>

Kentucky
Type: Digital images of a book; CW
Year Range: 1861–1865
Online: Ancestry
Title: Kentucky Confederate Volunteers
Notes, URL: From Adjutant General's Office, *Report of the Adjutant General of the State of Kentucky. Confederate Kentucky Volunteers. War 1861–1865.* <www.ancestry.com/search/rectype/inddbs/7046.htm>

Kentucky
Type: Transcripts; CW
Online: Free
Title: USGenWeb Archives Kentucky in the Civil War
Notes, URL: Union & Confederate army rosters. <www.rootsweb.com/~usgenweb/ky/military/civilwar.html>

Kentucky, Fayette Co.
Type: Digital images of a book; REV
Online: F&LH
Title: Revolutionary War pensions of soldiers who settled in Fayette County, Kentucky
Notes, URL: By Annie Walker Burns.

Kentucky, Greenup Co.
Type: Digital images of books; REV
Year Range: 1804–1902
CD-ROM: $30.50 (Mac/Win), Heritage Books, item #1424
Title: Heritage Books Archives: Kentucky Volume 2
Notes, URL: 6 books, including *Revolutionary War Pensions.* <www.heritagebooks.com>. Search on "1424."

Kentucky, Hardin Co.
Type: Digital images of a book containing abstracts; REV-1812
Online: F&LH
Title: Abstracts of pension papers, Revolutionary War, and 1812 War soldiers who settled in Hardin County, Ky.

Kentucky, Hickman Co.
Type: Digital images of a book containing abstracts; REV-1812
Online: F&LH
Title: Abstracts of pension papers of soldiers of the Revolutionary War, War of 1812, and Indian wars, who settled in Hickman County, Kentucky

Louisiana
Type: Digital images of books; CO-1812
Year Range: 1720–1812

CD-ROM: $29.99, Genealogy.com, CD #525
Online: Genealogy Library
Title: Early Louisiana Settlers, 1600s–1800s
Notes, URL: Includes *Louisiana Troops 1720–1770 & Louisiana Soldiers in the War of 1812*. <www.genealogy.com/525facd.html>

Louisiana
Type: Text of a book; 1812
Online: Ancestry
Title: Louisiana Soldiers in the War of 1812
Notes, URL: Nearly 15,000 soldiers. Source: Pierson, Marion, comp. *Louisiana Soldiers in the War of 1812*. <www.ancestry.com/search/rectype/inddbs/3339.htm>

Louisiana
Type: Index; CW
Online: Free
Title: Louisiana Archives Index of Confederate Pension Application Index
Notes, URL: <www.rootsweb.com/~usgenweb/la/military/civilwar/pensindex.htm> or <www.sec.state.la.us/archives/gen/cpa-index.htm>

Louisiana
Type: Text of a book; CW
Online: Ancestry
Title: Louisiana Confederate Soldiers
Notes, URL: Over 120,000 records. Source: Andrew B. Booth, *Records of Louisiana Confederate Soldiers & Confederate Commands*, vols. I-III. <www.ancestry.com/search/rectype/inddbs/3199.htm>

Louisiana, Claiborne Parish
Type: Digital images of a book; CW
Online: F&LH
Title: The history of Claiborne Parish, Louisiana: from its incorporation in 1828 to the close of the year 1885
Notes, URL: "Also the muster and death rolls of her sons in the late bloody war."

Louisiana, Orleans Parish, New Orleans
Type: Digital images of books; 1812
Year Range: 1720–1733
CD-ROM: $29.99, Genealogy.com, CD #525
Online: Genealogy Library
Title: Early Louisiana Settlers, 1600s–1800s
Notes, URL: Names 12,500 soldiers in the Battle of New Orleans & the War of 1812. Includes *Louisiana Troops 1720–1770 & Louisiana Soldiers in the War of 1812*. <www.genealogy.com/525facd-long.html>

Louisiana, Orleans Parish, New Orleans
Type: Transcript; CW
Year Range: 1861
Online: Free
Title: Register of Confederate Naval Patients in the Charity Hospital at New Orleans, Louisiana, 1861
Notes, URL: <http://hub.dataline.net.au/~tfoen/charity.htm>

Maine
Type: Digital images of books; REV
CD-ROM: $29.99, Genealogy.com, CD #523
Online: Genealogy Library
Title: Maine & New Hampshire Settlers, 1600s–1900s
Notes, URL: Includes *An Alphabetical Index of Revolutionary Pensioners Living in Maine* containing 5,000 names & *Names of Soldiers of the American Revolution from Maine*. <www.genealogy.com/523facd.html>

Maine
Type: Abstracts; REV
Year Range: 1835–1836
Online: Ancestry
Title: Maine Revolutionary War Bounty Applications, 1835–36
Notes, URL: Over 1,000 names. <www.ancestry.com/search/rectype/inddbs/4461.htm>

Maine
Type: Abstracts
Year Range: 1835
Online: Ancestry
Title: Maine Pensioners, 1835
Notes, URL: <www.ancestry.com/search/rectype/inddbs/3213.htm>

Maine
Type: Abstracts; AR
Year Range: 1839
Online: Ancestry
Title: Aroostook War (Maine) History and Roster
Notes, URL: Over 3,000 names. Source: *Historical Sketch and Roster of the Aroostook War*. <www.ancestry.com/search/rectype/inddbs/4518.htm>

Maine
Type: Abstracts; WWI
Year Range: 1917–1918
Online: Ancestry
Title: Maine Military Men, 1917–18
Notes, URL: About 36,300 names. Source: *Roster of Maine in the Military Service of the U.S. and Allies in World War 1917–1919*, vols. I-II. <www.ancestry.com/search/rectype/inddbs/4619.htm>

Maine, Cumberland Co., Portland
Type: Digital images of a book; CW
Online: F&LH
Title: Portland soldiers and sailors: a brief sketch of the part they took in the War of the Rebellion

Maine, York Co.
Type: Digital images of a book; REV
Year Range: 1775–1783
Online: F&LH
Title: A record of the services of the commissioned officers and enlisted men of Kittery and Eliot, Maine: who served their country on land and sea in the American Revolution, from 1775 to 1783

Maryland
Type: Digital images of a book containing abstracts; REV
Online: F&LH
Title: Maryland Revolutionary records: data obtained from 3,050 pension claims and bounty land applications

Maryland
Type: Index; REV
Year Range: 1778–1861
Online: Free
Title: Maryland Indexes (Pension Records, Revolutionary War, Index)
Notes, URL: Requires a password & the PaperPort Max file viewer. See <www.mdarchives.state.md.us/msa/refserv/indexes/html/howto.html> for help. <www.mdarchives.state.md.us/msa/refserv/stagser/ssu1400/html/ssu1421.html>

Maryland
Type: Abstracts; REV
Online: Ancestry
Title: Maryland Revolutionary War Records
Notes, URL: Over 3,000 pension & bounty applications & nearly 1,000 marriages of Maryland soldiers. Source: Newman, Harry Wright. *Maryland Revolutionary Records*. <www.ancestry.com/search/rectype/inddbs/4260.htm>

Maryland
Type: Digital images of books; REV-1812-CW

CD-ROM: $29.99, Genealogy.com, CD #521
Online: Genealogy Library
Title: Maryland Settlers & Soldiers, 1700s–1800s
Notes, URL: Includes *Muster Rolls and Other Records of Service of Maryland Troops in the American Revolution, 1775–1783, Orderly Book of the "Maryland Loyalists Regiment," June 18 & The British Invasion of Maryland, 1812–1815.* <www.geneal ogy.com/521facd.html>

Maryland
Type: Abstracts; CW
Online: Ancestry
Title: Maryland Soldiers in the Civil War, Vol. 1
Notes, URL: Over 36,000 records. <www.an cestry.com/search/rectype/inddbs/ 3087.htm>

Maryland
Type: Abstracts; CW
Online: Ancestry
Title: Maryland Soldiers in the Civil War, Vol. 2
Notes, URL: <www.ancestry.com/search/re ctype/inddbs/3088.htm>

Maryland
Type: Index
Year Range: 1898–1933
Online: Free
Title: Military Department: Service Records, Maryland National Guard, Index
Notes, URL: Index to the service records of the Maryland National Guard. <www.m darchives.state.md.us/msa/stagser/ s1400/s1499/html/ssi1499.html>

Maryland
Type: Text of books; WWI
Year Range: 1917–1918
Online: Ancestry
Title: Maryland Military Men, 1917–18
Notes, URL: Over 67,900 names. Source: *Maryland in the World War, 1917–1919; Military and Naval Service Records*, Vol. I-II. <www.ancestry.com/search/rectype/ inddbs/4545.htm>

Maryland, Baltimore (city)
Type: Abstracts; CW
Online: Free
Title: Civil War Prisons
Notes, URL: Confederate soldiers held prisoner at Fort McHenry & Union soldiers held prisoner at Andersonville. <www.itd.nps.gov/cwss/ prisoners.htm>

Maryland, Dorchester Co.
Type: Digital images of books; CW
CD-ROM: $31 (Mac/Win), Heritage Books, item #1623
Title: Heritage Books Archives: Maryland Volume 3
Notes, URL: Includes 5 volumes, including *History of Dorchester County, Maryland* with a list of Civil War soldiers. <www.he ritagebooks.com>. Search on "1623."

Maryland, St. Mary's Co.
Type: Abstracts; CW
Online: Free
Title: Point Lookout Confederate Cemetery: Point Lookout State Park, St. Mary's County, Maryland
Notes, URL: 3,053 records. <www.intermen t.net/data/us/md/stmarys/ptlookout/ index.htm>

Maryland, St. Mary's Co.
Type: Abstracts; CW
Online: Free
Title: Partial List of Point Lookout Dead
Notes, URL: <www.members.tripod.com/ ~PLPOW/POWDead_A-E.htm>

Massachusetts
Type: Compiled information; CO
Online: NEHGS
Title: Massachusetts Soldiers in the Colonial Wars
Notes, URL: More than 40,000 service records originally published in 7 volumes. <www.newenglandancestor s.org/research/database/ colonial_wars>

Massachusetts
Type: Compiled research; KP
Year Range: 1675–1677
Online: Genealogy Library
Title: Soldiers in King Philip's War
Notes, URL: Text of the book by George Madison Bodge. Select Subjects I Records I Colonial Lists I New England.

Massachusetts
Type: Digital images of books; KP
Year Range: 1675–1677
CD-ROM: $39.99, Genealogy.com, CD #504
Online: Genealogy Library
Title: (Genealogical Records:) Early New England Settlers, 1600s–1800s
Notes, URL: Includes the book, *Soldiers in King Philip's War: Official Lists of the Soldiers of Massachusetts Colony Serving in Philip's War.* <www.genealogy.com/ 504facd.html>

Massachusetts
Type: Digital images of books; KP-REV-1812
CD-ROM: $39.95, Genealogy.com, CD #526
Online: Genealogy Library
Title: Massachusetts, 1600s–1800s Genealogical Records
Notes, URL: Names over 5,000 soldiers in King Philip's War (1675–1677), 501 Loyalists of Massachusetts, & Massachusetts soldiers in the War of 1812. <www.genealogy.com/526facd. html>

Massachusetts
Type: Compiled information; REV
Year Range: 1765–1790
Online: NEHGS
Title: Divided Hearts: Massachusetts Loyalists, 1765–1790
Notes, URL: Information on 1,705 loyalists. From the book by David E. Maas. <www. newenglandancestors.org/research/ database/DividedHearts>

Massachusetts
Type: Transcript; REV
Year Range: 1775
Online: NEHGS
Title: Massachusetts Militia Companies and Officers in the Lexington Alarm
Notes, URL: Muster rolls. <www.newenglan dancestors.org/research/database/ lexingtonalarm>

Massachusetts
Type: Digital images; REV
Year Range: 1799–1807
Online: NEHGS
Title: Massachusetts Revolutionary War Pensioners' Receipts, 1799–1807
Notes, URL: <www.newenglandancestors. org/research/database/ mass_pension2>

Massachusetts
Type: Database; REV
Online: NEHGS
Title: The Massachusetts Society of the Cincinnati Profiles
Notes, URL: Officers of the Continental Army & their descendants. <www.newe nglandancestors.org/research/ database/msc>

Massachusetts
Type: Text of books; REV
CD-ROM: $29.95 (Win), Ancestry.com, item #2307, <http://shops.ancestry.co m>. Search on "Soldiers and Sailors." The CD is called "Massachusetts

Revolutionary War Soldiers and Sailors."
Online: Ancestry
Title: Massachusetts Soldiers and Sailors in the War of the Revolution, 17 Vols.
Notes, URL: Over 175,000 records. <www.ancestry.com/search/rectype/inddbs/3090.htm>

Massachusetts
Type: Digital images of books; REV
CD-ROM: $39.99, Genealogy.com, CD #147
Title: Massachusetts Revolutionary War Soldiers & Sailors, 1775–1782
Notes, URL: All 17 volumes of *Massachusetts Soldiers and Sailors of the Revolutionary War*. <www.genealogy.com/147facd.html>

Massachusetts
Type: Digital images; REV-1812
Year Range: 1829–1837
Online: NEHGS
Title: Massachusetts Revolutionary War Pensioners' Receipts, 1829–1837
Notes, URL: <www.newenglandancestors.org/research/database/mass_pension>

Massachusetts
Type: Digital images of a book containing abstracts; 1812
CD-ROM: $39.99, Genealogy.com, CD #526
Online: Genealogy Library
Title: Massachusetts, 1600s–1800s Genealogical Records
Notes, URL: Includes the names of Mass. soldiers in the War of 1812. <www.genealogy.com/526facd.html>

Massachusetts
Type: Digital images of a book; 1812
CD-ROM: $19.95, Willow Bend, item #A0797QP
Title: Records of Massachusetts Voluntary Militia
Notes, URL: <www.willowbendbooks.com>

Massachusetts
Type: Index; CW
Online: Free
Title: Canadians Who Served with Massachusetts Regiments During the Civil War
Notes, URL: <www.geocities.com/cancivwar/Massachusetts.html>

Massachusetts
Type: Text of a book; CW
Year Range: 1861–1865
Online: Ancestry
Title: Massachusetts Army & Navy, 1861–65
Notes, URL: Officers and soldiers killed in action. Source: Higginson, Thomas Wentworth. *Massachusetts in the Army and Navy during the war of 1861–1865*. <www.ancestry.com/search/rectype/inddbs/3082.htm>

Massachusetts
Type: Abstracts; CW
Online: Free
Title: Massachusetts Civil War Research Center
Notes, URL: Includes a database of over 150,000 soldiers, sailors, & marines who served in Massachusetts units and regiments during the Civil War. <www.massachusettscivilwar.com>

Massachusetts
Type: Text of a book; CW
Year Range: 1866–1888
Online: Ancestry
Title: Massachusetts Military Company History, Vol. 4
Notes, URL: Source: Roberts, Oliver Ayer. *History of the Military Company of Massachusetts*, vol. 4. <www.ancestry.com/search/rectype/inddbs/3100.htm>

Massachusetts
Type: Digital images of a book; CW
Year Range: 1866–1947
CD-ROM: $25 (Mac/Win), Heritage Books, item #2130
Title: Grand Army of the Republic: Civil War Veterans, Department of Massachusetts, 1866–1947
Notes, URL: Includes over 14,000 members' records with over 36,000 names. Also, 100,000 members of the Sons of Veterans and the Ladies Auxiliaries. <www.heritagebooks.com>. Search on "2130."

Massachusetts
Type: Digital images of a book; CW
Online: F&LH
Title: Massachusetts in the Army and Navy during the war of 1861–1865
Notes, URL: By Thomas Wentworth Higginson.

Massachusetts
Type: A book containing abstracts; CW
CD-ROM: $39.99, Genealogy.com, CD #134
Title: Massachusetts Civil War Soldiers and Sailors, 1861–1865 Military Records
Notes, URL: Information from the nine-volume *Massachusetts Soldiers, Sailors, and Marines in the Civil War*. <www.genealogy.com/134facd.html>

Massachusetts
Type: Abstracts; SA
Online: Ancestry
Title: Massachusetts Spanish American War Records
Notes, URL: Source: Harry E. Webber, compiler. *Twelve Months with the Eighth Massachusetts Infantry*. <www.ancestry.com/search/rectype/inddbs/5070.htm>

Massachusetts, Franklin Co., Ashfield
Type: Digital images of a book; REV
Online: F&LH
Title: Historical sketches of the times and men in Ashfield, Mass. during the Revolutionary War
Notes, URL: By Barnabas Howes.

Massachusetts, Hampden Co., Wales
Type: Pages images of a book; CW
Online: F&LH
Title: An address delivered in Wales, October 5, 1862
Notes, URL: Includes "a catalogue of the names, etc. of soldiers from this town who served in the armies of our governmemt [*sic*] in the late Civil War."

Massachusetts, Middlesex Co., Dracut
Type: Pages images of a book; REV
Online: F&LH
Title: In memoriam: citizen soldiers of Dracut, Mass. who served in the war of the American Revolution, 1775–1783

Massachusetts, Middlesex Co., Watertown
Type: Pages images of a book; CO-REV-CW-SA
Online: F&LH
Title: Watertown's military history

Massachusetts, Middlesex Co., Watertown
Type: Text of a book; CO-REV-CW-SA
Online: Genealogy Library
Title: Watertown's military history
Notes, URL: Select Records | Military | Massachusetts.

Massachusetts, Norfolk Co., Dover
Type: Digital images of a book; FI-REV-1812-MX-CW-SA
Online: F&LH

Title: Biographical sketch of the residents of that part of Dedham, which is now Dover, who took part in King Philip's War, the last French and Indian War, and the Revolution
Notes, URL: "Together with the record of the services of those who represented Dover in the War of 1812, the war with Mexico, the Civil War, and the war with Spain."

Massachusetts, Norfolk Co., Medway
Type: Digital images of a book; FI-REV-1812-CW
Year Range: 1745–1885
Online: F&LH
Title: The Military history of Medway, Mass., 1745–1885
Notes, URL: Includes soldiers' names.

Massachusetts, Plymouth Co., Hanover
Type: Digital images of a book; CW
Online: F&LH
Title: The record of the procession and of the exercises at the dedication of the monument (Wednesday, July 17, A.D. 1878) erected by the people of Hanover, Massachusetts
Notes, URL: "In grateful memory of the soldiers and sailors of that town who died in the war for the preservation of the union."

Massachusetts, Plymouth Co., Hingham
Type: Digital images of a book; CW
Online: F&LH
Title: The town of Hingham in the late Civil War: with sketches of its soldiers and sailors
Notes, URL: By Fearing Burr.

Massachusetts, Plymouth Co., Pembroke
Type: Digital images of a book; CW
Online: F&LH
Title: The record of the procession and of the exercises at the dedication of the monument: Wednesday, June 12th, A.D. 1889
Notes, URL: "Erected by the people of Pembroke, Mass. in grateful memory of the soldiers and sailors of that town who served in the war for the preservation of the Union."

Massachusetts, Suffolk Co., Boston
Type: Abstracts
Year Range: 1698
Online: Ancestry
Title: Boston, Massachusetts, Males in Major Townsend's Camp, 1698
Notes, URL: Source: *A Report of the Record Commissioners of the City of Boston Containing Miscellaneous Papers*. <www.ancestry.com/search/rectype/inddbs/6351.htm>

Massachusetts, Suffolk Co., Charlestown
Type: Digital images of a book; CW
Online: F&LH
Title: Register of the Charlestown men in the service during the Civil War, 1861–1865
Notes, URL: By James Edward Stone.

Massachusetts, Suffolk Co., Chelsea
Type: Digital images of a book; CW
Online: F&LH
Title: Roll of honor of the city of Chelsea
Notes, URL: "A list of the soldiers and sailors who served on the quota of Chelsea in the great Civil War."

Massachusetts, Worcester Co., Fitchburg
Type: Digital images of a book; CW
Online: F&LH
Title: Fitchburg in the war of the rebellion
Notes, URL: By Henry A. Willis.

Massachusetts, Worcester Co., Lancaster
Type: Digital images of a book; CO-REV-1812
Year Range: 1740–1865
Online: F&LH
Title: The military annals of Lancaster, Massachusetts, 1740–1865
Notes, URL: "Including lists of soldiers serving in the colonial and revolutionary wars for the Lancastrian towns, Berlin, Bolton, Harvard, Leominster, and Sterling."

Massachusetts, Worcester Co., North Brookfield
Type: Digital images of a book; CW
Online: F&LH
Title: A Historical record of the soldiers and sailors of North Brookfield.

Massachusetts, Worcester Co., Oakham
Type: Digital images of a book; REV-1812-CW
Online: F&LH
Title: Soldiers of Oakham, Massachusetts in the Revolutionary War, the War of 1812, and the Civil War
Notes, URL: By Henry Parks Wright.

Massachusetts, Worcester Co., Worcester
Type: Digital images of a book; CW
Online: F&LH
Title: History of Worcester in the War of the Rebellion
Notes, URL: By Abijah P. Marvin.

Michigan
Type: Abstracts
Year Range: 1775–1836
Online: Ancestry
Title: Michigan Military Records, 1775–1836
Notes, URL: Over 1,000 names. <www.ancestry.com/search/rectype/inddbs/4465.htm>

Michigan
Type: Digital images of a book of compiled information; REV
CD-ROM: $29.99, Genealogy.com, CD #508
Online: Genealogy Library
Title: Midwest Pioneers, 1600s–1800s
Notes, URL: Revolutionary War soldiers buried in Michigan. <www.genealogy.com/508facd.html>

Michigan
Type: Digital images of a book; 1812
Online: F&LH
Title: Soldiers of War of 1812: roster of soldiers of the War of 1812 who are buried in Michigan
Notes, URL: By Lynn T. Miller.

Michigan
Type: Text of a book; CW
Online: Genealogy Library
Title: Company K, Michigan Sharpshooters
Notes, URL: In Subject Directory select Places | United States | Michigan.

Michigan
Type: Digital images of a book.; CW
CD-ROM: $29.95 (Mac/Win), Willow Bend, item #A0799QP
Title: Michigan in the War
Notes, URL: Includes "a register of all commissioned officers from Michigan who took part in the war." <www.willowbendbooks.com>

Michigan
Type: Digital images of a book; CW
Online: F&LH
Title: Reminiscences, incidents, battles, marches and camp life of the old 4th Michigan Infantry in War of Rebellion, 1861 to 1864
Notes, URL: By O.S. Barrett.

Michigan
Type: Abstracts; CW

Year Range: 1883
Online: Free
Title: Michigan Civil War Files
Notes, URL: Civil War veterans in census records. <www.mifamilyhistory.org/civilwar/1883Pension/>

Michigan
Type: Abstracts; CW
Year Range: 1861–1865
CD-ROM: $20 (Mac/Win)
Online: Free
Title: Michigan in the Civil War 1861–1865
Notes, URL: Includes regimental rosters with over 88,500 names. <www.hometown.aol.com/dlharvey/cwmireg.htm>

Michigan
Type: CW
CD-ROM: $29.95 (Mac/Win), Willow Bend, item #A0800QP
Title: Michigan Soldiers and Sailors Individual Records
Notes, URL: 85,271 names. <www.willowbendbooks.com>

Michigan
Type: Abstracts; CW
Online: Free
Title: Roll of Honor: Names of Soldiers Who Died in Defense of the American Union, Interred in Michigan
Notes, URL: <www.mifamilyhistory.org/civilwar/interments/default.asp>

Michigan
Type: Digital images of a book; SA
Online: F&LH
Title: Letters from Michigan soldiers in the Spanish-American War

Michigan
Type: Digital images of a book; SA
Online: F&LH
Title: Michigan volunteers of '98: a complete photographic record of Michigan's part in the Spanish-American War of 1898

Michigan
Type: Digital images of a book; WWI
Online: F&LH
Title: History of the 126th Infantry in the war with Germany
Notes, URL: By Emil B. Gansser.

Michigan
Type: Transcript; WWI
Online: Free
Title: Michigan Soldiers: from the book *Soldiers of the Great War, WWI*
Notes, URL: Michigan soldiers who died in WWI. <www.rootsweb.com/~michippe/gwarsoldier.htm>

Michigan
Type: Digital images of a book; WWI
Online: F&LH
Title: The 32nd Division in the World War, 1917–1919

Michigan, Iosco Co.
Type: Index; WWI
Online: Ancestry
Title: Iosco County, Michigan WWI Veterans Index
Notes, URL: <www.ancestry.com/search/rectype/inddbs/5372.htm>

Michigan, Kent Co., Grand Rapids
Type: Text of a book
Year Range: 1885–1889
Online: Free
Title: Deaths of Inmates of the Soldiers' Home (Baxter 1891), Grand Rapids, Kent County, Michigan
Notes, URL: Source: Baxter, Albert, *History of the City of Grand Rapids, Michigan.* <www.rootsweb.com/~mikent/baxter1891/soldiershome.html>

Michigan, Livingston Co., Hartland Twp.
Type: Index; CW
Online: Free
Title: Civil War Soldiers who Resided in Hartland Twp., Livingston Co., Michigan
Notes, URL: <http://users.starpower.net/mkluskens/genealogy/HartlandCivilWarSoldiers.html>

Minnesota
Type: Abstracts; CW
Online: Ancestry
Title: Minnesota Civil War Soldiers
Notes, URL: Nearly 26,100 names. <www.ancestry.com/search/rectype/inddbs/3729.htm>

Minnesota
Type: Digital images of a book; SA-PI
Online: F&LH
Title: Minnesota in the Spanish-American War and the Philippine insurrection
Notes, URL: By Franklin F. Holbrook.

Minnesota
Type: Abstracts; SA-PI
Online: Ancestry
Title: Minnesota Volunteers in the Spanish American War and the Philippine Insurrection
Notes, URL: By Franklin F. Holbrook. 9,846 records. <www.ancestry.com/search/rectype/inddbs/4816.htm>

Minnesota, Becker Co.
Type: Abstracts; CW-SA-WWI-WWII-KO-VN
Online: Free
Title: Military Records
Notes, URL: Becker County veterans from the Civil War to the Vietnam War. <www.rootsweb.com/~mnbecker/military.htm>

Mississippi
Type: Text of books; CW
CD-ROM: $35, Eastern Digital Resources
Title: The Civil War in Mississippi
Notes, URL: Includes rosters of officers & enlisted men & biographies & genealogies of men from Mississippi who served in the war. <www.researchonline.net/catalog/msorder.htm>

Mississippi
Type: Abstracts; CW
Online: Free
Title: Mississippi Civil War Information
Notes, URL: Includes lists of Confederate casualties & graves. <www.misscivilwar.org>

Mississippi
Type: Index; WWI
Online: Free
Title: USGenWeb Mississippi Archives Index of WW1 Registrants
Notes, URL: <www.rootsweb.com/~usgenweb/ms/ww1reg.htm>

Mississippi, Warren Co., Vicksburg
Type: Abstracts; CW-MX-SA-WWI-WWII-KO
Online: Free
Title: Vicksburg National Cemetery
Notes, URL: Includes names of 5,000 of 17,000 Union veterans buried there. <www.nps.gov/vick/natcem/nat_cem.htm>

Missouri
Type: Abstracts; CW
Online: Ancestry
Title: Missouri Civil War Records
Notes, URL: A list of some Confederate soldiers from articles in the *St. Louis Republic* newspaper. <www.ancestry.com/search/rectype/inddbs/4122.htm>

Missouri
Type: Abstracts; CW
Online: Ancestry
Title: Missouri Confederate Death Records

Notes, URL: Over 1,700 names. <www.ancestry.com/search/rectype/inddbs/3697.htm>

Missouri
Type: Abstracts; CW
Online: Ancestry
Title: Missouri Confederate Volunteers
Notes, URL: Over 1,600 men who volunteered to fight in the 1st and 2nd Missouri Confederate Brigades. <www.ancestry.com/search/rectype/inddbs/3736.htm>

Missouri
Type: Abstracts, transcripts; CW
Online: Free
Title: Missouri in the Civil War
Notes, URL: Includes biographies & cemetery records. <www.rootsweb.com/~mocivwar/mocwindex.html>

Missouri
Type: Index; CW
Year Range: 1861–1866
Online: Free
Title: Missouri's Union Provost Marshal Papers: 1861–1866
Notes, URL: Papers dealing with citizens during the Civil War. <www.sos.state.mo.us/archives/provost>

Missouri
Type: Transcript; CW
Year Range: 1883
Online: Free
Title: 1883 Missouri Pensioners Online
Notes, URL: <www.arealdomain.com/missouri1883.html>

Missouri
Type: Abstracts
Year Range: 1916
Online: Ancestry
Title: Missouri National Guard, the Mexican Border, 1916
Notes, URL: Over 5,500 names. Source: *Report of the Adjutant General State of Missouri, 1915–16.* <www.ancestry.com/search/rectype/inddbs/4028.htm>

Missouri
Type: Abstracts; WWI
Online: Ancestry
Title: Missouri State Offices Political and Military Records, 1919–1920
Notes, URL: Includes the National Guard officers who served during World War I. Source: *Official Manual of the State of Missouri for the years 1919–1920.* <www.ancestry.com/search/rectype/inddbs/5594.htm>

Missouri
Type: Abstracts, digital images; WWI
Year Range: 1917–1919
Online: Free
Title: World War I Military Service Cards Database
Notes, URL: 145,000 service cards for Missouri men & women in the U.S. Army & Marines, as well as digitized images of 18,500 U.S. Navy service cards. <www.sos.state.mo.us/ww1>

Missouri, Audrain Co.
Type: Abstracts; WWI
Year Range: 1917
Online: Ancestry
Title: Audrain County, Missouri Draft Records, 1917
Notes, URL: Over 2,000 names. Source: Weant, Kenneth, ed. *Audrain County, Missouri, vol. 3.* <www.ancestry.com/search/rectype/inddbs/3981.htm>

Missouri, Callaway Co.
Type: Transcripts; 1812-WWI
Online: Ancestry
Title: Callaway County, Missouri Veterans
Notes, URL: Newspaper articles covering veterans of the War of 1812 to WWI. <www.ancestry.com/search/rectype/inddbs/3298.htm>

Missouri, Callaway Co.
Type: Transcripts; 1812-WWII
Online: Ancestry
Title: Callaway County, Missouri Veterans
Notes, URL: Newspaper articles covering over 5,000 veterans of the War of 1812 to WWII. <www.ancestry.com/search/rectype/inddbs/4042.htm>

Nebraska
Type: Digital images of a book; 1812-MX-CW
Online: F&LH
Title: Roster of soldiers, sailors, and marines of the War of 1812, the Mexican War, and the War of the Rebellion, residing in Nebraska, June 1, 1895

Nebraska
Type: Abstracts; CW
Year Range: 1861–1869
Online: Ancestry
Title: Nebraska Pawnee Scouts, 1861–69
Notes, URL: Native Americans who volunteered to aid Union forces. <www.ancestry.com/search/rectype/inddbs/3738.htm>

Nebraska
Type: Abstracts; CW
Year Range: 1861–1869
Online: Ancestry
Title: Nebraska Volunteers, 1861–69
Notes, URL: Over 5,100 names. <www.ancestry.com/search/rectype/inddbs/3734.htm>

Nebraska
Type: Abstracts
Year Range: 1891
Online: Ancestry
Title: Nebraska Resident Military Roster on June 1, 1891
Notes, URL: "Soldiers, Sailors, and Marines of the War of 1812, the Mexico War, and the War of the Rebellion, residing in Nebraska June 1, 1891." <www.ancestry.com/search/rectype/inddbs/4755.htm>

Nebraska
Type: Abstracts; CW
Year Range: 1893
Online: Free
Title: 1893 Nebraska Census of Civil War Veterans
Notes, URL: Many enlisted from other states. <www.usgennet.org/usa/ne/county/holt/1893/1893_search.html>

Nebraska
Type: Index; CW
Online: Free
Title: Nebraska Civil War Grand Army of the Republic; Nebraska Civil War Veterans
Notes, URL: <www.denver.lib.co.us/ebranch/whg/datafile.html#nebgar>

Nevada
Type: Index; CW
Year Range: 1863–1866
Online: Ancestry
Title: Nevada Civil War Volunteers
Notes, URL: <www.ancestry.com/search/rectype/inddbs/3349.htm>

New Hampshire
Type: Digital images; FI-REV
CD-ROM: $42.50 (Mac/Win), Heritage Books, item #1172
Title: Heritage Books Archives: New Hampshire Revolutionary War Rolls
Notes, URL: Contains 5 volumes of rolls & documents & a master index. <www.heritagebooks.com>. Search on "1172."

New Hampshire
Type: Abstracts
Year Range: 1835
Online: Ancestry
Title: New Hampshire Pensioners, 1835
Notes, URL: <www.ancestry.com/search/rectype/inddbs/3217.htm>

New Hampshire
Type: Transcripts; CW
Online: Free
Title: ALHN/AHGP New Hampshire Civil War History & Genealogy Project
Notes, URL: Regimental rosters. <www.usgennet.org/usa/nh/topic/civilwar>

New Hampshire
Type: Abstracts; CW
Online: Free
Title: New Hampshire Heritage
Notes, URL: Includes service rosters. <www.geocities.com/nh_heritage/Genealogy.htm#Rosters>

New Hampshire, Merrimack Co., Chichester
Type: Text of a book; CW
Online: Genealogy Library
Title: Pittsfield NH in the Great Rebellion
Notes, URL: By H.L. Robinson. Select Places | United States | New Hampshire. Pittsfield is now called Chichester.

New Hampshire, Rockingham Co., Exeter
Type: Digital images of a book; CW
Year Range: 1862
Online: F&LH
Title: A brief record of events in Exeter, N.H. during the year 1862: together with the names of the soldiers of this town in the war
Notes, URL: By Elias Nason.

New Hampshire, Rockingham Co., Exeter
Type: Digital images of a book; CW
Year Range: 1863
Online: F&LH
Title: A brief record of current events in Exeter, N.H. during the year 1863: together with the names of the soldiers of this town in the war
Notes, URL: By Elias Nason.

New Hampshire, Rockingham Co., Portsmouth
Type: Digital images of a book
Online: F&LH
Title: The Soldiers' Memorial, Portsmouth, N.H., 1893–1923: with indexed record of the graves we decorate

New Hampshire, Strafford Co.
Type: Digital images of a book; REV
Year Range: 1820–1832
Online: F&LH
Title: Revolutionary pension declarations, Strafford County, 1820–1832: comprising sketches of soldiers of the Revolution
Notes, URL: By Lucien Thompson.

New Hampshire, Strafford Co., Rochester
Type: Abstracts; CW
Online: Free
Title: Rochester Soldiers in the Civil War
Notes, URL: <www.geocities.com/powerofz7/civilwar.html>

New Hampshire, Sullivan Co., Claremont
Type: Digital images of a book; CW
Online: F&LH
Title: Claremont war history, April, 1861 to April, 1865
Notes, URL: "With sketches of New-Hampshire regiments, and a biographical notice of each Claremont soldier, etc."

New Jersey
Type: Digital images of a book; REV
Online: Free
Title: New Jersey State Library's CyberDesk: Register of Officers and Men of New Jersey in the Revolutionary War
Notes, URL: Stryker's *Officers and Men of New Jersey in the Revolutionary War.* <www.njstatelib.org/cyberdesk> Listed under "Searchable NJ Publications."

New Jersey
Type: Abstracts
Year Range: 1835
Online: Ancestry
Title: New Jersey Pensioners, 1835
Notes, URL: <www.ancestry.com/search/rectype/inddbs/3237.htm>

New Jersey, Bergen Co.
Type: Digital images of a book; REV
Online: F&LH
Title: Loyalty and reprisal: the loyalists of Bergen County, New Jersey, and their estates
Notes, URL: By Ruth M. Keesey.

New Jersey, Camden Co., Berlin
Type: Digital images of a book; WWII
Online: F&LH
Title: Berlin borough, Camden Co., New Jersey in WWII, 1941–1945

New Jersey, Essex Co., Newark
Type: Digital images of a book; WWI
Online: F&LH
Title: Official list of names of residents of the city of Newark, N.J., who served . . . April 6, 1917, to November 11, 1918

New Jersey, Monmouth Co.
Type: Index; REV
Year Range: 1779–1849
Online: Free
Title: Monmouth Co. Archives: Amer. Revolution Pension Requests
Notes, URL: <www.visitmonmouth.com/archives/morerevolution.asp>

New Jersey, Monmouth Co.
Type: Index; REV
Year Range: 1818–1829
Online: Free
Title: Monmouth Co. Archives: American Revolution Pension Requests
Notes, URL: <www.visitmonmouth.com/archives/penreq.asp>

New Jersey, Sussex Co.
Type: Transcript; REV
Year Range: 1787
Online: Free
Title: Nancy Pascal's Genealogy Page: Loyalists
Notes, URL: <www.gate.net/~pascalfl/index.html>

New Jersey, Sussex Co., Blairstown
Type: Digital images of a book; WWI
Online: F&LH
Title: Blair Academy and the Great War
Notes, URL: "A record of the part played by students and alumni in the world War of 1914–1919."

New Mexico
Type: Transcripts
Year Range: 1770–1816
Online: Free
Title: Spanish Enlistment Papers 1770–1816
Notes, URL: Based on the book, *New Mexico Archives Militia Papers.* <www.nmgs.org/artfil.htm>

New York
Type: Digital images of a book; FI
Year Range: 1755–1764
CD-ROM: $24.50 (Mac/Win), Long Island Genealogy
Online: Free
Title: Muster Rolls of New York Provincial Troops 1755–1764
Notes, URL: Online at <www.longislandgenealogy.com/MusterRolls/MainIndex.html>; CD at <http://genealogycds.com/sales/MusterRolls.htm>

New York
Type: Digital images of books; REV
Year Range: 1775–1840
CD-ROM: $29.99, Genealogy.com, CD #132
Title: New York Revolutionary War Records, 1775–1840
Notes, URL: Images of 32 sets of Revolutionary War records with 162,000 names. <www.genealogy.com/132facd.html>

New York
Type: Abstracts; REV
Year Range: 1775–1783
Online: Ancestry
Title: Muster and Pay Rolls of the War of the Revolution, 1775–1783: Misc. Records
Notes, URL: Source: Vols. XLVII & XLVIII of *Collections of the New-York Historical Society* for 1914 & 1915. <www.ancestry.com/search/rectype/inddbs/6154.htm>

New York
Type: Transcript; REV
Year Range: 1776–1783
Online: Free
Title: A Partial List of patriot civilian and military refugees from New York and Long Island
Notes, URL: From *New York State—The battleground of the Revolutionary War*, by Hamilton Fish. <www.longislandgenealogy.com/civmilref.html>

New York
Type: Abstracts; REV
Online: Ancestry
Title: New York Military in the Revolution
Notes, URL: "A collection of military records relating to the colonial militia during the war." Source: *New York in the Revolution as Colony and State, Vol. II.* <www.ancestry.com/search/rectype/inddbs/4674.htm>

New York
Type: Digital images of a book
Year Range: 1783–1821
Online: F&LH
Title: Military minutes of the Council of Appointment of the State of New York, 1783–1821
Notes, URL: Includes militia lists with thousands of names.

New York
Type: Abstracts; REV
Year Range: 1792–1795
Online: Free
Title: New York Revolutionary War Pension Lists of 1792–1795
Notes, URL: <www.rootsweb.com/~nydutche/pension2.htm>

New York
Type: Index; REV
Year Range: 1801–1815
Online: Free
Title: Index to New York Revolutionary War Invalid Pension Records 1801–1815
Notes, URL: <www.rootsweb.com/~nydutche/pension3.htm>

New York
Type: Digital images of books; REV-1812
CD-ROM: $29.99, Genealogy.com, CD #143
Online: Genealogy Library
Title: New York in the Revolution & War of 1812 Military Records
Notes, URL: 6 books with 217,000 names. <www.genealogy.com/143facd.html>

New York
Type: Index; 1812
Online: Free
Title: Index of Awards on Claims of the Soldiers of the War of 1812
Notes, URL: <www.usgennet.org/usa/ny/state/1812>

New York
Type: Index; 1812
Online: Ancestry
Title: New York Military Equipment Claims, War of 1812
Notes, URL: <www.ancestry.com/search/rectype/inddbs/3883.htm>

New York
Type: Abstracts
Year Range: 1835
Online: Ancestry
Title: New York Pensioners, 1835
Notes, URL: <www.ancestry.com/search/rectype/inddbs/3247.htm>

New York
Type: Abstracts; CW
Year Range: 1861–1865
Online: Ancestry
Title: New York Civil War Records (1861–65)
Notes, URL: Civil War infantrymen from southeastern New York (79th & 80th infantry units). <www.ancestry.com/search/rectype/inddbs/5519.htm>

New York
Type: Abstracts; CW
Online: Free
Title: The New York GenWeb Site of the Civil War
Notes, URL: Includes rosters & lists of soldiers killed. <www.rootsweb.com/~nycivilw>

New York
Type: Transcripts; CW
Year Range: 1891
Online: Free
Title: Roster No. 3, New York Soldiers, by the Organization of New York Soldiers Living in Michigan, July 1891
Notes, URL: <www.usgennet.org/usa/ny/state/cw/cwindex.htm>

New York
Type: Digital images of a book; SA
Online: F&LH
Title: New York in the Spanish-American War, 1898: part of the report of the adjutant-general of the state for 1900

New York
Type: Transcript; WWII
Online: Free
Title: World War II Honor Roll
Notes, URL: Soldiers from Allegany and Cattaraugus Counties in western New York who died in WWII. <www.members.tripod.com/~NSampson/ww2wny.html>

New York
Type: Transcript; KO
Year Range: 1950–1953
Online: Free
Title: WNY Genealogy: Residents of Western N.Y. killed in the Korean War (1950–1953)
Notes, URL: Source: *Buffalo News Almanac* of 1954. <http://samdecker.freeyellow.com/KoreanWar.html>

New York, Albany Co., Albany
Type: Digital images of a book; WWI
Online: F&LH
Title: Albany's part in the World War
Notes, URL: By Harry Cohen. Includes service & honor rolls.

New York, Broome Co.
Type: Digital images of a book; REV
Online: F&LH
Title: Revolutionary War veterans in Broome County

New York, Cattaraugus Co.
Type: Abstracts; 1812-CW-WWI-WWII
Online: Free

Title: Painted Hills Genealogy Society: Cattaraugus Co., NY: Military
Notes, URL: <www.paintedhills.org/cattco.html>

New York, Cattaraugus Co.
Type: Transcript; WWI
Year Range: 1917–1918
Online: Free
Title: Cattaraugus County Veterans of the Great War 1917–1918
Notes, URL: <www.members.aol.com/ny108thcompanyi/catwwi.html>

New York, Cayuga Co.
Type: Transcript; REV
Online: Free
Title: Revolutionary War Bounty Land in "The Military Tract of Central NY" for the Area Within Cayuga County, New York
Notes, URL: Revolutionary War veterans who received bounty land within the current boundaries of Cayuga County, N.Y. Source: *The Balloting Book and Other Documents Relating to Military Bounty Lands, In The State Of New York.* <www.rootsweb.com/~nycayuga/land/mtractac.html>

New York, Chautauqua Co.
Type: Compiled research; REV
Online: Free
Title: Revolutionary Soldiers of Chautauqua County
Notes, URL: Compiled from D.A.R. records at the NYS Archives at Albany. <www.rootsweb.com/~nychauta/MILITARY/REVSOL.HTM>

New York, Chautauqua Co.
Type: Text of a book; REV
Online: Genealogy Library
Title: Soldiers of the American Revolution
Notes, URL: Soldiers who lived in Chautauqua County, New York. Select Records | Military | New York.

New York, Chautauqua Co.
Type: Pages images of a book
Online: F&LH
Title: Soldiers of the American Revolution: who at one time were residents of, or whose graves are located in Chautauqua County, New York

New York, Chemung Co., Elmira
Type: Abstracts; CW
Online: Free
Title: Civil War Prison Camp, Elmira, Chemung County, New York
Notes, URL: Source: Chemung County Historical Society. <www.rootsweb.com/~nychemun/prison.htm>

New York, Clinton Co., Plattsburgh
Type: Digital images of a book; 1812
Online: F&LH
Title: A List of pensioners of the War of 1812
Notes, URL: Battle of Plattsburgh.

New York, Herkimer Co.
Type: Abstracts; WWI
Online: Ancestry
Title: Herkimer County, New York Soldiers, 1916–18
Notes, URL: Over 4,000 names. <www.ancestry.com/search/rectype/inddbs/3878.htm>

New York, Herkimer Co.
Type: Digital images of a book; WWI
Online: F&LH
Title: Herkimer County in the World War: 1916 to 1918
Notes, URL: By Franklin W. Cristman.

New York, Jefferson Co.
Type: Digital images of a book; WWI
Online: F&LH
Title: Jefferson County in the World War
Notes, URL: "Containing the honor roll of those who served in Army, Navy and Marine and the portraits of those who made the supreme sacrifice."

New York, Kings Co., Brooklyn
Type: Digital images of a book; REV
Online: F&LH
Title: Review, the Tomb of the Martyrs: adjoining the United States Navy Yard, Brooklyn City, in Jackson Street, who died in dungeons and pestilential prison ships, in and about the city of New York, during the seven years of our Revolutionary War
Notes, URL: By Benjamin Romaine.

New York, Montgomery Co.
Type: Transcript; REV
Year Range: 1766–1780
Online: Free
Title: Sir John Johnson's Rent Roll of the Kingsborough Patent
Notes, URL: Renters in Tryon County (now Montgomery County), New York. Many were Loyalists. <http://freepages.genealogy.rootsweb.com/~wjmartin/kingsbor.htm>

New York, New York (City)
Type: Abstracts; WWI
Online: Free
Title: New York City World War I Draft Board Data Base
Notes, URL: Over 13,000 names. <www.jgsny.org/WWI_Draft_1.HTML>

New York, Oneida Co.
Type: Digital images of a book; WWI
Online: F&LH
Title: Honor roll: Oneida County in the war, 1917–1919

New York, Oneida Co.
Type: Abstracts; WWI
Year Range: 1917–1919
Online: Ancestry
Title: Oneida County, New York Servicemen, 1917–19
Notes, URL: Nearly 9,000 names. <www.ancestry.com/search/rectype/inddbs/3900.htm>

New York, Onondaga Co.
Type: Digital images of a book; REV
Online: F&LH
Title: Revolutionary soldiers resident or dying in Onondaga County, N.Y.
Notes, URL: By William Martin Beauchamp.

New York, Ontario Co.
Type: Index; REV-CW
Online: Free
Title: Ontario County Records and Archives Center
Notes, URL: Also includes military commissions, 1802–1822. <www.raims.com/home.html>

New York, Orange Co., Newburgh
Type: Digital images of a book; WWI
Online: F&LH
Title: Newburgh in the World War
Notes, URL: "A review of the part played by residents of the city of Newburgh and the towns of Newburgh, New Windsor and vicinity in the great War."

New York, Oswego Co.
Type: Digital images of a book; CW
Online: F&LH
Title: Oswego County, New York, in the Civil War
Notes, URL: By Charles McCool Snyder.

New York, Steuben Co.
Type: Abstracts; REV
Online: Free
Title: Steuben County Rev. War Pensioners of 1835
Notes, URL: <www.rootsweb.com/~nysteube/rev1835.html>

New York, Suffolk Co., Islip
Type: Digital images of a book; WWII
Online: F&LH
Title: Islip town's World War II effort
Notes, URL: By Nathaniel R. Howell.

New York, Tompkins Co.
Type: Abstracts; REV
Online: Free
Title: Revolutionary War Bounty Land in "The Military Tract of Central NY" for the Area Within Tompkins County, New York
Notes, URL: Revolutionary War veterans who received bounty land within the current boundaries of Tompkins County, N.Y. <www.rootsweb.com/~ny tompki/bounty.htm>

New York, Wayne Co.
Type: Digital images of a book; CW
Online: F&LH
Title: Military history of Wayne County, N.Y.: the county in the Civil War
Notes, URL: By Lewis H. Clark.

New York, Westchester Co., New Rochelle
Type: Digital images of a book; WWI
Online: F&LH
Title: New Rochelle, her part in the great war
Notes, URL: "Historical and biographical sketches of individuals and organizations who rendered valuable service to their country during the great World War."

New York, Westchester Co., Rye
Type: Digital images of a book; WWI
Year Range: 1917–1918
Online: F&LH
Title: The "world war" history of the village of Rye
Notes, URL: By Chauncey Ives.

New York, Westchester Co., White Plains
Type: Digital images of a book; WWI
Online: F&LH
Title: The World War history of the city of White Plains, 1917–1918
Notes, URL: By Louisa C. Lockwood.

North Carolina
Type: Transcript; REV
Year Range: 1786–1831
Online: Free
Title: North Carolina Loyalists During the American Revolution
Notes, URL: <www.members.aol.com/Hose yGen/NCLOYAL.HTML>

North Carolina
Type: Abstracts; REV
Online: Ancestry
Title: North Carolina Revolutionary War Soldiers
Notes, URL: 36,000 names. Source: *Roster of Soldiers from North Carolina in the American Revolution.* <www.ancestry.com/search/rectype/inddbs/3185.htm>

North Carolina
Type: Abstracts; SA
Online: Ancestry
Title: North Carolina Volunteers, Spanish American War
Notes, URL: Over 3,900 names. Source: *Roster of the North Carolina Volunteers in the Spanish-American War, 1898–1899.* <www.ancestry.com/search/rectype/inddbs/4136.htm>

North Carolina
Type: Database; CW
Online: Free
Title: North Carolina Civil War Soldiers Records
Notes, URL: <www.censusdiggins.com/nc_civilwar.html>

North Carolina, Alamance Co.
Type: Digital images of a book; CW
Online: F&LH
Title: Confederate memoirs: Alamance County troops of the War Between the States, 1861–1865

North Carolina, Catawba Co.
Type: Digital images of a book; CW
Online: F&LH
Title: The Catawba soldier of the Civil War
Notes, URL: "A sketch of every soldier from Catawba County, North Carolina, with the photograph, biographical sketch, and reminiscence of many of them."

North Carolina, Lincoln Co.
Type: Digital images of a book; CW
Online: F&LH
Title: Roster of Confederate soldiers in the War Between the States
Notes, URL: By Alfred Nixon.

North Dakota
Type: Abstracts; WWI
Year Range: 1917–1918
Online: Ancestry
Title: North Dakota Military Men, 1917–18
Notes, URL: Over 32,000 names. Source: *Roster of the Men and Women Who Served in the Army or Naval Service (including the Marine Corps) of the United States of its Allies from the State of North Dakota in the World War, 1917–1918, Vol. I-IV.* <www.ancestry.com/search/re ctype/inddbs/4569.htm>

Ohio
Type: Digital images; REV
Online: F&LH
Title: The Official roster of the soldiers of the American Revolution buried in the state of Ohio
Notes, URL: By Frank D. Henderson, et al.

Ohio
Type: Abstracts; REV
Year Range: 1818–1819
Online: Free
Title: Revolutionary War Pensioners Living in the State of Ohio in 1818–1819
Notes, URL: <http://ezinfo.ucs.indiana.edu/~jetorres/ohiorev.html>

Ohio
Type: Digital images of books; 1812
CD-ROM: $29.99, Genealogy.com, CD #528
Online: Genealogy Library
Title: Early Ohio Settlers, 1700s–1900s
Notes, URL: Under Historical Records, select Genealogical Records: Early Ohio Settlers, 1700s–1900s. Includes the book *Roster of Ohio Soldiers in the War of 1812.* <www.genealogy.com/528facd.html>

Ohio
Type: Transcript; 1812
Online: Free
Title: The Ohio Historical Society: War of 1812 Roster of Ohio Soldiers
Notes, URL: 1,759 officers and 24,521 enlisted men from Ohio. Source: *Roster of Ohio Soldiers in the War of 1812.* Adjutant General of Ohio. <www.ohiohistory.org/resource/database/rosters.html>

Ohio
Type: Digital images of a book; 1812
Online: F&LH
Title: Roster of Ohio soldiers in the War of 1812
Notes, URL: By the Adjutant General of Ohio.

Ohio
Type: Digital images of a book; 1812-MX-CW-SA
Online: F&LH
Title: Ohio in four wars: a military history
Notes, URL: By Daniel J. Ryan.

Ohio
Type: Index; CW
Online: Free
Title: The Ohio Historical Society Civil War Documents: Civil War Guide Project, Guide to Primary Resource Collections at OHS
Notes, URL: <www.ohiohistory.org/resource/database/civilwar.html>

Ohio
Type: Index; CW
Year Range: 1864–1865
Online: Free
Title: The Ohio Historical Society Civil War Documents: Index to [Ohio] Prisoners at Andersonville, Georgia, and Salisbury, North Carolina Prisons, 1864–1865
Notes, URL: <www.ohiohistory.org/resource/database/civilwar.html>

Ohio
Type: Abstracts; SA
Year Range: 1898–1899
Online: Ancestry
Title: Ohio Soldiers in the War with Spain, 1898–99
Notes, URL: More than 19,000 names. Source: *The Official Roster of Ohio Soldiers in the War with Spain, 1898–99.* <www.ancestry.com/search/rectype/inddbs/5306.htm>

Ohio
Type: Digital images of a book; SA
Year Range: 1898–1899
Online: F&LH
Title: 6th Ohio Volunteer Infantry, war album
Notes, URL: "Historical events, reminiscences and views of the Spanish-American War, 1898–1899."

Ohio
Type: Digital images of books.; WWI
CD-ROM: $39.99, Genealogy.com, CD #549
Title: Ohio Soldiers in WWI Military Records
Notes, URL: 250,000 names. Source: all 23 volumes of *The Official Roster of Ohio Soldiers, Sailors and Marines in the World War, 1917–18.* <www.genealogy.com/549facd.html>

Ohio
Type: Text of books; WWI
Year Range: 1908–1928
CD-ROM: $29.95 (Win), Ancestry, item #2148, <http://shops.ancestry.com>. Search on "Ohio Enlistments."
Online: Ancestry
Title: Ohio Military Men, 1917–18
Notes, URL: Over 263,000 names. Source: *Official Roster of Ohio Soldiers, Sailors and Marines in the World War, 1917–1918, vols. I-XXIII.* <www.ancestry.com/search/rectype/inddbs/4520.htm>. The CD-ROM is called *Ohio Enlistments, 1908–1928.*

Ohio
Type: Digital images; WWII
Online: Free
Title: World War II Selective Service System Registration Cards
Notes, URL: "For Ohio Men born April 28, 1877 through February 16, 1897." <www.archives.gov>. Select Research Room | Archival Research Catalog | Search Hints for Genealogical Data in ARC.

Ohio, Franklin Co., Columbus
Type: Transcript; CW
Year Range: 1862–1865
Online: Ancestry
Title: Columbus, Franklin County, Ohio: Camp Chase Cemetery
Notes, URL: The burial place of 2,163 Confederate soldiers. <www.ancestry.com/search/rectype/inddbs/5642.htm>

Ohio, Greene Co.
Type: Digital images of a book; CW
Online: F&LH
Title: After thirty years: a complete roster, by townships, of Greene County, Ohio soldiers in the late Civil War
Notes, URL: By George F. Robinson.

Ohio, Lawrence Co.
Type: Index, transcripts; CW
Online: Free
Title: Lawrence County, Ohio Civil War Page
Notes, URL: Includes many obituaries & an index to the 1890 census of veterans & widows. <www.lawrencecountyohio.com/civilwar/index/>

Ohio, Trumbull Co.
Type: Compiled research; CW
Online: Free
Title: Trumbull Co. Ohio Civil War Vets
Notes, URL: <www.geocities.com/Heartland/Pointe/7056/tvintro.htm>

Oklahoma
Type: Index; CW
Online: Free
Title: Archives Division: Index to Oklahoma's Confederate Pension Records
Notes, URL: <www.odl.state.ok.us/oar/docs/pension.pdf>

Oklahoma
Type: Transcript; CW
Online: Free
Title: 1890 Union Veterans Census of Oklahoma
Notes, URL: <www.rootsweb.com/~okgarvin/kinard/1890unionvetsindex.html>

Oklahoma, Stephens Co.
Type: Abstracts; CW
Online: Free
Title: Civil War Veterans Buried in Stephens County, Oklahoma
Notes, URL: <www.geocities.com/sccwvets/>

Oregon
Type: Digital images of a book; SA-PI
Online: F&LH
Title: The official records of the Oregon volunteers in the Spanish War and Philippine Insurrection

Oregon
Type: Abstracts; SA-PI
Online: Ancestry
Title: Oregon Volunteers, Spanish American War and Philippine Insurrection
Notes, URL: 1,581 records. Source: *The Official Record of the Oregon Volunteers in the Spanish War and Philippine Insurrection.* <www.ancestry.com/search/rectype/inddbs/4830.htm>

Oregon
Type: Index; WWI
Year Range: 1848–1933
Online: Free
Title: Oregon Historical Records Index
Notes, URL: The search covers enlistment and service records, soldier home applications, soldier home histories, and WWI service histories. <http://arcweb.sos.state.or.us/banners/genlist.htm>

Oregon, Wasco Co.
Type: Index
Year Range: 1863–1872
Online: Free
Title: Oregon Historical Records Index: Wasco County: Military Lists
Notes, URL: 1863–1865, 1872. <http://arcweb.sos.state.or.us/banners/genlist/wasco.htm>

Pennsylvania
Type: Transcript

Year Range: 1744–1764
Online: Free
Title: Pennsylvania Archives, Second Series, Vol. II: Officers and Soldiers in the service of the Province of Pennsylvania 1744–1764
Notes, URL: <www.rootsweb.com/%7Eusgenweb/pa/1pa/paarchivesseries/series2/vol2/pass2-00.html>

Pennsylvania
Type: Digital images of abstracts; REV-WWI-SA-MXB-CW
Online: Free
Title: Pennsylvania State Archives Records Information Access System (ARIAS)
Notes, URL: 600,000 of 900,000 records of Pennsylvanians' military service. <www.digitalarchives.state.pa.us>

Pennsylvania
Type: Digital images of a book containing transcripts; REV
CD-ROM: F&LH
Online: Free
Title: Revolutionary soldiers' graves in Lower Merion Township, Montgomery County, Pennsylvania: and surrounding townships . . .

Pennsylvania
Type: Abstracts; 1812
Online: Ancestry
Title: Pennsylvania Volunteers in the War of 1812
Notes, URL: Source: Pennsylvania Archives. <www.ancestry.com/search/rectype/inddbs/3325.htm>

Pennsylvania
Type: Abstracts
Year Range: 1835
Online: Ancestry
Title: Pennsylvania Pensioners, 1835
Notes, URL: <www.ancestry.com/search/rectype/inddbs/3251.htm>

Pennsylvania
Type: Compiled research; CW
Online: Free
Title: Civil War Records of Bucks and Northampton Counties
Notes, URL: <www.geocities.com/Heartland/6508/DURHAM6.HTM>

Pennsylvania
Type: Digital images of books; CW
CD-ROM: $24 (Mac/Win), Heritage Books, item #1962
Title: Heritage Books Archives: The Penn. State Memorial at Gettysburg: Soldiers of the Commonwealth
Notes, URL: The names of over 34,000 Pennsylvanians who served at the Battle of Gettysburg. <www.heritagebooks.com>. Search on "1962."

Pennsylvania
Type: Digital images of books; CW
Online: Free
Title: History of Pennsylvania Volunteers, 1861–5
Notes, URL: Links to the 5-volume set by Samuel P. Bates at the Making of America Web site. <www.rootsweb.com/~pamercer/PA/Military/CivilWar/bates.htm>

Pennsylvania
Type: Index; CW
Online: Free
Title: Index to Compiled Service Records of Volunteer Union Soldiers from Pennsylvania (August Sungrist through Isaac Sweeney)
Notes, URL: This index covers only the names running alphabetically from *August Sungrist* through *Isaac Sweeney*. <www.archives.gov/research_room/genealogy/military/union_pennsylvania_records.html>

Pennsylvania
Type: Index, abstracts; CW
Online: Free
Title: Pennsylvania in the Civil War
Notes, URL: Includes regimental lists, a burial index, & a tool to search for names on the site. <www.pa-roots.com/~pacw>

Pennsylvania
Type: Transcript; CW
Online: Free
Title: Pennsylvania Volunteers of the Civil War
Notes, URL: <www.pacivilwar.com>

Pennsylvania
Type: Abstracts; SA
Year Range: 1898–1899
Online: Free
Title: Pennsylvania Volunteers of the Spanish-American War 1898–1899
Notes, URL: <www.paspanishamericanwar.com>

Pennsylvania, Berks Co.
Type: Abstracts; WWI
Year Range: 1917–1918
Online: Ancestry
Title: Berks County, Pennsylvania Service Roster, 1917–18
Notes, URL: 1,240 servicemen ages 18 to 31. <www.ancestry.com/search/rectype/inddbs/5065.htm>

Pennsylvania, Chester Co.
Type: Index; WWI
Online: Free
Title: Chester County Archives: World War I Servicemen Index/Chester County War Aid Association
Notes, URL: <www.chesco.org/archives/ww1_searchCriteria.asp>

Pennsylvania, Cumberland Co., Carlisle
Type: Digital images of a book; REV-MX-CW
Online: F&LH
Title: Military history of Carlisle and Carlisle Barracks
Notes, URL: By Thomas Grant Towsey.

Pennsylvania, Delaware Co.
Type: Transcript; CW
Year Range: 1883
Online: Free
Title: Pennsylvania Volunteers of the Civil War: Pension Roll of 1883 Delaware County, PA
Notes, URL: <www.pacivilwar.com/1883delaware.html>

Pennsylvania, Franklin Co.
Type: Digital images; CW
CD-ROM: $49.95 (Mac/Win), W.W. Norton & Co.
Title: The Valley of the Shadow: Two Communites in the American Civil War
Notes, URL: Newspapers, letters, diaries, photographs, maps, church records, population census, agricultural census, & military records from the period just before the Civil War. <http://valley.vcdh.virginia.edu/>

Pennsylvania, Montgomery Co.
Type: Abstracts; CW
Online: Free
Title: Civil War Burials in Montgomery County, PA
Notes, URL: <www.thefinalwaltz.com>

Pennsylvania, Philadelphia Co., Philadelphia
Type: Digital images of a book; CW
Online: F&LH
Title: Philadelphia in the Civil War, 1861–1865
Notes, URL: By Frank H. Taylor.

Pennsylvania, Potter Co.
Type: Transcript; MX-CW-SA-WWI-WWII-KO-VN
Online: Free
Title: Painted Hills Genealogy Society: Potter Co., PA: Military: Potter County Veterans
Notes, URL: Veterans buried in Potter County cemeteries. <www.paintedhills.org/potterco.html>

Pennsylvania, Somerset Co.
Type: Digital images of a book; WWI
Online: F&LH
Title: Survey of World War veterans of Somerset County, Pennsylvania

Pennsylvania, York Co.
Type: Digital images of a book; WWI
Online: F&LH
Title: York County and the World War
Notes, URL: By Clifford J. Hall.

Rhode Island
Type: Digital images of a book; CO-REV-1812-MX
Year Range: 1647–1800
Online: F&LH
Title: Civil and military list of Rhode Island, 1647–1800
Notes, URL: Lists officers. By Joseph Jencks Smith.

Rhode Island
Type: Digital images of a book; CO
Year Range: 1739–1748
Online: F&LH
Title: Rhode Island privateers in King George's war: 1739–1748
Notes, URL: By Howard M. Chapin.

Rhode Island
Type: Digital images of a book; CO
Year Range: 1740–1748
Online: F&LH
Title: Rhode Island in the colonial wars: a list of Rhode Island soldiers & sailors in King George's war, 1740–1748
Notes, URL: By Howard M. Chapin.

Rhode Island
Type: Abstracts; FI
Year Range: 1740–1762
Online: Ancestry
Title: Rhode Island Colonial War Servicemen, 1740–62
Notes, URL: Over 3,800 names. Source: Chapin, Howard. *Rhode Island in the Colonial Wars.* <www.ancestry.com/search/rectype/inddbs/4055.htm>

Rhode Island
Type: Abstracts
Year Range: 1835
Online: Ancestry
Title: Rhode Island Pensioners, 1835
Notes, URL: <www.ancestry.com/search/rectype/inddbs/3220.htm>

Rhode Island, Washington Co., Westerly
Type: Digital images of a book; REV-1812-CW
Year Range: 1710–1932
Online: F&LH
Title: Military history of Westerly
Notes, URL: By George R. Dowding.

South Carolina
Type: Text of a book; REV
Online: Genealogy Library
Title: South Carolinians in the Revolution
Notes, URL: By Sara Sullivan Ervin. Includes abstracts of Laurens County wills. Select Records | Military | South Carolina.

South Carolina
Type: Compiled research; CW
CD-ROM: $35, Eastern Digital Resources
Online: Free
Title: The Civil War in South Carolina
Notes, URL: Includes rosters of officers & enlisted men & biographies & genealogies of men from South Carolina who served in the war. The CD has more info than the Web site. <www.researchonline.net/sccw/index.htm>

South Carolina
Type: Abstracts; CW
Online: Free
Title: South Carolina in the Civil War Homepage
Notes, URL: Includes biographies, photos, & pension lists. <www.members.tripod.com/mwyckoff/index.html>

South Carolina
Type: Database; CW
Online: Free
Title: War Between the States in South Carolina
Notes, URL: Includes soldier biographies. <www.rootsweb.com/~scwbts>

South Carolina, Newberry Co.
Type: Database; CW
Online: Free
Title: War Between the States in Newberry County, S.C.
Notes, URL: Includes soldier biographies. <www.rootsweb.com/~scnewber/records/military/civilwar/index.htm>

South Carolina, Pickens Co.
Type: Index; REV-CW-WWI-WWII-KO-VN
Online: Free
Title: Military Pages for Pickens Co., S.C.
Notes, URL: <www.scgenealogy.com/pickens/records/military/index.htm>

South Carolina, York Co.
Type: Abstracts; CW
Online: Free
Title: York County, South Carolina in the Civil War
Notes, URL: Includes links to rosters & pension lists. <http://freepages.genealogy.rootsweb.com/~york/_indexYorkCivilWar.htm>

Tennessee
Type: Digital images of books; REV-1812
CD-ROM: $29.99, Genealogy.com, CD #511
Online: Genealogy Library
Title: Early Tennessee Settlers, 1700s–1900s
Notes, URL: Includes *Tennessee Soldiers in the Revolution, Some Tennessee Heroes of the Revolution,* & *Twenty-four Hundred Tennessee Pensioners, Revolution and War of 1812.* <www.genealogy.com/511facd.html>

Tennessee
Type: Transcript
Year Range: 1835
Online: Free
Title: TN Pension Roll of 1835
Notes, URL: <ftp://ftp.rootsweb.com/pub/usgenweb/tn/military/pen1835.txt>

Tennessee
Type: Transcript; CW
Year Range: 1863–1866
Online: Free
Title: 7th Regiment Colored Infantry/11th Regiment
Notes, URL: <www.genealogytoday.com/pub/7color.htm>

Tennessee
Type: Index; CW
Online: Free
Title: Tennessee Confederate Pension Applications: Soldiers and Widows
Notes, URL: <www.state.tn.us/sos/statelib/pubsvs/pension.htm>

Tennessee
Type: Abstracts; CW
Online: Free
Title: Death Roll: List of Tennessee Union Soldiers interred at Andersonville, Belle

Isle, Danville, Point of Rocks, and Camp Lawton, Milin, GA
Notes, URL: Extracted from *Report of the Adjutant General of the State of Tennessee, of the military forces of the state, from 1861 to 1866.* <www.tngenweb.org/civilwar/misc/dead1.html>

Tennessee
Type: Index; CW
CD-ROM: $29.99, Genealogy.com, CD #155
Online: Genealogy Library
Title: Civil War Confederate Pension Applications Index
Notes, URL: 28,000 names. Source: *Index to Tennessee Confederate Pension Applications.* <www.genealogy.com/155facd.html>

Tennessee
Type: Abstracts; CW
Online: Free
Title: Tennessee and the Civil War
Notes, URL: Includes Union & Confederate military rosters. <www.tngenweb.org/civilwar/>

Tennessee
Type: Text of a book; CW
Online: Ancestry
Title: Tennessee Civil War Regimental Histories
Notes, URL: "Includes names of commanders and important men." Source: Lindsley, John B. *The Military Annals of Tennessee Confederate.* <www.ancestry.com/search/rectype/inddbs/4528.htm>

Tennessee
Type: Index; CW
Online: Free
Title: Tennessee Civil War Veterans' Questionnaires
Notes, URL: <www.state.tn.us/sos/statelib/pubsvs/quest.htm>

Tennessee
Type: Index; CW
Online: Free
Title: Tennessee Confederate Physicians
Notes, URL: <www.state.tn.us/sos/statelib/pubsvs/docintro.htm>

Tennessee
Type: Index; CW
Online: Free
Title: Tennessee Confederate Soldiers' Home Applications
Notes, URL: <www.state.tn.us/sos/statelib/pubsvs/csh_intr.htm>

Tennessee
Type: Index; SA
Online: Free
Title: Index to Tennessee Volunteer Units in the Spanish American War
Notes, URL: <www.state.tn.us/sos/statelib/pubsvs/saw.htm>

Tennessee
Type: Index; WWI
Online: Free
Title: Tennessee World War I Veterans
Notes, URL: <www.state.tn.us/sos/statelib/pubsvs/ww1intro.htm>

Tennessee, Sumner Co.
Type: Transcript; CW
Online: Free
Title: 1890 Civil War Veterans Census Sumner County, Tennessee
Notes, URL: <www.rootsweb.com/~tnsumner/cwpens_1.htm>

Texas
Type: Index
Year Range: 1835–1900
Online: Free
Title: Republic Claims Search
Notes, URL: More than 48,500 indexed names in claims for payment, reimbursement, or restitution submitted by citizens to the Republic of Texas government, 1835–1846. Also, Republic pensions and claims against the Republic submitted as public debt claims after 1846. <www.tsl.state.tx.us/arc/repclaims/index.html>

Texas
Type: Index
Year Range: 1836–1935
Online: Free
Title: Texas Adjutant General Service Records 1836–1935
Notes, URL: <www.tsl.state.tx.us/arc/service/index.html>

Texas
Type: Index; CW
Year Range: 1863–1865
Online: Free
Title: Confederate Indigent Families Lists (1863–1865)
Notes, URL: <www.tsl.state.tx.us/arc/cif/index.html>

Texas
Type: Abstracts; CW
Online: Free
Title: Confederate Soldiers & the War Between the States in Northeast Texas
Notes, URL: Includes rosters of Confederate regiments. <http://gen.1starnet.com/civilwar/csamain.htm>

Texas
Type: Index; CW
Year Range: 1899–1975
Online: Free
Title: Confederate Pensions Search
Notes, URL: 54,634 approved, rejected, & home pensions issued by the Texas government. <www.tsl.state.tx.us/arc/pensions/index.html>

Texas
Type: Abstracts; CW
Online: Free
Title: Texas in the Civil War
Notes, URL: Includes links to muster rolls. <www.tarleton.edu/~kjones/CStx.html>

Texas
Type: Index; WWI
Online: Ancestry
Title: Camp Travis, Texas World War I Records
Notes, URL: Over 19,000 names. Source: Major E.B. Johns, U.S.A, compiler. *Camp Travis and Its Part in the World War.* <www.ancestry.com/search/rectype/inddbs/5073.htm>

Texas, Ellis Co.
Type: Abstracts; WWI
Online: Ancestry
Title: Ellis County, Texas World War I Veterans
Notes, URL: Names of 1,000 veterans. <www.ancestry.com/search/rectype/inddbs/3613.htm>

Texas, Hood Co.
Type: Database; ALL
Online: Free
Title: Military Veterans of Hood County, Texas
Notes, URL: <www.hcnews.com/depot/>

Texas, Milam Co.
Type: Index; CW
Online: Free
Title: Milam County, Texas in the Civil War
Notes, URL: Includes a list of Confederate pension applications. <www.members.tripod.com/~jamesewilliams/index-2.html>

Utah
Type: Index; IN
Year Range: 1865–1890
Online: Ancestry
Title: Utah Index to Indian War Service Affidavits, 1909–19
Notes, URL: <www.ancestry.com/search/rectype/inddbs/6887.htm>

Utah, Washington Co.
Type: Abstracts; WWII
Online: Free
Title: An Historical Index of Men and Women of Washington County Utah Who Served in the Military During World War II
Notes, URL: <www.lofthouse.com/USA/Utah/washington/military/index.html>

Vermont
Type: Digital images of a book; REV
Online: F&LH
Title: Vermont pension roll
Notes, URL: Register of Revolutionary War veterans residing in Vermont and receiving pensions from the federal government.

Vermont
Type: Abstracts
Year Range: 1835
Online: Ancestry
Title: Vermont Pensioners, 1835
Notes, URL: <www.ancestry.com/search/rectype/inddbs/3225.htm>

Vermont
Type: Transcripts, photos; CW
Online: Free
Title: Vermont in the Civil War
Notes, URL: Includes military rosters & a cemetery database. <www.vermontcivilwar.org/index.shtml>

Vermont, Caledonia Co., St. Johnsbury
Type: Digital images of a book
Online: F&LH
Title: Soldiers' record of the town of St. Johnsbury, Vermont in the War of the Rebellion, 1861–65
Notes, URL: By Albert G. Chadwick.

Vermont, Rutland Co., Rutland
Type: Digital images of a book; CW
Online: F&LH
Title: Official military and naval records of Rutland, Vermont, in the War of the Rebellion, 1861–1866
Notes, URL: By J.H. Goulding.

Vermont, Washington Co., Waitsfield
Type: Digital images; REV
Online: F&LH
Title: An address delivered at Waitsfield, Vt., Sept. 15, 1906: at the unveiling of a tablet erected in memory of soldiers of the American Revolution buried in that town
Notes, URL: By Matt B. Jones.

Vermont, Windsor Co., Hartland
Type: Digital images of a book; REV-1812-MX
Online: F&LH
Title: Hartland in the Revolutionary War: her soldiers, their homes, lives and burial places
Notes, URL: "The muster rolls of Captain Elias Weld's and Lieutenant Daniel Spooner's Hartland companies: also Hartland in the War of 1812 and in the Mexican War."

Virginia
Type: Abstracts
Year Range: 1651–1776
Online: Ancestry
Title: Virginia Colonial Militia, 1651–1776
Notes, URL: Over 4,000 names. Source: Crozier, William Armstrong. *Virginia Colonial Militia, 1651–1776*. <www.ancestry.com/search/rectype/inddbs/4596.htm>

Virginia
Type: Digital images of books; CO
Year Range: 1651–1776
CD-ROM: $29.99, Genealogy.com, CD #503
Online: Genealogy Library
Title: Virginia Colonial Records, 1600s–1700s
Notes, URL: Includes: *List of the Colonial Soldiers of Virginia, Virginia's Colonial Soldiers, & Virginia Colonial Militia, 1651–1776*. <www.genealogy.com/503facd.html>

Virginia
Type: Index
Year Range: Up to 1770s
Online: Ancestry (free)
Title: Virginia Colonial Soldiers
Notes, URL: Over 6,000 names. Source: Eckenrode, H.J. *Special Report of the Department of Archives and History for 1913*. <www.ancestry.com/search/rectype/inddbs/4006.htm>

Virginia
Type: Document images; DU-REV-1812-ME-CW-WWI
Online: Free
Title: The Library of Virginia: Military Records and Resources
Notes, URL: Databases include Revolutionary War Bounty Warrants, War of 1812 Pay Rolls and Muster Rolls, & Confederate Pension Rolls. <www.lva.lib.va.us/whatwehave/mil/index.htm>

Virginia
Type: Digital images of books; REV
CD-ROM: $31 (Mac/Win), Heritage Books, item #1382
Title: Heritage Books Archives: Revolutionary War Records, Volumes 1-6
Notes, URL: Includes *Virginia/West Virginia Revolutionary War Records, Volumes 1-6*. Extensive data derived from the pension & bounty land warrants in the National Archives. <www.heritagebooks.com>. Search on "1382."

Virginia
Type: Document images; REV
CD-ROM: $40 each (#1371, 1372, 1373) or $90/set of 3 CDs (#1370) (Mac/Win), Heritage Books
Title: Heritage Books Digital Microfilm: Virginia Half-Pay and Other Related Revolutionary War Pension Application Files, National Archives Microfilm Publication M910
Notes, URL: Virginia *state* pensions for Revolutionary War service in Virginia units (not to be confused with the main series of pensions originated by Congress). Soldiers A-M, Item #1371. Soldiers N-Z, #1372. Sailors A-Z, #1373. 3-CD set, #1370. <www.heritagebooks.com>. Search on "1370," "1371," "1372," or "1373."

Virginia
Type: Text of a book; REV
Online: Ancestry
Title: Virginia Militia in the Revolutionary War
Notes, URL: Source: McAllister, J.T., *Virginia Militia in the Revolutionary War*. <www.ancestry.com/search/rectype/inddbs/3076.htm>

Virginia
Type: Text of a book; REV
Online: Ancestry
Title: Virginia Navy in the Revolution
Notes, URL: Source: Stewart, Robert Armistead. *History of Virginia's Navy in the Revolution*. <www.ancestry.com/search/rectype/inddbs/3196.htm>

Virginia
Type: Text of a book; REV
Online: Ancestry
Title: Virginia Revolutionary War Records
Notes, URL: Source: Brumbaugh, Gaius Marcus. *Revolutionary War Records, Volume 1, Virginia.* <www.ancestry.com/search/rectype/inddbs/3206.htm>

Virginia
Type: Abstracts; REV
Year Range: 1775–1783
Online: Free
Title: 2nd Virginia Regiment, of the Continental Line "1775–1783"
Notes, URL: Over 400 officers and soldiers. <http://hammer.prohosting.com/~clrhodes/2ndVA.htm>

Virginia
Type: Text of a book; REV
Year Range: 1776
Online: Ancestry
Title: Virginia Soldiers of 1776, Vol. 1
Notes, URL: Source: Burgess, Louis Alexander. *Virginia Soldiers of 1776.* <www.ancestry.com/search/rectype/inddbs/1009.htm>

Virginia
Type: Digital images of books; REV-1812
CD-ROM: $29.99, Genealogy.com, CD #121
Online: Genealogy Library
Title: Virginia in the Revolution and War of 1812 Military Records
Notes, URL: Records of about 269,000 Virginia military personnel found in 11 books. <www.genealogy.com/121facd.html>

Virginia
Type: Abstracts
Year Range: 1802–1804
Online: Free
Title: Muster Rolls of Virginia Militia
Notes, URL: <www.genealogytoday.com/pub/vir11ros.htm>

Virginia
Type: Index; 1812
Online: Free
Title: Library of Va.: Index to War of 1812 Pay Rolls and Muster Rolls
Notes, URL: About 40,000 names. <www.lva.lib.va.us/whatwehave/mil/>

Virginia
Type: Abstracts
Year Range: 1835
Online: Free
Title: 1835 Federal Pension List for Virginia
Notes, URL: <www.rootsweb.com/~usgenweb/va/vapensio.htm>

Virginia
Type: Index
Year Range: 1839–1925
Online: Free
Title: Virginia Military Institute Archives
Notes, URL: Class rosters with the names of all students ever enrolled at VMI. <www.vmi.edu/archives>

Virginia
Type: Abstract; CW
Online: Free
Title: 54th Virginia Infantry Roster
Notes, URL: <www.genealogytoday.com/pub/va54ros.htm>

Virginia
Type: Abstract; CW
Online: Free
Title: 64th Virginia Infantry Roster
Notes, URL: <www.genealogytoday.com/pub/va64ros.htm>

Virginia
Type: Index; CW
Online: Free
Title: Library of Virginia: Confederate Pension Rolls, Veterans and Widows
Notes, URL: "Approved pension applications and amended applications filed by resident Virginia Confederate veterans and their widows." <www.lva.lib.va.us/whatwehave/mil/>

Virginia
Type: Abstracts; CW
Online: Free
Title: Virginia Roster Lists: 7th Battalion Confederate Cavalry
Notes, URL: <www.genealogytoday.com/pub/va7ros.htm>

Virginia
Type: Index; WWI
Year Range: 1917–1918
Online: Free
Title: World War I Draft Registrations for Northern Virginia
Notes, URL: 11,075 registrants from the City of Alexandria, Alexandria (now Arlington) County, & Fairfax County. <www.alexandria.lib.va.us/lhsc_genealogy_resources/draft/ww1draft.html>

Virginia, Augusta Co.
Type: Document images; CW
CD-ROM: $49.95 (Mac/Win), W.W. Norton & Co.
Title: The Valley of the Shadow: Two Communites in the American Civil War
Notes, URL: Includes military records. <http://valley.vcdh.virginia.edu/>

Virginia, Clarke Co.
Type: Digital images of a book; CW
Online: F&LH
Title: History of Clarke County, Virginia and its connection with the war between the states
Notes, URL: "With illustrations of colonial homes and of Confederate officers."

Virginia, Richmond
Type: Transcripts of newspaper articles, index of burials; CW
Online: Free
Title: Civil War Richmond
Notes, URL: Includes soldiers originally buried on Belle Isle & reinterred in Richmond National Cemetery. <www.mdgorman.com>

Virginia, Richmond
Type: Digital images of a book; CW
Online: F&LH
Title: Register of the Confederate dead, interred in Hollywood Cemetery, Richmond, Va.
Notes, URL: By the Hollywood Memorial Association of Richmond.

Virginia, Russell Co.
Type: Abstracts, transcripts; CW
Online: Free
Title: Russell County, Va., Civil War Web site
Notes, URL: Includes a list of soldiers, obituaries, & pension applications. <www.rhobard.com/russell/home.html>

Virginia, Spotsylvania Co.
Type: Index; CW
Online: Free
Title: Names of Men Buried in the Confederate Cemeteries of Fredericksburg and Spotsylvania Court House
Notes, URL: <http://freepages.genealogy.rootsweb.com/~helmsnc/FredCWCEM>

Washington
Type: Photographs; VN
Online: Free
Title: Faces from the Wall: Vietnam War: Washington State Web site
Notes, URL: Pictures of Washington soldiers killed in the Vietnam War. <www.facesfromthewall.com>

Washington, Snohomish Co.
Type: Trancripts; CW
Online: Free
Title: Civil War Veterans Project Snohomish County
Notes, URL: Includes the 1883 pensioners' roll & obituaries. <www.rootsweb.com/~wasnohom/scgarmus.htm>

West Virginia
Type: Digital images of books; REV
CD-ROM: $29.99, Genealogy.com, CD #520
Online: Genealogy Library
Title: Early West Virginia Settlers, 1600s–1900s
Notes, URL: Includes *West Virginians in the American Revolution* & *The Soldiery of West Virginia*. <www.genealogy.com/520facd.html>

West Virginia
Type: Abstracts; CW
Online: Free
Title: The Civil War in West Virginia
Notes, URL: Thousands of militia records. <www.rootsweb.com/~hcpd/civilwar.htm>

West Virginia
Type: Abstracts; CW
Online: Free
Title: The Civil War Medals of West Virginia. Where Are They?
Notes, URL: "In 1866, the state of West Virginia authorized the minting of over 26,000 medals to honor its Civil War Union soldiers." <www.lindapages.com/cwmedals.htm>

West Virginia
Type: Abstracts; CW
Online: Ancestry
Title: West Virginia 5th Cavalry Roster
Notes, URL: 1,100 names. Source: Reader, Frank S. *History of the Fifth West Virginia Cavalry*. <www.ancestry.com/search/rectype/inddbs/4148.htm>

Wisconsin
Type: Books; CW
Year Range: 1861–1865
Online: Free
Title: Roster of Wisconsin Volunteers, War of the Rebellion, 1861–1865
Notes, URL: Search by name or regiment. Images of *Roster of Wisconsin Volunteers, War of the Rebellion, 1861–1865* (2 vols.) & an index to the roster, *Wisconsin Volunteers, 1861–1865*. <www.wisconsinhistory.org/roster>

Wisconsin
Type: Digital images of a book; CW
Online: F&LH
Title: The Thirty-sixth Wisconsin Volunteer Infantry: 1st Brigade, 2d Division, 2d Army Corps, Army of the Potomac
Notes, URL: "A complete roster of its officers and men with their record, a full list of casualties."

Wisconsin
Type: Digital images of a book; WWI
Online: F&LH
Title: The 32nd Division in the World War, 1917–1919

Wisconsin
Type: Transcript of a book; WWI
Online: Free
Title: Wisconsin's Gold Star List Soldiers, Sailors, Marines, and Nurses Casualties for WWI
Notes, URL: <www.accessgenealogy.com/worldwarone/wisconsin/>

Wisconsin
Type: Digital images of a book; WWI
Online: F&LH
Title: Wisconsin's gold star list
Notes, URL: "Soldiers, sailors, marines, and nurses from the Badger State who died in the federal service during the World War."

Wisconsin, La Crosse Co.
Type: Index; 1812-SI-MX-CW-IN
Year Range: 1800–1900
Online: Free
Title: La Crosse, Wisconsin Military Veterans Buried in La Crosse County Cemeteries 1800–1900
Notes, URL: <http://my.execpc.com/~jblake47/research.html>

Wisconsin, Milwaukee Co.
Type: Index; WWI
Online: Free
Title: Milwaukee Public Library: World War I Military Portrait Index
Notes, URL: An index to persons pictured in 3,192 photographs of World War I military personnel from Milwaukee County. <www.mpl.org/File/hum_ww1_index.htm>

Wyoming
Type: Transcript
Year Range: 1883
Online: Free
Title: 1883 Pensioners on the Roll: Wyoming Territory
Notes, URL: <http://homepages.rootsweb.com/~godwin/reference/wyoming1883.html>

EIGHT

Land and Property Records

An 1826 deed records John Robertson's purchase of land in Worcester, Otsego County, New York, for $1,500. This information alone was interesting, but the deed also revealed his previous place of residence—Middleburgh, Schoharie County, New York—and that would prove to be an important clue, because it told me where to look for earlier records on John Robertson before he moved to Worcester.

Land records can help you track a person's movements and sometimes even identify a previous place of residence. **They often provide useful family information like occupations, the names of relatives, and other clues.**

Reminder

What land and property records are online or on CD-ROM?
County plat maps, tax lists, indexes to land grants, and indexes to a few county land records (see Figure 8-1 below).

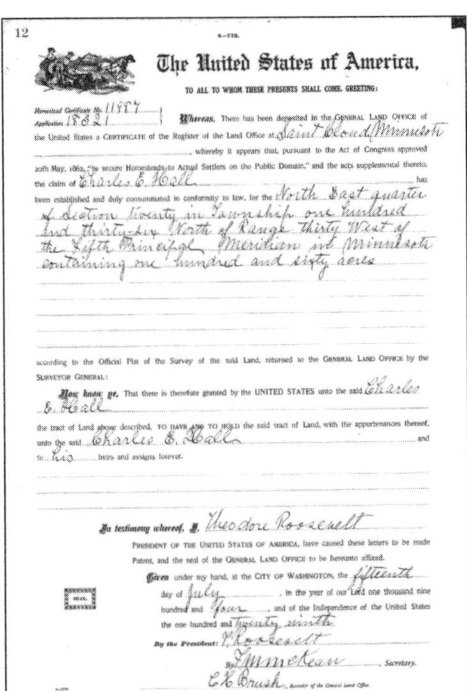

12

The United States of America,

TO ALL TO WHOM THESE PRESENTS SHALL COME, GREETING:

Homestead Certificate No. 11987
Application 18321

Whereas, There has been deposited in the General Land Office of the United States a Certificate of the Register of the Land Office at Saint Cloud, Minnesota whereby it appears that, pursuant to the Act of Congress approved 20th May, 1862, "To secure Homesteads to Actual Settlers on the Public Domain," and the acts supplemental thereto, the claim of Charles E. Hall has been established and duly consummated in conformity to law, for the North East quarter of Section twenty in Township one hundred and thirty-six North of Range thirty West of the Fifth Principal Meridian in Minnesota containing one hundred and sixty acres

according to the Official Plat of the Survey of the said Land, returned to the General Land Office by the Surveyor General:

Now know ye, That there is therefore granted by the UNITED STATES unto the said Charles E. Hall the tract of Land above described, TO HAVE AND TO HOLD the said tract of Land, with the appurtenances thereof, unto the said Charles E. Hall and to his heirs and assigns forever.

In testimony whereof, I, Theodore Roosevelt President of the United States of America, have caused these letters to be made Patent, and the seal of the General Land Office to be hereunto affixed.

Given under my hand, at the City of Washington, the fifteenth day of July, in the year of our Lord one thousand nine hundred and four, and of the Independence of the United States the one hundred and twenty-ninth.

By the President: T. Roosevelt
By F. M. McKean, Secretary.
C. H. Brush, Recorder of the General Land Office.

Figure 8-1
Homestead certificate issued 15 July 1904 granting Charles E. Hall 160 acres of land in Cass County, Minnesota. Document number 11,987, misc. doc. no. 18,321. Bureau of Land Management, General Land Office Records, <www.glorecords.blm.gov>.

What land and property records are not online or on CD-ROM?
The most useful land records are recorded at the county level, and very few of them are online.

KEY RESOURCES

Digital Images

The Official Federal Land Patent Records Site
<www.glorecords.blm.gov>

Were your ancestors homesteaders? Check out this database (see Figure 8-2 below) on the initial transfer of land titles from the federal government to individuals. You can view images of more than two million federal land title records issued between 1820 and 1908.

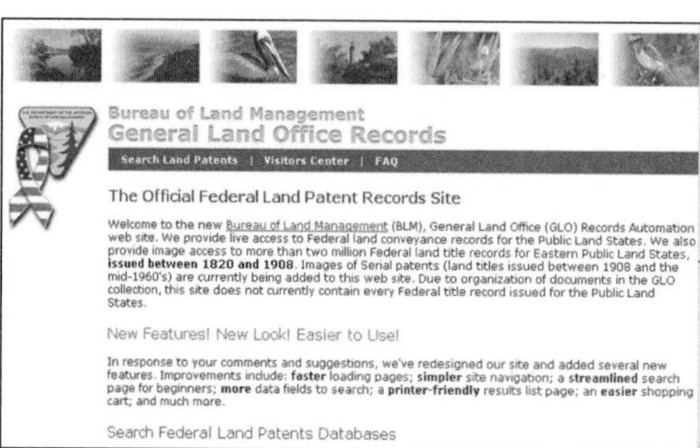

Figure 8-2
Official Federal Land Patent Records Site.

Indexes & Abstracts

USGenWeb Project State Pages
<www.usgenweb.org/statelinks-table.html>

Researchers have contributed indexes and abstracts of land records to USGenWeb's state pages and the county pages linked to them.

LINKS

Sources

Cyndi's List of Genealogy Sites on the Internet: Land Records, Deeds, Homesteads, Etc.
<www.cyndislist.com/land.htm>

SUGGESTED READING

Hatcher, Patricia Law. *Locating Your Roots: Discover Your Ancestors Using Land Records.* Cincinnati: Betterway Books, 2003.

Hone, E. Wade. *Land and Property Research in the United States.* Salt Lake City: Ancestry, 1997.

DATABASE DIRECTORY Land and Property Records

This directory does not include URLs for databases in the Family and Local Histories collection. See page 18 for instructions on "Searching an Individual Database" in Family and Local Histories. **Type**: Digital Images, Transcript, Database, Abstracts, or Index.

United States
Type: Index
Online: Free
Title: RootsWeb.com: Deed Records
Notes, URL: More than 2,312 records. <http://userdb.rootsweb.com/deeds>

United States
Type: Index
Online: Free
Title: RootsWeb.com: Land Records Database
Notes, URL: More than 1.3 million records, including many homestead records. <http://userdb.rootsweb.com/land records>

United States
Type: Index
Online: Free
Title: RootsWeb.com: Plat Records
Notes, URL: Over 11,000 records from Missouri. <http://userdb.rootsweb.com/plats>

United States
Type: Abstract
Year Range: 1790–1907
CD-ROM: $29.99, Genealogy.com, CD #255
Online: Genealogy Library
Title: AL, AR, FL, LA, MI, MN, OH, WI, 1790–1907 Land Records
Notes, URL: 1,645,000 recipients of land from the U.S. government. Records held by the General Land Office (GLO), Bureau of Land Management. <www.genealogy.com/255facd.html>

United States
Type: Abstract
Year Range: 1790–1907
Online: Ancestry
Title: BLM Land Records
Notes, URL: 1,846,743 records of land transfers in Ala., Ark., Fla., La., Mich., Minn., Miss., Ohio, & Wis. from the U.S. government. <www.ancestry.com/search/rectype/court/blm/main.htm>

United States
Type: Digital images
Year Range: 1790–1960s
Online: Free
Title: Bureau of Land Management, General Land Office Records
Notes, URL: Federal land conveyances for the Public Land States & more than 2 million federal land title records for Eastern Public Land States, 1820–1908. You can search only one state at a time on this site. <www.glorecords.blm.gov>

Arkansas
Type: Abstract
Year Range: Up to 1908
Online: Free
Title: Arkansas Land Records—Interactive Search
Notes, URL: <http://searches.rootsweb.com/cgi-bin/arkland/arkland.pl>

Arkansas
Type: Abstract
Year Range: Up to 1908
Online: Free
Title: Federal Land Records for Arkansas
Notes, URL: <www.rootsweb.com/~usgenweb/ar/fedland.htm>

California
Type: Index
Year Range: 1855–1875
Online: Free
Title: Spanish and Mexican Land Grant Maps, 1855–1875
Notes, URL: <www.ss.ca.gov/archives/level3_ussg3.html>

California, San Bernardino Co.
Type: Index
Year Range: 1980–pres.
Online: Free
Title: Auditor/Controller-Recorder: San Bernardino County Grantor/Grantee Index
Notes, URL: <www.co.san-bernardino.ca.us/acr/online.htm>

California, San Diego Co.
Type: Index
Year Range: 1982–pres.
Online: Free
Title: County of San Diego: Grantor/Grantee Index Search
Notes, URL: <http://arcc.co.san-diego.ca.us/services/grantorgrantee/>

Colorado
Type: Database
Year Range: 1862–1908
Online: Ancestry
Title: Denver Land Office Records, 1862–1908
Notes, URL: <www.ancestry.com/search/rectype/inddbs/3313.htm>

Colorado, Yuma Co.
Type: Index, images
Year Range: 1888–1922
Online: Free
Title: Yuma County, Colorado: Original Land Patents
Notes, URL: <www.rootsweb.com/~coyuma/data/landmap/blmpat.htm>

Connecticut, Hartford Co., Hartford
Type: Index
Year Range: 1639–1839
Online: NEHGS
Title: General Index of the Land Records of the Town of Hartford, Connecticut, 1639–1839
Notes, URL: <www.newenglandancestors.org/research/database/hartfordct/>

Delaware
Type: Transcript
Year Range: 1646–1680
CD-ROM: $30 (Mac/Win), Heritage Books, CD #1473
Title: Heritage Books Archives: Delaware and Pennsylvania
Notes, URL: Includes the Dutch grant of lands (1646–1657) & the Duke of York's grant of lands (1657–1680). <www.heritagebooks.com>. Search on "1473."

Delaware
Type: Transcript, digital images
Year Range: 1684–1686
Online: Free
Title: Documents Relating to William Penn
Notes, URL: Land owners in Kent & Sussex Counties. <www.state.de.us/sos/dpa/exhibits/17thcentury/docwp.htm>

Florida
Type: Digital images
Year Range: 1763–1821
Online: Free
Title: Confirmed Spanish Land Grant Claims

Notes, URL: <www.floridamemory.com/Collections/SpanishLandGrants/>

Florida
Type: Index
Year Range: 1842
Online: Free
Title: Florida Armed Occupation Land Permits
Notes, URL: Click on "Next" to view more entries. <www.anzwers.org/trade/research/armd.html>

Florida, Alachua Co.
Type: Digital images
Year Range: 1833–1927
Online: Free
Title: Alachua County Deed Book Index
Notes, URL: <www.clerk-alachua-fl.org/archive>

Florida, Calhoun Co.
Type: Index
Year Range: Up to 1908
Online: Free
Title: Calhoun County, Florida, Index to Reconstructed Federal Land Tract Book
Notes, URL: <www.geocities.com/Heartland/Bluffs/3010/calh-idx.htm>

Florida, Dade Co.
Type: Index
Year Range: 1974–2003
Online: Free
Title: County Recorder's Record Search
Notes, URL: <www.miami-dadeclerk.com/public-records/pubsearch1.asp>

Georgia
Type: Index
Year Range: 1789–1799
Online: Ancestry
Title: Georgia Tax Index, 1789–99
Notes, URL: Over 11,500 names. <www.ancestry.com/search/rectype/inddbs/3467.htm>

Georgia
Type: Database
Year Range: 1827
Online: Ancestry
Title: Georgia Land Lottery, 1827
Notes, URL: Originally published as *Official Register of the Land Lottery of 1827*. <www.ancestry.com/search/rectype/inddbs/2072.htm>

Georgia
Type: Database
Year Range: 1832
Online: Ancestry
Title: Georgia Cherokee Land Lottery, 1832
Notes, URL: <www.ancestry.com/search/rectype/inddbs/4242.htm>

Idaho, Idaho Co.
Type: Transcript
Year Range: 1886–1893
Online: Ancestry
Title: Idaho County, Idaho Newspaper Tax Lists, 1886–93
Notes, URL: Over 3,000 names. <www.ancestry.com/search/rectype/inddbs/3816.htm>

Illinois
Type: Abstracts
Year Range: 1813–1954
Online: Ancestry
Title: Illinois Public Land Purchase Records
Notes, URL: 538,000 land sales, most 1813-1870. <www.ancestry.com/search/rectype/inddbs/3780.htm>

Illinois
Type: Abstracts
Year Range: 1813–1954
Online: Free
Title: Illinois Public Domain Land Tract Sales
Notes, URL: "Nearly 550,000 land sales from the 54,740 square miles of the public domain sold within Illinois." Most 1813–1870. <www.sos.state.il.us/departments/archives/data_lan.html>

Illinois
Type: Abstracts
Year Range: 1817–1818
Online: Free
Title: War of 1812: Bounty Land Grants in the Illinois Military Tract
Notes, URL: <www.lineages.com/vault/BountyLands.asp>

Illinois, Hancock Co., Nauvoo
Type: Transcript
Year Range: 1842
Online: Ancestry
Title: Nauvoo, Illinois Tax Index, 1842
Notes, URL: <www.ancestry.com/search/rectype/inddbs/4221.htm>

Illinois, Ogle Co.
Type: Index
Year Range: 1878–1933
Online: Free
Title: Ogle County Almshouse Register Index, 1878–1933
Notes, URL: <www.library.sos.state.il.us/departments/archives/oglealms.html>

Illinois, Stephenson Co.
Type: Transcript
Year Range: 1917
Online: Ancestry
Title: Stephenson County, Illinois Farmer Directory, 1917
Notes, URL: About 13,200 names. <www.ancestry.com/search/rectype/inddbs/4371.htm>

Indiana
Type: Index
Year Range: 1823–1855
Online: Free
Title: Indiana State Archives: Databases—Archives Land Records Index
Notes, URL: <www.in.gov/icpr/archives/databases/land/landindx.html>

Indiana
Type: Database
Year Range: 1976–1994
Online: Free
Title: Hoosier Homestead Award Database
Notes, URL: Farms owned by the same family for 100 years or more. <www.in.gov/serv/icpr_homestead>

Indiana, Morgan Co.
Type: Abstracts
Online: Free
Title: Morgan County Public Library: Original Land Sales from U.S. Govt
Notes, URL: <www.scican.net/~morglib/genasist/genasist.html>

Indiana, Orange Co.
Type: Transcript
Online: Free
Title: Early Land Entries, Orange County, Indiana
Notes, URL: From Goodspeed's *1884 History of Orange County*. <www.usgennet.org/usa/in/county/orange/preland.htm>

Kansas
Type: Transcript
Year Range: 1854–1856
Online: Ancestry
Title: Kansas Voter Registration Lists, 1854–56
Notes, URL: Over 16,000 names. <www.ancestry.com/search/rectype/inddbs/3961.htm>

Kansas
Type: Database
Year Range: 1854–1879
Online: Ancestry
Title: Kansas Settlers, 1854–79
Notes, URL: Gives each settler's name, birthplace, birth date, & settlement

location. <www.ancestry.com/search/rectype/inddbs/4132.htm>

Kansas, Leavenworth Co.
Type: Transcript
Year Range: 1895–1900
Online: Ancestry
Title: Leavenworth, Kansas Tax List, 1895–97, 1899–1900
Notes, URL: Over 3,100 names. <www.ancestry.com/search/rectype/inddbs/3499.htm>

Kansas, Leavenworth Co.
Type: Transcript
Year Range: 1900–1920
Online: Ancestry
Title: Leavenworth County, Kansas Tax Payers, 1900–20
Notes, URL: Nearly 19,000 names transcribed from city directories. <www.ancestry.com/search/rectype/inddbs/3840.htm>

Kentucky
Type: Abstracts
Year Range: 1774–1924
CD-ROM: $29.99, Genealogy.com, CD #650
Online: Genealogy Library
Title: Kentucky, 1774–1924 Land Records
Notes, URL: Includes abstracts of 150,000 Kentucky land grants, 1782–1924; 17,000 landholders, 1787–1811; & 45,000 entries concentrated in Fayette, Lincoln, & Jefferson Counties. <www.genealogy.com/650facd.html>

Kentucky
Type: Digital images
Year Range: 1782–1787
Online: Free
Title: Revolutionary War Warrants
Notes, URL: "4,748 bounty land warrants issued by Virginia to veterans of the Revolutionary War." <www.kysos.com/admin/landoffi/revwaropen.asp>

Kentucky
Type: Index
Year Range: 1782–1924
Online: Ancestry
Title: Kentucky Land Grants
Notes, URL: Originally published as *The Kentucky Land Grants, vols. I-II*, by Willard Rouse Jillson. <www.ancestry.com/search/rectype/inddbs/2073d.htm>

Kentucky
Type: Digital images
Year Range: 1825–1826
Online: Free
Title: Kentucky Land Patents: West of Tennessee River Military Series
Notes, URL: <www.sos.state.ky.us/land/wtrm/>

Kentucky, Edmonson Co.
Type: Transcript
Year Range: 1825
Online: Free
Title: Edmonson County, Kentucky, Tax List For The Year 1825
Notes, URL: <www.tlc-gen.com/edmonson.cfm>

Louisiana
Type: Index
Year Range: Up to 1908
Online: Free
Title: Louisiana Land Records—Interactive Search
Notes, URL: Homestead & Cash Entry Patents from the Bureau of Land Management's General Land Office (GLO). <http://searches.rootsweb.com/cgi-bin/laland/laland.pl>

Maine
Type: Digital images, transcripts
Year Range: 1798
Online: NEHGS
Title: Massachusetts and Maine 1798 Direct Tax
Notes, URL: <www.newenglandancestors.org/research/database/mmt/>

Maine, Kennebec Co.
Type: Digital images of a book containing abstracts
Year Range: About 1763–1808
Online: F&LH
Title: Land titles in old Pittston

Maryland
Type: Index
Year Range: 1720–1917
Online: Free
Title: Maryland State Archives: Maryland Indexes (Boundary Records, Index)
Notes, URL: <www.mdarchives.state.md.us/msa/stagser/s1400/s1474/html/ssi1474.html>

Maryland
Type: Index
Year Range: 1783
Online: Free
Title: Maryland State Archives: Maryland Indexes (Assessment of 1783, Index)
Notes, URL: <www.mdarchives.state.md.us/msa/stagser/s1400/s1437/html/ssi1437e.html>

Maryland, Baltimore
Type: Index
Year Range: 1798–1808
Online: Ancestry
Title: Baltimore, Maryland Tax Records Index, 1798–1808
Notes, URL: 5,700 records. <www.ancestry.com/search/rectype/inddbs/4203.htm>

Maryland, Baltimore Co.
Type: Abstracts
Year Range: 1659–1775
CD-ROM: $29 (Mac/Win), Heritage Books, CD #1959
Title: Heritage Books Archives: Baltimore County, Maryland Deed Records, Volumes 1-4
Notes, URL: These deeds cover present-day Baltimore City, Cecil & Hartford Counties, & parts of Carroll, Anne Arundel, Howard, and Kent Counties. <www.heritagebooks.com>. Search on "1959."

Massachusetts
Type: Database
Year Range: 1600s
Online: Ancestry
Title: Massachusetts Freemen
Notes, URL: Originally published as "List of Freemen," by Lucius R. Paige, *New England Historical and Genealogical Register*, vol. 3, 1849. <www.ancestry.com/search/rectype/inddbs/1036.htm>

Massachusetts
Type: Database
Year Range: 1630–1691
Online: Ancestry
Title: Massachusetts Applications of Freemen, 1630–91
Notes, URL: Over 4,800 names. Originally published as *List of Freemen of Massachusetts*, by Lucius R. Paige. <www.ancestry.com/search/rectype/inddbs/4296.htm>

Massachusetts
Type: Digital images
Year Range: 1798
Online: NEHGS
Title: Massachusetts and Maine 1798 Direct Tax
Notes, URL: <www.newenglandancestors.org/research/database/mmt/>

Massachusetts, Berkshire Co., New Ashford
Type: Database
Year Range: 1842–1900
Online: Ancestry
Title: New Ashford, Massachusetts Land Owners, 1842–1900
Notes, URL: <www.ancestry.com/search/rectype/inddbs/3453.htm>

Massachusetts, Bristol Co.
Type: Digital image
Year Range: 1659
Online: Free
Title: Map of the Freemen's Purchase of 1659, Freetown/Fall River, MA
Notes, URL: <http://hometown.aol.com/troiscats/myhomepage/photo.html>

Massachusetts, Essex Co.
Type: Index, digital images
Year Range: 1981–pres.
Online: Free
Title: Essex County Registry of Deeds, Northern District
Notes, URL: Indexes, 1981–pres. Images, 1994–pres. Covers Andover, Lawrence, Methuen, & North Andover. <www.lawrencedeeds.com/dsSearch.asp>

Massachusetts, Essex Co.
Type: Index, digital images
Year Range: 1984–pres.
Online: Free
Title: Registry of Deeds: Southern Essex District
Notes, URL: Indexes, 1984–pres. Images, 1992–pres. <www.salemdeeds.com/goget.asp>

Massachusetts, Hampden Co.
Type: Transcripts
Year Range: About 1636–1650
Online: F&LH
Title: Indian deeds of Hampden County: being copies of all land transfers from the Indians recorded in the county of Hampden, Massachusetts

Massachusetts, Hampshire Co., Ware
Type: Digital images of a book containing transcripts
Online: F&LH
Title: Early land grants and incorporation of the town of Ware
Notes, URL: A book by Edward H. Gilbert.

Massachusetts, Middlesex Co., Groton
Type: Digital images of a book containing transcripts
Year Range: 1659–1681
Online: F&LH
Title: An account of the early land-grants of Groton, Massachusetts
Notes, URL: A book by Samuel A. Green.

Massachusetts, Middlesex Co., Watertown
Type: Abstracts
Year Range: 1863–1822
Online: Ancestry
Title: Watertown, Massachusetts Lands, Grants, and Possessions
Notes, URL: Digital images of a book, *Watertown Records: Lands Grants, Divisions, Allotments, Possessions, and Proprietors' Book.* <www.ancestry.com/search/rectype/inddbs/6350.htm>

Massachusetts, Middlesex Co., Woburn
Type: Abstracts
Year Range: 1649–1700
Online: F&LH
Title: Abstracts of early Woburn deeds: recorded at Middlesex County Registry, 1649–1700
Notes, URL: A book by Edward F. Johnson.

Massachusetts, Suffolk Co., Boston
Type: Index
Year Range: 1630–1822
CD-ROM: $39.99, NEHGS, Item #SCD-TH
Title: Inhabitants and Estates of the Town of Boston, 1630–1800 & The Crooked and Narrow Streets of Boston, 1630–1822
Notes, URL: Also known as "The Thwing Index," this CD has over 125,000 references to vital records, property holdings, occupation, town offices held, church affiliation, burial, and more for thousands of property holders. <www.newenglandancestors.org/rs1/store/browse/product.asp?sku=3119>

Michigan, Iosco Co.
Type: Abstracts
Year Range: 1841–1896
Online: Ancestry
Title: Iosco County, Michigan Early Land Owners, 1841–96
Notes, URL: About 3,000 early land purchases. <www.ancestry.com/search/rectype/inddbs/5473.htm>

Michigan, Iosco Co.
Type: Index
Year Range: 1869–1934
Online: Ancestry
Title: Iosco County, Michigan Paupers, 1869–1934
Notes, URL: <www.ancestry.com/search/rectype/inddbs/5243.htm>

Michigan, Iosco Co.
Type: Index
Year Range: 1903
Online: Ancestry
Title: Iosco County, Michigan Plat Book, 1903
Notes, URL: An index to the *1903 Plat Book of Iosco County, Michigan.* <www.ancestry.com/search/rectype/inddbs/5264.htm>

Minnesota, Becker Co.
Type: Index
Year Range: Up to 1908
Online: Free
Title: Land Records, Becker County, Minnesota GenWeb
Notes, URL: Homestead and cash entry land patents. <www.rootsweb.com/~mnbecker/land.htm>

Minnesota, Clay Co.
Type: Digital images, transcript
Year Range: 1905–1933
Online: Free
Title: Clay County Historical Society Archives
Notes, URL: 1905 personal property tax list, 1909 & 1920 plat maps, & 1933 lists of residents. <www.info.co.clay.mn.us/History/research_genealogy.htm>

Mississippi
Type: Abstracts
Year Range: 1789–1809
Online: F&LH
Title: First settlers of the Mississippi Territory: grants taken from the American state papers, class VIII, Public lands, volume I, 1789–1809
Notes, URL: A book by Mary Fagan Burr.

Mississippi
Type: Abstracts
Year Range: 1789–1834
Online: Ancestry
Title: Land Claims in Mississippi Territory, 1789–1834
Notes, URL: Originally published as *Early Settlers of Mississippi as Taken From Land Claims in the Mississippi Territory*, Walter Lowrie (ed.). <www.ancestry.com/search/rectype/inddbs/6232.htm>

Mississippi
Type: Digital images of a book containing transcripts
Year Range: 1833–1834
Online: F&LH
Title: A list of the purchasers of public lands at Columbus and Chocchuma,

Mississippi, from 1 Oct., 1833 to 1 Jan., 1834: report from the commissioner of the General Land Office, 1834

Mississippi, Madison Co.
Type: Transcript
Year Range: 1811–1812
Online: F&LH
Title: Tax lists 1811 & 1812, Madison County, Miss.: & a few Alabama land entries

Missouri, Buchanan Co.
Type: Database
Year Range: 1887–1890
Online: Ancestry
Title: Buchanan County, Missouri Taxpayers, 1887–90
Notes, URL: Nearly 10,000 taxpayers. <www.ancestry.com/search/rectype/inddbs/3870.htm>

Missouri, Buchanan Co.
Type: Database
Year Range: 1891–1901
Online: Ancestry
Title: Buchanan County, Missouri Taxpayers, 1891–95, 1901
Notes, URL: Over 21,200 taxpayers. <www.ancestry.com/search/rectype/inddbs/4254.htm>

Missouri, Buchanan Co.
Type: Database
Year Range: 1896–1900
Online: Ancestry
Title: Buchanan County, Missouri Taxpayers, 1896–1900
Notes, URL: Over 20,300 taxpayers. <www.ancestry.com/search/rectype/inddbs/4072.htm>

Missouri, Livingston Co.
Type: Index
Year Range: 1837–1855?
Online: Ancestry
Title: Livingston County, Missouri Deeds, Books 1 and 2
Notes, URL: More than 2,000 names. <www.ancestry.com/search/rectype/inddbs/5432.htm>

Missouri, Livingston Co.
Type: Index
Year Range: 1855–1857
Online: Ancestry
Title: Livingston County, Missouri Deeds, 1855–57, Volumes 2, 3, 5, 6
Notes, URL: More than 2,300 names. <www.ancestry.com/search/rectype/inddbs/5462.htm>

Nevada
Type: Transcript
Year Range: 1913–1918
Online: Ancestry
Title: Nevada Car Registration Records, 1913–18
Notes, URL: Over 24,500 names. <www.ancestry.com/search/rectype/inddbs/4328.htm>

New Jersey, Bergen Co.
Type: Abstracts
Year Range: 1689–1801
CD-ROM: $37.50 (Mac/Win), Heritage Books, item #1932
Title: Heritage Books Archives: New Jersey, Volume 2
Notes, URL: Includes *Bergen County, New Jersey, Deed Records, 1689–1801*, by John David Davis. <www.heritagebooks.com>. Search on "1932."

New Jersey, Salem Co.
Type: Abstracts
Year Range: About 1679–1840
Online: F&LH
Title: Old deeds belonging to the Salem County Historical Society: with an index of unrecorded deeds
Notes, URL: A book by Elmer Garfield Van Name.

New Jersey, Union Co., Elizabeth
Type: Abstracts
Year Range: 1660s
Online: F&LH
Title: Associates v. proprietors: early land disputes in Elizabeth, New Jersey: photocopy of typescript
Notes, URL: A book by David A. Roth.

New York
Type: Index
Year Range: 1643–1676
Online: Free
Title: New York Indorsed Land Papers, 1643–1676
Notes, URL: Land grant application files from the New York Secretary of State's Office. <www.tlc-gen.com/newyork.cfm> or <www.rootsweb.com/~nysuffol/land.html>

New York, Cayuga Co.
Type: Index
Year Range: Up to 1825
Online: Free
Title: Revolutionary War Bounty Land in "The Military Tract of Central NY" for the Area Within Cayuga County, New York
Notes, URL: <www.rootsweb.com/~nycayuga/land/mtractac.html>

New York, Erie Co., Buffalo
Type: Index
Year Range: 1806–1843
Online: Free
Title: Original Lot Holders, Buffalo, New York
Notes, URL: <www.rootsweb.com/~nyerie/buffalo/lots.htm>

New York, Kings Co., Brooklyn
Type: Digital images of a book containing abstracts
Year Range: 1645–1894
Online: F&LH
Title: Titles to land and land under water at Sea Gate, New York Harbor
Notes, URL: A book by Gherardi Davis.

New York, Montgomery Co.
Type: Transcript
Year Range: 1766–1780
Online: Free
Title: Sir John Johnson's Rent Roll of the Kingsborough Patent
Notes, URL: Renters in Tryon County (now Montgomery County), New York. <http://freepages.genealogy.rootsweb.com/~wjmartin/kingsbor.htm>

New York, Tompkins Co.
Type: Index
Year Range: Up to 1825
Online: Free
Title: Revolutionary War Bounty Land in "The Military Tract of Central NY" for the Area Within Tompkins County, New York
Notes, URL: <www.rootsweb.com/~nytompki/bounty.htm>

North Carolina
Type: Abstracts
Year Range: 1772
CD-ROM: $29.99, Genealogy.com, CD #524
Online: Genealogy Library
Title: Early North Carolina Settlers, 1700s–1900s
Notes, URL: Includes the book *North Carolina Land Grants in South Carolina.* <www.genealogy.com/524facd.html>

North Carolina
Type: Digital images of a book
Year Range: 1886
Online: F&LH
Title: Chas. Emerson's North Carolina tobacco belt directory: embracing the

counties of Alamance, Durham, Forsyth, Granville, Guilford, Orange, Rockingham, Vance, and Wake
Notes, URL: "A complete list of all landowners, number of acres owned." A book by Charles Emerson & Charles A. Horner.

North Carolina, Alamance Co.
Type: Index
Year Range: 1849–1902
Online: Free
Title: Alamance County Land Grant Recipients
Notes, URL: <www.rootsweb.com/~ncacgs/ala_nc_land_grants.html>

North Carolina, Chowan Co.
Type: Index
Year Range: 1696–1878
Online: Ancestry
Title: Chowan County, North Carolina Cross Index to Deeds-Grantees 1696–1878 Vol B
Notes, URL: 21,000 entries. <www.ancestry.com/search/rectype/inddbs/6203.htm>

North Dakota
Type: Index
Year Range: 1910–1937
Online: Free
Title: North Dakota Land Records
Notes, URL: County plat map indexes. <http://pixel.cs.vt.edu/library/land/nodak>

Ohio
Type: Digital images of a book
Year Range: 1775–1789?
Online: F&LH
Title: First ownership of Ohio lands
Notes, URL: A book by Albion Morris Dyer.

Ohio
Type: Digital images of a book
Year Range: 1778–1783
Online: F&LH
Title: Conquest of the country northwest of the river Ohio, 1778–1783, and life of Gen. George Rogers Clark: with numerous sketches of men who served under Clark, and full list of those allotted lands in Clark's Grant for service in the campaigns against the British posts, showing exact land allotted each
Notes, URL: A book by William Hayden English.

Ohio
Type: Abstracts, transcripts
Year Range: 1787–1840
CD-ROM: $29.99, Genealogy.com, CD #651
Online: Genealogy Library
Title: Ohio, 1787–1840 Land and Tax Records
Notes, URL: Abstracts of land purchases in southeastern Ohio, 1800–1840, & transcripts of tax lists, 1788–1825. <www.genealogy.com/651facd.html>

Ohio
Type: Transcript
Year Range: 1793
Online: Free
Title: Genealogy Quest: Ohio Company Land Grants, 1793
Notes, URL: <www.genealogy-quest.com/collections/ohland.html>

Ohio
Type: Transcript
Year Range: 1800s
Online: Ancestry
Title: Ohio Early Land Ownership Records
Notes, URL: Nearly 1,000 names. Originally published as *First Ownership of Ohio Lands*, by Albion Morris Dyer. <www.ancestry.com/search/rectype/inddbs/4642.htm>

Ohio
Type: Abstracts
Year Range: 1819
Online: Free
Title: Land Auction 1819
Notes, URL: Richland & Wayne Counties. <http://homepages.rootsweb.com/~maggieoh/land_act.html>

Ohio, Butler Co.
Type: Abstracts
Year Range: 1803–1823
CD-ROM: $34.50 (Mac/Win), Heritage Books, item #1640
Title: Heritage Books Archives: Ohio Vol. 2
Notes, URL: Includes Butler County, Ohio Land Records, Vols. 1 & 2: 1803–1823. <www.heritagebooks.com>. Search on "1640."

Ohio, Richland Co.
Type: Digital Images
Year Range: 1896
Online: Free
Title: Plat Book, 1896, Richland County, Ohio
Notes, URL: <www.rootsweb.com/~ohricha/PlatBook/PlatBook.htm>

Ohio, Wayne Co.
Type: Transcript
Year Range: 1913–1916
Online: Ancestry
Title: Wayne County, Ohio Tax Lists, 1913, 1914, and 1916
Notes, URL: Original data: *Assessment of Real Estate and Improvements Wayne County Ohio 1913, 1914, part of 1916.* <www.ancestry.com/search/rectype/inddbs/3944.htm>

Oklahoma
Type: Abstracts
Year Range: 1889–1907
Online: Free
Title: Oklahoma Land Openings 1889–1907
Notes, URL: Links to various lists. <http://marti.rootsweb.com/land/oklands.html>

Oregon
Type: Index
Online: F&LH
Title: Index to Oregon donation land claim files in the National Archives

Oregon
Type: Index
Year Range: 1845–1849
Online: Free
Title: Oregon Historical Records Index: Land Claims
Notes, URL: <http://arcweb.sos.state.or.us/banners/genlist.htm>

Pennsylvania
Type: Transcript
Year Range: 1685–1732
CD-ROM: $29.99, Genealogy.com, CD #512
Online: Genealogy Library
Title: Pennsylvania Colonial Records, 1600s–1800s
Notes, URL: Includes *Early Pennsylvania Land Records*, by William Henry Eagle. <www.genealogy.com/512facd.html>

Pennsylvania
Type: Transcript
Year Range: 1685–1732
Online: Ancestry
Title: Early Pennsylvania Land Records
Notes, URL: Originally published as *Early Pennsylvania Land Records. Minutes of the Board of Property of the Province of Pennsylvania*, by William Henry Eagle. <www.ancestry.com/search/rectype/inddbs/6041.htm>

Pennsylvania
Type: Digital images
Year Range: 1765–1788
CD-ROM: $98.95 (Win) or $19.95-24.95 per county
Title: Pennsylvania Archives, Third Series Volumes XI thru XXII: Pennsylvania Tax Lists
Notes, URL: 10,021 pages from vols. 11-22 of the Third Series of the Pennsylvania Archives. <www.retrospectpublishin g.com/Document/Disc.asp?disc= 3PA1>

Pennsylvania, Berks Co.
Type: Digital images
Year Range: 1876
Online: Free
Title: 1876 Atlas of Berks County
Notes, URL: <www.genealogy.lv/1876Berks>

Pennsylvania, Dauphin Co., Harrisburg
Type: Digital images
Year Range: 1889
Online: Free
Title: 1889 Atlas of the City of Harrisburg
Notes, URL: <www.genealogy.lv/1889Harri sburg>

Pennsylvania, Lancaster Co.
Type: Digital images
Year Range: 1864
Online: Free
Title: 1864 Atlas of Lancaster County
Notes, URL: <www.genealogy.lv/1864Lanc aster>

Pennsylvania, Washington Co.
Type: Abstracts
Year Range: 1782–1785
Online: F&LH
Title: Estate records, 1781–96, and deed records, 1782–85, in Washington County, Pennsylvania
Notes, URL: Both the 1967 & 1977 versions of the book by Raymond Martin Bell.

Pennsylvania, York Co.
Type: Index
Online: Free
Title: Pennsylvania Original Land Records Series for York County
Notes, URL: <www.innernet.net/hively/PAL and/index.htm>

Rhode Island
Type: Abstracts
Year Range: 1709
Online: F&LH
Title: Several purchases of the lands west of Wickford: sold by the committee of the colony for the sale of the vacant lans [*sic*] in 1709
Notes, URL: A book by Elisha R. Potter.

South Carolina
Type: Abstracts, transcript
Year Range: 1672–1772
CD-ROM: $29.99, Genealogy.com, CD #517
Online: Genealogy Library
Title: Early South Carolina Settlers, 1600s–1800s
Notes, URL: Includes *Warrants for Land in South Carolina, 1672–1711* (3 vols.) & *North Carolina Land Grants in South Carolina* (1772). Online: See Genealogical Records: Early South Carolina Settlers, 1600s–1800s.

South Dakota
Type: Abstracts
Year Range: 1867–1936
Online: Free
Title: South Dakota BLM Database
Notes, URL: Extracted from BLM data. <ww w.rootsweb.com/~usgenweb/sd/land/ sdland.htm>

South Dakota
Type: Index
Year Range: 1906–1913
Online: Free
Title: South Dakota Land Records
Notes, URL: County plat map indexes. <h ttp://pixel.cs.vt.edu/library/land/ sodak>

Tennessee
Type: Abstracts
Year Range: 1819–1833
CD-ROM: $11 (Mac/Win), Heritage Books, item #2192
Title: Blount County, Tennessee Deeds—1819–1833
Notes, URL: Digital images of the book by Jane Kizer Thomas. <www.heritagebook s.com>. Search on "2192."

Tennessee, Davidson Co.
Type: Transcript
Year Range: 1821–1835
CD-ROM: $28 (Mac/Win), Heritage Books, item #1495
Title: Heritage Books Archives: Tennessee Vol. 3
Notes, URL: Includes 2 books of deeds by Mary Sue Smith. <www.heritagebooks.c om>. Search on "1495."

Texas
Type: Abstracts
Year Range: 1700s–1900s
Online: Ancestry
Title: Texas Land Title Abstracts
Notes, URL: <www.ancestry.com/search/re ctype/inddbs/5112.htm>

Texas
Type: Index
Year Range: 1835–1888
Online: Free
Title: Name Index to Military Bounty and Donation Land Grants of Texas
Notes, URL: For service 1835–1846. From records of the Texas General Land Office as published in *Bounty and Donation Land Grants of Texas 1835–1888*, by Thomas Lloyd Miller. <www.mindspring .com/~dmaxey/rep_b&d.htm>

Texas
Type: Index, images
Year Range: 1950–pres.
Online: Title X
Title: titleX.com
Notes, URL: In order to search, view, & print records you must first purchase at least $20 in tokens. <www.titlex.com>

Virginia
Type: Narrative
CD-ROM: $31 (Mac/Win), Heritage Books, item #1522
Title: Heritage Books Archives: Virginia Volume 5
Notes, URL: Includes *Manors of Virginia in Colonial Times*, by Edith Tunis Sale. <ww w.heritagebooks.com>. Search on "1522."

Virginia
Type: Abstracts
Year Range: 1623–1704
CD-ROM: $29.99, Genealogy.com, CD #503
Online: Genealogy Library
Title: Virginia Colonial Records, 1600s–1700s
Notes, URL: Includes abstracts of Virginia land patents & grants, 1623–1666, & The Quit Rents Of Virginia, 1704.

Virginia
Type: Digital images, abstracts
Year Range: 1623–1992
Online: Free
Title: The Library of Virginia: Virginia Land Office Patents and Grants/Northern Neck Grants and Surveys
Notes, URL: <www.lva.lib.va.us/whatweh ave/land/>

Virginia
Type: Abstracts
Year Range: 1722–1800
CD-ROM: $39.99, Genealogy.com, CD #513
Online: Genealogy Library
Title: Virginia Land, Marriage, and Probate Records, 1639–1850
Notes, URL: Includes abstracts of deeds from Augusta County 1743–1800 & Spotsylvania County 1722–1799. <www.genealogy.com/513facd.html>

Virginia
Type: Abstracts
Year Range: 1728–1868
CD-ROM: $24.50 (Mac/Win), Heritage Books, item #1158
Title: Heritage Books Archives: Virginia, Vol. 1
Notes, URL: Includes *Accomack Land Causes, 1728–1825* and *Virginia Land Causes: Lancaster County, 1795–1848 & Northampton Co., 1731–1868*, by Stratton Nottingham. <www.heritagebooks.com>. Search on "1158."

Virginia, Bedford Co.
Type: Transcript
Year Range: 1795
Online: Free
Title: Land Processioners in Bedford County, Virginia, in August 1795
Notes, URL: <www.genealogymagazine.com/bedcounprocl.html>

Virginia, Brunswick Co.
Type: Abstracts
Year Range: 1744–1790
Online: Free
Title: Deeds, Brunswick County, Virginia
Notes, URL: <www.rootsweb.com/~vabrunsw/deeds.htm>

Virginia, Culpeper Co.
Type: Images of a book
Year Range: 1783
Online: F&LH
Title: Property tax list of Culpeper County, Virginia: and names of slaves, 1783
Notes, URL: A book by Mary Boldridge Norris.

Virginia, Fauquier Co.
Type: Abstracts
Year Range: 1759–1785
CD-ROM: $25 (Mac/Win), Heritage Books, item #1128
Title: *Fauquier County, Virginia*, by John K. Gott
Notes, URL: Includes *Fauquier County, Virginia: Deeds 1759–1778 & 1778–1785*, by John K. Gott. <www.heritagebooks.com>. Search on "1128."

Virginia, New Kent Co.
Type: Database
Year Range: 1782
Online: Ancestry
Title: New Kent County, Virginia Land Tax Records, 1782
Notes, URL: Almost 400 records. <www.ancestry.com/search/rectype/inddbs/3689.htm>

Virginia, Princess Anne Co.
Type: Abstracts
Year Range: 1691–1783
CD-ROM: $25 (Mac/Win), Heritage Books, item #1098
Title: Princess Anne County, Virginia, Deeds, Wills, and Guardianships
Notes, URL: Abstracted by Anne E. Maling. Includes *Princess Anne County, Virginia, Land and Probate Records Abstracted from Deed Books One to Eighteen, 1691–1783*. <www.heritagebooks.com>. Search on "1098."

Washington, Yakima Co.
Type: Index, images
Year Range: 1985–pres.
Online: Title X
Title: titleX.com
Notes, URL: In order to search, view, & print records you must first purchase at least $20 in tokens. <www.titlex.com>

West Virginia
Type: Digital images of a book containing an index
Year Range: 1772–1884
Online: F&LH
Title: Sims index to land grants in West Virginia
Notes, URL: Digital images of the book by Egdar B. Sims.

West Virginia, Monongalia Co.
Type: Abstracts
Year Range: 1784–1810
CD-ROM: $30.50 (Mac/Win), Heritage Books, item #1271
Title: Heritage Books Archives: West Virginia Volume 2
Notes, URL: Includes *Monongalia County, West Virginia Deedbook Records 1784–1810*, by Rick Toothman, with deeds & wills. <www.heritagebooks.com>. Search on "1271."

Wisconsin
Type: Abstracts
Year Range: Up to 1908
Online: Free
Title: Wisconsin Land Records—Interactive Search
Notes, URL: Homestead & cash entry patents from the Bureau of Land Management's General Land Office (GLO) Automated Records Project. <http://searches.rootsweb.com/cgi-bin/wisconsin/wisconsin.pl>

Wisconsin, Richland Co.
Type: Digital images
Year Range: 1874–1936
Online: Free
Title: The Hills and Hollows of Richland County
Notes, URL: Plat maps. <http://freepages.genealogy.rootsweb.com/~djnsl/Homepage.html>

Newspapers

Newspapers are an important source for birth, marriage, and death information, and local news items provide biographical details you won't find anywhere else. Jarvis A. Grant (1831–1917) is mentioned regularly in the "local gleanings" in the *Red River Valley News* of Glyndon, Clay County, Minnesota. He farmed in the summer, as reported in the August 14, 1879, issue:

> Mr. J. Grant has just completed the harvest of 200 acres of wheat and some oats on his fine farm. . . . The bulk of his land is bearing its first crop, and the yield varies greatly—some may reach 25 bushels, others not more than ten. . . . He uses one Wood self-binding machine and a McCormick Advance reaper.

In the winter he operated a logging camp, as reported on 18 December, 1879:

> Mr. J. Grant has taken the contract for hauling a million feet of logs, more or less, for Clark & McClure out of the pineries five miles from Perham, and with his three sons has gone thither for his winter's work.

Most old newspapers aren't indexed, so searching them can take a long time. Now several companies are scanning newspapers and placing the images online. **Every word in every issue is indexed so you can search through thousands of newspapers in an instant.**

Timesaver

What newspapers are online or on CD-ROM?
You'll find digital images of newspapers and collections of birth notices, marriage announcements, and obituaries (see Figure 9-1 on page 178).

What newspapers are not online or on CD-ROM?
While the number of online newspapers is growing fast, they still represent only a small percentage of newspapers ever published in the United States.

From. The Sturgeon Bay. (Wis.) Advocate. April 29. 1905.

F902
3LE
19

Celebrate Their 60th Wedding Anniversary

Rev. and Mrs. David Lewis of this city, who on Sunday April 30th, will be Married Sixty years.

On Sunday, April 30th, Rev. and Mrs. David Lewis celebrate the 60th anniversary of their wedding day, having been married at Fond du Lac on that date in the year 1845, Rev. W. H. Simpson performing the ceremony that bound this remarkable couple together.

Father Lewis will be 89 years of age if he lives until next November. While quite feeble he is able to get around when the weather is fair. Mrs.

Figure 9-1
Sturgeon Bay Advocate, Sturgeon Bay, Wisc., April 29, 1905. The Wisconsin Local History & Biography Articles digital collection <www.wisconsinhistory.org>. Used with permission of the Wisconsin Historical Society.

KEY RESOURCES

Digital Images

Ancestry.com Historical Newspapers

<www.ancestry.com>

This service gives you online access to selected years of hundreds of newspapers from across the United States (see Figure 9-2 below). The collection includes everything from *The New York Times* to the *Fairbanks Daily Times*, and it's constantly growing. Most titles date from the late 1800s and the early 1900s. You can search for any word, view digital images on your computer screen, zoom in on an article, and print it. A subscription costs $12.95 a month or $79.95 a year.

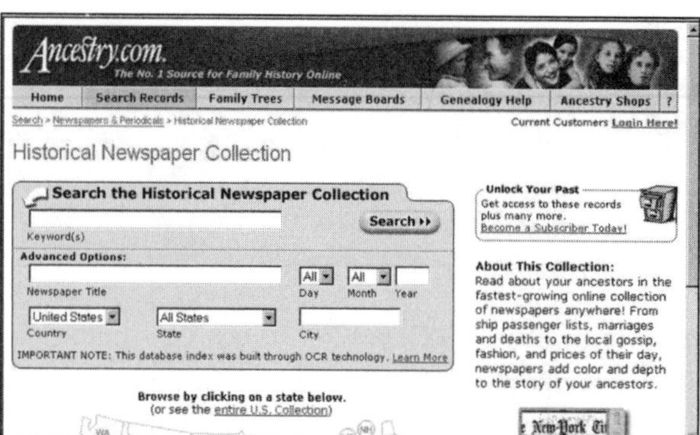

Figure 9-2
Ancestry.com Historical Newspapers.

Paper of Record
<www.paperofrecord.com>

This subscription service (see Figure 9-3 below) gives you online access to actual digital images of many newspapers published in Canada, as well as titles from Australia, England, Mexico, and the United States. Most date from the early 1800s to the mid-1900s. A subscription costs $16.75 a month or $99.99 a year.

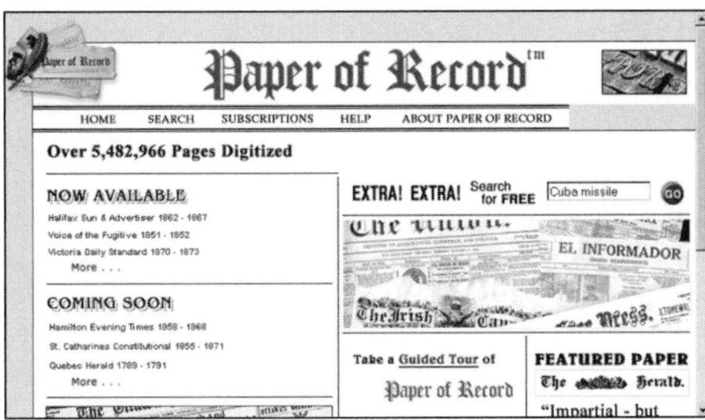

Figure 9-3
Paper of Record.

Transcripts

Accessible Archives
<www.accessible.com>

This subscription service (see Figure 9-4 below) gives you online access to the full text of major sources for research in the mid-Atlantic states. Newspaper databases include *The Pennsylvania Gazette*, 1728–1800, and African-American newspapers of the nineteenth century. You'll also find county histories from Delaware, New Jersey, and eastern Pennsylvania. $19.95 for 30 days or $59.95 per year.

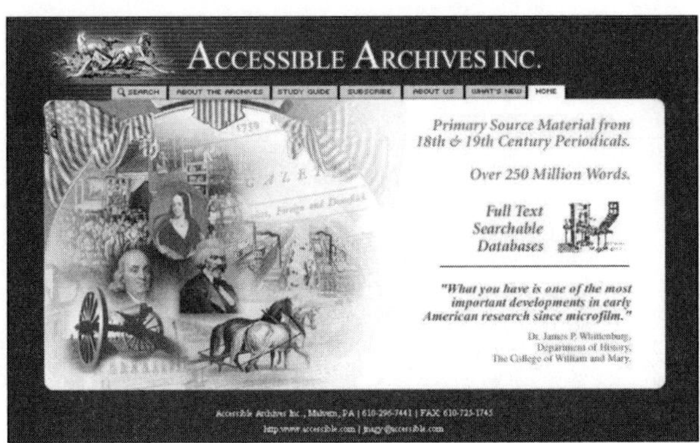

Figure 9-4
Accessible Archives.

ProQuest Newspaper Obituaries
<www.heritagequestonline.com>

Part of the HeritageQuest Online service geared toward libraries, this database will contain the full text of obituaries from over 150 newspapers from across the United States.

LINKS

ABYZ News Links
<www.abyznewslinks.com>

AllNewspapers.com
<www.allnewspapers.com>

Cyndi's List of Genealogy Sites on the Internet
<www.cyndislist.com>
See the categories for Newspapers and Obituaries.

Kidon Media-Link
<www.kidon.com/media-link>

NewsDirectory
<www.newsdirectory.com>

NewsLink
<http://newslink.org>

Newspaper Indexes/Archives/Morgues (Library of Congress)
<http://lcweb.loc.gov/rr/news/oltitles.html>

Obituary Links Page
<www.obitlinkspage.com>

Onlinenewspapers
<www.onlinenewspapers.com>

Online Obituaries for New England
<www.derrynh.50megs.com/obits.htm>

US Newspaper List
<www.usnpl.com>

DATABASE DIRECTORY Newspapers

This directory does not include URLs for databases in the Family and Local Histories Collection. See page 18 for instructions on "Searching an Individual Database" in Family and Local Histories. **Type**: Digital Images, Transcript, Database, Abstracts, or Index; Births (B), Marriages (M), Divorces (DI), Anniversaries (A), Deaths (D), Obituaries (O).

International
Type: Digital images
Year Range: 1748–pres.
Title: NewspaperArchive.com
Notes, URL: Newspapers from the U.S., Canada, Jamaica, & the British Isles. <www.newspaperarchive.com>. $79.95 Annually, $44.95 Quarterly, $12.95 Monthly, $3.95 Day Pass.

International
Type: Transcripts
Year Range: Up to 1923
Online: Free
Title: Newspaper Abstracts
Notes, URL: Newspaper abstracts from the U.S., Canada, & Ireland. <www.newspaperabstracts.com>

International
Type: Transcripts; O
Online: Free
Title: ObituariesOnTheNet.com
Notes, URL: <www.obituariesonthenet.com>

International
Type: Digital images; B-M-O
Year Range: 1788–1920
Online: Free
Title: The Olden Times: Historic Newspapers Online
Notes, URL: Newspapers from the U.S., England, Scotland, Ireland, & Australia. <www.theoldentimes.com>

International
Type: Digital images; B-M-D
Year Range: 1752–2002
Title: Paper of Record
Notes, URL: Search old newspapers from Australia, Canada, Mexico, the United Kingdom, & the U.S. <www.paperofrecord.com>. $16.75/month, $99.99/year.

United States
Type: Transcripts; O
Title: AmericanMemorials.com
Notes, URL: <www.obituaryregistry.com> and <www.americanmemorials.com>. $39.95/year.

United States
Type: Transcripts; O
Online: Free
Title: Current Obituary.com
Notes, URL: Obituaries from funeral homes in Conn., Ga., Mass., N.H., R.I., & Wyo. <www.currentobituary.com>

United States
Type: Transcripts; O
Online: Free
Title: Netmemories.com
Notes, URL: Extensive set of links to online obituaries. <www.netmemories.com>

United States
Type: Transcripts; O
Online: Free
Title: Obituary Central
Notes, URL: Extensive set of links to online obituaries. <www.obitcentral.com>

United States
Type: Index; O
Online: Free
Title: Obituary Daily Times
Notes, URL: Over 8 million obituaries. You can search on a woman's maiden or married name. <http://obits.rootsweb.com>

United States
Type: Index; O
Online: Free
Title: Obituary Depot
Notes, URL: Over 240,000 citations from hundreds of newspapers in the U.S., Canada, & Australia. <www.daddezio.com/obituary/index.html>

United States
Type: Transcripts; O
Year Range: 1995–pres.
Online: Free
Title: Obitz.us
Notes, URL: Over 67,000 obituaries in Washington and Oregon. <www.obitz.us>

United States
Type: Index
Online: Free
Title: RootsWeb.com Newspaper Indexes
Notes, URL: Over 130,000 records. <http://userdb.rootsweb.com/news>

United States
Type: Index; O
Online: Free
Title: RootsWeb.com Obituaries Database
Notes, URL: Over 73,000 records. <http://userdb.rootsweb.com/obituaries>

Alabama, Blount Co.
Type: Index; O
Year Range: 1915–1940
Online: Free
Title: Obituaries Taken From the Southern Democrat
Notes, URL: <www.members.aol.com/Blountal/Obit.html>

Alabama, Colbert Co., Muscle Shoals
Type: Abstracts; M-O
Year Range: 1985–1990
Online: Genealogy Library
Title: Times-Daily
Notes, URL: Includes marriages & wedding anniversaries, 1989, & obituaries, 1985–1990. Select Magazines, Publications, and Television I Newspapers.

Arkansas, Benton Co.
Type: Transcripts; O
Year Range: 1884–1933
CD-ROM: $47 (Mac/Win), Heritage Books, #1548
Title: Heritage Books Archives: Obituaries of Benton County, Arkansas
Notes, URL: 5,372 pages from 11 volumes. <www.heritagebooks.com>. Search on "1548."

California, Colusa Co., Colusa
Type: Transcripts; B-M-D
Year Range: 1876–1884
Online: Ancestry
Title: Colusa, California Newspaper Records, 1876–84
Notes, URL: Nearly 2,800 names. <www.ancestry.com/search/rectype/inddbs/3956.htm>

California, Sacramento Co., Sacramento
Type: Index; B-M-O
Year Range: 1859
Online: Ancestry
Title: Sacramento California, *Sacramento*

Bee newspaper 1859, Obituaries, Marriages, Births
Notes, URL: Over 6,000 names. <www.ancestry.com/search/rectype/inddbs/5724.htm>

California, Sacramento Co., Sacramento
Type: Index; B-M-D
Year Range: 1889
Online: Ancestry
Title: Sacramento [California] Bee Newspaper 1889: Vital Records
Notes, URL: <www.ancestry.com/search/rectype/inddbs/6857.htm>

California, Sacramento Co., Sacramento
Type: Index; B-M-DI-D
Year Range: 1889–1890
Online: Ancestry
Title: Sacramento California, Sacramento Bee Newspaper 1889–1890: vital records
Notes, URL: <www.ancestry.com/search/rectype/inddbs/6098.htm>

California, Sacramento Co., Sacramento
Type: Index; B-M-DI-D
Year Range: 1891
Online: Ancestry
Title: Sacramento California, Sacramento Bee Newspaper 1891: vital records
Notes, URL: <www.ancestry.com/search/rectype/inddbs/6841.htm>

California, San Diego Co., San Diego
Type: Abstracts; O
Year Range: 1993–1994
Online: Ancestry
Title: San Diego Union-Tribune (California) Obituaries, 1993–94
Notes, URL: Over 11,000 records & nearly 34,000 names. <www.ancestry.com/search/rectype/inddbs/4109.htm>

California, San Francisco Co.
Type: Transcripts; B-M-DI-D-O
Year Range: Up to 1920
Online: Free
Title: San Francisco Genealogy: Online Genealogy Databases containing records for the City & County of San Francisco
Notes, URL: Over 11,100 records, mostly before 1906. <www.sfgenealogy.com/sfdata.htm>

California, San Francisco Co., San Francisco
Type: Transcripts; DI
Year Range: 1856–1862
Online: Free
Title: San Francisco Divorces (1856–1862)
Notes, URL: From the *San Francisco Bulletin* & *Daily Alta California*. <www.sfgenealogy.com/sf/div1.htm>

California, San Francisco Co., San Francisco
Type: Index; B-M-D
Year Range: 1869–1895
Online: Free
Title: The *San Francisco Call* Database
Notes, URL: 277,396 records. <www.feefhs.org/fdb2/sfcalli.html>

California, San Francisco Co., San Francisco
Type: Index; B-M-DI-D
Year Range: 1869–1896
Online: Free
Title: *San Francisco Call* Database—Index 1869–1896
Notes, URL: 301,793 records, including 301 divorces, 1869–1870. <www.cefha.org/usa/ca/sf/sfcall/sfcalli.html>

California, Santa Cruz Co.
Type: Index; B-D
Year Range: 1896–1916
Online: Free
Title: Mountain Echo Index 1896–1916
Notes, URL: <www.santacruzpl.org/history/mtecho/index.shtml>

California, Tuolumne Co.
Type: Index; B
Year Range: 1863–1925
Online: Free
Title: Index to Tuolumne County, California Births—Newspaper Extractions
Notes, URL: <ftp://ftp.rootsweb.com/pub/usgenweb/ca/tuolumne/vitals/birth3.txt>

Colorado, Denver
Type: Index; O
Year Range: 1939–2000
Online: Free
Title: The Denver Public Library: Denver Obituary Index
Notes, URL: Obituary index, 1939–1940, 1942–1943, 1960–1974, 1990–2000. <www.denver.lib.co.us/ebranch/whg/datafile.html>

Colorado, Mineral Co.
Type: Transcript; B-M-DI-D-O
Year Range: 1892–1991
Online: Free
Title: Newspaper Extractions
Notes, URL: Vital records, 1892–1894, 1904–1906. Obituaries, 1892–1991. <www.comineral.homestead.com/extract.html>

Colorado, Rio Grande Co.
Type: Transcripts; B-M-DI-D-O
Year Range: 1888–1977
Online: Free
Title: Resources for Rio Grande County
Notes, URL: Vital records from the *Monte Vista Reporter*, 1899–1900. Obituaries, 1888–1977. <www.riograndeco.homestead.com/resources.html>

Delaware
Type: Index; O
Year Range: 1890–pres.
Online: Free
Title: News Journal Obituary & Marriage Index
Notes, URL: Info at <www.angelfire.com/de2/thomasgen/News_Journal_1.html>. Index at <http://userdb.rootsweb.com/news/>

District of Columbia, Washington
Type: Abstracts; M-D
Year Range: 1800–1850
Online: Free index, fee to view abstracts
Title: The National Intelligencer
Notes, URL: Contains news from across the U.S. <www.ngsgenealogy.org/intelligencer/intelligencer.htm>. Free to members of the National Genealogical Society ($55/year).

Florida
Type: Transcripts; O
Year Range: 1998–pres.
Online: Free
Title: The News-Press
Notes, URL: Over 37,000 obituaries, mostly from southwest Florida. <www.news-press.net/obitlegal/obituaries/search.php>

Florida, Hillsborough Co., Tampa
Type: Index; O
Year Range: 1905–pres.
Online: Free
Title: Hillsborough County Public Library Cooperative: TRAILS—Tampa History & Obituaries Index
Notes, URL: Includes an index to obituaries in the *Tampa Tribune*. <www.hcplc.org/hcplc/ig/genealogy.html>. Click on "TRAILS."

Georgia
Type: Digitized images
Year Range: 1828–1887
Online: Free

Title: Digital Library of Georgia: Georgia Historic Newspapers
Notes, URL: Contains the *Cherokee Phoenix* (1828–1833), the *Dublin Post* (1878–1881, 1884–1887), and the *Colored Tribune* (1876). <http://dlg.galileo.usg.edu>. Click on "Online Collections & Current Projects."

Idaho
Type: Index; O
Online: Free
Title: Idaho Falls Obituary Index
Notes, URL: 134,000 entries. <http://abish.byui.edu/specialCollections/fhc/Obit/searchForm.cfm>

Idaho, Idaho Co., Grangeville
Type: Transcript; B-M-DI-D
Year Range: 1886–1903
Online: Ancestry
Title: Idaho County Free Press, Vital Records, 1886–1903
Notes, URL: <www.ancestry.com/search/rectype/inddbs/3631.htm>

Illinois, Champaign Co., Champaign
Type: Index; B-M-D
Year Range: 1892
Online: Ancestry
Title: Champaign, Illinois Newspaper Index, 1892
Notes, URL: <www.ancestry.com/search/rectype/inddbs/4070.htm>

Illinois, Cook Co.
Type: Index; B-M-D
Year Range: 1833–1848
Online: Free
Title: CGS Online Library: Vital Records from Chicago Newspapers, 1833–1848
Notes, URL: <www.chgogs.org/Library.html>

Illinois, Cook Co., Chicago
Type: Index; O
Year Range: 1988–1995
Online: Ancestry
Title: Chicago Sun-Times Obituaries, 1988–95
Notes, URL: <www.ancestry.com/search/rectype/inddbs/5607.htm>

Illinois, Du Page Co.
Type: Index; B-M-D
Year Range: 1885–1887
Online: Free
Title: Wheaton Public Library: Vital Records Index
Notes, URL: <wpl.wheaton.lib.il.us>. Click on the Vital Records Index tab.

Illinois, Du Page Co., Elmhurst
Type: Index; O
Year Range: 1988–1998
Online: Ancestry
Title: Elmhurst Press (Elmhurst, Illinois) Obituaries, 1988–98
Notes, URL: More than 13,600 entries. <www.ancestry.com/search/rectype/inddbs/5341.htm>

Illinois, Du Page Co., Lombard
Type: Index; O
Year Range: 1929–1953
Online: Ancestry
Title: Lombard, Illinois Newspaper Obituaries, 1929–53
Notes, URL: 2,000 names. <www.ancestry.com/search/rectype/inddbs/3683.htm>

Illinois, Lake Co., Barrington
Type: Index; B-M-D
Year Range: 1890–2001
Online: Free
Title: Barrington Courier-Review Indexes
Notes, URL: Includes index to deaths, 1890–2001. <www.barringtonarealibrary.org/Local_Information/BCR/indexes.htm>

Illinois, Lake Co., Highland Park
Type: Index; O
Year Range: 1874–2002
Online: Free
Title: Highland Park, Illinois Obituary Index 1874–2002
Notes, URL: <www.highlandpark.org/obits>

Illinois, McHenry Co.
Type: Index; M-D
Year Range: 1856–1989
Online: Free
Title: McHenry County Illinois Genealogical Society: Indices
Notes, URL: Marriage and death notices indexes. <www.mcigs.org/indices.htm>

Illinois, St. Clair Co., Freeburg
Type: Index; O
Year Range: 1904–1939
Online: Free
Title: St. Clair County (Illinois) Genealogical Society: *Freeburg Tribune* Obituary Index
Notes, URL: <www.compu-type.net/rengen/stclair/stchome.htm>

Illinois, St. Clair Co., Mascoutah
Type: Index; O
Year Range: 1912–1971
Online: Free
Title: Mascoutah Historical Society: Mascoutah Herald Obituaries
Notes, URL: Does not include 1941. <www.mascoutah.com/Historical/WEBPG.HTM>

Illinois, Woodford Co.
Type: Index; O
Year Range: 1887–2000
Online: Ancestry
Title: Woodford County, Illinois, Prairie District Library, Obituaries, 1887–Present
Notes, URL: <www.ancestry.com/search/rectype/inddbs/6109.htm>

Indiana, Fulton Co.
Type: Transcripts; O
Year Range: 1914–2002
Online: Free
Title: Fulton County Indiana Obituaries
Notes, URL: 1914–1930, 1934–1985, 1997–2002. <www.fulco.lib.in.us/genealogy/fc_obits.htm>

Indiana, Grant Co.
Type: Transcripts; B-M-D
Year Range: 1889–1920
CD-ROM: $30 (Mac/Win), Heritage Books, #1168
Title: Heritage Books Archives: Indiana, Volume 1
Notes, URL: Vital statistics from Jonesboro & Gas City newspapers, biographies of Madison and Hancock Counties, history of Rush County. <www.heritagebooks.com>. Search on "1168."

Indiana, Grant Co., Fairmount
Type: Abstracts; B-M-D
Year Range: 1888–1905
CD-ROM: $34 (Mac/Win), Heritage Books, CD #1381
Title: Heritage Books Archives: Indiana Volume 2
Notes, URL: The CD-ROM also includes Indiana biographies. <www.heritagebooks.com>. Search on "1381."

Indiana, Howard Co.
Type: Index; D
Year Range: 1922–1947
Online: Free
Title: Kokomo-Howard County Public Library: Howard County Deaths
Notes, URL: From Kokomo, Indiana, Newspapers. <www.kokomo.lib.in.us/genealogy>

Indiana, Lake Co., Hammond
Type: Index; O
Year Range: 1939–2002
Online: Free
Title: Hammond Public Library: Times Obituaries Index
Notes, URL: 1939–1963 and 1998–2002. <www.hammond.lib.in.us/obits.htm>

Indiana, La Porte Co., Michigan City
Type: Index; O
Year Range: 1887–pres.
Online: Free
Title: Michigan City Public Library: Obituary File
Notes, URL: 75,000 entries. <www.mclib.org/obituary.htm>

Indiana, Madison Co.
Type: Index; O
Year Range: 1921–1967
Online: Free
Title: Madison County Area Obituary Database
Notes, URL: Over 67,000 obituaries from the *Anderson Daily Bulletin.* <www.and.lib.in.us/cemetery/obituary.asp>

Indiana, Porter Co.
Type: Index; O
Year Range: 1967–1994
Online: Free
Title: Porter County Public Library System
Notes, URL: Index to obituaries in the *Vidette-Messenger*, Valparaiso. <www.pcpls.lib.in.us>. Click on "Genealogy Dept."

Indiana, St. Joseph Co.
Type: Index; O
Year Range: 1920–1999
Online: Free
Title: Obituary Index
Notes, URL: Index of obituaries in the *South Bend Tribune.* <http://sjcpl.lib.in.us/databases/obituary/obituary.html>

Indiana, Vanderburgh Co., Evansville
Type: Index; O
Year Range: 1920–1990
Online: Free
Title: Browning Genealogy: Evansville, Indiana Area Obituary Search
Notes, URL: <http://browning.evcpl.lib.in.us>

Indiana, Vigo Co.
Type: Index; O
Year Range: 1900–2002
Online: Free
Title: Vigo County Public Library: Wabash Valley Obituary Index
Notes, URL: 1900–1966 & 2000–2002. Also includes listings for surrounding counties in Ind. & Ill. <http://165.138.44.12>

Kansas
Type: Index
Online: Free
Title: Kansas State Historical Society: Vertical File Index
Notes, URL: An index to newspaper clippings. <www.kshs.org/genealogists/individuals/vertical/>

Kansas
Type: Abstracts; B-M-D
Year Range: 1882–1906
Online: Genealogy Library
Title: Index to Northern Kansas Newspapers Vols. 1-2
Notes, URL: Vol. 1 covers the *Holton Recorder* 1882–1884, the *Denison Journal* 1895–1896, the *Hoyt Journal* 1896, the *Holton Weekly Signal* 1897. Vol. 2 covers the *Hoyt Sentinel* 1902–1906. Select Magazines, Publications and Television | Newspapers | Kansas.

Kansas
Type: Transcript; B-M-DI-D
Year Range: 1898–1900
Online: Ancestry
Title: Leavenworth Advertiser and McLouth Times (Kansas), 1898–1900
Notes, URL: <www.ancestry.com/search/rectype/inddbs/3376.htm>

Kansas, Chase Co.
Type: Index; O
Year Range: 1863–1999
Online: Free
Title: Chase County Death and Obituary Index
Notes, URL: <http://skyways.lib.ks.us/genweb/chase/deathindex.html>

Kansas, Leavenworth Co.
Type: Abstracts; B-M-DI-D
Year Range: 1900–1902
Online: Ancestry
Title: Western Life Newspaper Name Index, 1900–02
Notes, URL: Nearly 1,700 entries. <www.ancestry.com/search/rectype/inddbs/3522.htm>

Kansas, Leavenworth Co.
Type: Index; O
Year Range: 1947
Online: Ancestry
Title: Leavenworth County, Kansas Obituaries, 1947
Notes, URL: <www.ancestry.com/search/rectype/inddbs/6199.htm>

Kansas, Leavenworth Co.
Type: Index; O
Year Range: 1948
Online: Ancestry
Title: Leavenworth County, Kansas Obituaries, 1948
Notes, URL: More than 2,200 names. <www.ancestry.com/search/rectype/inddbs/5468.htm>

Kansas, Leavenworth Co.
Type: Index; O
Year Range: 1949–1953
Online: Ancestry
Title: Leavenworth Times (Kansas) Obituaries, 1949, 1951–53
Notes, URL: More than 7,200 names. <www.ancestry.com/search/rectype/inddbs/5000.htm>

Kansas, Leavenworth Co.
Type: Index; O
Year Range: 1950
Online: Ancestry
Title: Leavenworth Times (Kansas) Obituaries, 1950
Notes, URL: More than 1,900 names. <www.ancestry.com/search/rectype/inddbs/4144.htm>

Kansas, Leavenworth Co.
Type: Index; O
Year Range: 1954–1978
Online: Ancestry
Title: Leavenworth Times (Kansas) Obituaries, 1954, 1958, 1967–78
Notes, URL: More than 12,200 names. <www.ancestry.com/search/rectype/inddbs/4322.htm>

Kansas, Leavenworth Co.
Type: Index; O
Year Range: 1955–1956
Online: Ancestry
Title: Leavenworth Times (Kansas) Obituaries, 1955–56
Notes, URL: More than 5,000 names. <www.ancestry.com/search/rectype/inddbs/4386.htm>

Kansas, Leavenworth Co.
Type: Index; O
Year Range: 1957–1964
Online: Ancestry

Title: Leavenworth Times (Kansas) Obituaries, 1957–64
Notes, URL: More than 5,100 names. <www.ancestry.com/search/rectype/inddbs/4159.htm>

Kansas, Leavenworth Co.
Type: Index; O
Year Range: 1965–1982
Online: Ancestry
Title: Leavenworth Times (Kansas) Obituaries, 1965–66, 1979–82
Notes, URL: More than 5,400 names. <www.ancestry.com/search/rectype/inddbs/4081.htm>

Kansas, Leavenworth Co.
Type: Index; O
Year Range: 1987–1998
Online: Ancestry
Title: Leavenworth Times (Kansas) Obituaries, 1987–98
Notes, URL: More than 7,700 names. <www.ancestry.com/search/rectype/inddbs/3416.htm>

Kansas, Leavenworth Co.
Type: Index; O
Year Range: 1994–1998
Online: Ancestry
Title: Leavenworth Times (Kansas), Obituaries, 1994–1998
Notes, URL: Over 6,000 names. <www.ancestry.com/search/rectype/inddbs/3373.htm>

Kansas, Leavenworth Co.
Type: Index; O
Year Range: 1999
Online: Ancestry
Title: Leavenworth County, Kansas Obituaries, 1999
Notes, URL: <www.ancestry.com/search/rectype/inddbs/5009.htm>

Kansas, Leavenworth Co., Leavenworth
Type: Index; B-M-DI-D
Year Range: 1866–1868
Online: Ancestry
Title: Leavenworth, Kansas Newspaper Name Index, 1866–68
Notes, URL: Over 1,300 names. <www.ancestry.com/search/rectype/inddbs/3852.htm>

Kansas, Lyon Co.
Type: Index; O
Year Range: 1892–1989
Online: Free
Title: Index, Emporia Gazette Death Notices 1892–1989
Notes, URL: <www.rootsweb.com/~ksfhgslc/obithome.html>

Kansas, Lyon Co.
Type: Index; O
Year Range: 1990–1999
Online: Free
Title: Index, Emporia Gazette Death Notices 1990–1999
Notes, URL: <www.rootsweb.com/~ksfhgslc/obit1990s.html>

Kansas, Riley Co.
Type: Index; O
Year Range: 1994–1995
Online: Ancestry
Title: Riley County, Kansas Obituary Index, 1994–95
Notes, URL: 1,929 records. <www.ancestry.com/search/rectype/inddbs/4794.htm>

Kansas, Riley Co.
Type: Index; O
Year Range: 1998–1999
Online: Ancestry
Title: Riley County, Kansas Area Newspapers Obituaries, 1998–99
Notes, URL: 2,215 records. <www.ancestry.com/search/rectype/inddbs/5371.htm>

Kansas, Sedgwick Co., Wichita
Type: Index; O
Year Range: 1955–2003
Online: Free
Title: Midwest Historical and Genealogical Society: Obituary Scrapbooks Index
Notes, URL: *Wichita Eagle & Beacon* obituary indexes. <http://skyways.lib.ks.us/kansas/genweb/mhgs/obits.htm>

Kansas, Wyandotte Co., Kansas City
Type: Index; O
Year Range: 1998
Online: Ancestry
Title: Kansas City Kansan Obituaries, 1998
Notes, URL: Nearly 2200 names. <www.ancestry.com/search/rectype/inddbs/4027.htm>

Louisiana, Orleans Parish, New Orleans
Type: Index; D
Year Range: 1837–1870
Online: Free
Title: New Orleans Death Index: *Daily Picayune* 1837–1857; 1870
Notes, URL: <http://nutrias.org/~nopl/info/louinfo/deaths/deaths.htm>

Louisiana, Orleans Parish, New Orleans
Type: Index; D
Year Range: 1840–1970
Online: Ancestry
Title: New Orleans Deaths, 1840–1970
Notes, URL: 2,700 names from obituaries. <www.ancestry.com/search/rectype/inddbs/3528.htm>

Louisiana, Orleans Parish, New Orleans
Type: Index; O
Year Range: 1994–1999
Online: Free
Title: New Orleans Times-Picayune Obituaries Index
Notes, URL: <www.geocities.com/jeffersongenealogicalsociety/obits/deathnx.htm>

Louisiana, Richland Co., Rayville
Type: Abstracts
Year Range: 1872–1874
Online: Ancestry
Title: Rayville, Louisiana Newspaper Name Index, 1872–74
Notes, URL: Over 3,000 names from the *Richland Beacon*. <www.ancestry.com/search/rectype/inddbs/4187.htm>

Maine
Type: Abstracts; M-D
Year Range: 1785–1852
CD-ROM: $34 (Mac/Win), Heritage Books, CD #1423
Title: Heritage Books Archives: Maine Volume 2
Notes, URL: Includes vital records from 35 newspapers, 1785–1820, & marriage & death notices from the *Maine Farmer*, 1833–1852. <www.heritagebooks.com>. Search on "1423."

Maine, Knox Co., Rockland
Type: Abstracts; B-M-D
Year Range: 1845–1891
CD-ROM: $39.50, Picton Press, #1116
Title: Rockland Maine, Records of, Prior to 1892 published in the Lime Rock Gazette and Rockland Gazette
Notes, URL: Over 33,000 records. <www.pictonpress.com>

Maine, Penobscot Co., Dexter
Type: Transcripts; O
Year Range: 1837–2003
Online: Free
Title: Dexter, Maine Obituary Database
Notes, URL: <www.abbott-library.com>

Maryland
Type: Digital images of transcripts; M-D
Year Range: 1727–1839
CD-ROM: $29.99, Genealogy.com, CD #521
Online: Genealogy Library

Title: Maryland Settlers & Soldiers, 1700s–1800s
Notes, URL: Includes *Marriages and Deaths from the Maryland Gazette, 1727–1839.* <www.genealogy.com/521facd.html>

Maryland, Baltimore Co.
Type: Transcripts; M-D
Year Range: 1850–1859
Online: Free
Title: Baltimore County Newspapers: Marriage & Death Notice Archive
Notes, URL: <www.bcpl.net/~pely/archives/index.html>

Maryland, Baltimore City
Type: Digital images of transcripts; M-D
Year Range: 1796–1816
CD-ROM: $29.99, Genealogy.com, CD #521
Online: Genealogy Library
Title: Maryland Settlers & Soldiers, 1700s–1800s
Notes, URL: Includes *Marriages and Deaths from Baltimore Newspapers, 1796–1816.* <www.genealogy.com/521facd.html>

Maryland, Baltimore City
Type: Digital images of indexes; M-D
Year Range: 1837–1860
CD-ROM: $29.99, Genealogy.com, CD #521
Online: Genealogy Library
Title: Maryland Settlers & Soldiers, 1700s–1800s
Notes, URL: Includes *Index to Marriages and Deaths in the "Baltimore Sun," 1837–1850* & *Index to Marriages in the "Baltimore Sun," 1851–1860.* <www.genealogy.com/521facd.html>

Maryland, Charles Co.
Type: Transcripts; B-M-D
Year Range: 1844–1898
CD-ROM: $28 (Mac/Win), Heritage Books, CD #1356
Title: Port Tobacco Times and Charles County Advertiser, Vol. 1-6
Notes, URL: Also includes legal notices, names of people who had letters at the post office, & real estate listings. <www.heritagebooks.com>. Search on "1356."

Maryland, Prince George's County
Type: Transcripts; M-D
Year Range: 1800s
CD-ROM: $31 (Mac/Win), Heritage Books, CD #1623
Title: Heritage Books Archives: Maryland Volume 3
Notes, URL: The CD also includes histories of Dorchester County & Annapolis. <www.heritagebooks.com>. Search on "1623."

Massachusetts, Franklin Co., Greenfield
Type: Transcript; B-M-O
Year Range: 1870–1874
Online: Free
Title: The Franklin County Publication Archive Index
Notes, URL: Around 17,000 articles from the *Greenfield Courier and Gazette.* <http://fcpai.umassp.edu>

Massachusetts, Hampden Co., Springfield
Type: Transcript; M-D
Year Range: 1847
Online: NEHGS
Title: Marriages and Deaths from the *Springfield [MA] Republican*—1847
Notes, URL: <www.newenglandancestors.org/research/database/SpringfieldRep/>

Massachusetts, Suffolk Co., Boston
Type: Transcript; M
Year Range: 1784–1840
Online: Ancestry
Title: Massachusetts Centinal Marriage Notices
Notes, URL: Over 34,000 names, surnames A-D. <www.ancestry.com/search/rectype/inddbs/3393.htm>

Massachusetts, Suffolk Co., Boston
Type: Transcript; M
Year Range: 1785–1794
Online: Genealogy Library
Title: Marriage Notices for the United States, 1785–1794
Notes, URL: A book by Charles Knowles Bolton. Over 5,000 names from the *Massachusetts Centinel* and the *Columbian Centinel.* Select Records | Marriage | Massachusetts.

Massachusetts, Suffolk Co., Boston
Type: Abstracts; M
Year Range: 1827–1828
Online: NEHGS
Title: Marriages Reported in the *Boston Recorder and Telegraph*, 1827 and 1828
Notes, URL: <www.newenglandancestors.org/research/database/boston_marriages>

Massachusetts, Suffolk Co., Boston
Type: Abstracts; D
Year Range: 1827–1828
Online: NEHGS
Title: Deaths Reported in the *Boston Recorder and Telegraph*, 1827 and 1828
Notes, URL: <www.newenglandancestors.org/research/database/boston_deaths>

Massachusetts, Suffolk Co., Boston
Type: Transcripts
Year Range: 1831–1920
CD-ROM: $69.99 (Mac/Win), NEHGS, Item #SCDSMF
Title: The Search for Missing Friends: Irish Immigrant Advertisements Placed in the Boston Pilot 1831–1920
Notes, URL: These ads refer to Irish immigrants across the U.S. & often cite places of origin in Ireland and dates & places of arrival in North America. <www.newenglandancestors.org>. Search store for item #SCDSMF.

Massachusetts, Suffolk Co., Boston
Type: Index; O
Year Range: 1971–1997
Online: Free
Title: Boston Public Library's Obituary Database.
Notes, URL: Includes only obituaries, not death notices, that appeared in the *Boston Globe* & *Boston Herald* 1971–1974 & 1990–1997. <www.bpl.org/catalogs/frame_obits.htm>

Michigan
Type: Index; M-DI-D
Year Range: 1871–1929
Online: Ancestry (free)
Title: Northern Michigan, Newspaper Surname Index
Notes, URL: From Cheboygan & Mackinac counties. <www.ancestry.com/search/rectype/inddbs/3669.htm>

Michigan, Chippewa Co., Sault Ste. Marie
Type: Transcripts; B-M-D
Year Range: 1887–1900
Online: Free
Title: Sault Ste. Marie, Michigan, Newspaper Birth, Marriage, and Death Notices
Notes, URL: <http://freepages.genealogy.rootsweb.com/~wjmartin/democrat.htm>

Michigan, Ingham Co., Lansing
Type: Transcripts; M-D
Year Range: 1855–1870
Online: F&LH
Title: Marriages and deaths mentioned in the Lansing state republican, 1855–1870

Michigan, Iosco Co.
Type: Index; B-M-DI-D
Year Range: 1900–1910
Online: Ancestry (free)
Title: Iosco County, MI, *Iosco County Gazette* Index, 1900–10
Notes, URL: <www.ancestry.com/search/rectype/inddbs/5667.htm>

Michigan, Iosco Co.
Type: Index; O
Year Range: 1978–1990
Online: Ancestry (free)
Title: Iosco County, Michigan Obituaries, 1978–90
Notes, URL: About 2,200 obituaries. <www.ancestry.com/search/rectype/inddbs/5480.htm>

Michigan, Iosco Co., Tawas City
Type: Index; O
Year Range: 1892–1949
Online: Ancestry (free)
Title: Iosco County, Michigan, 1892–1949: Tawas Herald Obituaries
Notes, URL: About 2,400 obituaries. <www.ancestry.com/search/rectype/inddbs/5715.htm>

Michigan, Kent Co.
Type: Index; O
Year Range: 1910–pres.
Online: Free
Title: Western Michigan Genealogical Society: Kent County Obituaries
Notes, URL: <http://data.wmgs.org>

Michigan, Saginaw Co., Saginaw
Type: Index; O
Year Range: 1800s–pres.
Online: Free
Title: Public Libraries of Saginaw: Obituary Index
Notes, URL: Over 170,000 entries. <www.tricitynet.com/pls/obit.nsf>

Michigan, Sanilac Co., Fremont
Type: Abstracts; B-M-A-O
Year Range: 1882–pres.
Online: Free
Title: Freemont Area District Library: Local Records Database
Notes, URL: <http://fadl.ncats.net/Local%20History/gendatabase.html>

Minnesota
Type: Index; B-M-D
Year Range: 1865–1995
Online: Ancestry
Title: Minnesota Newspaper Headline Index
Notes, URL: Over 31,500 names. <www.ancestry.com/search/rectype/inddbs/3786.htm>

Minnesota, Clay Co.
Type: Index; O
Year Range: 1901–1995
Online: Free
Title: *The Forum* Obituaries Database
Notes, URL: Over 54,000 names from 1901–1902 & 1984–1995. Covers eastern N. Dak. & northwestern Minn. <www.lib.ndsu.nodak.edu/ndirs/bio&genealogy/forumobits.html>

Minnesota, Clay Co.
Type: Extracts; O
Year Range: 1995–2000
Online: Free
Title: Search the Fargo Forum
Notes, URL: Covers eastern N. Dak. & northwestern Minn. <http://dp3.lib.ndsu.nodak.edu/cgi-bin/forum/forum_art_start.pl>

Minnesota, Dakota Co.
Type: Index; O
Year Range: 1860s–pres.
Online: Free
Title: Dakota County Historical Society: Obituary Search
Notes, URL: <www.dakotahistory.org/Obit_Search.asp>

Minnesota, Stearns Co., St. Cloud
Type: O
Year Range: 1887–1926
Title: St. Cloud Area Genealogists, Inc.: Obituaries from the *St. Cloud Daily Times* 1887–1926
Notes, URL: To be published on CD-ROM in 2004. <www.rootsweb.com/~mnscag/SCAG/>

Minnesota, Stearns Co., St. Cloud
Type: Index; O
Year Range: 1928–pres.
Online: Free
Title: St. Cloud Times Index
Notes, URL: <http://grrl10.grrl.lib.mn.us:8080/index.htm>

Minnesota, Stearns Co., St. Cloud
Type: Index; O
Year Range: 1998–pres.
Online: Free
Title: St. Cloud Times Obituary Index
Notes, URL: <http://miva.sctimes.com/miva/cgi-bin/miva?News/Obits/index.mv>

Mississippi
Type: Transcript
Year Range: 1801–1863
CD-ROM: $25.50 (Mac/Win), Heritage Books, CD #2325
Title: Early Mississippi Records
Notes, URL: Includes 4 volumes on Attala, Carroll, Holmes, and Yazoo counties with information from newspapers and other sources. <www.heritagebooks.com>. Search on "2325."

Mississippi, Wilkinson Co., Woodville
Year Range: 1823–1883
CD-ROM: $27.50 (Mac/Win), Heritage Books, CD #1364
Title: The Woodville Republican Volumes 1-5
Notes, URL: <www.heritagebooks.com>. Search on "1364."

Missouri
Type: Index; D
Year Range: 1817–1997
CD-ROM: $26.95 (Win), Ancestry, item #2309
Title: Missouri Vital Records: Deaths Selected Counties
Notes, URL: 147,432 names from Missouri Newspaper Death Index 1822–1994 & Missouri Confederate Deaths 1861–1865. <http://shops.ancestry.com>. Search on "Missouri vital records."

Missouri
Type: Index; D
Year Range: 1846–1994
Online: Ancestry
Title: Missouri Newspaper Death Index
Notes, URL: 50,000 records from Callaway (1846–1926), Montgomery (1875–1994), & Cole (1884–1907) Counties. <www.ancestry.com/search/rectype/inddbs/3074.htm>

Missouri, Audrain Co.
Type: Abstracts; O
Year Range: 1885–1903
Online: Ancestry
Title: Audrain County, Missouri Obituaries, 1885–1903
Notes, URL: Over 5,400 names. <www.ancestry.com/search/rectype/inddbs/3927.htm>

Missouri, Audrain Co.
Type: Abstracts; O
Year Range: 1904–1916
Online: Ancestry
Title: Audrain County, Missouri Obituaries, 1904–16
Notes, URL: Over 5,400 names. <www.ance

stry.com/search/rectype/inddbs/4025.htm>

Missouri, Audrain Co.
Type: Abstracts; O
Year Range: 1917–1929
Online: Ancestry
Title: Audrain County, Missouri Obituaries, 1917–29
Notes, URL: Nearly 4,200 names. <www.ancestry.com/search/rectype/inddbs/3964.htm>

Missouri, Audrain Co.
Type: Abstracts; O
Year Range: 1930–1942
Online: Ancestry
Title: Audrain County, Missouri Obituaries, 1930–42
Notes, URL: About 4,900 names. <www.ancestry.com/search/rectype/inddbs/4100.htm>

Missouri, Boone Co.
Type: Abstracts; O
Year Range: 1871–1891
Online: Ancestry
Title: Boone County, Missouri Obituaries, 1871–91
Notes, URL: Over 5,500 obituaries from the *Columbia Missouri Herald*. <www.ancestry.com/search/rectype/inddbs/3497.htm>

Missouri, Boone Co.
Type: Abstracts; O
Year Range: 1892–1901
Online: Ancestry
Title: Boone County, Missouri Obituaries, 1892–1901
Notes, URL: Nearly 6,000 obituaries from the *Columbia Missouri Herald*. <www.ancestry.com/search/rectype/inddbs/3701.htm>

Missouri, Boone Co.
Type: Abstracts; O
Year Range: 1902–1913
Online: Ancestry
Title: Boone County, Missouri Obituaries, 1902–13
Notes, URL: Nearly 5,000 obituaries from the *Columbia Missouri Herald*. <www.ancestry.com/search/rectype/inddbs/3716.htm>

Missouri, Callaway Co.
Type: Index; O
Year Range: 1830–1910
Online: Ancestry
Title: Callaway County, Missouri Obituaries, 1830–1910
Notes, URL: Over 10,000 names. <www.ancestry.com/search/rectype/inddbs/3469.htm>

Missouri, Callaway Co.
Type: Index; O
Year Range: 1910–1930
Online: Ancestry
Title: Callaway County, Missouri Obituaries, 1910–30
Notes, URL: Over 10,000 names. <www.ancestry.com/search/rectype/inddbs/3474.htm>

Missouri, Callaway Co.
Type: Index; O
Year Range: 1920–1955
Online: Ancestry
Title: Callaway County, Missouri Obituaries, 1920–55
Notes, URL: Nearly 10,000 names. <www.ancestry.com/search/rectype/inddbs/3480.htm>

Missouri, Cole Co.
Type: Index; O
Year Range: 1871–1899
Online: Ancestry
Title: Cole County, Missouri Obituaries, 1871–99
Notes, URL: Nearly 4,700 names. <www.ancestry.com/search/rectype/inddbs/4075.htm>

Missouri, Jasper Co.
Type: Index; O
Year Range: 1999
Online: Ancestry
Title: Jasper County, Missouri Newspaper Obituaries, 1999
Notes, URL: Over 1,600 names. <www.ancestry.com/search/rectype/inddbs/4402.htm>

Missouri, Lafayette Co.
Type: Index; O
Year Range: 1891–1920
Online: Ancestry
Title: Lafayette County, Missouri Obituaries, 1891–1920
Notes, URL: Over 9,200 names. <www.ancestry.com/search/rectype/inddbs/4156.htm>

Missouri, Montgomery Co.
Type: Abstracts; M-D
Year Range: 1865–1962
CD-ROM: $26 (Mac/Win), Heritage Books, CD #1842
Title: Heritage Books Archives: Montgomery County, Missouri Volumes 8-13
Notes, URL: Newspaper abstracts, including deaths, 1882–1962, & marriages, 1865–1922. <www.heritagebooks.com>. Search on "1842."

Missouri, Montgomery Co.
Type: Abstracts; O
Year Range: 1889–1935
Online: Ancestry
Title: Montgomery Co., Missouri Obituaries, 1889–1935
Notes, URL: Over 3,800 names. <www.ancestry.com/search/rectype/inddbs/4298.htm>

Missouri, St. Clair Co.
Type: Abstracts; O
Year Range: 1888–1928
Online: Ancestry
Title: St. Clair County, Missouri Obituaries, 1888–1928
Notes, URL: Over 4,500 names. <www.ancestry.com/search/rectype/inddbs/4139.htm>

Missouri, St. Louis
Type: Index; O
Online: Free
Title: St. Louis Obituary Index
Notes, URL: <www.slpl.lib.mo.us/libsrc/obit.htm>

Nevada
Type: Index; B-M-D
Year Range: 1866–1867
Online: Ancestry
Title: Territorial Enterprise (Virginia City, Nevada), 1866–67
Notes, URL: Over 10,200 records. <www.ancestry.com/search/rectype/inddbs/3515.htm>

Nevada
Type: Abstracts; B-M-D
Year Range: 1870–1900
Online: Ancestry
Title: Nevada State Journal, 1870–1900
Notes, URL: Over 6,300 records <www.ancestry.com/search/rectype/inddbs/4768.htm>

Nevada
Type: Abstracts; B-M-D
Year Range: 1886–1892
Online: Ancestry
Title: Territorial Enterprise (Virginia City, Nevada), 1886–92
Notes, URL: Nearly 4,000 records. <www.an

cestry.com/search/rectype/inddbs/3457.htm>

Nevada, Ormsby Co., Carson City
Type: Index
Year Range: 1865–1886
Online: Free
Title: Carson Appeal Newspaper Index
Notes, URL: 1865–66, 1879–80, 1881, 1885–86. <http://dmla.clan.lib.nv.us/docs/nsla/archives/appeal/appeal.htm>

Nevada, Ormsby Co., Carson City
Type: Index; O
Year Range: 1996–pres.
Online: Free
Title: Nevada State Library and Archives: Obituaries from the *Nevada Appeal* Newspaper
Notes, URL: <http://dmla.clan.lib.nv.us/docs/nsla/services/genealres.htm>

New Hampshire
Type: Index; O
Year Range: 1993–pres.
Online: Free
Title: New Hampshire Newspapers Online
Notes, URL: Indexes to several newspapers. <www.state.nh.us/nhnews>

New Jersey, Mercer Co., Trenton
Type: Index; O
Year Range: 1901–1984
Online: Free
Title: Old Mill Hill Society: Trenton Obituary Indexes
Notes, URL: 1901–1918, 1984. <www.oldmillhillsociety.org/research/obits/obit-dex-index.htm>

New Mexico, Bernalillo Co., Albuquerque
Type: Transcripts; O
Year Range: 1998–pres.
Online: Free
Title: ABQjournal Obituaries
Notes, URL: Paid death notices from the *Albuquerque (N. Mex.) Journal* from 1 March 1998 to present. <www.albuquerquejournal.com/obits>

New York
Type: Abstracts; M
Year Range: 1800–1855
Online: Ancestry
Title: New York Marriage Notices, 1800–55
Notes, URL: From *Early Marriages From Newspapers Published in Central New York*, Pipe Creek Publications, 1992. <www.ancestry.com/search/rectype/inddbs/4244.htm>

New York, Albany Co., Albany
Type: Transcript; M-D
Year Range: 1826–1828
Online: NEHGS
Title: Record of Deaths and Marriages from *The Albany Argus*, 1826–1828
Notes, URL: <www.newenglandancestors.org/research/database/albany/>

New York, Columbia Co., Hudson
Type: Transcripts; M
Online: F&LH
Title: Marriages copied from the Rural repository

New York, Columbia Co., Hudson
Type: Transcripts; D
Online: F&LH
Title: Deaths copied from the Rural respository: published in Hudson, N.Y.

New York, Columbia Co., Hudson
Type: Transcripts; M-D
Year Range: 1823–1828
Online: F&LH
Title: Marriages and deaths from the Northern whig, published in Hudson, N.Y., 1823–1828

New York, Delaware Co.
Type: Transcripts; D
Year Range: 1819–1844
Online: F&LH
Title: Delaware gazette, published at Delhi, Delaware County, N.Y., from Nov. 1819 to Aug. 28, 1844, death notices

New York, Delaware Co.
Type: Digital images of books; M-D
Year Range: 1819–1879
CD-ROM: $24.50 (Mac/Win), Long Island Genealogy
Title: Vital Records Collection from Delaware County, New York
Notes, URL: Includes marriages 1844–1879, deaths 1819–1868, from the *Delaware Gazette*. <http://genealogycds.com/sales/Delaware.htm>

New York, Delaware Co.
Type: Transcripts; D
Year Range: 1844–1895
Online: F&LH
Title: Deaths taken from the Delaware gazette: Delhi, Delaware County, N.Y.

New York, Erie Co.
Type: Index; O
Year Range: 1960–pres.
Online: Free
Title: Erie County Public Library: Obituary Listings
Notes, URL: 1960–1969, 1987–pres. <www.erielibrary.org/obits/html>

New York, Greene Co.
Type: Index; O
Year Range: 1960–1994
Online: Free
Title: Greene County, NY Obituaries
Notes, URL: <http://ourworld.cs.com/pmorrowj/myhomepage/business.html>

New York, Kings Co., Brooklyn
Type: Digital images
Year Range: 1841–1902
Online: Free
Title: Brooklyn Daily Eagle Online
Notes, URL: <http://eagle.brooklynpubliclibrary.org/>

New York, Kings Co., Brooklyn
Type: Transcripts; B
Year Range: 1841–1846
Online: F&LH
Title: Miscellaneous vital statistics other than death and marriage notices taken from the "Brooklyn Eagle"

New York, Kings Co., Brooklyn
Type: Transcripts; B
Year Range: 1841–1846
CD-ROM: $19.50 (Mac/Win), Long Island Genealogy
Title: Miscellaneous vital statistics taken from the "Brooklyn Eagle"
Notes, URL: <http://genealogycds.com/sales/BrooklynEagle.htm>

New York, New York (City)
Type: Transcripts; M-D
Year Range: 1789–1796
Online: F&LH
Title: Marriage and death notices from the New York weekly museum, 1789–1796

New York, New York (City)
Type: Transcripts; M-D
Year Range: 1790–1793
Online: F&LH
Title: Marriage and death notices from the "New-York weekly museum," 1790–1793

New York, New York (City)
Type: Transcript; D
Year Range: 1801–1890
Online: NEHGS
Title: Death Notices from the *New York Evening Post*, 1801–1890

Notes, URL: <www.newenglandancestors.org/research/database/nypdeath>

New York, New York (City)
Type: Transcript; M
Year Range: 1801–1890
Online: NEHGS
Title: Marriage Notices from the *New York Evening Post*, 1801–1890
Notes, URL: <www.newenglandancestors.org/research/database/nypmarriages>

New York, New York (City)
Type: Images
Year Range: 1851–1999
Online: ProQuest, NYG, GML
Title: ProQuest Historical Newspapers: New York Times archive
Notes, URL: Available through libraries & universities <www.proquest.com> and free to NYG&BS members <www.newyorkfamilyhistory.org> and "Godfrey Scholars" <www.godfrey.org>.

New York, New York (City)
Type: Abstracts; M-O
Year Range: 1889
Online: Ancestry
Title: New York Times, Obituaries, & Marriage Notices, 1889
Notes, URL: <www.ancestry.com/search/rectype/inddbs/5662.htm>

New York, New York (City)
Type: Images
Year Range: 1889–1986
Online: ProQuest
Title: ProQuest Historical Newspapers: Wall Street Journal
Notes, URL: Available through libraries & universities. <www.proquest.com>

New York, New York (City)
Type: Abstracts; M-D
Year Range: 1890
Online: Ancestry
Title: New York Times (New York City, N.Y.) Death and Marriage Index, 1890
Notes, URL: About 10,000 names. <www.ancestry.com/search/rectype/inddbs/4523.htm>

New York, New York (City)
Type: Index; D
Year Range: 1929
Online: Free
Title: New York Times Death Notices Index
Notes, URL: Death notices from Jan.-Feb. 1929. <http://freepages.genealogy.rootsweb.com/~nytdn/nytimes_a_01.htm>

New York, New York (City)
Type: Abstracts; O
Year Range: 1929
Online: Free
Title: Early New York Times Obituaries Index
Notes, URL: Jan.-Feb. 1929. <www.obitcentral.com/obitsearch/obits/ny/nytimes>

New York, Onondaga Co., Skaneateles
Type: Abstracts; B-M-D
Year Range: 1831–1919
Online: Free
Title: The Skaneateles Historical Society
Notes, URL: Over 22,300 records from 4 newspapers. <http://skaneateles.com/historical/index.shtml>

New York, Ontario Co.
Type: Index; M
Year Range: 1794–1895
Online: Free
Title: Ontario County Marriages
Notes, URL: Marriages from newspapers. <www.usgennet.org/usa/ny/county/ontario/marriage/marriages.htm>

New York, Orange Co.
Type: Transcripts; D
Online: F&LH
Title: Orange Co., N.Y. deaths: from the Independent Republican, Goshen, N.Y.

New York, Orange Co.
Type: Transcripts; M-D
Year Range: 1828–1831
Online: F&LH
Title: Orange County patriot: a newspaper published at Goshen, N.Y.: marriages and deaths from May 1828 to Dec. 1831

New York, Orange Co., Goshen
Type: Digital images of a book containing transcripts
CD-ROM: $24.50 (Mac/Win), Long Island Genealogy
Title: Genealogy and History of Orange County, New York
Notes, URL: Graveyard inscriptions. *Orange County Patriot*, marriages & deaths, 1828–1831. St. James Protestant Episcopal Church records, Goshen. All by Gertrude A. Barber. <http://genealogycds.com/sales/Orange.htm>

New York, Otsego Co.
Type: Digital images of books containing transcripts; M-D
Year Range: 1795–1840
CD-ROM: $24.50 (Mac/Win), Long Island Genealogy
Title: Deaths, Marriages and Wills from Otsego County, New York
Notes, URL: Marriages, 1795–1850, & deaths, 1795–1840, from the *Otsego Herald*. Marriages & deaths from the *Cooperstown Federalist*, 1808–1812, & the *Watch Tower*, 1828–1831. All by Gertrude A. Barber. <http://genealogycds.com/sales/Otsego.htm>

New York, Otsego Co.
Type: Transcripts; M
Online: F&LH
Title: Marriages taken from the *Otsego Herald & Western Advertiser* and *Freeman's Journal*

New York, Otsego Co.
Type: Transcripts; D
Online: F&LH
Title: Deaths taken from the *Otsego Herald & Western Advertiser* and *Freeman's Journal*

New York, Otsego Co.
Type: Transcripts; B-M-D
Year Range: 1819–1950
Online: Free
Title: Rural New York State Family Research
Notes, URL: *Cherry Valley Gazette*, 1818–1830. Also newspapers from Oneonta, 1878–1902; Otego, 1868–1930; Schenevus, 1864–1899; and *The Worcester Times*, 1875–1950. <www.newyorkstate.research.com>, click on Newspaper Indexes.

New York, Otsego Co., Cooperstown
Type: Transcripts
Year Range: 1808–1831
Online: F&LH
Title: Death notices copied from the "Cooperstown federalist" from 1808–1809; Death notices copied from *Watch Tower* from 1828–1831, deaths pp. 1-11; Marriage notices copied from *Cooperstown Federalist* from 1808–1812; Marriage notices copied from *Watch Tower* from 1828–1831, marriages pp. 12-26

New York, Queens Co.
Type: Transcript; B-M-D
Year Range: 1858–1898
Online: Free
Title: Queens County Sentinel Records
Notes, URL: <www.longislandgenealogy.com/kristina/kristina.html>

New York, Saratoga Co.
Type: Index; M-D

Year Range: 1819–1837
Online: F&LH
Title: Index to marriage and death notices in the Saratoga Sentinel: 1819–1837

New York, Saratoga Co., Saratoga Springs
Type: Index; D
Year Range: 1840–1842
Online: Free
Title: Death Notices from *Saratoga Whig* Newspaper, 1840–1842
Notes, URL: <www.bfn.org/~ae487/awhig.html>

New York, Seneca Co., Ovid
Type: Transcripts; B-M-D
Year Range: 1822–1869
Online: F&LH
Title: Vital records from the Ovid bee

New York, Steuben Co., Dansville
Type: Transcripts; O
Year Range: 1985–2002
Online: Free
Title: Dansville Area Obituaries
Notes, URL: <www.dansville.lib.ny.us/cgi-bin/Obituary/obindex.pl>

New York, Suffolk Co.
Type: Transcripts; M
Online: F&LH
Title: Marriages of Suffolk Co., N.Y.: taken from the "Republican Watchman," a newspaper published at Greenport, N.Y.

New York, Suffolk Co.
Type: Digital images of books containing transcripts; M-D
Year Range: 1859–1901
CD-ROM: $24.50 (Mac/Win), Long Island Genealogy
Title: Genealogy and History of Suffolk County, New York
Notes, URL: Marriages, 1871–1901, & deaths, 1859–1900, from the *Republican Watchman*, copied by Gertrude A. Barber. <http://genealogycds.com/sales/SuffolkRecordsCombo.htm>

New York, Suffolk, Greenport
Type: Transcripts; D
Year Range: 1859–1900
Online: F&LH
Title: Deaths taken from *The Republican Watchman*: a newspaper published every Saturday morning at Greenport, Suffolk County, N.Y., covering death records for the whole county
Notes, URL: 1859–1861, 1867–1868, 1870–1878, 1880–1885, 1897, 1899–1900.

New York, Ulster Co., Saugerties
Type: Abstracts; D-O
Year Range: 1848–1870
CD-ROM: $24.50 (Mac/Win), Heritage Books, item #1414
Title: Heritage Books Archives: New York Volume 5
Notes, URL: Digital images of *Obituaries, Death Notices and Genealogical Gleanings from The Saugerties Telegraph*, Volumes 1-3, by Audrey M. Klinkenberg. <www.heritagebooks.com>. Search on "1414."

New York, Wayne Co., Lyons
Type: Transcripts; M-D
Online: F&LH
Title: Marriages and deaths from the Lyons Republican and inscriptions from the Lyons Rural Cemetery: Nelson, N.Y., and Aurora, N.Y.

New York, Wayne Co., Palmyra
Type: Transcripts; M-D
Online: F&LH
Title: Marriages and deaths from the Wayne Sentinel: a newspaper published in Palmyra, N.Y.

New York, Yates Co., Penn Yan
Type: Abstracts; M-D
Year Range: 1823–1867
CD-ROM: $28.50 (Mac/Win), Heritage Books, item #1251
Title: Heritage Books Archives: New York Volume 3
Notes, URL: Includes *Genealogical Gleanings Abstracted from the Early Newspaper of Penn Yan, Yates County, New York, 1823–1833 & 1841–1855* and *Genealogical Gleanings Abstracted from the "Yates County Chronicle" Penn Yan, New York, May 1856 to October 1867*, by Dianne Stenzel. <www.heritagebooks.com>. Search on "1251."

North Carolina
Type: Transcripts; M-D
Year Range: 1799–1867
CD-ROM: $29.99, Genealogy.com, CD #524
Online: Genealogy Library
Title: Early North Carolina Settlers, 1700s–1900s
Notes, URL: Includes *Marriage and Death Notices from Raleigh Register and North Carolina State Gazette, 1799–1825, 1826–1845, 1846–1867*. <www.genealogy.com/524facd.html>

North Carolina, Edgecombe Co.
Type: Transcripts; B-M-D
Year Range: 1720–1880
Online: Ancestry
Title: Edgecombe County, North Carolina Vital Records, 1720–1880
Notes, URL: Marriage records, obituaries, & gravestone inscriptions. <www.ancestry.com/search/rectype/inddbs/4990.htm>

North Carolina, Guilford Co., Greensboro
Type: Transcripts; D
Year Range: 1826–1899
Online: F&LH
Title: Death records from the files of the Greensboro, N.C. Patriot, 1826–1899

North Carolina, Mecklenburg Co.
Type: Index; D
Year Range: 1841–1849
Online: F&LH
Title: Death notices from the Mecklenburg Jeffersonian, Charlotte, N.C., 1841–1849: an index

North Carolina, Mecklenburg Co., Charlotte
Type: Transcripts; M-D
Year Range: 1835–1851
Online: F&LH
Title: Marriage notices from the Charlotte Journal, Charlotte, N.C., July 3, 1835–December 7, 1851

North Carolina, Mecklenburg Co., Charlotte
Type: Index; D
Year Range: 1841–1849
Online: F&LH
Title: Death notices from the Mecklenburg Jeffersonian, Charlotte, N.C., 1841–1849: an index

North Carolina, Mecklenburg Co., Charlotte
Type: Index; M
Year Range: 1853–1870
Online: F&LH
Title: Marriage notices from the Western Democrat, Charlotte, N.C., 1853–1870: an index

North Carolina, Wake Co., Raleigh
Type: Transcripts; M-D
Year Range: 1846–1893
Online: F&LH
Title: Marriage and death notices in Raleigh

register and North Carolina State gazette, 1846–1893

North Dakota, Cass Co., Fargo
Type: Index; O
Year Range: 1901–1995
Online: Free
Title: The Forum Obituaries Database
Notes, URL: Over 57,000 names from 1901–1904 & 1984–1995. Covers eastern N. Dak. & northwestern Minn. <www.lib.ndsu.nodak.edu/ndirs/bio&genealogy/forumobits.html>

North Dakota, Cass Co., Fargo
Type: Extracts; O
Year Range: 1995–2000
Online: Free
Title: Search the Fargo Forum
Notes, URL: <http://dp3.lib.ndsu.nodak.edu/cgi-bin/forum/forum_art_start.pl>

Ohio, Clark Co., Springfield
Type: Index; O
Year Range: 1926–pres.
Online: Free
Title: Clark County Public Library Obituary Index
Notes, URL: <http://guardian.ccpl.lib.oh.us/obits>

Ohio, Cuyahoga Co., Cleveland
Type: Transcript; O
Year Range: 1833–1975
Online: Free
Title: Cleveland Public Library: The Necrology File
Notes, URL: The database includes paid death notices published in the following newspapers: *The Cleveland Plain Dealer*, 1850–1975; *The Cleveland Herald*, 1833, 1847–1848, 1876, 1878–1879; & *The Cleveland Press*, 1941–1975. <www.cpl.org/Index.asp>

Ohio, Cuyahoga Co., Cleveland
Type: Index; O
Year Range: 1976–pres.
Online: Free
Title: Cleveland News Index: Obituaries from the *Plain Dealer* & the *Cleveland Press*
Notes, URL: <http://www-catalog.cpl.org/CLENIX> Note the hyphen (not a period) after the *www*.

Ohio, Fayette Co.
Type: Index; O
Year Range: 1911–1975
Online: Free
Title: Carnegie Public Library: Record Herald 1911–1930 & 1960–1975 Obituary Index
Notes, URL: <www.washington-ch.lib.oh.us/GenealogyLinks.asp>

Ohio, Hamilton Co.
Type: Transcripts; O
Year Range: 2000–pres.
Online: Free
Title: Cincinnati.Com: Obituary Search
Notes, URL: Over 10,000 obituaries, death notices, & related advertisements from the *Cincinnati Enquirer* & the *Cincinnati Post*, Oct. 2000–pres. <http://dunes.cincinnati.com/obits>

Ohio, Hamilton Co., Cincinnati
Type: Transcripts; M
Year Range: 1860–1869
CD-ROM: $18 (Mac/Win), Heritage Books, item #2262
Title: Restored Hamilton County, Ohio Marriages, 1860–1869
Notes, URL: Over 23,000 marriages from the *Cincinnati Volksblatt*, the *Protestantische Zeitblatter*, & church records. <www.heritagebooks.com>. Search on "2262."

Ohio, Lawrence Co.
Type: Index; O
Year Range: 1850–2001
Online: Free
Title: Lawrence County, Ohio Vital Statistics: Obituary Indexes
Notes, URL: 1850–1930, 1998–2001. <www.lawrencecountyohio.com/deaths/deathindex.html>

Ohio, Licking Co.
Type: Index; O
Year Range: 1880–1941
Online: Free
Title: Obituaries and Death Notices Published in *The Granville Times*
Notes, URL: <www.kinfinder.com/obits/GTObits.htm>

Ohio, Montgomery Co., Dayton
Type: Index; O
Year Range: 1985–pres.
Online: Free
Title: Dayton Newspaper and Obituary Index
Notes, URL: Dayton Daily News, 1985–present; *Dayton Journal Herald*, 1985–1990; *Dayton Magazine*, 1985–present. <http://home.dayton.lib.oh.us/html/welcome-newsdb.html>

Ohio, Preble Co.
Type: Index; O
Year Range: 1960–1982
Online: Free
Title: Preble County Obituary Index Search
Notes, URL: 1960–1968, 1970–1982. <www.pcdl.lib.oh.us/search.htm>

Ohio, Preble Co.
Type: Index; O
Year Range: 1980–1995
Online: Free
Title: Preble County Obituary Index
Notes, URL: An index of over 10,500 obituaries in the *Register-Herald*. <www.pcdl.lib.oh.us/getobit.htm>

Ohio, Preble Co., Eaton
Type: Transcripts; O
Year Range: 2001–pres.
Online: Free
Title: The *Register-Herald*: Resources: Obituaries
Notes, URL: <www.registerherald.com>

Ohio, Sandusky Co.
Type: Index; O
Year Range: 1830s–pres.
Online: Free
Title: Rutherford B. Hayes Obituary Index
Notes, URL: An index to over 230,000 obituaries, death, & marriage notices & other sources. <http://index.rbhayes.org/>

Ohio, Stark Co.
Type: Index; M-DI-O
Year Range: 1815–1840
Online: Free
Title: Ohio Repository Genealogical Records Index 1815-ca. 1840
Notes, URL: Indexes notices of marriage, divorce, death, & administration. <www.stark.lib.oh.us/newobitindex.html>

Ohio, Stark Co., Alliance
Type: Index; O
Year Range: 1871–pres.
Online: Free
Title: Alliance *Review* Obituaries Database
Notes, URL: Incomplete, 1871–1959. Complete, 1961–pres. <www.rodman.lib.oh.us/rpl/ref/obits/index.asp>

Ohio, Stark Co., Louisville
Type: Abstracts; O
Year Range: 1887–pres.
Online: Free
Title: Louisville (Ohio) Public Library Obituary Database

Notes, URL: Nearly 25,000 names. <www.louisville.lib.oh.us/genealogy/>

Ohio, Stark Co., Massillon
Type: Index; O
Year Range: 1863–pres.
Online: Free
Title: Massillon Public Library Online Obituary Database Project
Notes, URL: In progress. <www.massillon.lib.oh.us/dept/gene/default.htm>

Ohio, Wayne Co.
Type: Index; O
Year Range: 1890–pres.
Online: Free
Title: Wayne County Public Library: Wayne County, OH Newspaper Obituary Index
Notes, URL: Includes 1890–1959 and 2000s. <www.wayne.lib.oh.us/gen>

Ohio, Wood Co.
Type: Index; O
Year Range: 1848–pres.
Online: Free
Title: Wood County District Public Library: Obituary Index
Notes, URL: Over 60,000 records. <http://wcdpl.lib.oh.us/databases/>

Oklahoma, Tulsa Co., Tulsa
Type: Index, transcripts; O
Year Range: 1996–pres.
Title: Archive Tulsa
Notes, URL: Paid obituaries. <http://commerce.tulsaworld.com/search/searchformnew.asp>. Searches are free. $1.95 to view an article.

Oregon
Type: Digital images
Year Range: 1846–1934
Title: Heritage Trail Press: Newspapers
Notes, URL: 17 newspapers. <www.heritagetrailpress.com>. $39/year.

Pennsylvania
Type: Abstracts; O
Online: Free
Title: Eastern PA Obituaries Database
Notes, URL: 60,170 records. <http://userdb.rootsweb.com/paobits>

Pennsylvania
Type: Abstracts; M-D
Year Range: 1719–1748
CD-ROM: $29.99, Genealogy.com, CD #512
Online: Genealogy Library
Title: Pennsylvania Colonial Records, 1600s–1800s
Notes, URL: Includes abstracts from Ben Franklin's *Pennsylvania Gazette*, 1728–1748, & the *American Weekly Mercury*, 1719–1746. <www.genealogy.com/512facd.html>

Pennsylvania
Type: Transcripts; D
Year Range: 1826–1836
Online: Free
Title: Records of Marriages and Deaths 1826–1836
Notes, URL: Records from the *Susquehanna Democrat* of Wilkes-Barre, 1828–1831, the *Wyoming Republican* of Kingston, 1832–1835, & the *Wyoming Republican and Herald* of Kingston, 1835–1836. <www.geocities.com/Heartland/Plains/3558/voliv.htm>

Pennsylvania, Lebanon Co.
Type: Transcript; M-D
Year Range: 1832–1879
CD-ROM: $24.50 (Mac/Win), Heritage Books, item #1110
Title: Heritage Books Archives: Lebanon Valley, Pennsylvania, History & Genealogy
Notes, URL: Books by Robert A. Heilman cover *Der Libanon Demokrat* (1832–1864) & the *Lebanon Valley Standard* (1871–1879). <www.heritagebooks.com>. Search on "1110."

Pennsylvania, Washington Co., Washington
Type: Transcripts; O
Year Range: 1997–pres.
Online: Free
Title: Observer-Reporter Obituary Archive
Notes, URL: <www.savory.org/chartiers/wo robits>

South Carolina
Type: Transcript; D
Year Range: 1732–1775
Online: F&LH
Title: Death notices in the South-Carolina gazette, 1732–1775

South Carolina
Type: Transcript; M-D
Year Range: 1823–1888
CD-ROM: $35.95, Ancestry, item #1554
Title: South Carolina: Records and Reference
Notes, URL: Includes marriage & death notices from several newspapers. <http://shops.ancestry.com>. Search on "South Carolina Records."

South Carolina, Beaufort Co.
Type: Index; O
Year Range: 1862–1978
Online: Free
Title: Newspaper Obituary Index for Beaufort County, SC
Notes, URL: <www.co.beaufort.sc.us/bftlib/obit.htm>

South Carolina, Charleston Co., Charleston
Type: Transcript; M
Year Range: 1732–1801
Online: Ancestry
Title: South Carolina Newspaper Marriage Notices, 1732–1801
Notes, URL: <www.ancestry.com/search/rectype/inddbs/4665.htm>

South Carolina, Charleston Co., Charleston
Type: Abstracts; M-D
Year Range: 1827–1845
Online: Ancestry
Title: Charleston Observer (South Carolina), Marriages and Deaths
Notes, URL: 13,000 names. <www.ancestry.com/search/rectype/inddbs/3390.htm>

South Carolina, Charleston Co., Charleston
Type: Abstracts; M-D
Year Range: 1827–1845
CD-ROM: $24 (Mac/Win), Heritage Books, item #1164
Title: Heritage Books Archives: South Carolina, Vol. 1
Notes, URL: Includes *Marriage and Death Notices from the "Charleston Observer,"* 1827–1845, by Brent H. Holcomb. <www.heritagebooks.com>. Search on "1164."

South Carolina, Greenville Co., Greenville
Type: Transcript; M-D
Year Range: 1826–1863
Online: Ancestry
Title: Greenville, South Carolina Marriage and Death Notices, 1826–63
Notes, URL: <www.ancestry.com/search/rectype/inddbs/3407.htm>

South Carolina, Horry Co.
Type: Abstracts; O
Year Range: 1861–1914
Online: Free
Title: Horry County Historical Society Obituary Database

Notes, URL: <www.hchsonline.org/obits/index.html>

South Carolina, Pickens Co.
Type: Digital images; O
Online: Free
Title: Obituaries & Death Certificates for Pickens Co., SC
Notes, URL: <www.scgenealogy.com/pickens/records/obits/index.htm>

South Carolina, Richland Co., Columbia
Type: Transcript; M-D
Year Range: 1838–1860
Online: Ancestry
Title: Columbia, South Carolina Newspaper Marriage and Death Notices
Notes, URL: Over 8,000 names. <www.ancestry.com/search/rectype/inddbs/3399.htm>

South Carolina, Richland Co., Columbia
Type: Transcript; O
Year Range: 1859–1877
CD-ROM: South Carolina: Records and Reference, $35.95 (Win), Ancestry
Online: Ancestry
Title: Columbia, South Carolina Obituaries, 1859–77
Notes, URL: Over 1,500 names. <www.ancestry.com/search/rectype/inddbs/3417.htm>

South Carolina, Spartanburg Co., Spartanburg
Type: Index; O
Year Range: 1849–1893
Online: Free
Title: Carolina Spartan/Spartanburg Herald Death Index
Notes, URL: <www.spt.lib.sc.us/obits/carspartanherald/index.html>

South Carolina, Spartanburg Co., Spartanburg
Type: Index; O
Year Range: 1902–2003
Online: Free
Title: Spartanburg Herald and Herald-Journal Obituary Index
Notes, URL: 1902–1914, 1930, 1941–2003. <www.spt.lib.sc.us/obits/index.html>

South Carolina, York Co.
Type: Transcript; D
Year Range: 1823–1865
CD-ROM: South Carolina: Records and Reference, $35.95 (Win), Ancestry item #1554, <http://shops.ancestry.com>. Search on "South Carolina Records."
Online: Ancestry
Title: York County, South Carolina Marriage and Death Notices, 1823–65
Notes, URL: Over 5,000 names. From Brent H. Holcomb, *York, South Carolina, Newspapers Marriage and Death Notices, 1823–1865*. <www.ancestry.com/search/rectype/inddbs/3409.htm>

Tennessee
Type: Abstracts; M-D
Year Range: 1791–1828
CD-ROM: $25 (Mac/Win), Heritage Books, item #1156
Title: Tennessee Genealogical Records
Notes, URL: Includes 3 volumes of *Genealogical Abstracts from Tennessee Newspapers*, by Sherida K. Eddlemon. <www.heritagebooks.com>. Search on "1156."

Tennessee, Davidson Co., Nashville
Type: Index; O
Year Range: 1964–pres.
Online: Free
Title: Nashville Local History Indexes: Obituaries in Nashville Newspapers, 1964–
Notes, URL: <http://wendy.nashv.lib.tn.us:82/>. You need to include *http://* at the beginning.

Tennessee, Dickson Co.
Type: Abstracts; M
Year Range: 1817–1879
CD-ROM: $25 (Mac/Win), Heritage Books, item #1156
Title: Tennessee Genealogical Records
Notes, URL: Includes *Dickson County, Tennessee: Marriage Records 1817–1879*, by Sherida K. Eddlemon. <www.heritagebooks.com>. Search on "1156."

Tennessee, Lincoln Co.
Type: Index; M
Year Range: 1895–1910
Online: Free
Title: Lincoln County, Tennessee, Marriages—Interactive Search
Notes, URL: Source: *Fayetteville Observer*. <www.rootsweb.com/cgi-bin/tnlincoln/tnlincoln.pl>

Texas
Type: Abstracts; M-D
Year Range: 1890–1930
Online: Free
Title: Early Texas Newspaper Abstracts 1890–1930
Notes, URL: <www.censusdiggins.com/tx_news.html>

Utah
Type: Digital images
Year Range: 1850–1863
Title: Heritage Trail Press: Newspapers
Notes, URL: *Deseret News*. <www.heritagetrailpress.com>. $39/year.

Vermont, Windsor Co., Windsor
Type: Abstracts; O
Year Range: 1826–1898
Online: Free
Title: The Vermont Chronicle
Notes, URL: Published in Bellows Falls, Vt., 1826–1828. <http://community.middlebury.edu/~swilson/introvc.html>

Virginia
Type: Transcripts; O
Year Range: 1790–1940
Online: Free
Title: Old Virginia Obituaries, 1790–1940
Notes, URL: <www.virginiaobits.homestead.com>

Virginia, Alexandria
Type: Index; O
Year Range: 1916–1935
Online: Free
Title: Obituary Index to the Alexandria Gazette, 1916–1935
Notes, URL: Over 24,000 entries. <www.alexandria.lib.va.us/lhsc_genealogy_resources/obits/obits.html>

Virginia, Richmond
Type: Index; M-O
Year Range: 1780–1876
Online: Free
Title: Henley Marriage and Obituary Index
Notes, URL: More than 45,000 marriage & obituary notices. <www.lva.lib.va.us/whatwehave/vital/>

Virginia, Richmond
Type: Index; O
Year Range: 1804–1838
Online: Ancestry
Title: Richmond, Virginia Newspaper Obituaries, 1804–38
Notes, URL: Nearly 3,800 names. From Virginia State Library. *Index to Obituary Notices in the Richmond Enquirer from May 9, 1804, through 1828, and the Richmond Whig from January, 1824, through 1838*. <www.ancestry.com/search/rectype/inddbs/4183.htm>

Virginia, Richmond
Type: Index; O
Year Range: 1804–1860
Online: Free

Title: Obituary Index for *Richmond Enquirer*, 1804–1860 & *Richmond Visitor*, 1809–1810
Notes, URL: Over 11,000 names. <www.lva.lib.va.us/whatwehave/vital/>

Washington, Pierce Co., Tacoma
Type: Index; O
Year Range: 1930–pres.
Online: Free
Title: Tacoma Area Obituary Index
Notes, URL: More than 367,000 records. Complete, 1984–pres. Incomplete, 1930–1983. <http://search.tpl.lib.wa.us/obits/obitabout.asp>

Washington, Whatcom Co.
Type: Transcripts; O
Year Range: 1885–2002
Online: Free
Title: Obituaries of Whatcom County, WA
Notes, URL: <www.rootsweb.com/~wawhatco/obitindex.htm>

West Virginia, Jackson Co.
Type: Transcripts; O
Year Range: 1911–1947
Online: Free
Title: Jackson County Obituaries
Notes, URL: 1911–1915, 1922, & 1941–1947. <www.rootsweb.com/~wvjackso/obitpage.htm>

Wisconsin
Type: Index; O
Year Range: Up to 1970
Online: Free
Title: Wisconsin Name Index
Notes, URL: More than 100,000 obituaries, personal sketches, & other short biographies of WI people. <www.wisconsinhistory.org/wni/>

Wisconsin
Type: Digital images
Year Range: 1860–1940
Online: Free
Title: Wisconsin Local History & Biography Articles (WLHBA)
Notes, URL: 16,000 articles from 100s of newspapers. <www.wisconsinhistory.org/wlhba>

Wisconsin, Milwaukee Co., Wauwatosa
Type: Abstracts; M-D
Year Range: 1899–1904
CD-ROM: $28.50 (Mac/Win), Heritage Books, item #1267
Title: Heritage Books Archives: Wisconsin Volume 1
Notes, URL: Includes *Genealogical Abstracts from the Wauwatosa News, 1899–1904*, by Elizabeth Doherty Herzfeld. <www.heritagebooks.com>. Search on "1267."

Wisconsin, Portage Co., Stevens Point
Type: Index; O
Year Range: 1872–pres.
Online: Free
Title: Stevens Point Area Obituary Index
Notes, URL: <www.library.uwsp.edu/obits>

Wisconsin, Richland Co., Richland Center
Type: Index; B-M-D
Year Range: 1880–1885
Online: Free
Title: Richland Republican and Observer, Richland Center, Wisconsin
Notes, URL: <freepages.genealogy.rootsweb.com/~djnsl/RepOb/RepObHome.html>

Church Records

Records of new members dominate the minutes of the Presbyterian Church of Kortright, Delaware County, New York, but a lengthy 1809 entry concerning my immigrant ancestors from Scotland caught my eye. A nosy neighbor suspected Margaret Ferguson, age 23, and her boyfriend of unchaste behavior and brought the matter to the attention of church authorities. Neighbors and family members gave conflicting testimonies in the ensuing church trial. No verdict is recorded, but the case adds some color to my family history.

You don't often find such interesting accounts in church records, but they are a prime source for birth, marriage, and death information before most states began keeping such records around the year 1900.

What church records are online or on CD-ROM?

You'll find many church records, including transcribed records of baptism, marriage, burial, and membership, mostly from eastern states (see Figure 10-1 on page 197). Most date from the eighteenth and nineteenth centuries, but a few go back to the early 1600s in Massachusetts and Virginia. They cover all major denominations, but German Lutheran and Reformed churches from southeastern Pennsylvania and Dutch Reformed churches from New York are especially well represented.

What church records are not online or on CD-ROM?

Few Roman Catholic records have been published online or on CD-ROM.

Reminder

Keep in mind that some church record databases are only indexes. The original records might reveal more details like the sponsors in a baptism or the bride's and groom's places of residence.

KEY DATABASES

Transcripts & Abstracts

New York Births & Baptisms: Southeast Region, 1660–1916

<www.ancestry.com/search/rectype/inddbs/3711.htm>

The 75,000 transcribed birth and baptismal records in this database (see

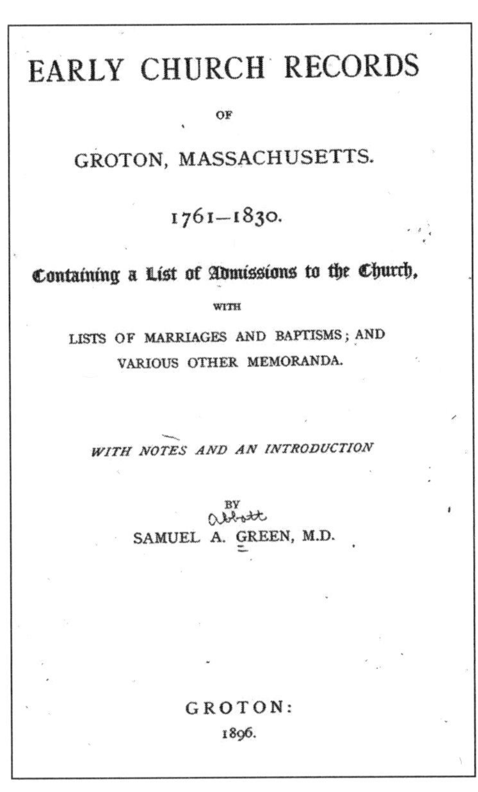

EARLY CHURCH RECORDS

OF

GROTON, MASSACHUSETTS.

1761–1830.

Containing a List of Admissions to the Church,

WITH

LISTS OF MARRIAGES AND BAPTISMS; AND VARIOUS OTHER MEMORANDA.

WITH NOTES AND AN INTRODUCTION

BY

SAMUEL A. GREEN, M.D.

GROTON:
1896.

Figure 10-1
Church records book available through Genealogy.com's Family and Local Histories collection and HeritageQuest Online.

Figure 10-2 below) provide details on more than 220,000 people in the New York counties of Dutchess, Greene, Putnam, Rockland, Ulster, and Westchester. You can also get the database on CD-ROM for $26.95 from Ancestry.com, item #1860.

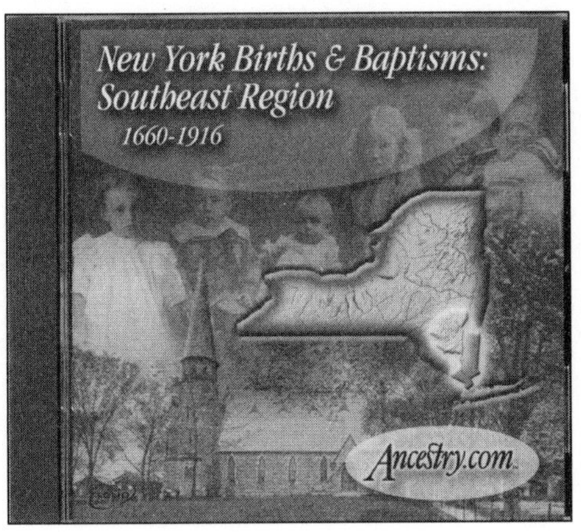

Figure 10-2
New York Births & Baptisms: Southeast Region, 1660–1916.

New York Births and Baptisms, Eastern Region, 1683–1928
<www.ancestry.com/search/rectype/inddbs/5538.htm>

Over 82,028 records from Columbia, Rensselaer, and Albany counties, New York.

Pennsylvania German Church Records, 1729–1870
<www.genealogy.com/130facd.html>

This CD-ROM, $29.99 from Genealogy.com, CD #130, has digital images of three volumes with 91,000 names (see Figure 10-3 below). The data is also available online with a subscription to Genealogy Library.

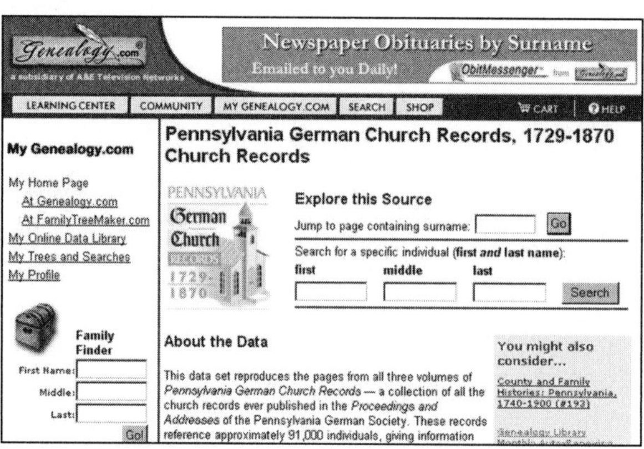

Figure 10-3
Pennsylvania German Church Records, 1729–1870.

Pennsylvania German Church Records on Ancestry.com

Ancestry.com has more than eighty databases with Pennsylvania church records, mostly from Lutheran and Reformed churches in southeastern Pennsylvania.

USGenWeb
<www.usgenweb.org/statelinks-table.html>

Researchers have contributed many indexes and abstracts of church records to USGenWeb's state pages and the county pages linked to them.

LINKS

Cyndi's List of Genealogy Sites on the Internet:

<www.cyndislist.com>

The site has links in these categories: Baptist, Catholic, Huguenot, Jewish, LDS & Family History Centers, Lutheran, Mennonite, Methodist, Presbyterian, Quaker, and Religion & Churches.

DATABASE DIRECTORY Church Records

This directory does not include URLs for databases in the Family and Local Histories Collection. See page 18 for instructions on "Searching an Individual Database" in Family and Local Histories. **Type**: Digital Images, Transcript, Database, Abstracts, or Index; Births (B), Baptisms (BA), Marriages (M), Divorces (DI), Deaths (D), Burials (BU).

United States
Type: Index
Year Range: 1786–1967
CD-ROM: $10 (Win)
Title: General Commission on Archives and History: The United Methodist Church: Conference Journal Memoirs
Notes, URL: An index to 97,000 biographies of pastors, their spouses, & lay leaders in pre–1968 Methodist & Evangelical United Brethren Church conference memoirs. <www.gcah.org/memoirscd.htm>.

United States
Type: Text of the books; B-M-D-BU
Online: Ancestry
Title: Encyclopedia of American Quaker Genealogy
Notes, URL: Vol. 1 (N.C.): <www.ancestry.com/search/rectype/inddbs/3215.htm>. Vol. 2 (Philadelphia): < . . ./3216.htm>. Vol. 3 (N.Y.): < . . ./3180.htm>. Vol. 4 (Ohio): < . . ./3219.htm>. Vol. 5 (Ohio & Ind.): < . . ./3222.htm>. Vol. 6 (Va. & Md.): < . . ./3226.htm>.

United States
Type: Digital images from books; B-M-D-BU
CD-ROM: $59.95, Genealogy.com, CD #192
Online: Genealogy Library
Title: The Encyclopedia of Quaker Genealogy, 1750–1930
Notes, URL: <www.genealogy.com/192facd.html>

United States
Type: Abstracts; M-DI-D
Year Range: 1811–1851
CD-ROM: $28 (Mac/Win), Heritage Books, CD #1109
Title: Heritage Books Archives: Freewill Baptist Vital Statistics, 1811–1851
Notes, URL: Vital statistics from Freewill Baptist publications. <www.heritagebooks.com>. Search on "1109."

United States
Type: Transcript; BA-M-BU
Online: Free
Title: RootsWeb.com: Church Records
Notes, URL: Over 17,000 records from several states. <http://userdb.rootsweb.com/churchrecords>

United States
Type: Transcripts; D
Year Range: 1862–1889
Online: Free
Title: Quaker Obituary Notices extracted from the *Friends' Intelligencer and Journal*
Notes, URL: <www.geocities.com/averys2002/quakerdth.htm>

United States
Type: Transcripts; M
Year Range: 1863–1889
Online: Free
Title: Quaker Marriage Notices extracted from the *Friends' Intelligencer and Journal*
Notes, URL: <www.geocities.com/averys2002/quakermrg.htm>

United States, Southern States
Type: Transcripts; M
Year Range: 1867–1878
CD-ROM: S.C.: Records and Reference, $35.95 (Win), Ancestry, item #1554, <http://shops.ancestry.com>. Search on "South Carolina Records."
Online: Ancestry
Title: Southern Christian Advocate Marriage Notices, 1867–78
Notes, URL: The official publication for the Methodist Conferences in South Carolina, Georgia, and Florida. <www.ancestry.com/search/rectype/inddbs/3319.htm>

United States, Southern States
Type: Transcripts; O
Year Range: 1867–1878
CD-ROM: S.C.: Records and Reference, $35.95 (Win), Ancestry, item #1554, <http://shops.ancestry.com>. Search on "South Carolina Records."
Online: Ancestry
Title: Southern Christian Advocate Obituaries, 1867–78
Notes, URL: The official publication for the Methodist Conferences in South Carolina, Georgia, and Florida. <www.ancestry.com/search/rectype/inddbs/3317.htm>

Alabama, Jefferson Co., Warrior
Type: Text of a book; BA-M-BU
Year Range: 1881–1987
Online: Genealogy Library
Title: Mt. Zion Baptist Church: The History of Mt. Zion Baptist Church 1881–1987
Notes, URL: Select Places | United States | Alabama

Connecticut, Fairfield Co., Greenwich
Type: Transcript; BA-M
Year Range: 1728–1909
Online: NEHGS
Title: Church Records of Greenwich, Connecticut, 1728–1909
Notes, URL: <www.newenglandancestors.org/research/database/greenwichchurch>

Connecticut, Hartford Co., Hartford
Type: Transcript; B-BA-M-D
Year Range: 1633–1885
Online: NEHGS
Title: Historical Catalogue of the First Church of Hartford, Connecticut, 1633–1885
Notes, URL: <www.newenglandancestors.org/researchdatabasehartfordfirstchurch>

Connecticut, Hartford Co., Hartford
Type: Images of pages containing transcripts
Year Range: 1904
Online: F&LH
Title: Year book of the First Church of Christ in Hartford: reports of the church for the year 1904

Connecticut, New Haven Co., Madison
Type: Transcript; BA-M-D
Year Range: 1791–1827
Online: NEHGS
Title: Church Records of Madison, CT
Notes, URL: <www.newenglandancestors.org/research/database/madisonchurch>

Connecticut, New Haven Co., Milford
Type: Transcript; BA
Year Range: 1635–1760
Online: NEHGS
Title: Records of the First Church of Milford, CT, 1635–1760

Notes, URL: <www.newenglandancestors.org/research/database/firstchurchmilford>

Connecticut, New Haven Co., Milford
Type: Transcript; BA-M
Year Range: 1749–1829
Online: NEHGS
Title: Records of the Second Church of Milford, Connecticut, 1749–1829
Notes, URL: <www.newenglandancestors.org/research/database/secondchurchmilford>

Connecticut, New London Co., Preston
Type: Digital images of a book
Year Range: 1698–1898
Online: F&LH
Title: First Congregational Church of Preston, Connecticut, 1698–1898: together with statistics of the church taken from church records
Notes, URL: By R.H. Gidman.

Connecticut, New London Co., Stonington
Type: Transcript; BA-M
Year Range: 1640–1975
Online: NEHGS
Title: Index to the Records of the First Church of Stonington, CT
Notes, URL: <www.newenglandancestors.org/research/database/stonington/>

Connecticut, Tolland Co., Mansfield
Type: Transcript
Year Range: 1744–1785
Online: Free
Title: Mansfield Marriages, 1744–1785, First Congregational Church
Notes, URL: Source: Bailey, Frederic W. *Early Connecticut Marriages as found on Ancient Church Records Prior to 1800*, Second book, pp. 126-131. <www.rootsweb.com/~ctcmansf/mansfieldbailey.html>

Delaware
Type: Transcript; B-BA-M-BU
Year Range: 1648–1899
CD-ROM: $29.99, Genealogy.com, CD #178
Online: Genealogy Library
Title: Maryland and Delaware, 1600s–1800s Church Records
Notes, URL: 263,000 names. <www.genealogy.com/178facd.html>

Delaware, Kent Co.
Type: Text of a book containing transcripts; B-M-D
Year Range: 1705–1865
Online: Genealogy Library
Title: Delaware Quaker Records: Duck Creek
Notes, URL: Click on Places | United States | Delaware.

Delaware, New Castle Co., New Castle
Type: Images of pages containing transcripts
Year Range: 1651–1890
CD-ROM: F&LH
Online: Sketch of early ecclesiastical affairs in New Castle, Delaware, and history of Immanuel Church

Georgia, Effingham Co.
Type: Images of pages containing transcripts
Year Range: 1754–1800
CD-ROM: F&LH
Online: Ebenezer record book: containing early records of Jerusalem Evangelical Lutheran Church, Effingham, Ga., more commonly known as Ebenezer Church
Title: By A.G. Voigt, et al. Translated from German.

Georgia, Liberty Co., Midway
Type: Transcript; B-BA-M-D
Year Range: 1743–1863
Online: Ancestry
Title: Midway Congregation[al] Church Records, Liberty County, Georgia
Notes, URL: <www.ancestry.com/search/rectype/inddbs/3448.htm>

Illinois
Type: Transcript; B-M-D
Online: Ancestry
Title: Illinois Quaker Records
Notes, URL: <www.ancestry.com/search/rectype/inddbs/4752.htm>

Indiana, Jennings Co.
Type: Transcript; B-BA-D
Year Range: 1822–1895
Online: Free
Title: Coffee Creek Baptist Church Records
Notes, URL: <http://members.cox.net/jefe19>

Maine
Type: Transcript; M
Year Range: 1854–1892
Online: NEHGS
Title: Record of Marriages Solemnized by H.F.A. Patterson in the State of Maine, 1854–1892
Notes, URL: <www.newenglandancestors.org/research/database/patterson>

Maine, Sagadahoc Co., Bath
Type: Transcript; M
Year Range: 1805–1817
Online: NEHGS
Title: Letter of Marriages of Bath, Maine, 1805–1817
Notes, URL: Marriages performed by Rev. William Jenk, a Congregationalist minister. <www.newenglandancestors.org/research/database/bath_maine>

Maryland
Type: Index; M
Year Range: 1634–1820
CD-ROM: $29.99 (Win/Mac), Genealogy.com, CD #195
Online: Genealogy Library
Title: Maryland Marriages and Genealogies, 1634–1820
Notes, URL: Marriage records compiled primarily from church records. <www.genealogy.com/195facd.html>

Maryland
Type: Transcript; B-BA-M-BU
Year Range: 1648–1899
CD-ROM: $29.99, Genealogy.com, CD #178
Online: Genealogy Library
Title: Maryland and Delaware, 1600s–1800s Church Records
Notes, URL: Covers many churches, including Catholic, Episcopal, Methodist, Presbyterian, & Quaker congregations. <www.genealogy.com/178facd.html>

Maryland
Type: Index; D-BU
Year Range: 1662–1958
Online: Free
Title: Maryland Indexes (Church Records, Deaths, and Burials Index)
Notes, URL: Records of 17 churches. <www.mdarchives.state.md.us/msa/stagser/s1400/s1402/html/ssi1402.html>

Maryland, Baltimore (City)
Type: Digital images of a book
Year Range: 1827–1859
Online: F&LH
Title: Register of the First English Lutheran Church, Baltimore: from February, 1827, to March, 1859

Maryland, Baltimore Co.
Type: Abstracts; B-BA-M-D
Year Range: 1787–1815
Online: Ancestry
Title: St. James Parish Register, Maryland, 1787–1815

Notes, URL: Over 3,200 names. <www.ancestry.com/search/rectype/inddbs/3641.htm>

Maryland, Cecil Co., Nottingham
Type: Transcript; B-M-D
Year Range: 1730–1880
Online: Ancestry
Title: Nottingham, Cecil County, Maryland Quaker Records
Notes, URL: <www.ancestry.com/search/rectype/inddbs/5025.htm>

Maryland, Dorchester Co., Cambridge
Type: Images of pages containing transcripts
Year Range: 1796–1893
CD-ROM: F&LH
Online: Records of Great Choptank Parish, Cambridge, Maryland

Maryland, Worcester Co., Worcester Parish
Type: Digital images of a book
Year Range: 1722–1839
Online: F&LH
Title: Register of St. Martin's Church, Worcester Parish, Worcester Co., Md., 1722–1839
Notes, URL: Typescript. By the Daughters of the American Revolution, California State Society.

Massachusetts, Berkshire Co., New Ashford
Type: Images of pages containing transcripts
Year Range: 1647–1889
CD-ROM: F&LH
Online: The "Register" of Dr. William H. Tyler: a manuscript notebook belonging to Mrs. Perry A. Smedley
Title: Families: Tyler, Clothier, Cole, Noble, Hall, Cook, Baldwin, Hamilton

Massachusetts, Berkshire Co., Pittsfield
Type: Images of pages containing transcripts
Year Range: 1834
CD-ROM: F&LH
Online: First Church in Pittsfield: confession of faith and catalogue of members, January 1, 1834

Massachusetts, Essex Co., Andover
Type: Images of pages containing transcripts
Year Range: 1711–1859
Online: F&LH
Title: Historical manual of the South Church in Andover, Mass.: August, 1859
Notes, URL: By George Mooar. Includes a catalog of members.

Massachusetts, Essex Co., Beverly
Type: Digital images of a book; BA
Year Range: 1667–1710
Online: F&LH
Title: The register of baptisms of the First Church in Beverly, 1667–1710
Notes, URL: By Augustus A. Galloupe.

Massachusetts, Essex Co., Ipswich
Type: Images of pages containing transcripts
Year Range: 1634–1862
Online: F&LH
Title: Concise history of the First Church of Christ in Ipswich
Notes, URL: Includes list of members.

Massachusetts, Essex Co., Lynn
Type: Images of pages containing transcripts
Year Range: 1845
CD-ROM: F&LH
Online: A catalogue of the members of the First Church in Lynn: embracing those who were members at the date of Jan. 1, 1845

Massachusetts, Essex Co., Methuen
Type: Transcript; M
Year Range: 1730–1788
Online: Free
Title: Record of Marriages Performed by Rev. Christopher Sargent
Notes, URL: <www.arches.uga.edu/~wprokasy/methuen/marriage.htm>

Massachusetts, Essex Co., Salem
Type: Transcript; BA
Year Range: 1702–1807
Online: NEHGS
Title: Eighteenth Century Baptisms in Salem, Massachusetts
Notes, URL: Published by James A. Emmerton in 1886. <www.newenglandancestors.org/research/database/vital_records_salem>

Massachusetts, Essex Co., Salem
Type: Transcript
Year Range: 1772–1827
Online: NEHGS
Title: A Catalogue of Members of North Church in Salem
Notes, URL: <www.newenglandancestors.org/research/database/nchurchsalem>

Massachusetts, Essex Co., Salisbury
Type: Transcript; M
Year Range: 1812–1835
Online: NEHGS
Title: Marriages by Elder Jabez True of Salisbury, MA, 1812–1835
Notes, URL: <www.newenglandancestors.org/research/database/jtrue>

Massachusetts, Hampden Co., Brimfield
Type: Images of pages containing transcripts
Year Range: 1724–1856
Online: F&LH
Title: Annals of the church in Brimfield
Notes, URL: Names of church members, 1724–1856.

Massachusetts, Hampden Co., Holyoke
Type: Transcript; D
Year Range: 1875
Online: Free
Title: May 27, 1875: The Tragedy of the Precious Blood Church Fire
Notes, URL: Transcripts of newspaper accounts. <www.rootsweb.com/~mahampde/towns/holyoke/pblood/index.html>

Massachusetts, Hampden Co., Westfield
Type: Transcript; BA
Year Range: 1679–1836
Online: NEHGS
Title: Baptisms Performed in the Church of Christ, Westfield, Massachusetts, 1679–1836
Notes, URL: <www.newenglandancestors.org/research/database/westfield>

Massachusetts, Hampden Co., Westfield
Type: Abstracts; BA
Year Range: 1679–1836
Online: NEHGS
Title: Baptisms Performed in the Church of Christ, Westfield, MA, 1679–1836
Notes, URL: <www.newenglandancestors.org/rs2/research/database/westfield/>

Massachusetts, Hampden Co., Westfield
Type: Abstracts; D
Year Range: 1728–1836
Online: NEHGS
Title: Register of Deaths of the First Church, Westfield, Massachusetts, 1728–1836
Notes, URL: <www.newenglandancestors.org/research/database/firstchurchdeaths/>

Massachusetts, Hampden Co., Westfield
Type: Digital images; B-M-D
Year Range: 1737–1774
CD-ROM: $33.50 (Mac/Win), Heritage Books, item #2109

Title: Rev. John Ballantine, Minister of Westfield, Massachusetts, Journal, 1737–1774
Notes, URL: 2,702 pp. <www.heritagebooks.com>. Search on "2109."

Massachusetts, Hampden Co., Westfield
Type: Abstracts; M
Year Range: 1781–1835
Online: NEHGS
Title: Marriage Records of the First Church, Westfield, MA, 1781–1835
Notes, URL: <www.newenglandancestors.org/research/database/firstchurchmarriages/>

Massachusetts, Hampshire Co., Northampton
Type: Images of pages containing transcripts
Year Range: 1661–1891
Online: F&LH
Title: Historical catalogue of the Northampton First Church, 1661–1891
Notes, URL: "Illustrated." Photocopy of original.

Massachusetts, Middlesex Co., Groton
Type: Digital images of a book; BA-M
Year Range: 1761–1830
Online: F&LH
Title: Early church records of Groton, Massachusetts, 1761–1830
Notes, URL: By Samuel A. Green.

Massachusetts, Middlesex Co., Malden
Type: Images of pages containing transcripts
Year Range: 1803–1915
Online: F&LH
Title: Directory of the First Baptist Church, Malden, MA

Massachusetts, Middlesex Co., Watertown
Type: Digital images of a book containing transcripts; BA-M
Year Range: 1686–1819
Online: Ancestry
Title: Watertown, Massachusetts, East Precinct Records, 1697–1737 and Pastors' Records, 1686–1819
Notes, URL: From *Watertown Records Comprising East Congregational and Precint Affairs 1697 to 1737 and Record Book of the Pastors 1686 to 1819*. <www.ancestry.com/search/rectype/inddbs/6357.htm>

Massachusetts, Middlesex Co., Wilmington
Type: Images of pages containing transcripts
Year Range: 1732–1933
CD-ROM: F&LH
Online: History, year book and church directory of the First Congregational Church, Wilmington, MA

Massachusetts, Norfolk Co., Dedham
Type: Transcript; BA-M-D-BU
Year Range: 1638–1845
Online: F&LH
Title: The record of baptisms, marriages and deaths and admissions to the church and dismissals therefrom, transcribed from the church records in the town of Dedham, MA, 1638–1845
Notes, URL: "Also all the epitaphs in the ancient burial place in Dedham, together with the other inscriptions before 1845 in the three parish cemeteries."

Massachusetts, Plymouth Co., East Bridgewater
Type: Transcript; M
Year Range: 1725–1803
Online: Free
Title: Record of Marriages Solemnized in the East Parish of Bridgewater, Mass.
Notes, URL: From the *New England Historical and Genealogical Register*, 45 [1891]: 12-14, 142-145, 244-246, 283-285; 46 [1892]: 55-57, 167-171). <www.rootsweb.com/~mabridge/nehgr/nehgr.html#ebrimar>

Massachusetts, Plymouth Co., Hanson
Type: Transcript; BA
Year Range: 1749–1825
Online: NEHGS
Title: Baptisms in the Second Religious Society of Pembroke, Massachusetts
Notes, URL: Now the First Congregational Church of Hanson. <www.newenglandancestors.org/research/database/hanson>

Massachusetts, Plymouth Co., Middleborough
Type: Images of pages containing transcripts
Year Range: 1694–1853
CD-ROM: F&LH
Online: First Church in Middleborough, Mass.: Mr. Putnam's century and half discourses, an historical account, and a catalogue of members
Title: Publ. 1852.

Massachusetts, Plymouth Co., Pembroke
Type: Transcript; BA
Year Range: 1749–1825
Online: NEHGS
Title: Baptisms in the Second Religious Society of Pembroke, Massachusetts
Notes, URL: Now the First Congregational Church of Hanson. <www.newenglandancestors.org/research/database/hanson>

Massachusetts, Plymouth Co., Plymouth
Type: Digital images of a book; BA-M-BU
Year Range: 1620–1859
Online: F&LH
Title: Plymouth church records, 1620–1859

Massachusetts, Plymouth Co., Plymouth
Type: Transcript; BA-M-BU
Year Range: 1620–1859
Online: Ancestry
Title: Plymouth, MA Church Records, Vols. I & II, 1620–1859
Notes, URL: From *Plymouth Church Records, 1620–1859*. <www.ancestry.com/search/rectype/inddbs/5261.htm>

Massachusetts, Plymouth Co., Plymouth
Type: Transcript; BA-M
Year Range: 1775–1803
Online: NEHGS
Title: Marriages and Baptisms of the Rev. Ivory Hovey of Plymouth, MA, 1775–1803
Notes, URL: <www.newenglandancestors.org/research/database/hovey>

Massachusetts, Worcester Co., Worcester
Type: Transcript; B-M-D
Year Range: 1785–1919
Online: NEHGS
Title: Records of First Unitarian Church of Worcester, Massachusetts, 1785–1919
Notes, URL: Copied & indexed by the Federal Writers Project, instituted by the WPA, in 1936. <www.newenglandancestors.org/research/database/firstunitchurch>

Michigan
Type: Digital images of pages containing transcripts; B-M-D
Year Range: 1843–1848
Online: F&LH
Title: Some MI vital records, arranged by counties, from the Expounder of primitive Christianity: Jackson, MI, Ann Arbor, MI, 1843–1848, an organ of the Universalist Church

Michigan
Type: Database; B-M

Year Range: 1843–1859
Online: Free
Title: Fr. Patrick O'Kelly Parish Registers
Notes, URL: Baptismal and matrimonial registers of Catholic congregations in Livingston, Oakland, and Ingham counties. <www.mifamilyhistory.org/frpok_registers/index.asp>

Michigan
Type: Transcript; M
Year Range: 1870–1887
Online: F&LH
Title: Michigan marriage records, 1870–1887, and the Coulter family records

Michigan, Chippewa Co., Sault Ste. Marie
Type: Transcript; BA-M-BU
Year Range: 1870–1910
Online: Free
Title: Precious Blood Cathedral
Notes, URL: <http://freepages.genealogy.rootsweb.com/~wjmartin/sacred.htm>

Michigan, Saginaw Co., Saginaw
Type: Transcript; B-BA-M-D
Year Range: 1856–1862
Online: Free
Title: St. John Lutheran Church Records
Notes, URL: English translation. <www.funstuffforgenealogists.com/html/databases.htm>

Michigan, Wayne Co., Grosse Pointe Woods
Type: Images of pages containing transcripts
Year Range: 1939–1951
Online: F&LH
Title: The new church register of the Grosse Pointe Woods Presbyterian Church

Missouri
Type: Abstracts; BA-M-BU
CD-ROM: $29.50 (Mac/Win), Heritage Books, CD #1369
Title: Heritage Books Archives: Missouri Volume 1
Notes, URL: Includes church records from 60 counties. <www.heritagebooks.com>. Search on "1369."

Missouri
Type: Abstracts; B-M-D
Year Range: 1800s
Online: Ancestry
Title: Missouri Quaker Records
Notes, URL: <www.ancestry.com/search/rectype/inddbs/4998.htm>

Nebraska
Type: Abstracts; B-M-D
Year Range: 1815–1936
Online: Ancestry
Title: Nebraska Monthly Meeting: Quaker Records
Notes, URL: <www.ancestry.com/search/rectype/inddbs/6027.htm>

New Hampshire, Merrimack Co.
Type: Images of pages containing transcripts
Year Range: 1791–1908
CD-ROM: F&LH
Online: Historical sketch & roll of membership of the First Congregational Church, Webster, N.H.
Title: Also, Westerly Religious Society (Boscawen, N.H.) Second Church of Christ (Boscawen, N.H.).

New Jersey
Type: Transcript; B-M-D
Year Range: 1710–1850
CD-ROM: Ancestry
Online: Hardwick and Mendham Monthly Meeting & Warren & Morris Counties, N.J.: Quaker Records
Title: <www.ancestry.com/search/rectype/inddbs/6190.htm>

New Jersey
Type: Abstracts
Online: Ancestry
Title: Historical and Genealogical Miscellany: New York and New Jersey, Vols. I-V
Notes, URL: Church and other records. <www.ancestry.com/search/rectype/inddbs/6248.htm>

New Jersey, Bergen Co., Mahwah
Type: Images of pages containing transcripts
Year Range: 1755–1944
CD-ROM: F&LH
Online: Ramapo Reformed Church, Ramapo Lutheran Church
Title: Introduction by Herbert S. Ackerman

New Jersey, Cape May Co.
Type: Digital images of a book; B-D
Year Range: 1600s–1700s
Online: F&LH
Title: Cape May meeting: minutes

New Jersey, Cape May Co.
Type: Images of pages containing transcripts; B-D
Year Range: 1600s–1700s
Online: F&LH
Title: Cape May meeting: minutes
Notes, URL: Includes 17th and 18th c. birth and death church records.

New Jersey, Essex Co.
Type: Abstracts; B-M-D
Year Range: About 1735–1868
Online: Ancestry
Title: Essex County, New Jersey Quaker Records
Notes, URL: <www.ancestry.com/search/rectype/inddbs/4575.htm>

New Jersey, Essex Co., Pinebrook
Type: Images of pages containing transcripts
Year Range: 1823–1904
Online: F&LH
Title: Pine Brook Methodist Church records
Notes, URL: Typescript. Lists of names of members, 1823–1865; Records of meetings of trustees, Feb. 13, 1843–June 6, 1904.

New Jersey, Hudson Co., Jersey City
Type: Images of pages containing transcripts; BU
Year Range: 1630–1915
Online: F&LH
Title: Yearbook of the Holland Society of New York, 1915: Bergen book
Notes, URL: Vol. 3 of the records of Bergen County, N.J. First settlers of Bergen, burials in Bergen, Church members in Bergen.

New Jersey, Hudson Co., Jersey City
Type: Transcript; BA-M-BU
Year Range: 1666–1788
CD-ROM: $37.50 (Mac/Win), Heritage Books, CD #1932
Title: HB Archives: New Jersey, Volume 2
Notes, URL: Records of the Reformed Protestant Dutch Church of Bergen (now Jersey City), originally published as *Yearbook of the Holland Society of New York: Bergen Book*. <www.heritagebooks.com>. Search on "1932."

New Jersey, Hudson Co., Jersey City
Type: Transcript; BA-M-BU
Year Range: 1666–1788
Online: Ancestry
Title: Reformed Protestant Dutch Church of Bergen [Jersey City], New Jersey, 1666–1788
Notes, URL: From the Holland Society of New York, *The Reformed Protestant Dutch Church of Bergen [Jersey City], New Jersey, 1666–1788*. <www.ancestry.

com/search/rectype/inddbs/6046.htm>

New Jersey, Hunterdon Co., Alexandria
Type: Abstracts; BA
Year Range: 1763–1802
Online: Ancestry
Title: New Jersey German Reformed Church Records, 1763–1802
Notes, URL: Nearly 600 baptismal records. <www.ancestry.com/search/rectype/inddbs/3315.htm>

New Jersey, Hunterdon Co., Kingwood
Type: Images of pages containing transcripts
Year Range: 1726–1868
CD-ROM: F&LH
Online: Record of the Kingwood monthly meeting of Friends, Hunterdon County, N.J.

New Jersey, Mercer Co., Lawrenceville
Type: Images of pages containing transcripts
Year Range: 1709–1850
CD-ROM: F&LH
Online: The church records of the Presbyterian Church of Lawrenceville, New Jersey, and the Bible records from the bibles in the library of the society

New Jersey, Mercer Co., Trenton
Type: Images of a book
Year Range: 1703–1726
Online: F&LH
Title: A history of St. Michael's Church, Trenton: in the diocese of New Jersey from its foundation in the year of our Lord, 1703 to 1726

New Jersey, Morris Co.
Type: Images of pages containing transcripts
Year Range: 1737–1873
Online: F&LH
Title: Reformed Dutch Church records of Pompton Plains, pages 1-210, records of Montville, pages 211-258
Notes, URL: Typescript.

New Jersey, Morris Co.
Type: Images of pages containing transcripts
Year Range: 1872–1965
Online: F&LH
Title: Records of the Millbrook and Walnut Grove (Mount Freedom) Methodist Episcopal Churches of Randolph Township, Morris County, New Jersey: Book One of church records beginning 1872
Notes, URL: By Helen M. Wright, et al.,1965.

New Jersey, Morris Co., Hanover
Type: Images of pages containing transcripts
Year Range: 1746–1796
Online: F&LH
Title: Church members, marriages & baptisms, at Hanover, Morris Co., N.J., during the pastorate of Rev. Jacob Green, and the settlement of Rev. Aaron Condit, 1746–1796

New Jersey, Morris Co., Mendham
Type: Images of pages containing transcripts
Year Range: 1738–1938
Online: F&LH
Title: The First Presbyterian Congregation, Mendham, Morris County, New Jersey, history and records, 1738–1938

New Jersey, Morris Co., Montville
Type: Images of pages containing transcripts
Year Range: 1824–1899
CD-ROM: F&LH
Online: Record of baptisms and members of the True Dutch Reformed Church at Montville, N.J.
Title: Typescript.

New Jersey, Morris Co., Morristown
Type: Images of pages containing transcripts; D
Year Range: 1768–1806
Online: F&LH
Title: Bill of mortality: being a register of all the deaths which have occured [*sic*] in the Presbyterian and Baptist congregations of Morris-town, New Jersey for thirty-eight years past

New Jersey, Morris Co., Pompton Plains
Type: Images of pages containing transcripts
Year Range: 1813–1931
CD-ROM: F&LH
Online: Records of the First Reformed Church at Pompton Plains, New Jersey
Title: Typescript.

New Jersey, Passaic Co.
Type: Transcript; BA-M-BU
Year Range: 1695–1902
Online: Ancestry
Title: Preakness and Preakness Reformed Church, Passaic County, New Jersey: Town History, 1695–1902
Notes, URL: From George Warne Labaw. *Preakness and the Preakness Reformed Church, Passaic County, New Jersey. A History. 1695–1902.* <www.ancestry.com/search/rectype/inddbs/6029.htm>

New Jersey, Passaic Co., Preakness
Type: Images of pages containing transcripts
Year Range: 1695–1902
CD-ROM: F&LH
Online: Preakness and the Preakness Reformed Church, Passaic County, New Jersey: a history 1695–1902:
Title: With genealogical notes, the records of the church, & tombstone inscriptions.

New Jersey, Passaic Co., Totowa
Type: Abstracts; B-BA
Year Range: 1755–1827
Online: Ancestry
Title: Totowa, New Jersey Old Dutch Church Records, 1755–1827
Notes, URL: Over 2,500 names. <www.ancestry.com/search/rectype/inddbs/3793.htm>

New Jersey, Passaic Co., West Milford
Type: Images of pages containing transcripts
Year Range: 1819–1884
Online: F&LH
Title: List of members and biptismal [*sic*] records found in the session book minutes of the West Milford Presbyterian Church (formerly called Long Pond & New Milford) West Milford, N.J., 1819–1884
Notes, URL: Typescript.

New Jersey, Somerset Co., Basking Ridge
Type: Images of pages containing transcripts; BA-M-D
Year Range: 1795–1817
Online: F&LH
Title: Dr. Robert Finley's [*sic*] marriages from June 1795 to 1817
Notes, URL: Typescript. "Basking Ridge Presbyterian Church baptisms from June 1795 to 1817" and "Deaths during Dr. Robert Finley's pastorate."

New Jersey, Sussex Co., Sparta
Type: Text of a book; Misc.
Year Range: Up to 1886
Online: Ancestry
Title: Sparta, New Jersey, Presbyterian Church Records
Notes, URL: From Theodore F. Chambers. *Proceedings of the Centennial Anniversary*

of the Presbyterian Church at Sparta, NJ, November 23, 1886. <www.ancestry.com/search/rectype/inddbs/4716.htm>

New Jersey, Union Co., Elizabeth
Type: Images of pages containing transcripts
Year Range: 1750–1855
CD-ROM: F&LH
Online: A register for the use of the missionary at St. John's [Church] at Elizabeth Town, N.J.
Title: Transcript, handwritten.

New Jersey, Union Co., Elizabeth
Type: Images of pages containing transcripts
Year Range: 1757–1815
Online: F&LH
Title: Records of the First Presbyterian Church, Elizabeth
Notes, URL: Typescript. "Members admitted, 1757–1800, 1802–1815; marriages, 1804–1817; children's baptisms, 1805–1813; adults [*sic*] baptisms, 1805–1813." Pages 10-13 lacking.

New Jersey, Union Co., New Providence
Type: Images of pages containing transcripts
Year Range: 1737–1860
CD-ROM: F&LH
Online: Copies and extracts of the old records of the Presbyterian Church at Turkey (now New Providence, Union County, N.J.)
Title: Typescript.

New Jersey, Union Co., Scotch Plains
Type: Images of pages containing transcripts
Year Range: 1747–1837
CD-ROM: F&LH
Online: The Records of the Baptist Church at the Scotch Plains in East New Jersey in the year of our Lord 1747
Title: Typescript.

New Jersey, Union Co., Westfield
Type: Images of pages containing transcripts; BA-M-BU
Year Range: 1867–1901
Online: F&LH
Title: Records of Saint Paul's Episcopal, 414 East Broad Street, Westfield, N.J., 07090, 1867–1901: baptisms, burials, marriages
Notes, URL: Typescript.

New York
Type: Images of pages containing transcripts
Year Range: 1707–1898
CD-ROM: F&LH
Online: The "Register" of Dr. William H. Tyler: a manuscript notebook belonging to Mrs. Perry A. Smedley
Title: Lanesboro, Hancock, & Otis families in Orleans & Chautauqua counties, N.Y. Congregational church records.

New York
Type: Transcript; B
Year Range: 1660–1916
CD-ROM: $26.95 (Win), Ancestry, item #1860, <http://shops.ancestry.com>. Search on "Southeast."
Online: Ancestry
Title: New York Births & Baptisms: Southeast Region
Notes, URL: Details on more than 220,000 individuals from over 75,000 records in Dutchess, Greene, Putnam, Rockland, Ulster, and Westchester counties. <www.ancestry.com/search/rectype/inddbs/3711.htm>

New York
Type: Transcript; B
Year Range: 1683–1928
Online: Ancestry
Title: New York Births and Baptisms, Eastern Region, 1683–1928
Notes, URL: Over 82,028 records from Columbia, Rensselaer, and Albany counties. <www.ancestry.com/search/rectype/inddbs/5538.htm>

New York
Type: Transcript; B-BA
Year Range: 1694–1906
Online: Ancestry
Title: New York Births and Baptisms, Schoharie and Mohawk Valleys, 1694–1906
Notes, URL: Over 56,000 records from Fulton, Herkimer, Montgomery, Schenectady, and Saratoga counties with details on more than 225,000 people. <www.ancestry.com/search/rectype/inddbs/6292.htm>

New York, Albany Co., Albany
Type: Transcript; BA-M-D
Year Range: 1683–1700
Online: Ancestry
Title: Albany, N.Y. Church Records, 1683–1700
Notes, URL: 3,000 names. <www.ancestry.com/search/rectype/inddbs/3850.htm>

New York, Albany Co., Albany
Type: Transcript; BA-M
Year Range: 1683–1809
Online: Free
Title: Records of the Reformed Dutch Church of Albany, N.Y., 1683–1809
Notes, URL: About 18,000 records. <http://aleph0.clarku.edu/~djoyce/gen/albany/refchurch.html>

New York, Chemung Co., Elmira
Type: Digital images of a book; M
Year Range: 1854–1900
Online: F&LH
Title: Marriage records: copy of the original records of marriage by Rev. Thomas K. Beecher of Park Church, Elmira, N.Y., from 1854 to 1900

New York, Columbia Co.
Type: Transcript; B-M-D
Year Range: About 1799–1865
Online: Ancestry
Title: Chatham & Hudson Monthly Meeting, Columbia County, New York: Quaker Records
Notes, URL: <www.ancestry.com/search/rectype/inddbs/5971.htm>

New York, Delaware Co., Kortright
Type: Transcript; BA-D
Year Range: 1813–1981
Online: Free
Title: Delaware County, N.Y.—Genealogy and History Site: Gilchrist Memorial Presbyterian Church
Notes, URL: Baptismal records, 1808–1886. Death records, 1873–1981. <www.rootsweb.com/~nydelawa/kortrightindex.html>

New York, Dutchess Co.
Type: Transcript; B-M-D
Year Range: About 1746–1861
Online: Ancestry
Title: Dutchess County, New York Quaker Records
Notes, URL: Over 4,200 names. <www.ancestry.com/search/rectype/inddbs/4702.htm>

New York, Dutchess Co., Fishkill
Type: Digital images of a book
Year Range: 1731–1850
Online: F&LH
Title: Records of the Dutch Reformed Church of Fishkill: Dutchess Co., N.Y., 1731–1850

New York, Dutchess Co., Pleasant Valley
Type: Digital images of a book
Year Range: 1746–1905
CD-ROM: F&LH
Online: A manual of the Presbyterian Church of Pleasant Valley, N.Y.
Title: By Frank W. Townsend. Includes church registers.

New York, Greene Co., Catskill
Type: Images of pages containing transcripts
Year Range: 1802–1881
CD-ROM: F&LH
Online: Records of the Presbyterian Church: Catskill, Greene County, New York
Title: Typescript.

New York, Herkimer Co., Ilion
Type: Transcript
Year Range: 1895–1923
Online: Ancestry
Title: Ilion, New York Baptists, 1895 and 1923
Notes, URL: Membership directories. <www.ancestry.com/search/rectype/inddbs/4088.htm>

New York, Kings Co., Brooklyn
Type: Images of pages containing transcripts
Year Range: 1660–1719
Online: F&LH
Title: Index to the First book of records of the Dutch Reformed Church of Brooklyn, New York

New York, Kings Co., Brooklyn
Type: Images of pages containing transcripts
Year Range: 1873–1903
Online: F&LH
Title: History, year book, and register of the Dutch Evangelical Reformed Church of Canarsie, Brooklyn, New York

New York, Kings Co., Flatbush
Type: Transcript; BA-M
Year Range: 1787–1872
Online: Free
Title: The Olive Tree Genealogy: Flatbush RDC Consistory Books, Kings Co. Long Island N.Y.
Notes, URL: <www.olivetreegenealogy.com/nn/church/flatbush_intro.shtml>

New York, Kings Co., Flatlands
Type: Transcript; BA
Year Range: 1747–1802
Online: Free
Title: The Olive Tree Genealogy: Baptismal Records of the Reformed Dutch Church of Flatlands, L.I. 1747–1802
Notes, URL: <www.olivetreegenealogy.com/nn/church/flatlands1.shtml>

New York, Kings Co., New Utrecht
Type: Images of pages containing transcripts; BA
Year Range: 1718–1741
Online: F&LH
Title: The baptismal records of the Reformed Protestant Dutch Church of New Utrecht, Long Island: 1718–1741
Notes, URL: Typescript.

New York, Monroe Co., Rochester
Type: Abstract; B-M-D
Year Range: About 1775–1929
Online: Ancestry
Title: Rochester Monthly Meeting, Monroe County, New York: Quaker Records
Notes, URL: From *Quaker Records: Rochester Monthly Meeting Monroe County, New York.* <www.ancestry.com/search/rectype/inddbs/5987.htm>

New York, Montgomery Co.
Type: Images of pages containing transcripts; BA-M
Online: F&LH
Title: Records of marriages and baptisms of the Rev. James Dempster
Notes, URL: Typescript.

New York, Montgomery Co., Fonda
Type: Images of pages containing transcripts
Year Range: 1758–1779
Online: F&LH
Title: Fonda church records: from 1758 to Jan. 1779
Notes, URL: Includes Vrooman and allied families.

New York, Montgomery Co., Fort Hunter
Type: Images of pages containing transcripts; BA-M-D
Year Range: 1734–1746
Online: F&LH
Title: Register of baptisms, marriages, communicants, & funerals begun by Henry Barclay at Fort Hunter, January 26th, 1734/5: register book, Fort Hunter 1734

New York, Montgomery Co., Fort Plain
Type: Digital images of a book; B-BA-M-D
Year Range: 1788–1851
Online: F&LH
Title: Fort Plain Reformed Church records
Notes, URL: Births & baptisms, 1809–1851. Marriages, 1788–1849. Deaths, 1814–1832.

New York, Montgomery Co., Palatine
Type: Images of pages containing transcripts
Year Range: 1739–1866
CD-ROM: F&LH
Online: Records of the Lutheran Trinity Church of Stone Arabia: in the town of Palatine, Montgomery County, N.Y.
Title: Typescript. By Royden Woodward Vosburgh.

New York, Nassau Co.
Type: Transcript
Year Range: 1747–1844
Online: Free
Title: George M. Easter's Collection of Marriage Records
Notes, URL: <www.longislandgenealogy.com/records.html>

New York, Nassau Co., Hempstead
Type: Images of pages containing transcripts
Year Range: 1725–1813
CD-ROM: F&LH
Online: Adventures for God: a history of St. George's Episcopal Church, Hempstead, Long Island

New York, Nassau Co., Hempstead
Type: Transcript; BA-M
Year Range: 1725–1813
Online: Free
Title: Marriage and Baptismal Records of St. George's Episcopal Church
Notes, URL: <www.longislandgenealogy.com/StGeorge/GeorgesIndex.html>

New York, Nassau Co., Hempstead
Type: Transcript; BA-M-D
Year Range: 1805–1893
Online: Free
Title: History and Vital Records of Christ's First Presbyterian Church of Hempstead, Long Island, New York
Notes, URL: <www.longislandgenealogy.com/firstPresHempstead/July1922.htm>

New York, Nassau Co., Jericho
Type: Digital images of a book; B-M-D
Year Range: 1790–1900
Online: F&LH
Title: Quaker Marriages, Jericho Monthly Meeting, Long Island, New York
Notes, URL: Births, 1812–1887. Marriages, 1790–1900. Deaths, 1813–1888.

New York, Nassau Co., Jericho
Type: Digital images of a book; B-M-D
Year Range: 1790–1900
Online: Free
Title: Quaker Marriages, Jericho Monthly Meeting, Long Island, New York
Notes, URL: Births, 1812–1887. Marriages, 1790–1900. Deaths, 1813–1888. <http://freepages.genealogy.rootsweb.com/~longislandgenealogy/QuakerMarriages.pdf>

New York, Nassau Co., Manhasset
Type: Digital images of a book; M-D
Year Range: 1785–1878
Online: F&LH
Title: Marriages recorded at Reformed Dutch Church, Manhasset, Long Island: 1785–1878, also a few deaths 1841–1878

New York, Nassau Co., Manhasset
Type: Digital images of a book; M-D
Year Range: 1785–1878
Online: Free
Title: Marriages Recorded at Reformed Dutch Church, Manhasset, Long Island: 1785–1878, also a few deaths 1841–1878
Notes, URL: <http://freepages.genealogy.rootsweb.com/~longislandgenealogy/DutchChurchManhasset.pdf>

New York, Nassau Co., North Hempstead
Type: Digital images of a book; M
Year Range: 1826–1859
Online: F&LH
Title: Marriages by Rev. Henry Hermance at Reformed Dutch Church of North Hempstead, Long Island (formerly Success) 1826–1859

New York, Nassau Co., North Hempstead
Type: Digital images of a book; M
Year Range: 1826–1859
Online: Free
Title: Marriages by Rev. Henry Hermance at Reformed Dutch Church of North Hempstead, Long Island (formerly Success) 1826–1859
Notes, URL: <http://freepages.genealogy.rootsweb.com/~longislandgenealogy/MarriagesReformed.pdf>

New York, New York (City)
Type: Abstracts; BU
Year Range: Up to 1899
Online: Ancestry
Title: New York City, Dutch Church Burials
Notes, URL: Over 3,600 names. <www.ancestry.com/search/rectype/inddbs/4494.htm>

New York, New York (City)
Type: Transcript; M
Year Range: 1639–1695
Online: Ancestry
Title: New York City Reformed Dutch Marriage Records, 1639–95
Notes, URL: Over 2600 names. In Dutch. <www.ancestry.com/search/rectype/inddbs/3799.htm>

New York, New York (City)
Type: Transcript; BA
Year Range: 1639–1730
Online: Free
Title: New Amsterdam Baptisms from 1639–1730
Notes, URL: <www.longislandgenealogy.com/baptisms/bapsoptions.html>

New York, New York (City)
Type: Transcript; BA
Year Range: 1639–1760
Online: Free
Title: The Olive Tree Genealogy: New Amsterdam/New York Reformed Dutch Church: Baptisms
Notes, URL: <www.olivetreegenealogy.com/nn/church/rdcbapt.shtml>

New York, New York (City)
Type: Transcript; M
Year Range: 1639–1760
Online: Free
Title: The Olive Tree Genealogy: Records of the Reformed Dutch Church in New Amsterdam/New York—Marriages
Notes, URL: <www.olivetreegenealogy.com/nn/church/rdcmarr1639.shtml>

New York, New York (City)
Type: Transcript; M
Year Range: 1639–1801
Online: Free
Title: Marriage Records of the Reformed Dutch Church in New Amsterdam and New York
Notes, URL: <www.longislandgenealogy.com/Marriage/marroptions.html>

New York, New York (City)
Type: Abstracts; BA-M-BU
Year Range: 1834–1854
Online: Ancestry
Title: New York City, Lutheran Church Records, 1834–54
Notes, URL: Over 17,000 names. <www.ancestry.com/search/rectype/inddbs/4095.htm>

New York, New York (City)
Type: Images of pages containing transcripts
Year Range: 1836–1907
Online: F&LH
Title: A short history of the Church of the Holy Apostles (P.E.): 9th Ave. & 28th St., New York City, 1836–1907: also records of the church, 1845–1862
Notes, URL: Typescript.

New York, Onondaga Co., Syracuse
Type: Digital images of a book; BA-M
Year Range: 1826–1850
Online: F&LH
Title: Early records of the First Presbyterian Church of Syracuse, N.Y.

New York, Orange Co., Chester
Type: Images of pages containing transcripts
Year Range: 1798–1898
Online: F&LH
Title: The First Presbyterian Church, Chester, N.Y.: 1798–1898

New York, Orange Co., Goshen
Type: Images of pages containing transcripts
Year Range: 1814–1874
CD-ROM: F&LH
Online: St. James Protestant Episcopal Church records: Goshen, Orange County, N.Y.
Title: Typescript.

New York, Orange Co., Goshen
Type: Digital images of a book containing transcripts
CD-ROM: $24.50 (Mac/Win), Long Island Genealogy
Title: Genealogy and History of Orange County, New York
Notes, URL: Graveyard inscriptions. *Orange County Patriot*, marriages & deaths, 1828–1831. St. James Protestant Episcopal Church records, Goshen. All by Gertrude A. Barber. <www.genealogycds.com/sales/Orange.htm>

New York, Orange Co., Goshen
Type: Images of pages containing transcripts
Year Range: 1720–1895
Online: F&LH
Title: The First Presbyterian Church, Goshen, New York, 1720–1895

New York, Orange Co., Goshen
Type: Images of pages containing transcripts

Year Range: 1767–1885
Online: F&LH
Title: The early records of the First Presbyterian Church at Goshen, N.Y.: from 1767 to 1885

New York, Orange Co., Montgomery
Type: Images of pages containing transcripts
Year Range: 1732–1907
CD-ROM: F&LH
Online: German Reformed Church of Montgomery, Orange Co., N.Y. records, Orange Co., N.Y.
Title: Also called the Montgomery Dutch Reformed Church.

New York, Orange Co., Montgomery
Type: Images of pages containing transcripts
Year Range: 1770–1880
CD-ROM: F&LH
Online: The Goodwill memorial, or, The first one hundred and fifty years of the Goodwill Presbyterian Church: Montgomery, Orange Co., N.Y.
Title: Includes a roll of church membership.

New York, Orange Co., Newburgh
Type: Images of pages containing transcripts
Year Range: 1856–1881
Online: F&LH
Title: Calvary Presbyterian Church, Newburgh, N.Y., 1856–1881
Notes, URL: Contains church membership lists.

New York, Orange Co., Newburgh
Type: Images of pages containing transcripts
Year Range: 1858–1958
Online: F&LH
Title: The centennial anniversary of Calvary Presbyterian Church of Newburgh, New York
Notes, URL: List of members.

New York, Orange Co., New Windsor
Type: Images of pages containing transcripts
Year Range: 1774–1827
CD-ROM: F&LH
Online: New Windsor Presbyterian Church record

New York, Orange Co., Warwick
Type: Images of pages containing transcripts
Year Range: 1801–1860
CD-ROM: F&LH
Online: Records of the Dutch Reformed Church: Warwick, Orange County, N.Y.
Title: Typescript.

New York, Otsego Co., Cooperstown
Type: Images of pages containing transcripts
Year Range: 1845–1875
CD-ROM: F&LH
Online: Records of Christ Church at Cooperstown, Otsego County, N.Y.
Title: Typescript.

New York, Otsego Co., Cooperstown
Type: 1792–1850
Year Range: $24.50 (Mac/Win), Long Island Genealogy
Online: Digital images of a book containing an index & abstracts
Title: Deaths, Marriages, and Wills from Ostego County, New York
Notes, URL: Records of Christ Church. Also includes vital records from newspapers, will indexes & abstracts, & tombstone inscriptions. All by Gertrude A. Barber. <www.genealogycds.com/sales/Otsego.htm>

New York, Otsego Co., Cooperstown
Type: Images of typescript pages; B-BA
Year Range: 1797–1827
Online: F&LH
Title: Record of births and baptisms, 1797–1827
Notes, URL: Records of Christ Church, compiled by Gertrude A. Barber & Daniel Nash.

New York, Queens Co., Flushing
Type: Transcript; BA
Year Range: 1788–1834
Online: Free
Title: Baptisms at St. George's of Flushing, N.Y.
Notes, URL: <www.longislandgenealogy.com/BaptismsGeorges.html>

New York, Richmond Co., Staten Island
Type: Abstracts; B-M-D
Year Range: 1749–1828
Online: Ancestry
Title: Staten Island, New York Church Records, 1749–1828
Notes, URL: About 11,000 names. <www.ancestry.com/search/rectype/inddbs/4272.htm>

New York, Richmond Co., Staten Island
Type: Images of pages containing transcripts; B-M-D-BU
Year Range: 1752–1923
Online: F&LH
Title: The Church of St. Andrew, Richmond, Staten Island: its history, vital records and gravestone inscriptions

New York, Rockland Co., Clarkstown
Type: Images of pages containing transcripts
Year Range: 1794–1857
CD-ROM: F&LH
Online: Reformed Dutch Church, Clarkstown, Rockland County, New York
Title: Typescript.

New York, Saratoga Co.
Type: Images of pages containing transcripts
Year Range: 1810–1811
CD-ROM: F&LH
Online: Methodist Episcopal Church, Saratoga County circuit

New York, Saratoga Co., Ballston Spa
Type: Images of pages containing transcripts
Year Range: 1793–1915
Online: F&LH
Title: Records of Christ Church (Episcopal): at Ballston Spa, New York.

New York, Saratoga Co., Clifton Park
Type: Images of pages containing transcripts
Year Range: 1795–1850
Online: F&LH
Title: Clifton Park Reformed Church: (the North Church), ca. 1795–1850

New York, Saratoga Co., Schuylerville
Type: Images of pages containing transcripts
Year Range: 1851–1884
Online: F&LH
Title: Records of Methodist Episcopal Church at Schuylerville, Saratoga Co.: 1851–1884
Notes, URL: Typescript.

New York, Schenectady Co., Schenectady
Type: Images of pages containing transcripts; BA
Online: F&LH
Title: Index of mothers mentioned in baptisms of First Protestant Dutch Reformed Church of Schenectady, N.Y.
Notes, URL: Typescript.

New York, Suffolk Co., East Hampton
Type: Images of pages containing transcripts
Year Range: 1696–1884

Online: F&LH
Title: Presbyterian Church, East Hampton, N.Y., church records 1696–1884: extract from printed records of the town of East Hampton, N.Y., Vol. 5, 1905
Notes, URL: Text in typescript and print.

New York, Suffolk Co., Greenport
Type: Images of pages containing transcripts
Year Range: 1833–1845
CD-ROM: F&LH
Online: Names of the officers and members of the Presbyterian Church, Greenport, L.I.
Title: From a pamphlet published in 1846.

New York, Suffolk Co., Huntington
Type: Images of pages containing transcripts; BA-M
Year Range: 1723–1799
Online: Free
Title: Records of the First church in Huntington, Long Island, 1723–1799
Notes, URL: By Ebenezer Prine. <www.longislandgenealogy.com/Huntington/MainIndex.html>

New York, Suffolk Co., Mattituck
Type: Transcripts; BA-M-D-BU
Year Range: 1751–1809
Online: Free
Title: Mattituck Parish Burying-Ground: Parish Registers of Mattituck and Aquedogue
Notes, URL: <www.longislandgenealogy.com/MattituckBurying/mattituckIndex.html>

New York, Suffolk Co., Middle Island
Type: Transcripts; M
Year Range: 1818–1887
Online: Free
Title: Middle Island, Long Island Presbyterian Church
Notes, URL: <www.longislandgenealogy.com/MIPresbyterianMarr.html>

New York, Suffolk Co., Southold
Type: Transcripts; BA-M
Year Range: 1807–1832
Online: Free
Title: Records of the First Church of Southold, Long Island
Notes, URL: <www.longislandgenealogy.com/SoutholdChurches/FirstChurchJan1935.htm>

New York, Suffolk Co., Southold
Type: Transcripts; M
Year Range: 1812–1891
Online: Free
Title: Marriage Records of the Southold Presbyterian Church of Southold, Suffolk Co., Long Island, N.Y., Vol. 2
Notes, URL: <www.longislandgenealogy.com/SoutholdChurches/SoutholdPresbyterian.htm>

New York, Sullivan Co.
Type: Images of pages containing transcripts
Year Range: 1765–1929
CD-ROM: F&LH
Online: Records of the Dutch Reformed Congregation of Mamakating: later known as the Dutch Reformed Church of Wurtsboro (Rome), Sullivan County, New York
Title: Typescript.

New York, Sullivan Co.
Type: Images of pages containing transcripts
Year Range: 1844–1889
CD-ROM: F&LH
Online: Record of the Methodist Episcopal Church, Half Way Brook Village, Sullivan Co., N.Y., now known as Pond Eddy, N.Y.
Title: Typescript.

New York, Sullivan Co.
Type: Images of pages containing transcripts
Year Range: 1858–1929
CD-ROM: F&LH
Online: Records of the Baptist Church at Parksville and Liberty, N.Y., Sullivan County, N.Y.
Title: Typescript.

New York, Sullivan Co.
Type: Images of pages containing transcripts
Year Range: 1859—1929
CD-ROM: F&LH
Online: Record of Bridgeville Circuit, which includes Glen Wild, Rockhill & Bridgeville, N.Y., Sullivan Co., N.Y., Methodist Episcopal Church
Title: Typescript.

New York, Sullivan Co.
Type: Images of pages containing transcripts
Year Range: 1868–1929
CD-ROM: F&LH
Online: Records of the Methodist Episcopal Church at Swan Lake, Sullivan County, N.Y., White Sulphur Springs, Sullivan County, N.Y., Harris, Sullivan County, N.Y.
Title: Typescript.

New York, Sullivan Co.
Type: Images of pages containing transcripts
Year Range: 1883–1909
CD-ROM: F&LH
Online: Methodist Episcopal Church records: charges, Fallsburgh, N.Y., South Fallsburgh, N.Y., Neversink, N.Y., Hurleyville, N.Y., all in Sullivan Co., N.Y.
Title: Typescript.

New York, Sullivan Co., Barryville
Type: Images of pages containing transcripts
Year Range: 1836–1927
CD-ROM: F&LH
Online: Records of the Barryville Congregational Church of Barryville, Sullivan Co., N.Y.
Title: Typescript.

New York, Sullivan Co., Barryville
Type: Images of pages containing transcripts
Year Range: 1889–1929
CD-ROM: F&LH
Online: Record of the Methodist Episcopal Church, Barryville, N.Y. (Sullivan Co.)
Title: Typescript.

New York, Sullivan Co., Bethel
Type: Images of pages containing transcripts
Year Range: 1805–1891
CD-ROM: F&LH
Online: Records of the White Lake Presbyterian Church of Bethel, Sullivan Co., N.Y.
Title: Typescript.

New York, Sullivan Co., Bloomingburgh
Type: Images of pages containing transcripts
Year Range: 1820–1925
CD-ROM: F&LH
Online: Records of the Reformed Protestant Dutch Church of Bloomingburgh, Sullivan County, N.Y.
Title: Typescript.

New York, Sullivan Co., Cochecton
Type: Images of pages containing transcripts
Year Range: 1812–1928
CD-ROM: F&LH
Online: Records of the Presbyterian Church

of Cochecton, Sullivan County, New York
Title: Typescript.

New York, Sullivan Co., Ferndale
Type: Images of pages containing transcripts
Year Range: 1894–1896
CD-ROM: F&LH
Online: Records of the Free Methodist Church, Ferndale, Sullivan County, N.Y.
Title: Typescript.

New York, Sullivan Co., Grahamsville
Type: Images of pages containing transcripts
Year Range: 1844–1927
CD-ROM: F&LH
Online: Records of the Reformed Dutch Church of Grahamsville, Sullivan County, N.Y.

New York, Sullivan Co., Lake Huntington
Type: Images of pages containing transcripts
Year Range: 1910–1928
CD-ROM: F&LH
Online: Records of the First Presbyterian Church, Lake Huntington, Sullivan County, N.Y.
Title: Typescript.

New York, Sullivan Co., Mongaup Valley
Type: Images of pages containing transcripts
Year Range: 1830–1919
CD-ROM: F&LH
Online: Records of the Associated Reformed Church of Mongaup Valley, Sullivan County, New York
Title: Typescript.

New York, Sullivan Co., Monticello
Type: Images of pages containing transcripts
Year Range: 1862–1907
CD-ROM: F&LH
Online: Records of the Methodist Episcopal Church: Monticello, Sullivan Co., N.Y.
Title: Typescript.

New York, Sullivan Co., Rock Hill
Type: Images of pages containing transcripts
Year Range: 1867–1891
CD-ROM: F&LH
Online: Records of the Methodist Episcopal Church, Rock Hill, Sullivan County, N.Y.
Title: Typescript.

New York, Sullivan Co., Sandburgh
Type: Images of pages containing transcripts
Year Range: 1863–1881
CD-ROM: F&LH
Online: Records of the Methodist Episcopal Church, Sandburgh, Sullivan County, N.Y.
Title: Typescript.

New York, Sullivan Co., Unionville
Type: Images of pages containing transcripts
Year Range: 1880–1912
CD-ROM: F&LH
Online: Records of Consistory of the Union Tabernacle Reformed Church, Unionville, Sullivan County, N.Y.
Title: Typescript.

New York, Sullivan Co., Woodbourne
Type: Images of pages containing transcripts
Year Range: 1858–1929
CD-ROM: F&LH
Online: Records of the Reformed Dutch Church, Woodbourne, Sullivan County, New York
Title: Typescript.

New York, Tioga Co., Spencer
Type: Images of pages containing transcripts
Year Range: 1815–1915
Online: F&LH
Title: Book of remembrance, Presbyterian Church, Spencer, N.Y., 1815–1915

New York, Ulster Co., Gardiner
Type: Images of pages containing transcripts
Online: F&LH
Title: Guilford church records
Notes, URL: Typescript.

New York, Ulster Co., Kingston
Type: Transcript; BA-M
Year Range: 1660–1809
Online: Genealogy Library
Title: Baptismal and marriage registers of the Old Dutch Church of Kingston
Notes, URL: Text of the book. Select Records | Church.

New York, Ulster Co., Kingston
Type: Images of pages containing transcripts; BA-M
Year Range: 1660–1809
Online: F&LH
Title: Baptismal and marriage registers of the Old Dutch Church of Kingston: Ulster County, New York, 1660–1809
Notes, URL: Publ. by the De Vinne Press, 1891.

New York, Ulster Co., Kingston
Type: Digital images; BA-M
Year Range: 1660–1809
CD-ROM: $24.50 (Mac/Win), Long Island Genealogy
Title: Ulster County N.Y. Genealogical & Historical Information
Notes, URL: Also includes gravestone inscriptions. <www.genealogycds.com/sales/Ulster.htm>

New York, Ulster Co., Kingston
Type: Images of pages containing transcripts; BA
Year Range: 1810–1877
Online: F&LH
Title: Baptisms of the old Dutch Church of Kingston, New York, 1810–1877

New York, Ulster Co., Wawarsing
Type: Transcript; B-BA-M
Year Range: 1745–1850
Online: Ancestry
Title: Wawarsing, New York Reformed Dutch Church Records
Notes, URL: English translation. <www.ancestry.com/search/rectype/inddbs/4737.htm>

New York, Westchester Co., Amawalk
Type: Digital images of typescript; B-M-D
Year Range: 1724–1908
Online: F&LH
Title: Amawalk, Westchester County, New York, Friends Monthly Meeting records

New York, Westchester Co., Chappaqua
Type: Transcript; B-M-D-BU
Year Range: About 1790–1917
Online: Ancestry
Title: Chappaqua Monthly Meeting, Westchester County, New York: Quaker Records
Notes, URL: <www.ancestry.com/search/rectype/inddbs/5955.htm>

New York, Westchester Co., Chappaqua
Type: Transcript; B-M-D
Year Range: 1800s
Online: Ancestry
Title: Chappaqua, Westchester County, New York Quaker Records
Notes, URL: <www.ancestry.com/search/rectype/inddbs/4968.htm>

New York, Westchester Co., North Tarrytown

Type: Digital images of a book
Year Range: 1785–1836
CD-ROM: F&LH
Online: First English record book of the Dutch Reformed Church in Sleepy Hollow: formerly the Manor Church of Philipsburgh, now the First Reformed Church of Tarrytown
Title: By Edgar M. Bacon.

New York, Westchester Co., Pound Ridge
Type: Images of pages containing transcripts; M
Year Range: 1837–1886
Online: F&LH
Title: Poundridge Presbyterian Church, Westchester County, N.Y.
Notes, URL: Marriages performed by Rev. William Patterson. Typescript.

New York, Westchester Co., Purchase
Type: Abstracts; B-M-D
Year Range: About 1737–1941
Online: Ancestry
Title: Purchase Monthly Meeting, Westchester County, New York: Quaker Records
Notes, URL: <www.ancestry.com/search/rectype/inddbs/5975.htm>

New York, Westchester Co., Tarrytown
Type: Images of pages containing transcripts; BA-M
Year Range: 1697–1791
Online: F&LH
Title: First record book of the "Old Dutch Church of Sleepy Hollow," organized in 1697, and now the First Reformed Church of Tarrytown, N.Y.
Notes, URL: English translation. By David Cole, et al.

New York, Westchester Co., Tarrytown
Type: Images of pages containing transcripts; BA-M
Year Range: 1697–1791
CD-ROM: $24.50 (Mac/Win), Long Island Genealogy
Title: First record book of the "Old Dutch Church of Sleepy Hollow"
Notes, URL: English translation. By David Cole, et al. <www.genealogycds.com/sales/sleepyhollow.htm>

New York, Westchester Co., Yorktown
Type: Images of pages containing transcripts; M
Year Range: 1784–1825
Online: F&LH
Title: The journal of the Reverend Silas Constant: pastor of the Presbyterian Church at Yorktown, New York
Notes, URL: "With some of the records of the church and a list of his marriages, 1784–1825, together with notes on the Nelson, Van Cortlandt, Warren, and some other families mentioned in the journal."

North Carolina
Type: Transcript; M
Year Range: 1677–1800
CD-ROM: $28 (Mac/Win), Heritage Books, item #1157
Title: Quaker Marriage Certificates
Notes, URL: Based on 3 books by Gwen Boyer Bjorkman. One covers Pasquotank, Perquimans, Piney Woods, & Suttons Creek Monthly Meetings. <www.heritagebooks.com>. Search on "1157."

Ohio, Darke Co., Greenville
Type: Images of pages containing transcripts; B-M-D
Year Range: 1852–1900
Online: F&LH
Title: Marriages, births, deaths, 1852–1900, St. John Lutheran Church
Notes, URL: Typescript.

Oklahoma, Lincoln Co.
Type: Transcript; M
Year Range: 1896–1961
Online: Free
Title: Lincoln County, Oklahoma Early Marriages
Notes, URL: "Over 600 marriage ceremonies performed by Rev. James Grant Cansler [d. May 13, 1962], a non-denominational pastor, living in Chandler, Oklahoma." <www.rootsweb.com/~oklincol/marriage.html>

Pennsylvania
Type: Images of pages from a book; BA-M
Online: F&LH
Title: Register of marriages and baptisms kept by the Rev. Traugott Frederick Illing in connection with the churches of St. Peter's (Lutheran), Middletown, and Caernarvon (Episcopal), Lancaster

Pennsylvania
Type: Abstracts; M
Year Range: Up to 1810
Online: Genealogy Library
Title: Record of PA Marriages Vol. II
Notes, URL: Source: Pennsylvania Archives, 2nd Series, vol. 9. In the Subjects Directory, select Places | United States | Pennsylvania.

Pennsylvania
Type: Transcript; M
Year Range: 1679–1808
CD-ROM: $28 (Mac/Win), Heritage Books, item #1157
Title: Quaker Marriage Certificates
Notes, URL: Based on 3 books by Gwen Boyer Bjorkman. They include the *Concord Monthly Meeting, Delaware Co., PA, 1679–1808*, & the *New Garden Monthly Meeting, Chester Co., PA, 1704–1799*. <www.heritagebooks.com>. Search on "1157."

Pennsylvania
Type: Transcript; B
Year Range: 1680–1800
CD-ROM: $39.99, Genealogy.com, CD #196
Title: Southeastern Pennsylvania, 1680–1800, Birth Index
Notes, URL: 476,000 births or baptisms. "These records, found in 213 church, meeting, and pastoral records and compiled by John T. Humphrey, were originally published in a thirteen-volume set entitled *Pennsylvania Births*." <www.genealogy.com/196facd.html>

Pennsylvania
Type: Transcript; B-BA-MA-BU
Year Range: 1729–1870
CD-ROM: $29.99, Genealogy.com, CD #130
Online: Genealogy Library
Title: Pennsylvania German Church Records, 1729–1870
Notes, URL: Digital images of 3 volumes of *Pennsylvania German Church Records*. 91,000 names. <www.genealogy.com/130facd.html>

Pennsylvania
Type: Abstracts; B-BA-M-D
Year Range: 1729–1881
CD-ROM: $39.99, Genealogy.com, CD #129
Online: Genealogy Library
Title: Adams, Berks & Lancaster Counties, PA 1729–1881 Church Records
Notes, URL: 180,000 names in registers of more than 50 churches. <www.genealogy.com/129facd.html>

Pennsylvania
Type: Abstracts; BA-M
Year Range: 1730–1779
Online: Ancestry

Title: Pennsylvania, Lutheran Baptisms and Marriages
Notes, URL: Over 6,000 names. Records kept by Rev. John Casper Stoever in southeastern Pa. <www.ancestry.com/search/rectype/inddbs/4640.htm>

Pennsylvania
Type: Text of a book containing abstracts; B-M-D
Year Range: mid 1800s–early 1900s
Online: Ancestry
Title: Pennsylvania Quaker Records
Notes, URL: From *Pennsylvania Quaker Records: Warrington, York County; Little Brittain, Lancaster County; Centre, Centre County; West Branch, Clearfield County; Dunnings Creek, Bedford County.* <www.ancestry.com/search/rectype/inddbs/5996.htm>

Pennsylvania
Type: Text of a book
Year Range: 1908
Online: Ancestry
Title: Pennsylvania Methodist Church Records, 1908
Notes, URL: A directory of ministers & widows of ministers. From *Central Pennsylvania Conference of the Methodist Episcopal Church, 1908.* <www.ancestry.com/search/rectype/inddbs/5038.htm>

Pennsylvania, Adams Co., Arendtsville
Type: Transcript; BA
Year Range: 1785–1874
Online: Ancestry
Title: Adams County, PA, 1785–1874: Lutheran and Reformed Congregations
Notes, URL: 6,300 records. <www.ancestry.com/search/rectype/inddbs/5375.htm>

Pennsylvania, Adams Co., Gettysburg
Type: Images of pages containing transcripts
Online: F&LH
Title: Burial record of Lower Marsh Creek Presbyterian Church
Notes, URL: Foreword by Rev. Joseph W. Woods.

Pennsylvania, Berks Co., Fleetwood
Type: Images of pages containing transcripts; M-D-BU
Online: F&LH
Title: An early nineteenth century constitution of a union church
Notes, URL: St. Paul's Union Church. By Irwin H. DeLong.

Pennsylvania, Berks Co., Lower Heidelberg Township
Type: Transcript; BA
Year Range: 1745–1805
Online: Ancestry
Title: Berks County, Pennsylvania, 1745–1805: Cacusi or Hain's Reformed Church
Notes, URL: More than 7,100 records. <www.ancestry.com/search/rectype/inddbs/5319.htm>

Pennsylvania, Berks Co., Mertztown
Type: Transcript; BA
Year Range: 1762–1810
Online: Ancestry
Title: Berks County, PA, 1762–1810: Longswamp Reformed Church records
Notes, URL: <www.ancestry.com/search/rectype/inddbs/5682.htm>

Pennsylvania, Bucks Co., Bedminster Township
Type: Transcript; B-MA-BU
Year Range: 1744–1801
Online: Ancestry
Title: Bucks County, PA, 1744–1801: Tohickon Union Reformed Church
Notes, URL: 9,400 entries. <www.ancestry.com/search/rectype/inddbs/4933.htm>

Pennsylvania, Bucks Co., Bedminster Township
Type: Abstracts; BA-M-BU
Year Range: 1750–1800
Online: Ancestry
Title: Tohickon Union Lutheran Church, Bucks County, Pennsylvania, 1750–1800
Notes, URL: 4,000 entries. From William J. Hinke. *A history of the Tohickon Union Church, Bedminster Township, Bucks County, Pennsylvania.* <www.ancestry.com/search/rectype/inddbs/4931.htm>

Pennsylvania, Bucks Co., Bedminster Township
Type: Transcript; B-M-BU
Year Range: 1751–1798
Online: Ancestry
Title: Bucks County, Pennsylvania, 1751–98: Keller's Lutheran Church Records
Notes, URL: <www.ancestry.com/search/rectype/inddbs/4926.htm>

Pennsylvania, Bucks Co., Nockamixon Township
Type: Transcript; BA-M-D
Year Range: 1770–1820
Online: Ancestry
Title: Bucks County, Pennsylvania Church Records, 1770–1820: Nockamixon Township
Notes, URL: <www.ancestry.com/search/rectype/inddbs/4923.htm>

Pennsylvania, Bucks Co., Solebury Township
Type: Transcript; BA-M-BU
Year Range: 1812–1867
Online: Ancestry
Title: Solebury Presbyterian Church, Bucks County, Pennsylvania, 1812–67
Notes, URL: <www.ancestry.com/search/rectype/inddbs/5995.htm>

Pennsylvania, Bucks Co., Southampton Township
Type: Transcript; BA-M
Year Range: 1710–1800
Online: Ancestry
Title: Bucks County, PA, 1710–1800: Southampton Dutch Reformed Church
Notes, URL: More than 4,700 records. <www.ancestry.com/search/rectype/inddbs/5464.htm>

Pennsylvania, Bucks Co., Springfield Township
Type: Transcript; BA-M-D
Year Range: 1751–1800
Online: Ancestry
Title: Bucks County, PA, 1751–1800: Trinity Union Lutheran and Reformed Church
Notes, URL: <www.ancestry.com/search/rectype/inddbs/5506.htm>

Pennsylvania, Bucks Co., Springfield Township
Type: Abstracts; BA-M-D
Year Range: 1760–1829
Online: Ancestry
Title: Trinity Union Church, Bucks County, Pennsylvania, 1760–1829
Notes, URL: <www.ancestry.com/search/rectype/inddbs/4925.htm>

Pennsylvania, Bucks Co., Springfield Township
Type: Abstracts; BA-M-BU
Year Range: 1801–1829
Online: Ancestry
Title: Trinity Union Reformed Church, Bucks County, Pennsylvania, 1801–29
Notes, URL: <www.ancestry.com/search/rectype/inddbs/5692.htm>

Pennsylvania, Bucks Co., Warwick
Type: Transcript; BA-M-BU

Year Range: 1788–1885
Online: Ancestry
Title: Bucks County, PA, 1788–1885: Neshaminy Presbyterian Church
Notes, URL: More than 5,900 records. <www.ancestry.com/search/rectype/inddbs/5386.htm>

Pennsylvania, Cumberland Co.
Type: Transcript; BA-M-BU
Year Range: 1737–1923
Online: Ancestry
Title: Cumberland County, Pennsylvania Church Records
Notes, URL: <www.ancestry.com/search/rectype/inddbs/4921.htm>

Pennsylvania, Cumberland Co., Lemoyne Township
Type: Abstracts; BA-M-BU
Year Range: 1896–1936
Online: Ancestry
Title: Trinity Evangelical Lutheran Church, Cumberland County, PA, 1896–1936
Notes, URL: <www.ancestry.com/search/rectype/inddbs/5717.htm>

Pennsylvania, Dauphin Co.
Type: Transcript; B-M-BU
Year Range: 1756–1844
Online: Ancestry
Title: Dauphin County, Pennsylvania Church Records
Notes, URL: <www.ancestry.com/search/rectype/inddbs/4934.htm>

Pennsylvania, Dauphin Co., Derry
Type: Images of pages containing transcripts; BA-BU
Year Range: 1757–1825
Online: F&LH
Title: Records of the "Hill" Lutheran Church in Derry Township, Dauphin County, Pennsylvania
Notes, URL: Record of baptisms, 1757–1825, inscriptions in the graveyard, etc.

Pennsylvania, Dauphin Co., Harrisburg
Type: Transcript; BA-M-D
Year Range: 1860–1997
Online: Ancestry
Title: Harrisburg, Pennsylvania, St. Paul's United Methodist Church Records
Notes, URL: <www.ancestry.com/search/rectype/inddbs/3369.htm>

Pennsylvania, Dauphin Co., Lykens Township
Type: Transcript; BA-M-BU
Year Range: 1800–1855
Online: Ancestry
Title: Dauphin County, Pennsylvania, 1800–55: Hoffman Reformed Church
Notes, URL: More than 8,400 records. <www.ancestry.com/search/rectype/inddbs/5271.htm>

Pennsylvania, Franklin Co.
Type: Transcript; BA-D
Year Range: 1834–1906
Online: Ancestry
Title: Mount Zion Evangelical Lutheran Church, Franklin County, Pennsylvania, 1834–1906
Notes, URL: <www.ancestry.com/search/rectype/inddbs/5999.htm>

Pennsylvania, Fulton Co., Ayr Township
Type: Abstracts; BA-M-BU
Year Range: 1849–1906
Online: Ancestry
Title: St. Paul's Lutheran Church, Fulton County, PA, 1849–1906
Notes, URL: <www.ancestry.com/search/rectype/inddbs/6003.htm>

Pennsylvania, Fulton Co., McConnellsburg
Type: Transcript; BA-M-BU
Year Range: 1805–1930
Online: Ancestry
Title: Fulton County, Pennsylvania, 1805–1930: St. Paul's Church
Notes, URL: <www.ancestry.com/search/rectype/inddbs/5452.htm>

Pennsylvania, Lancaster Co.
Type: Images of pages containing transcripts
Online: F&LH
Title: Register of marriages and baptisms kept by the Rev. Traugott Frederick Illing: in connection with the churches of St. Peter's (Lutheran), Middletown, and Caernarvon (Episcopal), Lancaster County, Penn'a
Notes, URL: Middletown is in Dauphin County. Edited by E.W.S. Parthemore.

Pennsylvania, Lancaster Co., Maytown
Type: Transcript; BA-M-BU
Year Range: 1765–1819
Online: Ancestry
Title: Reformed Church of Maytown, Lancaster County, PA, 1765–1819
Notes, URL: <www.ancestry.com/search/rectype/inddbs/6004.htm>

Pennsylvania, Lancaster Co., West Cocalico Township
Type: Abstracts; B-BA
Year Range: 1788–1822
Online: Ancestry
Title: Swamp Reformed (Little Cocalico) Church, Lancaster County, Pennsylvania, 1788–1822
Notes, URL: <www.ancestry.com/search/rectype/inddbs/5545.htm>

Pennsylvania, Lebanon Co., Bethel Township
Type: Transcript; BA-M-BU
Year Range: 1794–1906
Online: Ancestry
Title: Lebanon County, Pennsylvania, 1794–1906: Zoar Evangelical Lutheran Church
Notes, URL: <www.ancestry.com/search/rectype/inddbs/5302.htm>

Pennsylvania, Lebanon Co., Bethel Township
Type: Transcript; BA-M-BU
Year Range: 1879–1957
Online: Ancestry
Title: Goshert's Zion Lutheran Church, Lebanon County, Pennsylvania, 1879–1957
Notes, URL: <www.ancestry.com/search/rectype/inddbs/5735.htm>

Pennsylvania, Lebanon Co., Jackson Township
Type: Transcript; M
Year Range: 1769–1864
Online: Ancestry
Title: Lebanon County, PA Marriages, 1769–1864: Trinity Tulpehocken Reformed Congregation
Notes, URL: <www.ancestry.com/search/rectype/inddbs/4919.htm>

Pennsylvania, Lebanon Co., Jackson Township
Type: Abstracts; BA
Year Range: 1800–1856
Online: Ancestry
Title: Trinity Tuplehocken Reformed Congregation Births, Lebanon County, PA, 1800–56
Notes, URL: <www.ancestry.com/search/rectype/inddbs/4917.htm>

Pennsylvania, Lebanon Co., Millardsville
Type: Images of pages containing transcripts; BU
Online: F&LH
Title: Tuplehocken Trinity Reformed Church, Millardsville, Pa.
Notes, URL: Church bulletins containing tombstone inscriptions.

Pennsylvania, Lebanon Co., Millbach Township
Type: Transcript; B-M-D
Year Range: 1747–1875
Online: Ancestry
Title: Lebanon County, PA, 1747–1875: Millbach Reformed Congregation
Notes, URL: More than 4,600 names. <www.ancestry.com/search/rectype/inddbs/5487.htm>

Pennsylvania, Lebanon Co., Schaefferstown
Type: Transcript; BA-M-D
Year Range: 1765–1864
Online: Ancestry
Title: Heidelberg Congregation, 1765–1864, Schaefferstown, Lebanon County, PA
Notes, URL: <www.ancestry.com/search/rectype/inddbs/4918.htm>

Pennsylvania, Lehigh Co.
Type: Transcript; BA-M-BU
Year Range: 1790–1862
Online: Ancestry
Title: Lehigh County, Pennsylvania: Hilffrich Pastoral Records
Notes, URL: <www.ancestry.com/search/rectype/inddbs/4915.htm>

Pennsylvania, Lehigh Co., Allentown
Type: Images of pages containing transcripts
Year Range: 1762–1937
Online: F&LH
Title: History of Zion Reformed Church, Allentown, Pennsylvania, 1762–1937

Pennsylvania, Lehigh Co., Hanover Township
Type: Transcript; BA-M-BU
Year Range: 1782–1856
Online: Ancestry
Title: Lehigh County, Pennsylvania, 1782–1856: Christ Lutheran Congregation
Notes, URL: More than 4,600 records. <www.ancestry.com/search/rectype/inddbs/4914.htm>

Pennsylvania, Lehigh Co., New Tripoli
Type: Images of pages containing transcripts
Online: F&LH
Title: A history of Weisenberg Church
Notes, URL: Includes a history, brief biographies, & church records.

Pennsylvania, Lehigh Co., Rittersville
Type: Images of pages containing transcripts
Year Range: 1842–1912
Online: F&LH
Title: Seventy years history of Saint Peter's Lutheran & Reformed Congregations of Rittersville, Lehigh Co., PA
Notes, URL: Includes a history, brief biographies, and church records.

Pennsylvania, Lehigh Co., Salisbury
Type: Images of pages containing transcripts; BA-M-BU
Online: F&LH
Title: History of Jerusalem Lutheran and Reformed Church of Western Salisbury, Lehigh Co., Penn.
Notes, URL: "With complete records of all members of both congregations, baptisms, confirmations, marriages and burials."

Pennsylvania, Lehigh Co., Shoenersville
Type: Images of pages containing transcripts; BU
Online: F&LH
Title: Centennial of Christ Church at Shoenersville, Pa.
Notes, URL: Contains a short history of the Lutheran and Reformed congregations.

Pennsylvania, Lehigh Co., Shoenersville
Type: Images of pages containing transcripts; BU
Year Range: 1780–1910
Online: F&LH
Title: History of Christ Lutheran and Reformed Church, Shoenersville, Pa.
Notes, URL: Includes a history, brief biographies, & church records.

Pennsylvania, Lehigh Co., South Whitehall Township
Type: Transcript; BA-M-D
Year Range: 1765–1858
Online: Ancestry
Title: Lehigh County, Pennsylvania, 1765–1858: Jordan Reformed Congregation
Notes, URL: <www.ancestry.com/search/rectype/inddbs/4913.htm>

Pennsylvania, Lehigh Co., Upper Macungie Township
Type: Abstracts; BA-M
Year Range: 1784–1882
Online: Ancestry
Title: Trexlertown Union Church, Lehigh County, Pennsylvania, 1784–1882
Notes, URL: <www.ancestry.com/search/rectype/inddbs/4916.htm>

Pennsylvania, Lehigh Co., Upper Milford Township
Type: Transcript; BA-M
Year Range: 1757–1885
Online: Ancestry
Title: Lehigh County, Pennsylvania, 1757–1885: Upper Milford Reformed Congregation
Notes, URL: <www.ancestry.com/search/rectype/inddbs/4912.htm>

Pennsylvania, Montgomery Co., Franconia Township
Type: Abstracts; BA-M
Year Range: 1753–1851
Online: Ancestry
Title: Montgomery County, Pennsylvania, 1753–1851: Indian Creek Reformed Church
Notes, URL: <www.ancestry.com/search/rectype/inddbs/5348.htm>

Pennsylvania, Montgomery Co., New Hanover Township
Type: Abstracts; B-M-D
Year Range: 1748–1854
Online: Ancestry
Title: Montgomery County, Pennsylvania, 1748–1854: Falckner Swamp Reformed Congregation
Notes, URL: More than 15,000 entries. <www.ancestry.com/search/rectype/inddbs/4910.htm>

Pennsylvania, Montgomery Co., North Wales Township
Type: Abstracts; B-M-D
Year Range: 1787–1856
Online: Ancestry
Title: Montgomery County, Pennsylvania, 1787–1856: St. Peter's Yellow Church
Notes, URL: More than 4,800 records. <www.ancestry.com/search/rectype/inddbs/5422.htm>

Pennsylvania, Montgomery Co., Pottstown
Type: Abstracts; B-M-D
Year Range: 1770–1865
Online: Ancestry
Title: Montgomery County, Pennsylvania, 1770–1865: Trinity Reformed Church of Pottstown
Notes, URL: <www.ancestry.com/search/rectype/inddbs/4911.htm>

Pennsylvania, Northampton Co.
Type: Digital images of a book; BA-M-D
Year Range: 1897–1912
Online: F&LH

Title: A history of Grace Reformed Church, Northampton, Pennsylvania

Pennsylvania, Northampton Co., Bethlehem
Type: Transcript, digital images; BA-M-D
Year Range: 1742–1854
Online: Free
Title: Bethlehem Digital History Project
Notes, URL: Records of the Bethlehem Moravian Congregation. Baptisms, 1742–1756. Marriages, 1742–1854. Deaths, 1746–1849. <http://bdhp.moravian.edu/community_records/register/register.html>

Pennsylvania, Northampton Co., Hamilton Township
Type: Transcript; BA-M-D
Year Range: 1800–1830
Online: Ancestry
Title: Hamilton Township, Northampton County, Pennsylvania, 1800–30: Union Church
Notes, URL: More than 17,000 entries. <www.ancestry.com/search/rectype/inddbs/4909.htm>

Pennsylvania, Northampton Co., Howertown
Type: Images of pages containing transcripts
Year Range: 1835–1885
Online: F&LH
Title: A brief sketch of the principle events of St. John's Church, Howertown, Pa.: together with a burial record, from 1835 to 1885

Pennsylvania, Northampton Co., Lowhill Township
Type: Transcript; BA-M-BU
Year Range: 1769–1881
Online: Ancestry
Title: Lowhill Reformed Congregation, Northampton County, Pennsylvania, 1769–1881
Notes, URL: <www.ancestry.com/search/rectype/inddbs/5557.htm>

Pennsylvania, Northampton Co., Moore Township
Type: Transcript; BA-M-D
Year Range: 1774–1840
Online: Ancestry
Title: Northampton County, Pennsylvania Church Records, 1774–1840
Notes, URL: <www.ancestry.com/search/rectype/inddbs/5210.htm>

Pennsylvania, Northampton Co., Nazareth Township
Type: Transcript; BA-M-BU
Year Range: 1763–1832
Online: Ancestry
Title: Dryland Union Lutheran Church, Northampton County, Pennsylvania, 1763–1832
Notes, URL: <www.ancestry.com/search/rectype/inddbs/5630.htm>

Pennsylvania, Northampton Co., Northampton
Type: Images of pages containing transcripts; BA-M-D
Year Range: 1897–1912
Online: F&LH
Title: A history of Grace Reformed Church, Northampton, Pennsylvania
Notes, URL: By Preston D. Borger, et al.

Pennsylvania, Northampton Co., Saucon Township
Type: Transcript; B-M-D
Year Range: 1756–1845
Online: Ancestry
Title: Northampton County, Pennsylvania, 1756–1845: Christ Union Church
Notes, URL: <www.ancestry.com/search/rectype/inddbs/5239.htm>

Pennsylvania, Northumberland Co., Lower Mahanoy Township
Type: Transcript; BA-M-BU
Year Range: 1777–1854
Online: Ancestry
Title: Northumberland County, Pennsylvania, 1777–1854: Stone Valley Lutheran and Reformed Congregations
Notes, URL: <www.ancestry.com/search/rectype/inddbs/5236.htm>

Pennsylvania, Northumberland Co., Sunbury Township
Type: Transcript; BA-M-BU
Year Range: 1851–1892
Online: Ancestry
Title: Northumberland County, Pennsylvania, 1851–92: Zion Evangelical Lutheran Church
Notes, URL: <www.ancestry.com/search/rectype/inddbs/5395.htm>

Pennsylvania, Northumberland Co., Washington Township
Type: Transcript; BA-M-BU
Year Range: 1774–1846
Online: Ancestry
Title: Northumberland County, Pennsylvania, 1774–1846: Schwaben Creek
Notes, URL: <www.ancestry.com/search/rectype/inddbs/5226.htm>

Pennsylvania, Philadelphia Co., Philadelphia
Type: Text of a book
Year Range: 1682–1750
Online: Ancestry
Title: Philadelphia Quaker Arrivals, 1682–1750
Notes, URL: From Albert Cook Myers. *Quaker Arrivals at Philadelphia, 1682–1750.* <www.ancestry.com/search/rectype/inddbs/4444.htm>

Pennsylvania, Philadelphia Co., Philadelphia
Type: Transripts; BA-BU
Year Range: 1709–1760
Online: Ancestry
Title: Philadelphia, Pennsylvania Church Records, 1709–60
Notes, URL: Over 20,000 names from records of Christ Church. From Charles R. Hildeburn, ed. *Baptisms and Burials From the Records of Christ Church, Philadelphia, 1709–1760*. Philadelphia: Pennsylvania Magazine of History and Biography, 1877–1893. <www.ancestry.com/search/rectype/inddbs/4030.htm>

Pennsylvania, Philadelphia Co., Philadelphia
Type: Transcript; M
Year Range: 1745–1760
Online: Free
Title: St. Michael's & Zion Lutheran Church, Marriages 1745–1760: Philadelphia, PA
Notes, URL: Does not include witnesses. <ftp://ftp.rootsweb.com/pub/usgenweb/pa/philadelphia/church/stmikeandzion01.txt>

Pennsylvania, Snyder Co., Kratzerville Township
Type: Transript; BA-M-BU
Year Range: 1889–1943
Online: Ancestry
Title: Zion Lutheran Church, Snyder County, Pennsylvania, 1889–1943
Notes, URL: <www.ancestry.com/search/rectype/inddbs/5580.htm>

Pennsylvania, Westmoreland Co., Greensburg
Type: Images of pages containing transcripts
Year Range: 1792–1853
Online: F&LH
Title: Births, baptisms (3683) of the First

Lutheran Church, Westmoreland County, Greensburg, Pennsylvania, 1792–1853: Rev. J.M. Steck, 1792–1830, Rev. M.J. Steck, 1830–1848, Rev. Jonas Mechling, 1840–1853

Pennsylvania, York Co.
Type: Transcript; BA-M-BU
Year Range: 1730–1800
Online: Ancestry
Title: Private Church Registers to 1800, York County, Pennsylvania
Notes, URL: <www.ancestry.com/search/rectype/inddbs/4948.htm>

Pennsylvania, York Co.
Type: Transcript; BA
Year Range: 1744–1769
Online: Ancestry
Title: York County, Pennsylvania Church Records, 1744–69: Jacob Lischy's Private Pastoral Record
Notes, URL: More than 8,400 names. <www.ancestry.com/search/rectype/inddbs/4935.htm>

Pennsylvania, York Co.
Type: Transcript; BA-M-BU
Year Range: 1754–1800
Online: Ancestry
Title: York County, Pennsylvania Church Records to 1800
Notes, URL: <www.ancestry.com/search/rectype/inddbs/4952.htm>

Pennsylvania, York Co., Chanceford Township
Type: Transcript; BA-M-BU
Year Range: 1754–1800
Online: Ancestry
Title: Chanceford Township, York County, Pennsylvania Church Records
Notes, URL: <www.ancestry.com/search/rectype/inddbs/4950.htm>

Pennsylvania, York Co., Chanceford Township
Type: Transcript; BA-M-BU
Year Range: 1773–1835
Online: Ancestry
Title: St. Luke's Lutheran and Reformed Congregations, York County, Pennsylvania, 1773–1835
Notes, URL: <www.ancestry.com/search/rectype/inddbs/6089.htm>

Pennsylvania, York Co., Codorus Township
Type: Transcript; B-BA
Year Range: 1760–1800
Online: Ancestry
Title: York County, Pennsylvania Church Records, 1760–1800: Codorus Township
Notes, URL: More than 6,400 records. <www.ancestry.com/search/rectype/inddbs/4949.htm>

Pennsylvania, York Co., Conewago Township
Type: B-BA
Year Range: 1765–1803
Online: Ancestry
Title: York County, PA, 1765–1803: Quickel's (Zion) Lutheran and Reformed Church
Notes, URL: English translation from German. More than 5,500 names. <www.ancestry.com/search/rectype/inddbs/4940.htm>

Pennsylvania, York Co., Dover Township
Year Range: 1764–1800
Online: Ancestry
Title: York County, PA, 1764–1800: Strayer's (Salem) Reformed Church
Notes, URL: English translation from German. More than 5,900 names. <www.ancestry.com/search/rectype/inddbs/4943.htm>

Pennsylvania, York Co., Fairview Township
Type: Transcript; BA-M-BU
Year Range: 1868–1938
Online: Ancestry
Title: Mt. Zion Lutheran Church at Cedar Point, York County, PA, 1868–1938
Notes, URL: <www.ancestry.com/search/rectype/inddbs/6015.htm>

Pennsylvania, York Co., Freysville
Type: Transcript; BA-M-BU
Year Range: 1871–1889
Online: Ancestry
Title: Evangelical Lutheran Congregation of Freysville, York County, Pennsylvania, 1871–89
Notes, URL: <www.ancestry.com/search/rectype/inddbs/6013.htm>

Pennsylvania, York Co., Hanover Township
Type: BA-M
Year Range: 1800–1856
Online: Ancestry
Title: York County, Pennsylvania, 1800–56: Emmanuel's Reformed Church
Notes, URL: Translation from German to English. More than 7,000 names. <www.ancestry.com/search/rectype/inddbs/4937.htm>

Pennsylvania, York Co., Hellam Township
Type: Transcript; BA-M-BU
Year Range: 1757–1855
Online: Ancestry
Title: York County, Pennsylvania: Creutz Creek Church Records
Notes, URL: <www.ancestry.com/search/rectype/inddbs/4947.htm>

Pennsylvania, York Co., Hopewell Township
Type: Transcript; BA
Year Range: 1792–1861
Online: Ancestry
Title: Saddler's Lutheran Church Baptisms, York County, Pennsylvania, 1792–1861
Notes, URL: <www.ancestry.com/search/rectype/inddbs/5723.htm>

Pennsylvania, York Co., Jackson Township
Type: Transcript; BA
Year Range: 1818–1900
Online: Ancestry
Title: Pennsylvania: Reformed Congregation of Roth's Church Baptisms, York County 1818–1900
Notes, URL: <www.ancestry.com/search/rectype/inddbs/5647.htm>

Pennsylvania, York Co., Lower Windsor Township
Type: Transcript; BA-M-BU
Year Range: 1801–1873
Online: Ancestry
Title: York County, PA, 1801–73: Canadochly Lutheran and Reformed Congregations
Notes, URL: <www.ancestry.com/search/rectype/inddbs/5300.htm>

Pennsylvania, York Co., Manheim Township
Type: Transcript; BA
Year Range: 1855–1887
Online: Ancestry
Title: Reformed Congregation at Dub's Union Church Baptisms, York County, Pennsylvania, 1855–1887
Notes, URL: From *Registers of the Reformed Congregation at Dubs's Union Church, Manheim Township, York County, Pennsylvania, 1855–1887.* <www.ancestry.com/search/rectype/inddbs/5727.htm>

Pennsylvania, York Co., North Codorus Township
Type: Transcript; BA
Year Range: 1773–1901
Online: Ancestry
Title: York County, Pennsylvania,

1773–1901: Lischy's Reformed Church
Notes, URL: Translation from German to English. 6,700 names. <www.ancestry.com/search/rectype/inddbs/4939.htm>

Pennsylvania, York Co., Paradise Township
Type: Transcript; BA
Year Range: 1833–1935
Online: Ancestry
Title: York County, Pennsylvania, 1833–1935: Holtzschwamm Church (Reformed)
Notes, URL: <www.ancestry.com/search/rectype/inddbs/5522.htm>

Pennsylvania, York Co., Penn Township
Type: Abstracts; B-BA
Year Range: 1743–1799
Online: Ancestry
Title: St. Matthew's Lutheran Church, York County, Pennsylvania, 1743–99
Notes, URL: 4,391 names. <www.ancestry.com/search/rectype/inddbs/4942.htm>

Pennsylvania, York Co., Rossville
Type: Transcript; BA-M-BU
Year Range: 1843–1888
Online: Ancestry
Title: Evangelical Lutheran Congregation at Rossville, York County, Pennsylvania, 1843–88
Notes, URL: <www.ancestry.com/search/rectype/inddbs/5708.htm>

Pennsylvania, York Co., Springfield Township
Type: Transcript; B-BA
Year Range: 1755–1801
Online: Ancestry
Title: Springfield Township Church Records, York County, Pennsylvania, 1755–1801
Notes, URL: Over 3,900 names. <www.ancestry.com/search/rectype/inddbs/4951.htm>

Pennsylvania, York Co., West Manchester Township
Type: Transcript; BA-M-BU
Year Range: 1764–1894
Online: Ancestry
Title: York County, Pennsylvania, 1764–1894: Wolf's (St. Paul's) Reformed and Lutheran Church
Notes, URL: <www.ancestry.com/search/rectype/inddbs/5337.htm>

Pennsylvania, York Co., West Manchester Township
Type: Transcript; BA-M-BU
Year Range: 1764–1936
Online: Ancestry
Title: York County, Pennsylvania, 1764–1936: Reformed Congregation of St. Paul's/Wolf's Church
Notes, URL: <www.ancestry.com/search/rectype/inddbs/5293.htm>

Pennsylvania, York Co., West Manheim Township
Type: Transcript; B-BA-M
Year Range: 1751–1800
Online: Ancestry
Title: Sherman's (St. David's) Union Church, York County, Pennsylvania, 1751–1800
Notes, URL: Translation from German. Over 4,000 names. <www.ancestry.com/search/rectype/inddbs/4941.htm>

Pennsylvania, York Co., West Manheim Township
Type: Transcript; BA
Year Range: 1763–1869
Online: Ancestry
Title: York County, Pennsylvania, 1763–1869: St. David's/Sherman's Reformed and Lutheran Church
Notes, URL: <www.ancestry.com/search/rectype/inddbs/5346.htm>

Pennsylvania, York Co., Windsor Township
Type: Transcript; BA
Year Range: 1809–1862
Online: Ancestry
Title: Reformed and Lutheran Congregations of Frey's Church, York County, Pennsylvania, 1809–32, 1861–62
Notes, URL: <www.ancestry.com/search/rectype/inddbs/6011.htm>

Pennsylvania, York Co., York
Type: Transcript; B-M-D-BU
Year Range: 1733–1800
Online: Ancestry
Title: York County, PA, 1733–1800: Christ Evangelical Lutheran Church
Notes, URL: 17,565 names. From F.J.C. Hertzog. *Records, Christ Evangelical Lutheran Church, City of York, York County, Pennsylvania, 1733–1800.* <www.ancestry.com/search/rectype/inddbs/4936.htm>

Pennsylvania, York Co., York
Type: Transcript; B-BA
Year Range: 1745–1800
Online: Ancestry
Title: York County, Pennsylvania, 1745–1800: First Reformed (Trinity) Church
Notes, URL: More than 7,000 names. <www.ancestry.com/search/rectype/inddbs/4946.htm>

Pennsylvania, York Co., York
Type: Transcript; B-M-D-BU
Year Range: 1758–1800
Online: Ancestry
Title: York County, PA, 1758–1800: First Moravian Church
Notes, URL: More than 6,300 names. <www.ancestry.com/search/rectype/inddbs/4944.htm>

Pennsylvania, York Co., York
Type: Transcript; M
Year Range: 1800–1846
Online: Ancestry
Title: York County, Pennsylvania Marriages, 1800–46: First Trinity Reformed Church
Notes, URL: More than 5,400 names. <www.ancestry.com/search/rectype/inddbs/4938.htm>

Pennsylvania, York Co., York
Type: Transcript; BA-M-BU
Year Range: 1801–1853
Online: Ancestry
Title: York County, PA, 1801–53: Trinity Reformed Church
Notes, URL: More than 16,500 names. <www.ancestry.com/search/rectype/inddbs/4945.htm>.

Pennsylvania, York Co., York Township
Type: Transcript; B-BA-M-BU
Year Range: 1766–1851
Online: Ancestry
Title: Lutheran and Reformed Blimyer's Union Church, York County, Pennsylvania, 1766–1851
Notes, URL: <www.ancestry.com/search/rectype/inddbs/5702.htm>

Rhode Island, Kent Co., Warwick
Type: Images of pages containing transcripts; M
Online: F&LH
Title: Historical sketches of the churches of Warwick, Rhode Island

Rhode Island, Providence Co., Providence
Type: Images of pages containing transcripts
Online: F&LH
Title: List of members of the First Baptist Church in Providence, R.I.: with biographical sketches of the pastors

Rhode Island, Providence Co., Smithfield
Type: Transcript; M
Year Range: 1725–1905
Online: Free
Title: Society of Friends, Smithfield Monthly Meetings Vol.30
Notes, URL: <http://freepages.genealogy.rootsweb.com/~fullercaleb/smithfieldmar.htm>

South Carolina
Type: Transcript; M-D
Year Range: 1835–1865
CD-ROM: SC: Records and Reference, $35.95 (Win), Ancestry, item #1554, <http://shops.ancestry.com>. Search on "South Carolina Records."
Online: Ancestry
Title: South Carolina Baptist Marriages and Deaths, 1835–65
Notes, URL: <www.ancestry.com/search/rectype/inddbs/3414.htm>

South Carolina
Type: Transcript; M-D
Year Range: 1843–1863
Online: Ancestry
Title: Reformed Presbyterian Marriages and Deaths, 1843–63
Notes, URL: 3,600 names from throughout the South. <www.ancestry.com/search/rectype/inddbs/3395.htm>

South Carolina
Type: Transcript; M-D
Year Range: 1866–1868
Online: Ancestry
Title: Reformed Presbyterian Marriages and Deaths, 1866–68
Notes, URL: 4,200 names from throughout the South. <www.ancestry.com/search/rectype/inddbs/3403.htm>

South Carolina
Type: Transcript; M-D
Year Range: 1866–1887
CD-ROM: South Carolina: Records and Reference, $35.95 (Win), Ancestry, item #1554 <http://shops.ancestry.com>. Search on "South Carolina Records."
Online: Ancestry
Title: South Carolina Baptist Deaths and Marriages, 1866–87
Notes, URL: <www.ancestry.com/search/rectype/inddbs/3322.htm>

South Carolina, Berkeley Co., St. Thomas
Type: Abstracts; B-BA-M-D
Year Range: 1680–1884
Online: Ancestry
Title: St. Thomas Parish Register, South Carolina, 1680–1884
Notes, URL: Over 3,000 names. From *The Annals and Parish Register of St. Thomas and St. Denis Parish, in South Carolina, from 1680 to 1884.* <www.ancestry.com/search/rectype/inddbs/4672.htm>

South Carolina, Chester Co.
Type: Transcript
Year Range: 1799–1859
CD-ROM: $24 (Mac/Win), Heritage Books, item #1164
Title: Heritage Books Archives: South Carolina, Vol. 1
Notes, URL: Includes *Early Records of Fishing Creek Presbyterian Church, Chester Co., South Carolina, 1799–1859*, by Brent H. Holcomb & Elmer O. Parker. Also, a cemetery roster, 1762–1979. <www.heritagebooks.com>. Search on "1164."

Vermont, Franklin Co., Swanton
Type: Abstracts; BA-M
Year Range: 1858–1884
Online: Ancestry
Title: Swanton, Vermont Church Records, 1858–84
Notes, URL: Over 7,500 names. <www.ancestry.com/search/rectype/inddbs/4265.htm>

Vermont, Franklin Co., Swanton
Type: Abstracts; BA-M
Year Range: 1865–1898
Online: Ancestry
Title: Swanton, Vermont Church Records, 1865–1908
Notes, URL: Nearly 7,600 names. <www.ancestry.com/search/rectype/inddbs/4317.htm>

Vermont, Franklin Co., Swanton
Type: Abstracts; D
Year Range: 1872–1934
Online: Ancestry
Title: Swanton, Franklin county, Vermont, Church Records, 1872–1934: Saint Mary's Church Death Records
Notes, URL: Over 1,800 names. <www.ancestry.com/search/rectype/inddbs/5703.htm>

Vermont, Rutland Co., Rutland
Type: Transcripts; BA-M-D
Year Range: 1788–1842
Online: NEHGS
Title: Records of the Congregational Church of Rutland, Vermont (East Parish), 1788–1842
Notes, URL: <www.newenglandancestors.org/research/database/rutlandvt/>

Vermont, Windsor Co., Springfield
Type: Transcripts; M-D
Year Range: 1840–1902
Online: NEHGS
Title: Records of the Rev. George W. Bailey of Springfield, Vermont, 1840–1902
Notes, URL: <www.newenglandancestors.org/research/database/georgebailey>

Virginia
Type: Abstracts; B-M-D
Year Range: 1673 & later
Online: Ancestry
Title: Virginia Early Quaker Records
Notes, URL: Records of Nansemond and Isle of Wight counties. <www.ancestry.com/search/rectype/inddbs/1035.htm>

Virginia
Type: Up to about 1857
CD-ROM: Ancestry
Online: Text of a book
Title: Virginia Old Churches, Vol. 1
Notes, URL: Over 11,000 names. From William Meade. *Old Churches, Ministers, and Families of Virginia, Volume I.* <www.ancestry.com/search/rectype/inddbs/4579.htm>

Virginia
Type: Up to about 1857
CD-ROM: Ancestry
Online: Text of a book
Title: Virginia Old Churches, Vol. 2
Notes, URL: Over 9,000 names. From William Meade. *Old Churches, Ministers, and Families of Virginia, Volume II.* <www.ancestry.com/search/rectype/inddbs/4602.htm>

Virginia, Arlington Co.
Type: Transcript; M
Year Range: 1801–1852
CD-ROM: $9.50 (Mac/Win), Heritage Books, item #2208
Title: Alexandria & Alexandria (Arlington) County, Virginia: Minister Returns & Marriage Bonds, 1801–1852
Notes, URL: Digital images of the book by T. Michael Miller. <www.heritagebooks.com>. Search on "2208."

Virginia, Frederick Co.
Type: Text of a book; B-D
Year Range: 1734–1934
Online: Ancestry
Title: Frederick County, Virginia Hopewell Friends History
Notes, URL: <www.ancestry.com/search/rectype/inddbs/1048.htm>

Virginia, Goochland Co., St. James Northam Parish
Type: Images of pages containing transcripts; B-M-D
Year Range: 1750–1797
Online: F&LH
Title: The Douglas register: being a detailed record of births, marriages and deaths together with other interesting notes, as kept by the Rev. William Douglas, from 1750–1797

Virginia, Henrico Co.
Type: Images of pages containing transcripts
Online: F&LH
Title: The annals and history of Henrico Parish, Diocese of Virginia: and St. John's P.E. Church
Notes, URL: Reprint (without R.A. Brock's transcription of The Vestry book of Henrico Parish, Virginia) originally published Richmond: Williams Print. Co., 1904.

Virginia, Henrico Co.
Type: Transcript
Year Range: 1611–1904
CD-ROM: $30.50 (Mac/Win), Heritage Books, item #1448
Title: Heritage Books Archives: Virginia Vol. 4
Notes, URL: Includes *History of Henrico Parish and Old St. John's Church, Richmond, Virginia, 1611–1904*, by J. Staunton Moore. <www.heritagebooks.com>. Search on "1448."

Virginia, Henry Co.
Type: Images of pages containing transcripts
Online: F&LH
Title: Copy of the history of Bever Creek Church, 1786, Henry County, Virginia
Notes, URL: Reproduced from typewritten copy.

Virginia, Middlesex Co., Christ Church Parish
Type: Transcript; B
Year Range: 1653–1812
Online: Ancestry
Title: Christ Church Parish, Virginia Births, 1653–1812
Notes, URL: 5,900 names. <www.ancestry.com/search/rectype/inddbs/4306.htm>

Virginia, Middlesex Co., Christ Church Parish
Type: Transcript; D
Year Range: 1653–1812
Online: Ancestry
Title: Christ Church Parish, Virginia Deaths, 1653–1812
Notes, URL: Over 17,000 names. <www.ancestry.com/search/rectype/inddbs/4239.htm>

Virginia, Middlesex Co., Christ Church Parish
Type: Transcript; M
Year Range: 1653–1812
Online: Ancestry
Title: Christ Church Parish, Virginia Marriages, 1653–1812
Notes, URL: Over 4,700 names. <www.ancestry.com/search/rectype/inddbs/4307.htm>

Virginia, Middlesex Co., Christ Church Parish
Type: Transcript; B-BA
Year Range: 1653–1812
Online: Ancestry
Title: Christ Church Parish, Virginia Records, 1653–1812
Notes, URL: Over 4800 records. <www.ancestry.com/search/rectype/inddbs/4194.htm>

Virginia, New Kent Co.
Type: Abstracts; B-BA-M-D
Year Range: 1680–1787
CD-ROM: $30.50 (Mac/Win), Heritage Books, item #1448
Title: Heritage Books Archives: Virginia Volume 4
Notes, URL: Includes *The Parish Register of Saint Peter's, New Kent County, Virginia, from 1680 to 1787*, by the National Soc. of the Colonial Dames of America in the State of Virginia. <www.heritagebooks.com>. Search on "1448."

Virginia, New Kent Co., St. Peter's
Type: Abstracts; B-BA
Year Range: 1680–1787
Online: Ancestry
Title: St. Peter's, Virginia Parish Records, 1680–1787
Notes, URL: Over 12,000 names. <www.ancestry.com/search/rectype/inddbs/4045.htm>

Virginia, Northumberland Co.
Type: Images of pages containing transcripts; B
Year Range: 1661–1810
Online: F&LH
Title: Northumberland Co. record of births, 1661–1810
Notes, URL: The register of St. Stephen's Parish, Northumberland County, Virginia.

Virginia, Williamsburg
Type: Digital images of a book; B-D
Year Range: 1662–1797
CD-ROM: $30.50 (Mac/Win), Heritage Books, item #1448
Title: Heritage Books Archives: Virginia Volume 4
Notes, URL: Includes *Historical Sketch of Bruton Church, Williamsburg, Virginia*, by Rev. W.A.R. Goodwin. It has birth records, 1739–1797, & death records, 1662–1751. <www.heritagebooks.com>. Search on "1448."

Washington
Type: Transcript
Online: Genealogy Library
Title: Catholic Church Records—Washington
Notes, URL: By Warner and Minnick. Primarily covers American Indians. Select Records | Church | American-Indian.

West Virginia, Kanawha Co., Saint Albans
Type: Images of pages containing transcripts; BA-M-D
Year Range: 1838–1906
Online: F&LH
Title: Register of the St. Albans Presbyterian Church : organized August 22, 1868: Seventh Avenue and E Street, St. Albans, W. Va.

Books, Journals, and Manuscripts

Once upon a time, in the not-so-distant past, researching your family history meant spending many hours at a library, paging through dusty books, tattered journals, and nearly illegible manuscripts. A book without an index was virtually useless. **Today, sitting at your home computer, you can find a word anywhere in online and CD-ROM versions of books, journals, and manuscripts in just seconds.**

Timesaver

What books, journals, and manuscripts are online or on CD-ROM?
You'll find everything from Bible records and family papers to rare genealogical journals dating back to the very first issue. Though they fall outside the scope of this book, many published family histories and county histories are also available in online and CD-ROM versions.

What books, journals, and manuscripts are not online or on CD-ROM?
Only a small percentage of genealogical books, journals, and manuscripts have been published online or on CD-ROM. Online library catalogs will help you locate print versions at libraries and archives whose Web sites are listed in these directories:

- COSHRC State Archives and Records Management Programs <www.coshrc.org/arc/states.htm>
- Library of Congress: State Libraries <www.loc.gov/global/library/statelib.html>
- LibDex: The Library Index <www.libdex.com>

For help using library catalogs, public libraries, and state libraries, take a look at my articles published in *Family Tree Magazine* and summarized online:

- "Your Virtual Library Card." *Family Tree Magazine*, Apr. 2000 <www.familytreemagazine.com/articles/librarylinks.html>
- "Top 10 Public Libraries." *Family Tree Magazine*, Oct. 2002 <www.familytreemagazine.com/articles/oct02/top10libraries.html>
- "State Secrets." *Family Tree Magazine*, Aug. 2003, on state libraries <www.familytreemagazine.com/articles/aug03/libraries.html>

You can order back issues at <www.familytreemagazine.com/mags/>.

KEY RESOURCES

Digital Images

American Memory from the Library of Congress

<http://memory.loc.gov>

This site features more than seven million digitized items, including rare books, manuscripts, and maps, as well as photographs, recorded sound, and moving pictures. While you probably won't find anything on your ancestors, material like maps from the Revolutionary War era, Civil War photographs, and slave narratives will put your genealogy in historical context.

The Complete Mayflower Descendant, Vols. 1-46 and Other Sources

In addition to the only electronic publication of the entire forty-six volumes of *The Mayflower Descendant*, this database also includes *Middleborough, Massachusetts Vital Records*, Volumes 1-2, and *Pilgrim Notes and Queries*, Volumes 1-5. Altogether, these resources include about 200,000 names. $49.99 on CD-ROM from Genealogy.com <www.genealogy.com/203facd.html> or on Genealogy Library <www.genealogy.com/ifa/co_cd203.html>.

Family and Local Histories

This subscription database from Genealogy.com features page images from almost 8,000 family histories, over 12,000 local histories, and over 250 primary sources. $14.99/month or $79.99/year. See chapter two for a more complete description.

HeritageQuest Online: ProQuest's Genealogy & Local History Collection.

Identical to Genealogy.com's Family and Local Histories Collection, this database is geared toward libraries. You can search every word in over 25,000 family and local history books and view images of the original pages. HeritageQuest Online <www.heritagequestonline.com>.

Making of America

<http://moa.umdl.umich.edu> and <http://moa.cit.cornell.edu/moa>

This collaborative effort between the University of Michigan and Cornell University features more than 4 million page images from 8,767 books and over 150,000 journal articles. Most date from 1850 to 1877. The two sites have different collections, including a few genealogy titles. Many other works like *Iowa as it is in 1855* and articles such as "History of the Presbyterian Church in Kentucky" (1847) will help put your family history in historical context.

Mayflower Descendant Legacy

This CD has 34 volumes of the *Mayflower Descendant*, 1899-1937, plus several other sources. It includes town vital records, cemetery records, wills and probates, diaries, and research notes. Mac or Windows, $27. Search & Re-Search Publishing, Inc. <www.searchresearchpub.com/mayflower.html>.

National Genealogical Society Quarterly

This resource contains every page from volumes 1 through 85 of the *NGS Quarterly* published between 1908 and 1997. Included are guides to research, compiled family histories, and an index of names. Online on Genealogy Library or on 2 CD-ROMs for Mac or Windows, $49.99 <www.genealogy.com/210fa cd.html>.

New England Historical and Genealogical Register

This database includes all 56,000 pages of volumes 1 through 148 of the quarterly journal published from 1847 to 1994. It contains in-depth articles on history and genealogy, cemetery, church, Bible, and vital records, and an index of names. Free online access for NEHGS members. Issues of the *NEHGS Nexus* newsletter, published from 1983 to 1999, and *New England Ancestors* magazine are also being placed on the Web site. New England Historic Genealogical Society <www.newenglandancestors.org>, (888) 296-3447.

The New York Genealogical and Biographical Record

This CD-ROM has digital images of every page from the first thirty years of the quarterly journal. Originally published between 1870 and 1899, these 120 issues contain compiled genealogies of New York families, transcripts of New York sources, and book reviews. The first in a series, this CD-ROM for Mac or Windows costs $42 ($32 for members) from the New York Genealogical and Biographical Society <www.newyorkfamilyhistory.org>, (212) 755-8532.

The Virginia Genealogist

This CD contains a graphic image of every page from the first twenty-seven volumes of this quarterly published between 1957 and 1983, as well as an index to names, locations, and subjects. Mac or Windows, $60, Heritage Books, Inc. <www.heritagebooks.com> (search on "2323"), (800) 398-7709.

Transcripts & Abstracts

Accessible Archives

<www.accessible.com>

This subscription service gives you online access to the full text of major sources for research in the mid-Atlantic states. Newspaper databases include *The Pennsylvania Gazette 1728-1800* and *African American Newspapers: The 19th Century*. You'll also find county histories from Delaware, New Jersey, and eastern Pennsylvania. $19.95 for 30 days or $59.95 per year.

Bible Records from the Manuscript Collections of the New England Historic Genealogical Society

This CD includes 2,536 separate files, many of which contain records from more than one Bible. Mac or Windows, item #SCDBR, $39.99, New England Historic Genealogical Society <www.newenglandancestors.org>, (888) 296-3447.

Directories & Member Lists

<www.ancestry.com/search/rectype/directories/main.htm>

Ancestry.com's collection of over 700 U.S. city directories date from 1786 to 1979. Many were published around 1890 and substitute for the lost 1890 federal census. You can also buy the city directories on CD-ROM for Massachusetts ($26.95) and the Southern Midwest, the Northern Midwest, New England, New York, and Pennsylvania ($29.95 each).

Genealogy Library

<www.genealogy.com/glsub.html>

This subscription database from Genealogy.com features digitized books, passenger lists, and census images. $9.99/month or $49.99/year. See chapter two for a more detailed description.

William and Mary College Quarterly Historical Magazine

<www.rootsweb.com/~usgenweb/special/wmmaryqtr/index.htm>

This site has the text of many pages from the first twenty-seven volumes of this journal dated 1892 to 1919, as well as indexes to volumes 1 (A-L) and 2 (M-Z). The quarterly is indexed in the Periodical Source Index (PERSI) online <www.ancestry.com/search/rectype/periodicals/persi/main.htm> or on CD-ROM annually from Ancestry.com.

Indexes

Rootsweb.com Book Indexes

<http://userdb.rootsweb.com/bookindexes/>

This index of over 240,000 names covers 70 U.S. local history and genealogy books and over 50 from Australia.

World Biographical Index

<www.saur-wbi.de>

This mammoth database from Germany indexes over 3.2 million biographies in 5,700 reference works published around the world. When you find a promising reference, take it to your local public library to request a copy of the biography on interlibrary loan.

Sources

LINKS

Cyndi's List of Genealogy Sites on the Internet

<www.cyndislist.com>

See especially these categories: Books; Family Bibles; and Magazines, Journals, Columns & Newsletters.

GeneaLinks: Family Bible Records

<www.genealinks.com/bible.htm>

DATABASE DIRECTORY Books, Journals, and Manuscripts

Type: Digital Images, Transcript, Database, Abstracts, or Index; Bible (BI), Journal (JO), Photos (PH), Documents (DO), Family papers (FP), Diaries (DI), Manuscripts (MS), Books (BO), Genealogy (GE).

International
Type: Transcripts; BI
Online: Free
Title: The Bible Archives (TBA)
Notes, URL: <www.geocities.com/Heartland/Fields/2403/>

International
Type: Page images, transcripts; BI
Year Range: 1621–1999
Online: Free
Title: Bible Records Online
Notes, URL: Over 900 Bibles. <www.biblerecords.com>

United States
Type: Index; BI
Online: Free
Title: National Society Daughters of the American Revolution: DAR GRC Index
Notes, URL: An index to unpublished genealogical materials, largely Bible and cemetery transcriptions, in 180,000 volumes of Genealogical Records Committee Reports. <www.dar.org>. Click on "DAR Library" and then on "GRC National Index."

United States
Type: Index; BI
Online: Free index
Title: NGS Bible Records
Notes, URL: <www.ngsgenealogy.org/library/biblerecords.htm>. $15 for a copy of a record, plus $5 for nonmembers.

United States
Type: Index; JO
CD-ROM: $39.95 (Win), Picton Press, #1866
Title: The American Genealogist Index
Notes, URL: An index to 172,513 names in volumes 9-41 of *The American Genealogist*. <www.pictonpress.com>. Search on "1866."

United States
Type: Index; PH-BI-DO
Online: Free index
Title: Ford & Nagle
Notes, URL: 3,000 photos & many family Bibles & family documents. <http://my.erinet.com/~fordnag/FordNagle.htm>

Delaware
Type: Transcriptions; BI
Year Range: 1652–1960
CD-ROM: $23.50 (Mac/Win), Heritage Books, CD #1412
Title: Heritage Books Archives: Delaware Bible Records, Volumes 1-4
Notes, URL: <www.heritagebooks.com>. Search on "1412."

Georgia
Type: Digital images; FP-DI
Online: Free
Title: Digital Library of Georgia
Notes, URL: <http://dlg.galileo.usg.edu>

Maryland
Type: Page images; JO
CD-ROM: $39.99, Genealogy.com, CD #208
Online: Genealogy Library
Title: Maryland Genealogical Society Bulletin, Volumes 1-38
Notes, URL: <www.genealogy.com/208facd.html>

Massachusetts
Type: Transcripts, page images; DI
Online: NEHGS
Title: NEHGS Databases: Diaries from the NEHGS Manuscript Collections
Notes, URL: <www.newenglandancestors.org/research/database>

Massachusetts
Type: Text of the journal; JO
Year Range: 1800s & earlier
Online: Ancestry
Title: Genealogical Advertiser: A quarterly Magazine of Family History, Vol. 1-4
Notes, URL: Miscellaneous probate, court, church, and vital records from Massachusetts and Maine. <www.ancestry.com/search/rectype/inddbs/6156.htm>

Massachusetts, Essex Co., Newburyport
Type: Transcripts, images; DI
Year Range: 1762–1806
Online: NEHGS
Title: The Diaries of the Rev. Thomas Cary of Newburyport, Massachusetts, 1762–1806
Notes, URL: <www.newenglandancestors.org/rs0/research/database/diary/Default.asp>

Massachusetts, Hampshire Co.
Type: Transcripts; MS
CD-ROM: $55 (Mac/Win), NEHGS, item #SCD-CC1
Title: The Corbin Collection: Volume 1: Records of Hampshire County, Massachusetts
Notes, URL: Vital records, cemeteries, town histories, town records. <www.newenglandancestors.org>

Missouri
Type: Transcripts; BI
Online: Ancestry
Title: Missouri Bible Records, Volume 1
Notes, URL: <www.ancestry.com/search/rectype/inddbs/5401.htm>

New Mexico
Type: Digital images; JO
CD-ROM: $55.00, New Mexico Genealogical Society
Title: The *New Mexico Genealogist*: The First Forty Years
Notes, URL: Images of all issues, 1962–2001, with an index to 100,000 names. <www.nmgs.org/NMG-CD.htm>

New York
Type: Transcripts; BI
Year Range: 1581–1917
Online: Ancestry
Title: New York, Family Bible Records, 1581–1917
Notes, URL: From Jeannie Floyd Jones Robison. *Genealogical Records Taken from Family Bibles, 1581–1917*. <www.ancestry.com/search/rectype/inddbs/4615.htm>

New York
Type: Index; JO
CD-ROM: $27, $22 for members
Title: Worden's Index to The New York Genealogical and Biographical Record 1870–1998
Notes, URL: A CD-ROM with more than 1 million names. Order from the New York Genealogical & Biographical Society. <www.nygbs.org/info/worden.html>

New York
Type: Page images; JO
CD-ROM: $44.95
Title: Western New York Genealogical Society Journal, Vol. 1-27
Notes, URL: Western New York Genealogical Society, Inc., P.O. Box 338, Hamburg, NY 14075-0338. <www .wnygs.org>

New York, Dutchess Co.
Type: Compiled research; BO
Year Range: 1700s
Online: NEHGS
Title: The Settlers of the Beekman Patent
Notes, URL: Detailed family histories of the 18th-century residents of the Patent, by Frank J. Doherty. <www.newenglandan cestors.org/research/database/ beekman>

North Carolina, Union Co.
Type: Transcript; DI
Year Range: 1800–1821
Online: Free
Title: John Osborn Diary: January 1, 1800–October 2, 1802; March 7, 1819–September 19, 1821
Notes, URL: <http://freepages.history.roots web.com/~helmsnc/osborndiary>

Ohio
Type: Index; BI
Online: OGS
Title: OGS Databases: OGS Bible Records Index
Notes, URL: For Ohio Genealogical Society members. <www.ogs.org>. Click on Databases.

Pennsylvania
Type: Page images; JO
Year Range: 1650–1900s
CD-ROM: $39.99, Genealogy.com, CD #213
Online: Genealogy Library
Title: The Pennsylvania Genealogical Magazine, Vols. 1-39
Notes, URL: <www.genealogy.com/213fac d.html>

Rhode Island
Type: Text & images; BO
CD-ROM: $39.99, NEHGS, item #SCD-RRI
Title: Records of the Colony and State of Rhode Island and Providence Plantations
Notes, URL: 10 vols. & a supplement. John Russell Bartlett, ed. Includes lists of town freemen, colonial officers, & military records. <www.newenglandancestors .org>

South Carolina
Type: Text of the journal; JO
CD-ROM: South Carolina: Records and Reference, $35.95 (Win), Ancestry
Online: Ancestry
Title: South Carolina Magazine of Ancestral Research, Vols. 1-20
Notes, URL: <www.ancestry.com/search/re ctype/inddbs/4084.htm>

Tennessee
Type: Digital images of a book containing transcriptions; BI
Year Range: 1700s–1900s
CD-ROM: $29.99, Genealogy.com, CD #511
Online: Genealogy Library
Title: Early Tennessee Settlers, 1700s–1900s
Notes, URL: Includes Tennessee Records: Bible Records and Marriage Bonds with 15,000 names from Dickson, Knox, Lebanon, & Wilson counties. <www.gen ealogy.com/511facd.html>

Tennessee
Type: Description; FP
Year Range: 1326–2002
Online: Free
Title: Tennessee State Library and Archives: Manuscript Collection Finding Aids
Notes, URL: <www.state.tn.us/sos/statelib/ techsvs/manu.htm>

Virginia
Type: Text of a periodical; GE
Online: Ancestry
Title: Virginia County Records, Volume VI
Notes, URL: Includes wills, land grants, & marriage bonds. From William Armstrong Crozier. *Virginia County Records, Volume VI*. <www.ancestry. com/search/rectype/inddbs/ 6280.htm>

Virginia
Type: Text of a periodical; GE
Online: Ancestry
Title: Virginia County Records, Volume VII
Notes, URL: Includes wills, land grants, & marriage bonds. From William Armstrong Crozier. *Virginia County Records, Volume VII*. <www.ancestry. com/search/rectype/inddbs/ 6286.htm>

Virginia
Type: Text of a periodical; GE
Online: Ancestry
Title: Virginia County Records, Volume IX
Notes, URL: Includes wills, land grants, & marriage bonds. From William Armstrong Crozier. *Virginia County Records, Volume IX*. <www.ancestry. com/search/rectype/inddbs/ 6293.htm>

Virginia
Type: Text of a periodical; GE
Online: Ancestry
Title: Virginia County Records, Volume X
Notes, URL: Includes wills, land grants, & marriage bonds. From William Armstrong Crozier. *Virginia County Records, Volume X*. <www.ancestry. com/search/rectype/inddbs/ 6325.htm>

Virginia
Type: Digital images of a journal; JO
Online: Ancestry
Title: Virginia Genealogical Society Quarterly
Notes, URL: Vols. 1-35, containing tombstone & Bible records, military records, account books, tithable lists, & unrecorded or lost wills. <www.ancestry .com/search/rectype/inddbs/ 6131.htm>

Virginia, Westmoreland Co.
Type: Text of a periodical; GE
Online: Ancestry
Title: Virginia County Records: Westmoreland County, Volume I
Notes, URL: Includes wills, land grants, & marriage bonds. From William Armstrong Crozier. *Virginia County Records, New Series, Volume I, Westmoreland County*. <www.ancestry. com/search/rectype/inddbs/ 6277.htm>

Wyoming
Type: Index; JO
Year Range: Up to 1994
Online: Free
Title: Annals of Wyoming: The Wyoming History Journal: Index of the Annals of Wyoming, 1923–1994
Notes, URL: <www.wyshs.org/annals.htm>

Documenting Digital Sources

Genealogists find family information in many sources, some more reliable than others. You can usually trust a record made by a witness to the event soon after the event took place. The further removed the record is from the original event in time and place, the more likely errors will creep in. A marriage record made by a clergyman soon after he performed the ceremony is more likely to be reliable than a marriage record in a database compiled from various unnamed sources.

Citing Sources

When documenting sources, your primary objective is to include enough information so you or someone else can find the book, record, or other source. You may also want to quote or summarize the source in your citation so you have the key information handy.

Most genealogists use software like Family Tree Maker, Personal Ancestral File, and RootsMagic to organize their findings. All popular programs let you record where you found each piece of information. Most also let you attach a digitized image of the original document to each source citation.

Keep in mind that an index isn't a source. Many online and CD-ROM databases are indexes that point you toward an original document. Citations to an index like the International Genealogical Index (IGI) should be used just temporarily until you consult the original record and can cite it. Even if the database has an abstract or transcription of the original record, you should check the original source to verify that the information was copied correctly and to find additional clues. Then cite the original document instead of the database.

Many online and CD-ROM sources were originally published in book form. Database descriptions on Ancestry.com and Genealogy.com usually give bibliographic information for the source. Your source citation should include bibliographic information describing both the original source and the electronic publication where you found it, as in these three examples:

Ancestry.com U.S. Records Collection

Title: Indiana Marriages, 1845–1920
Author: Original Data: Indiana Works Progress Administration, Index to Marriage Records Indiana.
Publication Information: 1938–1940
Repository/Source Location: Ancestry.com U.S. Records Collection
Call No.: <www.ancestry.com/search/rectype/inddbs/5059a.htm>
Actual text:
Comments: Compiled by Wabash County Historical Museum.
Citation Detail
Film/Vol./Page No.: Pt. III (1842–1854)
Date Record Was Made:

Actual Text/Citation Text: County: Wabash. Name: Mark G. Crenna. Spouse: Elizabeth Shaubhut. Marriage Date: 09 April 1846. Performed By: M.G. [minister of the gospel]. Name: W.R. Love. Book: A. Original Source Page: 14.
Comments: Marks G. Crume's name must have been misread as Mark G. Crenna.

Genealogy Library

Title: Chronicles of the Scotch-Irish Settlement of Virginia
Author: Chalkley, Lyman
Publication Information: Originally published in three volumes by Mary S. Lockwood, 1912.
Repository/Source Location: Genealogy Library
Call No.: <www.genealogy.com>
Actual text:
Comments:
Citation Detail
Film/Vol./Page No.: Vol. III, p. 26.
Date Record Was Made:
Actual Text/Citation Text: Page 440. 20 August 1752. Elizabeth Thomas's bond as administratrix of John Windlekite, her former husband, with witnesses John Crum, Jacob Miller.
Comments: This section of the book has abstracts of wills of Augusta County. "John Crum" must be John Crume.

New England Ancestors

Title: Massachusetts Vital Records
Author:
Publication Information: Original source: Vital Records of Haverhill, Massachusetts, to the Year 1850 (Topsfield, Mass.: Topsfield Historical Society, 1910).
Repository/Source Location: New England Ancestors
Call No.: <www.newenglandancestors.org>
Actual text:
Comments:
Citation Detail
Film/Vol./Page No.:
Date Record Was Made:
Actual Text/Citation Text: Snow, James, s[on of] Isaac and Elisabeth (Bowditch). 21 September 1756, Birth, Haverhill, Mass.
Comments:

The three books below provide guidelines and examples for citing genealogical sources, both traditional and electronic.

SUGGESTED READING

Croom, Emily Anne. *The Sleuth Book for Genealogists: Strategies for More Successful Family History Research.* Cincinnati, Ohio: Betterway Books, 2000. See especially Appendix B, an excellent guide to documentation style.

Mills, Elizabeth Shown. *Evidence! Citation & Analysis for the Family Historian.* Baltimore: Genealogical Publishing Co., 1997.

Silicon Valley PAF Users Group. *Family History Documentation Guidelines.* San Jose, Calif.: Silicon Valley PAF Users Group, 2000.

Saving Files

If you print every Web page, census record, and book reference that mentions your family, you may soon find yourself drowning in a sea of paper and unable to locate the record you need. Saving this information as electronic files on your computer saves space and makes it easier to organize your files and share them via e-mail. (Just be sure you back up your data regularly.)

Most genealogy software lets you not only describe where you found your family information, but also attach an image of the original record to your source citations. You can get digital images by scanning paper documents, downloading image files from the Internet, or copying them from a CD-ROM.

To keep these files organized, you may want to create a separate Genealogy folder within your general documents folder. Then create folders within the Genealogy folder for surnames, like Adams and Brown, and places, like New York and New York Chenango Co (for Chenango County, New York).

SAVING DOCUMENT IMAGES

Follow these steps to save images from the major genealogy Web sites:

Ancestry.com

Historical Newspaper Collection, U.S. Census Records, and other image databases using the Advanced Image Viewer

1. Display the page image on your computer screen and click on Save.
2. Choose a folder on your hard drive and type in a name for the file. You might include a newspaper article's name, date, and page number (e.g., *Appleton (WI) Post Crescent 1914 Nov 8 p 4*) or a census year, state, county, town, and page number (e.g., *1930 ND Cass Rochester p 2B*).
3. Click on the Save button. The entire page will be saved.

U.S. Census Records using MrSID

1. Display a census page on your computer screen and click on View Full Screen.
2. Click on the Other Options icon left of the question mark (or right-click on the image) and select Save Image As.
3. Under Save as Type select JPEG.
4. Beside Save In select a folder on your hard drive.
5. Type in a name for the file with the year, state, county, town, and page number, like *1840 NY Ontario South Bristol p 253*.
6. Click on the Save button. Keep in mind that the saved image will show only the part of the page that was visible on your computer screen.

Genealogy.com

Family and Local Histories (same as Genealogy & Local History Online <www .heritagequestonline.com>)

1. Display a page image and click on Download Images.
2. Select the entire book, sections, or a page range.
3. Click on the Download button to save the files to disk or on the View button to view the pages in Adobe Acrobat.
4. If you choose to download the file, a File Download window will appear. Click on Save.
5. Select a folder, enter a file name, and click on Save. The image will be saved as an Adobe Acrobat file.
6. When it says, "Download complete," click on either Open to view the file or on Close to close the window.

Follow these steps to save part of the Adobe Acrobat file as a graphics file:

1. Double-click on the PDF file to open it in the Adobe Acrobat Reader.
2. Click on the Graphics Select Tool on the toolbar. To select an area of the page, place the mouse cursor in the upper left-hand corner of the area you want to select, hold down the left mouse button, drag to the lower right-hand corner, and release the mouse button.
3. Select Copy from the Edit menu or hold down Ctrl and press the C key.
4. Open a graphics program such as Windows' Paint (Start | All Programs | Accessories | Paint). Select Paste from the Edit menu or hold down Ctrl and press the V key.
5. Select Save As from the File menu in Paint and select a folder by "Save in," enter a file name, select a file type like JPEG, and click on Save.

New England Ancestors

The New England Historical and Genealogical Register

1. Right-click on the page image and select Save Picture As from the pop-up menu.
2. Select a folder, enter a file name like *NEHGR v 25 p 291,* and choose a file type (GIF). You may want to save the entire article or at least the first page so you have the title and author's name.

SAVING TEXT FILES AND HTML FILES

Instead of printing Web pages, you can save them as text or HTML files. If you just want to save some text from a Web page, cut and paste it into a text or word processing document. (Sometimes it's easier to cut and paste text from the printer-friendly version of the page.) Be sure to include the Web site's title, URL, and the date you visited the site.

Web pages come and go, so you may want to save an entire Web page on your hard drive. Internet Explorer version 6 gives you two options:

- **Make available offline.** Visit the Web page and select Add to Favorites from the Favorites menu. Select a folder and give the file a descriptive name. Then check the box for "Make available offline." Now you can select the site from your list of Favorites and view it offline just as it was when you saved it.

- **Save as a Web archive.** Select Save As from the File menu. Choose an appropriate folder and give the file a meaningful name. Then under "Save as type," select "Web archive, single file (*.mht)" and click on Save. Now you can double-click on the file to view it in Internet Explorer.

Either option lets you view the Web page without connecting to the Internet.

IDENTIFYING THE FILE'S SOURCE

Include enough information with the file you have saved so that, when you return to it at a later date, you can tell where you got it. Be sure to give the file a meaningful name and save it in an appropriate surname or place name folder on your computer's hard drive.

In Windows XP, you can add descriptive information to a Microsoft Word file and many types of image files. Open the folder where you saved the file, right-click on the file name, and click on Properties and then on the Summary tab. You can type information in several fields: Title, Subject, Author, Category, Keywords, and Comments. The Category field could hold the name of the online service like Ancestry.com Historical Newspaper Collection or New England Ancestors. You might enter surnames or place names in the Keywords field.

Online Services and CD-ROM Publishers

COMPANY OR SERVICE	CONTACT AND SUBSCRIPTION INFORMATION
Accessible Archives	Accessible Archives, $19.95/30 days or $59.95/year <www.accessible.com>.
AmericanMemorials.com	<www.obituaryregistry.com> and <www.americanmemorials.com>, $39.95/year
AncestorStuff	AncestorStuff.com <www.ancestorstuff.com>.
Ancestry	Ancestry.com <www.ancestry.com>, (800) 262-3787. • U.S. Records Collection, $12.95 per month or $79.95 per year. • U.S. Federal Census Collection, $12.95 per month or $99.95 per year. • U.S. Immigration Collection, $19.95 per month or $79.95 per year. • Historical Newspapers, $12.95 per month or $79.95 per year. • U.S. Premiere Collection, $29.95 per month or $199.95 per year, provides access to the three U.S. Collections and Historical Newspapers. • U.K. and Ireland Records Collection, $12.95 per month or $99.95 per year. The U.S. Federal Census Collection, the U.S. Records Collection and the U.K. & Ireland Records Collection are also available through libraries subscribing to AncestryPlus.
Archive Publishing	Archive Publishing <www.archivepublishing.com>, (801) 818-0881.
Archive Tulsa	<http://commerce.tulsaworld.com/search/searchformnew.asp>.
Broadfoot	Broadfoot Publishing Company <www.broadfootpublishing.com>, (910) 686-9591.
Eastern Digital Resources	Eastern Digital Resources <www.researchonline.net/catalog/index.htm>, (803) 439-2938.
FamilySearch	FamilySearch <www.familysearch.org> or Salt Lake Distribution Center, (800) 537-5971, ldscatalog@ldschurch.org. The online databases are free.
F&LH	Family and Local Histories, $14.99 a month or $79.99 a year, Genealogy.com <www.genealogy.com>, (800) 548-1806. This database is also accessible through libraries subscribing to HeritageQuest Online <www.heritagequestonline.com> where the service is known as ProQuest's Genealogy & Local History Collection.
Family Tree Magazine	<www.familytreemagazine.com>.
Genealogy.com	Genealogy.com <www.genealogy.com>, (800) 548-1806. Family and Local Histories, $14.99 a month or $79.99 a year. Genealogy Library, $9.99 a month or $49.99 a year. International and Passenger Records, $14.99 a month or $79.99 a year. U.S. Census Collection, $19.99 a month or $99.99 a year.
Genealogy Library	Genealogy Library, $9.99/month or $49.99/year, Genealogy.com <www.genealogy.com>, (800) 548-1806.
Global Data	Global Data CD Publishers, LLC <www.gencd.com>.
Godfrey Memorial Library	<www.godfrey.org>. As a "Godfrey Scholar" ($35/year), you gain access to HeritageQuest Online (census images and indexes and the Genealogy & Local History collection) as well as newspapers and other databases.
GPC	Genealogical Publishing Company <www.genealogical.com>, (800) 296-6687.
Heritage Books	Heritage Books <www.heritagebooks.com>, (800) 398-7709.
Heritage Quest	Heritage Quest <www.heritagequest.com>, (800) 760-2455. See Heritage Quest's census guide at <www.censussearch.com>.
Heritage Trail Press: Newspapers	<www.heritagetrailpress.com>, $39/year.

COMPANY OR SERVICE	CONTACT AND SUBSCRIPTION INFORMATION
Historical Data Systems	Historical Data Systems, $10 visitor pass or $25 a year for the American Civil War Research Database <www.civilwardata.com>, (800) 244-3446.
IPR	International and Passenger Records, $14.99 a month or $79.99 a year, Genealogy.com <www.genealogy.com>, (800) 548-1806.
Long Island Genealogy	<www.longislandgenealogy.com>, click on "Long Island History & Genealogy Reference Collections on CD." Or enter the store directly at <http://genealogycds.com/altmenu.html>.
MilitaryUSA.com	MilitaryUSA.com <www.militaryusa.com>, $9.95/week, $19.95/month, or $39.95/year.
MOCA	Maine Old Cemetery Association <www.rootsweb.com/~memoca/moca.htm>, P.O. Box 641, Augusta, ME 04332-0641.
MyTrees	MyTrees.com <www.mytrees.com>, $5 for 10 days, $15 for one month, $100 for one year.
Newspaper Archive.com	<www.newspaperarchive.com>, $149.95/year, $44.95/quarter, $19.95/month, $4.95/day.
NEHGS	New England Historic Genealogical Society <www.newenglandancestors.org>, (888) 296-3447, $75 annual membership.
NYG&B	New York Genealogical & Biographical Society <www.nygbs.org>, (212) 755-8532, $60 annual membership.
Ohio Genealogical Society	<www.ogs.org>.
Paper of Record	<www.paperofrecord.com>, $16.75/month or $99/year.
Progeny Software	Progeny Software <www.progenysoftware.com>, (800) 565-0018.
ProQuest	<www.proquest.com>.
Quintin	Quintin Publications <www.quintinpublications.com>, (800) 747-6687.
Search & ReSearch	Search and ReSearch Publishing, Inc. <www.searchresearchpub.com>, (800) 284-8380.
titlex.com	<www.titlex.com>. $20 minimum token purchase.
Vitalsearch	Vitalsearch Company Worldwide, Inc. <www.vitalsearch-worldwide.com>. Access to most databases is free. Paying customers ($24.95/quarter or $57.95/year) avoid pop-up ads and can view more indexes.
Willow Bend	Willow Bend Books <www.willowbendbooks.com>, (800) 876-6103.
W. W. Norton & Co.	W. W. Norton & Company <www.wwnorton.com>, (800) 233-4830.

Index